Creative Developments in Psychotherapy

Volume 1

Creative

Developments in

Psychotherapy

Volume 1

Edited by

Alvin R. Mahrer

and

Leonard Pearson

The Press of Case Western Reserve University
Cleveland and London / 1971

*We wish to dedicate this volume to Abraham H. Maslow—
to the memory of a life of creative development*

CONTRIBUTORS

GENERAL EDITORS

Alvin R. Mahrer
Miami University
Oxford, Ohio

Leonard Pearson
Sonoma State College
Rohnert Park, California

CONTRIBUTORS OF REPRINTED MATERIALS

Franz Alexander
deceased

John Elderkin Bell
Mental Research Institute
Palo Alto, California

J. F. T. Bugental
Educational Policy Research
    Center
Stanford Research Institute

Jerome D. Frank
The Johns Hopkins University
    School of Medicine
Baltimore, Maryland

Eugene T. Gendlin
University of Chicago
Chicago, Illinois

Abraham H. Maslow
deceased

Rollo May
William Alanson White Institute
    of Psychiatry, Psychoanalysis,
    and Psychology
New York, New York

Carl R. Rogers
Center for the Study of
    the Person
La Jolla, California

Albert E. Scheflen
Bronx State Hospital
Bronx, New York

Hans H. Strupp
Vanderbilt University
Nashville, Tennessee

Charles B. Truax
University of Arkansas
Fayetteville, Arkansas

CONTRIBUTORS OF ORIGINAL COMMENTARIES

Frank Auld
University of Windsor
Windsor, Ontario, Canada

Allen E. Bergin
Teachers College, Columbia
    University
New York, New York

Arthur Burton
Sacramento State College
Sacramento, California

James L. Framo
Eastern Pennsylvania Psychiatric
    Institute
Philadelphia, Pennsylvania

Jerome D. Frank
The Johns Hopkins University
    School of Medicine
Baltimore, Maryland

Sol. L. Garfield
Washington University
Saint Louis, Missouri

Arnold P. Goldstein
Syracuse University
Syracuse, New York

Robert MacGregor
Mental Health Center
Chicago, Illinois

Joseph D. Matarazzo
University of Oregon Medical
    School
Portland, Oregon

Rollo May
William Alanson White Institute
    of Psychiatry, Psychoanalysis,
    and Psychology
New York, New York

Norman A. McQuown
University of Chicago
Chicago, Illinois

O. Hobart Mowrer
University of Illinois
Urbana, Illinois

Vincent F. O'Connell
Volusa County Mental Health
    Center
Daytona, Florida

Fred E. Spaner
National Institute of Mental
    Health
Bethesda, Maryland

Carl A. Whitaker
University of Wisconsin
Madison, Wisconsin

Frederick Wyatt
University of Michigan
Ann Arbor, Michigan

Contents

Introduction

Alvin R. Mahrer and Leonard Pearson

The purpose of this series of volumes, developed under the auspices of the Division of Psychotherapy, American Psychological Association, is to stimulate creative thinking about psychotherapy. We hope to accomplish this by engaging in a continuing process of searching out, openly discussing, and re-examining creative contributions to the psychotherapy literature. This series of volumes is dedicated to such identification. In the contemporary literature on psychotherapy there seems to be no forum explicitly reserved for discussion of such works. Our aim is to provide that specific forum, using varying procedures and formats to identify and elaborate creative developments in psychotherapy.

Any application of the label "creative" is bound to overlap with related labels such as "significant," "popular," "innovative," etc. Without seeking definitive criteria, we recognize a quality which differentiates the creative from the popular, unusual, etcetera, and for us this distinguishing quality involves the ability of an idea to answer basic questions, open up new directions for research or practice, lead us to ask new questions, or phrase old and gnawing questions in a new and productive way. We believe that such developments have long-range consequences and must be identified in the open forum. In this manner, significant changes in therapeutic research, practice, or theory can subsequently be related to the influence of the earlier "creative" expression.

The basic objective of this particular volume, the first, is to take a retrospective look at recent publications in therapy and flag the landmark ones, note them closely and clearly, and describe their impact and contribution. For whom are we publishing this book? Our object is to reach a wide range of students of psychotherapy, from intense, cynical graduate students, to curious undergraduates, to "old-timers" who may recall their own excitement when reading or hearing about these articles five, seven, or ten years ago and may want to recapture their own earlier involvement, or carry it even further.

The book is organized around reprinted publications over a ten-year period that have been selected as meeting the criteria for being "creative developments" in the field of psychotherapy. Each of the three major sections is preceded by an interpretive overview by the editors, and is followed by three or four reprinted articles, with from four to six original commentaries and discussions of these articles. Each of the members of our Editorial Board was provided with a loose definition of what constituted a "creative development" in the field and was asked to nominate one or two outstanding articles or chapters in books to which the criteria applied and which had appeared within the period stipulated. As might have been expected, a few gave one nomination, the majority suggested two, and several made as many as six nominations. Forty articles and chapters were ultimately nominated. These were then randomly divided into groups of six and seven and distributed back to the Editorial Board for final selection on the basis of rank-order voting. From the pool of forty nominated publications, eleven were chosen to appear in this volume.

Our next problem was to obtain suggestions for names of discussants. We invited the authors of the selected works to recommend possible discussants, and also prevailed upon our patient Editorial Board to suggest possibilities. Using the resulting pool of names we chose the final group of discussants; the responsibility for this choice is thus ours.

The guidelines given the discussants were not the ordinary ones, since our purpose was not to seek negative or pedantic critiques. Instead, reviewers were urged to provide serious, partisan commentaries, to describe from their own perspectives and experiences the creative impact, richness, and significance of the selection with relation to the development of the field of therapy. These reviews were to be creative contributions in their own right, and the writers were invited to examine implications, look further into the future of the field, and extend the horizons of the article under discussion. This proved to be a fairly new posture for many of the discussants, and a challenging one for all.

In sum, our focus has been on psychotherapy as an exciting process, one that has been profoundly altered from time to time by writers such as the ones in this volume. Our contributors were selected because of the value and force of their ideas. We believe that the completed volume contains "creative developments" of two kinds: those selected by our Editorial Board for reprinting and the original discussions that will be judged in the course of time for their own creative influence.

The next volume in this series will deal with "creative developments" without regard to time of publication—gems that have been overlooked or neglected or are little-known for whatever reason. Readers are invited to send suggestions for this category to the editors.

Alvin R. Mahrer   Leonard Pearson
Oxford, Ohio   *Berkeley, California*

Creative Developments in Psychotherapy

Volume 1

Part I

The Directions of Psychotherapeutic Change

CHAPTER 1

The Directions of Psychotherapeutic Change: Creative Developments

Alvin R. Mahrer and Leonard Pearson

The purpose of these introductory chapters is to summarize and provide interpretive frameworks for the following contributions and their discussions, although references will be made to other writings in the volume. We intend in the present chapter to look at recent creative answers to the old question of direction of change in psychotherapy.

OPTIMAL PERSONALITY FUNCTIONING

Traditionally, psychotherapy was a method of treating psychological problems and pathological conditions with a special focus on the symptoms. The patient might be a man with *a throbbing headache*, a wife with *growing uncertainties of her abilities as a mother*, or a hospitalized veteran *dejectedly withdrawn from the world about him*.

Today psychotherapy is expanding. It is becoming a means whereby persons can undergo positive changes toward optimal personality functioning (Frank; Strupp). Individuals without major psychopathology or severe emotional problems may make full use of psychotherapeutic changes to enrich their personal lives. Others without disruptive pathology or symptomatology may begin to feel increasingly happy and worthwhile, and may come to function more fully and richly. Psychotherapy has expanded from a means of treating problems, symptoms, and pathology to a means of facilitating positive and constructive personality change.

PERSONALITY POTENTIALS AND CAPACITIES

Psychotherapy is coming to be understood as a means of opening up personality potentials and capacities (Maslow; May; O'Connell; Rogers; Spaner). In addition to curing an illness, treating a maladjustment, or reducing symptomatic behavior, the psychotherapist's role is beginning to include that of facilitating or enhancing positive personality changes (O'Connell). Successful therapy now usually refers to the facilitation of positive potentials instead of movement from a diagnostic category considered pathological to one considered normal (Rogers).

Symptom reduction and elimination. The very process of opening up personality potentials and capacities includes that of reducing and eliminating symptoms (May). In fact, May asserts that such an opening-up process is a highly effective means of resolving symptomatology. For example, opening up the capacity for aggressive forthrightness may sweep away such symptoms of contained or avoided aggression as headaches, stuttering, fatigue, and the like. According to this view, symptoms are reduced or eliminated by unlocking the underlying potentials and capacities which are responsible for symptomatic behavior when they are blocked.

UNIVERSAL VERSUS IDIOSYNCRATIC CHANGE

The method of opening up inner potentialities and capacities is offered as universally applicable; this *process* is the same for everyone. But what emerges will vary with the idiosyncratic nature of the given person's personality structure. To the extent that persons share similar inner potentials and capacities, they would tend to become similar in the course of psychotherapeutic change. If these potentials and capacities are different, then the process of psychotherapy would effect increased differences. For Maslow, this means that the first stage of therapeutic change will be one of increasing similarity, because universal basic *deficiency needs* must first be satisfied; the next step is one of increasing individuality, because *growth* (self-actualization) *needs* are idiosyncratic.

For O'Connell, psychotherapy becomes a process of facilitating the idiosyncratic change of each personality. Further, psychotherapy places the means of undergoing change at the person's own disposal, and must depend on his active role in allowing change to occur. Responsibility is thereby assigned to the individual for much of his own changing process (Maslow; May; O'Connell; Spaner). Both Maslow and May envision that individuals may be given the means for psychotherapeutic methods of change so that they may undertake an individual process of self-searching and inner-directed personality change.

THE STRUCTURE AND CONTENTS OF PERSONALITY

The directions of psychotherapeutic change are related, at least in part, to the posited structure and contents of personality. In our view, the contributions in this section reflect changing conceptions of the structure and contents of personality, with accompanying changes in the directions of psychotherapeutic aims and goals. Our intent is to capture what we see as a new way of viewing personality structure and contents.

ACTUALIZATION

Personality is characterized by inner capabilities and potentialities (Burton; Gendlin; Maslow; May; O'Connell; Rogers), and therapeutic personality change occurs in realizing or actualizing what is within. Movement is toward growth, individuation, or actualization (Maslow; Rogers).

Internal experiencing. The actualizing of inner resources is accompanied by a conscious process of "experiencing" (Burton; Gendlin). The person experiences something substantially new when he finally actualizes a potential or capacity for loving another human being, becoming wholesomely angry, or carrying out a lifelong wish to write poetry. This flow of bodily experienced feelings is one of the major features of actualization. As long as the potentiality or capacity is unactualized, such a sense of vital experiencing is absent (Gendlin), but when the personality process is pushed into empirical realization, the person feels throughout his body.

According to Maslow, it is the sheer experiencing of actualization which constitutes the desired, welcomed, pleasurable state. Full or complete experiencing of a given need leads to the emergence of a still higher need which likewise must be experienced. But the essential pleasure is the internal bodily experiencing which accompanies the actualizing of potentials and capacities.

Actualization of a capability or potential is manifested in the form of certain behaviors, but these behaviors are not the same as the internal experiencings. The internal bodily experiences refer instead to a different realm of events—a buoyancy in the chest, a tingling throughout the skin, an internal sensation of aliveness; these constitute the heightened flow of internal experiencing.

Goal-directionality of all behavior. Actualization of one potential or capability can lead to another wave of actualization of the next potential or capability. A need for affection is functionally related to the next underlying need—for example, a deeper need for care and protection. Actualization of the need for affection opens the way for the emergence of a deeper need for the giving and receiving of care and protection. In other words, a personality need (or potential or capability) is goal-directed by virtue of its functional relation to a deeper personality need. Affection behavior is understood as motivated, goal-directed, and having intention (Bergin; Burton). The process of actualization creates a motivational goal-directedness toward bringing into actual experience the next underlying need (or potential or capability).

So-called psychopathological behavior is reinterpreted in terms of a goal-directionality toward the actualization of some personality need, potential, or capability. Being depressed, having a skin rash, not being able to maintain a job, avoiding being touched, having an ulcer, getting low grades, believing that others are plotting to control oneself, or suffering amnesia are reconceptualized as psychological behaviors which have been motivated by a given need, and which are intentionally directed toward the goal of actualizing that next motivational need. What have heretofore been regarded as pathological departures from reality are also reconceptualized as efforts to actualize intentions (Burton). Behavioral indications of a state of flux, interpreted by some diagnosticians as pathology or verging "psychosis," are reinterpreted as goal-directed changes toward the actualization of personality potentials and capacities (Spaner).

INTEGRATION

In addition to the process of actualizing potentials and capacities, personality change flows out of the relationships among personality forces (May). The relationships among such basic personality forces as sex and eros, anger and rage, and the craving for power vary from integrated (assimilated, accepted) to disintegrated (avoided, defended against) (May). The optimal state is one of integration among basic personality forces.

Maslow describes some basic personality forces as deficiency needs and explains their operation in terms of tension-reduction, need-reduction, or drive-reduction. The end state, according to Maslow, is one of equilibrium or homeostasis, characterized by quiescence and an absence of tension. For May, the end state is beyond that of a static equilibrium or tension-reduction, toward an active and vital acceptance and assimilation. More than the absence of tension, integration is a positive acceptance of one's self (May), characterized by unconditioned self-worth, value, understanding, and freedom from inner barriers (Rogers). Internal integration includes a sense of harmony, peace, and tranquility together with a sense of unity, wholeness, and oneness. Internal integration, which is to be differentiated from tension-reduction, joins with actualization as the two basic organizing principles of personality structure, content, and change.

No school of personality or psychotherapy, according to May, has achieved an adequate basis for dealing with the relationships among basic personality forces, or the relationship of a self to itself. A concept of internal integration is a step toward this goal.

Internal experiencing. Characteristic internal bodily experiencings occur in conjunction with the process of integration. The nature of this internal experiencing is given in such words as: unconditioned self-worth, self-understanding, self-acceptance, freedom from inner barriers, harmony, peace, tranquility, unity, wholeness, and oneness. These words refer to the bodily feelings which accompany integrative relations among personality needs.

When relationships among personality needs are disintegrated, the nature of the internal experiencing is given in such words as: disjointed, in pieces, in parts, separated from oneself, incomplete, in turmoil, distressed. Guilt and anxiety are internal experiencings which accompany particular kinds of disintegrative relations among personality needs. For example, two personality forces may be so related that one threatens to replace (dissolve, eclipse) the other (May). A person's manifest cooperative behavior may be so related to deeper potentials for competition that the merest upsurge of the underlying competition leads to internal experiencing of anxiety and guilt. Anxiety occurs when the deeper need (competition) threatens to dissolve or replace the way the person typically behaves (cooperative behavior), and guilt occurs when the person denies the deeper potential (May). Gendlin likewise describes the emergence of feelings of badness, guilt, and shame as responses which occur instead of the experiences for which we feel guilt, shame, or badness. For example, instead of feeling competition, the person tends to deny or avoid it and therefore experiences a feeling of guilt, shame, or badness.

Locus of control. When the person is integrated with his personality needs, forces, or felt meanings, there is a sense of ownership, a sense of self (Gendlin), of being in control, of being the director, activator, initiator, the controller, the one who determines or who is responsible. As May puts it, the person accrues to himself the power of all the personality forces.

When personality needs bear disintegrative relationships with one another, the locus is no longer within the person himself. It may be external to the individual so that the control (determination, responsibility, power, activation, initiation, direction) lies in other individuals, groups, or social forces: I am not the one who initiates action; my husband does. I do not determine how I behave; I respond to stimuli in the external world. The responsibility for how I am is not within me; it is within the social group. The power lies out there, not within me. I am activated to behave the way I do by external forces. Things out there control me. I am directed by other persons to be the way I am.

When personality needs are disintegrated, the locus of control may be located not in the external world, but in alien and remote internal personality processes: Something else inside me forced me to do that. My condition determined that I should behave that way. The responsibility for my behavior lies in constitutional or neurophysiological variables, not in me. I have little power; the power lies in my problems or id or impulses or drives or needs. I am controlled by things inside me and beyond my control. The real control over the way I am lies in my childhood problems or my neurosis or my physical condition.

THE SUBJECT MATTER OF PSYCHOTHERAPY: BEYOND BEHAVIOR

It is not enough to define the subject matter of psychotherapy simply as behavior. It must be redefined to incorporate the realm of inner experience (Bergin). Thus, the person is not only behaving; his behaviors are accompanied by internal experiencings. In addition, his behavings are motivationally directional and include an internal subjective state of desiring, wanting, or lacking (Maslow). For the psychotherapist, then, the subject matter consists of motivationally directed behavior accompanied by ongoing inner experiencings. One patient is pleading for help, with internal feelings of desperation. Another patient is finally standing up to an authority, with internal bodily feelings of exhilarated excitement. A third patient is being close to a loved person, with internal bodily feelings of fullness and yielding. Each patient is exhibiting behaviors which, together with the motivational directionality and internal bodily feelings, comprise the subject matter of personality.

THERAPEUTIC APPROACHES AND RANGES OF CONVENIENCE

Different therapeutic approaches are appropriate for different kinds of treatment needs. One approach relies upon affective experiencing, relationship variables, and a growth model of personality (Bergin; Rogers). This approach seems particularly suited to overly inhibited, intellectualized persons, with dependency deprivation, independence-striving, social inhibition, and value-system narrowness—personalities in the process of unfreezing and becoming open to experience (Bergin), including the acceptance and assimilation of their own rejected internal impulses (May). The approach accommodates relatively mature and well-adjusted persons seeking to move into more advanced stages of growth and actualization (O'Connell).

For deviant behavior, phobias, compulsions, and similar problems of automatic, conditioned responding, the appropriate approach is becoming that of behavior therapy (Bergin). Many problems call for the acquisition of new behaviors, a forte of the behavior therapies. Maslow is somewhat skeptical about the prospects of adding new behaviors to the same old personality, but Bergin finds self-actualization and behavior therapies so different in ranges of convenience that it is difficult to compare one with the other.

For problems of self-regulation and life style, Bergin claims that no appropriate therapy has as yet proven itself. Mowrer champions ego psychological methods stressing learning (rather than extinction) and progression (rather than regression) for this category of problems.

There appears to be no single therapeutic approach applicable to all patients and problems (Bergin; Goldstein). Instead, the direction, according to Bergin, is away from monolithic schools and toward a continually changing body of research-derived and research-confirmed principles. The trend is toward multiple therapeutic approaches with varied and different ranges of convenience (Bergin; Frank). Certainly, we welcome this liberalizing of treatment principles and methods which are dealing with a far broader range of problems than are usually dealt with by therapists.

PRETHERAPEUTIC PSYCHOLOGICAL UNDERSTANDING

We believe that the above considerations pave the way toward comprehensive and intensive psychological understanding prior to the selection of a particular treatment approach, program, or modality. Such a thorough psychological study would consist of effective techniques to provide the data necessary for making treatment decisions. If the person is best conceptualized in terms of a process of unfreezing and opening up to experience, perhaps a growth model of psychotherapy, with its relationship variables and experiential techniques, is most appropriate. On the other hand, a phobia may be most effectively treated by behavior modification methods. We call for a thorough psychological understanding of the person followed by joint planning on the selection and initiation of an appropriate treatment. We urge against accepting patients into treatment without a systematic consideration of whether the patient might be better treated by some other approach. Too many practitioners learn a great deal about a tiny corner of their patients' personalities by rushing past careful psychological understanding into whatever brand of therapy they offer. One innovative and, we believe, valuable approach is to organize a community's complete treatment resources behind a psychological center of highly skilled clinicians who undertake the initial depth contact with patients. Following a thorough psychological understanding, the most appropriate and effective community treatment facility may be utilized in a careful person-relevant therapeutic program. The more we are coming to know of the varying ranges of convenience for varying therapeutic approaches, the more mandatory it becomes to undertake pre-therapeutic psychological understanding. Simply to launch a person into any therapeutic course is not only wasteful and unproductive, but may be deleterious to the welfare of the patient.

THERAPEUTIC-PROGRAMMING AND PROFESSIONAL ETHICS

It is important to consider the right of the patient to know the value systems and therapeutic philosophy of the treatment approach (i.e., of the therapist) he selects (Bergin). Is the approach geared toward the practical treatment of his facial tic? Will he find himself pressured to alter the entire foundations of his personality and life-style? Or will he be seen through a psychiatric classification system as a borderline psychotic who must be cured of a mental illness? Does the patient have a right to know whether or not the therapist adheres to an existential philosophy? If it is true, as Alexander and Frank both claim, that various schools of psychotherapy differ only slightly in terms of short- or long-term results, does a patient have the right to know whether the therapist is inclined toward a short treatment duration of three months or so, or a "career" of up to five years or even more? It seems that the future holds increasing prospects of therapist selection as a function of knowledge about, and relative attractiveness of, the overall goals and philosophical value systems of the various approaches (Bergin).

THE CRITERIA OF OUTCOME

The acknowledgment that there are varying therapeutic approaches and varying directions and goals raises the usual knotty question: What kinds of criteria are appropriate for evaluating the outcome of treatment? Until recently, we have acted as if psychotherapy were a method of curing a mental illness, and should therefore be evaluated in terms of its effectiveness in curing the symptoms and the underlying responsible condition. From this conventional viewpoint, treatment would be successful if it cures the person's symptomatic facial tic (Strupp). Treatment would be more successful if it succeeded not only in curing the symptom but also the cause (e.g., the anxiety reaction of which the facial tic is symptomatic). From another viewpoint, behavior modification, for example, the elimination of the facial tic per se would be considered successful and not merely the alleviation of a token symptom. From still another viewpoint, success would hinge on the actualization of the potential underlying the facial tic. The current trend is toward abandoning the conventional narrow criteria in favor of sets of criteria linked with specific approaches to psychotherapy. These are increasingly serious considerations for research employing loose, general-outcome criteria as if all psychotherapy were aimed at the same goals and the same directions. The availability and appropriateness of different sets of outcome criteria mean that research, and clinical practice as well, must clearly identify the criteria of outcome (and not presume that all treatment has similar outcomes), and must have different criteria for different treatment approaches.

PSYCHOTHERAPY, SOCIAL CHANGE, AND SOCIAL CLASH

The internal frame of reference, in approaches such as those of Rogers and Maslow, constitutes a challenge to societal values (Bergin). More positively, we are coming to appreciate that intrapsychic changes in individuals will lead to social change (Frank). Psychotherapeutic principles bear the seeds of contagious social clash and change.

INTERNAL INTEGRATION

The internal frame of reference involves integration (acceptance, assimilation) with one's own needs (motivations, drives, impulses, tendencies). We do not just cope with or adjust to our distantiated needs; we become positively assimilated (integrated) with them (May). A state of internal integration means that changes will occur between the individual and society, for there is now no basis for the individual coping with or adjusting to a fundamentally separated or alien external world. As May says, by assimilating our own devil-parts we no longer have to fight with or adjust to them in the external world. The powerful implication is that massive social change is achieved from inside; by assimilating with and integrating with our own internal parts, society itself is changed. By integrating with and assimilating our own violence, rebellion against authority, homosexuality, lust, power, independence, etc., we are changing social relationships from inside out.

By changing ourselves, we change others. Whitaker finds this principle most appropriate for defining the aim of the therapist as not that of helping a patient directly, but as that of trying to help *himself* with— or in the context of—the patient. This process makes both patient and therapist "come alive" (Whitaker), as we change others by undergoing change ourselves.

The internal frame of reference asks a great deal of one's own internal, and correspondingly less of the external, world. Both the responsibility and the resources for effecting integration with others lie in the struggle to achieve integration with oneself. This inward-turning takes the place of our culture's massive turning to other persons and to society, which is essentially the urge to achieve acceptance of oneself through acceptance from others. By moving in the direction of an assimilative integration with our own deeper needs, we reject a psychotherapy which places a premium upon adjustment and the inculcation of given patterns of behavior (May). We also reject a psychotherapy which tries to relieve the anxiety of potential change by enforcing a conforming "adjustment to reality" (May). Thus, an internal frame of reference challenges society by replacing external seeking with internal seeking.

Are there any parts of the external real world for which the category of adjustment is relevant? According to May, one adjusts to an external world of objects and conditions (sidewalks, cold weather, etc.) which are unaffected by our adjustment or lack of adjustment to them: I cannot change a sidewalk; to that I must adjust. But I can change your relationship to me; I do not merely adjust to you. I become more integrated with myself and thereby I change what you are to me and what I am to you. There is, then, a small corner of the external world for which the concept of adjustment is relevant.

Internal integration modifies the external world and sets into motion social change processes in at least two other ways. First, by integrating with or assimilating our own "demonic" needs, we expand the external reality in which we live (May). The integrative assimilation of one's own violence will expand the external world to include more than our externalized fragments of violence. Instead of adjusting to an external world of our own projected creation, there is a continuous unfolding of increasing possibilities from within each of us. Through integration we may open up our own needs for love and affection, and society is thereby expanded to include love and affection relationships. The process of internal integration acts as a burgeoning wellspring of expanding potentialities for society. Secondly, by integrating with our own internal needs we come into increasing contact with the real external world. We relate less to our own projected distortions of external society, and more to the reality of what is out there. We become better able to know the external real world by being fully receptive and passively letting it reach us (Maslow). This process brings into bold relief the realities of the external world, other persons and society—its real ugliness and beauty, its shallowness and true depths, its hypocrisy and exciting possibilities. Thus, internal integration sets social change processes in motion by tearing away our own defenses and making us available (or vulnerable) to the impacts of the real external social world.

THE EXPERIENTIAL ACTUALIZATION OF INTEGRATED NEEDS

Focus on the internal frame of reference leads to the open expression of one's needs (drives, motivations, or impulses). Once the need is wholly integrated with the balance of personality, the next step is to actualize the need, to experience it, to express the need in behavior. Thus, the guide to behavior is internal, not external, and depends on the rightness of the feeling to the person himself (Bergin; Rogers; Spaner). The issue is whether experiencing the actualization of such internally integrated needs will or will not lead inevitably to a clash with social values. Rogers acknowledges that behaving on the basis of internal criteria, being maximally open and responsive to one's internal and external experiencings, will be seen by others as being deviant. The person who is open to his experience and behaves on the basis of internal criteria will be fluid and not rigid, apparently unpredictable rather than statically predictable, and able to express all of his needs, not just a narrow few (Rogers; Spaner). Furthermore, Maslow asserts that a self-actualizing process will include increased functioning on the basis of growth needs which do not require gratification by other people and will therefore pull the person even farther away from the usual social values and supposed needs for other individuals. Going still farther, Bergin sees the espousing of an internal frame of reference as leading inevitably to a clash of personal values with those of society. According to our view, the experiential actualization of *integrated* needs will indeed bring about significant social change, but without inducing violent societal opposition or catastrophic clashes. That the expressive experiencing of integrated needs will lead to social change seems quite clear; every real contact between such individuals and society is a challenge to present social values.

THE EXPERIENTIAL ACTUALIZATION OF DISINTEGRATED NEEDS

Some needs are disintegrated from one another. The disintegrative relationship is manifested in bad feelings such as fear, anxiety, inner trembling, or guilt. A serious issue is whether a personality model can provide for the wholesale acting out (or acting through) of all needs, including those described as disintegrated (Bergin; Burton; Mowrer). The wholesale expression of internal impulses paired with the reduction of the effects of conscience (superego) will, Mowrer asserts, arouse little but grinding resistance and violent retaliation because it violates long ingrained values and standards of society. Furthermore, therapy geared toward a weakening of (superego) controls will produce regression, and since the (neurotic) patient needs (ego-) strengthening, it is understandable that treatment lasting many years has proven ineffective (Mowrer). Referring to forbidden impulses and highly motivated but previously punished acts, Mowrer draws a sharp distinction between (a) the capacity to experience fear *before* the expression of such behavior, and (b) the fear of impending punishment *after* the performance of the forbidden behavior. Rather than freewheeling expression of (forbidden) behavior, optimal functioning involves an increasing capacity to restrain infantile, animalistic gratification of immediate impulses, and, Mowrer continues, the model should include greater resistance to temptation and greater (ego) control of one's self. Such a model of optimal functioning is congruent with the overall objectives of socialization and education and avoids any significant clash with social values.

On the question of whether all impulses (needs, drives), including forbidden (disintegrated) ones, are to be expressed in behavior, we see that the internal frame of reference is open to at least two positions. One position places a premium on open, full expressiveness. Impulses and behavioral tendencies are to be openly expressed, including those surrounded with disintegrative discomfort. It is important to show one's anger, jealousy, sexual impulses, and responsive affection. A second position, which is closer to our own, maintains equally high premium on the expressive experiencing of needs and impulses but clearly distinguishes between those which are integrated with the balance of personality and those which, as Mowrer implies, are severely at odds and disintegrated; some needs and impulses are ready for expressive experiencing without disintegrative discomfort, and some are not.

What is to be done with forbidden impulses and disintegrative needs which are not ready for experiencing or carrying out in behavior? As mentioned before, Mowrer favors a personality model which provides for greater (ego) control and resistance to temptation. Forbidden impulses are to be controlled and resisted. An alternative position, again closer to our own, is that these forbidden impulses and disintegrative needs should eventually be openly and freely expressed (acted out, experienced), but that they must first undergo a change from forbidden impulses to accepted impulses, from being separated from one another to becoming assimilated, from being accompanied by distressing feelings to being accompanied by good feelings—from being disintegrated to being integrated with the balance of personality needs. An important step in this direction is precisely the process described by both Mowrer and May, viz., the acquiring of control over one's forbidden impulses or demonic needs. Stated in another way, the increasing capacity to control forbidden, demonic impulses and needs is a step toward their eventual open experiencing. It seems necessary, however, that this process be initiated by an acceptance of one's disintegrated needs.

In summary, a position which holds that all impulses and needs, including those which are forbidden and disintegrative, are to be openly expressed will lead to an inevitable clash with social values. A position which holds that forbidden and disintegrative impulses and needs are to be mastered and controlled, but not expressed, will not lead to a clash with social values. A third position which holds that forbidden and disintegrative impulses and needs are first to be converted to accepted and integrated impulses and needs, and then openly expressed, may also lead eventually to a clash with social values. However, we accept this type of conflict with established values as a constructive outcome of growth therapy. If the integrated person who is realizing his potential and is directed from his inner resources clashes with external values, this is a decision he chooses. He is not driven to it. And we are in accord with this latter position on the issue of the internal frame of reference.

CHAPTER 2

Deficiency Motivation and Growth Motivation

Abraham H. Maslow

The concept "basic need" can be defined in terms of the questions which it answers and the operations which uncovered it (17). My original question was about psychopathogenesis. "What makes people neurotic?" My answer (a modification of and, I think, an improvement upon the analytic one) was, in brief, that neurosis seemed at its core, and in its beginning, to be a deficiency disease; that it was born out of being deprived of certain satisfactions which I called needs in the same sense that water and amino acids and calcium are needs, namely that their absence produces illness. Most neuroses involved, along with other complex determinants, ungratified wishes for safety, for belongingness and identification, for close love relationships and for respect and prestige. My "data" were gathered through twelve years of psychotherapeutic work and research and twenty years of personality study. One obvious control research (done at the same time and in the same operation) was on the effect of replacement therapy which showed, with many complexities, that when these deficiencies were eliminated, sicknesses tended to disappear. Still another necessary long-time control research was on the family backgrounds of both neurotic and healthy people establishing, as many others have also done, that people who are later healthy are not deprived of these essential basic-need-satisfactions, i.e., the prophylactic control (17, Chapter 5).

These conclusions, which are now in effect shared by most clinicians, therapists, and child psychologists (many of them would not phrase it as I have) make it more possible year by year to define need, in a natural, easy, spontaneous way, as a generalization of actual experiential data (rather than by fiat, arbitrarily and prematurely, prior to the accumulation of knowledge rather than subsequent to it (22) simply for the sake of greater objectivity).

The long-run deficiency characteristics are then the following. It is a basic or instinctoid need if

1. its absence breeds illness,
2. its presence prevents illness,
3. its restoration cures illness,
4. under certain (very complex) free choice situations, it is preferred by the deprived person over other satisfactions,
5. it is found to be inactive, at a low ebb, or functionally absent in the healthy person.

Two additional characteristics are subjective ones, namely, conscious or unconscious yearning and desire, and feeling of lack or deficiency, as of something missing on the one hand, and, on the other, palatability. ("It tastes good.")

One last word on definition. Many of the problems that have plagued writers in this area, as they attempted to define and delimit motivation, are a consequence of the exclusive demand for behavioral, externally observable criteria. The original criterion of motivation and the one that is still used by all human beings except behavioral psychologists is the subjective one. I am motivated when I feel desire or want or yearning or wish or lack. No objectively observable state has yet been found that correlates decently with these subjective reports, i.e., no good behavioral definition of motivation has yet been found.

Now of course we ought to keep on seeking for objective correlates or indicators of subjective states. On the day when we discover such a public and external indicator of pleasure or of anxiety or of desire, psychology will have jumped forward by a century. But *until* we find it we ought not make believe that we have. Nor ought we neglect the subjective data that we do have. It is unfortunate that we cannot ask a rat to give subjective reports. Fortunately, however, we *can* ask the human being, and there is no reason in the world why we should refrain from doing so until we have a better source of data.

It is these needs which are essentially deficits in the organism, empty holes, so to speak, which must be filled up for health's sake, and furthermore must be filled from without by human beings *other* than the subject, that I shall call deficits or deficiency needs for purposes of this exposition and to set them in contrast to another and very different kind of motivation.

It would not occur to anyone to question the statement that we "need" iodine or vitamin C. I remind you that the evidence that we "need" love is of exactly the same type.

In recent years more and more psychologists have found themselves compelled to postulate some tendency to growth or self-perfection to supplement the concepts of equilibrium, homeostasis, tension-reduction, defense and other conserving motivations. This was so for various reasons.

1. *Psychotherapy.* The pressure toward health makes therapy possible. It is an absolute *sine qua non.* If there were no such trend, therapy would be inexplicable to the extent that it goes beyond the building of defenses against pain and anxiety (2, 8, 10, 23).

2. *Brain-injured soldiers.* Goldstein's work (9) is well known to all. He found it necessary to invent the concept of self-actualization to explain the reorganization of the person's capacities after injury.

3. *Psychoanalysis.* Some analysts, notably Fromm (8) and Horney (10), have found it impossible to understand even neuroses unless one postulates that they are a distorted version of an impulse toward growth, toward perfection of development, toward the fulfillment of the person's possibilities.

4. *Creativeness.* Much light is being thrown on the general subject of creativeness by the study of healthy growing and grown people, especially when contrasted with sick people. Especially does the theory of art and art education call for a concept of growth and spontaneity (31, 32).

5. *Child Psychology.* Observation of children shows more and more clearly that healthy children *enjoy* growing and moving forward, gaining new skills, capacities and powers. This is in flat contradiction to that version of Freudian theory which conceives of every child as hanging on desperately to each adjustment that it achieves and to each state of rest or equilibrium. According to this theory, the reluctant and conservative child has continually to be kicked upstairs, out of its comfortable, preferred state of rest *into* a new frightening situation.

While this Freudian conception is continually confirmed by clinicians as largely true for insecure and frightened children, and while it is partially true for all human beings, in the main it is *untrue* for healthy, happy, secure children. In these children we see clearly an eagerness to grow up, to mature, to drop the old adjustment as outworn, like an old pair of shoes. We see in them with special clarity not only the eagerness for the new skill but also the most obvious delight in repeatedly enjoying it, the so-called *Funktionslust* of Karl Buhler (6).

For the writers in these various groups, notably Fromm (8), Horney (10), Jung (13), C. Buhler (5), Angyal (2), Rogers (24), G. Allport (1), Schachtel (25), and Lynd (16), and recently some Catholic psychologists (3, 21), growth, individuation, autonomy, self-actualization, self-development, productiveness, self-realization, are all crudely synonymous, designating a vaguely perceived area rather than a sharply defined concept. In my opinion, it is *not* possible to define this area sharply at the present time. Nor is this desirable either, since a definition which does not emerge easily and naturally from well-known facts is apt to be inhibiting and distorting rather than helpful, since it is quite likely to be wrong or mistaken if made by an act of the will, on a priori grounds. We just don't know enough about growth yet to be able to define it well.

Its meaning can be *indicated* rather than defined, partly by positive pointing, partly by negative contrast, i.e., what is *not*. For example, it is not the same as equilibrium, homeostasis, tension-reduction, etc.

Its necessity has presented itself to its proponents partly because of dissatisfaction (certain newly noticed phenomena simply were not covered by extant theories); partly by positive needs for theories and concepts which would better serve the new humanistic value systems emerging from the breakdown of the older value systems.

This present treatment, however, derives mostly from a direct study of psychologically healthy individuals. This was undertaken not only for reasons of intrinsic and personal interest but also to supply a firmer foundation for the theory of therapy, of pathology and therefore of values. The true goals of education, of family training, of psychotherapy, of self-development, it seems to me, can be discovered only by such a direct attack. The end product of growth teaches us much about the processes of growth. In a recent book (17), I have described what was learned from this study and in addition theorized very freely about various possible consequences for general psychology of this kind of direct study of good rather than bad human beings, of healthy rather than sick people, of the positive as well as the negative. (I must warn you that the data cannot be considered reliable until someone else repeats the study. The possibilities of projection are very real in such a study and of course are unlikely to be detected by the investigator himself.) I want now to discuss some of the differences that I have observed to exist between the motivational lives of healthy people and of others, i.e., people motivated by growth needs contrasted with those motivated by the basic needs.

So far as motivational status is concerned, healthy people have sufficiently gratified their basic needs for safety, belongingness, love, respect and self-esteem so that they are motivated primarily by trends to self-actualization (defined as ongoing actualization of potentials, capacities and talents, as fulfillment of mission (or call, fate, destiny, or vocation), as a fuller knowledge of, and acceptance of, the person's own intrinsic nature, as an unceasing trend toward unity, integration or synergy within the person).

Much to be preferred to this generalized definition would be a descriptive and operational one which I have already published (17). These healthy people are there defined by describing their clinically observed characteristics. These are:

1. Superior perception of reality.
2. Increased acceptance of self, of others and of nature.
3. Increased spontaneity.
4. Increase in problem-centering.
5. Increased detachment and desire for privacy.
6. Increased autonomy, and resistance to enculturation.
7. Greater freshness of appreciation, and richness of emotional reaction.
8. Higher frequency of peak experiences.
9. Increased identification with the human species.
10. Changed (the clinician would say, improved) interpersonal relations.
11. More democratic character structure.
12. Greatly increased creativeness.
13. Certain changes in the value system.

Furthermore, in this book are described also the limitations imposed upon the definition by unavoidable shortcomings in sampling and in availability of data.

One major difficulty with this conception as so far presented is its somewhat static character. Self-actualization, since I have found it only in older people, tends to be seen as an ultimate or final state of affairs, a far goal, rather than a dynamic process, active throughout life, Being, rather than Becoming.

If we define growth as the various processes which bring the person toward ultimate self-actualization, then this conforms better with the observed fact that it is going on *all* the time in the life history. It discourages also the stepwise, *all* or none, saltatory conception of motivational progression toward self-actualization in which the basic needs are completely gratified, one by one, before the next higher one emerges into consciousness. Growth is seen then not only as progressive gratification of basic needs to the point where they "disappear," but also in the form of specific growth motivations over and above these basic needs, e.g., talents, capacities, creative tendencies, constitutional potentialities. We are thereby helped also to realize that basic needs and self-actualization do not contradict each other any more than do childhood and maturity. One passes into the other and is a necessary prerequisite for it.

The differentiation between these growth-needs and basic needs which we shall explore here is a consequence of the clinical perception of qualitative differences between the motivational lives of self-actualizers and of other people. These differences, listed below, are fairly well though not perfectly described by the names deficiency-needs and growth-needs. For instance, not all physiological needs are deficits, e.g., sex, elimination, sleep and rest.

At a higher level, needs for safety, belongingness, love and respect are all clearly deficits. But the need for self-respect is a doubtful case. While the cognitive needs for curiosity-satisfaction and for a system of explanation can easily be considered deficits to be satisfied, as can also the hypothetical need for beauty, the need to create is another matter, as is also the need to express. Apparently not all basic needs are deficits but the needs whose frustration is pathogenic are deficits. (Clearly also the sensory satisfactions that Murphy (19) has emphasized can not be considered deficits, perhaps not even needs at all.)

In any case, the psychological life of the person, in many of its aspects, is lived out differently when he is deficiency-need-gratification-bent and when he is growth-dominated or "metamotivated" or growth-motivated or self-actualizing. The following differences make this clear.

1. ATTITUDE TOWARD IMPULSE:
IMPULSE-REJECTION AND IMPULSE-ACCEPTANCE

Practically all historical and contemporary theories of motivation unite in regarding needs, drives and motivating states in general as annoying, irritating, unpleasant, undesirable, as something to get rid of. Motivated behavior, goal seeking, consummatory responses are all techniques for reducing these discomforts. This attitude is very explicitly assumed in such widely used descriptions of motivation as need reduction, tension reduction, drive reduction, and anxiety reduction.

This approach is understandable in animal psychology and in the behaviorism which is so heavily based upon work with animals. It may be that animals have *only* deficiency needs. Whether or not this turns out to be so, in any case we have treated animals *as if* this were so for the sake of objectivity. A goal object has to be something outside the animal organism so that we can measure the effort put out by the animal in achieving this goal.

It is also understandable that the Freudian psychology should be built upon the same attitude toward motivation that impulses are dangerous and to be fought. After all, this whole psychology is based upon experience with sick people, people who in fact suffer from bad experiences with their needs, and with their gratifications and frustrations. It is no wonder that such people should fear or even loathe their impulses which have made so much trouble for them and which they handle so badly, and that a usual way of handling them is repression.

This derogation of desire and need has, of course, been a constant theme throughout the history of philosophy, theology and psychology. The Stoics, most hedonists, practically all theologians, many political philosophers and most economic theorists have united in affirming the fact that good or happiness or pleasure is essentially the consequence of amelioration of this unpleasant state-of-affairs of wanting, of desiring, of needing.

To put it as succinctly as possible, these people all find desire or impulse to be a nuisance or even a threat and therefore will try generally to get rid of it, to deny it or to avoid it.

This contention is sometimes an accurate report of what is the case. The physiological needs, the needs for safety, for love, for respect, for information are in fact often nuisances for many people, psychic trouble-makers, and problem-creators, especially for those who have had unsuccessful experiences at gratifying them and for those who cannot now count on gratification.

Even with these deficiencies, however, the case is very badly overdrawn: one can accept and enjoy one's needs and welcome them to consciousness if (a) past experience with them has been rewarding, and (b) if present and future gratification can be counted on. For example, if one has in general enjoyed food and if good food is now available, the emergence of appetite into consciousness is welcomed instead of dreaded. ("The trouble with eating is that it kills my appetite.") Something like this is true for thirst, for sleepiness, for sex, for dependency needs and for love needs. However, a far more powerful refutation of the "need-is-a-nuisance" theory is found in the recently emerging awareness of, and concern with, growth (self-actualization) motivation.

The multitude of idiosyncratic motives which come under the head of "self-actualization" can hardly be listed since each person has different talents, capacities, potentialities. But some characteristics are general to all of them. And one is that these impulses are desired and welcomed, are enjoyable and pleasant, that the person wants more of them rather than less, and that if they constitute tensions, they are *pleasurable* tensions. The creator ordinarily welcomes his creative impulses, the talented person enjoys using and expanding his talents.

It is simply inaccurate to speak in such instances of tension-reduction, implying thereby the getting rid of an annoying state. For these states are not annoying.

2. DIFFERENTIAL EFFECTS OF GRATIFICATION

Almost always associated with negative attitudes toward the need is the conception that the primary aim of the organism is to get rid of the annoying need and thereby to achieve a cessation of tension, an equilibrium, a homeostasis, a quiescence, a state of rest, a lack of pain.

The drive or need presses toward its own elimination. Its only striving is toward cessation, toward getting rid of itself, toward a state of not wanting. Pushed to its logical extreme, we wind up with Freud's death-instinct.

Angyal, Goldstein, G. Allport, C. Buhler, Schachtel and others have effectively criticized this essentially circular position. If the motivational life consists essentially of a defensive removal of irritating tensions, and if the only end product of tension-reduction is a state of passive waiting for more unwelcome irritations to arise and in their turn, to be dispelled, then how does change, or development or movement or direction come about? Why do people improve? Get wiser? What does zest in living mean?

Charlotte Buhler (5) has pointed out that the theory of homeostasis is different from the theory of rest. The latter theory speaks simply of removing tension which implies that zero tension is best. Homeostasis means coming not to a zero but to an optimum level. This means sometimes reducing tension, sometimes increasing it, e.g., blood pressure may be too low as well as too high.

In either case the lack of constant direction through a lifespan is obvious. In both cases, growth of the personality, increases in wisdom, self-actualization, strengthening of the character, and the planning of one's life are not and cannot be accounted for. Some long-time vector, or directional tendency, must be invoked to make any sense of development through the lifetime (12).

This theory must be put down as an inadequate description even of deficiency motivation. What is lacking here is awareness of the dynamic principle which ties together and interrelates all these separate motivational episodes. The different basic needs are related to each other in a hierarchical order such that gratification of one need and its consequent removal from the center of the stage brings about not a state of rest or Stoic apathy, but rather the emergence into consciousness of another "higher" need; wanting and desiring continues but at a "higher" level. Thus the coming-to-rest theory isn't adequate even for deficiency motivation.

However, when we examine people who are predominantly growth-motivated, the coming-to-rest conception of motivation becomes completely useless. In such people gratification breeds increased rather than decreased motivation, heightened rather than lessened excitement. The appetites become intensified and heightened. They grow upon themselves and instead of wanting less and less, such a person wants more and more of, for instance, education. The person rather than coming to rest becomes more active. The appetite for growth is whetted rather than allayed by gratification. Growth is, *in itself,* a rewarding and exciting process, e.g., the fulfilling of yearnings and ambitions, like that of being a good doctor; the acquisition of admired skills, like playing the violin or being a good carpenter; the steady increase of understanding about people or about the universe, or about oneself; the development of creativeness in whatever field, or, most important, simply the ambition to be a good human being.

Wertheimer (30) long ago stressed another aspect of this same differentiation by claiming, in a seeming paradox, that true goal-seeking activity took up less than 10% of his time. Activity can be enjoyed either intrinsically, for its own sake, or else have worth and value only because it is instrumental in bringing about a desired gratification. In the latter case it loses its value and is no longer pleasurable when it is no longer successful or efficient. More frequently, it is simply *not enjoyed at all,* but only the goal is enjoyed. This is similar to that attitude toward life which values it less for its own sake than because one goes to Heaven at the end of it. The observation upon which this generalization is based is that self-actualizing people enjoy life in general and in practically all its aspects, while most other people enjoy only stray moments of triumph, of achievement or of climax or peak experience.

Partly this intrinsic validity of living comes from the pleasurableness inherent in growing and in being grown. But it also comes from the ability of healthy people to transform means-activity into end-experience, so that even instrumental activity is enjoyed as if it were end activity (17). Growth motivation may be long-term in character. Most of a lifetime may be involved in becoming a good psychologist or a good artist. All equilibrium or homeostasis or rest theories deal only with short-term episodes, each of which has nothing to do with each other. Allport particularly has stressed this point. Planfulness and looking into the future, he points out, are of the central stuff of healthy human nature. He agrees (1) that "Deficit motives do, in fact, call for the reduction of tension and restoration of equilibrium. Growth motives, on the other hand, maintain tension in the interest of distant and often unattainable goals. As such they distinguish human from animal becoming, and adult from infant becoming."

3. CLINICAL EFFECTS OF GRATIFICATION

Deficit-need gratifications and growth-need gratifications have differential subjective and objective effects upon the personality. If I may phrase what I am groping for here in a generalized way, it is this: satisfying deficiencies avoids illness; growth satisfactions produce positive health. I must grant that this will be difficult to pin down for research purposes at this time. And yet there is a real *clinical* difference between fending off threat or attack and positive triumph and achievement, between protecting, defending and preserving oneself and reaching out for fulfillment, for excitement and for enlargement. I have tried to express this as a contrast between living fully and *preparing* to live fully, between growing up and being grown.

4. DIFFERENT KINDS OF PLEASURE

Erich Fromm (8) has made an interesting and important effort to distinguish higher from lower pleasures, as have so many others before him. This is a crucial necessity for breaking through subjective ethical relativity and is a prerequisite for a scientific value theory.

He distinguishes scarcity-pleasure from abundance-pleasure, the "lower" pleasure of satiation of a need from the "higher" pleasure of production, creation and growth of insight. The glut, the relaxation, and the loss of tension that follow deficiency-satiation can at best be called "relief" by contrast with the *Funktions-lust*, the ecstasy, the serenity that one experiences when functioning easily, perfectly and at the peak of one's powers—in overdrive, so to speak.

"Relief," depending so strongly on something that disappears, is itself more likely to disappear. It must be less stable, less enduring, less constant than the pleasure accompanying growth, which can go on forever.

5. ATTAINABLE (EPISODIC) AND UNATTAINABLE GOAL STATES

Deficiency-need gratification tends to be episodic and climactic. The most frequent schema here begins with an instigating, motivating state which sets off motivated behavior designed to achieve a goal-state, which, mounting gradually and steadily in desire and excitement, finally reaches a peak in a moment of success and consummation. From this peak curve of desire, excitement and pleasure fall rapidly to a plateau of quiet tension-release, and lack of motivation.

This schema, though not universally applicable, in any case contrasts very sharply with the situation in growth-motivation, for here, characteristically, there is no climax or consummation, no orgasmic moment, no end-state, even no goal if this be defined climactically. Growth is instead a continued, more or less steady upward or forward development. The more one gets, the more one wants, so that this kind of wanting is endless and can never be attained or satisfied.

It is for this reason that the usual separation between instigation, goal-seeking behavior, the goal object and the accompanying effect breaks down completely. The behaving is itself the goal, and to differentiate the goal of growth from the instigation to growth is impossible. They too are the same.

6. SPECIES-WIDE GOALS AND IDIOSYNCRATIC GOALS

The deficit-needs are shared by all members of the human species and to some extent by other species as well. Self-actualization is idiosyncratic since every person is different. The deficits, i.e., the species requirements, must ordinarily be fairly well satisfied before real individuality can develop fully.

Just as all trees need sun, water, and foods from the environment, so do all people need safety, love and status from *their* environment. However, in both cases this is just where real development of individuality can begin, for once satiated with these elementary, species-wide necessities, each tree and each person proceeds to develop in his own style, uniquely, using these necessities for his own private purposes. In a very meaningful sense, development then becomes more determined from within rather than from without.

7. DEPENDENCE ON, AND INDEPENDENCE FROM, THE ENVIRONMENT

The needs for safety, belongingness, love relations and for respect can be satisfied only by other people, i.e., only from outside the person. This means considerable dependence on the environment. A person in this dependent position cannot really be said to be governing himself, or in control of his own fate. He *must* be beholden to the sources of supply of needed gratifications. Their wishes, their whims, their rules and laws govern him and must be appeased lest he jeopardize his sources of supply. He *must* be, to an extent, "other-directed," and *must* be sensitive to other people's approval, affection and good will. This is the same as saying that he must adapt and adjust by being flexible and responsive and by changing himself to fit the external situation. *He* is the dependent variable; the environment is the fixed, independent variable.

Because of this, the deficiency-motivated man must be more afraid of the environment, since there is always the possibility that it may fail or disappoint him. We now know that this kind of anxious dependence breeds hostility as well. All of which adds up to a lack of freedom, more or less, depending on the good fortune or bad fortune of the individual.

In contrast, the self-actualizing individual, by definition gratified in his basic needs, is far less dependent, far less beholden, far more autonomous and self-directed. Far from needing other people, growth-motivated people may actually be hampered by them. I have already reported (17) their special liking for privacy, for detachment and for meditativeness.

Such people become far more self-sufficient and self-contained. The determinants which govern them are now primarily inner ones, rather than social or environmental. They are the laws of their own inner nature, their potentialities and capacities, their talents, their latent resources, their creative impulses, their needs to know themselves and to become more and more integrated and unified, more and more aware of what they really are, of what they really want, of what their call or vocation or fate is to be.

Since they depend less on other people, they are less ambivalent about them, less anxious and also less hostile, less needful of their praise and their affection. They are less anxious for honors, prestige and rewards.

Autonomy or relative independence of environment means also relative independence of adverse external circumstances, such as ill fortune, hard knocks, tragedy, stress, deprivation. As Allport has stressed, the notion of the human being as essentially reactive, the S-R man, we might call him, who is set into motion by external stimuli, becomes completely ridiculous and untenable for self-actualizing people. The sources of *their* actions are more internal than reactive. This *relative* independence of the outside world and its wishes and pressures, does not mean of course, lack of intercourse with it or respect for its "demand-character." It means only that in these contacts, the self-actualizer's wishes and plans are the primary determiners, rather than stresses from the environment. This I have called psychological freedom, contrasting it with geographical freedom.

Allport's expressive contrast (1) between "opportunistic" and "propriate" determination of behavior parallels closely our outer-determined, inner-determined opposition. It reminds us also of the uniform agreement among biological theorists in considering increasing autonomy and independence of environmental stimuli as *the* defining characteristics of full individuality, of true freedom, of the whole evolutionary process (27).

8. Interested and Disinterested Interpersonal Relations

In essence, the deficit-motivated man is far more dependent upon other people than is the man who is predominantly growth-motivated. He is more "interested," more needful, more attached, more desirous.

This dependency colors and limits interpersonal relations. To see people primarily as need-gratifiers or as sources of supply is an abstractive act. They are seen not as wholes, as complicated, unique individuals, but rather from the point of view of usefulness. What in them is not related to the perceiver's needs is either overlooked altogether, or else bores, irritates, or threatens. This parallels our relations with cows, horses, and sheep, as well as with waiters, taxicab drivers, porters, policemen or others whom we *use*.

Fully disinterested, desireless, objective and holistic perception of another human being becomes possible only when nothing is needed from him, only when *he* is not needed. Idiographic, aesthetic perception of the whole person is far more possible for self-actualizing people (or in moments of self-actualization), and furthermore approval, admiration, and love are based less upon gratitude for usefulness and more upon the objective, intrinsic qualities of the perceived person. He is admired for objectively admirable qualities rather than because he flatters or praises. He is loved because he is love-worthy rather than because he gives out love. This is what will be discussed below as un-needing love, e.g., for Abraham Lincoln.

One characteristic of "interested" and need-gratifying relations to other people is that to a very large extent these need-gratifying persons are interchangeable. Since, for instance, the adolescent girl needs admiration per se, it therefore makes little difference who supplies this admiration; one admiration-supplier is about as good as another. So also for the love-supplier or the safety-supplier.

Disinterested, unrewarded, useless, desireless perception of the other as unique, as independent, as end-in-himself—in other words, as a person rather than as a tool—is the more difficult, the more hungry the perceiver is for deficit satisfaction. A "high-ceiling" interpersonal psychology, i.e., an understanding of the highest possible development of human relationships, cannot base itself on deficit theory of motivation.

9. Ego-Centering and Ego-Transcendence

We are confronted with a difficult paradox when we attempt to describe the complex attitude toward the self or ego of the growth-oriented, self-actualized person. It is just this person, in whom ego-strength is at its height, who most easily forgets or transcends the ego, who can be most problem-centered, most self-forgetful, most spontaneous in his activities, most homonomous, to use Angyal's term (2). In such people, absorption in perceiving, in doing, in enjoying, in creating can be very complete, very integrated and very pure.

This ability to center upon the world rather than to be self-conscious, egocentric and gratification-oriented becomes the more difficult the more need-deficits the person has. The more growth-motivated the person is the more problem-centered can he be, and the more he can leave self-consciousness behind him as he deals with the objective world.

10. Interpersonal Psychotherapy and Intrapersonal Psychology

A major characteristic of people who seek psychotherapy is a former and/or present deficiency of basic-need gratification. Neurosis can be seen as a deficiency-disease. Because this is so, a basic necessity for cure is supplying what has been lacking or making it possible for the patient to do this himself. Since these supplies come from other people, ordinary therapy *must* be interpersonal.

But this fact has been badly over-generalized. It is true that people whose deficiency needs have been gratified and who are primarily growth-motivated are by no means exempt from conflict, unhappiness, anxiety, and confusion. In such moments they too are apt to seek help and may very well turn to interpersonal therapy. And yet it is unwise to forget that frequently the problems and the conflicts of the growth-motivated person are solved by himself by turning inward in a meditative way, i.e., self-searching, rather than seeking for help from someone. Even in principle, many of the tasks of self-actualization are largely intrapersonal, such as the making of plans, the discovery of self, the selection of potentialities to develop, the construction of a life-outlook.

In the theory of personality improvement, a place must be reserved for self-improvement and self-searching, contemplation and meditation. In the later stages of growth the person is essentially alone and can rely only upon himself. This improvement of an already well person, Oswald Schwarz (26) has called psychogogy. If psychotherapy makes sick people not-sick and removes symptoms, then psychogogy takes up where therapy leaves off and tries to make not-sick people healthy. I was interested to notice in Rogers (23) that successful therapy raised the patient's average score in The Willoughby Maturity Scale from the twenty-fifth to the fiftieth percentile. Who shall then lift him to the seventy-fifth percentile? Or the one hundredth? And are we not likely to need new principles and techniques to do this with?

11. INSTRUMENTAL LEARNING AND PERSONALITY CHANGE

So-called learning theory in this country has based itself almost entirely on deficit-motivation with goal objects usually external to the organism, i.e., learning the best way to satisfy a need. For this reason, among others, our psychology of learning is a limited body of knowledge, useful only in small areas of life and of real interest only to other "learning theorists."

This is of little help in solving the problem of growth and self-actualization. Here the techniques of repeatedly acquiring from the outside world satisfactions of motivational deficiencies are much less needed. Associative learning and canalizations give way more to perceptual learning (20), to the increase of insight and understanding, to knowledge of self and to the steady growth of personality, i.e., increased synergy, integration and inner consistency. Change becomes much less an acquisition of habits or associations one by one, and much more a total change of the total person, i.e., a new person rather than the same person with some habits added like new external possessions.

This kind of character-change-learning means changing a very complex, highly integrated, holistic organism, which in turn means that many impacts will make no change at all because more and more such impacts will be rejected as the person becomes more stable and more autonomous.

The most important learning experiences reported to me by my subjects were very frequently single life experiences such as tragedies, deaths, traumata, conversions, and sudden insights, which forced change in the life-outlook of the person and consequently in everything that he did. (Of course the so-called "working through" of the tragedy or of the insight took place over a longer period of time but this, too, was not primarily a matter of associative learning.)

To the extent that growth consists in peeling away inhibitions and constraints and then permitting the person to "be himself," to emit be-havior—"radioactively," as it were—rather than to repeat it, to allow his inner nature to express itself, to this extent the behavior of self-actualizers is unlearned, created and released rather than acquired, ex-pressive rather than coping (17, p. 180).

12. DEFICIENCY-MOTIVATED AND GROWTH-MOTIVATED PERCEPTION

What may turn out to be the most important difference of all is the greater closeness of deficit-satisfied people to the realm of Being (29). Psychologists have never yet been able to claim this vague jurisdiction of the philosophers, this area dimly seen but nevertheless having un-doubted basis in reality. But it may now become feasible through the study of self-fulfilling individuals to have our eyes opened to all sorts of basic insights, old to the philosophers but new to us.

For instance, I think that our understanding of perception and there-fore of the perceived world will be much changed and enlarged if we study carefully the distinction between need-interested and need-disinterested or desireless perception. Because the latter is so much more concrete and less abstracted and selective, it is possible for such a person to see more easily the intrinsic nature of the percept. Also, he can perceive simultaneously the opposites, the dichotomies, the polari-ties, the contradictions and the incompatibles (17, p. 232). It is as if less developed people lived in an Aristotelian world in which classes and concepts have sharp boundaries and are mutually exclusive and in-compatible, e.g., male-female, selfish-unselfish, adult-child, kind-cruel, good-bad. A is A and everything else is not-A in the Aristotelian logic, and never the twain shall meet. But seen by self-actualizing people is the fact that A and not-A interpenetrate and are one, that any person is simultaneously good *and* bad, male *and* female, adult *and* child. One cannot place a whole person on a continuum, only an abstracted aspect of a person.

We may not be aware when *we* perceive in a need-determined way. But we certainly are aware of it when *we* ourselves are perceived in this way, e.g., simply as a money-giver, a food-supplier, a safety-giver, someone to depend on, or as a waiter or other anonymous servant or means-object. When this happens we don't like it at all. We want to be taken for ourselves, as complete and whole individuals. We dislike being perceived as useful objects or as tools. We dislike being "used."

Because self-actualizing people ordinarily do not have to abstract need-gratifying qualities nor see the person as a tool, it is much more possible for them to take a non-valuing, non-judging, non-interfering, non-condemning attitude towards others, a desirelessness, a "choiceless awareness" (14). This permits much clearer and more insightful perception and understanding of what is there. This is the kind of un-tangled and uninvolved, detached perception that surgeons and thera-pists are supposed to try for and which self-actualizing people attain *without* trying for.

Especially when the structure of the person or object seen is difficult, subtle, and not obvious is this difference in style of perception most im-portant. Especially then must the perceiver have respect for the nature of the object. Perception must then be gentle, delicate, unintruding, undemanding, able to fit itself passively to the nature of things as water gently soaks into crevices. It must *not* be the need-motivated kind of perception which *shapes* things in a blustering, over-riding, exploiting, purposeful fashion, in the manner of a butcher chopping apart a carcass.

The most efficient way to perceive the intrinsic nature of the world is to be more receptive than active, determined as much as possible by the intrinsic organization of that which is perceived and as little as possible by the nature of the perceiver. This kind of detached, Taoist, passive, non-interfering awareness of all the simultaneously existing aspects of the concrete, has much in common with some descriptions of the aesthetic experience and of the mystic experience. The stress is the same. Do we see the real, concrete world or do we see our own system of rubrics, motives, expectations and abstractions which we have projected onto the real world? Or, to put it very bluntly, do we see or are we blind?

13. NEEDING LOVE AND UNNEEDING LOVE

The love need as ordinarily studied, for instance by Bowlby (4), Spitz (28), and Levy (15), is a deficit need. It is a hole which has to be filled, an emptiness into which love is poured. If this healing necessity is not available, severe pathology results; if it *is* available at the right time, in the right quantities and with proper style, then pathology is averted. Intermediate states of pathology and health follow upon intermediate states of thwarting or satiation. If the pathology is not too severe and if it is caught early enough, replacement therapy can cure. That is to say the sickness, "love-hunger," can be cured in certain cases by making up the pathological deficiency. Love hunger is a deficiency disease, like salt hunger or the avitaminoses.

The healthy person, not having this deficiency, does not need to receive love except in steady, small, maintenance doses and he may even do without these for periods of time. But if motivation is entirely a matter of satisfying deficits and thus getting rid of needs, then a contradiction appears. Satisfaction of the need should cause it to disappear, which is to say that people who have stood in satisfying love relationships are precisely the people who should be *less* likely to give and to receive love! But clinical study of healthier people, who have been love-need-satiated, show that although they need less to *receive* love, they are more able to *give* love. In this sense, they are *more* loving people.

This finding in itself exposes the limitation of ordinary (deficiency-need-centered) motivation theory and indicates the necessity for "meta-motivation theory" (or growth-motivation or self-actualization theory).

I have already described in a preliminary fashion (17) the contrasting dynamics of B-love (love for the Being of another person, unneeding love, unselfish love) and D-love (deficiency-love, love need, selfish love). At this point, I wish only to use these two contrasting groups of people to exemplify and illustrate some of the generalizations made above.

1. B-love is welcomed into consciousness, and is completely enjoyed. Since it is non-possessive and is admiring rather than needing, it makes no trouble and is practically always pleasure-giving.

2. It can never be sated; it may be enjoyed without end. It usually grows greater rather than disappearing. It is intrinsically enjoyable. It is end rather than means.

3. The B-love experience is often described as being the same as, and having the same effects as the aesthetic experience or the mystic experience (18).

4. The therapeutic and psychogogic effects of experiencing B-love are very profound and widespread. Similar are the characterological

effects of the relatively pure love of a healthy mother for her baby, or the perfect love of their God that some mystics have described (7, 11).

5. B-love is, beyond the shadow of a doubt, a richer, "higher," more valuable subjective experience than D-love (which all B-lovers have also previously experienced). This preference is also reported by my other older, more average subjects, many of whom experience both kinds of love simultaneously in varying combinations.

6. D-love *can* be gratified. The concept "gratification" hardly applies at all to admiration-love for another person's admiration-worthiness and love-worthiness.

7. In B-love there is a minimum of anxiety-hostility. For all practical human purposes, it may even be considered to be absent. There *can*, of course, be anxiety-for-the-other. In D-love one must always expect some degree of anxiety-hostility.

8. B-lovers are more independent of each other, more autonomous, less jealous or threatened, less needful, more individual, more disinterested, but also simultaneously more eager to help the other toward self-actualization, more proud of his triumphs, more altruistic, generous and fostering.

9. The truest, most penetrating perception of the other is made possible by B-love. It is as much a cognitive as an emotional-conative reaction, as I have already emphasized (17, p. 257). So impressive is this, and so often validated by other people's later experience, that, far from accepting the common platitude that love makes people blind, I become more and more inclined to think of the *opposite* as true, namely that non-love makes us blind.

10. Finally, I may say that B-love, in a profound but testable sense, creates the partner. It gives him a self-image, it gives him self-acceptance, a feeling of love-worthiness and respect-worthiness, all of which permit him to grow. It is a real question whether the full development of the human being is possible without it.

REFERENCES

1. Allport, G. *Becoming*. New Haven: Yale University Press, 1955.
2. Angyal, A. *Foundations for a science of personality*. New York: Commonwealth Fund, 1941.
3. Arnold, M, & Gasson, J. *The human person*. New York: Ronald Press, 1954.
4. Bowlby, J. *Maternal care and mental health*. Geneva: World Health Organization, 1952.

5. Buhler, C. Maturation and motivation. *Dialectica*, 1951, 5, 312–361.
6. Buhler, K. *Die geistige Entwickling des Kindes.* (4th ed.) Jena: Fischer, 1924.
7. D'Arcy, M. C. *The mind and heart of love.* New York: Holt, 1947.
8. Fromm, E. *Man for himself.* New York: Rinehart, 1947.
9. Goldstein, K. *The organism.* New York: American Book Co., 1939.
10. Horney, K. *Neurosis and human growth.* New York: W. W. Norton & Co., 1950.
11. Huxley, A. *Heaven & hell.* New York: Harper, 1955.
12. Jourard, S. M. *Personal adjustment.* New York: Macmillan, 1958.
13. Jung, C. C. *Modern man in search of a soul.* New York: Harcourt, Brace, 1933.
14. Krishnamurti, J. *The first and last freedom.* New York: Harper, 1954.
15. Levy, D. M. *Maternal overprotection.* New York: Columbia University Press, 1943.
16. Lynd, H. M. *On shame and the search for identity.* New York: Harcourt, Brace, 1958.
17. Maslow, A. H. *Motivation and personality.* New York: Harper, 1954.
18. Maslow, A. H. Lessons from the peak-experiences. *Journal of Humanistic Psychology*, 1962, 2, 9–18.
19. Murphy, G. *Personality.* New York: Harper, 1947.
20. Murphy, G., & Hochberg, J. Perceptual development: Some tentative hypotheses. *Psychological Review*, 1951, 58, 332–349.
21. Nuttin, J. *Psychoanalysis and personality.* Chicago: Sheed & Ward, 1953.
22. Ritchie, B. F. Comments on Professor Farber's paper. In Marshall R. Jones (Ed.), *Nebraska symposium on motivation.* Omaha: University of Nebraska Press. Pp. 46–50.
23. Rogers, C. R. *Psychotherapy and personality change.* Chicago: University of Chicago Press, 1954.
24. Rogers, C. R. A theory of therapy, personality and interpersonal relationships as developed in the client-centered framework. In S. Koch (Ed.), *Psychology: A study of a science.* Vol. 3. New York: McGraw-Hill, 1959.
25. Schachtel, E. *Metamorphosis.* New York: Basic Books, 1959.
26. Schwarz, O. *The psychology of sex.* New York: Pelican Books, 1951.
27. Sinnott, E. W. *Matter, mind and man.* New York: Harper, 1957.
28. Spitz, R. Anaclitic depression. *Psychoanalytic Study of the Child*, 1946, 2, 313–342.
29. Tillich, P. *The courage to be.* New Haven: Yale University Press, 1952.
30. Wertheimer, M. Unpublished lectures at the New School for Social Research, 1935–36.
31. Wilson, F. Human nature and esthetic growth. In C. Moustakas (Ed.), *The self.* New York: Harper, 1956.
32. Wilson, F. Unpublished manuscripts on Art Education.

CHAPTER 3

Person and Personality: Sketch for a Psychotherapy of Self-Actualization

Vincent F. O'Connell

INTRODUCTION

Until the advent of the "Third Force" school, psychologists faced a forced choice in their theory and model of man. They could elect for the "approach from below" of behaviorism and the positivism which that implies; or they could opt for psychoanalytic theory and choose a model derived from the study of human illness. In basing itself in a psychology of human health, the "Third Force" school opens up a third pathway to the empirical study of man. It offers another approach to human illness and human health, a model and theory in which the higher motivations of man may be studied and understood, and an addition also to psychotherapy theory which enlarges the horizon of therapeutic procedures.

It is not my intention to spell out here how the "Third Force" school differs from behaviorism and psychoanalysis, nor shall I discuss to any extent how these three theories of man complement and complete each other. Following Maslow's observation that the "Third Force" school "adds to and supplements" the two other approaches rather than denying their findings, I shall address myself rather to the "supplementary" function of Maslow's theory, and show how it relates to a psychotherapy which is pertinent to the self-actualization process.

Oddly enough, Maslow might disagree on this point—that there is a therapy approach which is helpful at the self-actualization stage of the growth process. He says, for example:

This chapter is a discussion-commentary, written especially for the present volume, of Chapter 2: "Deficiency Motivation and Growth Motivation," by Abraham H. Maslow.

It is true that people whose deficiency needs have been gratified and who are primarily growth-motivated are by no means exempt from conflict, unhappiness, anxiety, and confusion. In such moments they too are apt to seek help and may very well turn to interpersonal therapy. And yet it is unwise to forget that frequently the problems and the conflicts of the growth-motivated person are solved by himself by turning inward in a meditative way, i.e., self-searching, rather than seeking help from someone. Even in principle, many of the tasks of self-actualization are largely intrapersonal, such as the making of plans, the discovery of self, the selection of potentialities to develop, the construction of a life-outlook. . . . In the later stages of growth the person is essentially alone and can rely only upon himself [Maslow, 1962].

I agree with Maslow when he says that interpersonal therapy (what he calls "ordinary" therapy) may be of little help at the later stages of growth, and the person does often need at this time to rely on himself. Where we may disagree is on whether the person is alone at this period of his development and can rely, then, only upon himself. For a person does not have to be thrown back upon himself, even at the later stages of his growth, if there is a therapy which is sympathetic to "full humanness." Such a therapy approach already exists, and it is now quietly finding a place for itself alongside behavior therapy and psychoanalysis. It thus offers the supplement that Maslow calls for, and therefore the possibility of an eventual comprehensive psychotherapy theory. Following Martin Buber (1958, 1966) I call this third form of therapy *dialogical psychotherapy*. In the following sections of this paper I shall attempt to sketch in some of the factors in this therapy approach and to show how it applies in the self-actualization stage of the growth process.

PERSON AND PERSONALITY

In the formulation I will be discussing, *person* and *personality* are not equivalent terms. When I speak of *person,* I am referring to the *central core,* or *center,* of the human organism, and to what Maslow calls *species-virtue*: the "deep down inside" feeling, the inner nature which "is in part unique . . . and in part species-wide" (Maslow, 1962). When a human individual experiences himself as person he knows himself a human being (*Mensch*) who is integrated with the world, a world to which he gives himself and to which he is responsible (able to respond). As person, which is to say, as one centered in the being which is himself, he knows no division between conscience and consciousness. For his awareness then is the awareness of what is: of the imperative with which species-virtue addresses each man as he comes forward in his development in community. At the level of his center, his inner nature, the person is a whole man who is at home in the world, and a partner in creation who lives with others in the life of community—and knows himself to be simply this!

Personality is something other than this central core. For as personality, the human individual functions on the periphery of himself, and his awareness is then of division in his consciousness.

When the human person experiences himself on the level of his personality he is still integrated with the world, but his integration is distant now from his centered awareness as person. As personality, his concern becomes the matter of his individuality. And his mode of integration with the world is the individual one (*der Mann*), that of individuality rather than of community (Buber, 1966). In this distance from his center, his lack of contact with his central integrity, resides much of his confusion, his anxiety, his fears, and his suffering. For the realm of personality is the realm of the transient and the popular, and the illusions that come and go in society, seemingly without order or plan; whereas the life of the center is the knowledge of what comes and goes, and also the peace which happens to the person when he "wakes up to" and "understands" what is.

The more the person gives himself to the concerns of personality, the more he gets caught up in the peripheral illusions we now call the "game" of social relations. He lives in society, it is true, but as an individual who "relates" to other single ones with whom he "communicates," and whom he seems forever unable to sound out. In this resides his loneliness, his aloneness, his alienation from himself and others, and his vulnerability to emptiness.

The individual who confuses his person with his personality may be aware to some extent of his organismic confusion (which emerges as symptoms of insecurity, anxiety, depression, etc.). He is less likely to realize that his confusion arises from the fact he is off on the periphery of himself and out of touch with his inner integrity. But what is even more unlikely is that he will realize that his present pattern of peripheral living is a circular one and that he lives for much of the time in a hypnotized state, much like the rat in the maze who has become so confused by conditioning that he jumps to the left on the sound of a buzzer.

No, person and personality are not the same. For while person (self) is just this simple awareness of what changes and is reborn (namely, centered consciousness which is free of attachments), personality is the state of illusion and attachment, the figment of imaginations which arise on the periphery of the person in the situation of conditioned deficiency needs.

PROBLEM AND MYSTERY

Because our time is a time of confusion regarding essential goals, it is also a time wherein *sensation* is becoming one of the primary modes of distraction from that confusion. The life of sensation is the life of the merry-go-round, one in which the deep in oneself is avoided and the peripheral factors in personality are cultivated. The life of sensation is the search for pleasure, the circular mode of escape. Followed to its limit, it becomes the kind of tragic life from which the *mystery* of the inner integrity has been dispelled and the individual encounters himself as a *problem* he cannot reconcile.

The existential writers have declared that ours is the time when men have become problematical for themselves. This formulation can be interpreted from many viewpoints. What I wish to draw from it now is Marcel's consideration that mystery and problem are different realms of being and that, when we reduce the former to the latter (that is, when we attempt to approach mystery on the level of a "scientific construct" in order to explain it), we end up, not in explaining mystery, but in explaining it away. In the Marcellian sense, the existence of mystery is not the consequence of insufficient data—something, in other words, that an enlightened science will eventually dispel. Science does dispel superstition and ignorance, but it does not dispel mystery, since the latter is the matter of the lived life rather than of genetic data. Mystery is the matter composing the foundation on which a person places his feet so he can look at, and take to himself, what is above, around, and below him. It is the substance of how he looks to the cosmos and the atom, how he can behold all and discover his life as something good and worthwhile—an event that is going somewhere other than into absurdity and nothingness (Marcel, 1965).

What happens to men when they explain away the mystery of their lives as a problem instead of giving themselves to their mystery and living it out? They then come upon the absurd: first, as an objective phenomenon that is "something out there"; and next, as a phenomenon that is "something in here," within oneself. The experience of that confrontation has been described by Sartre in *Nausea* (1947), and by Camus in *The Stranger* (1946) and *The Fall* (1957). Both writers describe a contemporary kind of life: that is to say, the life of men who have, so to speak, fallen from grace, men who have become alienated from their inner nature. As such, they are models of individuals who have become emptied of mystery; they become homeless wanderers, who pass the time with lives that are full of problems and explanations. When such an individual comes for psychotherapy today he is much like the character in *Waiting for Godot* (Beckett, 1954) who waits for something, he knows not what. And, as with the latter, who is "tired of breathing," we always find in some measure the flaccid breathing and the psychic scotomata which are the symptoms of present-day emptiness and alienation.

As I understand it, a life in which the awareness of mystery is no longer present is the situation which Buber calls the "absence of God" (1958), and which Maslow might call "the life without values." It is this life that *is* vulnerable to experiences of emptiness and alienation, and it is my opinion that a person living such a life (having rejected or lost touch with his central core and its mystery) must perforce fill himself with sensations. Yet sensations are the primary experiences of elemental living, *sans* the intuitional orientation and valuing which give "sense data" a purpose and a direction. In that situation resides the circularity of such a person's life, and the fact that his living seems to be going nowhere—except toward more of the same. Even intense sensations will eventually become dull and blunt until the moment he is "burned out": waiting for Godot!

Problems are solved and dissolved. Mysteries are not solved and dissolved: they are lived. Until now our classic question has been, "What is your problem?" Perhaps we can begin to interpose a more essential question, "What is your mystery?" as the starting point for what Maslow calls "the turning inward in a meditative way." For in the latter is to be found the path to the center, and the threshold to the self.

BEHAVIOR THERAPY

I mentioned earlier that Maslow understands his theory and the "Third Force" psychology as adding to and supplementing the approaches of psychoanalysis and behaviorism rather than denying their findings. But growth, or being, psychology is not just a supplement; it is also a corrective of some of the limitations of the other two approaches, and particularly of the deficiencies in their theories of man. I want to emphasize the latter aspect now, because it will be from this viewpoint that I shall discuss behavior therapy and psychoanalysis in order to highlight the corrective function in dialogical therapy. Although this will inevitably slight much that is valid in behavior therapy and psycho-analysis, and oversimplify their limitations in the bargain, a more comprehensive comparison now of the three theories is not possible.

Behavior therapy has its roots in learning theory, and it is a begin-ning attempt to generalize from the psychology of learning to a theory of motivated behavior in the human individual. In this resides its pres-ent limitation as a therapy approach. Behavior therapy seems to be primarily a straightforward reconditioning method in which the person is approached as a natural phenomenon in need of retraining. Insofar as it roots its theory and its approach in a form of positivism, it is a strictly *problem-oriented* approach; the individual is perceived, at least theo-retically, as a Humean bundle of associations in a state of complex conditioning. To that extent it ignores the so-called inner reality of the person, and his inner integrity as well, except as this central core is demonstrable in his observed behavior. Behavior therapy orients its approach toward modifying what Maslow calls deficiency-needs, and particularly as those needs are associated with fear, and most especially the fear of punishment. In the behavior-therapy approach the person is perceived again, at least theoretically, as a complex machine which is determined and unfree. And the approach, by and large, is a mechani-cal one, which attempts to condition the person to new stimuli, predom-inantly under the command of the therapist.

The behavior-therapy approach is valid when it perceives the mechanical and conditioned factors in the personality: namely, that the individual, at one level of his being, is a natural phenomenon which is conditioned and unfree; that he can be studied in his determinism, manipulated by determining environmental stimulation, and shaped or changed on that level of his phenomenology by determining techniques of reward and punishment. Inasmuch as behavior therapy hews to that line it is an approach of human engineering, and the individual is essentially an engineering problem (which is to say, a system of dy-namics and stresses which can be systematized), so it can be regarded as valid.

I see two principal limitations in the approach, both of which flow from limitations of its theory and method. In the first place, while the approach is correct in its assumption that the individual is conditioned and unfree on the bio-psychological level, it fails to take into account that the human organism, as person, is integrated and free, particularly when the person comes to full awareness of his pattern of conditioning (his "history"). In approaching the person as if he is merely a complex machine and an engineering problem, the behavior therapist discards the very levels of being that differentiate the human being from the universe of natural phenomena, namely, his potentiality for awareness, for transcendence, and for change in the present on the basis of his freedom.

The second limitation of the approach is its failure to realize that behavior therapy replaces one conditioned *trancelike state* with another conditioned, and equally *trancelike, state.*[1]

The situation, as I see it, is not just that of substituting one conditioned pattern for another but of replacing trancelike, unconsciously motivated behavior with unconditional behavior and wakefulness. That event does not occur on the basis of techniques, but with encounter on the personal level and between persons. Engineers, not therapists, build bridges, and to approach the person as if he is such an object is to condition him to become one.

PSYCHOANALYSIS

While the final limitation of behavior therapy is its positivism and a certain lack of humanity, the limitation of psychoanalysis is of a different order. The analytic approach has always placed the human individual at the center of its inquiry, even when, as in the early days of theory building, the couch may have become on occasion a Procrustean bed! Those days are now past, and the modifications of analytic theory up to the present help to keep it a viable, complex, and often elegant theory of man. It continues to be, at least in our time, the benchmark against which we measure psychological theories, whether the theory is an essentially new breakthrough or a supplement which describes a dimension of psychology which psychoanalysis ignores.

The place at which the analytic approach becomes limited and limiting (and where it demands the kind of supplement that Maslow asks for) is when it sees the terminus or goal of therapy as residing primarily in the ego and the personality, i.e., in coming to understand the peripheral levels of the self. But even when the goal is such, the analytic approach can be nonetheless instrumental, as far as it goes, in moving the person in the direction of his center, particularly when the analyst emphasizes creative adaptation to one's being motivations. What can be lacking at the end of the analysis (and this can be the function of the person himself as much as the philosophical approach of the analyst) is the full breakthrough to the center, and the realization, therefore, that the sense of individuality is a culturally determined phenomenon which is factual only when one lives on the periphery of oneself. Failing that breakthrough, the person continues to experience himself as individual, and an individual, moreover, who believes his life rests primarily in his own hands. True, in understanding his deficiency motivations through analysis the person does come to experience himself with a sense of immediacy and powerfulness that was lacking originally. In this, at least, he is freer, freer and ultimately more responsible to himself and others. But what he may still not realize is that his sense of individuality is an illusion, an illusion that will dissolve the moment he makes his first real contact with the center of himself! As long as that threshold is not in sight and understood as the goal toward which he directs himself, the person remains incapable of actualizing his sense of individuality and his personality.

It is not until the ego and its attachments (the self-concept, that which he prides himself on being, etc.) dissolve, and the sense of egoless understanding comes upon him that the person can be said to have come to terms with his conditioned pattern of behavior, and to have reached wakefulness. Until then, he is in varying stages of being a dreamer who imagines himself free (Perls, 1957; Rednick, 1962).

DIALOGICAL THERAPY

With the advent of the "Third Force" psychology we are beginning at last to have *three* theories which describe three of the possible modes of man's being in the world. We can study the person, via behaviorism, as a *bio-psychological mechanism* which is determined and unfree; we can approach him via psychoanalysis as an *interpersonal phenomenon* in his circumscribed individuality in society; and finally, now, via self-actualization theory, we can begin to know him as person, which is to say as *an open and transcending system of consciousness.*

In the "Third Force" therapy approach, which I have tentatively labelled dialogical therapy, there is much that is very old and little that is radically new. Many people have contributed to the approach, including psychoanalysts like Jung, Goldstein, Horney, Fromm, and Perls; theologians like Tillich and Buber; philosophers like Heidegger, Marcel, and Husserl; and several psychologists, of whom Maslow and Rogers are perhaps the best known. Maslow has been at the center of this movement from the beginning, and it would probably not be an exaggeration to say he has been one of its progenitors, as well as one of its most farsighted American theoreticians.

What, then, is dialogical therapy? And how does it differ from what Maslow calls ordinary therapy? It is not a *therapist* telling a *patient,* or *client*, what to do with his life, but rather an investigation into a person's ways of traveling about the world with himself and others. As an exploratory approach, it is phenomenological rather than analytic, experimental rather than theory-bound, and democratic rather than egalitarian (in the sense that the inequality of the persons is appreciated, where it exists, rather than being denied).

Dialogical therapy is not *treatment* in the medical sense that some pathological structure or process in the person is eliminated or changed by techniques—even including the technique of relationship. It is a dialogue of two (or more) persons, who come forward in their development, each in his own way and in the face of his limitations and potentialities, be these symptoms of "health" or of "illness."

It is necessary to set off both of these terms if the therapist is to address himself to the integrity of the person, and to permit the person to suffer through the crises of his growing without hindrance. Moreover, what may be "health" for the person may be "illness" for the therapist or for someone else. This is not a mere nosological relativism, but the recognition that growth implies crisis, and crisis, in turn, implies symptoms and suffering for the person who is doing the growing. Although this would apply, ideally, at any stage of the therapy process, it becomes an essential consideration when an ego aspect of the personality is in the process of dissolution. Since the crisis becomes acute at this time (and the symptoms can on occasion be alarming), a therapist who is not freed from his own conditioned state may then perceive the peripheral symptoms instead of the whole person. If, in his fears, he then reverts to his own periphery, difficulty in classification may occur (Maslow, 1962). However, when the approach is dialogical, the emphasis is not so much on *what the person is* as on *what needs to be done*. The focus is where it more properly belongs, namely, on paying attention to the growing possibilities of the person instead of classifying him under a rubric that diminishes the therapist's fears, as well as his participation.

As the person's individuality and his personality (his *ego*) can at times obstruct the path to his center, the dialogic approach views the therapist's personality and individuality as having little importance. The therapist realizes that he is involved in what happens and that what transpires in the dialogue with the other deepens his own understanding of himself and the other. He also knows that in his work of enabling the other to awaken to his conditioned state he too develops, deepening his contact with the center of himself. Dialogue is what enables this contact, not personality or individuality.

Dialogical psychotherapy differs from interpersonal psychotherapy to the extent that its mode of relationship is that of compassion, or impersonal sympathy. Impersonal sympathy implies full commitment to the other person, but at the same time serves to prevent the taking on of the other's symptoms, primarily because the therapist does not function at the level of *emotional* participation, where the need to interfere, to overwhelm, to change the other person is sometimes found.

Interpersonal psychotherapies root their procedures at the level of emotional participation insofar as they use the transference situation, among other means, to resolve the deficiency conflicts of the patient. This is perfectly appropriate when it is the *emotional factors* in the patient's living which require the work. The emotional component is found in dialogical therapy as well, specifically when it begins where interpersonal therapy leaves off. But the emotional component is seen here as a way station, where the person's tendency to identify himself with his emotions is worked through. This is not to say that emotions are frowned on, or that emotions are viewed pejoratively. Rather it is the recognition that much of what the person considers "emotional" may in fact be a conditioned response to his sense of individuality, namely, his sense of prior right to feel anything "he" pleases, and to express "himself" in the face of others as his mood demands. Dialogical therapy would see such a situation as an obstruction in the path to the center; it would work toward enabling the person to see how his *ego* (his conditioned pattern, his self-concept, etc.) continually draws him back to the periphery of his being in moments of fear, threat, suffering, etc.

A factor in a person's growth in therapy is the willingness of the therapist to allow him to suffer through to the end of his crisis as he becomes aware of his pattern of conditioning. In that regard, I believe Maslow is correct when he highlights the function of suffering (pain) in the growth process (Maslow, 1962). In suffering, the person confronts the habitual patterns of behavior that have stood in the way of his development. Suffering is *processing*: the person's confrontation with what he is, with how he is limited, and with how he is limiting himself in failing to meet the demands that his inner nature has created for him. To suffer in this way is to become aware of himself as a conflicted organism and to realize that the conflict has come into being because of his involvement with the periphery of himself. Suffering is the pain, the agony, of that realization, and, on occasion, the resistance to facing the situation in full awareness! But suffering is also, even in the moment of agony, the possibility that the person can take upon himself the responsibility for his own growth, that even in this suffering he may wake up to himself as center, as person.

Using the word "suffer" in this context is returning to an earlier etymological meaning of the word, "to allow," in the sense that the person allows himself to be aware of some present aspect of his behavior. To be aware of behavior is one thing; to change and modify that behavior is something else. And it is often a difficult, painful procedure because patterns of behavior exist as conditioned responses that "contain" systems of reward and punishment, that is to say, a "history."

Suffering (or what I call processing) is waking up to the realization of one's "history," one's conditioned state. It is to become aware of the hypnotic state of conditioned behavior and to acknowledge that, on that level of oneself, one is presently a machine which is determined and unfree. But wakefulness, awareness, self-actualization, involves not only the limiting structures that interpose and channel growth; awareness, self-actualization, also entails the discovery of the means whereby the personal situation may be changed. In suffering, which is the confrontation with one's conditioned pattern, the person makes this discovery. And in this discovery hope becomes a reality, hope for the present and hope for the future. (As psychologists, we have yet to take up the function and necessity of hope in the individual life. Does it not have something to do with suffering?)

Insofar as the therapist is willing to allow the person to suffer to the end of his crisis so he may grow, the dialogical-therapy approach intends that the therapist himself suffers as well. He does not suffer the person's symptoms. He suffers in his own way, much as we suffer the tragedy and pain of another in sympathy but not in kind. From the therapist's side this is often an active process rather than a passive one (though it can be this as well) of listening, reflecting, and interpreting what the other says and does. For dialogue, commitment to and involvement with the other, always entails in some measure the possibility that the therapist himself comes to understand some aspect of his own conditioned state even as he confronts the hypnotic state and suffering of the other. Dialogical therapy is to this extent a "no-holds-barred" approach, save that it does not transgress the absolute worth of the persons involved—their right to come forward in their development in their own way, at their own pace, and according to their own rhythm.

A "no-holds-barred" approach could be a harrowing and an even dangerous approach for the therapist and his partner if the therapist functioned at the level of emotional participation rather than that of impersonal sympathy. A kind of emotional contagion could happen then which would draw the therapy into a confluent situation so that one or the other of the partners could become a means to an end rather than an end in himself. Interpersonal therapy deals with that situation by always maintaining some barrier between the persons. And wisely so, because on the level of emotional participation there is the possibility of some unconscious conflict or attitude being transferred from one partner to the other as the dialogue moves into deeper levels of the person's conditioned state. When the therapist roots himself in impersonal sympathy, this confluent difficulty does not occur, for in impersonal sympathy, he is at his center. There he is enabled to remain open to what transpires in the relationship and to work with the person in the depth of his conditioned state, yet to remain free of the hypnotic trance of the other. In that way, through impersonal sympathy, he becomes the kind of presence and center of consciousness which makes change and growth more possible.

I have called this the mode of impersonal sympathy, the mode of compassion. It is the mode of loving too as it flows out from the center of the self and touches the heart of the other. But it is a loving that is now freed from deficiency-needs, and which is therefore the essential solvent of the state of hypnosis (because it is free, undetermined, and unconditional). Maslow describes that condition as Taoist, as non-interfering, as more disinterested, yet more generous, more eager to help, more fostering—the loving that creates the partner: "So impressive is this, and so often validated by other people's later experiences, that, far from accepting the common platitude that love makes people blind, I become more and more inclined to think of the *opposite* as true, namely that non-love makes us blind." (Maslow, 1962). I can only echo that, as non-love makes the person blind, loving enables him to see: the loving which sees to the center of the other, the loving which sounds out the other, the loving which cuts through the peripheral personality and the conditioned state until the heart of the other is touched and opens.

In essence, that is what dialogical therapy is: to wake the person up from his dreaming state of being on the periphery of himself, to journey with him in loving compassion as his partner, to experience with him the suffering, joys, and conflicts of his journey, to be there with him in the peak experiences which come from his center and which orient him eventually to himself, to the other, and to the universe which is his being—to do this and to be this until he steps over the threshold of his blindness, of his dreaming, until he wakes up and sees.

NOTE

1. I am referring now to the fact that conditioned behaviors work as such on the level of unconsciousness; and that the person is, so to speak, run by his conditioned pattern of behavior up to the moment he becomes aware of how these mechanical aspects of his organism operate. The therapy approach is limited if it fails to place the therapy itself at the person's disposal, to teach the patient how he is machinelike in certain of his responses. Since he does not do such teaching, the therapist works *on* the patient, but not *with* him, and fails to get complete cooperation, since, though the therapist has the theory, the patient lacks it. In my view, it is better to help the person to study the theory as it manifests itself in the present, in himself here and now. How else can he possibly become aware of the mechanical factors in himself and *choose* to let go of his repetition compulsion?

REFERENCES

Beckett, S. *Waiting for Godot*. New York: Grove Press, 1954.

Buber, M. *I and thou*. New York: Scribners, 1958.

Buber, M. *Knowledge of man*. New York: Harper & Row, 1966.

Camus, A. *The stranger*. New York: Alfred A. Knopf, 1946.

Camus, A. *The fall*. New York: Alfred A. Knopf, 1957.

cummings, e.e. *Poems, 1923–1954*. New York: Harcourt, Brace, 1954.

Marcel, G. *Being and having*. New York: Harper & Row, 1965.

Maslow, A. H. *Toward a psychology of being*. New York: Van Nostrand, 1962.

Perls, F. S. Personal communication. 1957.

Rednick, H. Personal communication. 1962.

Sartre, J. P. *Nausea*. Norfolk, Conn.: New Directions, 1947.

CHAPTER 4

A Commentary on Maslow's "Deficiency Motivation and Growth Motivation" from the Point of View of Humanistic Psychotherapy

Arthur Burton

As advances are made over the years on other fronts of behavioral psychology, concepts of human motivation in psychology show remarkably little change. Whether this is because scientific observations on motivation have historically been made on infrahuman specimens and basically continue to be made in this way, I do not know. But I do suspect that the flight from the human being in research on motivation is in some way influenced by Hebrew-Christian morality which determines what one should and should not study. It is by now well known that the areas of the person we select for study, and the hypotheses we select to prove or disprove, are often unconsciously determined. Indeed, the history of the ethical and religious aspects of man is one of cultural taboos and injunctions, and these surreptitiously creep into science. Nowhere are they so influential as in what we know as pure motivational research. To take one or two examples: The Hebrew-Christian outlook, antedated by its Greco-Roman origins, extols growth, learning, and purposiveness. But growth, learning, and purposiveness, in addition to being good, integrative, adaptive, satisfying, and healthy, have their negative aspects: they can be bad, maladaptive, arbitrary, frustrating, and unhealthy. For this reason a very real but hidden corpus of approved and

---

This chapter is a discussion-commentary, written especially for the present volume, of Chapter 2: "Deficiency Motivation and Growth Motivation," by Abraham H. Maslow.

disapproved areas of study of the motives of men appeared. How otherwise can one explain the serious lag in the study of the sexual drives of man and the extremely late appearance in science of Kinsey and Masterson, not to speak of Freud? The core of this reserve is a value judgment that the "impulse" is something to eradicate and that Christian guilt must follow expression of impulse. Impulses and drives in rats, and even anthropoid apes, are acceptable for study for they cannot in any sense be interpreted as human impulses; the species gap is the safety valve!

As we look at pure research on motivation today we find it minuscule, redundant, and defensive when it comes to describing higher-order behavior in man. What motivational psychologist, for example, has studied in his laboratory the creation of a poem or the making of a hero? What does the laboratory have to say about the experience of suffering and ecstasy, both of which have an exalted place in the history of man? Indeed, the most useful understanding of human behavior today comes from the very much maligned Sigmund Freud, and also from the industrial psychologists who, willy-nilly, have to help improve profits for the entrepreneur. If I am overstating the case somewhat, it is because the awakening has been so long in coming and a counter-reaction is sorely needed.

One of the first to sense and respond to this condition was Abraham Maslow. Maslow said, in effect, Let us look at what motivates human beings without epistemological prejudices of any sort, not even those belonging to science itself. Let us consider normal people as well as diseased ones, and let us search for wider parameters to describe their motives. Above all, let us recognize that the humanity of the individual is so unique and so purposeful as to color and abridge—in ways not yet known—the urgencies of even the most basic biological drives. We must study higher-order human motives without assuming a negation of lower-order ones, and without assuming the existence of an unvarying causal chain from lower motives to higher ones. The essential motivation of the person is truly that critical aspect of him which leads him to either freedom or bondage, to meaning or nihilism, to mental illness or health, and cannot be treated in so cavalier a fashion. All of this Maslow has in effect said, but he has not been content with merely saying it. He has offered new concepts—albeit few techniques—for approaching a proper investigation of human motivation in this way. That his approach is a first approximation and is incomplete is simply because understanding comes in stages and is not to be seized upon at any one creative moment.

To come back to our topic, self-deficit or self-immolation in the ascetic tradition or for modern political purposes would indeed be difficult to explain by present-day deficit-frustration hypotheses. Such asceticism in the history of man has often been purifying, ecstatic, and satisfying, and cannot be wished away by calling it mystical. The violence which deficit motivation does to contemporary understanding is that it totally ignores the intrasubjective interpretation one gives to a press need and, obversely, the intrasubjective interpretation of the fulfillment of that need. The equation of press need to satiation is not as direct as the motivational people would have us believe. Why do we know so little today about satiation (and its blood brother, boredom) when surfeit rather than deficit is becoming the learning problem par excellence in the modern world? Satiation does not necessarily lead to quietism and can indeed produce revolutions against entire cultures and societies, something that even hunger fails at times to do. Do we not therefore need a subdiscipline of surfeit motivation as well as deficit motivation?

What is involved here, of course, is a confusion of the levels of motivational description. Classical need psychology does without question operate in all organisms, including the human ones, but its usefulness tails off as the possibilities of the biological cortex increase. We might rather put it that, as the cortex becomes more organized, a highly complex relationship between basic needs and the multiple higher ones becomes operative. Symbolization in human beings, for example, integrates and capsulates a number of simultaneous motives and places them in a time/space framework not necessarily seen in a rat learning a maze problem. Symbols can themselves become second-, third-, or fourth-order motivating systems and have tremendous evocative power. They can even lead to the giving up of self-preservation or, on the other side, to the most significant engagements of life. The biological energy model obviously breaks down on the symbolic level; our tools are even insufficient to make adequate notations of processes on this level. It is one thing, however, to state frankly one's scientific inadequacies and another to assume gratuitously, as the motivational people have assumed, that need psychology applies across the board because this is what we know about motivation at this moment.

A secondary problem is our orientation toward the negative. No clinical psychologist, nor anyone in the healing arts, can, in my opinion, be adequately trained today until he has examined or treated some normal or, better yet, what I call non-diseased people. Similarly, no animal psychologist today is fully competent until he has observed his animals in their natural habitat, as has recently been done with anthropoid apes. Observations made in highly confining situations always have elements of the neurotic about them.

Motivation from such a positivistic/normative framework will, I believe, provide us with data we could hardly appreciate classically. We will find less deficit, less pathology, fewer needs, and more satisfaction than present research leads us to expect. As we become less deficit-seeking, optimism replaces pessimism as the tone of our research. One senses this in the naturalistic work of ethnologists such as Lorenz and Portmann. Although nature is apparently cruel and merciless with its species, the natural animal world is an optimistic, non-neurotic one, and deficit is not so overdetermined as it is in the affluent society. In some curious way deficit psychology has become unconsciously permeated with the subtle influences of Thanatos, so that "meeting needs" is a defensive oversubscription to the great need of staying alive, i.e., adaptation. The *quality* of the aliveness, however, has not been the concern of traditional motivational insight. Need psychology has very little to say about psychological time, psychological space, forlornness, nothingness, or even so prosaic a subject as money, which comes up in every single psychotherapy session and at every cocktail party. These are the basic parameters of human existence and motivation, but they become lost in traditionalism. Money motivation in American life, for example, pervades every aspect of individual and group living and is the symbolic if not the actual basis for the power and security struggles we all experience. It is also the way other nations see us. Every neurotic, specifically, is concerned in some way with money, and war, criminality, and divorce, as a few examples, are intimately involved with it. Yet we assume that tokens (or candy) from a mechanical feeding machine in conditioning experiments analogically explain John Paul Getty's drive to wealth and his specific being-in-the-world.

In all of this, Maslow's is the original cry against the classical views of motivation, and for this reason I place him in the humanistic camp. I concur almost completely with what he says in the chapter reviewed here but would update it in the following way, according to the new humanistic psychology. My formulations are obviously incomplete and exploratory, but they do have a rough validation in my work with non-diseased and neurotic/psychotic people.

1. *Ontogenetic Thrust.* The greatest motivator of all in the human being is some indigenous, forward-going impetus which drives the person into experience. This is not a search for homeostasis, equilibrium, or similar states, but a need for experiencing and involvement. It is

more than keeping sensory inputs loaded, and more than an exploratory or creative instinct. It is in a sense the urgency to escape from nothingness: the need for being-in-the-world and engaging it as the basic purpose of existence and as the fundamental premise of life. If existence precedes essence, as we believe, then every person must psychologically structure his life as a project, since nothing we know instinctually ordains him to it. His thrust in the direction of project we call ontogenetic thrust.

Depression and elation are the polarities by which ontogenetic thrust is pathologically distinguished, for on the one hand it is diminished and on the other, exaggerated. It is the force behind the individual life-style. Energy plays a part in it but does not explain it. The most creative people manifest it, but it is not limited merely to the creative. In psychotherapy one client persists because of it and recovers, and another is everlastingly frozen into a neurotic life-style he cannot live with. It is the motivational foundation of beauty and of cultural attainment in that it forces one to go beyond oneself, that is, into transcendence. Eros as a comprehensive instinct does not fully describe it, for Eros operates epiphenomenally on the side of ontogenetic thrust but not in place of it.

Ontogenetic thrust is fostered by a favorable maternal milieu but is not limited to it. Autism counters it, but it comes through idiosyncrasies of this kind. It is a form of "push" or qualitative "will to live" which gives low weighting to obstacles and detours or incorporates them into successive goals, one by one, until death intervenes. It is necessary to say again that such life thrust is not the equivalent of the need for rest, for homeostasis, or for equilibrium, since stasis or the lack of irritability and tension goes counter to its function. It is instead a general, propelling life force with the goal of ever higher successful resolutions of complex life designs which provide a meaning and purpose to existence. It is in essence the implicit recognition and acceptance of the self in the total cosmic setting, unification with it, and the assumption of the task of human centeredness in all things regardless of their absurdity.

2. *Intentionality.* The phenomenologists—I include Husserl here—were possibly the first to insist on the importance of this purely philosophical construct as it relates to the project which is life. As a derivation of this construct, I construe intentionality as intimately coupled with ontogenetic thrust to provide the basis for that being-in-the-world which we know as existence. Intentionality is thus for me that aspect of organized human perception which congeals the natural world into

a specific style of being sometimes known as "personality." It is that aspect of the sensing/knowing part of the person which distinguishes and organizes the world so that existence can be congealed into an identity. Ontogenetic thrust by itself is formless, but intentionality serves to give it specific direction. Such a conception of motivation is quite different from that we describe in terms of values, needs, and attitudes. These also serve to give direction, but are dependent on the more fundamental intentionality and seem to be indigenous to life rather than acquired by it. Intentionality is the basis for self-realization (and similar conceptions) in that it offers the basic need to be fully human. The human organism "intends" it as such and spends its life actualizing its intention. When the self cannot be human in this way, it becomes self-dystonic and falls into despair and anxiety.

Perception is thus not merely the act of apprehending the world, and it is not even using the products of perception for adaptational purposes. It is rather a numinous act of being which operates to bring ontic closure to the perceiver in that which he has perceived. It makes him fully what he is and is the fundamental structure for his ability to grow and change.

The primacy and universality of intentionality makes it mandatory that we consider it a drive in the conventional sense—albeit one below the level of consciousness—but this really begs the question. It is rather that the push for realization and fulfillment are the indigenous intention of the person, and the human condition is both the struggle for, and the sign of, it. Those perceptual distortions which we come to recognize as departures from reality in neurosis/psychosis are simply attempts to actualize the intentionality of the person when the most serious obstacles obtrude. They are in this sense not necessarily intrusive or sick, but salutary in that this is the only way actualization can occur.

Without intentionality, ontogenetic thrust by itself can assume ascetic or psychopathic qualities. On the other hand, intentionality without ontogenetic thrust results in the stasis, loneliness, and longing which are the nihilistic form, and are again seen in a variety of psychopathologies. The two have a fundamental relationship to each other which has not yet been satisfactorily defined.

It would be interesting and helpful to locate the intentionality function either in the nature of the person himself, possibly as one of his instincts, or as a learned process on a conditioning or similar basis. Even better yet would be some isomorphic physiological principle related to the cortex itself. In this way we could anchor what seems to be a mystical principle. It is true that intentionality is still only an inference, but it is one that is based not only upon philosophical investigations but on perception studies as well. The human being is a screening device in which the purpose of the screening is to further not only survival but a coherent style of existence as well as a total body-mind gestalt. This is also precisely the need of the newborn infant. It is never lost until death itself.

3. *Freedom-to-Be.* The word "freedom" has been much abused, particularly by those political scientists who use it for their own ends. It would be appropriate to our work as behavioral scientists to relinquish the word forever, but I see no way this can be done at present. It is the fundament of any humanistic system and also of any approach which claims to be meliorative. Without falling into a semantic morass, I interpret the freedom-to-be as the possibilities and potentialities for fully being. The freedom of the psyche is that comfort which permits one *to experience*—particularly those experiences which are denied one for one inhibitory reason or another. Humanness is reaching beyond the reflexes and instincts, the everlasting desire for those processes and events which are seen mostly in fantasy. The fact that one can allow oneself "to see" and "to reach" for what is distinctly human, even if frustration is inevitable, is freedom. The greatest constriction of all is the inability to allow oneself even to conceive of the Promised Land, and the neurotic fixation is just such a constriction. Fascism must "burn the books" for its own survival, for books open windows to freedom from the Fascistic structure. In this regard, Maslow correctly points out that healthy people are distinguished from the unhealthy by the following characteristics:

1) Superior perception of reality
2) Increased acceptance of self, of others, and of nature
3) Increased spontaneity
4) Increase in problem-centering
5) Increased detachment and desire for privacy
6) Increased autonomy, and resistance to enculturation
7) Greater freshness of appreciation, and richness of emotional reaction
8) Higher frequency of peak experiences
9) Increased identification with the human species
10) Changed (a clinician would say, improved) interpersonal relations
11) More democratic character structure
12) Greatly increased creativeness
13) Certain changes in the value system

But what Maslow fails specifically to note is that all these indicators of health are the products of a freedom-to-be and are derived from it. Once the person attains such an admittedly nirvana-like state, his creativeness, peak experiences, spontaneity, interpersonal relationships, human identifications, democratic attitudes, etc., all flower in the way described. He no longer has any need to suppress or inhibit them. They are the result rather than the cause of a new way of being-in-the-world and of experiencing it. The "little goals" of mankind, with their attendant anxieties, exert less pull when the major parameters of existence are uncovered in the freedom-to-be. Sooner or later all clients in treatment make this discovery.

The freedom-to-be has no marked distinguishing features as such and must once again be inferred from observed behavior and subjective report. On a collective basis, whether a nation is free-to-be is similarly determined, not by the size of its gross national product or its standing army, or even by the number of its Nobel laureates, but by its internal spirit and well-being and its contribution to the evolution of man, that is, the carrying forward of the humanism of man itself first remarkably keynoted by the Hellenic culture 2500 years ago (Hadas, 1967). In psychotherapy freedom-to-be evolves in a natural, predictable way as the therapy progresses, but the reason we have such a difficult time with the end point of treatment is that it is hampered by the refusal of both participants to recognize and act upon this sense of freedom. The therapist is invariably behind his client in this regard and sometimes actually keeps the client from it.

It happens again and again that even so-called unremitting psychosomatic symptoms drop by the wayside as the freedom-to-be grows in treatment. The resistances to such state of being are of course tremendous, which is why few people ever attain it and why it tends to come late in life. One clings not only to the security of the compelling culture but to the passions which limit and bind and which, at any rate, are momentarily titillating. Fromm pointed this out in cogent fashion some time ago, and I can only add that it is even more true today than when he wrote. The hippie, flower, and wider-consciousness movements reveal the individual and social need for this freedom-to-be and the price young people, at least, are willing to pay for it. That becoming a hippie is not the proper route to the freedom I am speaking of is only my opinion. So far as I know, no respectable clinician has called the hippie movement sick, and I myself do not believe it is. For me, it is the first non-sick indication on a large scale of the failure of Western civilization.

To find the self—to find authenticity, self-realization, individuation, or whatever term may be used to describe it—is not only a need but the entire basis for existence. Since death is so much more imminent in our century, the need for freedom, the will-to-meaning, and the cry for authenticity is that much greater. Apparently, the twentieth-century "battle of the symptom" has really been only a skirmish; the campaign itself is now on!

Thus my critical comment on Maslow's position is that it does not go far enough. I believe that if the chapter had been written today he would go beyond it in the way I have indicated above. Similarly, Maslow's B-love and D-love are in the true sense abstractions like all the others he condemns. Loving oneself and loving another are of one genre and pale in comparison to what I call F-love, love of freedom, in which love is merely the epiphenomenal aspect of authenticity, that is, ontogenetic thrust, intentionality, and the freedom-to-be.

REFERENCE

Hadas, M. *The living tradition.* New York: The New American Library, 1967.

CHAPTER 5

The Concept of the Fully Functioning Person

Carl R. Rogers

INTRODUCTION

I wrote this paper on one of our winter quarter "escapes" from the rigors of the Chicago winter. If my memory is correct, I wrote it in 1952–53 in a cottage (more accurately "shack") at the tip end of the island of Grenada, in the Caribbean, where we could look out on the angry Atlantic to the east, and toward the calmer, more colorful Caribbean to the west. When I had finished it I liked the paper.

Considerably later, I submitted it to a prominent psychological journal, whose editor wrote me in kindly fashion. It was clear he was dubious about its publication value; as a beginning he suggested that it be completely rewritten in much more objective terms. I knew I did not want to do this, but I was also aware of how remote it was from orthodox psychological thinking, so I simply had it duplicated for personal distribution.

As time went on, I drew on it very heavily for later, and perhaps more polished, articles. Consequently the reader may find large portions of this paper which he has met in some other context. Nevertheless, as I re-read it now, I am pleased to have it come out in its original form. I realize that many of the things I said very tentatively then I would say with more conviction, and with more objective evidence, now.

This chapter was voted, by the Editorial Board of the present volume, as one of the creative developments in psychotherapy, 1958–1968. From *Psychotherapy: Research, Theory and Practice*, 1963, 1, 17–26.

THE PROBLEM

I suspect that each one of us, from time to time, speculates on the general characteristics of the person who has completed psychotherapy. If we were as successful as therapists as we could wish to be, what sort of persons would have developed in our therapy? What is the hypothetical end-point, the ultimate, of the therapeutic process?

I have often asked myself this kind of question and have felt an increasing dissatisfaction with the kind of answers which are current. They seem too slippery, too relativistic, to have much value in a developing science of personality. They often contain too, I believe, a concealed bias which makes them unsatisfactory. I think of the commonly held notion that the person who has completed therapy will be adjusted to society. But what society? Any society, no matter what its characteristics? I cannot accept this. I think of the concept, implicit in much psychological writing, that successful therapy means that a person will have moved from a diagnostic category considered pathological to one considered normal. But the evidence is accumulating that there is so little agreement on diagnostic categories as to make them practically meaningless as scientific concepts. And even if a person becomes "normal," is that a suitable outcome of therapy? Furthermore recent years have made me wonder whether the term psychopathology may not be simply a convenient basket for all those aspects of personality which diagnosticians as a group are most afraid of in themselves. For these and other reasons, change in diagnosis is not a description of therapeutic outcome which is satisfying to me. If I turn to another type of concept I find that the person, after therapy, is said to have achieved a positive mental health. But who defines mental health? I suspect that the Menninger Clinic and the Counseling Center of the University of Chicago would define it rather differently. I am sure that the Soviet state would have still another definition.

Pushed about by questions such as these I find myself speculating about the characteristics of the person who comes out of therapy, if therapy is maximally successful. I should like to share with you some of these tentative personal speculations. What I wish to do is to formulate a theoretical concept of the end-point, or asymptote, of therapy. I would hope that I could state it in terms which would be free from some of the criticisms I have mentioned, terms which might eventually be given operational definition and objective test.

The Background from Which the Problem Is Approached

I shall have to make it clear at the outset that I am speaking from a background of client-centered therapy. Quite possibly all successful psychotherapy has a similar personality outcome, but I am less sure of that than formerly, and hence wish to narrow my field of consideration. So I shall assume that this hypothetical person whom I describe has had an intensive and extensive experience in client-centered therapy, and that the therapy has been as completely successful as is theoretically possible. This would mean that the therapist has been able to enter into an intensely personal and subjective relationship with this client—relating not as a scientist to an object of study, not as a physician expecting to diagnose and cure, but as a person to a person. It would mean that the therapist feels this client to be a person of unconditional self-worth; of value no matter what his condition, his behavior, or his feelings. It means that the therapist is able to let himself go in understanding this client; that no inner barriers keep him from sensing what it feels like to be the client at each moment of the relationship; and that he can convey something of his empathic understanding to the client. It means that the therapist has been comfortable in entering this relationship fully, without knowing cognitively where it will lead, satisfied with providing a climate which will free the client to become himself.

For the client, this optimal therapy has meant an exploration of increasingly strange and unknown and dangerous feelings in himself; the exploration proving possible only because he is gradually realizing that he is accepted unconditionally. Thus he becomes acquainted with elements of his experience which have in the past been denied to awareness as too threatening, too damaging to the structure of the self. He finds himself experiencing these feelings fully, completely, in the relationship, so that for the moment he *is* his fear, or his anger, or his tenderness, or his strength. And as he lives these widely varied feelings, in all their degrees of intensity, he discovers that he has experienced *himself*, that he *is* all these feelings. He finds his behavior changing in constructive fashion in accordance with his newly experienced self. He approaches the realization that he no longer needs to fear what experience may hold, but can welcome it freely as a part of his changing and developing self.

This is a thumbnail sketch of what client-centered therapy might be at its optimum. I give it here simply as an introduction to my main concern: What personality characteristics would develop in the client as a result of this kind of experience?

THREE CHARACTERISTICS OF THE PERSON AFTER THERAPY

What then is the end-point of optimal psychotherapy? I shall try to answer this question for myself, basing my thinking upon the knowledge we have gained from clinical experience and research, but pushing this to the limit in order better to see the kind of person who would emerge if therapy were maximal. As I have puzzled over the answer, the description seems to me quite unitary, but for clarity of presentation I shall break it down into three facets.

1. This person would be open to his experience. This is a phrase which has come to have increasingly definite meaning for me. It is the polar opposite of defensiveness. Defensiveness we have described in the past as being the organism's response to experiences which are perceived or anticipated as incongruent with the structure of the self. In order to maintain the self-structure, such experiences are given a distorted symbolization in awareness, which reduces the incongruity. Thus the individual defends himself against any threat of alteration in the concept of self.

In the person who is open to his experience, however, every stimulus, whether originating within the organism or in the environment, would be freely relayed through the nervous system without being distorted by a defensive mechanism. There would be no need of the mechanism of "subception" whereby the organism is forewarned of any experience threatening to the self. On the contrary, whether the stimulus was the impact of a configuration of form, color, or sound in the environment on the sensory nerves, or a memory trace from the past, or a visceral sensation of fear or pleasure or disgust, the person would be "living it," would have it completely available to awareness.

Perhaps I can give this concept a more vivid meaning if I illustrate it from a recorded interview. A young professional man reports in the 48th interview the way in which he has become more open to some of his bodily sensations, as well as other feelings.

Client: It doesn't seem to me that it would be possible for anybody to relate all the changes that you feel. But I certainly have felt recently that I have more respect for, more objectivity toward my physical makeup. I mean I don't expect too much of myself. This is how it works out: It feels to me that in the past I used to fight a certain tiredness that I felt after supper. Well now I feel pretty sure that I really am *tired*—that I am not making myself tired—

that I am just physiologically lower. It seemed that I was just constantly criticizing my tiredness.

Therapist: So you can let yourself *be* tired, instead of feeling along with it a kind of criticism of it.

Client: Yes, that I shouldn't be tired or something. And it seems in a way to be pretty profound that I can just not fight this tiredness, and along with it goes a real feeling of *I've* got to slow down, too, so that being tired isn't such an awful thing. I think I can also kind of pick up a thread here of why I should be that way in the way my father is and the way he looks at some of these things. For instance, say that I was sick, and I would report this, and it would seem that overtly he would want to do something about it but he would also communicate, "Oh, my gosh, more trouble." You know, something like that.

Therapist: As though there were something quite annoying, really, about being physically ill.

Client: Yeah, I am sure that my father has the same disrespect for his own physiology that I have had. Now last summer I twisted my back, I wrenched it, I heard it snap and everything. There was real pain there all the time at first, real sharp. And I had the doctor look at it and he said it wasn't serious, it should heal by itself as long as I didn't bend too much. Well this was months ago—and I have been noticing recently that—hell, this is a real pain and it's still there—and it's not my fault, I mean it's—

Therapist: It doesn't prove something bad about you—

Client: No—and one of the reasons I seem to get more tired than I should maybe is because of this constant strain and so on—I have already made an appointment with one of the doctors at the hospital that he would look at it and take an X-ray or something. In a way I guess you could say that I am just more accurately sensitive—or objectively sensitive to this kind of thing. I can say with certainty that this has also spread to what I eat and how much I eat. And this is really a profound change as I say—and of course my relationship with my wife and the two children is—well you just wouldn't recognize it if you could see me inside—as you have—I mean—there just doesn't seem to be anything more wonderful than really and genuinely— really *feeling* love for your own children and at the same time *receiving* it. I don't know how to put this. We have such an increased respect—both of us— for Judy and we've noticed just—as we participated in this—we have noticed such a tremendous change in her—it seems to be a pretty deep kind of thing.

Therapist: It seems to me you are saying that you can listen more accurately to yourself. If your body says it's tired, you listen to it and believe it, instead of criticizing it; if it's in pain you can listen to that; if the feeling is really loving your wife or children, you can *feel* that, and it seems to show up in the differences in them too.

Here, in a relatively minor but symbolically important excerpt, can be seen much of what I have been trying to say about openness to experience. Formerly he could not freely feel pain or illness, because being ill meant being unacceptable. Neither could he feel tenderness and love for his child, because such feelings meant being weak, and he had to maintain his facade of being strong. But now he can be genuinely open to the experience of his organism—he can be tired when he is tired, he can feel pain when his organism is in pain, he can freely experience the love he feels for his daughter, and he can also feel and express annoyance toward her, as he goes on to say in the next portion of the interview. He can fully live the experiences of his total organism, rather than shutting them out of awareness.

I have used this concept of availability to awareness to try to make clear what I mean by openness to experience. This might be misunderstood. I do not mean that this individual would be self-consciously aware of all that was going on within himself, like the centipede who became aware of all of his legs. On the contrary, he would be free to live a feeling subjectively, as well as be aware of it. He might experience love, or pain, or fear, living in this attitude subjectively. Or he might abstract himself from this subjectivity and realize in awareness, "I am in pain," "I am afraid," "I do love." The crucial point is that there would be no barriers, no inhibitions, which would prevent the full experiencing of whatever was organismically present, and availability to awareness is a good measure of this absence of barriers.

2. *This person would live in an existential fashion.* I believe it would be evident that for the person who was fully open to his experience, completely without defensiveness, each moment would be new. The complex configuration of inner and outer stimuli which exists in this moment has never existed before in just this fashion. Consequently our hypothetical person would realize that "What I will be in the next moment, and what I will do, grows out of that moment, and cannot be predicted in advance either by me or by others." Not infrequently we find clients expressing this sort of feeling. Thus one, at the end of therapy, says in rather puzzled fashion, "I haven't finished the job of integrating and reorganizing myself, but that's only confusing, not discouraging, now that I realize this is a continuing process. . . . It is exciting, sometimes upsetting, but deeply encouraging to feel yourself in action and apparently knowing where you are going even though you don't always consciously know where that is."

One way of expressing the fluidity which would be present in such existential living is to say that the self and personality would emerge *from* experience, rather than experience being translated or twisted to fit a preconceived self-structure. It means that one becomes a participant in and an observer of the ongoing process of organismic experience, rather than being in control of it. On another occasion I have tried to describe how this type of living seems to me. "This whole train of experiencing, and the meaning that I have thus far discovered in it, seem to have launched me on a process which is both fascinating and at times a little frightening. It seems to mean letting my experience carry me on, in a direction which appears to be forward, toward goals that I can but dimly define, as I try to understand at least the current meaning of that experience. The sensation is that of floating with a complex stream of experience, with the fascinating possibility of trying to comprehend its everchanging complexity" (Rogers, 1958).

Such living in the moment, then, means an absence of rigidity, of tight organization, of the imposition of structure on experience. It means instead a maximum of adaptability, a discovery of structure *in* experience, a flowing, changing organization of self and personality.

The personality and the self would be continually in flux, the only stable elements being the physiological capacities and limitations of the organism, the continuing or recurrent organismic needs for survival, enhancement, food, affection, sex, and the like. The most stable personality traits would be openness to experience, and the flexible resolution of the existing needs in the existing environment.

3. This person would find his organism a trustworthy means of arriving at the most satisfying behavior in each existential situation. He would do what "felt right" in this immediate moment and he would find this in general to be a competent and trustworthy guide to his behavior.

If this seems strange, let me explain the reasoning behind it. Since he would be open to his experience he would have access to all of the available data in the situation, on which to base his behavior; the social demands, his own complex and possibly conflicting needs; his memories of similar situations, his perception of the uniqueness of this situation, etc., etc. The "dynamic system" of each situation, as Krech (1951) would term it, would be very complex indeed. But he could permit his total organism, his consciousness participating, to consider each stimulus, need, and demand, its relative intensity and importance, and out of this complex weighing and balancing, discover that course of action which would come closest to satisfying all his needs in the situation. An analogy which might come close to a description would be to compare this person to a giant electronic computing machine. Since he is open to his experience, all of the data from his sense impressions, from his memory, from previous learning, from his visceral and internal states, is fed into the machine. The machine takes all of these multitudinous pulls and forces which were fed in as data, and quickly computes the course of action which would be the most economical vector of need satisfaction in this existential situation. This is the behavior of our hypothetical person.

The defects which in most of us make this process untrustworthy are the inclusion of non-existential material, or the absence of data. It is when memories and previous learnings are fed into the computation as if they were *this* reality, and not memories and learnings, that erroneous behavioral answers arise. Or when certain threatening experiences are inhibited from awareness, and hence are withheld from the computation or fed into it in distorted form, this too produces error. But our hypothetical person would find his organism thoroughly trustworthy, because all the available data would be used, and it would be present in accurate rather than distorted form. Hence his behavior would come as close as possible to satisfying all his needs—for enhancement, for affiliation with others, and the like.

In this weighing, balancing, and computation, his organism would not by any means be infallible. It would always give the best possible answer for the available data, but sometimes data would be missing. Because of the element of openness to experience however, any errors, any following of behavior which was not satisfying would be quickly corrected. The computations, as it were, would always be in process of being corrected, because they would be continually checked in behavior.

Perhaps you will not like my analogy of an electronic computing machine. Let me put it in more human terms. The client I previously quoted found himself expressing annoyance to his daughter when he "felt like it," as well as affection. Yet he found himself doing it in a way which not only released tension in himself, but which freed this small girl to voice her annoyances. He describes the differences between communicating his annoyance and directing his feelings of anger at, or imposing them on her. He continues, "Because it just doesn't feel like I'm imposing my feelings on her, and it seems to me I must show it on my face. Maybe she sees it as 'Yes, daddy is angry, but I don't have to cower.' Because she never *does* cower. This in itself is a topic for a novel, it just feels that good." In this instance, being open to his experience, he selects, with astonishing intuitive skill, a subtly guided course of behavior which meets his need for release of angry tension, but also satisfies his need to be a good father, and his need to find satisfaction in his daughter's healthy development. Yet he achieves all this by simply doing the thing that feels right to him.

On quite another level, it seems to be this same kind of complex organismic selection that determines the scientific behavior of a man like Einstein, holding him toward a given direction, long before he can give any completely conscious and rational basis for it. During this initial period he is simply trusting his total organismic reaction. And he says, "During all those years there was a feeling of direction, of going straight toward something concrete. It is, of course, very hard to express that feeling in words; but it was decidedly the case, and clearly to be distinguished from later considerations about the rational form of the solution" (Wertheimer, 1945). This is the type of behavior which is also, I believe, characteristic of the person who has gained greatly from therapy.

THE FULLY FUNCTIONING PERSON

I should like to pull together these three threads into one more unified descriptive strand. It appears that the person who emerges from a theoretically optimal experience of client-centered therapy is then a fully functioning person. He is able to live fully in and with each and all of his feelings and reactions. He is making use of all his organic equipment to sense, as accurately as possible, the existential situation within and without. He is using all of the data his nervous system can thus supply, using it in awareness, but recognizing that his total organism may be, and often is, wiser than his awareness. He is able to permit his total organism to function in all its complexity in selecting, from the multitude of possibilities, that behavior which in this moment of time will be most generally and genuinely satisfying. He is able to trust his organism in this functioning, not because it is infallible, but because he can be fully open to the consequences of each of his actions and correct them if they prove to be less than satisfying.

He is able to experience all of his feelings, and is afraid of none of his feelings; he is his own sifter of evidence, but is open to evidence from all sources; he is completely engaged in the process of being and becoming himself, and thus discovers that he is soundly and realistically social; he lives completely in this moment, but learns that this is the soundest living for all time. He is a fully functioning organism, and because of the awareness of himself which flows freely in and through his experiences, he is a fully functioning person.

SOME IMPLICATIONS OF THIS DESCRIPTION

This, then, is my tentative definition of the hypothetical end-point of therapy, my description of the ultimate picture which our actual clients approach but never fully reach. I have come to like this description, both because I believe it is rooted in and is true of our clinical experience, and also because I believe it has significant clinical, scientific, and philosophical implications. I should like to present some of these ramifications and implications as I see them.

A. APPROPRIATE TO CLINICAL EXPERIENCE

In the first place it appears to contain a basis for the phenomena of clinical experience in successful therapy. We have noted the fact that the client develops a locus of evaluation within himself; this is consistent with the concept of the trustworthiness of the organism. We have commented on the client's satisfaction at being and becoming himself, a satisfaction associated with functioning fully. We find that clients tolerate a much wider range and variety of feelings, including feelings which were formerly anxiety-producing; and that these feelings are usefully integrated into their more flexibly organized personalities. In short, the concepts I have stated appear to be sufficiently broad to contain the positive outcomes of therapy as we know it.

B. LEADS TOWARD OPERATIONAL HYPOTHESES

While the formulation as given is admittedly speculative, it leads, I believe, in the direction of hypotheses which may be stated in rigorous and operational terms. Such hypotheses would be culture-free or universal, I trust, rather than being different for each culture.

It is obvious that the concepts given are not easily tested or measured, but with our growing research sophistication in this area, their measurability is not an unreasonable hope. We are already making one very crude attempt to get at the concept of openness to experience.

C. EXPLAINS PERPLEXING CONTRADICTIONS

Over the last several years there have been an accumulation of several perplexing bits of evidence regarding the relationship between therapy and projective tests. They are the stubborn facts that simply cannot be fitted comfortably into the overall trend of research findings. I will describe each of these in general terms, so as not to embarrass the persons involved.

a. On an early case which was regarded by several criteria as very successful, a young diagnostician studied the post-therapy Rorschach and exclaimed, "My God! Does the therapist realize this client is still psychotic!"

b. Rorschachs on ten cases were submitted to an experienced psychodiagnostician. He found no evidence of constructive change in the Rorschachs, only slight fluctuations. This result was published. Later a more experienced clinician who was also a Freudian therapist analyzed the Rorschachs on the same ten cases. She found decided evidence of therapeutic progress. This seemed confusing, and was never published.

c. When a clinician studied the pre and post Rorschachs of fifty-six clients, her impression as a diagnostician studying the Rorschachs was that no progress was shown. Later, when objective rating scales had been developed, measuring traits which theoretically should change in client-centered therapy, it was found that significant change has occurred in terms of these scales.

d. On one case, studied and analyzed in great detail, the TATs were analyzed by a clinician who was experienced in projective tests and strongly oriented toward therapy, but who knew nothing of the case. She found striking evidence of progress. When the same set of TATs was later analyzed on the basis of objective scales set up by a diagnostician, no change was found.

e. On a series of cases judged by therapists to range from little to much success, there was a highly negative correlation between the therapist's ratings and the analysis of the TATs on the basis of objective scales set up by a diagnostician. The cases judged most successful by the therapist were rated least successful on the TAT scales. The cases rated most successful on the TAT scales were regarded by the therapists as still decidedly defensive.

These contradictions now begin to fall into a sensible pattern, in terms of the theory I have been presenting. It would appear, though at the moment I state this very tentatively, that when projective tests are analyzed following therapy the very elements which the therapeutically oriented worker sees as evidence of progress, are seen by the diagnostically oriented worker as evidence of disorganization. What one sees as fluidity, openness to experience, existential rather than rigid organization, may be seen by another as extreme lack of defense, disorganization, near-chaos. This, at any rate, is what is tentatively suggested by our evidence.

It seems possible then that the openness, adaptability, and existential living which is characteristic of the person who has received maximal aid from therapy, may be seen by a diagnostician, operating in terms of population norms, as signs that the person is "falling apart." What to the client are deeply enriching qualities in his life, may in terms of population norms be seen as deviant pathology. This is a meaningful possible explanation of what otherwise are disconnected and contradictory facts.

D. CREATIVITY AS AN OUTCOME

One of the elements which pleases me in the theoretical formulation I have given is that this is a creative person. This person at the hypothetical end-point of therapy could well be one of Maslow's "self-actualizing people." With his sensitive openness to his world, his trust of his own ability to form new relationships with his environment, he would be the type of person from whom creative products and creative living emerge. He would not necessarily be "adjusted" to his culture, and he would almost certainly not be a conformist. But at any time and in any culture he would live constructively, in as much harmony with his culture as a balanced satisfaction of needs demanded. In some cultural situations he might in some ways be very unhappy, but he would continue to be himself, and to behave in such a way as to provide the maximum satisfaction of his deepest needs.

Such a person would, I believe, be recognized by the student of evolution as the type most likely to adapt and survive under changing environmental conditions. He would be able creatively to make sound adjustments to new as well as old conditions. He would be a fit vanguard of human evolution.

E. BUILDS ON TRUSTWORTHINESS OF HUMAN NATURE

It will have been evident that one implication of the view I have been presenting is that the basic nature of the human being, when functioning freely, is constructive and trustworthy. For me this is an inescapable conclusion from a quarter century of experience in psychotherapy. When we are able to free the individual from defensiveness, so that he is open to the wide range of his own needs, as well as the wide range of environmental and social demands, his reactions may be trusted to be positive, forward-moving, constructive. We do not need to ask who will socialize him, for one of his own deepest needs is for affiliation with and communication with others. When he is fully himself, he cannot help but be realistically socialized. We do not need to ask who will control his aggressive impulses, for when he is open to all of his impulses, his need to be liked by others and his tendency to give affection are as strong as his impulses to strike out or to seize for himself. He will be aggressive in situations in which aggression is realistically appropriate, but there will be no runaway need for aggression. His total behavior, in these and other areas, when he is open to all his experience, is balanced and realistic, behavior which is appropriate to the survival and enhancement of a highly social animal.

I have little sympathy with the rather prevalent concept that man is basically irrational, and thus his impulses, if not controlled, would lead to destruction of others and self. Man's behavior is exquisitely rational, moving with subtle and ordered complexity toward the goals his organism is endeavoring to achieve. The tragedy for most of us is that our defenses keep us from being aware of this rationality, so that consciously we are moving in one direction, while organismically we are moving in another. But in our hypothetical person there would be no such barriers, and he would be a participant in the rationality of his organism. The only control of impulses which would exist or which would prove necessary, is the natural and internal balancing of one need against another, and the discovery of behaviors which follow the vector most closely approximating the satisfaction of all needs. The experience of extreme satisfaction of one need (for aggression, or sex, etc.) in such a way as to do violence to the satisfaction of other needs (for companionship, tender relationship, etc.)—an experience very common in the defensively organized person—would simply be unknown in our hypothetical individual. He would participate in the vastly complex self-regulatory activities of his organism—the psychological as well as physiological thermostatic controls—in such a fashion as to live harmoniously, with himself and with others.

F. BEHAVIOR DEPENDABLE BUT NOT PREDICTABLE

There are certain implications of this view of the optimum human being which have to do with predictability, which I find fascinating to contemplate. It should be clear from the theoretical picture I have sketched that the particular configuration of inner and outer stimuli in which the person lives at this moment has never existed in precisely this fashion before; and also that his behavior is a realistic reaction to an accurate apprehension of all this internalized evidence. It should therefore be clear that this person will seem to himself to be dependable but not specifically predictable. If he is entering a new situation with an authority figure, for example, he cannot predict what his behavior will be. It is contingent upon the behavior of this authority figure, and his own immediate internal reactions, desires, etc., etc. He can feel confident that he will behave appropriately, but he has no knowledge in advance of what he will do. I find this point of view often expressed by clients, and I believe it is profoundly important.

But what I have been saying about the client himself, would be equally true of the scientist studying his behavior. The scientist would find this person's behavior lawful, and would find it possible to post-dict it, but could not forecast or predict the specific behavior of this individual. The reasons are these. If the behavior of our hypothetical friend is determined by the accurate sensing of all of the complex evidence which exists in this moment of time, and by that evidence only, then the data necessary for prediction is clear. It would be necessary to have instruments available to measure every one of the multitudinous stimuli of the input, and a mechanical computer of great size to calculate the most economical vector of reaction. While this computation is going on our hypothetical person has already made this complex summation and appraisal within his own organism, and has acted. Science, if it can eventually collect all this data with sufficient accuracy, should theoretically be able to analyze it and come to the same conclusion and thus postdict his behavior. It is doubtful that it could ever collect and analyze the data instantaneously and this would be necessary if it were to predict the behavior before it occurred.

It may clarify this if I borrow and extend some of the thinking of my colleague, Dr. Hedda Bolgar, and point out that it is the maladjusted person whose behavior can be specifically predicted, and some loss of predictability should be evident in every increase in openness to experience and existential living. In the maladjusted person, behavior is predictable precisely because it is rigidly patterned. If such a person has learned a pattern of hostile reaction to authority, and if this "badness of authority" is a part of his conception of himself-in-relation-to-authority, and if because of this he denies or distorts any experience which should supply contradictory evidence, *then* his behavior is specifically predictable. It can be said with assurance that when he enters a new situation with an authority figure, he will be hostile to him. But the more that therapy, or any therapeutic type of experience, increases the openness to experience of this individual, the less predictable his behavior will be. This receives some crude confirmation from the Michigan study (Kelley, 1951) attempting to predict success in clinical psychology. The predictions for the men who were in therapy during the period of investigation were definitely less accurate than for the group as a whole.

What I am saying here has a bearing on the common statement that the long range purpose of psychology as a science is "the prediction and control of human behavior," a phrase which for me has had disturbing philosophical implications. I am suggesting that as the individual approaches this optimum of complete functioning his behavior, though always lawful and determined, becomes more difficult to predict; and though always dependable and appropriate, more difficult to control. This would mean that the science of psychology, at its highest levels, would perhaps be more of a science of understanding than a science of prediction; an analysis of the lawfulness of that which has occurred, rather than primarily a control of what is about to occur.

In general this line of thought is confirmed by our clients, who feel confident that what they will do in a situation will be appropriate and comprehensible and sound, but who cannot predict in advance how they will behave. It is also confirmed by our experience as therapists, where we form a relationship in which we can be sure the person will discover himself, become himself, learn to function more freely, but where we cannot forecast the specific content of the next statement, of the next phase of therapy, or of the behavioral solution the client will find to a given problem. The general direction is dependable, and we can rest assured it will be appropriate; but its specific content is unpredictable.

G. RELATES FREEDOM AND DETERMINISM

I should like to stray still further afield, and give one final philosophical implication which has meaning for me. For some time I have been perplexed over the living paradox which exists in psychotherapy between freedom and determinism. In the therapeutic relationship some of the most compelling subjective experiences are those in which the client feels within himself the power of naked choice. He is *free*—to become himself or to hide behind a facade; to move forward or to retrogress; to behave in ways which are destructive of self and others, or in ways which are enhancing; quite literally free to live or die, in both the physiological and psychological meaning of those terms. Yet as we enter this field of psychotherapy with objective research methods, we are, like any other scientist, committed to a complete determinism. From this point of view every thought, feeling, and action of the client is determined by what precedes it. The dilemma I am trying to describe is no different than that found in other fields—it is simply brought to sharper focus. I tried to bring this out in a paper written a year ago contrasting these two views. In the field of psychotherapy, "Here is the maximizing of all that is subjective, inward, personal; here a relationship is lived, not examined, and a person, not an object, emerges, a person who feels, chooses, believes, acts, not as an automaton, but as a person. And here too is the ultimate in science—the objective exploration of the most subjective aspects of life; the reduction to hypotheses, and eventually to theorems, of all that has been regarded as most personal, most completely inward, most thoroughly a private world" (Rogers, 1952).

Now I am not so naive as to suppose that I have resolved the dilemma between the subjective and the objective, between freedom and determinism. Nevertheless, in terms of the definition I have given of the fully functioning person, that relationship can be seen in a fresh perspective. We could say that in the optimum of therapy the person rightfully experiences the most complete and absolute freedom. He wills or chooses to follow the course of action which is the most economical vector in relation to all the internal and external stimuli, because it is that behavior which will be most deeply satisfying. But this is the same course of action which from another vantage point may be said to be determined by all the factors in the existential situation. Let us contrast this with the picture of the person who is defensively organized. He wills or chooses to follow a given course of action, but finds that he *cannot* behave in the fashion that he chooses. He is determined by the factors in the existential situation, but these factors include his defensiveness, his denial or distortion of some of the relevant data. Hence it is certain that his behavior will be less than fully satisfying. His behavior is determined, but he is not free to make an effective choice. The fully functioning person, on the other hand, not only experiences, but utilizes, the most absolute freedom when he spontaneously, freely, and voluntarily chooses and wills that which is absolutely determined.

I am quite aware that this is not a new idea to the philosopher, but it has been refreshing to come upon it from a totally unexpected angle, in analyzing a concept in personality theory. For me it provides the rationale for the subjective reality of absolute freedom of choice, which is so profoundly important in therapy, and at the same time the rationale for the complete determinism which is the very foundation stone of science. With this framework I can enter subjectively the experience of naked choice which the client is experiencing; I can also as a scientist, study his behavior as being absolutely determined.

CONCLUSION

Here then is my theoretical model of the person who emerges from therapy—a person functioning freely in all the fullness of his organismic potentialities; a person who is dependable in being realistic, self-enhancing, socialized and appropriate in his behavior; a creative person, whose specific formings of behavior are not easily predictable; a person who is ever-changing, ever developing, always discovering himself and the newness in himself in each succeeding moment of time. This is the person who in an imperfect way actually emerges from the experience of safety and freedom in a therapeutic experience, and this is the person whom I have tried to describe for you in "pure" form.

My purpose has not been to convince you of the correctness of this view. Indeed I would have to confess that I have written this paper primarily for my own satisfaction, to clarify the thoughts which have been stirring in me. But if this presentation causes you to formulate your view of the person who emerges from therapy, or enables you to point out flaws in my own thinking which I have not yet seen, or arouses in you the desire to put to objective test either this picture or one which you paint for yourself, then it will have fully served both its primary and its secondary purpose.

REFERENCES

Kelley, E. L., & Fiske, Donald W. *The Prediction of Performance in Clinical Psychology.* Ann Arbor: University of Michigan Press, 1951.

Krech, D. Notes toward a psychological theory. *J. Pers.*, Sept. 1949, 18, 66–87.

Rogers, C. R. Personal thoughts on teaching and learning. *Merrill-Palmer Quart.*, Summer, 1957, 3, pp. 241–243. Also published in *Improving College and University Teaching*, 1958, 6, 4–5.

Rogers, C. R. Persons or Science: A Philosophical Question. *Amer. Psychologist*, 1955, 10, 267–278.

Wertheimer, M. *Productive Thinking.* New York: Harper, 1945, 183–4.

CHAPTER 6

Carl Rogers' Contribution to a Fully Functioning Psychology

Allen E. Bergin

This brief treatise on the fully functioning person runs deep. It reflects its author's character in its prominent characteristics—the same characteristics that thread their way as dominant themes through the humanistic psychology which today vies with mechanistic, cognitive, and psychodynamic theories. Its style as a highly personal, yet scientifically oriented, document is characteristic of Rogers and of the movement in psychology which he represents. Its global character is consistent with the gestalt quality of much of his thinking, and it confronts the reader with the problem of coping with the full complex of pithy issues in psychotherapy all at once—the nature of personality change, the definition of positive outcome, the sources of personal values, the nature of psychology (and of science itself), and the philosophy of man and the role of the individual in society.

One does not confidently approach the task of evaluating such a gigantic and impressive sweep of thought, nor is it easy to criticize a man who states himself so directly and openly without pretense and without defensiveness. It would be unfair and irrelevant to react to this paper in an excessively cognitive manner, and for this reason I begin by responding to the man himself, violating Boring's dictum and commenting *ad hominem* rather than merely *ad verbum*. One tends to feel that Rogers, the humanist, would rather have it this way—the whole man responding to him, rather than the detached intellect.

This highly personal, almost autobiographical, document reveals Carl Rogers as a man in the tradition of the Emersonian ideal. Emerson at-

---

This chapter is a discussion-commentary, written especially for the present volume, of Chapter 5: "The Concept of the Fully Functioning Person," by Carl R. Rogers.

tacked the professional specializations of human society in that they make of men

walking monsters—a good finger, a neck, a stomach, an elbow, but never a *Man*. . . . The Planter, who is *Man* sent out into the field to gather food, is seldom cheered by an idea of the true dignity of his ministry. He sees his bushel and his cart, and nothing beyond, and sinks into the farmer, instead of *Man* on the farm. . . . In this distribution of functions the scholar is the delegated intellect. In the right state he is *Man* thinking [1837, p. 46].

Carl Rogers has never permitted himself to be fenced in or subjugated by common orthodoxies and demands of professional convention. He is *Man*, to quote Emerson, living "with the privilege of the immeasurable mind." His standards, originating from within his own fully functioning self, permit him to say of this paper:

"I have written this paper primarily for my own satisfaction."
"When I had finished it I liked [it]."
[The editor] was dubious about its publication value."
"I was . . . aware of how remote it was from orthodox psychological thinking, so I simply had it duplicated for personal distribution."

And, commenting on its publication ten years later:

"I am pleased to have it come out in its original form."

The uneasy relationship which Rogers' stance has created with organized psychology is well conveyed by these statements, as is his tendency to become the eventual victor in each confrontation with established views. Indeed, it may be said that Rogers' kind of psychologist, once rare, is coming to have an increasing influence in American psychology; and, as this occurs, his other battle—that with organized psychiatry and psychoanalysis over the practice of psychotherapy—is simultaneously being won.

It is ironic that a person so dedicated to the study of human psychology and so respected by a large segment of the profession should be criticized by editors and leaders in the field. A former president of APA once said, "Why, Rogers isn't even a psychologist!" Little did he realize that Rogers had long before rejected that president's meaning of psychology. He states in his autobiography,

I have never really *belonged* to *any* professional group. . . . Because of this attitude, I was deeply touched, to the point of tears, when I was awarded one of the first three Scientific Contribution Awards by the APA. I was astonished that psychologists deeply and significantly regarded me as "one of them" [1967, p. 375].

This is also a measure of Rogers' influence. If he did not confront the very essence of psychology, as habitually practiced, with freshness, he would be no trouble to it and would thus have less impact upon it. As it is, intense pursuing of his deepest intuitions has led him to challenge the definitions both of psychology and of science itself.

A SCIENCE OF THE PERSON

In the description of the fully functioning person we observe a characteristic attempt by Rogers to describe human experience and behavior in its complexity. The most notable feature of this attempt is the focus on internal experience as felt and conceptualized by the individual. While such attempts to describe and conceptualize the experimental world are characteristic of the existential avant-garde in American psychology, Rogers goes one giant step beyond this and calls for objectification of the subjective. The significance of his so doing cannot be underestimated, because it places the phenomenological world of private experience within the empirical domain, at least logically and conceptually. The experimental implementation of such a notion is another thing; but in years subsequent to the writing of this paper, substantial progress has been made in this direction (Bergin, 1964; Rogers, 1964; Rogers, Gendlin, Kiesler, & Truax, 1967). These methodological advances, derived from the daring conceptualization of the "private" as objectifiable, set Rogers apart from his phenomenological comrades and mark an advance in psychology of very substantial proportions. Rogers, in this paper, adds substance and momentum to a redefinition of psychology as "a science of inner experience."

While laboratory-bred psychologists might react with horror to the thought that this paper has any *scientific* characteristics at all—as the editor to whom it was originally submitted apparently did—it is important to recognize that the obvious looseness of the paper is its most redeeming quality, even in scientific terms. For here we find an honest and vigorous conceptual grappling with the very essence of the inner man. To reshape these initial conceptualizations into refined and operationalized hypotheses, akin to those of laboratory research, would be an injustice to the phenomena, a travesty on inquiry, and would blunt and truncate the whole effort to grapple with essences of life instead of mere forms.

If it were not for all the controversy that has surrounded the relationships between phenomenologists and neobehaviorists over the years, one might think that it would be self-evident that a psychology of the inner life should be *different*, not only in its content but in its style of theoretical conception and its manner of empirical inquiry. So powerful does this thought become as one conceives of the range and dimension of the experiential world, as described by Rogers in this and other papers, that it becomes almost logically impossible to avoid the notion that the effect of such a work is to engender an entirely new attitude toward what science is, let alone what psychology is.

Such a conclusion has not escaped Dr. Rogers and, indeed, it has been his own work which has given this notion prominence. The present paper appears in the context of a flow of work which has continued to be productive. We find hints and allusions to something new in the way of science here, such as: "This would mean that the science of psychology, at its highest levels, would perhaps be more of a science of understanding than a science of prediction; an analysis of the lawfulness of that which has occurred, rather than primarily a control of what is about to occur." One does not wonder at some people's stating that Rogers is not a psychologist when he writes like this, but what is not indicated by such judgments is any understanding that they imply the redefinition of psychology rather than the labeling of an outcast. That this redefinition carries implications for the whole of science should not be too surprising in light of the kind of phenomena being examined. Indeed, Koch (1959) has made it convincingly clear that the most original scientists have been bound by neither theoretical nor methodological codes, but have shaped their work around phenomena, not around the dogma of science and its philosophers. Geology, astronomy, and biology have all profitably borrowed from chemistry and physics, but each has benefited most from casting its approach to science in terms convenient and fruitful to the raw material under consideration.

The ultimate value of a view of science and its attendant methodologies is measured by its fruitfulness or yield in new knowledge and derivative technologies. By this measure, experimental psychology has yielded much, but not in the realm of the subjective life processes, where meaning and the quality of life are largely determined. It is to Rogers' great credit that he presages in this paper views now more fully evident. His original contribution to the philosophy and methodology of the behavioral sciences has gained considerable momentum by the publication of "Toward a Science of the Person" (1964), and this is now one of his primary foci of interest (1967). This growing effort must be measured by its ultimate yield rather than by comparisons with some common definitions of what psychological science ought to be.

A fuller analysis of Rogers' developing thought in this domain is beyond the scope of this paper, but it is appropriate to note the sweeping character of his work as evidenced by his contribution here, for we observe that as he sets out to describe conceptually what he has experienced in the consulting room, the canons and codes of psychology—and of science itself—are totally reexamined, and we realize that this is no common man making a common description—this is *Man thinking,* "with the privilege of the immeasurable mind."

THE CRITERION PROBLEM IN PSYCHOTHERAPY

It is to Rogers' credit that he does not back off from the criterion problem as so many have in their ventures into process research. This persistence and honesty have had significant consequences, in that new criteria of an experiential and self-concept type have been developed to measure the kinds of change Rogers is talking about. Thus, he seems to have solved the criterion problem for himself, if not for the field, by taking a position of deep commitment based on immersion in the flow of data peculiar to his experience and has then stimulated the development of methods for measuring the kinds of change he has observed and promoted. There is then, for him, little or no criterion problem. He has selected what he values and has developed a congenial procedure for promoting it.

There is little question, from Rogers' account in this paper, that he has strong views of what a fully functioning person is or ought to be. There is also little doubt that he does everything in his power to promote personality change in this direction. The paper is therefore a profound response to the criterion problem in psychotherapy. While we may discover a variety of techniques for producing given kinds of personality change, how do we decide which changes are desirable? In analyzing this question, Perry London (1964) convincingly argues that therapists promote what they personally value and that because of this they are to a substantial degree secular moralists.

As Rogers implies, it is doubtful that his "fully functioning person" would fit the Menninger Clinic's concept of the "normal" personality or the Soviet state's view of the adjusted person. This simply proves that he follows the bias that grows out of his special set of experiences in defining the positive end point of therapy. He seems to argue that the fully functioning person is *the* necessary product of a therapy which allows the actualization of the basic human potential in each individual and that he simply observes such a transcendent development in the course of therapy. We might argue, on the other hand, that he "causes" this development in his patients and that he is merely observing the consequences of implementing his own belief system in the therapeutic hour. It seems likely, though, that while he would agree that he strongly espouses a view of what the healthy personality should be, he would disagree that he promotes it rather than permits its occurrence.

He suggests elsewhere (1956) that the effect of his work is to increase the number of alternatives available to the client at a choice-point, even though the structure of therapy is determined by the therapist. This may be so, but it is also true that systematic desensitization has such an effect, and certainly, no one sees Wolpe describing anything like the fully functioning person as an outcome of behavior therapy. This must mean that there are additional effects of the therapy and that these are results of some type of social-influence process. Perhaps an important contribution of Rogers' work will be the ultimate conclusion that it is impossible *not* to influence people in directions you value even if you try not to do so.

This section would be incomplete if no mention were made of the fact that Rogers has selected a growth type of criterion, rather than the cure type of criterion that behavior therapists use. The difference between these views is profound, and the differing implications are great. In the one case, the therapist takes it upon himself to organize conditions that will assist the client in developing a sense of personal identity and a satisfying life-style that will develop into a continuing sense of personal progress. Concern with specific symptoms is incidental to the larger enterprise. In the "treat and cure" approach, which more closely follows a medical model, the therapist's role is seen as one of creating in the individual a reasonable adjustment to his environment, a reduction of symptomatic pain, and a focusing on being able to function. Treatment, then, does not presume to enter into the entire life-style or experiential world of the individual, but rather concerns itself only with the professional's assistance of his client to maintain psychological integrity and adequacy within his own life stream.

The difference this makes is both technical and social. The work of the symptom remover fits well within current societal views of the practitioner as serving society by keeping its members functioning equably.

Rogers and others like him confront society, through their work, with value-system conflicts, in that they assume the role of change agents with a particular goal orientation that may or may not be consistent with that of the larger society. Rogers describes the fully functioning person: "He would not necessarily be 'adjusted' to his culture, and he would almost certainly not be a conformist." Thus it is obvious that those who take a "growth" view of personality change have assumed the role of socialization agents in society without society's having given assent to it or even knowing about it. This inexplicitness is probably not as bad as the fact that many therapists are unaware of it themselves.

This casting of the therapist into a role of secular priest may be argued to be necessary, as by London; its validity may be denied, as it might be by Rogers; or it may occasion eventual open conflict between the psychological socializing agents and those that currently hold sway. In any event, therapists of Rogers' kind, who explicitly define their work in terms of promoting particular styles of living such as that of the "fully functioning person," produce consequences that are fraught with problems for the field—problems that are not easily resolved and that do not permit a comfortable and secure existence for the professional therapist.

Whether this entire development tends toward good or ill may eventually depend upon how honest and explicit therapists are about their preferences and aspirations for patients. It would seem to be to the patient's advantage to know, before selecting his therapist, which kind of world view he will be subjected to or which end point of therapy is espoused by the one treating him. It is to Rogers' credit that he is explicit on this point, and it would be well for all therapists to be more informative toward their clients about such matters.

The views of goals, of health, and of positive change are diverse, and it would be a valuable outgrowth of Rogers' careful description of the well-functioning personality if others were inspired to be so explicit. It would then be possible for the rest of society, including the clinical population, to support and select that which they prefer rather than accept each preferred brand of secular morals because it is offered by an "expert."

It is ironic that Rogers' writings should give credence to the notion that therapists are, to varying degrees, promoters of moral systems, in the light of his conscientious desire to avoid exactly this. The important fact is that his *openness* has tended to reveal information, on a number of occasions, that was strange even to himself. If, as he has argued, "the facts are friendly," then perhaps it is valuable to know that life is like that. No one exists in, nor can he create, a moral vacuum. Thus, we have learned one lesson from Rogers that he did not plan to teach, and a profound one it is.

PHILOSOPHICAL IMPLICATIONS

There is a willful inclination in this paper to generalize from a small sample to the whole of the fully functioning life. It is at this juncture that the author's personal philosophy tends to take over from empirical observation.

It is evident that Rogers' style has been similar to that of Freud, specifically in extrapolating deep insights gained from intensive case experience to the psychology of the population in general. In Freuds case it leads to a relatively negative view of the nature of man, and in Rogers' case to a positive one. While some differences in the two populations sampled may have been present, it is doubtful that they were significant enough to account for these disparate views of man.

It seems that every great man feels that his particular experience carries a message of import to mankind in general, and perhaps this is a measure of his genius; but it also becomes gradually evident that the experience of even a person of great insight, when confined to a small and biased sampling of humanity, yields truth mostly relevant to that special subpopulation or to a restricted set of dimensions of all men's lives which that sample magnifies in some way.

It would be highly debatable, though, to say that this work is nonsense because it lacks the general validity attributed to it by its author. It would be more correct to assert that its implications are significant, but related chiefly to certain kinds of people with certain kinds of problems. The idea of the locus of evaluation as being within the self, of the existential, momentary experience as being the chief source of direction; the idea of ultimate authority as being within one's organismic experience; and the idea of oneself as part of an ongoing process rather than as in control of it—all seem vividly descriptive of the coerced or overprotected personality during the process of unfreezing and becoming a person open to experience, capable of adequate self-awareness, and able to set an independent course of action. But to declare this brilliantly conceived process to be appropriate for all pathologies or to be the crux of growth in all men is an enormous overexercise of some useful facts.

Despite such limitations, the philosophical character of the paper places it well ahead of the psychological existentialism that has since become an important part of American psychology and psychiatry. Probably the most important philosophical contribution made here is the description of an organismic valuing process as the ultimate source of authority, of conceptions of right and wrong, and of valid decision making. There is a definite philosophical appeal to this proposition, for it poses a solution to one of the most difficult of dilemmas: the sources of value and the appropriateness or applicability of a given value in a given situation.

As a result of complete openness to all internal and external stimuli, the fully functioning individual makes at any given moment the choice or response most satisfying to *all* his needs (i.e., survival, enhancement, food, affection, sex, etc.). Thus, rather than imposing a structure on experience, this process constitutes finding "structure *in* experience," and the person finds "his organism a trustworthy means of arriving at the most satisfying behavior in each existential situation." Not only is this an interesting *psychological* resolution of an old philosophical dilemma, it also represents one of the strongest endorsements of individualism in any literature. It is one, but only one, approach to the problem of authority and its sources.

This description is almost more effective philosophically than it is psychologically. In psychological terms, the organismic valuing process remains a mystical, unverified entity. Philosophically it would be a neat solution, if only it were so. That there are other equally or even more appealing philosophical views, and that there are loopholes in the psychological structure of this viewpoint, should not deter us from observing that there is another implication that is greater than either of these. This is that Rogers, in his willingness to advocate such views flatly, assumes a role of secular moralist and in so doing, whether or not by intention, sets himself in competition with or in substitution for traditional sources of value. It is this point that exceeds the rest and illustrates well the degree to which psychotherapists have assumed the role of purveyors of values rather than that, simply, of curers of symptoms.

Herein lie both opportunity and the danger of folly for the helping professions, for if they can show the effects of value deficiencies upon psychopathology, they will have contributed well; but, if they proceed to institute a "new morality" and thus establish a secular priesthood, their identity as empirically based professions is lost, and they enter the public maelstrom of moral politics—a place where no scientific profession is likely to survive intact.

Another danger lies in this direction of movement, namely, that we may well take ourselves too seriously and be taken too seriously by the community. The danger in this is that our empirical base is more likely to be a correlate of our values than a cause of them, and we may thus impose our wills onto the society by a superfluous association that gives us an authority we ought not to have. Our views thus convey a special status and bear an influence that will have consequences for which we may not wish to accept responsibility. We would do well to learn early that there is an enormous difference between *what is* and *what ought to be.* As scientists, we are experts on the former but have no special status in relation to the latter. That is, we may be able to specify which conditions lead to which behaviors, but intuitive value judgments are still necessary to decide which behaviors we consider good.

This paper thus illustrates Rogers' statement that "what is most personal is most general," for by intensive reflection upon the experience of his clients and himself in psychotherapy he derives conceptions which confront psychology, in the most general sense, with one of its most profound dilemmas, that of being reluctantly cast into the role of moral arbiter. Perhaps unintentionally, Rogers has made it clear that this implication of our work must be accepted and acted upon. It can no longer be denied that our values influence our work, and also the attitudes and convictions of our clients. Logically, we are thereby compelled to argue more explicitly our views for and against the values of the social milieu in which we live, as Rogers has done.

If, then, we publicly expose what we privately promote in the solitude of our consulting rooms, we will be less guilty of a most hypocritical form of subtle brainwashing, and we will open the way for a more sophisticated kind of patient-therapist pairing than now exists. We would suggest that the therapists of the future will be selected by their clientele partly on the basis of similarity of values or ideology. Such a possibility seems essential in light of the increasing evidence that issues of value are frequently crucial in clinical treatment, and also because of the pluralistic nature of values in our culture. Thus, while one person might prefer to be treated by a therapist who advocates the fully functioning person, another might prefer a Skinnerian philosophy, and still another might elect to be influenced by staff members of Norman Vincent Peale's Academy of Religion and Mental Health. That such selections already occur is evident. That they could be made more systematically with less stress on therapists and patients and with more successful outcomes (Jasper, 1967) is equally evident.

CONTRIBUTIONS OF THE CLIENT-CENTERED APPROACH TO A
MULTIPHASIC SYSTEM OF PSYCHOTHERAPY

It seems likely that no one of the extant therapies is all right or all wrong, but rather that each will contribute in some measure to the eventual development of a refined system of treatment. Our own view is that the outlines of such an approach are presently taking shape (Bergin, 1967). The description of this view is too complex to undertake here, but, in rough outline it suggests that there are approximately three types of clinical problems for which psychotherapy is the treatment of choice: (1) problems in human relating or emotional need-satisfaction; (2) problems of conditioned responding; and (3) problems of life-style and self-regulation. We argue elsewhere that the relationship variables isolated by the client-centered tradition are of most positive value with problems of human relating, that behavioral therapies are most applicable to problems of conditioned responding, and that there is currently no adequate therapy for problems of life-style and self-regulation, although reality therapy (Glasser, 1965), integrity therapy (Mowrer, 1967), and the other traditional therapies all contribute in this area. It has been our experience that there are many clients whose problems lie primarily in *one* of these domains and that there are others whose problems cut across all three domains and for whom all three kinds of therapy are necessary.

It appears to me, then, that the therapy of the near future will be a "multiphasic" therapy, and that practitioners will base their work on a body of evidence that will permit them to use the treatment indicated for each case rather than determine their practices by identification with a school of thought. It has come to my attention, since espousing this view, that there are a number of practitioners besides myself who are conscientiously attempting to do just this. Though these people have been trained as psychoanalysts, behavior therapists, and client-centered therapists, they now prefer to do what they think "works" with each patient. The idea of a multiphasic therapy provides a good context for our view of the contributions and future significance of the work of Carl Rogers and his associates. Rogers' conception of positive personality functioning and the conditions which bring it about is an unusually clear example of the advantages of a school-type approach. In spite of the many problems which such an approach has created in the field of psychotherapy, its one enormous advantage is that it has permitted and promoted the study of a few complex variables in relative isolation.

It is evident that Rogers describes in embryo, in this paper, the theory of personality change he developed more fully in later publications, a theory of therapy which we might characterize as *relationship therapy*. All of the significant change agents are seen as relationship variables. The domains of existence and meaning of which Rogers also writes are byproducts of this process and come in part from his own weltanschauung rather than solely from the therapy and his observations of it. I characterize his description as one of relationship therapy also because it is from within the safety, warmth, and empathy of the relationship that the fully functioning personality emerges with its newborn sense of freedom to experience, perceive, and actualize. I characterize it thus also because it helps to distinguish the unique contribution of Rogers' work from that of others whose emphasis has focused more on processes of conditioning, on self-regulation, or on existence and life-styles.

Another salient fact in Rogers' paper, and in his work generally, is that he focuses almost entirely upon affective experience, and where he does not, he implies that affective experiencing is the crucial nexus from which all other dimensions of human functioning receive their ultimate direction and meaning. While this may be the most appropriate response to certain kinds of overly inhibited and intellectualized neurotics, it has less crucial relevance to the broader range of human problems and possibilities. It illustrates another instance of how thinking in terms of schools permits the isolation of important variables and reveals connections with significant life events. At the same time it makes equally clear the danger of extrapolating too broadly from the particular to the general. This problem has been a common one for all traditional therapies. They have continued to proceed as though the affective life functioned independently and was more generic than the domains of cognition, thought, anticipation, etc. It is these latter functions that are coming to have more prominent play in the new therapies, in the continuing modifications of psychoanalytic ego psychology, and in the field of general experimental psychology.

It has sometimes been argued that psychopathology consists chiefly of disturbances in the affect life of the individual, but it is becoming increasingly clear that the domain of thought, problem solving, planning, intellectual commitment, etc., is of equal significance. The contributions of Rogers and others like him thus seem to be receiving their rightfully important, but restricted, place in the total scheme of human experience.

It is in his focusing on a few relationship variables which have powerful effects, to the exclusion of other considerations, that Rogers has produced useful results in terms of both technique and theory. This seemingly narrow focusing may have been the best way to discover that set of technical procedures and theoretical concepts which now characterize client-centered therapy and personality theory. These discoveries are much less likely to have been made in other ways.

It is a most interesting observation that the various schools, while attempting to embrace everything within a single, homogeneous framework, in actuality create an isolation of variables which bears scientific fruit and which, in turn, ironically, makes evident the fallacious pretensions of the individual school to be the answer to everything. For example, we observe in client-centered therapy that its technical operations and the research which supports them suggest their special relevance to particular types of problems in which matters of dependency-need deprivation, independence striving, social inhibition, and value-system narrowness are dominant. But they seem to be less relevant for deviant behavior, phobias, compulsions, and the like.

Thus, in proving itself, such an orientation demonstrates the salient value of relationship variables with regard to some kinds of pathology, but at the same time lays bare the fact that it is not all things to all men. The issue is, in essence, whether Rogers' "conditions" are necessary and sufficient for all therapeutic change or whether they are necessary for some and not others, and sufficient for still others. The ultimate consequence of the school approach is thus to refine the meaning and usefulness of given variables and also to specify the population for which they are most useful.

The client-centered group have succeeded in isolating and formulating into a practical technique a few variables most germane to human relating and deficiencies therein. These they have called vividly to the attention of therapists from all persuasions and professions. What is more, they have successfully demonstrated, on an empirical level, significant correlations between therapist utilization of these variables and positive change in clients. This contribution is substantial and compelling. There is little doubt that this work will eventually be considered the first scientific foundation for developing potent relationship variables in therapeutic change and will be classed among the foremost contributions to the general psychology of human relationships as they occur in all their natural contexts. Certainly, any multiphasic therapy of the future will have to provide a significant role for the types of factors and methods emerging from this framework.

It has become increasingly evident that the client-centered viewpoint, while persuasive and often crucial in the clinic, must give way to a broader view. This is perhaps most clearly demonstrated by the behavior of prominent client-centered therapists who have moved dramatically away from the commonly held notion of their therapeutic style. William U. Snyder has incorporated the style suggested by Dollard and Miller into his work to the point where he accepts and uses a methodology considerably influenced by both psychoanalysis and learning theory. Nicholas Hobbs (1966) has devised a technology for treating children which has a strong cognitive base to it. Truax and Carkhuff (1967) advocate appropriate utilization of Wolpean methods. None of these men may be considered defectors to other schools. They remain committed to the value of essential relationship variables derived from the client-centered approach, but each has found additional variables and methods to be of great value and, in particular cases, of more value than the ones with which they have been traditionally associated. Their behavior simply testifies to the validity of the conclusions regarding the importance of a multiphasic approach which includes a relationship therapy component stated in the foregoing paragraphs.

It is well to distinguish here the relationship factors of client-centered therapy from the purported existential and philosophical aspects. There is substantial evidence that the conditions of therapy posited by Rogers have potency with many disorders and particularly with those he has treated most extensively, but there is little *evidence* that the philosophical overlay he postulates is a consistent correlate of the change process so induced.

The contribution of this school to a theory and technique of life-style therapy, as partially described in "The Concept of the Fully Functioning Person," is small in comparison to its contribution to an effective relationship therapy. While significant thoughts are proposed in this domain, and while they are bound to have an important influence, it seems doubtful that they will dominate the future psychology of life-style and self-regulation with anything like the influence that pertains in the relationship domain. They currently lack precise articulation, empirical support, and a sense of general application to the human population.

While one can see independence of thought, creativity, and openness to experience in extremely well-functioning persons, it has also been our experience that they practically never live in a moment-to-moment flow of subtle, hardly discerned, private affective experience. Their consciousness of being goal-oriented, of imposing structure on their lives, of deriving direction and focus from a highly conscious and intellectual process, and of finding meaning through action and thought, rather than feeling alone, seems fairly obvious.

On the other hand, the creative insights or intuitive breakthroughs experienced by an Einstein or a Rogers seem real enough and probably do occur on occasion among all persons, including neurotics, at that special moment when a profound swell of affectively loaded insight occurs. It is for all of these people a powerful "living in the moment," as Rogers describes it—and a brilliant and apt description it is. But to suggest that such moments of existential "peaking" are or should be the essence of the full life seems limited. It is one thing to assert that such momentary fullness, if continued, will yield a pattern of fruitful action, a sense of social responsibility, or an ability to delay and to time self-gratification, and quite another thing to prove it.

It would seem that recent research on prosocial behavior, on self-regulation, and on cognitive processes would suggest otherwise. It also seems evident that the type of cases we encounter clinically are increasingly problems of undercontrol, and it is of considerable interest that several newer therapies (Glasser, 1965; Mowrer, 1967) have come into being in specific response to the fact that traditional therapies simply are not adequate for handling them. In these instances, it is frequently the therapist's intent to *teach* self-control rather than, as Rogers puts it, "floating with a complex stream of experience. . . "(!)

We see then, again in this domain, the fruitful analysis of a profoundly important dimension of human experience and an overgeneralization of it. This does not take away from the significance of the conceptualization of those phenomena which have been directly observed, such as insight into change in the neurotic, or creativity in the scientist, but it does suggest that the further the concepts get from data the more tentative and subject to drastic revision they become. It seems likely that a person theorizing about consistency and stability in human personality and basing his concepts on observations of consistent and stable people would project a very different fully functioning person than the one described in this paper, which is part of a theory of change and is based on observations of people who are changing. It is Rogers' theory of the change process and of the conditions which promote it that will have its most enduring impact. Whether he eventually stands alongside or in opposition to Freud, his name will be especially known for this contribution and for his giving it empirical substance.

The extent to which he has succeeded in capturing both the subjective inner life and the process of personality change within the net of science is a remarkable and enduring achievement. Because of this influence, the study and practice of therapy can never again be so thoroughly subjected to the narrowness and dogmatism which psychoanalysis imposed upon it from roughly 1930 to 1960. For that we must all be grateful.

CLIENT-CENTERED, BEHAVIORAL, AND PSYCHOANALYTIC THERAPIES

This commentary would be incomplete without referring to the competition which has existed among the client-centered, psychoanalytic, and behavioral therapies. It is our view, documented more fully elsewhere (Bergin, 1967; Strupp & Bergin, 1969), that disputations among schools are gradually dissipating, largely owing to an influx of empirical information which makes certain kinds of pronouncements less appealing than they once were. Rogers himself (1959) foresaw this development and welcomed the demise of his own "school":

> In concluding this chapter I would like to comment on the question "Where does this lead? To what end is all this research?"
>
> Its major significance, it seems to me, is that a growing body of objectively verified knowledge of psychotherapy will bring about the gradual demise of "schools" of psychotherapy, including this one. As solid knowledge increases as to the conditions which facilitate therapeutic change, the nature of the therapeutic process, the conditions which block or inhibit therapy, the characteristic outcomes of therapy in terms of personality or behavioral change, then there will be less and less emphasis upon dogmatic and purely theoretical formulations. Differences of opinion, different procedures in therapy, different judgments as to outcome, will be put to empirical test rather than being simply a matter of debate or argument.
>
> In medicine today we do not find a "penicillin school of treatment" versus some other school of treatment. There are differences of judgment and opinion, to be sure, but there is confidence that these will be resolved in the foreseeable future by carefully designed research. Just so I believe will psychotherapy turn increasingly to the facts rather than to dogma as an arbiter of differences.
>
> Out of this should grow an increasingly effective, and continually changing psychotherapy which will neither have nor need any specific label. It will have incorporated whatever is factually verified from any and every therapeutic orientation.

We feel that the data increasingly support the need for such changes and the development of a multiphasic approach.

It seems clear from what evidence is available that behavior therapy has superior effects in cases where specific conditioned symptoms, particularly involving avoidance responses, are at issue. But where complex neuroses are involved, various relationship and life-style techniques must be invoked by behavior therapists (Davison, 1967; Lazarus, 1967; Wolpe & Lazarus, 1966) during the course of treatment. This, then, limits their approach and makes it clear that these other two classes of variables have not been well isolated, nor have techniques relevant to them been developed, by those who operate within a learning and conditioning framework. As previously stated, Rogers has contributed the basic foundation for research and therapy on relationship factors, and to my mind, the debate between Rogers and the behaviorists boils down to the fact that there are two classes of human phenomena under discussion, Rogers being relevant to one class and the behaviorists to the other. Both have contributed enormously to these classes of phenomena: namely, human relating and automatic, conditioned responding. Obviously, learning and conditioning processes can influence certain aspects of the manner of human relating, but when we speak of relationship variables, we are referring primarily to those in which love and empathy are consistently communicated—where the phenomenological world of need for affection and worth predominate rather than reinforcement and conditioned emotional responding.

Unfortunately, therapists from both of these schools tend to engage in implementing *both* sets of variables while asserting that they are using only one. Rogers, e.g., makes the following statement: "We find that clients tolerate a much wider range and variety of feelings, including feelings which were formerly anxiety-producing; and that these feelings are usefully integrated into their more flexibly organized personalities" [p. 66]. This description also fits beautifully the effects of systematic desensitization, and it seems entirely likely that the client-centered relationship can serve unwittingly as a counterconditioner of anxiety responses. It is also evident from published research that client behavior can be and is shaped by the differential use of warmth and empathy on the part of client-centered therapists (Murray, 1956; Truax, 1966). At the same time, it is equally evident from case reports that behavior therapists use empathy and warmth to directly evoke comfort responses, cooperation, and confidence in the therapist (Wolpe & Lazarus, 1966), all of which can have direct therapeutic effects as well as indirectly enhancing the potency of conditioning by making the patient more receptive to the necessary manipulations.

These overlapping behaviors on the part of adherents to different schools need to be isolated and tested for the independent contributions they make to therapeutic change. At the same time practitioners would do well to be more explicit about which they are doing and when. If they were so explicit, it would probably be more apparent how many therapists are already using a multiphasic approach by differentially applying relationship and conditioning factors to their client's problems.

It might seem, from the foregoing exposition, that psychoanalysis would have special relevance to life-style and self-regulation problems, but analysts have not counted this to be their prime objective and, indeed, there is no evidence to date to support any notion of analytical superiority in this realm. We must then ask, what is the contribution of the psychoanalytic tradition to this discussion, and how does it stand in relation to Rogers' position?

We are discussing here psychoanalytic technique and theory of technique, not the whole of psychoanalytic thought. In the realm of treatment methods, it is clear enough that the psychoanalytic tradition has made contributions which overlap those of the other therapies under discussion, but in no case can it be said that this viewpoint has produced a technique of value comparable to the client-centered approach in relationship factors or the behavioral approach in conditioning factors. What efficacy this approach has is probably due to the application of principles better developed within these other persuasions.

While the analytic tradition has spawned many concepts relevant to a life-style therapy, especially in its existential variants, these developments are currently tenuous and unverified. Certainly, the advocates of reality and integrity therapy seem more vigorous at the moment. It cannot be denied that psychoanalysis has laid much of the groundwork for the newer therapies which are flourishing and seem to have surpassed it. But psychoanalysis can hardly take credit for these productive and influential innovations, any more than Catholicism can take credit for some of the creative developments of Protestantism, or orthodox Judaism for the contributions of the reform movement. While they have similar roots, these modern developments owe more to their protesting inventors than they do to the historical conditions from which they sprang. Thus, we view psychoanalysis as a creative eruption whose contribution has substantially passed, whereas the work represented by "the fully functioning person" retains its vitality and continues to tend toward its full promise as a lasting theme in the complex picture of therapeutic change. Lest this evaluation of psychoanalysis seem too pessimistic, we cite the following from Rogers' autobiography (1967) regarding his year at the Center for Advanced Study in the Behavioral Sciences:

Another important influence was my contact with Erik Erikson, a splendid person whose very appearance is therapeutic, and several other psychoanalysts, foreign as well as American. From them I learned what I had strongly suspected—that psychoanalysis as a school of thought is dead—but that out of loyalty and other motives, none but the very brave analysts mention this fact as they go on to develop theories and ways of working very remote from, or entirely opposed to, the Freudian views [p. 372].

It can always be asked why we think Rogers' view will last, at least in some form, in the psychology of the future. Perhaps the best evidence for this lies in the positive experiential power of a relationship characterized by the qualities Rogers proposes and implements. This evidence could be presented statistically, historically, or theoretically, but we prefer to present it as an experience, in other words, at the level of discourse which Rogers so well represents. I believe that, when the following description by Rogers can be fully stated objectively, we finally shall have an adequate measure of his real impact upon psychology and also a conclusive witness that a "science of the fully functioning person" is possible:

This book is about the suffering and the hope, the anxiety and the satisfaction, with which each therapist's counseling room is filled. It is about the uniqueness of the relationship each therapist forms with each client, and equally about the common elements which we discover in all these relationships. This book is about the highly personal experiences of each one of us. It is about a client in my office who sits there by the corner of the desk, struggling to be himself, yet deathly afraid of being himself—striving to see his experience as it is, wanting to *be* that experience, and yet deeply fearful of the prospect. This book is about me, as I sit there with that client, facing him, participating in that struggle as deeply and sensitively as I am able. It is about me as I try to perceive his experience, and the meaning and the feeling and the taste and the flavor that it has for him. It is about me as I bemoan my very human fallibility in understanding that client, and the occasional failures to see life as it appears to him, failures which fall like heavy objects across the intricate, delicate web of growth which is taking place. It is about me as I rejoice at the privilege of being a midwife to a new personality—as I stand by with awe at the emergence of a self, a person, as I see a birth process in which I have had an important and facilitating part. It is about both the client and me as we regard with wonder the potent and orderly forces which are evident in this whole experience, forces which seem deeply rooted in the universe as a whole. The book is, I believe, about life, as life vividly reveals itself in the therapeutic process—with its blind power and its tremendous capacity for destruction, but with its overbalancing thrust toward growth, if the opportunity for growth is provided [Rogers, 1951, pp. x–xi].

REFERENCES

Bergin, A. E. Psychology as a science of inner experience. *Journal of Humanistic Psychology*, 1964, *4*, 95–103.

Bergin, A. E. A multiphasic experimental approach to psychotherapy. Paper presented at colloquium of the Department of Behavioral Science, Temple University Medical School. Philadelphia, March 1967.

Davidson, G. C. Personal communication. State University of New York at Stony Brook, 1967.

Emerson, R. W. The American scholar. Delivered at Harvard University in 1837. In B. Atkinson (Ed.), *The complete essays and other writings of Ralph Waldo Emerson.* New York: The Modern Library, 1950. Pp. 45–66.

Glasser, W. *Reality therapy.* New York: Harper & Row, 1965.

Hobbs, N. Helping disturbed children: Psychological and ecological strategies. *American Psychologist*, 1966, *21*, 1105–1115.

Jasper, L. Patient-therapist pairing in psychotherapy. Unpublished manuscript, Teachers College, Columbia University, 1967.

Koch, S. Some trends of study I (Vols. 1–3) Epilogue. In S. Koch (Ed.), *Psychology: A study of a science.* Vol. 3. New York: McGraw-Hill, 1959. Pp. 729–788.

Lazarus, A. A. In support of technical eclecticism. Manuscript submitted for publication, Temple University Medical School, 1967.

London, P. *The modes and morals of psychotherapy.* New York: Holt, Rinehart & Winston, 1964.

Mowrer, O. H. *Morality and mental health.* Chicago: Rand McNally, 1967.

Murray, E. J. A content-analysis method for studying psychotherapy. *Psychological Monographs*, 1956, *70* (13, Whole No. 420).

Rogers, C. R. *Client-centered therapy.* Boston: Houghton Mifflin, 1951.

Rogers, C. R. Some issues concerning the control of human behavior. *Science*, 1956, *124*, No. 3231, 1057–1066.

Rogers, C. R. Client-centered therapy in its context of research. In C. R. Rogers & G. M. Kinget, *Psychotherapie en menselyke verhoudingen: Theorie an praktyk van de non-directeve therapie.* Utrecht, Holland: Uitgeverij het Spectrum, 1959. Chapter 12.

Rogers, C. R. The concept of the fully functioning person. *Psychotherapy: Research, Theory and Practice*, 1963, *1*, 17–26. Reprinted in this collection, pp. 57–73; page numbers cited in the text refer to this volume.

Rogers, C. R. Toward a science of the person. In T. W. Wann (Ed.), *Be-*

haviorism and phenomenology. Chicago: University of Chicago Press, 1964. Pp. 109–133.

Rogers, C. R. Carl R. Rogers. In E. G. Boring & G. Lindzey (Eds.) *A history of psychology in autobiography.* Vol. 5. New York: Appleton-Century-Crofts, 1967. Pp. 341–384.

Rogers, C. R., Gendlin, E. T., Kiesler, D. J., & Truax, C. B. (Eds.) *The therapeutic relationship and its impact.* Madison: University of Wisconsin Press, 1967.

Snyder, W. U. *The psychotherapy relationship.* New York: Macmillan, 1961.

Strupp, H. H., & Bergin, A. E. Some empirical and conceptual bases for psychotherapy: A critical review of issues, trends, and evidence. *International Journal of Psychiatry,* 1969, 7, 18–90.

Truax, C. B. Reinforcement and nonreinforcement in Rogerian therapy. *Journal of Abnormal Psychology,* 1966, 71, 1–9.

Truax, C. B., & Carkhuff, R. R. *Toward effective counseling and psychotherapy.* Chicago: Aldine, 1967.

Wolpe, J., & Lazarus, A. A. *Behavior therapy techniques.* New York: Pergamon Press, 1966.

CHAPTER 7

What Man Should Be

Fred E. Spaner

Carl Rogers describes the "fully functioning person" as the intended end product of client-centered therapy. He could have similarly described the kind of person we would want our child to become, or what man should be. In his article we are presented not only with the objectives of client-centered therapy, but also with a concept of man. This concept concerns man's perceptions and attitudes toward himself and his experiences, rather than specific characteristics or traits. In it the goal of man's behavior is not fixed; it is evolving. Hence, "fully functioning" is not so much what a person does, but how he goes about doing. This may be akin to saying that psychotherapy does not necessarily solve problems, but rather enables the person to learn how to solve them. The solutions are not so important as the acquisition of the problem-solving orientation.

It seems that what Rogers says about a client's "fully functioning" state also applies to the therapist. In creating a therapeutic relationship the therapist may very well be involved in experiencing or functioning as such rather than in a specific experience or a specific function. Consequently, "fully functioning," as (1) being open to one's experience, (2) living in an existential fashion, and (3) finding one's organism trustworthy in arriving at the most satisfying behavior at each moment, applies equally to the therapist in his experience with the client and to the client in his experience with the therapist.

The therapist, the therapeutic process, and the goals of the client in this process all attempt to achieve greater awareness by the individual of his experiences and relationships. This, it is believed, will lead to optimal effectiveness in day-to-day living. This follows from observa-

This chapter is a discussion-commentary, written especially for the present volume, of Chapter 5: "The Concept of the Fully Functioning Person," by Carl R. Rogers.

tions that, as an individual is able to receive and experience a fuller range of communications, both from within and without, he may become better able to select judiciously among them and respond competently. When he is unable to do this, his range of awareness narrows and he begins to protect himself from experiencing, since he expects to be overwhelmed. When one opens oneself to communications, one encounters both satisfying and dissatisfying experiences and becomes more keenly aware of the antecedents to each. Thus, with continued openness one tends to avoid behavior which leads to dissatisfying experience and begins to experience more satisfying consequences. This develops a trust in one's ability to select among communications and respond competently. Openness to communications, and trust in oneself as a capable instrument for selecting and responding, go together. They are inversely related to defensiveness and apprehension. The greater the openness and trust in oneself, the less one is defensive and apprehensive. The opposite is equally true: the greater the defensiveness and apprehension, the less openness and trust. This holds for the psychotherapist as much as it does for his client. In the psychotherapeutic relationship, the psychotherapist's defensiveness may be related to his concern over his competence to deal with his client and over whether or not he will be an effective agent to produce the desired change. The psychotherapist who is able to reduce his anxiety about himself in relation to his client is free to be more open with him and to trust himself in the relationship. This, then, can have the effect of freeing him to be more attentive and attuned to the client's feelings since he is not so preoccupied with his own. In this way he becomes more open to the communications in the psychotherapeutic transactions and can trust himself to respond appropriately. The entire process becomes more open and provides the client with a moment-to-moment model of the openness and trust in oneself which will help him to become a "fully functioning person." The psychotherapist thus enables his client to approach the objective of becoming a "fully functioning person" as he himself is able to move in that direction.

The concept of the "fully functioning person" is similar to the concept of the "self-actualized person" or the person engaged in "authentic living." These, too, have been noted as applicable to the therapist and have been considered as relevant to a therapist's effectiveness. These concepts applied to man in general, client or therapist, have been enunciated by others; Rogers, however, helps us to relate them to an understanding of personality. His explanation of the contradiction between a diagnostic impression of psychosis from projective tests and a therapist's simultaneous evaluation of great progress presents an interesting perspective to this seeming dilemma. The extrapolation of Rogers' analysis could bring to light other differences between diagnosticians and therapists which relate to the phenomenon. The mission of the diagnostician is to seek identifiable balances and imbalances in the personality. He examines the forces and movements to determine the directions behavior will take. Consequently when the diagnostician is confronted with an amorphous, ill-defined configuration, he is unable to identify its direction. He has associated unpredictable personality configurations with psychosis. This may be due to the diagnostician's exposure to a select population. His usual clientele consists of individuals who have established a protective, but less than fully effective, personality organization to cope with their doubts, fears, lack of direction, and vague searchings. In many instances this configuration has been observed in individuals who subsequently are identified as "psychotic." The psychotherapist has seen in his select population similar inner stirrings, doubts, and searchings as indicative of a breakup of the less than fully effective protective personality organization with the potential for achieving greater effectiveness. Thus, the state of flux which the *diagnostician* relates to psychosis has been seen by him most frequently in persons who have then manifested psychotic reactions. The *psychotherapist* has witnessed a seemingly similar state of flux, which he relates to greater progress, most frequently in persons who have then gone on to acquire more effective behavior patterns.

Rogers' discussion of the diagnostic-psychotherapeutic dilemma has been reexamined with a somewhat different explanation from the one he has offered, because it illustrates other implications. The expectancies which man has about himself are related to his experience in a manner similar to that of the interpretations of the expectancies of the diagnostician and the psychotherapist. These different interpretations, perceptions, or expectancies determine whether he will welcome new experiences and expect to be effective, or fear them because he may be incompetent. Trust produces an active anticipation of each new moment. One expects the new to be a desirable experience, and thus becomes more open, which permits fuller involvement in each moment. This openness grows with each new experience which is associated with desirable outcomes. As one anticipates that each new experience will be worthwhile, one becomes more open and involved in experiencing and trusting oneself. This in turn permits more experiences, each of which has the potential to further develop the trust in oneself. Consequently, the anticipation of worthwhile experiences and openness, involvement in each momentary occurrence, and trust in oneself go hand in hand, each supporting and reaffirming the other. This may be akin to a self-fulfilling prophecy.

The psychotherapeutic process is an experience which can provide the client with anticipations which will enable him to become open, existential, and trusting in himself. As the process acquires these same "fully functioning" attributes intended for the person, it leads to an awareness by those involved that they are more effective people. The relationship between client and psychotherapist assumes a dimension of intensity and involvement which makes this experience meaningful regardless of whether it is pleasant or unpleasant. This promotes greater trust, which then leads to further expectancies that it will be meaningful. Both parties through these expectancies become more open, involved, and trusting. The total psychotherapeutic experience begins to produce a "fully functioning" dyad. Rogers' objective for the client, which has been noted as applicable also to the psychotherapist, is actually an objective for the therapeutic process. The client does not move toward achieving a "fully functioning" condition alone; he does it in a special situation which provides the client with a sample of the fruits to be derived from being open and existential, and from trusting his own organism.

"Fully functioning" is not a state or condition in a static sense; it is an evolving set of attitudes toward oneself. These attitudes and ways of dealing with experiences continue to change, and with each new experience the individual obtains verification or refutation of its effectiveness. Hence, "fully functioning" permits the personality to develop under conditions in which the individual has knowledge of the impact of his responses and their consequences. This promotes adaptability: when one is aware of oneself, one is able to modify responses accordingly. Being able to focus fully on each moment becomes more significant, since it increases one's knowledge and awareness. The organism becomes more adept at responding to each new occurrence, which makes reactions more immediate and seemingly automatic. The individual meets each new circumstance as it occurs in a more effective manner. This adaptability enables one to trust one's own organism as being capable of producing the most satisfying behavior at each moment. The "fully functioning person" is constantly changing. He has faith in his ability to adapt to each new occurrence without requiring knowledge in advance of either the nature of the occurrence or the necessary adaptation.

This relates to Rogers' discussion of the dependability of behavior in spite of its unpredictability. His point is that a "fully functioning person" lives each moment and responds to each configuration of relationships and events on its present merits; thus it is impossible to predict his response. Yet the response, as Rogers notes, is dependable. The requirement of advance knowledge and the desire to predict indicate an apprehension and a desire to forestall or prepare for potentially disastrous events. Fears arise because the inability to predict has been associated with undesirable consequences. Since the "fully functioning person" expects to meet any event in an effective manner, prediction for him becomes less important.

If we relate this to psychotherapeutic orientations, it is similar to the idea that psychotherapy does not need to be planned, since the therapist responds to the client as he presents himself at each moment. There are those who feel that a therapeutic objective has to be determined, that goals have to be listed, that ways of achieving the goals must be identified for each client. There are others who feel that the general objectives are basically the same for all clients and that specific objectives will emerge in the course of therapy. For them, the psychotherapist does not predetermine what these specific objectives will be, but works them out with the client as their therapeutic relationship develops. It may be that in the latter orientation the therapist depends on himself and the process, and thus does not feel the need to anticipate or predict what the client will do next. This orientation is also based on the belief that a preoccupation with predicting may lessen his attending to the existential moment.

The concept of the "fully functioning person" has been applied here more broadly than to just the product of client-centered psychotherapy. Rogers, however, limits his discussion to the objectives of client-centered psychotherapy. In that context, he observes that one of the implications of this concept is the trustworthiness of human nature. But it would seem that, rather than this implication being derived from the concept, the concept is based on an assumption. The trustworthiness of human nature is fundamental to experiencing openness, existential living, and trust in one's organism. In client-centered therapy there is the implicit assumption that, if the individual is freed from the inhibiting influence of defensiveness, basic resources within the individual will be permitted to grow. The trustworthiness of human nature is a restatement of this assumption.

This seems similar to the "trust one's organism" attitude of the "fully functioning person." Trusting oneself is the basic characteristic of the three which Rogers gives. The other two, "openness" and "existential living," would appear to be dependent on it. It is highly improbable that one could be either open or existential without such trust. Since becoming a "fully functioning person" is part of a process, all of these characteristics emerge as the individual is able to incorporate them. A discussion of assumptions does not imply that a sequence exists. All of these attitudes toward oneself, as well as the orientations toward experiences and expectancies or anticipations, interact. It is just as appropriate to assume that, as one becomes more open, one then becomes more existential and more trusting of oneself as to assume that, as one becomes more trusting of oneself, one becomes more open and more existential. Other arrangements of these characteristics are equally relevant. The psychotherapeutic experience involves all of them as a part of achieving the "fully functioning" state. If we seek some basic philosophical characteristic, it would seem that trust in human nature is fundamental to trust in oneself, which in turn is basic to permitting openness and existential living. This philosophical ordering does not determine experiences, but is derived from experiences to help us interpret and understand them.

Let us accept, then, the basic assumption of the trustworthiness of human nature. If it is applied to personality, it supports the thesis that personality development is dependable. It also implies that the individual is an effective instrument for determining his own well-being. And it follows from this assumption that psychotherapy is a process which encourages or promotes the individual's use of himself as the best determiner of his behavior.

Creativity as a consequence of psychotherapy also follows logically from the ability of the individual to trust his organism to react competently. If one can trust oneself, then one is free to respond in new and previously untried fashions when they feel right. In this way, new relationships, experiences, thoughts, and actions come into being. The creative aspect of personality is dependent on the degree of trust the individual has in himself. Thus the more new configurations or relationships of previously unrelated events one permits, the more creative one may become. Similarly, expressions of inner experiences which previously were not a part of awareness can also promote creativity. Whether the individual's new arrangement of responses is to external or internal experiences, it can occur only if he is open to them and can focus on them fully when they do occur. This full involvement in the moment requires the faith that one can handle whatever will emerge, regardless of whether it has been previously experienced.

Rogers' discussion of the relationship between freedom and determinism contains many other implications. This philosophical problem has many dimensions, and one which was not discussed by Rogers is pertinent here. Freedom seems to relate to choices preceding behavior, whereas determinism seems to be based on post hoc interpretations. It may be that only when we examine events in retrospect do their logical sequences emerge and provide us with the impression that they were determined. The difficulty we have with prediction of behavior is testimony to its freedom. Freedom may, therefore, be observable only as we contemplate the future, for it is then that we can weigh alternatives and respond in a manner which denotes a choice. If this is later analyzed, with retrospective knowledge of the forces involved, it becomes understandable and the reason for the particular course of behavior can be explained. Only then do the behavior and the events which led up to it become so obvious that we conclude that the choice was not free but determined. Freedom of choice or determinism of behavior becomes a function of perspective and the time at which one views events. If one views behavior as it evolves, one becomes aware of the freedom involved; freedom is an existential phenomenon. If one views behavior only after it has occurred and then engages in the historical process of tracing its antecedents, one becomes aware of its determinants. Thus, determinism can only be retrospective and consequently finds itself frustrated when tested as a predictive concept.

The distance between freedom of choice and predetermination can be lessened if the number of choices is limited. The greater the number of choices, the greater the freedom and the more difficult it is to predict behavior. As one narrows the range, one increases the predictive odds, and if only one choice is available, a predetermined outcome can be assured. Narrowing or widening the range of choices will therefore affect predictability. A person's behavior becomes less predictable as he approaches the state of "fully functioning." As he opens himself and permits fuller existential involvement, he increases the range of choices since he is responding on a moment-to-moment basis, with complete freedom to select among all available alternatives. It is this freedom that is both dependable and creative. It is also this freedom which does not permit identification of a specific outcome and thus appears to leave the individual without any directedness. In this state of freedom, trust in one's organism becomes the reference point. It would appear that this is indicated in Rogers' discussion of the dependability and unpredictability of behavior.

Rogers has asked man to regard his uncertainties, lack of predictability, and freedom as desirable. He recognizes that these are conditions long associated with apprehension. Those who seek psychotherapy, probably more than others, have found these conditions to be fraught with anxiety and suffering. Thus, the psychotherapeutic process must reverse these unfavorable associations and provide a new set of expectancies. As the person becomes more "fully functioning," he can welcome the uncharted course and be open, respond on a moment-to-moment basis, and trust himself to make the most satisfying response to each situation. Teaching the person to react in this manner becomes the purpose of psychotherapy. Consequently, Rogers has helped us to define psychotherapy as a process in which the therapist enables the person to become more "fully functioning."

Yet if the therapist is to communicate to his client this orientation toward oneself and one's relationship to experiences, he himself must have achieved a reasonable degree of openness, existential living, and trust in his own organism. We might even assume that the more the therapist approaches the condition of a "fully functioning person" the more successfully he can communicate this state and enable his client to evolve in that direction. Thus, we may extend Rogers' discussion of the "fully functioning person" to an objective in the training and development of psychotherapists.

Rogers' concept has presented us not only with an understanding of the nature of psychotherapy and its purpose but with implications derived from the concept. It has enabled us to appreciate more fully the connection between a concept of man and the explanations of how he becomes what he is. Personality theory and psychotherapy theories seem to be an outgrowth of such concepts. These are not culture-free, nor are they independent of our philosophies. An explanation of how personality develops and the psychotherapeutic procedures which will promote this development are implicitly, if not explicitly, consistent with some concept of what man should be. Rogers has illustrated this in his examination of client-centered psychotherapy and the end product to be derived from it. The concept of the "fully functioning person" is consistent with the personality theory and psychotherapy from which it is spawned. It may even be that this concept, on an implicit level, enabled client-centered psychotherapy to evolve.

It would be an interesting exercise to take some other psychotherapeutic orientations and the theories of personality with which they are associated and derive a concept of man which would be consistent with them. The psychotherapy we practice relates not only to what we think man should be but also to what we think man is.

CHAPTER 8

Contributions of Existential Psychotherapy

Rollo May

The fundamental contribution of existential therapy is its understanding of man as *being*. It does not deny the validity of dynamisms and the
study of specific behavior patterns in their rightful places. But it holds
that drives or dynamisms, by whatever name one calls them, can be
understood only in the context of the structure of the existence of the
person we are dealing with. The distinctive character of existential
analysis is, thus, that it is concerned with *ontology*, the science of being,
and with *Dasein*, the existence of this particular being sitting opposite
the psychotherapist.

Before struggling with definitions of *being* and related terms, let us
begin existentially by reminding ourselves that what we are talking
about is an experience every sensitive therapist must have countless
times a day. It is the experience of the instantaneous encounter with
another person who comes alive to us on a very different level from
what we know *about* him. "Instantaneous" refers, of course, not to the
actual time involved but to the quality of the experience. We may know
a great deal about a patient from his case record, let us say, and may
have a fairly good idea of how other interviewers have described him.
But when the patient himself steps in, we often have a sudden, sometimes powerful, experience of here-is-a-new-person, an experience that
normally carries with it an element of surprise, not in the sense of perplexity or bewilderment, but in its etymological sense of being "taken
from above." This is of course in no sense a criticism of one's colleagues'
reports; for we have this experience of encounter even with persons we

This chapter was voted, by the Editorial Board of the present volume, one of the
creative developments in psychotherapy, 1958–1968. Chapter II of *Existence*, edited
by Rollo May, Ernest Angel, and Henri F. Ellenberger, © 1958 by Basic Books, Inc.,
Publishers, New York.

have known or worked with for a long time.[1] The data we learned *about* the patient may have been accurate and well worth learning. But the point rather is that *the grasping of the being of the other person occurs on a quite different level from our knowledge of specific things about him.* Obviously a knowledge of the drives and mechanisms which are in operation in the other person's behavior is useful; a familiarity with his patterns of interpersonal relationships is highly relevant; information about his social conditioning, the meaning of particular gestures and symbolic actions is of course to the point, and so on *ad infinitum.* But all these fall on to a quite different level when we confront the overarching, most real fact of all—namely, the immediate, living person himself. When we find that all our voluminous knowledge about the person suddenly forms itself into a new pattern in this confrontation, the implication is not that the knowledge was wrong; it is rather that it takes its meaning, form, and significance from the reality of the person of whom these specific things are expressions. Nothing we are saying here in the slightest deprecates the importance of gathering and studying seriously all the specific data one can get about the given person. This is only common sense. But neither can one close his eyes to the experiential fact that this data forms itself into a configuration given in the encounter with the person himself. This also is illustrated by the common experience we all have had in interviewing persons; we may say we do not get a "feeling" of the other person and need to prolong the interview until the data "breaks" into its own form in our minds. We particularly do not get this "feeling" when we ourselves are hostile or resenting the relationship—that is, keeping the other person out—no matter how intellectually bright we may be at the time. This is the classical distinction between *knowing* and *knowing about.* When we seek to know a person, the knowledge *about* him must be subordinated to the overarching fact of his actual existence.

In the ancient Greek and Hebrew languages the verb "to know" is the same word as that which means "to have sexual intercourse." This is illustrated time and again in the King James translation of the Bible— "Abraham knew his wife and she conceived . . ." and so on. Thus the etymological relation between knowing and loving is exceedingly close. Though we cannot go into this complex topic, we can at least say that knowing another human being, like loving him, involves a kind of union, a dialectical participation with the other. This Binswanger calls the "dual mode." One must have at least a readiness to love the other person, broadly speaking, if one is to be able to understand him.

The encounter with the being of another person has the power to shake one profoundly and may potentially be very anxiety-arousing. It may also be joy-creating. In either case, it has the power to grasp and move one deeply. The therapist understandably may be tempted for his own comfort to abstract himself from the encounter by thinking of the other as just a "patient" or by focusing only on certain mechanisms of behavior. But if the technical view is used dominantly in the relating to the other person, obviously one has defended himself from anxiety at the price not only of the isolation of himself from the other but also of radical distortion of reality. For one does not then really *see* the other person. It does not disparage the importance of technique to point out that technique, like data, must be subordinated to the fact of the reality of two persons in the room.

This point has been admirably made in a slightly different way by Sartre. If we "consider man," he writes, "as capable of being analyzed and reduced to original data, to determined drives (or 'desires'), supported by the subject as properties of an object," we may indeed end up with an imposing system of substances which we may then call mechanisms or dynamisms or patterns. But we find ourselves up against a dilemma. Our human being has become "a sort of indeterminate clay which would have to receive [the desires] passively—or he would be reduced to a simple bundle of these irreducible drives or tendencies. In either case the *man* disappears; we can no longer find 'the one' to whom this or that experience has happened."[2]

I To Be and Not To Be

It is difficult enough to give definitions of "being" and *Dasein*, but our task is made doubly difficult by the fact that these terms and their connotations encounter much resistance. Some readers may feel that these words are only a new form of "mysticism" (used in its disparaging and quite inaccurate sense of "misty") and have nothing to do with science. But this attitude obviously dodges the whole issue by disparaging it. It is interesting that the term "mystic" is used in this derogatory sense to mean anything we cannot segmentize and count. The odd belief prevails in our culture that a thing or experience is not real if we cannot make it mathematical, and somehow it must be real if we can reduce it to numbers. But this means making an abstraction out of it—mathematics is the abstraction par excellence, which is indeed its glory and the reason for its great usefulness. Modern Western man thus finds himself in the strange situation, after reducing something to an abstraction, of having then to persuade himself it is real. This has much to do with the sense of isolation and loneliness which is endemic in the modern Western world; for the only experience we let ourselves believe in as real is that which precisely is not. Thus we deny the reality of our own experience. The term "mystic," in this disparaging sense, is generally used in the service of obscurantism; certainly avoiding an issue by derogation is only to obscure it. Is not the scientific attitude rather, to try to see clearly what it is we are talking about and then to find whatever terms or symbols can best, with least distortion, describe this reality? It should not so greatly surprise us to find that "being" belongs to that class of realities, like "love" and "consciousness" (for two other examples), which we cannot segmentize or abstract without losing precisely what we set out to study. This does not, however, relieve us from the task of trying to understand and describe them.

A more serious source of resistance is one that runs through the whole of modern Western society—namely, the psychological need to avoid and, in some ways, repress, the whole concern with "being." In contrast to other cultures which may be very concerned with being—particularly Indian and Oriental—and other historical periods which have been so concerned, the characteristic of our period in the West, as Marcel rightly phrases it, is precisely that the awareness of "the sense of the ontological—the sense of being—is lacking. Generally speaking, modern man is in this condition; if ontological demands worry him at all, it is only dully, as an obscure impulse."[3] Marcel points out what many students have emphasized, that this loss of the sense of being is related on one hand to our tendency to subordinate existence to function: a man knows himself not as a man or self but as a ticket-seller in the subway, a grocer, a professor, a vice president of A. T. & T., or by whatever his economic function may be. And on the other hand, this loss of the sense of being is related to the mass collectivist trends and widespread conformist tendencies in our culture. Marcel then makes this trenchant challenge: *"Indeed I wonder if a psychoanalytic method, deeper and more discerning than any that has been evolved until now, would not reveal the morbid effects of the repression of this sense and of the ignoring of this need."*[4]

"As for defining the word 'being,'" Marcel goes on, "let us admit that it is extremely difficult; I would merely suggest this method of approach: being is what withstands—or what would withstand—an exhaustive analysis bearing on the data of experience and aiming to reduce them step by step to elements increasingly devoid of intrinsic or significant value. (An analysis of this kind is attempted in the theoretical works of Freud.)"[5] This last sentence I take to mean that when Freud's analysis is pushed to the ultimate extreme, and we know, let us say, everything about drives, instincts, and mechanisms, we have everything *except* being. Being is that which remains. It is that which constitutes this infinitely complex set of deterministic factors into a person *to whom* the experiences happen and who possesses some element, no matter how minute, of freedom to become aware that these forces are acting upon him. This is the sphere where he has the potential capacity to pause before reacting and thus to cast some weight on whether his reaction will go this way or that. And this, therefore, is the sphere where he, the human being, is never merely a collection of drives and determined forms of behavior.

The term the existential therapists use for the distinctive character of human existence is *Dasein*. Binswanger, Kuhn, and others designate their school as *Daseinsanalyse*. Composed of *sein* (being) plus *da* (there), *Dasein* indicates that man is the being who *is there* and implies also that he *has* a "there" in the sense that he can know he is there and can take a stand with reference to that fact. The "there" is moreover not just any place, but the particular "there" that is mine, the particular point *in time* as well as space of my existence at this given moment. Man is the being who can be conscious of, and therefore responsible for, his existence. It is this capacity to become aware of his own being which distinguishes the human being from other beings. The existential therapists think of man not only as "being-in-itself," as all beings are, but also as "being-for-itself." Binswanger and other authors in the chapters that follow speak of "*Dasein* choosing" this or that, meaning "the person-who-is-responsible-for-his-existence choosing. . . ."

The full meaning of the term "human being" will be clearer if the reader will keep in mind that "being" is a participle, a verb form implying that someone is in the process of *being something*. It is unfortunate that, when used as a general noun in English, the term "being" connotes a static substance, and when used as a particular noun such as *a* being, it is usually assumed to refer to an entity, say, such as a soldier to be counted as a unit. Rather, "being" should be understood, when used as a general noun, to mean *potentia*, the source of potentiality; "being" is the potentiality by which the acorn becomes the oak or each of us becomes what he truly is. And when used in a particular sense, such as *a* human being, it always has the dynamic connotation of someone in process, the person being something. Perhaps, therefore, *becoming* connotes more accurately the meaning of the term in this country. We can understand another human being only as we see what he is moving toward, what he is becoming; and we can know ourselves only as we "project our *potentia* in action." The significant tense for human beings is thus the *future*—that is to say, the critical question is what I am pointing toward, becoming, what I will be in the immediate future.

Thus, being in the human sense is not given once and for all. It does not unfold automatically as the oak tree does from the acorn. For an intrinsic and inseparable element in being human is self-consciousness. Man (or *Dasein*) is the particular being who has to be aware of himself, be responsible for himself, if he is to become himself. He also is that particular being who knows that at some future moment he will not be; he is the being who is always in a dialectical relation with non-being, death. And he not only knows he will sometime not be, but he can, in his own choices, slough off and forfeit his being. "To be and not to be"— the "and" in our subtitle to this section is not a typographical error—is not a choice one makes once and for all at the point of considering suicide; it reflects to some degree a choice made at every instant. The profound dialectic in the human being's awareness of his own being is pictured with incomparable beauty by Pascal:

Man is only a reed, the feeblest reed in nature, but he is a thinking reed. There is no need for the entire universe to arm itself in order to annihilate him: a vapour, a drop of water, suffices to kill him. But were the universe to crush him, man would yet be more noble than that which slays him, because he knows that he dies, and the advantage that the universe has over him; of this the universe knows nothing.[6]

In the hope of making clearer what it means for a person to experience his own being, we shall present an illustration from a case history. This patient, an intelligent woman of twenty-eight, was especially gifted in expressing what was occurring within her. She had come for psychotherapy because of serious anxiety spells in closed places, severe self-doubts, and eruptions of rage which were sometimes uncontrollable.[7] An illegitimate child, she had been brought up by relatives in a small village in the southwestern part of the country. Her mother, in periods of anger, often reminded her as a child of her origin, recounted how she had tried to abort her, and in times of trouble had shouted at the little girl, "If you hadn't been born, we wouldn't have to go through this!" Other relatives had cried at the child, in family quarrels, "Why didn't you kill yourself?" and "You should have been choked the day you were born!" Later, as a young woman, the patient had become well-educated on her own initiative.

In the fourth month of therapy she had the following dream: "I was in a crowd of people. They had no faces; they were like shadows. It seemed like a wilderness of people. Then I saw there was someone in the crowd who had compassion for me." The next session she reported that she had had, in the intervening day, an exceedingly important experience. It is reported here as she wrote it down from memory and notes two years later.

I remember walking that day under the elevated tracks in a slum area, feeling the thought, "I am an illegitimate child." I recall the sweat pouring forth in my anguish in trying to accept that fact. Then I understood what it must feel like to accept, "I am a Negro in the midst of privileged whites," or "I am blind in the midst of people who see." Later on that night I woke up and it came to me this way, "I accept the fact that I am an illegitimate child." But "I am not a child anymore." So it is, "I am illegitimate." That is not so either: "I was born illegitimate." Then what is left? What is left is this, "I Am." This act of contact and acceptance with "I am," once gotten hold of, gave me (what I think was for me the first time) the experience "Since I Am, I have the right to be."

What is this experience like? It is a primary feeling—it feels like receiving the deed to my house. It is the experience of my own aliveness not caring whether it turns out to be an ion or just a wave. It is like when a very young child I once reached the core of a peach and cracked the pit, not knowing what I would find and then feeling the wonder of finding the inner seed, good to eat in its bitter sweetness. . . . It is like a sailboat in the harbor being given an anchor so that, being made out of earthly things, it can by means of its anchor get in touch again with the earth, the ground from which its wood grew; it can lift its anchor to sail but always at times it can cast its anchor to weather the storm or rest a little. . . . It is my saying to Descartes, "I Am, therefore I think, I feel, I do."

It is like an axiom in geometry—never experiencing it would be like going through a geometry course not knowing the first axiom. It is like going into my very own Garden of Eden where I am beyond good and evil and all other human concepts. It is like the experience of the poets of the intuitive world, the mystics, except that instead of the pure feeling of and union with God it is the finding of and the union with my own being. It is like owning Cinderella's shoe and looking all over the world for the foot it will fit and realizing all of a sudden that one's own foot is the only one it will fit. It is a "Matter of Fact" in the etymological sense of the expression. It is like a globe before the mountains and oceans and continents have been drawn on it. It is like a child in grammar finding the subject of the verb in a sentence—in this case the subject being one's own life span. It is ceasing to feel like a theory toward one's self. . . .

We shall call this the "I-am" experience.[8] This one phase of a complex case, powerfully and beautifully described above, illustrates the emergence and strengthening of the sense of being in one person. The experience is etched the more sharply in this person because of the more patent threat to her being that she had suffered as an illegitimate child and her poetic articulateness as she looked back on her experience from the vantage point of two years later. I do not believe either of these facts, however, makes her experience different in fundamental quality from what human beings in general, normal or neurotic, go through.

We shall make four final comments on the experience exemplified in this case. First, the "I-am" experience is not in itself the solution to a person's problems; it is rather the *precondition* for their solution. This patient spent some two years thereafter working through specific psychological problems, which she was able to do on the basis of this emerged experience of her own existence. In the broadest sense, of course, the achieving of the sense of being is a goal of all therapy, but in the more precise sense it is a relation to one's self and one's world, an experience of one's own existence (including one's own identity), which is a prerequisite for the working through of specific problems. It is, as the patient wrote, the "primary fact," a *ur* experience. It is not to be identified with any patient's discovery of his or her specific powers—when he learns, let us say, that he can paint or write or work successfully or have successful sexual intercourse. Viewed from the outside, the discovery of specific powers and the experience of one's own being may seem to go hand in hand, but the latter is the underpinning, the foundation, the psychological precondition of the former. We may well be suspicious that solutions to a person's specific problems in psychotherapy which do not presuppose this "I-am" experience in greater or lesser degree will have a pseudo quality. The new "powers" the patient discovers may well be experienced by him as merely compensatory— that is, as proofs that he is of significance despite the fact that he is certain on a deeper level that he is not, since he still lacks a basic conviction of "*I Am*, therefore I think, I act." And we could well wonder whether such compensatory solutions would not represent rather the patient's simply exchanging one defense system for another, one set of terms for another, without ever experiencing himself as existing. In the second state the patient, instead of blowing up in anger, "sublimates" or "introverts" or "relates," but still without the act being rooted in his own existence.

Our second comment is that this patient's "I-am" experience is not to be explained by the transference relationship. That the positive transference, whether directed to therapist or husband,[9] is obviously present in the above case is shown in the eloquent dream the night before in which there was one person in the barren, depersonalized wilderness of the crowd who had compassion for her. True, she is showing in the dream that she could have the "I-am" experience only if she could trust some other human being. But this does not account for the experience itself. It may well be true that for any human being the possibility of acceptance by and trust for another human being is a necessary condition for the "I-am" experience. But the awareness of one's own being occurs basically on the level of the grasping of one's self; it is an experience of *Dasein*, realized in the realm of self-awareness. It is not to be explained *essentially* in social categories. The acceptance by another person, such as the therapist, shows the patient that he no longer needs to fight his main battle on the front of whether anyone else, or the world, can accept him; the acceptance *frees* him to experience his own being. This point must be emphasized because of the common error in many circles of assuming that the experience of one's own being will take place automatically if only one is accepted by somebody else. This is the basic error of some forms of "relationship therapy." The attitude of "If-I-love-and-accept-you, this-is-all-you-need," is in life and in therapy an attitude which may well minister to increased passivity. The crucial question is what the individual himself, in his own awareness of and responsibility for his existence, does with the fact that he can be accepted.

The third comment follows directly from the above, that *being* is a category which cannot be reduced to introjection of social and ethical norms. It is, to use Nietzsche's phrase, "beyond good and evil." To the extent that my sense of existence is authentic, it is precisely *not* what others have told me I should be, but is the one Archimedes point I have to stand on from which to judge what parents and other authorities demand. Indeed, *compulsive and rigid moralism arises in given persons precisely as the result of a lack of a sense of being.* Rigid moralism is a compensatory mechanism by which the individual persuades himself to take over the external sanctions because he has no fundamental assurance that his own choices have any sanction of their own. This is not to deny the vast social influences in anyone's morality, but it is to say that the ontological sense cannot be wholly reduced to such influences. The ontological sense *is not a superego* phenomenon. By the same token the sense of being gives the person a basis for a self-esteem which is not merely the reflection of others' views about him. For if your self-esteem must rest in the long run on social validation, you have, not self-esteem, but a more sophisticated form of social conformity. It cannot be said too strongly that the sense of one's own existence, though interwoven with all kinds of social relatedness, is in basis not the product of social forces; it always presupposes *Eigenwelt,* the "own world" (a term which will be discussed below).

Our fourth comment deals with the most important consideration of all, namely that the "I-am" experience must not be identified with what is called in various circles the "functioning of the ego." That is to say, it is an error to define the emergence of awareness of one's own being as one phase of the "development of the ego." We need only reflect on what the concept of "ego" has meant in classical psychoanalytic tradition to see why this is so. The ego was traditionally conceived as a relatively weak, shadowy, passive, and derived agent, largely an epiphenomenon of other more powerful processes. It is "derived from the Id by modifications imposed on it from the external world" and is "representative of the external world."[10] "What we call the ego is essentially passive," says Groddeck, a statement which Freud cites with approval.[11] The developments in the middle period of psychoanalytic theory brought increased emphasis on the ego, to be sure, but chiefly as an aspect of the study of defense mechanisms; the ego enlarged its originally buffeted and frail realm chiefly by its negative, defensive functions. It "owes service to three masters and is consequently menaced by three dangers: the external world, the libido of the Id, the severity of the Super-ego."[12] Freud often remarked that the ego does very well indeed if it can preserve some semblance of harmony in its unruly house.

A moment's thought will show how great is the difference between this ego and the "I-am" experience, the sense of being which we have been discussing. The latter occurs on a more fundamental level and is a precondition for ego development. The ego is a *part* of the personality, and traditionally a relatively weak part, whereas the sense of being refers to one's whole experience, unconscious as well as conscious, and is by no means merely the agent of awareness. The ego is a reflection of the outside world; the sense of being is rooted in one's own experience of existence, and if it is a mirroring of, a reflection of, the outside world alone, it is then precisely not one's own sense of existence. My sense of being is *not* my capacity to see the outside world, to size it up, to assess reality; it is rather my capacity to see myself as a being in the world, *to know myself as the being who can do these things.* It is in this sense a precondition for what is called "ego development." The ego is the *subject* in the subject-object relationship; the sense of being occurs on a level prior to this dichotomy. Being means not "I am the subject," but "I am the being who can, among other things, know himself as the subject of what is occurring." The sense of being is not in origin set against the outside world but it must include this capacity to set one's self against the external world if necessary, just as it must include the capacity to confront non-being, as we shall indicate later. To be sure, both what is called the ego and the sense of being presuppose the emergence of self-awareness in the child somewhere between the first couple of months of infancy and the age of two years, a developmental process often called the "emergence of the ego." But this does not mean these two should be identified. The ego is said normally to be especially weak in childhood, weak in proportion to the child's relatively weak assessment of and relation to reality; whereas the sense of being may be especially strong, only later to diminish as the child learns to give himself over to conformist tendencies, to experience his existence as a reflection of others' evaluation of him, to lose some of his originality and primary sense of being. Actually, the sense of being—that is, the ontological sense—is presupposed for ego development, just as it is presupposed for the solution of other problems.[13]

We are of course aware that additions and elaborations are occurring in ego theory of late decades in the orthodox psychoanalytic tradition. But one cannot strengthen such a weak monarch by decking him with additional robes, no matter how well-woven or intricately tailored the robes may be. The real and fundamental trouble with the doctrine of the ego is that it represents, par excellence, the subject-object dichotomy in modern thought. Indeed, it is necessary to emphasize that *the very fact that the ego is conceived of as weak, passive, and derived is itself an evidence and a symptom of the loss of the sense of being in our day, a symptom of the repression of the ontological concern.* This view of the ego is a symbol of the pervasive tendency to see the human being primarily as a passive recipient of forces acting upon him, whether the forces be identified as the Id or the vast industrial juggernaut in Marxian terms or the submersion of the individual as "one among many" in the sea of conformity, in Heidegger's terms. The view of the ego as relatively weak and buffeted about by the Id was in Freud a profound symbol of the fragmentation of man in the Victorian period and also a strong corrective to the superficial voluntarism of that day. But the error arises when this ego is elaborated as the basic norm. The sense of being, the ontological awareness, must be assumed below ego theory if that theory is to refer with self-consistency to man as man.

We now come to the important problem of *non-being* or, as phrased in existential literature, *nothingness*. The "and" in the title of this section, "To Be *and* Not To Be," expresses the fact that non-being is an inseparable part of being. To grasp what it means to exist, one needs to grasp the fact that he might not exist, that he treads at every moment on the sharp edge of possible annihilation and can never escape the fact that death will arrive at some unknown moment in the future. Existence, never automatic, not only can be sloughed off and forfeited but is indeed at every instant threatened by non-being. Without this awareness of non-being—that is, awareness of the threats to one's being in death, anxiety, and the less dramatic but persistent threats of loss of potentialities in conformism—existence is vapid, unreal, and characterized by lack of concrete self-awareness. But with the confronting of non-being, existence takes on vitality and immediacy, and the individual experiences a heightened consciousness of himself, his world, and others around him.

Death is of course the most obvious form of the threat of non-being. Freud grasped this truth on one level in his symbol of the death instinct. Life forces (being) are arrayed at every moment, he held, against the forces of death (non-being), and in every individual life the latter will ultimately triumph. But Freud's concept of the death instinct is an ontological truth and should not be taken as a deteriorated psychological theory. The concept of the death instinct is an excellent example of our earlier point that Freud went beyond technical reason and tried to keep open the tragic dimension of life. His emphasis on the inevitability of hostility, aggression, and self-destructiveness in existence also, from one standpoint, has this meaning. True, he phrased these concepts wrongly, as when he interpreted the "death instinct" in chemical terms. The use of the word "thanatos" in psychoanalytic circles as parallel to libido is an example of this deteriorated phraseology. These are errors which arise from trying to put ontological truths, which death and tragedy are, into the frame of technical reason and reduce them to specific psychological mechanisms. On that basis Horney and others could logically argue that Freud was too "pessimistic" and that he merely rationalized war and aggression. I think that is a sound argument against the usual oversimplified psychoanalytic interpretations, which are in the form of technical reason; but it is not a sound argument against Freud himself, who tried to preserve a real concept of tragedy, ambivalent though his frame of reference was. He had indeed a sense of non-being, despite the fact that he always tried to subordinate it and his concept of being to technical reason.

It is also an error to see the "death instinct" only in biological terms, which would leave us hobbled with a fatalism. The unique and crucial fact, rather, is that the human being is the one who *knows* he is going to die, who anticipates his own death. The critical question thus is how he relates to the fact of death: whether he spends his existence running away from death or making a cult of repressing the recognition of death under the rationalizations of beliefs in automatic progress or providence, as is the habit of our Western society, or obscuring it by saying "one dies" and turning it into a matter of public statistics which serve to cover over the one ultimately important fact, that he himself at some unknown future moment will die.

The existential analysts, on the other hand, hold that the confronting of death gives the most positive reality to life itself. It makes the individual existence real, absolute, and concrete. For "death as an irrelative potentiality singles man out and, as it were, individualizes him to make him understand the potentiality of being in others [as well as in himself], when he realizes the inescapable nature of his own death."[14] Death is, in other words, the one fact of my life which is not relative but absolute, and my awareness of this gives my existence and what I do each hour an absolute quality.

Nor do we need to go as far as the extreme example of death to see the problem of non-being. Perhaps the most ubiquitous and ever-present form of the failure to confront non-being in our day is in *conformism*, the tendency of the individual to let himself be absorbed in the sea of collective responses and attitudes, to become swallowed up in *das Man*, with the corresponding loss of his own awareness, potentialities, and whatever characterizes him as a unique and original being. The individual temporarily escapes the anxiety of non-being by this means, but at the price of forfeiting his own powers and sense of existence.

On the positive side, the capacity to confront non-being is illustrated in the ability to accept anxiety, hostility, and aggression. By "accept" we mean here to tolerate without repression and so far as possible to utilize constructively. Severe anxiety, hostility, and aggression are states and ways of relating to one's self and others which would curtail or destroy being. But to preserve one's existence by running away from situations which would produce anxiety or situations of potential hostility and aggression leaves one with the vapid, weak, unreal sense of being—what Nietzsche meant in his brilliant description we quoted in the previous chapter of the "impotent people" who evade their aggression by repressing it and thereupon experience "drugged tranquillity" and free-floating resentment. Our point does not at all imply the sloughing over of the distinction between the *neurotic* and *normal* forms of anxiety, hostility, and aggression. Obviously the one constructive way to confront neurotic anxiety, hostility, and aggression is to clarify them psychotherapeutically and so far as possible to wipe them out. But that task has been made doubly difficult, and the whole problem confused, by our failure to see the normal forms of these states—"normal" in the sense that they inhere in the threat of non-being with which any being always has to cope. Indeed, is it not clear that *neurotic* forms of anxiety, hostility, and aggression develop precisely because the individual has been unable to accept and deal with the *normal* forms of these states and ways of behaving? Paul Tillich has suggested far-reaching implications for the therapeutic process in his powerful sentence, which we shall quote without attempting to elucidate, "The self-affirmation of a being is the stronger the more non-being it can take into itself."

II ANXIETY AND GUILT AS ONTOLOGICAL

Our discussion of being and non-being now leads to the point where we can understand the fundamental nature of anxiety. Anxiety is not an affect among other affects such as pleasure or sadness. It is rather an ontological characteristic of man, rooted in his very existence as such. It is not a peripheral threat which I can take or leave, for example, or a reaction which may be classified beside other reactions; it is always a threat to the foundation, the center of my existence. Anxiety is *the experience of the threat of imminent non-being*.[15]

In his classical contributions to the understanding of anxiety, Kurt Goldstein has emphasized that anxiety is not something we "have" but something we "are." His vivid descriptions of anxiety at the onset of psychosis, when the patient is literally experiencing the threat of dissolution of the self, make his point abundantly clear. But, as he himself insists, this threat of dissolution of the self is not merely something confined to psychotics but describes the neurotic and normal nature of anxiety as well. Anxiety is the subjective state of the individual's becoming aware that his existence can become destroyed, that he can lose himself and his world, that he can become "nothing."[16]

This understanding of anxiety as ontological illuminates the difference between anxiety and fear. The distinction is not one of degree nor of the intensity of the experience. The anxiety a person feels when some-one he respects passes him on the street without speaking, for example, is not as intense as the fear he experiences when the dentist seizes the drill to attack a sensitive tooth. But the gnawing threat of the slight on the street may hound him all day long and torment his dreams at night, whereas the feeling of fear, though it was quantitatively greater, is gone forever as soon as he steps out of the dentist's chair. The difference is that the anxiety strikes at the center core of his self-esteem and his sense of value as a self, which is one important aspect of his experience of himself as a being. Fear, in contrast, is a threat to the periphery of his existence; it can be objectivated, and the person can stand outside and look at it. In greater or lesser degree, anxiety overwhelms the person's awareness of existence, blots out the sense of time, dulls the memory of the past, and erases the future[17]—which is perhaps the most com-pelling proof of the fact that it attacks the center of one's being. While we are subject to anxiety, we are to that extent unable to conceive in imagination how existence would be "outside" the anxiety. This is of course why anxiety is so hard to bear, and why people will choose, if they have the chance, severe physical pain which would appear to the outside observer much worse. Anxiety is ontological, fear is not. Fear can be studied as an affect among other affects, a reaction among other reactions. But anxiety can be understood only as a threat to *Dasein*.

This understanding of anxiety as an ontological characteristic again highlights our difficulty with words. The term which Freud, Binswanger, Goldstein, Kierkegaard (as he is translated into German) use for anx-iety is *Angst*, a word for which there is no English equivalent. It is first cousin to anguish (which comes from Latin *angustus*, "narrow," which in turn comes from *angere*, "to pain by pushing together," "to choke"). The English term *anxiety*, such as in "I am anxious to do this or that," is a much weaker word.[18] Hence some students translate *Angst* as "dread," as did Lowrie in his translations of Kierkegaard and as the translators of Ellen West have done in *Existence*. Some of us have tried to preserve the term "anxiety" for *Angst*[19] but we were caught in a dilemma. It seemed the alternative was either to use "anxiety" as a watered-down affect among other affects, which will work scientifically but at the price of the loss of power of the word; or to use such a term as "dread," which carries literary power but has no role as a scientific category. Hence so often laboratory experiments on anxiety have seemed to fall woefully short of dealing with the power and devastating qualities of anxiety which we observe every day in clinical work, and also even clinical discussions about neurotic symptoms and psychotic conditions seem often to coast along the surface of the problem. The upshot of the existential understanding of anxiety is to give the term back its original power. It is an experience of threat which carries both anguish and dread, indeed the most painful and basic threat which any being can suffer, for it is the threat of loss of existence itself. In my judgment, our psychological and psychiatric dealings with anxiety phenomena of all sorts will be greatly helped by shifting the concept to its ontological base.

Another significant aspect of anxiety may now also be seen more clearly, namely, the fact that anxiety always involves inner conflict. Is not this conflict precisely between what we have called being and non-being? Anxiety occurs at the point where some emerging potentiality or possibility faces the individual, some possibility of fulfilling his existence; but this very possibility involves the destroying of present security, which thereupon gives rise to the tendency to deny the new potentiality. Here lies the truth of the symbol of the birth trauma as the prototype of all anxiety—an interpretation suggested by the etymological source of the word "anxiety" as "pain in narrows," "choking," as though through the straits of being born. This interpretation of anxiety as birth trauma was, as is well known, held by Rank to cover all anxiety and agreed to by Freud on a less comprehensive basis. There is no doubt that it carries an important symbolic truth even if one does not take it as connected with the literal birth of the infant. If there were not some possibility opening up, some potentiality crying to be "born," we would not experience anxiety. This is why anxiety is so profoundly connected with the problem of freedom. If the individual did not have some freedom, no matter how minute, to fulfill some new potentiality, he would not experience anxiety. Kierkegaard described anxiety as "the dizziness of freedom," and added more explicitly, if not more clearly, "Anxiety is the reality of freedom as a potentiality before this freedom has materialized." Goldstein illustrates this by pointing out how people individually and collectively surrender freedom in the hope of getting rid of unbearable anxiety, citing the individual's retreating behind the rigid stockade of dogma or whole groups collectively turning to fascism in recent decades in Europe.[20] In whatever way one chooses to illustrate it, this discussion points to the positive aspect of *Angst*. For the experience of anxiety itself demonstrates that some potentiality is present, some new possibility of being, threatened by non-being.

We have stated that the condition of the individual when confronted with the issue of fulfilling his potentialities is *anxiety*. We now move on to state that when the person denies these potentialities, fails to fulfill them, his condition is *guilt*. That is to say, guilt is also an ontological characteristic of human existence.

This can be no better illustrated than to summarize a case Medard Boss cites of a severe obsessional-compulsive which he treated.[21] This patient, a physician suffering from washing, cleaning compulsions, had gone through both Freudian and Jungian analyses. He had had for some time a recurrent dream involving church steeples which had been interpreted in the Freudian analysis in terms of phallic symbols and in the Jungian in terms of religious archetype symbols. The patient could discuss these interpretations intelligently and at length, but his neurotic compulsive behavior, after temporary abeyance, continued as crippling as ever. During the first months of his analysis with Boss, the patient reported a recurrent dream in which he would approach a lavatory door which would always be locked. Boss confined himself to asking each time only why the door needed to be locked—to "rattling the doorknob," as he put it. Finally the patient had a dream in which he went through the door and found himself inside a church, waist deep in faeces and being tugged by a rope wrapped around his waist leading up to the bell tower. The patient was suspended in such tension that he thought he would be pulled to pieces. He then went through a psychotic episode of four days during which Boss remained by his bedside, after which the analysis continued with an eventual very successful outcome.

Boss points out in his discussion of this case that the patient was guilty because he had locked up some essential potentialities in himself. *Therefore* he had guilt feelings. If, as Boss puts it, we "forget being"—by failing to bring ourselves to our entire being, by failing to be authentic, by slipping into the conformist anonymity of *das Man*— then we have in fact missed our being and to that extent are failures. "If you lock up potentialities, you are guilty against (or *indebted to*, as the German word may be translated) what is given you in your origin, in your 'core.' In this existential condition of being indebted and being guilty are founded all guilt feelings, in whatever thousand and one concrete forms and malformations they may appear in actuality." This is what had happened to the patient. He had locked up both the bodily and the spiritual possibilities of experience (the "drive" aspect and the "god" aspect, as Boss also phrases it). The patient had previously accepted the libido and archetype explanations and knew them all too well; but that is a good way, says Boss, to escape the whole thing.

Because the patient did not accept and take into his existence these two aspects, he was guilty, indebted to himself. This was the origin (*Anlass*) of his neurosis and psychosis.

The patient, in a letter to Boss sometime after the treatment, pointed out that the reason he could not really accept his anality in his first analysis was that he "sensed the ground was not fully developed in the analyst himself." The analyst had always attempted to reduce the dream of the church steeple to genital symbols and the "whole weight of the holy appeared to him as a mere sublimation mist." By the same token, the archetypal explanation, also symbolic, never could be integrated with the bodily, and for that matter never did really mesh with the religious experience either.

Let us note well that Boss says the patient *is* guilty, not merely that he *has guilt feelings*. This is a radical statement with far-reaching implications. It is an existential approach which cuts through the dense fog which has obscured much of the psychological discussion of guilt—discussions that have proceeded on the assumption that we can deal only with some vague "guilt feelings," as though it did not matter whether guilt was real or not. Has not this reduction of guilt to mere guilt feelings contributed considerably to the lack of reality and the sense of illusion in much psychotherapy? Has it not also tended to confirm the patient's neurosis in that it implicitly opens the way for him not to take his guilt seriously and to make peace with the fact that he has indeed forfeited his own being? Boss's approach is radically existential in that it takes the real phenomena with respect, here the real phenomenon being guilt. Nor is the guilt exclusively linked up with the religious aspect of this, or any patient's, experience: we can be as guilty by refusing to accept the anal, genital, or any other corporeal aspects of life as the intellectual or spiritual aspects. This understanding of guilt has nothing whatever to do with a judgmental attitude toward the patient. It has only to do with taking the patient's life and experience seriously and with respect.

We have cited only one form of ontological guilt, namely, that arising from forfeiting one's own potentialities. There are other forms as well. Another, for example, is ontological guilt against one's fellows, arising from the fact that since each of us is an individual, he necessarily perceives his fellow man through his own limited and biased eyes. This means that he always to some extent does violence to the true picture of his fellow man and always to some extent fails fully to understand and meet the other's needs. This is not a question of moral failure or slackness—though it can indeed be greatly increased by lack of moral sensitivity. It is an inescapable result of the fact that each of us is a separate individuality and has no choice but to look at the world through his own eyes. This guilt, rooted in our existential structure, is one of the most potent sources of a sound humility and an unsentimental attitude of forgiveness toward one's fellow men.

The first form of ontological guilt mentioned above, namely, forfeiting of potentialities, corresponds roughly to the mode of world which we shall describe and define in the next section called *Eigenwelt*, or own-world. The second form of guilt corresponds roughly to *Mitwelt*, since it is guilt chiefly related to one's fellow men. There is a third form of ontological guilt which involves *Umwelt* as well as the other two modes, namely, "separation guilt" in relation to nature as a whole. This is the most complex and comprehensive aspect of ontological guilt. It may seem confusing, particularly since we are unable in this outline to explicate it in detail; we include it for the sake of completeness and for the interest of those who may wish to do further research in areas of ontological guilt. This guilt with respect to our separation from nature may well be much more influential (though repressed) than we realize in our modern Western scientific age. It was originally expressed beautifully in a classical fragment from one of the early Greek philosophers of being, Anaximander: "The source of things is the boundless. From whence they arise, thence they must also of necessity return. For they do penance and make compensation to one another for their injustice in the order of time."

Ontological guilt has, among others, these characteristics. *First*, everyone participates in it. No one of us fails to some extent to distort the reality of his fellow men, and no one fully fulfills his own potentialities. Each of us is always in a dialectical relation to his potentialities, dramatically illustrated in the dream of Boss's patient being stretched between faeces and bell tower. *Second*, ontological guilt does not come from cultural prohibitions, or from introjection of cultural mores; it is rooted in the fact of self-awareness. Ontological guilt does not consist of I-am-guilty-because-I-violate-parental-prohibitions, but arises from the fact that I can see myself as the one who can choose or fail to choose. Every developed human being would have this ontological guilt, though its *content* would vary from culture to culture and would largely be given by the culture.

Third, ontological guilt is not to be confused with morbid or neurotic guilt. If it is unaccepted and repressed, it may turn into neurotic guilt. Just as neurotic anxiety is the end-product of unfaced normal ontological anxiety, so neurotic guilt is the result of unconfronted ontological guilt.

If the person can become aware of it and accept it (as Boss's patient later did), it is not morbid or neurotic. *Fourth*, ontological guilt does not lead to symptom formation, but has constructive effects in the personality. Specifically, it can and should lead to humility, as suggested above, sharpened sensitivity in relationships with fellow men, and increased creativity in the use of one's own potentialities.

III BEING-IN-THE-WORLD

Another one of the major and far-reaching contributions of the existential therapists—to my mind second in importance only to their analysis of being—is the understanding of the person-in-his-world. "To understand the compulsive," writes Erwin Straus, "we must first understand his world"—and this is certainly true of all other types of patients as well as any human being, for that matter. For *being together* means *being together in the same world*; and knowing means knowing in the context of the same world. The world of this particular patient must be grasped from the inside, be known and seen so far as possible from the angle of the one who exists in it. "We psychiatrists," writes Binswanger, "have paid far too much attention to the deviations of our patients from life in the world which is common to all, instead of focusing primarily upon the patients' own or private world, as was first systematically done by Freud."[22]

The problem is how we are to understand the other person's world. It cannot be understood as an external collection of objects which we view from the outside (in which case we never really understand it), nor by sentimental identification (in which case our understanding doesn't do any good, for we have failed to preserve the reality of our own existence). A difficult dilemma indeed! What is required is an approach to world which undercuts the "cancer," namely, the traditional subject-object dichotomy.

The reason this endeavor to rediscover man as being-in-the-world is so important is that it strikes directly at one of the most acute problems of modern human beings—namely, that they have *lost their world*, lost their experience of community. Kierkegaard, Nietzsche, and the existentialists who followed them perdurably pointed out that the two chief sources of modern Western man's anxiety and despair were, first, his loss of sense of being and, secondly, his loss of his world. The existential analysts believe there is much evidence that these prophets were correct and that twentieth-century Western man not only experiences an alienation from the human world about him but also suffers an inner, harrowing conviction of being estranged (like, say, a paroled convict) in the natural world as well.

The writings of Frieda Fromm-Reichmann and Sullivan describe the state of the person who has lost his world. These authors, and others like them, illustrate how the problems of loneliness, isolation, and alienation are being increasingly dealt with in psychiatric literature. The assumption would seem likely that there is an increase not only in awareness of these problems among psychiatrists and psychologists but also in the presence of the conditions themselves. Broadly speaking, the symptoms of isolation and alienation reflect the state of a person whose relation to the world has become broken. Some psychotherapists have pointed out that more and more patients exhibit schizoid features and that the "typical" kind of psychic problem in our day is not hysteria, as it was in Freud's time, but the schizoid type—that is to say, problems of persons who are detached, unrelated, lacking in affect, tending toward depersonalization, and covering up their problems by means of intellectualization and technical formulations.

There is also plenty of evidence that the sense of isolation, the alienation of one's self from the world, is suffered not only by people in pathological conditions but by countless "normal" persons as well in our day. Riesman presents a good deal of sociopsychological data in his study *The Lonely Crowd* to demonstrate that the isolated, lonely, alienated character type is characteristic not only of neurotic patients but of people as a whole in our society and that the trends in that direction have been increasing over the past couple of decades. He makes the significant point that these people have only a *technical* communication with their world; his "outer-directed" persons (the type characteristic of our day) relate to everything from its technical, external side. Their orientation, for example, was not "I liked the play," but "The play was *well done*," "the article *well written*," and so forth. Other portrayals of this condition of personal isolation and alienation in our society are given by Fromm in *Escape from Freedom*, particularly with respect to sociopolitical considerations; by Karl Marx, particularly in relation to the dehumanization arising out of the tendency in modern capitalism to value everything in the external, object-centered terms of money; and by Tillich from the spiritual viewpoint. Camus's *The Stranger* and Kafka's *The Castle*, finally, are surprisingly similar illustrations of our point: each gives a vivid and gripping picture of a man who is a stranger in his world, a stranger to other people whom he seeks or pretends to love; he moves about in a state of homelessness, vagueness, and haze as though he had no direct sense connection with his world but were in a foreign country where he does not know the language and has no hope of learning it but is always doomed to wander in quiet despair, incommunicado, homeless, and a stranger.

Nor is the problem of this loss of world simply one of lack of interpersonal relations or lack of communication with one's fellows. Its roots reach below the social levels to an alienation from the natural world as well. It is a particular experience of isolation which has been called "epistemological loneliness."[23] Underlying the economic, sociological, and psychological aspects of alienation can be found a profound common denominator, namely, the alienation which is the ultimate consequence of four centuries of the outworking of the separation of man as subject from the objective world. This alienation has expressed itself for several centuries in Western man's passion to gain power *over* nature, but now shows itself in an estrangement from nature and a vague, unarticulated, and half-suppressed sense of despair of gaining any real relationship with the natural world, including one's own body.

These sentences may sound strange in this century of apparent scientific confidence. But let us examine the matter more closely. In his excellent chapter in *Existence*, Straus points out that Descartes, the father of modern thought, held that ego and consciousness were separated from the world and from other persons.[24] That is to say, consciousness is cut off and stands by itself alone. Sensations do not tell us anything directly about the outside world; they only give us inferential data. Descartes is commonly the whipping boy in these days and made to shoulder the blame for the dichotomy between subject and object; but he was of course only reflecting the spirit of his age and the underground tendencies in modern culture, about which he saw and wrote with beautiful clarity. The Middle Ages, Straus goes on to say, is commonly thought of as other-worldly in contrast to the "present world" concerns of modern man. But actually the medieval Christian's soul was considered, while it did exist in the world, to be really related to the world. Men experienced the world about them as directly real (*vide* Giotto) and the body as immediate and real (*vide* St. Francis). Since Descartes, however, the soul and nature have had nothing to do with each other. Nature belongs exclusively to the realm of *res extensa*, to be understood mathematically. We know the world only indirectly, by inference. This of course sets the problem we have been wrestling with ever since, the full implications of which did not emerge until the last century. Straus points out how the traditional textbooks on neurology and physiology have accepted this doctrine, and have endeavored to demonstrate that what goes on neurologically has only a "sign" relation to the real world.

Only "unconscious inferences lead to the assumption of the existence of an outside world."[25]

Thus it is by no means accidental that modern man feels estranged from nature, that each consciousness stands off by itself, alone. This has been "built in" to our education and to some extent even into our language. It means that the overcoming of this situation of isolation is not a simple task and requires something much more fundamental than merely the rearrangement of some of our present ideas. This alienation of man from the natural and human world sets one of the problems which writers in this volume try to meet.

Let us now inquire how the existential analysts undertake to rediscover man as a being interrelated with his world and to rediscover world as meaningful to man. They hold that the person and his world are a unitary, structural whole; the hyphenation of the phrase being-in-the-world expresses precisely that. The two poles, self and world, are always dialectically related. Self implies world and world self; there is neither without the other, and each is understandable only in terms of the other. It makes no sense, for example, to speak of man in his world (though we often do) as primarily a *spatial* relation. The phrase "match *in* a box" does imply a spatial relation, but to speak of a man *in* his home or in his office or in a hotel at the seashore implies something radically different.[26]

A person's world cannot be comprehended by describing the environment, no matter how complex we make our description. As we shall see below, environment is only one mode of world; and the common tendencies to talk of a person *in* an environment or to ask what "influence the environment has upon him" are vast oversimplifications. Even from a biological viewpoint, Von Uexküll holds, one is justified in assuming as many environments (*Umwelten*) as there are animals; "there is not one space and time only," he goes on to say, "but as many spaces and times as there are subjects."[27] How much more would it not be true that the human being has his own world? Granted that this confronts us with no easy problem: for we cannot describe world in purely objective terms, nor is world to be limited to our subjective, imaginative participation in the structure around us, although that too is part of being-in-the-world.

World is the structure of meaningful relationships in which a person exists and in the design of which he participates. Thus world includes the past events which condition my existence and all the vast variety of deterministic influences which operate upon me. But it is these *as I relate to them,* am aware of them, carry them with me, molding, inevitably forming, building them in every minute of relating. For to be aware of one's world means at the same time to be designing it.

World is not to be limited to the past determining events but includes also all the possibilities which open up before any person and are not simply given in the historical situation. World is thus not to be identified with "culture." It includes culture but a good deal more, such as *Eigen-welt* (the own-world which cannot be reduced merely to an introjection of the culture), as well as all the individual's future possibilities.[28] "One would get some idea," Schachtel writes, "of the unimaginable richness and depth of the world and its possible meanings for man, if he knew all languages and cultures, not merely intellectually but with his total personality. This would comprise the historically knowable world of man, but not the infinity of future possibilities."[29] It is the "openness of world" which chiefly distinguishes man's world from the closed worlds of animals and plants. This does not deny the finiteness of life; we are all limited by death and old age and are subject to infirmities of every sort; the point, rather, is that these possibilities are given within the context of the contingency of existence. In a dynamic sense, indeed, these future possibilities are the most significant aspect of any human being's world. For they are the potentialities with which he "builds or designs world"—a phrase the existential therapists are fond of using.

World is never something static, something merely given which the person then "accepts" or "adjusts to" or "fights." It is rather a dynamic pattern which, so long as I possess self-consciousness, I am in the process of forming and designing. Thus Binswanger speaks of world as "that toward which the existence has climbed and according to which it has designed itself,"[30] and goes on to emphasize that whereas a tree or an animal is tied to its "blueprint" in relation to the environment, "human existence not only contains numerous possibilities of modes of being, but is precisely rooted in this manifold potentiality of being."

The important and very fruitful use the existential analysts make of analyzing the patient's "world" is shown in Roland Kuhn's chapter in this volume, the case study of Rudolf, the butcher boy who shot a prostitute. Noting that Rudolf was in mourning in this period following the death of his father, Kuhn goes to considerable lengths to understand the "world of the mourner." At the conclusion of this chapter, the reader is left with a clear and convincing picture of the fact that Rudolf's shooting of the prostitute was an act of mourning for his mother, who died when he was four. I do not think this clarity and completeness of understanding could be gained by any method other than this pains-taking description of the patient-in-his-world.

IV The Three Modes of World

The existential analysts distinguish three modes of world, that is, three simultaneous aspects of world which characterize the existence of each one of us as being-in-the-world. First, there is *Umwelt*, literally meaning "world around"; this is the biological world, generally called the environment. There is, second, the *Mitwelt*, literally the "with-world," the world of beings of one's own kind, the world of one's fellow men. The third is *Eigenwelt*, the "own-world," the mode of relationship to one's self.

The first, *Umwelt*, is of course what is taken in general parlance as world, namely, the world of objects about us, the natural world. All organisms have an *Umwelt*. For animals and human beings the *Umwelt* includes biological needs, drives, instincts—the world one would still exist in if, let us hypothesize, one had no self-awareness. It is the world of natural law and natural cycles, of sleep and awakeness, of being born and dying, desire and relief, the world of finiteness and biological determinism, the "thrown world" to which each of us must in some way adjust. The existential analysts do not at all neglect the reality of the natural world; "natural law is as valid as ever," as Kierkegaard put it. They have no truck with the idealists who would reduce the material world to an epiphenomenon or with the intuitionists who would make it purely subjective or with anyone who would underestimate the importance of the world of biological determinism. Indeed, their insistence on taking the objective world of nature seriously is one of their distinctive characteristics. In reading them I often have the impression that they are able to grasp the *Umwelt*, the material world, with greater reality than those who segment it into "drives" and "substances," precisely because they are not limited to *Umwelt* alone, but see it also in the context of human self-awareness.[31] Boss's understanding of the patient with the "faeces and church steeple" dream cited above is an excellent example. They insist strongly that it is an oversimplification and radical error to deal with human beings as though *Umwelt* were the only mode of existence or to carry over the categories which fit *Umwelt* to make a procrustean bed upon which to force all human experience. In this connection, the existential analysts are *more empirical*, that is, more respectful of actual human phenomena, than the mechanists or positivists.

The *Mitwelt* is the world of interrelationships with human beings. But it is not to be confused with "the influence of the group upon the individual," or "the collective mind," or the various forms of "social determinism." The distinctive quality of *Mitwelt* can be seen when we note the difference between a herd of animals and a community of people. Howard Liddell has pointed out that for his sheep the "herd instinct consists of keeping the environment constant." Except in mating and suckling periods, a flock of collie dogs and children will do as well for the sheep providing such an environment is kept constant. In a group of human beings, however, a vastly more complex interaction goes on, with the meaning of the others in the group partly determined by one's own relationship to them. Strictly speaking, we should say animals have an *environment*, human beings have a *world*. For world includes the structure of meaning which is designed by the interrelationship of the persons in it. Thus the meaning of the group for me depends in part upon how I put myself into it. And thus, also, love can never be understood on a purely biological level but depends upon such factors as personal decision and commitment to the other person.[32]

The categories of "adjustment" and "adaptation" are entirely accurate in *Umwelt*. I adapt to the cold weather and I adjust to the periodic needs of my body for sleep; the critical point is that the weather is not changed by my adjusting to it nor is it affected at all. Adjustment occurs between two objects, or a person and an object. But in *Mitwelt*, the categories of adjustment and adaptation are not accurate; the term "relationship" offers the right category. If I insist that another person adjust to me, I am not taking him as a person, as *Dasein*, but as an instrumentality; and even if I adjust to myself, I am using myself as an object. One can never accurately speak of human beings as "sexual objects," as Kinsey for one example does; once a person is a sexual object, you are not talking about a person any more. *The essence of relationship is that in the encounter both persons are changed.* Providing the human beings involved are not too severely ill and have some degree of consciousness, relationship always involves mutual awareness; and this already is the process of being mutually affected by the encounter.

The *Eigenwelt*, or "own world," is the mode which is least adequately dealt with or understood in modern psychology and depth-psychology; indeed, it is fair to say that it is almost ignored. *Eigenwelt* presupposes self-awareness, self-relatedness, and is uniquely present in human beings. But it is not merely a subjective, inner experience; it is rather the basis on which we see the real world in its true perspective, the basis on which we relate. It is a grasping of what something in the world—this bouquet of flowers, this other person—means to *me*. Suzuki has remarked that in Eastern languages, such as Japanese, adjectives always include the implication of "for-me-ness." That is to say, "this

flower is beautiful" means *"for me* this flower is beautiful." Our Western dichotomy between subject and object has led us, in contrast, to
assume that we have said most if we state that the flower is beautiful
entirely divorced from ourselves, as though a statement were the more
true in proportion to how little we ourselves have to do with it! This
leaving of *Eigenwelt* out of the picture not only contributes to arid
intellectualism and loss of vitality but obviously also has much to do
with the fact that modern people tend to lose the sense of reality of
their experiences.

It should be clear that these three modes of world are always interrelated and always condition each other. At every moment, for example,
I exist in *Umwelt,* the biological world; but how I relate to my need for
sleep or the weather or any instinct—how, that is, I see in my own self-
awareness this or that aspect of *Umwelt*—is crucial for its meaning for
me and conditions how I will react to it. The human being lives in
Umwelt, Mitwelt, and *Eigenwelt* simultaneously. They are by no means
three different worlds but three simultaneous modes of being-in-the-
world.

Several implications follow from the above description of the three
modes of world. One is that the reality of being-in-the-world is lost if
one of these modes is emphasized to the exclusion of the other two. In
this connection, Binswanger holds that classical psychoanalysis deals
only with the *Umwelt.* The genius and the value of Freud's work lies in
uncovering man in the *Umwelt,* the mode of instincts, drives, contingency, biological determinism. But traditional psychoanalysis has only
a shadowy concept of *Mitwelt,* the mode of the interrelation of persons
as subjects. One might argue that such psychoanalysis does have a
Mitwelt in the sense that individuals need to find each other for the
sheer necessity of meeting biological needs, that libidinal drives require
social outlets and make social relationships necessary. But this is simply
to derive *Mitwelt* from *Umwelt,* to make *Mitwelt* an epiphenomenon
of *Umwelt*; and it means that we are not really dealing with *Mitwelt* at
all but only another form of *Umwelt.*

It is of course clear that the interpersonal schools do have a theoretical basis for dealing directly with *Mitwelt.* This is shown, to take only
one example, in Sullivan's interpersonal theory. Though they should not
be identified, *Mitwelt* and interpersonal theory have a great deal in
common. The danger at this point, however, is that if *Eigenwelt* in turn
is omitted, interpersonal relations tend to become hollow and sterile.
It is well known that Sullivan argued against the concept of the individual personality, and went to great efforts to define the self in

terms of "reflected appraisal" and social categories, *i.e.*, the roles the person plays in the interpersonal world.[33] Theoretically, this suffers from considerable logical inconsistency and indeed goes directly against other very important contributions of Sullivan. Practically, it tends to make the self a mirror of the group around one, to empty the self of vitality and originality, and to reduce the interpersonal world to mere "social relations." It opens the way to the tendency which is directly opposed to the goals of Sullivan and other interpersonal thinkers, namely, social conformity. *Mitwelt* does not automatically absorb either *Umwelt* or *Eigenwelt*.

But when we turn to the mode of *Eigenwelt* itself, we find ourselves on the unexplored frontier of psychotherapeutic theory. What does it mean to say, "the self in relation to itself"? What goes on in the phenomena of consciousness, of self-awareness? What happens in "insight" when the inner gestalt of a person reforms itself? Indeed, what does the "self knowing itself" mean? Each of these phenomena goes on almost every instant with all of us; they are indeed closer to us than our breathing. Yet, perhaps precisely because they are so near to us, no one knows what is happening in these events. This mode of the self in relation to itself was the aspect of experience which Freud never really saw, and it is doubtful whether any school has as yet achieved a basis for adequately dealing with it. *Eigenwelt* is certainly the hardest mode to grasp in the face of our Western technological preoccupations. It may well be that the mode of *Eigenwelt* will be the area in which most clarification will occur in the next decades.

Another implication of this analysis of the modes of being-in-the-world is that it gives us a basis for the psychological understanding of love. The human experience of love obviously cannot be adequately described within the confines of *Umwelt*. The interpersonal schools, at home chiefly in *Mitwelt*, have dealt with love, particularly in Sullivan's concept of the meaning of the "chum" and in Fromm's analysis of the difficulties of love in contemporary estranged society. But there is reason for doubting whether a theoretical foundation for going further is yet present in these or other schools. The same general caution given above is pertinent here—namely, that without an adequate concept of *Umwelt*, love becomes empty of vitality, and without *Eigenwelt*, it lacks power and the capacity to fructify itself.[34]

In any case, *Eigenwelt* cannot be omitted in the understanding of love. Nietzsche and Kierkegaard continually insisted that to love presupposes that one has already become the "true individual," the "Solitary One," the one who "has comprehended the deep secret that also in loving another person one must be sufficient unto oneself."[35] They, like other existentialists, do not attain to love themselves; but they help perform the psycho-surgical operations on nineteenth-century man which may clear blockages away and make love possible. By the same token, Binswanger and other existential therapists speak frequently of love. And though one could raise questions about how love is actually dealt with by them in given therapeutic cases, they nonetheless give us the theoretical groundwork for ultimately dealing with love adequately in psychotherapy.

V Of Time and History

The next contribution of the existential analysts we shall consider is their distinctive approach to *time*. They are struck by the fact that the most profound human experiences, such as anxiety, depression, and joy, occur more in the dimension of time than in space. They boldly place time in the center of the psychological picture and proceed to study it not in the traditional way as an analogy to space but in its own existential meaning for the patient.

An example of the fresh light this new approach to time throws upon psychological problems is seen in the engaging case study by Minkowski published in *Existence*.[36] Coming to Paris after his psychiatric training, Minkowski was struck by the relevance of the time dimension then being developed by Bergson to the understanding of psychiatric patients.[37] In his study of this depressed schizophrenic in this case, Minkowski points out that the patient could not relate to time and that each day was a separate island with no past and no future, the patient remaining unable to feel any hope or sense of continuity with the morrow. It was obvious, of course, that this patient's terrifying delusion that his execution was imminent had much to do with his being unable to deal with the future. Traditionally, the psychiatrist would reason simply that the patient cannot relate to the future, cannot "temporize," *because* he has this delusion. Minkowski proposes the exact opposite. "Could we not," he asks, "on the contrary suppose *the more basic disorder is the distorted attitude toward the future*, while the delusion is only one of its manifestations?" Minkowski goes on to consider this possibility carefully in his case study. How this approach should be applied in different cases would be, of course, debated by clinicians. But it is indisputable that Minkowski's original approach throws a beam of illumination on these dark, unexplored areas of time, and introduces a new freedom from the limits and shackles of clinical thought when bound only to traditional ways of thinking.

This new approach to time begins with observing that the most crucial fact about existence is that it *emerges*—that is, it is always in the process of becoming, always developing in time, and is never to be defined at static points.[38] The existential therapists propose a psychology literally of *being*, rather than "is" or "has been" or fixed inorganic categories. Though their concepts were worked out several decades ago, it is highly significant that recent experimental work in psychology, such as that by Mowrer and Liddell, illustrates and bears out their conclusions. At the end of one of his most important papers, Mowrer holds that time is the distinctive dimension of human personality. "Time-binding"—that is, the capacity to bring the past into the present as part of the total causal nexus in which living organisms act and react, together with the capacity to act in the light of the long-term future—is "the essence of mind and personality alike."[39] Liddell has shown that his sheep can keep time—anticipate punishment—for about fifteen minutes and his dogs for about half an hour; but a human being can bring the past of thousands of years ago into the present as data to guide his present actions. And he can likewise project himself in self-conscious imagination into the future not only for a quarter of an hour but for weeks and years and decades. This capacity to transcend the immediate boundaries of time, to see one's experience self-consciously in the light of the distant past and the future, to act and react in these dimensions, to learn from the past of a thousand years ago and to mold the long-time future, is the unique characteristic of human existence.

The existential therapists agree with Bergson that "time is the heart of existence" and that our error has been to think of ourselves primarily in spatialized terms appropriate to *res extensa*, as though we were objects which could be located like substances at this spot or that. By this distortion we lose our genuine and real existential relation with ourselves, and indeed with other persons around us. As a consequence of this overemphasis on spatialized thinking, says Bergson, "the moments when we grasp ourselves are rare, and consequently we are seldom free."[40] Or, when we have taken time into the picture, it has been in the sense of Aristotle's definition, the dominant one in the tradition of Western thought, "For the time is this: what is counted in the movement in accordance with what is earlier and later." Now the striking thing about this description of "clock time" is that it really is an analogy from space, and one can best understand it by thinking in terms of a line of blocks or regularly spaced points on a clock or calendar. This approach to time is most fitting in the *Umwelt*, where we view the human being as an entity set among the various conditioning and determining forces of the natural world and acted upon by instinctual drives. But in the *Mitwelt*, the mode of personal relations and love, quantitative time has much less to do with the significance of an occurrence; the nature or degree of one's love, for example, can never be measured by the number of years one has known the loved one. It is true of course that clock time has much to do with *Mitwelt*: many people sell their time on an hourly basis and daily life runs on schedules. We refer rather to the inner meaning of the events. "No clock strikes for the happy one," says a German proverb quoted by Straus. Indeed, the most significant events in a person's psychological existence are likely to be precisely the ones which are "immediate," breaking through the usual steady progression of time.

Finally, the *Eigenwelt*, the own world of self-relatedness, self-awareness, and insight into the meaning of an event for one's self, has practically nothing whatever to do with Aristotle's clock time. The essence of self-awareness and insight are that they are "there"—instantaneous, immediate—and the moment of awareness has its significance for all time. One can see this easily by noting what happens in oneself at the instant of an insight or any experience of grasping oneself; the insight occurs with suddenness, is "born whole," so to speak. And one will discover that, though meditating on the insight for an hour or so may reveal many of its further implications, the insight is not clearer—and disconcertingly enough, often not as clear—at the end of the hour as it was at the beginning.

The existential therapists also observed that the most profound psychological experiences are peculiarly those which shake the individual's relation to time. Severe anxiety and depression blot out time, annihilate the future. Or, as Minkowski proposes, it may be that the disturbance of the patient in relation to time, his inability to "have" a future, gives rise to his anxiety and depression. In either case, the most painful aspect of the sufferer's predicament is that he is unable to imagine a future moment in time when he will be out of the anxiety or depression. We see a similar close interrelationship between the disturbance of the time function and neurotic symptoms. Repression and other processes of the blocking off of awareness are in essence methods of ensuring that the usual relation of past to present will not obtain. Since it would be too painful or in other ways too threatening for the individual to retain certain aspects of his past in his present consciousness, he must carry the past along like a foreign body *in* him but not *of* him, as it were, an encapsulated fifth column which thereupon compulsively drives to its outlets in neurotic symptoms.

However one looks at it, thus, the problem of time has a peculiar importance in understanding human existence. The reader may agree at this point but feel that, if we try to understand time in other than spatial categories, we are confronted with a mystery. He may well share the perplexity of Augustine who wrote, "When no one asks me what time is, I know, but when I would give an explanation of it in answer to a man's question I do not know."[41]

One of the distinctive contributions of the existential analysts to this problem is that, having placed time in the center of the psychological picture, they then propose that the *future*, in contrast to present or past, is the dominant mode of time for human beings. Personality can be understood only as we see it on a trajectory toward its future; a man can understand himself only as he projects himself forward. This is a corollary of the fact that the person is always becoming, always emerging into the future. The self is to be seen in its potentiality; "a self, every instant it exists," Kierkegaard wrote, "is in process of becoming, for the self . . . is only that which it is to become." The existentialists do not mean "distant future" or anything connected with using the future as an escape from the past or present; they mean only to indicate that the human being, so long as he possesses self-awareness and is not incapacitated by anxiety or neurotic rigidities, is always in a dynamic self-actualizing process, always exploring, molding himself, and moving into the immediate future.

They do not neglect the past, but they hold it can be understood only in the light of the future. The past is the domain of *Umwelt*, of the contingent, natural historical, deterministic forces operating upon us; but since we do not live exclusively in *Umwelt*, we are never merely the victims of automatic pressures from the past. *The deterministic events of the past take their significance from the present and future.* As Freud put it, we are anxious *lest* something happen in the future. "The word of the past is an oracle uttered," remarked Nietzsche. "Only as builders of the future, as knowing the present, will you understand it." All experience has a historical character, but the error is to treat the past in mechanical terms. The past is not the "now which was," nor any collection of isolated events, nor a static reservoir of memories or past influences or impressions. The past, rather, is the domain of contingency in which we accept events and from which we select events in order to fulfill our potentialities and to gain satisfactions and security in the immediate future. This realm of the past, of natural history and "thrownness," Binswanger points out, is the mode which classical psychoanalysis has, *par excellence*, made its own for exploration and study.

But as soon as we consider the exploration of a patient's past in psychoanalysis, we note two very curious facts. First is the obvious phenomenon observed every day, that the events in the past which the patient carries with him have very little, if any, necessary connection with the quantitative events that actually happened to him as a child. One single thing that occurred to him at a given age is remembered and thousands of things are forgotten, and even the events that occurred most frequently, like getting up in the morning, are most apt obviously to leave no impression. Alfred Adler used to point out that memory was a creative process, that we remember what has significance for our "style of life," and that the whole "form" of memory is therefore a mirror of the individual's style of life. What an individual seeks *to become* determines what he remembers of his *has been*. In this sense the future determines the past.

The second fact is this: *whether or not a patient can even recall the significant events of the past depends upon his decision with regard to the future.* Every therapist knows that patients may bring up past memories *ad interminum* without any memory ever moving them, the whole recital being flat, inconsequential, tedious. From an existential point of view, the problem is not at all that these patients happened to have endured impoverished pasts; it is rather that they cannot or do not commit themselves to the present and future. Their past does not become alive because nothing matters enough to them in the future. Some hope and commitment to work toward changing something in the immediate future, be it overcoming anxiety or other painful symptoms or integrating one's self for further creativity, is necessary before any uncovering of the past will have reality.

One practical implication of the above analysis of time is that psychotherapy cannot rest on the usual automatic doctrines of historical progress. The existential analysts take history very seriously,[42] but they protest against any tendency to evade the immediate, anxiety-creating issues in the present by taking refuge behind the determinism of the past. They are against the doctrines that historical forces carry the individual along automatically, whether these doctrines take the form of the religious beliefs of predestination or providence, the deteriorated Marxist doctrine of historical materialism, the various psychological doctrines of determinism, or that most common form of such historical determinism in our society, faith in automatic technical progress. Kierkegaard was very emphatic on this point:

Whatever the one generation may learn from the other, that which is genuinely human no generation learns from the foregoing. . . . Thus no generation has learned from another to love, no generation begins at any other point than at the beginning, no generation has a shorter task assigned to it than had the previous generation. . . . In this respect every generation begins primitively, has no different task from that of every previous generation, nor does it get further, except in so far as the preceding generation shirked its task and deluded itself.[43]

This implication is particularly relevant to psychotherapy, since the popular mind so often makes of psychoanalysis and other forms of psychotherapy the new technical authority which will take over for them the burden of learning to love. Obviously all any therapy can do is to help a person remove the blocks which keep him from loving; it cannot love for him, and it is doing him ultimate harm if it dulls his own responsible awareness at this point.

A last contribution of this existential analysis of time lies in its understanding of the process of insight. Kierkegaard uses the engaging term *Augenblick*, literally meaning the "blinking of an eye" and generally translated "the pregnant moment." It is the moment when a person suddenly grasps the meaning of some important event in the past or future in the present. Its pregnancy consists of the fact that it is never an intellectual act alone; the grasping of the new meaning always presents the possibility and necessity of some personal decision, some shift in gestalt, some new orientation of the person toward the world and future. This is experienced by most people as the moment of most heightened awareness; it is referred to in psychological literature as the "aha" experience. On the philosophical level, Paul Tillich describes it as the moment when "eternity touches time," for which moment he has developed the concept of *Kairos*, "time fulfilled."

VI TRANSCENDING THE IMMEDIATE SITUATION

A final characteristic of man's existence (*Dasein*) which we shall discuss is the capacity to transcend the immediate situation. If one tries to study the human being as a composite of substances, one does not of course need to deal with the disturbing fact that existence is always in process of self-transcending. But if we are to understand a given person as existing, dynamic, at every moment becoming, we cannot avoid this dimension. This capacity is already stated in the term "exist," that is, "to stand out from." Existing involves a continual emerging, in the sense of emergent evolution, a transcending of one's past and present in terms of the future. Thus *transcendere*—literally "to climb over or beyond"— describes what every human being is engaged in doing every moment when he is not seriously ill or temporarily blocked by despair or anxiety. One can, of course, see this emergent evolution in all life processes. Nietzsche has his old Zarathustra proclaim, "And this secret spake Life herself to me, 'Behold' said she, 'I am that which must ever surpass itself.' " But it is much more radically true of human existence, where the capacity for self-awareness qualitatively increases the range of consciousness and therefore greatly enlarges the range of possibilities of transcending the immediate situation.

The term "transcending," appearing often in the following papers, is open to much misunderstanding, and indeed often calls forth violent antagonism.[44] In this country the term is relegated to vague and ethereal things which, as Bacon remarked, are better dealt with in "poesy, where transcendences are more allowed," or associated with Kantian *a priori* assumptions or with New England Transcendentalism or religious other-worldliness, or with anything unempirical and unrelated to actual experience. We mean something different from all of these. It has been suggested that the word has lost its usefulness and another should be found. That would be fine if another were available which would adequately describe the exceedingly important empirical, immediate human experience to which this term, when used by Goldstein and the existential writers, refers; for any adequate description of human beings requires that the experience be taken into account. Some suspicion of the term obviously is sound to the extent that the word serves to elevate any given topic out of any immediate field in which it can be discussed. It must be confessed that occasional usages of the term in some of the papers which follow do have this effect, particularly when the "transcendental categories" of Husserl are assumed without explanation of how they apply. Other objections to the term, less justifiable, may arise from the fact that the capacity to transcend the present situation introduces a disturbing fourth dimension, a *time* dimension, and this is a serious threat to the traditional way of describing human beings in terms of static substances. The term is likewise rejected by those who seek to make no distinction between animal and human behavior or to understand human psychology in terms only of mechanical models. This capacity we are about to discuss does in actual fact present difficulties to those approaches since it is uniquely characteristic of human beings.

The neurobiological base for this capacity is classically described by Kurt Goldstein. Goldstein found that his brain-injured patients—chiefly soldiers with portions of the frontal cortex shot away—had specifically lost the ability to abstract, to think in terms of "the possible." They were tied to the immediate concrete situation in which they found themselves. When their closets happened to be in disarray, they were thrown into profound anxiety and disordered behavior. They exhibited compulsive orderliness—which is a way of holding one's self at every moment rigidly to the concrete situation. When asked to write their names on a sheet of paper, they would typically write in the very corner, any venture out from the specific boundaries of the edges of the paper representing too great a threat. It was as though they were threatened with dissolution of the self unless they remained related at every moment to the immediate situation, as though they could "be a self" only as the self was bound to the concrete items in space. Goldstein holds that the distinctive capacity of the normal human being is precisely this capacity to abstract, to use symbols, to orient one's self beyond the immediate limits of the given time and space, to think in terms of "the possible." The injured, or "ill," patients were characterized by loss of range of possibility. Their world-space was shrunk, their time curtailed, and they suffered a consequent radical loss of freedom.

The capacity of the normal human being to transcend the present situation is exemplified in all kinds of behavior. One is the capacity to transcend the boundaries of the present moment in time—as we pointed out in our discussion above—and to bring the distant past and the long-term future into one's immediate existence. It is also exemplified in the human being's unique capacity to think and talk in symbols. Reason and the use of symbols are rooted in the capacity to stand outside the particular object or sound at hand, say these boards on which my typewriter sits and the two syllables that make up the word "table," and agreeing with each other that these will stand for a whole class of objects.

The capacity is particularly shown in social relationships, in the normal person's relation to the community. Indeed, the whole fabric of trust and responsibility in human relations presupposes the capacity of the individual to "see himself as others see him," as Robert Burns puts it in contrasting himself with the field mouse, to see himself as the one fulfilling his fellow men's expectations, acting for their welfare or failing to. Just as this capacity for transcending the situation is impaired with respect to the *Umwelt* in the brain-injured, it is impaired with respect to the *Mitwelt* in the psychopathic disorders which are described as the disorders of those in whom the capacity to see themselves as others see them is absent or does not carry sufficient weight, who are then said to lack "conscience." The term "conscience," significantly enough, is in many languages the same word as "consciousness," both meaning *to know with*. Nietzsche remarked, "Man is the animal who can make promises." By this he did not mean promises in the sense of social pressure or simply introjection of social requirement (which are oversimplified ways of describing conscience, errors which arise from conceiving of *Mitwelt* apart from *Eigenwelt*). Rather, he meant that man can be aware of the fact that he has given his word, can see himself as the one who makes the agreement. Thus, to make promises presupposes conscious self-relatedness and is a very different thing from simple conditioned "social behavior," acting in terms of the requirements of the group or herd or hive. In the same light, Sartre writes that dishonesty is a uniquely human form of behavior: "the lie is a behavior of transcendence."

It is significant at this point to note the great number of terms used in describing human actions which contain the prefix "re"—*re*-sponsible, *re*-collect, *re*-late, and so on. In the last analysis, all imply and rest upon this capacity to "come back" to one's self as the one performing the act. This is illustrated with special clarity in the peculiarly human capacity to be *responsible* (a word combining *re* and *spondere*, "promise"), designating the one who can be depended upon, who can promise to give back, to answer. Erwin Straus describes man as "the questioning being," the organism who at the same moment that he exists can question himself and his own existence.[45] Indeed, the whole existential approach is rooted in the always curious phenomenon that we have in man a being who not only *can* but *must*, if he is to realize himself, question his own being. One can see at this point that the discussion of dynamisms of social adjustment, such as "introjection," "identification," and so forth is oversimplified and inadequate when it omits the central fact of all, namely, the person's capacity to be aware at the moment that he is the one responding to the social expectation, the one choosing (or not choosing) to guide himself according to a certain model. This is the distinction between rote social conformity on one hand and the freedom, originality, and creativity of genuine social response on the other. The latter are the unique mark of the human being acting in the light of "the possible."

Self-consciousness implies self-transcendence. The one has no reality without the other. It will have become apparent to many readers that the capacity to transcend the immediate situation uniquely presupposes *Eigenwelt*, that is, the mode of behavior in which a person sees himself as subject and object at once. The capacity to transcend the situation is an inseparable part of self-awareness, for it is obvious that the mere awareness of one's self as a being in the world implies the capacity to stand outside and look at one's self and the situation and to assess and guide one's self by an infinite variety of possibilities. The existential analysts insist that the human being's capacity for transcending the immediate situation is discernible in the very center of human experience and cannot be sidestepped or overlooked without distorting and making unreal and vague one's picture of the man. This is particularly cogent and true with respect to data we encounter in psychotherapy. All of the peculiarly neurotic phenomena, such as the split of unconsciousness from consciousness, repression, blocking of awareness, self-deceit by way of symptoms, *ad interminum*, are misused, "neurotic" forms of the fundamental capacity of the human being to relate to himself and his world as subject and object at the same time. As Lawrence Kubie has written, "The neurotic process is always a symbolic process: and the split into parallel yet interacting streams of conscious and unconscious processes starts approximately as the child begins to develop the rudiments of speech. . . . It may be accurate to say, therefore, that the neurotic process is the price that we pay for our most precious human heritage, namely our ability to represent experience and communicate our thoughts by means of symbols. . . ."[46] The essence of the use of symbols, we have tried to show, is the capacity to transcend the immediate, concrete situation.

We can now see why Medard Boss and the other existential psychiatrists and psychologists make this capacity to transcend the immediate situation the basic and unique characteristic of human existence. "Transcendence and being-in-the-world are names for the identical structure of Dasein, which is the foundation for every kind of attitude and behavior."[47] Boss goes on in this connection to criticize Binswanger for speaking of different kinds of "transcendences"—the "transcendence of love" as well as the "transcendence of care." This unnecessarily complicates the point, says Boss; and it makes no sense to speak of "transcendences" in the plural. We can only say, holds Boss, that man has the capacity for transcending the immediate situation because he has the capacity for *Sorge*—that is, for "care" or, more accurately, for understanding his being and taking responsibility for it. (This term is from Heidegger and is basic to existential thought; it is used often in the form of *Fürsorge*, meaning "care for," "concerned for the welfare of.") *Sorge* is for Boss the encompassing notion and includes love, hate, hope, and even indifference. All attitudes are ways of behaving in *Sorge* or lack of it. In Boss's sense the capacity of man to have *Sorge* and to transcend the immediate situation are two aspects of the same thing.

We need now to emphasize that this capacity to transcend the immediate situation is not a "faculty" to be listed along with other faculties. It is rather given in the ontological nature of being human. To abstract, to objectivate, are evidences of it; but as Heidegger puts it, "transcendence does not consist of objectivation, but objectivation presupposes transcendence." That is to say, the fact that the human being can be self-related gives him, as one manifestation, the capacity to objectify his world, to think and talk in symbols and so forth. This is Kierkegaard's point when he reminds us that to understand the self we must see clearly that "imagination is not one faculty on a par with others, but, if one would so speak, it is the faculty *instar omnium* [for all faculties]. What feeling, knowledge or will a man has depends in the last resort upon what imagination he has, that is to say, upon how these things are reflected. . . . Imagination is the possibility of all reflection, and the intensity of this medium is the possibility of the intensity of the self."[48]

It remains to make more specific what is implicit above, namely, that this capacity for transcending the immediate situation is the basis of human freedom. The unique characteristic of the human being is the vast range of possibilities in any situation, which in turn depend upon his self-awareness, his capacity to run through in imagination the different ways of reacting he can consider in a given situation. Binswanger, in his discussion of Von Uexküll's metaphor of the contrasting environments of the tree in the forest, the jigger in the tree, the woodsman who comes to chop the tree, the romantic girl who comes to walk in the forest, and so on, points out that the distinctive thing about the human being is that he can one day be the romantic lover, another day the woodchopper, another day the painter. In a variety of ways the human being can select among many self-world relationships. The "self" is the capacity to see one's self in these many possibilities. This freedom with respect to world, Binswanger goes on to point out, is the mark of the psychologically healthy person; to be rigidly confined to a specific "world," as was Ellen West, is the mark of psychological disorder. What is essential is "freedom in designing world," or "letting world occur," as Binswanger puts it. "So deeply founded," he observes indeed, "is the essence of freedom as a necessity in existence that it can also dispense with existence itself."[49]

VII SOME IMPLICATIONS FOR PSYCHOTHERAPEUTIC TECHNIQUE

Those who read works on existential analysis as handbooks of technique are bound to be disappointed. They will not find specifically developed practical methods. The chapters in this book, for example, have much more the character of "pure" than of applied science. The reader will also sense that many of the existential analysts are not greatly concerned with technical matters. Part of the reason for this is the newness of the approach. Roland Kuhn wrote, in answer to our inquiry about technique in some of his significant cases, that since existential analysis is a relatively new discipline, it has not yet had time to work out its therapeutic applications in detail.

But there is another, more basic reason for the fact that these psychiatrists are not so concerned with formulating technique and make no apologies for this fact. Existential analysis is a way of understanding human existence, and its representatives believe that one of the chief (if not *the* chief) blocks to the understanding of human beings in Western culture is precisely the overemphasis on technique, an overemphasis which goes along with the tendency to see the human being as an object to be calculated, managed, "analyzed."[50] Our Western tendency has been to believe that *understanding follows technique*; if we get the right technique, then we can penetrate the riddle of the patient, or, as said popularly with amazing perspicacity, we can "get the other person's number." The existential approach holds the exact opposite; namely, that *technique follows understanding*. The central task and responsibility of the therapist is to seek to understand the patient as a being and as being-in-his-world. All technical problems are subordinate to this understanding. Without this understanding, technical facility is at best irrelevant, at worst a method of "structuralizing" the neurosis. With it, the groundwork is laid for the therapist's being able to help the patient recognize and experience his own existence, and this is the central process of therapy. This does not derogate disciplined technique; it rather puts it into perspective.

When editing this volume, therefore, we had difficulty piecing together information about what an existential therapist would actually *do* in given situations in therapy, but we kept asking the question, for we knew American readers would be particularly concerned with this area. It is clear at the outset that what distinguishes existential therapy is not what the therapist would specifically do, say, in meeting anxiety or confronting resistance or getting the life history and so forth, but rather the *context* of his therapy. How an existential therapist might interpret a given dream, or an outburst of temper on the patient's part, might not differ from what a classical psychoanalyst might say, if each were taken in isolated fashion. But the context of existential therapy would be very distinct; it would always focus on the questions of how this dream throws light on this particular patient's existence in his world, what it says about *where* he is at the moment and what he is moving toward, and so forth. The context is the patient not as a set of psychic dynamisms or mechanisms but as a human being who is choosing, committing, and pointing himself toward something right now; the context is dynamic, immediately real, and present.

I shall try to block out some implications concerning therapeutic technique from my knowledge of the works of the existential therapists and from my own experience of how their emphases have contributed to me, a therapist trained in psychoanalysis in its broad sense.[51] Making a systematic summary would be presumptuous to try and impossible to accomplish, but I hope the following points will at least suggest some of the important therapeutic implications. It should be clear at every point, however, that the really important contributions of this approach are its deepened understanding of human existence, and one gets no place talking about isolated techniques of therapy unless the understanding we have sought to give in the earlier portions of these chapters is presupposed at every point.

The *first* implication is the variability of techniques among the existential therapists. Boss, for example, uses couch and free association in traditional Freudian manner and permits a good deal of acting out of transference. Others would vary as much as the different schools vary anyway. But the critical point is that the existential therapists have a definite reason for using any given technique with a given patient. They sharply question the use of techniques simply because of rote, custom, or tradition. Their approach also does not at all settle for the air of vagueness and unreality that surrounds many therapeutic sessions, particularly in the eclectic schools which allegedly have freed themselves from bondage to a traditional technique and select from all schools as though the presuppositions of these approaches did not matter. Existential therapy is distinguished by a sense of reality and concreteness.

I would phrase the above point positively as follows: existential technique should have flexibility and versatility, varying from patient to patient and from one phase to another in treatment with the same patient. The specific technique to be used at a given point should be decided on the basis of these questions: What will best reveal the existence of this particular patient at this moment in his history? What will best illuminate his being-in-the-world? Never merely "eclectic," this flexibility always involves a clear understanding of the underlying assumptions of any method. Let us say a Kinseyite, for example, a traditional Freudian, and an existential analyst are dealing with an instance of sexual repression. The Kinseyite would speak of it in terms of finding a sexual object, in which case he is not talking about sex in human beings. The traditional Freudian would see its psychological implications, but would look primarily for causes in the past and might well ask himself how this instance of sexual repression *qua* repression can be overcome. The existential therapist would view the sexual repression as a holding back of *potentia* of the existence of this person, and though he might or might not, depending on the circumstances, deal immediately with the sex problem as such, it would always be seen not as a mechanism of repression as such but as a limitation of this person's being-in-his-world.

The *second* implication is that psychological dynamisms always take their meaning from the existential situation of the patient's own, immediate life. The writings of Medard Boss, whose small book on existential psychotherapy and psychoanalysis was published just as this chapter went to press, are very pertinent at this point.[52] Boss holds that Freud's practice was right but his theories explaining his practice were wrong. Freudian in technique, Boss places the theories and concepts of traditional psychoanalysis on a fundamental existential basis. Take *transference*, for example, a discovery which Boss greatly values. What really happens is not that the neurotic patient "transfers" feelings he had toward mother or father to wife or therapist. Rather, the neurotic is one who in certain areas never developed beyond the limited and restricted forms of experience characteristic of the infant. Hence in later years he perceives wife or therapist through the same restricted, distorted "spectacles" as he perceived father or mother. The problem is to be understood in terms of perception and relatedness to the world. This makes unnecessary the concept of transference in the sense of a displacement of detachable feelings from one object to another. The new basis of this concept frees psychoanalysis from the burden of a number of insoluble problems.

Take, also, the ways of behaving known as *repression* and *resistance*. Freud saw repression as related to bourgeois morality, specifically, as the patient's need to preserve an acceptable picture of himself and therefore to hold back thoughts, desires, and so forth which are unacceptable according to bourgeois moral codes. Rather, says Boss, the conflict must be seen more basically in the area of the patient's acceptance or rejection of his own potentialities. We need to keep in mind the question—What keeps the patient from accepting in freedom his potentialities? This may involve bourgeois morality, but it also involves a lot more: it leads immediately to the existential question of the person's freedom. Before repression is possible or conceivable, the person must have some possibility of accepting or rejecting—that is, some margin of freedom. Whether the person is aware of this freedom or can articulate it is another question; he does not need to be. To repress is precisely to make one's self unaware of freedom; this is the nature of the dynamism. Thus, to repress or deny this freedom already presupposes it as a possibility. Boss then points out that psychic determinism is always a secondary phenomenon and works only in a limited area. The primary question is how the person relates to his freedom to express potentialities in the first place, repression being one way of so relating.

With respect to *resistance*, Boss again asks the question: What makes such a phenomenon possible? He answers that it is an outworking of the tendency of the patient to become absorbed in the *Mitwelt*, to slip back into *das Man*, the anonymous mass, and to renounce the particular unique and original potentiality which is his. Thus "social conformity" is a general form of resistance in life; and even the patient's acceptance of the doctrines and interpretations of the therapist may itself be an expression of resistance.

We do not wish here to go into the question of what underlies these phenomena. We want only to demonstrate that at each point in considering these dynamisms of transference, resistance, and repression Boss does something critically important for the existential approach. *He places each dynamism on an ontological basis.* Each way of behaving is seen and understood in the light of the existence of the patient as a human being. This is shown, too, in his conceiving of drives, libido, and so forth always in terms of *potentialities* for existence. Thus he proposes "to throw overboard the painful intellectual acrobatic of the old psychoanalytic theory which sought to derive the phenomena from the interplay of some forces or drives behind them." He does not deny forces as such but holds that they cannot be understood as "energy transformation" or on any other such natural science model but only as the person's *potentia* of existence. "This freeing from unnecessary constructions facilitates the understanding between patient and doctor. Also it makes the pseudo-resistances disappear which were a justified defense of the analysands against a violation of their essence." Boss holds that he thus can follow the "basic rule" in analysis—the one condition Freud set for analysis, namely, that the patient give forth in complete honesty whatever was going on in his mind—more effectively than in traditional psychoanalysis, for he listens with respect and takes seriously and without reserve the contents of the patient's communication rather than sieving it through prejudgments or destroying it by special interpretations. Boss holds himself to be entirely loyal to Freud in all of this and to be simply engaged in bringing out the underlying meaning of Freud's discoveries and placing them on their necessary comprehensive foundation. Believing that Freud's discoveries have to be understood below their faulty formulation, he points out that Freud himself was not merely a passive "mirror" for the patient in analysis, as traditionally urged in psychoanalysis, but was "translucent," a vehicle and medium through which the patient saw himself.

The *third* implication in existential therapy is the emphasis on *presence*. By this we mean that the relationship of the therapist and patient is taken as a real one, the therapist being not merely a shadowy reflector but an alive human being who happens, at that hour, to be concerned not with his own problems but with understanding and experiencing so far as possible the being of the patient. The way was prepared for this emphasis on presence by our discussion of the fundamental existential idea of truth-in-relationship.[53] It was there pointed out that existentially truth always involves the relation of the person to something or someone and that the therapist is part of the patient's relationship "field." We indicated, too, that this was not only the therapist's best avenue to understanding the patient but that he cannot really *see* the patient unless he participates in the field.

Several quotations will make clearer what this presence means. Karl Jaspers has remarked, "What we are missing! What opportunities of understanding we let pass by because at a single decisive moment we were, with all our knowledge, lacking in the simple virtue of a *full human presence!*"[54] In similar vein but greater detail Binswanger writes as follows, in his paper on psychotherapy, concerning the significance of the therapist's role of the relationship:

If such a [psychoanalytic] treatment fails, the analyst inclines to assume that the patient is not capable of overcoming his resistance to the physician, for example, as a "father image." Whether an analysis can have success or not is often, however, not decided by whether a patient is capable *at all* of overcoming such a transferred father image but by the opportunity *this particular physician* accords him to do so; it may, in other words, be the rejection of the therapist as a person, the impossibility of entering into a genuine communicative rapport with him, that may form the obstacle against breaking through the "eternal" repetition of the father resistance. Caught in the "mechanism" and thus in what inheres in it, *mechanical repetition*, the psychoanalytic doctrine, as we know, is altogether strangely blind toward the entire category of the *new*, the properly *creative* in the life of the psyche everywhere. Certainly it not always is true to the facts if one attributes the failure of treatment only to the patient; the question always to be asked first by the physician is whether the fault may not be his. What is meant here is not any technical fault but the far more fundamental failure that consists of an impotence to wake or rekindle that divine "spark" in the patient which only true communication from existence to existence can bring forth and which alone possesses, with its light and warmth, also the fundamental power that makes any therapy work—the power to liberate a person from the blind isolation, the *idios kosmos* of Heraclitus, from a mere vegetating in his body, his dreams, his private wishes, his conceit and his presumptions, and to ready him for a life of *koinonia*, of genuine community.[55]

Presence is not to be confused with a sentimental attitude toward the patient but depends firmly and consistently on how the therapist conceives of human beings. It is found in therapists of various schools and differing beliefs—differing, that is, on anything except one central issue —their assumptions about whether the human being is an object to be analyzed or a being to be understood. Any therapist is existential to the extent that, with all his technical training and his knowledge of transference and dynamisms, he is still able to relate to the patient as "one existence communicating with another," to use Binswanger's phrase. In my own experience, Frieda Fromm-Reichmann particularly had this power in a given therapeutic hour; she used to say, "'The patient needs an experience, not an explanation." Erich Fromm, for another example, not only emphasizes presence in a way similar to Jasper's statement above but makes it a central point in his teaching of psychoanalysis.

Carl Rogers is an illustration of one who, never having had, so far as I know, direct contact with the existential therapists as such, has written a very existential document in his *apologia pro vita sua* as a therapist:

I launch myself into the therapeutic relationship having a hypothesis, or a faith, that my liking, my confidence, and my understanding of the other person's inner world, will lead to a significant process of becoming. I enter the relationship not as a scientist, not as a physician who can accurately diagnose and cure, but as a person, entering into a personal relationship. Insofar as I see him only as an object, the client will tend to become only an object.

I risk myself, because if, as the relationship deepens, what develops is a failure, a regression, a repudiation of me and the relationship by the client, then I sense that I will lose myself, or a part of myself. At times this risk is very real, and is very keenly experienced.

I let myself go into the immediacy of the relationship where it is my total organism which takes over and is sensitive to the relationship, not simply my consciousness. I am not consciously responding in a planful or analytic way, but simply in an unreflective way to the other individual, my reaction being based (but not consciously) on my total organismic sensitivity to this other person. I live the relationship on this basis.[56]

There are real differences between Rogers and the existential therapists, such as the fact that most of his work is based on relatively shorter-time therapeutic relationships whereas the work of the existential therapists in this volume is generally long-time, Rogers' viewpoint is more optimistic, whereas the existential approach is oriented more to the tragic crises of life, and so forth. What are significant, however, are Rogers' basic ideas that therapy is a "process of becoming," that the freedom and inner growth of the individual are what counts, and the implicit assumption pervading Rogers' work of the dignity of the human being. These concepts are all very close to the existentialist approach to the human being.

Before leaving the topic of *presence*, we need to make three caveats. One is that this emphasis on relationship is in no way an oversimplification or short cut; it is not a substitute for discipline or thoroughness of training. It rather puts these things in their context—namely, discipline and thoroughness of training directed to understanding human beings as human. The therapist is assumedly an expert; but, if he is not first of all a human being, his expertness will be irrelevant and quite possibly harmful. The distinctive character of the existential approach is that understanding *being human* is no longer just a "gift," an intuition, or something left to chance; it is the "proper study of man," in Alexander Pope's phrase, and becomes the center of a thorough and scientific concern in the broad sense. The existential analysts do the same thing with the structure of human existence that Freud did with the structure of the unconscious—namely, take it out of the realm of the hit-and-miss gift of special intuitive individuals, accept it as the area of exploration and understanding, and make it to some extent teachable.

Another caveat is that the emphasis on the reality of presence does not obviate the exceedingly significant truths in Freud's concept of transference, rightly understood. It is demonstrable every day in the week that patients, and all of us to some extent, behave toward therapist or wife or husband as though they were father or mother or someone else, and the working through of this is of crucial importance. But in existential therapy "transference" gets placed in the new context of *an event occurring in a real relationship between two people.* Almost everything the patient does vis-à-vis the therapist in a given hour has an element of transference in it. But nothing is ever "just transference," to be explained to the patient as one would an arithmetic problem. The concept of "transference" as such has often been used as a convenient protective screen behind which both therapist and patient hide in order to avoid the more anxiety-creating situation of direct confrontation. For me to tell myself, say when especially fatigued, that the patient-is-so-demanding-because-she-wants-to-prove-she-can-make-her-father-love-her may be a relief and may also be in fact true. But the real point is that she is doing this to me in this given moment, and the reasons it occurs at this instant of intersection of her existence and mine are not exhausted by what she did with her father. Beyond all considerations of unconscious determinism—which are true in their partial context—she is at some point choosing to do this at this specific moment. Furthermore, the only thing that will grasp the patient, and in the long run make it possible for her to change, is to experience fully and deeply that she is doing precisely this to a real person, myself, in this real moment.[57] Part of the *sense of timing* in therapy—which, as Ellenberger indicates in the next chapter, has received special development among the existential therapists—consists of letting the patient experience what he or she is doing until the experience really grasps him.[58] Then and only then will an explanation of *why* help. For the patient referred to above to become aware that she is demanding this particular unconditioned love from this real person in this immediate hour may indeed shock her, and thereafter—or possibly only hours later—she should become aware of the early childhood antecedents. She may well explore and re-experience then how she smoldered with anger as a child because she couldn't make her father notice her. But if she is simply told this is a transference phenomenon, she may have learned an interesting intellectual fact which does not existentially grasp her at all.

Another caveat is that *presence* in a session does not at all mean the therapist imposes himself or his ideas or feelings on the patient. It is a highly interesting proof of our point that Rogers, who gives such a vivid picture of presence in the quotation above, is precisely the psychologist who has most unqualifiedly insisted that the therapist not project himself but at every point follow the affect and leads of the patient. Being alive in the relationship does not at all mean the therapist will chatter along with the patient; he will know that patients have an infinite number of ways of trying to become involved with the therapist in order to avoid their own problems. And he, the therapist, may well be silent, aware that to be a projective screen is one aspect of his part of the relationship. The therapist is what Socrates named the "midwife"— completely real in "being there," but being there with the specific purpose of helping the other person to bring to birth something from within himself.

The *fourth* implication for technique in existential analysis follows immediately from our discussion of presence: therapy will attempt to "analyze out" the ways of behaving which destroy presence. The therapist, on his part, will need to be aware of whatever in him blocks full presence. I do not know the context of Freud's remark that he preferred that patients lie on the couch because he could not stand to be stared at for nine hours a day. But it is obviously true that any therapist—whose task is arduous and taxing at best—is tempted at many points to evade the anxiety and potential discomfort of confrontation by various devices. We have earlier described the fact that real confrontation between two people can be profoundly anxiety-creating. Thus it is not surprising that it is much more comfortable to protect ourselves by thinking of the other only as a "patient" or focusing only on certain mechanisms of behavior. The *technical* view of the other person is perhaps the therapist's most handy anxiety-reducing device. This has its legitimate place. The therapist is presumably an expert. But technique must not be used as a way of blocking presence. Whenever the therapist finds himself reacting in a rigid or preformulated way, he had obviously best ask himself whether he is not trying to avoid some anxiety and as a result is losing something existentially real in the relationship. The therapist's situation is like that of the artist who has spent many years of disciplined study learning technique; but he knows that if specific thoughts of technique preoccupy him when he actually is in the process of painting, he has at that moment lost his vision; the creative process, which should absorb him, transcending the subject-object split, has become temporarily broken; he is now dealing with objects and himself as a manipulator of objects.

The *fifth* implication has to do with the goal of the therapeutic process. The aim of therapy is that the patient *experience his existence as real.* The purpose is that he become aware of his existence fully, which includes becoming aware of his potentialities and becoming able to act on the basis of them. The characteristic of the neurotic is that his existence has become "darkened," as the existential analysts put it, blurred, easily threatened and clouded over, and gives no sanction to his acts; the task of therapy is to illuminate the existence. The neurotic is over-concerned about the *Umwelt*, and underconcerned about *Eigenwelt*.[59] As the *Eigenwelt* becomes real to him in therapy, the patient tends to experience the *Eigenwelt* of the therapist as stronger than his own. Binswanger points out that the tendency to take over the therapist's *Eigenwelt* must be guarded against, and therapy must not become a power struggle between the two *Eigenwelten*. The therapist's function is to *be there* (with all of the connotation of *Dasein*), present in the relationship, while the patient finds and learns to live out his own *Eigenwelt*.

An experience of my own may serve to illustrate one way of taking the patient existentially. I often have found myself having the impulse to ask, when the patient comes in and sits down, not "*How* are you?" but "*Where* are you?" The contrast of these questions—neither of which would I probably actually ask aloud—highlights what is sought. I want to know, as I experience him in this hour, not just how he feels, but rather *where he is*, the "where" including his feelings but also a lot more—whether he is detached or fully present, whether his direction is toward me and toward his problems or away from both, whether he is running from anxiety, whether this special courtesy when he came in or appearance of eagerness to reveal things is really inviting me to overlook some evasion he is about to make, where he is in relation to the girl friend he talked about yesterday, and so on. I became aware of this asking "where" the patient was several years ago, before I specifically knew the work of the existential therapists; it illustrates a spontaneous existential attitude.

It follows that when mechanisms or dynamisms are interpreted, as they will be in existential therapy as in any other, it will always be in the context of this person's becoming aware of his existence. This is the only way the dynamism will have reality for him, will affect him; otherwise he might as well—as indeed most patients do these days—read about the mechanism in a book. This point is of special importance because precisely the problem of many patients is that they think and talk about themselves in terms of mechanisms; it is their way, as well-taught citizens of twentieth-century Western culture, to avoid confronting their own existence, their method of repressing ontological awareness. This is done, to be sure, under the rubric of being "objective" about one's self; but is it not, in therapy as well as in life, often a systematized, culturally acceptable way of rationalizing detachment from one's self? Even the motive for coming for therapy may be just that, to find an acceptable system by which one can continue to think of himself as a mechanism, to run himself as he would his motor car, only now to do it successfully. If we assume, as we have reason for doing, that the fundamental neurotic process in our day is the repression of the ontological sense—the loss of the sense of being, together with the truncation of awareness and the locking up of the potentialities which are the manifestations of this being—then we are playing directly into the patient's neurosis to the extent that we teach him new ways of thinking of himself as a mechanism. This is one illustration of how psychotherapy can reflect the fragmentation of the culture, structuralizing neurosis rather than curing it. Trying to help the patient on a sexual problem by explaining it merely as a mechanism is like teaching a farmer irrigation while damming up his stream.

This raises some penetrating questions about the nature of "cure" in psychotherapy. It implies that it is not the therapist's function to "cure" the patients' neurotic symptoms, though this is the motive for which most people come for therapy. Indeed, the fact that this is their motive reflects their problem. Therapy is concerned with something more fundamental, namely, helping the person experience his existence; and any cure of symptoms which will last must be a by-product of that. The general ideas of "cure"—namely, to live as long as possible and as satisfactorily adjusted as possible—are themselves a denial of *Dasein*, of this particular patient's being. The kind of cure that consists of adjustment, becoming able to fit the culture, can be obtained by technical emphases in therapy, for it is precisely the central theme of the culture that one live in a calculated, controlled, technically well-managed way. Then the patient accepts a confined world without conflict, for now his world is identical with the culture. And since anxiety comes only with freedom, the patient naturally gets over his anxiety; he is relieved from his symptoms because he surrenders the possibilities which caused his anxiety. This is the way of being "cured" by giving up being, giving up existence, by constricting, hedging in existence. In this respect, psychotherapists become the agents of the culture whose particular task it is to adjust people to it; psychotherapy becomes an expression of the fragmentation of the period rather than an enterprise for overcoming it. As we have indicated above, there are clear historical indications that this is occurring in the different psychotherapeutic schools, and the historical probability is that it will increase. There is certainly a question how far this gaining of release from conflict by giving up being can proceed without generating in individuals and groups a submerged despair, a resentment which will later burst out in self-destructiveness, for history proclaims again and again that sooner or later man's need to be free will out. But the complicating factor in our immediate historical situation is that the culture itself is built around this ideal of technical adjustment and carries so many built-in devices for narcotizing the despair that comes from using one's self as a machine that the damaging effects may remain submerged for some time.

On the other hand, the term "cure" can be given a deeper and truer meaning, namely, becoming oriented toward the fulfillment of one's existence. This may include as a by-product the cure of symptoms—obviously a desideratum, even if we have stated decisively that it is not the chief goal of therapy. The important thing is that the person discovers his being, his *Dasein*.

The *sixth* implication which distinguishes the process of existential therapy is the importance of *commitment*. The basis for this was prepared at numerous points in our previous sections, particularly in our discussion of Kierkegaard's idea that "truth exists only as the individual himself produces it in action." The significance of commitment is not that it is simply a vaguely good thing or ethically to be advised. It is a necessary prerequisite, rather, for seeing truth. This involves a crucial point which has never to my knowledge been fully taken into account in writings on psychotherapy, namely, that *decision precedes knowledge*. We have worked normally on the assumption that, as the patient gets more and more knowledge and insight about himself, he will make the appropriate decisions. This is a half truth. The second half of the truth is generally overlooked, namely, that *the patient cannot permit himself to get insight or knowledge until he is ready to decide, takes a decisive orientation to life, and has made the preliminary decisions along the way.*

We mean "decision" here not in the sense of a be-all-and-end-all jump, say, to get married or to join the foreign legion. The possibility or readiness to take such "leaps" is a necessary condition for the decisive orientation, but the big leap itself is sound only so far as it is based upon the minute decisions along the way. Otherwise the sudden decision is the product of unconscious processes, proceeding compulsively in unawareness to the point where they erupt, for example, in a "conversion." We use the term decision as meaning a *decisive attitude toward existence*, an attitude of commitment. In this respect, *knowledge and insight follow decision rather than vice versa.* Everyone knows of the incidents in which a patient becomes aware in a dream that a certain boss is exploiting him and the next day decides to quit his job. But just as significant, though not generally taken into account because they go against our usual ideas of causality, are the incidents when the patient cannot have the dream *until* he makes the decision. He makes the jump to quit his job, for example, and then he can permit himself to see in dreams that his boss was exploiting him all along.

One interesting corollary of this point is seen when we note that a patient cannot recall what was vital and significant in his past until he is ready to make a decision with regard to the future. Memory works not on a basis simply of what is there imprinted; it works rather on the basis of one's decisions in the present and future. It has often been said that one's past determines one's present and future. Let it be underlined that one's present and future—how he commits himself to existence at the moment—also determines his past. That is, it determines what he can recall of his past, what portions of his past he selects (consciously but also unconsciously) to influence him now, and therefore the particular gestalt his past will assume.

This commitment is, furthermore, not a purely conscious or voluntaristic phenomenon. It is also present on so-called "unconscious" levels. When a person lacks commitment, for example, his dreams may be staid, flat, impoverished; but when he does assume a decisive orientation toward himself and his life, his dreams often take over the creative process of exploring, molding, forming himself in relation to his future or—what is the same thing from the neurotic viewpoint—the dreams struggle to evade, substitute, cover up. The important point is that either way the issue has been joined.

With respect to helping the patient develop the orientation of commitment, we should first emphasize that the existential therapists do not at all mean activism. This is no "decision as a short cut," no matter of premature jumping because to act may be easier and may quiet anxiety more quickly than the slow, arduous, long-time process of self-exploration. They mean rather the attitude of *Dasein*, the self-aware being taking his own existence seriously. The points of commitment and decision are those where the dichotomy between being subject and object is overcome in the unity of readiness for action. When a patient discusses intellectually *ad interminum* a given topic without its ever shaking him or becoming real to him, the therapist asks, what is he doing existentially by means of this talk? The talk itself, obviously, is in the service of covering up reality, rationalized generally under the idea of unprejudiced inquiry into the data. It is customarily said that the patient will break through such talk when some experience of anxiety, some inner suffering or outer threat, shocks him into committing himself really to getting help and gives him the incentive necessary for the painful process of uncovering illusions, of inner change and growth. True; this of course does occur from time to time. And the existential therapist can aid the patient in absorbing the real impact of such experiences by helping him develop the capacity for silence (which is another form of communication) and thus avoid using chatter to break the shocking power of the encounter with the insight.

But in principle I do not think the conclusion that we must wait around until anxiety is aroused is adequate. If we assume that the patient's commitment depends upon being pushed by external or internal pain, we are in several difficult dilemmas. Either the therapy "marks time" until anxiety or pain occurs, or we arouse anxiety ourselves (which is a questionable procedure). And the very reassurance and quieting of anxiety the patient receives in therapy may work against his commitment to further help and may make for postponement and procrastination.

Commitment must be on a more positive basis. The question we need to ask is: What is going on that the patient has not found some point in his own existence to which he can commit himself unconditionally? In the earlier discussion of non-being and death, it was pointed out that everyone constantly faces the threat of non-being if he lets himself recognize the fact. Central here is the symbol of death, but such threat of destruction of being is present in a thousand and one other guises as well. The therapist is doing the patient a disservice if he takes away from him the realization that it is entirely within the realm of possibility that he forfeit or lose his existence and that may well be precisely what he is doing at this very moment. This point is especially important because patients tend to carry a never-quite-articulated belief, no doubt connected with childhood omnipotent beliefs associated with parents, that somehow the therapist will see that nothing harmful happens to them, and therefore they don't need to take their own existence seriously. The tendency prevails in much therapy to water down anxiety, despair, and the tragic aspects of life. Is it not true as a general principle that we need to engender anxiety only to the extent that we already have watered it down? Life itself produces enough, and the only real, crises; and it is very much to the credit of the existential emphasis in therapy that it confronts these tragic realities directly. The patient can indeed destroy himself if he so chooses. The therapist may not say this: it is simply a reflection of fact, and the important point is that it not be sloughed over. The symbol of suicide as a possibility has a far-reaching positive value; Nietzsche once remarked that the thought of suicide has saved many lives. I am doubtful whether anyone takes his life with full seriousness until he realizes that it is entirely within his power to commit suicide.[60]

Death in any of its aspects is the fact which makes of the present hour something of absolute value. One student put it, "I know only two things—one, that I will be dead someday, two, that I am not dead now. The only question is what shall I do between those two points." We cannot go into this matter in further detail, but we only wish to emphasize that the core of the existential approach is the taking of existence seriously.

We conclude with two final caveats. One is a danger that lies in the existential approach, the danger of *generality*. It would indeed be a pity if the existential concepts were tossed around among therapists without regard for their concrete, real meaning. For it must be admitted that there is temptation to become lost in words in these complex areas with which existential analysis deals. One can certainly become philosophically detached in the same way as one can be technically detached. The temptation to use existential concepts in the service of intellectualizing tendencies is especially to be guarded against, since, because they refer to things that have to do with the center of personal reality, these concepts can the more seductively give the illusion of dealing with reality. It must be confessed that some of the writers in the papers in this volume may not have fully resisted this temptation, and some readers may feel that I myself have not. I could plead the necessity of having to explain a great deal within a short compass; but extenuating circumstances are not the point. The point is that to the extent that the existential movement in psychotherapy becomes influential in this country—a desideratum which we believe would be very beneficial—the adherents will have to be on guard against the use of the concepts in the service of intellectual detachment. It is, of course, precisely for the above reasons that the existential therapists pay much attention to making clear the verbal utterances of the patient, and they also continually make certain that the necessary interrelation of verbalizing and acting is never overlooked. The "logos must be made flesh." The important thing is *to be* existential.

The other caveat has to do with the existential attitude toward the *unconscious*. In principle most existential analysts deny this concept. They point out all the logical as well as psychological difficulties with the doctrine of the unconscious, and they stand against splitting the being into parts. What is called unconscious, they hold, is still part of this given person; *being*, in any living sense, is at its core indivisible. Now it must be admitted that the doctrine of the unconscious has played most notoriously into the contemporary tendencies to rationalize behavior, to avoid the reality of one's own existence, to act as though one were not himself doing the living. (The man in the street who has picked up the lingo says, "My unconscious did it.") The existential analysts are correct, in my judgment, in their criticism of the doctrine of the unconscious as a convenient blank check on which any causal explanation can be written or as a reservoir from which any deterministic theory can be drawn. But this is the "cellar" view of the unconscious, and objections to it should not be permitted to cancel out the great contribution that the historical meaning of the unconscious had in Freud's terms. Freud's great discovery and his perdurable contribution was to enlarge the sphere of the human personality beyond the immediate voluntarism and rationalism of Victorian man, to include in this enlarged sphere the "depths," that is, the irrational, the so-called repressed, hostile, and unacceptable urges, the forgotten aspects of experience, *ad infinitum*. The symbol for this vast enlarging of the domain of the personality was "the unconscious."

I do not wish to enter into the complex discussion of this concept itself; I wish only to suggest a position. It is right that the blank check, deteriorated, cellar form of this concept should be rejected. But the far-reaching enlargement of personality, which is its real meaning, should not be lost. Binswanger remarks that, for the time being, the existential therapists will not be able to dispense with the concept of the unconscious. I would propose, rather, to agree that being is at some point indivisible, that unconsciousness is part of any given being, that the cellar theory of the unconscious is logically wrong and practically unconstructive; but that the meaning of the discovery, namely, the radical enlargement of being, is one of the great contributions of our day and must be retained.

NOTES

1. We may have it with friends and loved ones. It is not a once-and-for-all experience; indeed, in any developing, growing relationship it may—probably should, if the relationship is vital—occur continually.

2. Jean-Paul Sartre, *Being and Nothingness*, trans. by Hazel Barnes (1956), p. 561. Sartre goes on, ". . . either in looking for the *person* we encounter a useless, contradictory metaphysical substance—or else the being whom we seek vanishes in a dust of phenomena bound together by external connections. But what each of us requires in this very effort to comprehend another is that he should never resort to this idea of substance, which is inhuman because it is well this side of the human" (p. 52). Also, "If we admit that the person is a

totality, we can not hope to reconstruct him by an addition or by an organization of the diverse tendencies which we have empirically discovered in him. . . ." Every attitude of the person contains some reflection of this totality, holds Sartre. "A jealousy of a particular date in which a subject posits himself in history in relation to a certain woman, signifies for the one who knows how to interpret it, the total relation to the world by which the subject constitutes himself as a self. In other words this *empirical attitude* is by itself the expression of the 'choice of an intelligible character.' There is no mystery about this" (p. 58).

3. Gabriel Marcel, *The Philosophy of Existence* (1949), p. 1.

4. *Ibid.* Italics mine. For data concerning the "morbid effects of the repression" of the sense of being, cf. Fromm, *Escape from Freedom*, and David Riesman, *The Lonely Crowd*.

5. *Ibid.*, p. 5.

6. Pascal's *Penseés*, Gertrude B. Burfurd Rawlings, trans. and ed. (Peter Pauper Press), p. 35. Pascal goes on, "Thus all our dignity lies in thought. By thought we must raise ourselves, not by space and time, which we cannot fill. Let us strive, then, to think well,—therein is the principle of morality." It is perhaps well to remark that of course by "thought" he means not intellectualism nor technical reason but self-consciousness, the reason which also knows the reasons of the heart.

7. Since our purpose is merely to illustrate one phenomenon, namely, the experience of the sense of being, we shall not report the diagnostic or other details of the case.

8. Some readers will be reminded of the passage in Exodus 3:14 in which Moses, after Yahweh had appeared to him in the burning bush and charged him to free the Israelites from Egypt, demands that the God tell his name. Yahweh gives the famous answer, "I am that I am." This classical, existential sentence (the patient, incidentally, did not consciously know this sentence) carries great symbolic power because, coming from an archaic period, it has God state that *the quintessence of divinity is the power to be.* We are unable to go into the many rich meanings of this answer, nor the equally intricate translation problems, beyond pointing out that the Hebrew of the sentence can be translated as well, "I shall be what I shall be." This bears out our statement above that being is in the future tense and inseparable from becoming; God is creative *potentia*, the essence of the power to become.

9. We omit for purposes of the above discussion the question whether this rightly should be called "transference" or simply human trust at this particular point in this case. We do not deny the validity of the concept of transference rightly defined (see p. 149), but it never makes sense to speak of something as "just transference," as though it were all carried over simply from the past.

10. Healy, Bronner and Bowers, *The Meaning and Structure of Psychoanalysis* (1930), p. 38. We give these quotations from a standard summary from the classical middle period of psychoanalysis, not because we are not aware of refinements made to ego theory later, but because we wish to

show the essence of the concept of the ego, an essence which has been elaborated but not basically changed.

11. *Ibid.*, p. 41.

12. *Ibid.*, p. 38.

13. If the objection is entered that the concept of the "ego" at least is more precise and therefore more satisfactory scientifically than this sense of being, we can only repeat what we have said above, that precision can be gained easily enough on paper. But the question always is the bridge between the concept and the reality of the person, and the scientific challenge is to find a concept, a way of understanding, which does not do violence to reality, even though it may be less precise.

14. This is an interpretation of Heidegger, given by Werner Brock in the introduction to *Existence and Being* (Regnery, 1949), p. 77. For those who are interested in the logical aspects of the problem of being vs. non-being, it may be added that the dialectic of "yes vs. no," as Tillich points out in *The Courage to Be*, is present in various forms throughout the history of thought. Hegel held that non-being was an integral part of being, specifically in the "antithesis" stage of his dialectic of "thesis, antithesis, and synthesis." The emphasis on "will" in Schelling, Schopenhauer, Nietzsche, and others as a basic ontological category is a way of showing that being has the power of "negating itself without losing itself." Tillich, giving his own conclusion, holds that the question of how being and non-being are related can be answered only metaphorically: "Being embraces both itself and non-being." In everyday terms, being embraces non-being in the sense that we can be aware of death, can accept it, can even invite it in suicide, in short, can by self-awareness encompass death.

15. The points in this summary of ontological anxiety are given in epigrammatic form, since for reasons of space we are forced to omit the considerable empirical data which could be cited at each point. A fuller development of some aspects of this approach to anxiety will be found in my book, *The Meaning of Anxiety* (New York: Ronald Press, 1950).

16. We speak here of anxiety as the "subjective" state, making a distinction between subjective and objective that may not be entirely justified logically but shows the viewpoint from which one observes. The "objective" side of the anxiety experience, which we can observe from the outside, shows itself in severe cases in disordered, catastrophic behavior (Goldstein) or in cases of neurotics in symptom-formation or in cases of "normal" persons in ennui, compulsive activity, meaningless diversions, and truncation of awareness.

17. See discussion of this phenomenon in connection with Minkowski's chapter in R. May, E. Angel, & H. F. Ellenberger (Eds.), *Existence: A New Dimension in Psychiatry and Psychology* (New York: Basic Books, Inc., 1958), pp. 66 and 127.

18. It is an interesting question whether our pragmatic tendencies in English-speaking countries to avoid reacting to anxiety experiences—by being stoical in Britain and by not crying or showing fear in this country, for

examples—is part of the reason we have not developed words to do justice to the experience.

19. See *Meaning of Anxiety*, p. 32.

20. *Human Nature in the Light of Psychopathology* (Cambridge: Harvard University Press, 1940).

21. Medard Boss, *Psychoanalyse und Daseinsanalytik* (Bern and Stuttgart: Verlag Hans Huber, 1957). I am grateful to Dr. Erich Heydt, student and colleague of Boss, for translating parts of this work for me as well as discussing at length with me the viewpoint of Boss.

22. "The Existential Analysis School of Thought," R. May, et al., *op. cit.*, p. 197.

23. This phrase, "epistemological loneliness," is used by David Bakan to describe Western man's experience of isolation from his world. He sees this isolation as stemming from the skepticism which we inherited from the British empiricists, Locke, Berkeley, and Hume. Their error specifically, he holds, was in conceiving of the "thinker as essentially alone rather than as a member and participant of a thinking community" ("Clinical Psychology and Logic," *The American Psychologist*, December 1956, p. 656). It is interesting that Bakan, in good psychological tradition, interprets the error as a social one, namely, separation from the community. But is this not more symptom than cause? More accurately stated, is not the isolation from the community simply one of the ways in which a more basic and comprehensive isolation shows itself?

24. *Existence*, p. 142.

25. Readers interested in this history of ideas will recall the important and imposing symbol of the same situation in Leibnitz' famous doctrine that all reality consists of *monads*. The monads had no doors or windows opening to each other, each being separated, isolated. "Each single unit is lonely in itself, without any direct communication. The horror of this idea was overcome by the harmonistic presupposition that in every monad the whole world is potentially present and that the development of each individual is in a natural harmony with the development of all the others. This is the most profound metaphysical situation in the early periods of bourgeois civilization. It fitted this situation because there was still a common world, in spite of the increasing social atomization." (Paul Tillich, *The Protestant Era*, p. 246.) This doctrine of "pre-established harmony" is a carry-over of the religious idea of providence. The relation between the person and the world was somehow "pre-ordained." Descartes, in similar vein, held that God—whose existence he believed he had proved—guaranteed the relation between consciousness and the world. The socio-historical situation in the expanding phases of the modern period were such that the "faith" of Leibnitz and Descartes *worked*, that is, it reflected the fact that there was still a common world (Tillich). But now that God is not only "dead," but a requiem has been sung over his grave, the stark isolation and alienation inherent in the relation between man and the world has become apparent. To put the matter less poetically, when the humanistic

and Hebrew-Christian values disintegrated along with the cultural phenomena we have discussed above, the inherent implications of the situation
emerged.

26. Thus Heidegger uses the terms "to sojourn" and "to dwell" rather than
"is" when he speaks of a person being some place. His use of the term "world"
is in the sense of the Greek *kosmos*, that is, the "uni-verse" with which we act
and react. He chides Descartes for being so concerned with *res extensa* that
he analyzed all the objects and things *in* the world and forgot about the
most significant fact of all, namely, that there is world *itself*, that is, a meaningful relationship of these objects with the person. Modern thought has followed Descartes almost exclusively at this point, greatly to the impairment of
our understanding of human beings.

27. See Binswanger, in *Existence*, p. 196.

28. The term "culture" is generally in common parlance set over against
the individual, *e.g.*, "the influence of the culture on the individual." This
usage is probably an unavoidable result of the dichotomy between subject and
object in which the concepts of "individual" and "culture" emerged. It of
course omits the very significant fact that the individual is at every moment
also forming his culture.

29. "World-openness is the distinctively human characteristic of man's
awake life," Schachtel continues. He discusses cogently and clearly the life-
space and life-time which characterize the human being's world in contrast to
that of plants and animals. "In the animals, drives and affects remain to a very
large extent ties to an inherited instinctive organization. The animal is embedded in this organization and in the closed world (J. v. Uexküll's 'Werk-
welt' and 'Wirkwelt') corresponding to this organization. Man's relation to
his world is an open one, governed only to a very small extent by instinctive
organization, and to the largest extent by man's learning and exploration, in
which he establishes his complex, changing and developing relations with his
fellow men and with the natural and cultural world around him." So closely
interrelated are man and his world, Schachtel demonstrates, that "all our
affects arise from . . . spatial and temporal gaps which open between us and
our world." "On Affect, Anxiety and the Pleasure Principle," paper to be published, pp. 101–104.

30. *Existence*, p. 191. In this chapter, it is significant to note the parallels
Binswanger draws between his conception of "world" and that of Kurt
Goldstein.

31. In this respect it is significant to note that Kierkegaard and Nietzsche,
in contrast to the great bulk of nineteenth-century thinkers, were able to take
the body seriously. The reason was that they saw it not as a collection of
abstracted substances or drives, *but as one mode of the reality of the person*.
Thus when Nietzsche says "We think with our bodies," he means something
radically different from the behaviorists.

32. Martin Buber has developed implications of *Mitwelt* in his *I and Thou*
philosophy. See his lectures at the Washington School of Psychiatry, printed

in *Psychiatry*, May 1957, Vol. 20, No. Two, and especially the lecture on "Distance and Relation."

33. This concept was originally formulated by William James as "the self is the sum of the different roles the person plays." Though the definition was a gain in its day in overcoming a fictitious "self" existing in a vacuum, we wish to point out that it is an inadequate and faulty definition. If one takes it consistently, one not only has a picture of an *unintegrated*, "neurotic" self but falls into all kinds of difficulty in adding up these roles. We propose, rather, that the self is not the sum of the roles you play but your capacity *to know that you are the one playing these roles*. This is the only point of integration, and rightly makes the roles *manifestations* of the self.

34. One feels in many of the psychological and psychiatric discussions of love a lack of the *tragic* dimension. Indeed, to take tragedy into the picture in any sense requires that the individual be understood in the three modes of world—the world of biological drive, fate, and determinism (*Umwelt*), the world of responsiblity to fellow men (*Mitwelt*), and the world in which the individual can be aware (*Eigenwelt*) of the fate he alone at that moment is struggling with. The *Eigenwelt* is essential to any experience of tragedy, for the individual must be conscious of his own identity in the midst of the vast natural and social forces operating upon him. It has been rightly said that we lack a sense of tragedy in the modern world—and hence produce few real tragedies in drama or other forms of art—because we have lost the sense of the individual's own identity and consciousness in the midst of the overwhelming economic, political, social, and natural forces acting upon him. One of the significant things about the existential psychiatric and psychological approach is that tragedy comes back into the human realm and is to be looked at and understood in its own right.

35. Sören Kierkegaard, *Fear and Trembling*, trans. by Walter Lowrie (New York: Doubleday & Co., 1954), p. 55.

36. "Findings in a Case of Schizophrenic Depression," R. May, et al., *op. cit.*, p. 127. Minkowski's book, *Le Temps Vécu* (Paris: J. L. L. d'Artrey, 1933), a presentation of his concepts of "lived time," is unfortunately not translated into English.

37. This understanding of time is also reflected in "process philosophies," such as Whitehead's, and has obvious parallels in modern physics.

38. Cf. Tillich, "Existence is distinguished from essence by its temporal character." Also Heidegger, referring to one's awareness of his own existence in time, "Temporality is the genuine meaning of Care." Tillich, "Existential Philosophy," *Journal of the History of Ideas*, 5:1 ,61, 62, 1944.

39. "Time as a Determinant in Integrative Learning," in *Learning Theory and Personality Dynamics*, selected papers by O. Hobart Mowrer (New York: Ronald Press, 1950).

40. Bergson, *Essai sur les Données Immédiates de la Conscience*, quoted by Tillich, "Existential Philosophy," p. 56.

41. Heidegger's *Being and Time* is devoted, as its title indicates, to an

analysis of this interrelationship. His over-all theme is "the vindication of time for being" (Straus). He calls the three modes of time, namely, past, present, and future, the "three ecstasies of time," using the term ecstasy in its etymological meaning of "to stand outside and beyond." For the essential characteristic of the human being is the capacity to transcend a given mode of time. Heidegger holds that our preoccupation with objective time is really an evasion; people much prefer to see themselves in terms of objective time, the time of statistics, of quantitative measurement, of "the average," etc., because they are afraid to grasp their existence directly. He holds, moreover, that objective time, which has its rightful place in quantitative measurements, can be understood only on the basis of time as immediately experienced rather than vice versa.

42. Not only the existential psychologists and psychiatrists but the existential thinkers in general are to be distinguished precisely by the fact that they do take seriously the historical cultural situation which conditions the psychological and spiritual problems for any individual. But they emphasize that to know history we must act in it. Cf. Heidegger: "Fundamentally history takes its start not from the 'present' nor from what is 'real' only today, but from the future. The 'selection' of what is to be an object of history is made by the actual, 'existential' choice . . . of the historian, in which history arises." Brock, op. cit., p. 110. The parallel in therapy is that what the patient selects from the past is determined by what he faces in the future.

43. *Fear and Trembling*, p. 130. What we do learn from previous generations are of course facts; one may learn them by repetition, like the multiplication table, or remember facts or experiences on their "shock" basis. Kierkegaard is not denying any of this. He was well aware that there is progress from one generation to the next in *technical areas*. What he is speaking of above is "that which is genuinely human," specifically, love.

44. This antagonism was illustrated to me when a recent paper of mine was read by a discussant prior to its presentation. I had included in the paper a paragraph discussing Goldstein's concept of the neurobiological aspects of the organism's capacity to transcend its immediate situation, not at all under the impression that I was saying anything very provocative. My using the word "transcending" in introducing the topic, however, was like waving a red flag in my discussant's face, for he printed a huge "No!!" in red crayon replete with exclamation marks on the margin before even getting to the discussion of what the word meant. The very word, indeed, seems to carry some inciting-to-riot quality.

45. Erwin W. Straus, "Man, a Questioning Being," UIT *Tijdschrift voor Philosophie*, 17e Jaargang, No. 1, Maart 1955.

46. *Practical and Theoretical Aspects of Psychoanalysis* (New York: International Universities Press, 1950), p. 19.

47. Medard Boss, *op. cit.*

48. *The Sickness Unto Death*, p. 163. The quote continues, "Imagination is the reflection of the process of infinitizing, and hence the elder Fichte

quite rightly assumed, even in relation to knowledge, that imagination is the origin of the categories. The self is reflection, and imagination is reflection, it is the counterfeit presentment of the self, which is the possibility of the self."

49. Ludwig Binswanger, "The Case of Ellen West," in R. May, et al., *op. cit.*, p. 308.

50. The term "analyzed" itself reflects this problem, and patients may be doing more than using a semantic difficulty as a way of expressing resistance when they aver that the idea of "being analyzed" makes them objects being "worked upon." The term is carried over into the phrase "existential analysis" partly because it has become standard for deep psychotherapy since the advent of psychoanalysis and partly because existential thought itself (following Heidegger) is an "analysis of reality." This term is of course a reflection of the tendency in our whole culture, called "The Age of Analysis" in the title of a recent survey of modern Western thought. Though I am not happy about the term, I have used the identification "existential analyst" for the writers in *Existence* because it is too clumsy to say "phenomenological and existential psychiatrists and psychologists."

51. I am indebted to Dr. Ludwig Lefebre and Dr. Hans Hoffman, students of existential therapy, for correspondence and discussion of techniques of *Daseinsanalyse*.

52. *Psychoanalyse und Daseinsanalytik.* The quotations which follow are rough translations from this book by Dr. Erich Heydt.

53. See "The Origins and Significance of the Existential Movement in Psychology," R. May, et al., *op. cit.*, p. 26.

54. Ulrich Sonnemann, in *Existence and Therapy* (New York: Grune & Stratton, 1954), p. 343, quoted from Kolle. Sonnemann's book, we may add, was the first in English to deal directly with existential theory and therapy and contains useful and relevant material. It is therefore the more unfortunate that the book is written in a style which does not communicate.

55. Quoted by Sonnemann, *op. cit.*, p. 255, from L. Binswanger, "Uber Psychotherapie," in *Ausgewählte Vorträge und Aufsätze*, pp. 142–143.

56. C. R. Rogers, "Persons or Science? A Philosophical Question," *American Psychologist*, 10:267–278, 1955.

57. This is a point the phenomenologists make consistently, namely, that to know fully *what* we are doing, to feel it, to experience it all through our being, is much more important than to know *why*. For, they hold, if we fully know the *what*, the *why* will come along by itself. One sees this demonstrated very frequently in psychotherapy: the patient may have only a vague and intellectual idea of the "cause" of this or that pattern in his behavior, but as he explores and experiences more and more the different aspects and phases of this pattern, the cause may suddenly become real to him not as an abstracted formulation but as one real, integral aspect of the total understanding of what he is doing. This approach also has an important cultural significance: is not the *why* asked so much in our culture precisely as a way of detaching ourselves, a way of avoiding the more disturbing and anxiety-creating alternative

of sticking to the end with the *what?* That is to say, the excessive preoccupation with causality and function that characterizes modern Western society may well serve, much more widely than realized, the need to abstract ourselves from the reality of the given experience. Asking *why* is generally in the service of a need to get power *over* the phenomenon, in line with Bacon's dictum, "knowledge is power" and specifically, knowledge of nature is power over nature. Asking the question of *what,* on the other hand, is a way of *participating* in the phenomenon.

58. This could well be defined as "existential time"—*the time it takes for something to become real.* It may occur instantaneously, or it may require an hour of talk or some time of silence. In any case, the sense of timing the therapist uses in pondering when to interpret will not be based only on the negative criterion—How much can the patient take? It will involve a positive criterion—Has this become real to the patient? As in the example above, has what she is doing in the present to the therapist been sharply and vividly enough experienced so that an exploration of the past will have dynamic reality and thus give the power for change?

59. The point in this and the rest of the sentences in this paragraph is Binswanger's, interpreted by Dr. Hoffman.

60. We are of course not speaking here of the practical question of what to do when patients actually threaten suicide; this introduces many other elements and is a quite different question. The conscious awareness we are speaking of is a different thing from the overwhelming and persistent depression, with the self-destructive impulse unbroken by self-conscious awareness, which seems to obtain in actual suicides.

CHAPTER 9

Psychotherapy and the Daimonic

Rollo May

Amid the feelings of honor I have at being asked to take part in this symposium, I must confess to another feeling, an emergence of an old conviction which rises up to haunt me. This is the conviction that there is always something "dead" about trying to summarize one's previous contributions, especially if that summary is put into a collection of summaries of others' previous contributions. Try as I will, I cannot forget that pithy remark by Gibbon in his *Decline and Fall of the Roman Empire,* when he speaks of writing and distribution of works in ancient Rome: "From one end of the land to the other, the empire was flooded with collections, anthologies and symposia; but of original poetry or true oratory there was none."

Since summaries of my viewpoint, moreover, are available in paperback, and since it would be doubly dead to make a "summary of a summary," I shall use this space to demonstrate my approach to psychotherapy by offering an original contribution. This contribution rests upon and presupposes everything I have thought and written before. But it reaches out, I trust, into new areas. I believe such a chapter will give the reader the best and most immediate experience of my approach to therapy.

The poet Rilke once wrote, on withdrawing from psychotherapy after having one session in which the therapist explained the goals to which therapy aspired, "If my devils are to leave me, I am afraid my angels will take flight as well." Taking off from that text, this chapter will explore the place of the daimonic[1] in psychotherapy.

This chapter is a discussion-summary of Chapter 8 of the present volume: "Contributions of Existential Psychotherapy," by Rollo May. Reprinted from *Love and Will* by Rollo May. By permission of W. W. Norton & Company, Inc. Copyright © 1969 by W. W. Norton & Company, Inc. And by permission of the Souvenir Press, Ltd., of London.

1. DEFINITION OF THE DAIMONIC

I define "the daimonic" as *any natural function in the individual which has the power of taking over the whole person.* Sex and eros, anger and rage, and the craving for power are examples. The daimonic element always has its biological base; indeed, Goethe, who knew modern man's daimonic urges intimately, as is shown so eloquently in *Faust*, remarks, "The daimon is the power of nature." But the important characteristic of the daimonic is that the one element within the person which has its rightful function as part of the personality can itself usurp power over the *whole* self and thus drive the person into disintegrative behavior. The erotic-sexual urge, as one illustration of the daimonic, pushes the person toward physical union with the partner, but it may, when it takes command over the total person, drive him in many diverse directions and into all kinds of relationships without regard for the integration of the self. The Karamazov father has coitus with the idiot woman in the ditch; on a more erotic level, Antony dallies in Egypt with Cleopatra to his own destruction.

The daimonic can be either destructive or creative. When this power goes awry and one element takes over the total personality, we have "daimon possession," the traditional term through history for psychosis. The destructive activities of the daimonic are only the reverse side of vitality and of potentially constructive activities that it also motivates.

"Eros is a daimon," said Diotima, the authority on love among Plato's banqueting friends.[2] True, the daimonic is correlated with eros rather than with libido or sex as such. Antony presumably had all his sexual needs well taken care of by concubines, but the daimonic power which seized him in his meeting with Cleopatra was a very different thing. When Freud introduced eros as the opposite to and adversary of libido, i.e., as the force which stood against the death instinct and fought for life, he was using eros in a way that included the daimonic. The daimonic fights against death, fights always to assert its own vitality, accepts no "three-score and ten" or other timetable of life. It is this daimonic which is referred to when we adjure someone seriously ill not to give up the "fight," or when we sadly acknowledge some indication that a friend will die as the fact that he "has given up the fight." The daimonic will never take a rational "no" for an answer.

In this respect the daimonic is the enemy of technology. It will accept no clock-time, or nine-to-five schedule, or assembly line to attach ourselves to as robots.

The daimonic needs to be directed, channeled; this is where human consciousness becomes so important. We initially experience (whether in awareness or not) the daimonic as a blind push; it is impersonal in the sense that it makes us nature's tool; it pushes us toward the blind assertion of ourselves, as in rage, or toward the triumph of the species by impregnating the female, as in sex. When I am in a rage, it couldn't matter to me less who I am or who you are; I want only to strike out and destroy you. When a man is in intense sexual excitement, he loses his personal sense and wants only to "make" or "lay" (as the verbs of forcing so clearly put it) the woman, regardless of who she is.

2. THE DAIMONIC IN PRIMITIVE PSYCHOTHERAPY

Native psychotherapy often shows us exceedingly interesting and revealing ways of dealing with the daimonic. Dr. Raymond Prince, a psychiatrist who lived with and studied the natives of Yoruba for a number of years, filmed a fascinating ceremony which I offer here as an illustration.[3] When the tribal mental healer is to treat some members of the community for what we would call psychological ailments, the whole village participates. After the usual rituals of the casting of bones and a ceremony which is believed to transfer the problem—be it sexual impotence or depression or what not—to a goat who then (as the "scape-goat") is ceremonially slaughtered, everybody in the village joins together for several hours of frenzied dancing. In the dancing, which constitutes the main part of the healing, the significant point is that *the native who wants to be cured identifies with the figure he believes has demonic possession of him.*

A man in Dr. Prince's film who had the problem of sexual impotence put on the clothes of his mother and danced around at length *as though he were her.* This reveals to us that the natives had insight into the fact that such a man's impotence is connected with his relationship to his mother, ostensibly an overdependence on her which he, in his own self-system, has denied. What is necessary for the "cure," thus, is that he confront and come to terms with this "demon" in himself. Now, needing and clinging to mother are a normal part of the experience of everyone of us, absolutely essential for our survival when we are infants and the source of much of our tenderness and sensitivity in later years. If this clinging is felt by the person to be too great, or for some other reason he must repress it, he projects it outside: it is the *woman he goes to bed with who is the evil one, the devil who would castrate him.* So he is thereupon impotent, thus castrating himself. Presumably such a man has become preoccupied with women—"possessed" by them—and has found himself fighting off this obsession to no avail. Whether he visualizes his mother specifically as the demon or not, I would not know; usually we would expect some *symbolic* expression of the "demon." Accurately speaking, the demon is his own inner morbid relationship to his mother. In the frenzied dance he then "invites the daimonic," welcomes it. He not only confronts the devil toe to toe, but accepts her, identifies with her, assimilates and integrates her as a constructive part of himself—and hopefully becomes both more gentle and sensitive as a man and sexually potent.

In Dr. Prince's film of this healing dance, we see also a late-teen-age girl of the village who had a problem with male authority and had felt herself "possessed." In the ceremony she danced wearing the hat and coat of the British census taker of the region, apparently the symbol of her daimonic problem with authority. We would expect that, after the healing frenzy of the ceremony, she would hopefully be more assertive in her own right, less "mousy," more able to deal with authorities; and I would expect able to give herself with less ambivalence to a man in sexual love.

They both boldly identified with what they feared, with what they had been previously struggling so hard to deny. The principle is: *Identify with that which haunts you, not in order to fight it off, but to take it into your self, for it must represent some rejected element in you.* The man identifies with his feminine component; he does not become homosexual but heterosexually potent. As he dances wearing the hat and dress of a woman, and the girl the officer's hat and jacket, you would think you are seeing a masquerade in the film. But not at all: no one of the villagers smiles a bit; they are there to perform a significant ceremony for members of their community. The girl and man were emboldened to "invite" the daimonic by the support of their group.

I note, now, that both of these persons happen to be identifying with someone of the opposite sex. We are reminded of Jung's idea that the shadow side of the self which is denied in a person is of the opposite sex, the *anima* in the case of men, or in the case of women the *animus*. What is especially interesting is that the term animus is related both to "animosity," a feeling of hostility, a violent, malevolent intention, and to "animate," to give spirit, to enliven. All of these terms have their root in the Latin *anima*, soul or spirit. Thus the wisdom of the words, distilled through man's history, is that the denied part of you is the source of hostility and aggression, but when you can through consciousness integrate it into your self-system, it becomes the source of energy and spirit which enlivens you. You take in the daimonic which would possess *you* if you didn't. The one way to get over daimonic possession is to possess *it*, by frankly confronting it, coming to terms with it, integrating it into the self-system. This process yields several benefits. It strengthens the self because it brings in what had been left out. It overcomes the "split" which has consisted of the paralyzing ambivalence in the self. And it renders the person more "human" by breaking down the self-righteousness and aloof detachment which are the usual defenses of the human being who denies the daimonic.

3. Confronting the Daimonic

"If my devils leave me," we have quoted Rilke as writing, "I am afraid my angels will take flight as well." Those of us to whom Rilke's poems have given special pleasure and meaning may well be glad he did not continue with *that* particular therapist, the consultation with whom was the occasion for this note in his letter to a friend. I say this, believing though I do that therapy can be the most meaningful experience in a human being's life. But we must admit that the kind of therapy that seeks first of all "adjustment," or that strives to inculcate certain pre-ordained behavior patterns cannot escape being manipulating and de-humanizing. In this sense Rilke was right; if the aim is to take the devils away, we had better be prepared to bid goodbye to our angels as well.

It is the task of the therapist, in my judgment, to conjure up the devils rather than put them to sleep. For the devils are there—in modern man as well as in ancient. Our technology and our widespread education and our vaunted rationalism change the form of the devils but not their essential character: and a good thing, too, for in them lie not only our problems but our strength, our animation, our spirit.

The function of the therapist is to disturb homeostasis. To speak practically, most patients come to us already in a state of disturbed homeostasis. Our initial task is to make available an interpersonal world—consisting chiefly of the therapist-patient relationship—in which they are able to confront the despair, the daimonic, as fully and directly as possible. The therapist must at least not participate in drugging the disturbed homeostasis into unawareness. The Furies are called in Aeschylus' *Oresteia* the "disturbers of sleep." When one stops to think about it, if Orestes had slept soundly in that month after he killed his mother, something tremendously important would have been lost. Sleep is possible only after the pattern of fate-guilt-personal responsibility-new integration is worked through, as it is in the last drama of the trilogy, the *Eumenides*. In the working-through, dreams then can have not only a regressive but a progressive function. For dreams boldly conjure up the devils. If we can dare the daimonic, our dreams can be a reaching out to find the world again with its angels *and* devils: dreams then are a looking-around with an eye that can conceive in order to perceive, to see what new possibilities there are in the world.

We have seen that there is good practical reason for the psychologists to admit the concept of the daimonic into their systems of thought and therapy. There is good logical reason also. Take, for example, the pathological form of the daimonic: a patient comes into a clinic with the conviction that the priest across the street or the policeman on the corner has designs against him and has been for some weeks thinking up a complicated plan to give him a fatal disease. We would find that most therapists and psychologists would interpret the phenomenon as the patient's projection of his inner reality on the outside world. The therapist in the clinic would then try to get the patient, not to focus on what is going on out there in the priest's mind or policeman's mind, but to look into his own inner state to find what and why he needs to "project" on the outside world. If so, there should be no objection in principle to what I am proposing, namely, to bring back the entire experience of the daimonic into the inner life of the individual, and to ask what we and our patients are trying to deny in ourselves, which we then have to "project" on someone else. My example, of course, represents in actuality a symptom of fairly serious psychopathology. But instead of merely calling it "paranoid schizophrenic projection" and assuring ourselves we have said something, could we therapists not devote some concern to exploring why the patient has worked out this quite elaborate scheme for the *other person's* mind, what he is trying to say about his own lost potentialities in the process?

The daimons are here, surely not as entities but as symbols of tendencies within ourselves which obsess us. If we are forced to run from them and deny them, they have us in their power; if we stand, recognizing them, their power becomes available for us. Rilke's devils contributed as much to his poetry as his angels.

Turning now to the question of how to deal with the daimonic in therapy, we find that our first consideration has already been implied. This is the simple necessity to confront and accept the existence of daimonic trends in the experience of the patient and in each one of us. This confronting sounds easy; but it is the hardest step of all, for not only does our clock-ruled, committee-managed, and computer-directed society make a religion of denying the daimonic in general, but most of our psychological theory denies it specifically. We assume that an individual *ought* to be able to direct his life by rational rules that make him "productive, efficient and happy," to use Professor Skinner's words—so, *mirabile dictu*, we find ourselves assuming that is the way he does live, or could if he had enough sense to let us change a few of his unproductive, inefficient, unhappy habits. This denial of the daimonic is most egregious in behavior therapy, where it is maintained that man's habits can be changed in the same manner as conditioning Pavlov's dogs.

But the denial is also present in such therapy as that of Carl Rogers, which is the diametric opposite to Pavlovian. I wish to refer here to a significant research done by Rogers and his associates (1967) in psychotherapy with schizophrenics, of which I had the honor to be one of the judges. It came out, as a negative aspect of otherwise generally constructive therapy, that these therapists had great difficulty even *hearing*, let alone dealing with, the hostile, aggressive, destructive feelings and tendencies of the patients. In the observation of all the judges who listened to the tapes, almost every time the patient brought up something genuinely hostile and destructive toward the therapist or the hospital, the therapist missed the point and interpreted the patient's reaction as loneliness, or isolation, or some other form of dependency need. These therapists were not stupid or prevaricating: they simply could not *hear* the feelings with this aggressive character, and consequently tended to turn off the patient whenever these "devils" put in an appearance. Now we regularly find in supervising students in psychotherapy that they do not "hear" the patient when he is talking about some kind of experience that they have not been able to deal with in their own lives. Carl Rogers is perspicacious and straightforward when, in his discussion of this fact that the judges of his therapeutic project were all but unanimous in finding this flaw in the work of the Rogerian therapists, he asks whether this does not indicate that these therapists have failed to come to terms with their own aggression, anger, and negative feelings. The answer is obviously yes. We can presume that such feelings represented daimonic trends in the therapists—otherwise why the avoidance of them?

The reader may wonder why I single out feelings of aggression and hostility and call them daimonic in this therapy. Because they are the elements denied in Rogerian therapy. Rogers makes much of his belief that man is by nature good.[4] I am arguing that a feeling or tendency is denied because, first, it is perceived as daimonic to start with (and therefore a threat to one's self-image and faith in life). Second, that it becomes more daimonic by virtue of being denied. Loneliness surely can be daimonic when it preoccupies the person, as for example in borderline schizophrenic patients, and I suspect at some time in all of our lives, loneliness rises to a panic which can drive us literally to frenzied behavior. I judge that loneliness is less apt to be repressed by the patient working with Rogerian therapists. But there are kinds of therapy in which the patient and therapist seem to be *in love with aggression and hostility.* In this therapy, presumably, loneliness is repressed and—in line with our culture as a whole—*tenderness* would be especially denied.

What does it mean to confront the daimonic? This illustration is from a patient who suffered bouts of acute loneliness which sometimes developed into temporary panic bordering on the schizophrenic. In the panics he could not orient himself, could not hang on to his sense of time, and became, as long as the bout lasted, numb in his reactions to the world. The ghostlike character of this loneliness was shown in the fact that it could vanish instantaneously with his hearing a step in the hall of someone coming or a ring on the phone. The patient customarily tried to fight off these attacks, as we all do—not surprising, since acute loneliness, as Fromm-Reichmann used to emphasize, is the most painful form of anxiety which can attack the human psyche. This patient would try to think about something else, get busy doing something, or go out to a movie, but no matter what escape he essayed, there would remain the haunting menace hovering behind him like a hated presence waiting to plunge a rapier into his lungs.[5] If he was working, he could practically hear the Mephistophelean laugh behind him that the device would not succeed; sooner or later he would have to stop, more fatigued than ever—and immediately the rapier would be there. If he was in the movies, the awareness would return as soon as the scene changed; his ache would come back again as soon as he stepped out on the street.

One day this patient came in reporting he had made a surprising discovery. When an acute attack of loneliness was beginning, it occurred to him not to try to fight it off, but to accept it, breathe with it, not turn away from it. Amazingly, the loneliness did not overwhelm him but seemed to diminish. Emboldened, he even began to invite it by imagining situations in the past when he was acutely lonely, memories which had always been sure to cue off the panic. But strangely, he reported, the loneliness had lost its power. He could not feel the panic even when he tried. The more he turned on it and welcomed it, the more impossible it was even to imagine how he had ever been lonely in that unbearably painful way before.[6]

The patient had discovered—and was teaching me that day—that he felt the acute loneliness only as he ran; when he turned on the devil, he vanished, to use the language of this chapter. Running never works, anyway. As I have said above, the very running itself is a response which assures the daimonic of its continuing power. Whether or not we agree with the James-Lange theory (1890) of emotions[7] it is surely true that anxiety (or loneliness) has the upper hand as long as we continue to run. In the language of this chapter, the repression of the daimonic has the power of a ghost: so long as it is locked in the closet, we are afraid of it; let the devil out, turn on him, and he vanishes—at least as a devil—and in his place we find a source of energy we can use.

To put the matter in more psychological terminology, anxiety (of which we here take loneliness or "abandonment anxiety" to be the most painful form) overcomes the organism to the extent that the person loses orientation to the objective world. The function of anxiety is to destroy the self-world relationship, i.e., to disorient the victim from space and time, and so long as it succeeds, the person remains in the state of anxiety. Anxiety remains the dominant state precisely by virtue of the preservation of the disorientation. If the person can reorient himself, however, and again relate to the world directly, experientially, with his senses alive, he destroys the anxiety. My slightly anthropomorphic terminology comes out of my work as a therapist and is not out of place there. Though the patient and I are entirely aware of the symbolic nature of this (anxiety does not *do* anything, as libido and sex drives do not), it is often helpful for the patient to see himself struggling against an "adversary." For then, instead of waiting forever for the therapy to analyze away the anxiety, he himself can help in his own treatment by taking practical steps, when he experiences anxiety, to stop and ask just what it was that occurred in reality or in his phantasies that preceded the disorientation cueing the anxiety. He not only opens the doors of his closet where the ghosts hide, but he then can often take practical steps to reorient himself.

4. THE WORD IN THERAPY

"In the beginning was the Word," and the Word was what man could set against the daimonic. It is of utmost importance that we examine this idea in order to avoid an egregious mistake of much contemporary psychotherapy, namely the illusion that merely *experiencing* or *acting out* is all that is necessary for cure. Experiencing is absolutely essential, but if it occurs without changing the patient's concepts, symbols, and myths, the "experiencing" is truncated and has a masturbatory rather than fully procreative character.

William James (1890) has some pithy sentences when he writes about the curing effect of the patient getting the right concept, the right *name* for his problem. Referring specifically to the drunkard's proclivity for evading his problem through calling it everything else in the world, he writes,

But if he once gets able to pick out that way of conceiving, from all possible ways of conceiving the various opportunities which occur, if through thick and thin he holds to it that this is being a drunkard and is nothing else, he is not likely to remain one long. The effort by which he succeeds in keeping the right *name* unwaveringly present to his mind proves to be his saving moral act [p. 565].

The way man has gained power over the daimonic historically is by the Word. This is demonstrated in the crucial importance of knowing the *name* of the demon in order to overcome him. Jesus calls out "Beelzebub!" in the Bible, or some other presumably accurate name, and the devil leaves the possessed unfortunate immediately. In the medieval casting-out of devils, if you could find the name of the demon you could conjure the evil spirit out and away. The naming gives a power over the other person or thing. In ancient Israel the Jews were not permitted to pronounce the name of God: Yahweh, or Jehovah, means "no name," and is a device to get around saying the name of God.[8]

There is an obvious but nonetheless interesting parallel here to contemporary medical and psychological therapy. Everyone must have sometime been aware how relieved he was when he went to the doctor with a troublesome illness and the doctor pronounced a *name* for it. A name for the virus or germ; a name for the disorder process; and the doctor could make a statement or two about the disease on the basis of this name. Diagnosis (literally "knowing through") may be thought of as our modern form of calling the name of the offending demon.

I suggest that something deeper is going on in this phenomenon than one's relief at whether or not the doctor can predict a quick cure, or at least a cure of some kind. Some years ago when, after weeks of undetermined illness, I heard from a specialist the diagnosis that my sickness was tuberculosis, I was, I recall, distinctly relieved to know it, even though I was fully aware that this, in those days, meant that medicine could find no cure. A number of explanations will leap to the reader's tongue: I was glad to have the relief from responsibility; any patient is reassured because he has the authority of the doctor to give himself to; the naming of the disorder takes away the mystery of it. But these explanations are surely too simple. Even the last mentioned, that the naming reduces the mystery, will be seen on further thought to be an illusion: the bacillus, or the virus or germ, is still as much a mystery to me as ever. May I make bold to suggest that these explanations, no matter how true in themselves, all miss the fundamental point at issue.

I suggest that the relief comes from the power and the act of confronting the daimonic world of illness with its names. The doctor and I stand together, he knowing more names in this purgatory than I do and being therefore, technically, my guide through hell. It is not that the rational information about the disease is unimportant; it most certainly is. But it adds up to something more inclusive and significant than the information itself: it becomes for me a symbol of a new way of life. The names are symbols to me of a certain attitude I must take toward this daimonic situation of illness; the disorder is a myth which communicates to me a way I must now orient and order my life. Whether for two weeks with a cold, or twelve years with tuberculosis, the quantity of time is not the point; it is a quality of life. In short, the myth by which I identify myself changes by its contact, on a new depth, with the myth portraying the daimonic in the processes of disease.[9]

The reader may wonder whether I have gotten away from the relation of psychology to the daimonic. By no means; the parallel of this point to psychotherapy is even closer than to medicine. Many therapists, like Allan Wheelis, speak of their task as *naming* the unconscious." Every therapist must be impressed almost every hour with the strange power the names of the psychological "complexes" or patterns have for the patient. If the therapist says to the patient that he is afraid of the "primal scene," or has an "inverted Oedipus," or that he is an "introvert" or "extrovert" or has an "inferiority complex," or that he is angry at his boss because of "transference," or that the reason he cannot talk this morning is "resistance," it is amazing how the word itself seems to help the patient. He relaxes and acts as though he already has gotten something of great value. Indeed, one could burlesque psychoanalysis or therapy of any sort with the statement that the patient pays money to hear certain seemingly magic words; and he seems to feel he has received his money's worth if he hears a few esoteric terms. This relief *does* seem to have the characteristics of "the magic of words."

It has been argued that the relief the patient gets is that the naming gets him off the hook; it relieves him of responsibility by making a technical process to blame; he is not doing it but his "unconscious" is. There is truth in this. Furthermore, on the positive side, the naming helps the patient feel himself allied with a great movement which is "scientific" and also that he is not isolated since all kinds of other people have the same problems as he does. The naming also assures him that the therapist has an interest in him and is willing to act as his guide through purgatory. Naming the problem is tantamount to the therapist's saying, "Your problem can be known, it has causes; you can stand outside and look at it."

We are here able to go deeper than these customary explanations. We find that some of the important functions of therapy rest on fundamental aspects of the structure of language itself. The Word does give man a power over the daimonic. The Word discloses the daimonic, forces it out into the open where we can confront it directly.

But the greatest danger in the therapeutic process lies right here: that the naming will take the place of changing; we stand off and get a temporary security by diagnoses, labels, talking about symptoms, and are relieved of the necessity of using will in action or of loving. This plays into the hands of modern man's central defense, namely intellectualization—using words as substitutes for feelings and experience. The Word skates always on the edge of the danger of *covering up* the daimonic as well as disclosing it. When Apollo, the intellectual, argues in the *Oresteia* that the Furies be banished, he is using the cultural arts to fragmentize man, to suppress the daimonic and to truncate human experience. But Athena, who "reconciles the opposites in her own being," rightly refuses. By accepting the daimonic Furies, welcoming them into Athens, the community itself is enriched. And the Furies have their *name changed!* They are now the Eumenides, the makers of grace.

This ambivalent character of language requires our asking what the ancients meant by the Word which has power over the daimonic. They were referring to the *logos*, the structure of reality. "In the beginning was the Word" is true experientially as well as theologically. For the beginning of man as man is the capacity for language.[10] This Word can be communicated only by symbols and myths. It is important not to forget that any healing process—even whatever each of us with a common cold may do about his viruses—is a myth, a way of looking at one's self, including one's body, in relation to the world. Unless my illness changes my myth of myself I shall not have distilled from the trauma of illness the opportunity for new insight into myself and self-realization in life, and I shall not attain anything that can be rightly called a cure.

The daimonic in an individual pushes him toward the *logos*. That is to say, the more I come to terms with my daimonic tendencies, the more I will find myself conceiving and living by a more universal structure of reality. This *logos* in this sense is *trans*personal. We saw that the daimonic begins as *im*personal: my gonads clamor that I have sexual relations with someone, *any*one. But by deepening my consciousness I make my daimonic tendencies personal: I will make this sexual appetite a motivation to make love to, and be loved by, a woman I desire and choose. Then beyond that the daimonic pushes me to a more sensitive understanding of bodies (to use a physical analogy) and of the meaning of love toward all people as well (to use a psychological and ethical concept). We move thus from an impersonal through a personal to a transpersonal dimension.

NOTES

1. This term could be spelled "demonic" (the popularized vulgar form) or "daemonic" (the medieval form often used by poets, Yeats for example) or "daimonic" (the derivative from the ancient Greek word *daimon*). Since this last is the origin of the concept and since I don't want to have the reader confused with images of little creatures with horns flying around, I use the Greek term.

2. *The Symposium*, in Plato's *Dialogues*.

3. Dr. Prince, we should add for those who tend to take the usual pejorative view of primitive therapy and ceremonies, had a high regard for the skill of the native mental healers. Several times, when a native could not be helped by the psychiatric facilities of the hospital, Dr. Prince sent him to a native mental healer. These healers seemed to have quite a good idea of the different types of ailments we call schizophrenia and had some idea of which types they could cure and which not. I believe we should not judge this kind of therapy by comparing it to our contemporary techniques or see it simply as "primitive" healing, but consider it as an expression of archetypal ways of dealing with human problems which were to some extent adequate for their tribal situation as our methods are relatively adequate for us.

4. I should add that I am not arguing the opposite—that man is by nature evil. I am saying that on the experiential level, which is the level psychology works on, man is both good and evil, both destructive and altruistic. Our goal is the heightened consciousness and deepened meaning in human relationships which is created by the way the person uses the dialectical tension between these two.

5. I say lungs because the anxiety in loneliness seems to affect the breathing apparatus, and the pain seems a sharp stab of constriction of the lungs rather than, as we say in grief or sadness, a pain "in the heart." There is a greater basis for this usage than mere localization of felt pain, for anxiety in general has been connected with the narrow passage the infant must go through in birth, and the difficulties in breathing that may be associated (whether "caused by" or not we don't need to go into for this purpose) with the confined channel, the "straitened gate." The French root for anxiety—*angoisse*—is connected literally with the meaning of going through a narrow

channel, as is the English word "anguish" (L. *angustia*, narrowness, distress, fr. *angere*, to press together). Cf. R. May, *The Meaning of Anxiety* (New York: Ronald Press, 1950).

6. It is literally true that, when a neurotic symptom changes, it becomes almost impossible for a person *to recall the feeling as a feeling.* He can recall the situations in which he felt lonely, or anxious, but not the feeling. This seems to be a trick of memory: neurotic phenomena have strange effects upon one's sense of time and memory. The problem, however, hinges on the meaning of intentionality. To recall the feeling of the symptom, to reexperience it, which this remembering would require, involves still having the neurosis, or, more accurately, the intentionality which showed itself in the neurosis. We shall later point out that to remember requires being able to reexperience the intentionality involved in the memory.

7. That we are afraid because we run, rather than running because we are afraid. James believed that the experiencing of an emotion was our awareness of the inner chemical and muscular changes in the body produced by our action such as running away.

8. In my clinical work, I have come to the hypothesis that this danger in words, the prohibition of naming, has something important to do with the symptom of writer's block.

9. It is part of our myth of the technological man that we believe that rational explanation is what does us good in situations like this. I suggest that this explanation takes its place, and has its cogency, within a context of myth: we are assuming a myth we try to deny, and it is this myth which gives the explanation the power. It does this by the power of the name.

10. The contemporary revolt of the hippies and other groups against talking does not gainsay our point. They are protesting—and I have genuine empathy for the protest—against the use of language to rob us of immediate experiencing.

REFERENCES

James, W. *The principles of psychology.* New York: Holt, Rinehart & Winston, 1890.

Rogers, C., et al. *The therapeutic relationship.* Madison, Wis.: The University of Wisconsin Press, 1967.

CHAPTER 10

A Commentary on Rollo May's "Contributions of Existential Psychotherapy"

Carl A. Whitaker

Psychotherapy is a new discipline. It emerged twenty years ago as an illegitimate child (technical byproduct) of the evolution of the Freud-instigated study of psychopathology. Once we had learned how the psyche operated we became anxious (responsible) to put that knowledge to work. However, the arrival of psychotherapy as a discipline and its gradual separation from the parent science have brought complications and the usual parent-child rebellion problems. Just as philosophy challenged religion, so psychotherapy challenged psychopathology. One of the major discoveries in this battle was the rediscovery of the therapist as a person. Ten years ago countertransference was talked of in whispers and identified as pathology in the therapist. When Rollo May began to seed psychotherapy with the thoughts of the existential theologians he made a major move toward freeing the therapist to be a person. It was time to move on from being a mirror for reflection. The therapist was a person, and a live one. The new attitude of "I take my stand" was a kind of hallmark of Rollo's just as it had been the hallmark of Soren Kierkegaard. A person is a person is a person. The days of therapist-worship or patient-worship were coming to an end. To be with another you have to be with yourself; to be with yourself you have to be with another.

To assay a discussion of Rollo May's article one needs to establish the framework from which Dr. May speaks. I knew Rollo May in 1935 as an idealistic youth headed for the ministry. As I study his work now, I get a deep sense of the seeds that idealistic youth planted. They have

---

This chapter is a discussion-commentary, written especially for the present volume, of Chapter 8: "Contributions of Existential Psychotherapy," by Rollo May.

developed into the profound thought and significant contribution made by Dr. May as adult. To read and study his work now is to meet the person. He talks about psychotherapy and he talks about himself. Through it you see the idealism of his early faith in and hope for the future of man through religion transformed and expanded to faith in man as a self. This sense of worth frees such a person to produce seminal thought about man as man. He fights off the morphine of the past and the LSD of the future and takes a position on today which is uniquely his own though centered in a common understanding with colleagues and teachers.

Today, ten years later, Dr. May's writing is very much alive. He moves from a search into the state of dasein to a concern with the relationship of the therapist to the person. He sees therapy as a *two*-person event with many inferences to be drawn from this. He does battle with the schools of psychotherapy as he did with the schools of religion and the schools of philosophy. He very beautifully portrays the defeat of each technique by the next technique in almost the same way that we are now learning to kill painful microorganisms by overfeeding. At times, I get a sense that Rollo is almost struggling to unify Zoroaster's philosophical God-Devil split by his own inner unification. It is as though his stance on his own two feet were a model for man's right to exist.

Dr. May has made a major contribution to man's sense of himself. Not only does he picture man but he gives evidence that man is more than an object of research and more than a researcher. Dr. May sets a definition of time and its relationship to past, to future, to the symptom role as time-binding and to anxiety as time-destroying. Likewise, he shows beautifully how our worship of the image of the self or image of the future can deny the self as a unique being. He gives us the dream that man, by learning to love himself, can recall the image he worshiped in the past and in destroying that image and his image of the future find the self that is today.

The Dr. May of 1958 points up one of the great struggles in contemporary psychiatry. We are dated. Margaret Mead once said that we cannot move to a new generation. "When my car met a threshing machine on a New England road I expected it to rear up in fright as my team of horses did years ago." Dr. May speaks about the therapist trying to *avoid* his own anxiety. He thereby points the way for the new generation. Yet now and again he talks about "the patient's needs" or says that "the therapist must understand." In this he is showing us the depth of his struggle to get away from the old "therapist-acting-upon" model. He assumes that the therapist has found his own beingness at some past time and that the existential struggle for him is not a live, current one as it must be for the patient (poor thing).

Now, ten years later, building on his groundwork, I sense that my struggle with myself in a certain hour with a certain patient has all the stress of my inner battle of that past time. The battle for my own growth, the echoes in my body may be different, and my fantasies may be less chaotic—but my struggle is with me. I, too, battle to quit "functioning" and break free to exist. Tom Malone said to a patient once, "Don't be mad at me. I'm not trying to help you." Now I struggle to say, "Can you see? I'm trying to help me. Watch! Jump in! Maybe you can help you."

I find myself struggling with an effort to extend Rollo's pattern, that of understanding man in the therapeutic arena, to an effort to portray how I become me in each therapeutic hour. I want to define my experience of myself. I assume that this me is vital to my patient: the significant other. During that hour, dasein includes the existence of the patient who is with me. He comes alive to me, and hopefully I come alive to him. This is the perception of a third dimension of beingness and of we-ness. Socrates said to the father, "I cannot teach your son because he doesn't love me." I wonder if it is possible that the reason the son didn't love Socrates was because Socrates didn't love the son. We talk about transference coming first, or transference being present without countertransference. I wonder which arises first. Is it possible that there is no psychotherapy without countertransference, that there is no psychotherapy without first a sense on the part of the therapist of what is possible with the patient and what is possible in the relationship that he and the patient, as a twosome, could have? The being of the patient may be a reflection of the fullness of being-me-in-myself with that patient-as-a-self, the experiencing of myself and of myself in relationship to another, and the difference that is brought about in me by the fact of experiencing that other. Many times the patient does not seem to sense the bilaterality in the therapeutic set. His aloneness with me is identical to my aloneness with him. As he is distant from me, to that degree I am distant from him. It is as far from my side to him as it is from his side to me. In this sense, psychotherapy does not rest on the acceptance by the therapist of the other, but the acceptance by the therapist of himself. My accepting the patient still leaves him where he is. However, if I experience myself in me during that hour, then that may help him experience himself. It is not a doing-ness in either of us but a sense of self-ness which is like the sense of body-ness after a good tiring game of handball. Psychotherapy might then be defined as a dialectical relationship with a significant other. The thesis is we-ness; the antithesis is separateness, defined by the therapist as "I am me." The synthesis is a time-bound, dynamic, joint being-ness, and a realization that the death of the therapeutic relationship will take place for each. "When I am me, you can be you. Then we can be us, and this is now. This now will end, and then I will be more me, and you will be more you. If I can love me and accept me, then you can dare accept the right to be you." Am-ness cannot be given or taken; it is a "leap of faith," in the theological sense, a leap into the unknown with the chance of death and the possibility of finding the self.

Hopefully the patient is to be part of my lighting up and fading out in this hour. I exist and I die in front of his eyes. I exist with him and I die of loneliness without him. I yearn for a we-ness, and I despair of it. I relish it and dread it. To a greater or lesser degree I enjoy a me-ness; I despair at the possibility of losing myself and am joyous at being me again. Thus death is relative in the interview and absolute at the end of our time together. To dare to confront his neurotic anxiety and hostility and aggression, the patient must be a we with me as I confront my neurotic anxiety, my hostility, and my aggression. If I dare non-be-ness in our relationship and be-ness in myself he may dare to leap to his own self-ness. The tingling in the hair on the back of my neck is clearly related to our relationship in this time, and at this place; and he had better not try to avoid responsibility for his participation in it. As I demand he share my anxiety, which is non-neurotic for him, he may dare to demand I share his neurotic anxiety, which is non-neurotic for me, and then dare to wallow in his own be-ness in the face of the living-end dread.

In psychotherapy I battle to face, in the presence of the patient, my guilt at not being all I can with him. Can I force him to face his guilt at not being himself with me and to face his guilt at denying his selfhood? Will this open for him a rebuttal-like opportunity to accuse me of similar guilt and thus establish a we-ness in guilt with a sense of imminent separation and thereby a greater sense of self in each of us?

The sense of knowingness in the experience seems to be variable and at times unnecessary. When it does arrive, it seems serendipitous, a kind of byproduct of growth, and of be-ness. I focus on me in my world as a prototype for his leap into his world. Then I can focus on him in relation to his inner and his outer world and in the paradigm of our two-person world. My first-person world in this interview and his first-person world in this interview equal a first-person-plural world. I and I together equal a we.

In our relationship in that hour I get lonely. I try to drag him out of his *Umwelt* into our *Mitwelt* with the hope that it will increase the *Eigenwelt* in me *and* in him. I always fear lest I am using the patient as a him instead of relating in an I-Thou mode. I think I do not do so if I do it on the basis of my increasing loneliness without him in the time-place of our hour. I see myself as breaking up by a direct attack the graven image of the self in each of us with the hope that out of this will emerge a unity of self in me and in us and a sense of our own-ness —an emergence of am-ness and of self-presence. I doubt seriously whether the experience of self is identical to the awareness of self or with insight into self. Certainly, insight may be full and vivid, and the experience of the self, in the sense of intimacy with the wholeness of self, very fragmentary. It is as though by questioning, promising, lying, I search for myself and thereby for the patient. To be in and out of the relationship and in a kind of double consciousness, pushing myself and the other for my greater *Eigenwelt* and our *Mitwelt*, and thereby his *Eigenwelt*, is my only way of freedom from the pain he precipitated by inducing me to care by his presence and by his simulation and stimulation of my loneliness.

My being-ness in the world has been challenged by his presence. Now I demand or plead that we unite for my, no, our sake and to incorporate this state of non-being-ness that hurts me so. His non-being impairs my being-ness, and our being-ness is a route back toward a relationship in which I can be and we can be and hopefully out of which he can be. Rollo quotes from Freida Fromm-Reichmann: "The patient needs an experience not an explanation." Am I presumptuous in wanting to expand this and say "I need an experience not an understanding"? Rollo talks about care for, or concern with, and in general relates this to the concern of the therapist for the patient. For me this is a foreshortened description. I think of my care for the patient as being a byproduct of my care and my concern for myself, and that essentially the patient perceives my care for him in the framework of my care for myself. Likewise, if I am responsible and responsive in my life, then he is free to sense not only that I would also be responsive to his living, but more important, that I open up for him the prototype of his being concerned with his life, of his being willing to care, *positively* or *negatively*, about his own being-ness. In the same sense it seems to me that variations in technique, in reality, and in concreteness are based on means to reveal the patient's existence to him. I prefer to reveal my own existence and thereby, hopefully, reveal our joint existence, so that the patient is thus free to perceive and move into his own existing. My sense of my own presence and the dignity of my being is a quality of any other whom I see as an extension of myself. In 1958 Rollo, it seemed, was still confusing understanding with living; yet, as he writes, one can sense the struggle to break away from the old one-to-one object study. The proper study of man is no substitute for being one's self.

In the realm of time I perceive the therapeutic process as being a sequential set of relationships, a rising transference arch which moves on to a crescendo and then quiets down so that the therapist is more and more free to be himself as a person and to be less concerned with the patient's wishful projected image of him. The patient must then begin to face the therapist as the person he is. This second ascending arch, which overlaps before the first has faded, also mounts to a high point and then becomes less resonant and less a required component in the patient's need for a significant other.

Rollo makes a beautiful differentiation between the "what" and the "why." The why is a way of objectifying, of thinking and remembering about, a way of leaving the scene, of elaborating memory and relieving anxiety. The what, in contrast, is a way of participating, a way of being real with, of intensifying the experience, of precipitating the therapist and the patient into a deeper relationship. I perceive myself as being in considerable contrast with the Rollo May of 1958 in reference to the sense of presence. I *do* mean to impose myself and my presence on the patient. I try to lead; I think of myself as an usher in a dark theater. I know where I'm going and I hope he's free to follow. I believe in confrontation to the limit of the patient's anxiety tolerance, and sometimes beyond it: confrontation with myself, my anxiety, and my despair, with every "what" of my existing at that time in that place and with that person. To me, Rollo is at his best when he says that the technical view of the patient is the handiest anxiety-reducing device the therapist can use, or when he says that decision precedes knowledge. This leap of faith precedes being-ness, and being-ness is one-ness, and that precedes growth. And what of insight? I see insight as an incidental byproduct of growth, almost unimportant.

Is the patient's leap of faith based on a double bond with the therapist, who makes his own decision and his own leap, or do they make the leap conjoined but separate? Maybe the therapist commits his all to himself and in that moment the patient may, as a result of a long cue and counter-cue series, make his leap, commit himself to the unknown of his being-ness or his death. What greater adventure could life offer except death itself?

Part II

The Expanded Context of Psychotherapy

CHAPTER 11

The Expanded Context of Psychotherapy: Creative Developments

Alvin R. Mahrer and Leonard Pearson

The selections in Part II place psychotherapy in a broader perspective than that of the relationship between therapist and patient. There is, these contributors say, a larger context which impels us to think differently about what occurs in the psychotherapeutic situation. In this chapter we aim not only to introduce and to summarize the contributions of Part II, but also to provide a perspective within which the contributions may be discussed.

If we accept the premise that the individual acts upon his environment as well as being acted on by it, then the context in which therapy takes place assumes new meaning. Family therapy and group therapy take cognizance of the individual's role in a larger society, of his ability to have an impact on, and be influenced by, broader patterns of relationships. Individual therapy, as well, becomes a more valuable and powerful experience. This expanded view allows us to conceive of a different dimension of therapy—i.e., the influence that the individual patient has on his therapist as part of his (the patient's) psychological world—which is relevant to the relationship between them. It becomes a new and exciting two-way relationship, one in which both participants make distinctive contributions.

THE INDIVIDUAL AND THE EXTERNAL WORLD

An individual's personality transcends his physical body to include his own larger field of psychologically significant events (Framo). Thus, the definition of an individual's personality includes his own encompassing psychological field (Framo) and is not limited by his physical bodily boundaries. The meaning of such a position is given in implications such as the following:

The individual as determiner of his external world. The individual is a powerfully active participant in the molding and designing of his own meaningful external world (Auld; May). He participates actively in structuring the psychological world which encompasses him to include understanding and close friends, external forces attempting to control him, situations offering nurture and dependence, and violent oppositional forces. I determine my own external world in the playing out of my own personality: such a model is in contrast (May) to that of a static entity, the person, in a separated external world which he must accept, fight, or adjust to in some way; it rejects the concept of two static entities, the person and the external world, in interaction. The factors that determine a psychologically meaningful external world are localized within each person, conceived as an actively structuring personality in mutual interaction with other personalities. That is, my current motivations and needs lead me to design (structure, select) this particular external world.

The external world as expression of the individual. The full range of an individual's personality includes the encompassing field of psychologically meaningful figures and objects (Framo). A mother's anger may manifest itself in her own angry behavior or in that of her child. A man's antisocial tendencies may be expressed through his own behavior or the psychopathic practices of his business partner. Other significant persons can carry out meaningful psychological functions for each other (Framo) according to the paradigm: My needs are expressed in your behavior. An individual's personality processes are manifested in the kind of external situation he constructs around himself.

The long-suffering wife's fuller personality is manifested in the form of her irresponsible alcoholic husband to whom she has unhappily tied herself. The full exposition of the irresponsible alcoholic's personality includes the criticalness of a complaining wife. The husband and the wife play out each other's needs, for better or for worse. The external psychological world of a given individual is a function of his own selection and construction and represents a fuller exposition of his personality (Auld; Framo).

PSYCHOPATHOLOGICAL BEHAVIOR

AND THE PATIENT-DETERMINED LIFE SITUATION

A patient's behavior has a particular meaning when it is understood within the larger psychological field (Auld; Framo).

Mental illness vs. motivated behavior. Framo replaces a mental-illness conception of behavior with an understanding of behavior as being motivationally directed toward determining a particular life situation. Depression and bizarre speech have conventionally been understood as signs of mental illness. For Auld and Framo, being depressed becomes understandable as behavior motivated toward determining a particular life situation, for example, as a means of withdrawing from a family or punishing a wife. Talking bizarrely is a method of creating another kind of life situation, for example, avoiding responsibility for a particularly impulsive act or exerting superiority over those who are now unable to hurt or reach one. Behavior is not to be classified as "mentally ill" or "not mentally ill," but to be understood as motivationally directed toward determining a particular life situation.

Localizing the problem. The patient actively participates in the construction of his own life situation, a segment of which he identifies as a problem. Thus, the "problem" may refer to his own behavior or to that of another person (Framo). Problems with aggression may take the form of complaints about one's own aggressiveness or complaints about the aggression of other persons significant in one's own psychological field. The wife or the child may manifest the aggression, but we look for the person who is building this aggression into his own determined life situation. The wife's aggression is one building block in the husband's personality. He gets the aggression going, and he is the motivational resource, even though he is the one who calls the practitioner or clinic about his wife's aggression. This process is more evident in the case of children, as when a mother provokes the aggressive behavior manifested by her child. She is the motivating agent as well as the one who identifies the problem. We trace the problem to its motivational source by identifying the person behind the behavior and the complaint. Accordingly, treatment is now focused upon the complainant, not the complainee; upon the husband rather than the wife about whom he complains, upon the mother rather than the child about whom she complains (Framo).

Psychotherapy research and patient-determined situations. The patient's own personality processes play a considerable role in determining what is to occur in psychotherapy. Indeed, the patient's motivations determine that he will seek out a therapist, that therapy will have a particular meaning in his life, even that therapy shall occur at this given time and in this particular manner. The patient is a motivationally active person, not a static experimental subject. His active motivations give therapy its meaning and particular significance. If we do research on psychotherapy, it is crucial to preserve the patient's role as the determiner of much of what goes on. This kind of research involves a live patient, motivationally determining much of what is happening, interacting with the experimenter-therapist who seeks to maintain the patient's motivational determination. If the patient is understood as possessing motivations which determine the context, then psychotherapy research must focus on live people in live treatment.

The bulk of therapy research deprives the patient of motivation, of a sense of collaboration in a mutually significant task, and often includes elements of deception or secretiveness which are antithetical to an honest, open, healing relationship. In such research, the motivation behind what is going on lies within the experimenter, not the subject (patient); the focus of study is a situation determined by the experimenter, not the subject. The patient is deprived of and disengaged from his own motivational determination because he is not allowed to structure the situation. The situation is a function of what the experimenter structures, determines, and is motivated to bring about. Such a research approach assumes that patients' motivationally determined situations are irrelevant. But we believe that a subject disengaged from his own motivation is an inadequate source of study; research which replaces motivational determination on the part of the patient with experimenter motivations and experimenter-determined situations has little relevance to the psychotherapeutic process (Auld).

A PERSON AS A COMPONENT OF
THE PSYCHOLOGICAL FIELD OF ANOTHER INDIVIDUAL

My personality extends to the significant persons about me. I structure and mold them actively to play certain kinds of roles congruent with my personality, and they are moving me to assume roles meaningful to them. According to Frank, we are coming to acknowledge the considerable degree to which personality forces in two interacting individuals tend to evoke certain classes of behavior in each other. For example, my motivations and needs construct an external psychological world in which you are seductive and I pull back from your invitations; your motivations and needs construct a psychological world in which I encourage and then reject you. As a component of my psychological field, I cause (stimulate, determine, motivate) your seductiveness toward me. You are a component of my psychological field. This relationship is germane to psychotherapy when I am the therapist and also when I am the patient. But before we discuss this expanded motivational context of psychotherapy, we must describe three implications of this general idea.

The child as a component of the psychological field of the parents. One implication is that of parental figures actively structuring their external world to include the infant-child as a singularly important component of that world. The infant-child is so structured and molded that his behavior serves as part of the fuller exposition of the personalities of his parents. Thus, a parent will force his infant-child to assume roles meaningfully related to the motivations of the parent (e.g., the "parentification" of the child) (Framo). A child's temper tantrums can reflect the mother's buried anger (Framo); otherwise stated, the mother will actively structure her external psychological world (i.e., her child) to represent a fuller exposition of her own personality (i.e., to manifest a temper tantrum). The implication is that much of the behavior of the infant-child is a function and an expression of the motivational determinants of the parental figures, who in turn respond to the behavior of the growing, developing child they have structured and shaped.

The therapeutic potential of an individual. Reasoning from Truax's findings that effective therapist characteristics include accurate empathy, mature integration, and non-possessive warmth, Garfield suggests that we may some day be able to identify persons with high "therapeutic potential" for other individuals. Many persons, even without professional training, possess these characteristics and represent an available cadre for treatment purposes. For example, Goldstein envisages the mobilized therapeutic potential of many nonprofessional change agents: nurses, aides, parents, college undergraduates, psychological technicians, auxiliary counselors, friends, physicians, and so on. Their therapeutic potential lies in their use of the effective characteristics—empathy, warmth, and mature integration.

Psychological families. We foresee the eventual expansion of the usual roles of patient and therapist toward maximum utilization of the therapeutic potential of one person for the other. Both theoretically and practically, the personality of one individual bears a potentially good or poor therapeutic fit with regard to another. On this basis, a group of persons with optimal therapeutic fit for each other can be brought together. In addition to a good relationship between patient and psychotherapist or patient and hospital, or person and friend or person and spouse, there may be more optimal interweaving of the needs, wants, and tendencies of one individual and those of another. We conceive of a therapeutic mutual interdependence between a maternal-providing woman bereft of her family and a maternal-needing child, also without a family, or between a person who needs structure and control and another who needs open expressiveness. Optimal therapeutic relationships may be established among two to eight individuals with interdependent and mutual need relationships. In addition to patient and therapist, we envisage mutual, interdependent therapeutic groups whose personality processes mesh optimally with one another. A full psychological understanding of each individual would reveal the personality needs and processes to be complemented, facilitated, and developed in an optimal therapeutic group, and such groups can be used diagnostically as well as therapeutically. The criterion is the best possible fit of mutual, interdependent need relationships among persons who represent the highest degree of therapeutic potential for one another. These groups may be termed *psychological families,* and we conceive of psychological treatment as including the establishing of such families. We can view any individual's personality as including a social interacting identity and then determine groups or families significant for him. The therapeutic potential of carefully implemented psychological families goes beyond the treatment of problems to encompass the facilitation of optimal and constructive personality change of groups of individuals. In other words, psychological families are useful for resolving "problems" and also for optimal personality change.

The group as the focus of treatment. The expanding view of an individual's personality to encompass his psychological environment raises the issue of whether the focus of treatment is the individual or the group. The group is identified, not biologically or sociologically, but psychologically—i.e., in terms of the unit formed by interacting personalities (Bell; Framo). Perhaps the creative development lies in the explicit identification of the group as the direct focus of treatment. The rich implications of such a position are not yet unfolded.

By identifying the group as the "target," Bell and Framo differentiate the visible patient from the effective motivating agent. Thus, the group may move the mother to seek treatment as if she were the group's ambassador, and treatment is aimed, therefore, at the family group rather than at the mother alone.

THE EXPANDED MOTIVATIONAL CONTEXT OF PSYCHOTHERAPY

The personality of the therapist transcends his physical body to include his patient and the psychotherapeutic situation; similarly, the patient's personality extends outward to include both the therapist and the psychotherapeutic situation. Their personalities include the interaction each has with the other. Because the motivations and needs of both therapist and patient are instrumental in designing (structuring, selecting) the psychotherapeutic situation, the whole context of that situation is enlarged. Both patient and therapist use the situation (and each other) to act out the expression of their respective personalities. We turn first to the patient and then to the therapist in order to follow the implications of this expanded context of psychotherapy.

The expanded context of psychotherapy for the patient. We may identify many kinds of motivations and needs which lead the patient to assume a particular role in treatment, to assign a particular role to the therapist, and to attribute a given meaning to the psychotherapeutic situation. For some patients, the psychotherapeutic situation is merely one of a larger class of help-seeking situations; accordingly, the patient is under help-seeking motivations, and the therapist is induced to be the help-provider (Frank). For other patients, the psychotherapeutic situation is an arena for needs either to oppose or win over an external force, the therapist (Frank). Many patients seek out the psychotherapeutic situation as a means of having a relationship with a person (therapist) whom they endow with qualities of mature integration, nonpossessive warmth, and accurate empathy (Truax). For still other patients, the therapy situation offers a means of relating to an omniscient, saintly individual who exacts awe and magical fantasies (Wyatt).

Matarazzo describes the typical patient as being in the midst of a moderate crisis, the major motivation being to seek some way out of the crisis (Bell) by means of the psychotherapy situation. Many patients in Freud's time presented so-called hysterical problems; this is analogous to the frequency with which persons turn to psychotherapy today as a way out of their loneliness, isolation, alienation, and feelings of being detached, unrelated, unfeeling, and depersonalized (May). Under these motivations, patients turn to psychotherapy to establish a relationship with an open, fully disclosing, available human being, quite willing to "be there," to open himself up as a model of authenticity and genuineness (Bugental).

Psychotherapy also serves as a means of acting out stress-ridden motivational needs. For some patients, the therapy situation serves as a means of suffering as the scapegoat of accusations from others or receiving punishment from family members who force the person into treatment (Bell). Clinics, hospitals, and private practitioners often unwittingly serve as a punitive disciplinary arm of a spouse, family, church, court, or society, and the patient assumes the role of the guilty culprit (Bell). By focusing diagnostic or therapeutic attention upon a given person (frequently a child), the clinic (hospital, practitioner) is part of a larger situational context in which the person is identified and designated as the "bad guy," the source of the problem, the one who is to be "treated" (Framo). Some patients are motivated to use the psychotherapeutic situation as a means of making another individual (the therapist) feel guilty because he has not fulfilled all of the hopes and desires (and demands) invested in him with a full measure of faith and trust (Bugental). According to Sandor Rado, psychoanalytic therapy is frequently an expression of a covert pact between patient and therapist wherein the patient assumes the role of the child and the therapist is the punitive parent (Alexander).

The motivations and needs of the *patient* invest the expanded context of psychotherapy with identifiable meaning and significance. We now turn to the ways in which the motivations and needs of the *therapist* also contribute to the expanded context of psychotherapy.

The expanded context of psychotherapy for the therapist. The motivational needs of the therapist actively participate in the design and construction of the psychotherapeutic situation. Some therapists find the psychotherapy situation important as a means of fulfilling their own motivational needs to be help-providers to help-seekers (Bugental; Frank). Only in their relationships with patients are such therapists able to manifest maturity, integration, and genuineness, and highly charged personal feelings (Truax). Within their relationship with patients, therapists can also play out their own motivational needs for deep human experiences, for the continuous realization of their own personal growth and for participating in the growth of another individual (Bugental). According to Bugental, additional motivational needs are frequently played against the backdrop of the psychotherapeutic situation by the therapist. The therapist may, for example, find such a situation appropriate for gaining a safe, one-way intimacy. Often, he may use the treatment situation to be the omnipotent helper, to have patients undergo that which allays his own anxiety, to dispense tenderness and love without arousing his own anxiety, to be both omniscient and saintly, or to revolt against society while in the cloak of an authority figure (Bugental; Wyatt). The motivational needs of the therapist may dovetail with the community's efforts to change given attitudes and behaviors, in which case the psychotherapeutic situation takes its place as another avenue whereby authority figures alter the behavior of others (Frank). In fact, Frank finds the therapist functioning frequently as one of society's persuaders and influencers. Within this context, psychotherapy becomes an interpersonal influencing process, i.e., persuasion mediated by methods of interpersonal influence. As such, it grows out of the heritage of primitive forms of persuasion and healing (Goldstein).

Bugental describes the patient as serving the vicarious needs of the therapist by undergoing experiences for the unrealized parts of the therapist's personality. Wyatt carries this theme further; the patient represents the

naïve, or helpless, or foolish part of the therapist's self. The other part, the knowing and self-assured one, laughs at the wayward and ignorant child, thus settling, at least temporarily, memories of defeat and embarrassment. . . . At least in his therapeutic activity he can behave (or imagine himself behaving) as he always wanted and expected himself to. . . . By guiding the patient through the wasteland of unredeemed conflict the therapist also attempts to resolve his own unsettled problems. . . . [He] treats his patient in some respects as he wishes he had been treated when he himself was a child [p. 300].

For other therapists, psychotherapy offers an enormously rich resource for study and information. It provides these therapists with direct access to: (a) long-term personality trends and their genetic basis; (b) deep feelings of other persons; (c) the relationship of motivation to behavior over time; (d) a situation more real than psychological testing or laboratory experimentation; (e) the patient's inner world and his real external world; and (f) the ways in which external events are phenomenally perceived (Strupp).

To the extent that patient and therapist are motivationally geared toward the therapy situation as a means of implementing their respective needs, psychotherapy is embedded within an encompassing psychological context reflecting the motivational needs of both interacting parties, patient(s) and therapist.

Therapist motivations and patient selection. The motivational needs of therapists determine that some kinds of patients will be better patients than others (i.e., have good prognosis or high therapeutic potential).

For therapists seeking to use the therapeutic situation to play out the motivational need to be an influencer, the qualities of a good patient include high accessibility to influence, viz., high degree of distress, anxiety, self-dissatisfaction, and feelings of social or personal inferiority (Frank). Each major motivational need of the therapist translates into a requirement for patient acceptability. For example, certain therapist motivations call for patients who place high premium upon a relationship with an almost godlike figure who is maturely integrated, offers non-possessive warmth, and provides accurate empathy. Other therapist motivations require patients in a high state of help-seeking; the patients must want to be helped, and make manifest their help-needing desires. Still other therapist motivations call for patients who evidence needs for love and tenderness from a figure such as the therapist. In large measure, the characteristics of a "good" patient are those which implement the motivational needs of the therapist.

A therapist is understandably more favorably inclined to select patients with a high potential for the kind of therapeutic relationship important to him, the therapist. According to Strupp, therapists carry out subtle value judgments about the kinds of patients with whom they would like to relate. For example, the better-trained therapists generally practice in large cities and are surrounded with an aura of prestige; able to command high fees, they most often treat patients who have education, money, and the more subtly sophisticated needs for psychotherapy (Frank). Therapist motivations are incisive determinants of the kind of patients with whom they will relate.

Therapists can require that, in order for a person to become a patient, he must manifest certain classes of behavior which vary from culture to culture (Frank). In general, he must behave so as to signify that he needs whatever the therapist offers. To gain the status of a psychotherapy candidate from a hospital therapist, one must manifest behaviors different from those called for by a private practitioner. Not only do therapist motivations and needs play a part in determining the very clinical behaviors which will succeed or fail to gain entry into psychotherapy, but these motivations and needs also serve as criteria for identifying patients as good prospects, acceptable candidates, with good prognosis and high motivation for treatment. For the motivations and needs of the typical class of psychotherapists, these good patients tend to be:

young, physically attractive, well-educated, members of the upper middle class, possessing a high degree of ego-strength, some anxiety which impels them to seek help, no seriously disabling neurotic symptoms, relative absence of deep characterological distortions or strong secondary gains, a willingness to talk about their difficulties, an ability to communicate well, some skill in the social-vocational area, a value system relatively congruent with that of the therapist, and a certain psychological-mindedness which makes them see their problems as emotional rather than physical [Strupp, p. 497].

Our picture of the determining role of therapist motivations and needs is consistent with Frank's observation that the intensity of a patient-therapist relationship is primarily a function of the therapist himself. As a patient reveals himself as having close, warm, affectionate needs for a deeply personal relationship with an understanding older man, the therapist's own motivations and needs determine whether he will tend to enter into or withdraw from such a prospective relationship.

Thus, the therapist is a significant determinant of the patient's movement, from initial selection to the very outcome of treatment (Strupp). As Strupp puts it, patients who impress the therapist favorably (who appear to be appropriately motivated for treatment and have expectations for therapy congruent with those of the therapist) seem to "do well" in treatment. If it is accurate that psychotherapy does have a significant impact upon the patient, either beneficial or harmful (Garfield; Matarazzo; Truax), then the therapist's motivations and needs play a large part in determining the outcome. It is becoming clear that the therapist's motivations and needs are significant determiners of major therapeutic phenomena.

THERAPIST SELF-CONCEPT RELATIVE TO PATIENT'S MOTIVATIONS

Regardless of the role the therapist assumes for himself, there is a growing consensus that the patient invests the therapist with human qualities and attempts to respond to him as a relating human being. The therapist may conceptualize himself as the patient's ego-supporter, behavior-modifier, or psyche-analyst, but the patient's motivations, in league with the therapist's motivations, betray the therapist as a real person with, for instance, a rather poor sense of humor, a genuine tolerance of human frailties, a sore spot about his high fees, a stubborn persistence, and a little skittishness about being attacked personally. He is highly perceptive, well-read, and subject to the usual human mood changes. The growing recognition of the patient's motivations leaves the therapist with at least four options, four positions to take with regard to the patient's motivation. Take, for example, the case of a patient in love with his therapist:

First, the therapist may avoid being the target of the motivation. He removes himself as love object by assuming some other role, refusing to respond, or punishing the patient for his overtures. Thus, the therapist may strive to appear as the patient's helper, or friend, or analyzer, or authority—or any other role which the therapist prefers to that of the patient's love object. The therapist frequently avoids being the target of the patient's love by struggling to interpret or to provide insight; in the light of the patient's motivation, these tactics are usually sensed as ways of refusing the patient, being annoyed with him, or otherwise saying that the patient should not be that way. In taking this posture, the therapist says, "I will not respond to you. . . . Do not be that way. . . . I will never do what you want. . . . Sooner or later you must stop being that way." The locus of the therapist's response is out of the channel of the patient's motivation.

Secondly, the therapist may be the complete object of the patient's motivations. The therapist and psychotherapy become the major (and often sole) fulfillment of the patient's motivations. No one but the therapist is the object of love. All the love motivation is systematically funneled into the relationship with the therapist, who either basks (positive transference) or writhes (negative transference) in the role of the exclusive object of the patient's deepest love motivations. The patient's motivations are easily channeled into and deposited with the therapist who places himself in this position. In this role, the therapist says, "*I* am the object of your love. . . . I know you want to love *me*. . . . Sooner or later you will be in love with *me*." The locus of the therapist is the complete object of the motivation.

Thirdly, the therapist may actively facilitate the full presence of the patient's motivation in the therapeutic relationship. But instead of truncating or stopping the motivation as it comes to life with the therapist, the motivation is continued through the therapist and develops with greater intensity with an even more critically significant person. The therapist places himself squarely in the path of the motivation as it proceeds to and through him. He serves as the stimulant or catalyst by being its object. But, instead of culminating the motivation with him, the motivation proceeds on through him to the more critical figure toward whom it is more genuinely directed. In assuming this position, the therapist says, "Your love is reaching and affecting me and wants to proceed on through me to reach and affect your mother [or husband, or father, or lover]. . . . Yes, I will respond to you, and through me your mother will respond to you. . . . Your love can come to life with me and proceed on to your mother." The locus of the therapist is that of the wholly accessible intermediary between the motivation and the critically significant figure.

Fourthly, the therapist is located at the existential point of origin of the motivation within the patient's internal personality structure. The therapist is the patient's own inner voice, reflecting and clarifying with respect to the internal roots of the motivation. He is the patient's closest ally, the spokesman of deeper personality processes and the voice of the motivation itself. When the therapist can be located, together with the patient, at the point of origin of the motivation within the personality, the direct object of the motivation is the critically significant other person or component of the patient himself. Therapist and patient are conjoined in experiencing the motivation directed toward the patient's real object. In assuming this position, the therapist says, "The love reaches out to mother, and tears are coming. . . . Perhaps mother will respond. . . . This is scary and tense. . . . It is all so new and different to start to hold mother's face in your hands; there is an uncontrollable tingling and trembling all over."

We propose the above fourfold schema to describe the potential loci of the therapist relative to the motivations of the patient. Clearly our preference is for the latter two loci. Such a schema acknowledges the role of the patient's motivations and needs in an enlarged context of psychotherapy.

THE IMPLICATIONS OF FAMILY THERAPY FOR INDIVIDUAL THERAPY

Family therapy has become a creative new development in the field of psychotherapy (Bell; Framo; MacGregor). Arising out of both individual and group procedures, family therapy is establishing and revising its own body of theory and techniques. As is common, a developing area within a larger field synergizes change throughout the field. Thus, it is possible to speculate about the creative impact of the theory and techniques of family therapy on the theory and techniques of individual treatment. One way to bridge the two fields is to conceive of the family unit as analogous to an individual personality. Members or components of the family have available to them an almost infinite fabric of interactions with the larger unit. In a similar way, a component of an individual's personality can relate in a complex and changing way to his own total personality or "family of component parts."

In family therapy, the referrent is the family itself rather than outside individuals (Bell). Discussion about a person outside the family is diverted back to a focus on the family. The linkage to individual therapy is that a patient's focus upon external persons can best be understood and treated as referring to components of himself. Thus, a patient's vilification of his grasping neighbor can often be understood and treated as a vilification of his own grasping tendencies. All discussion is to be brought home, so to speak, whether "home" is the family unit or the individual himself.

The therapist does not fill a specific role in the family (Bell). He does not meet the customary image of the strong male, the omniscient one, the helper, the understanding one. If these roles are pertinent, the therapist facilitates the fulfilling of the roles by one or another of the family members rather than accepting that role for himself (Bell). For individual therapy, the implication is that the therapist does not step into a role which the patient seeks to impose on him. If the patient seeks to treat the therapist as a strong male, an omniscient one, a helper, an understanding individual, the therapist facilitates the patient's awareness and, in some cases, the patient's own fulfilling of these tendencies for himself. The family and the individual patient often are themselves to assimilate the roles they seek to assign to the therapist.

In family therapy, the therapist aims to facilitate communication among family members (Bell). The therapist is quite sensitive to the truncated and narrowed lines of communication among family members and the therapeutic desirability of opening up the interactional relationships among members of the family unit (Bell). As to individual treatment, the therapist seeks to facilitate the communicative interaction between the personality components of the patient himself. Thus, the patient's intellectual and detached component is to be brought into communication with his giddiness and silliness. His submissiveness is to interact with his own capacity for dominance. The therapist is to facilitate communication and interaction between component members of the family and among personality components of each individual patient.

In family therapy, the therapist is to be keenly alert to the family member who is now ready or beginning to communicate, and then facilitates his speaking out (Bell). The therapist is perceptually vigilant, scans the family and tries to be sensitive to the cues which indicate that one or another family member is beginning to communicate at a given moment (Bell). The therapist knows how difficult and subtle communication is and that achieving clear and honest communication is one of the prime goals of family therapy. In a sense, the therapist is also trying to teach the family members a therapeutic skill or function, that of receptivity to what is being communicated. Similarly, in individual therapy the therapist continuously asks himself what the patient is trying to say. Is his affection and love trying to act? Is his suffering and hurt attempting to express itself? In both family and individual therapy, the therapist is continuously aware of that component or facet of self which is making overtures to communicate at any moment.

In family therapy, it is perhaps more effective not to see one of the members in individual treatment as well (Framo). Such a practice prevents that member from interacting with the family as a whole and focuses needless therapeutic attention on a single member (Framo). As applied to individual therapy, the therapist is to be on guard against an exclusive or possessive involvement with any single component of the patient's personality and rather to be attuned to the "family" of vociferous as well as shy feelings, etc.

According to Bell, the aim of family therapy is to change the relationship among family members, rather than attempt to change the personality of any one member. This focus on the relationship among components implies, for individual treatment, that the relationships among personality components are the target of psychotherapeutic change rather than the expunging of an undesirable or pathological aspect. The relationship between a person's needs for affection and his own homosexual tendencies must be the arena of change, rather than "doing" something about either personality component alone.

In summary, we have seen that the emergence of an expanded context of psychotherapy has led to several creative developments in practice as well as theory and research. The traditional model of the patient-therapist interaction has been magnified and expanded to include the psychological fields that encompass them both. The therapist can now function as a more genuine human being, rather than being restricted to a role image with rigid boundaries, shutting off a dimension of important feelings and thoughts. Research that takes account of the patient as an active participant in a meaningful process is now part of the expanded context of therapy, and family therapy has added conceptual advances that also take account of this new context.

CHAPTER 12

A Theoretical Position for
Family Group Therapy

John Elderkin Bell

I want to take this opportunity to talk about my work and the evolution of my thoughts on family group therapy over the past eleven years. There is an immense gap between that which I believed when I first began and that to which I hold at this point. I recognize this transition in myself and know that others who start from the orientation I once held must make a big leap, a radical shift, if they are immediately to understand my present position. I cannot expect others to achieve in an hour, or a few days or months, what I have had the privilege of reaching gradually and progressively over a decade. This creates its own difficulties in our talking together about family group therapy.

There are some who are simply tempted to say, "This isn't so new. I've always had a family emphasis. This is just a way of rephrasing old ideas that others advanced a long time ago." I will not argue for the originality of the ideas which I discuss here. However, their application to the family, and particularly to therapeutic effort with disturbed families, is new. May I request you, then, to approach my remarks with the set that there is a new idea here that requires a reorientation in thinking and in practice.

Put yourself in my position when I started. I was acquainted with individual psychotherapy and had worked many years with children, college students, and adults. I was facing for the first time a family group consisting of a father, mother, a 16 year old boy, and a 13 year old girl who was the reason for the referral. I wished no escape, because

This chapter was voted, by the Editorial Board of the present volume, as one of the creative developments in psychotherapy, 1958–1968. From *Family Process*, 1963, 2, 1–14.

I had said to myself, "Yes, I will try to work with a whole family." Now, what would I do? How would I help this family to deal with its problems?

Let me share with you some of the experiences I had with them. First of all, without knowing it, I had accepted the idea that the girl about whom the referral originated was *the* problem. I heard mother and father, particularly mother, who was one of those women, to quoke Saki, who would have been "enormously improved by death," tell about the difficulties she and the family were having with this girl. The parents always spoke with firmness and often with rancor. Somewhat non-plussed by their attack, I would try to put myself in the place of the girl, to think about how it must feel to hear herself talked about in this way. I tried to see her father, mother, brother, and world through her eyes, to uncover the past so I could answer the question how she became the problem she is, and to engage her in a relationship through which I could understand and help her. I was full of good will. I had had indi-vidual patients like her before. I concluded that as a step towards the ultimate therapeutic goals I must help a transference relationship to develop, so I began to increase my concentration on her.

Theoretically this was fine. Practically it did not work. What had happened? The first sign it was not working came from the brother. He was restless; he began to protest that he could not see any point in com-ing, that he was not the problem, and besides he had many other things to do that he had given up to come to the conferences. Should I let him go or not? I scarcely knew then that whether I did or not, I would be lost. Now I know that if he went I would lose the chance to have an impact on him, and that if he stayed he would block me from continuing to work with the others in the family since he would only become more intransigent. He left.

Secondly, I found the problem girl did not seem to welcome my help nearly as much as I thought she should. She seemed unconcerned about the things mother and father said about her. I thought she should have been unhappy and felt I would have been in her place. She was no more enthusiastic about coming than her brother. She seemed indifferent. Later I came to understand that she was showing that her parents were reciting an old familiar story against which she had long ago contrived effective ways to defend herself. In addition, however, elements of anxiety appeared that seemed primarily associated with her relation-ship to me and that seemed to be impelling her to the safe course of running away from the conferences.

Later, I began to hear a detailed elaboration of the story of her difficulties from mother, father, and her—and I began to think I was getting to the foundation of the problem. But then little happened. She was not much different; her attitudes to her parents were relatively unchanged, and least of all was there any shift in the ways the parents were acting.

What to do? Where to turn? I was often reasoning that the transference problems were so great that I had better arrange an individual therapist for each of the family members. "Yes," I would say, "that would seem simpler, and then all the therapists could come together and compare notes—which would seem to be a good sound way to keep a family point of view."

At other times an alternative would appear more attractive. I now seemed to have such a good understanding of the family situation that if I were only to tell the family what I knew about them and give them some prescriptions or psychological sermonettes, they would surely be able to solve their problems. This indeed some families would do, although if the truth were known their solutions would probably be little related to my advice or even to the fact of their having come to me, there being in any family group strong pressures to work out the problems with one another. Giving advice was foreign to my usual therapeutic approach, however, so I was reluctant to use it, even though others have advocated it for family work.

THE BASIC SET

Fortunately, the solution for the difficulties I seemed to experience, if not to create, came rather soon. I continued to see total families together and arrived at the point where I had a kind of intuitive grasp of what was needed. I had to wipe clean the blackboard of my mind and find a fresh piece of chalk to write large: "The *family* is the problem." I learned to reject the notion that the child who brought the family to treatment presented the problem with which I was to work. The child might be *a* problem, his behavior having provided the occasion for starting the treatment, but I learned that I must not regard him as the problem for therapy, not even at the moment of beginning the therapy. *The problem is the family.* Here was the crux of the matter. Here was the transition in thought that I must make. This is the new idea, seemingly so small, but actually so major. "The family is the problem!"

Translated into technical language, one is substituting a social psychological orientation for a clinical psychological orientation. One is now thinking "group" rather than "individual." Therefrom follow the goals for the therapy—to change the structure and functions of the family group—and the technical steps through which the therapist introduces optimal conditions for producing group change.

Contrast with Group Therapy

If I, who had turned my back on the individual therapist, seemed now to be courting the group therapist, it was only an illusion. Let me hasten to point out the gulf between the usual practice of group therapy and family group therapy. Group therapy is treatment of a number of individuals at one time in a group setting. Its orientation is the individual. The group exists as an instrument for accomplishing certain purposes with the series of individuals who compose it, but not as an end in itself. We construct the group for the therapy and are unconcerned about its ultimate fate as a group, expecting it to dissolve when the therapy concludes. The group retains its identity as a group only as an accident—not as a conscious goal of the therapist.

With the family we do not construct the group. That began as a natural process many years ago. The group existed before the therapy, it continues through the therapy, and, most important of all, it will move into the future as a group. It is not only an instrument of the therapy, it is an end in itself. We are to promote its well-being.

Beyond this, in family group therapy the group life persists throughout the whole week. Whereas in group therapy a group comes together for the therapy hour and then disperses, with the family, the group is together in one way or another all the time. The therapy hour is a continuation of family life. Thus change that is initiated in a therapy hour is likely to have a direct and immediate transfer into the continuing work of the family. Immediate support or reinforcement for changes can be available on a 24-hour-a-day basis.

Family group therapy is an independent therapy, distinct from both the individual and group therapies we knew formerly. It differs because of the relationships among those who come for treatment, it differs in the definition of the problem they bring, it differs in the therapeutic techniques, and finally in the goals towards which it moves.

I hope that I have alerted you to listen with care, so that you may hear the distinctive in what I am trying to say. If so, we may proceed to deal with a number of issues that are tied in with the fundamental point I am making. To be absolutely sure that we start from the same premise, however, let me restate it. I am averring that family group therapy is a social psychological treatment method to provide help so that the natural family group may solve its problems and continue to function more efficiently as a group. From this base let us now take up a number of further considerations.

QUESTIONS OF TECHNIQUE

First, we shall give our attention to some practical matters. Regarding the family as the problem, what are the implications for technique? Or, how do we promote the changes that take place during the course of family group therapy?

WHO IS THE FAMILY

Let us examine the matter of who makes up the family with whom we work. About this we have no inflexible rules. It may be a matter of discussion with the parents or other family members. I have found that for the most part children younger than nine years of age are not mature enough verbally and intellectually to undertake the communication demanded in this group method. "Family" does not necessarily mean a biological relationship. It probably is best to think of the family in terms of the functioning group living together in one household and to bring together all those individuals who seem to be the functioning members of this immediate group. In choosing the group to treat, it is helpful to remember that each potential member who is excluded will be a force working against changes in the family; or he will be driven away from the rest of the family, since the distance between him and those in the group will be accentuated as cohesive processes bind the family into a group organized in new ways.

RELATING TO THE FAMILY AS A GROUP

Having decided who will make up the family group, we now are able to operate according to a firm principle in dealing with the efforts of individuals to retreat or to manipulate the composition of the group in other ways. It sounds simple-minded to say that if we are going to work on the group problem, we must work with the group, but this is our first rule. If we really believe in the family as the problem, we will insist on having all members of the family come to all sessions. I expect attendance, and postpone meetings if someone cannot come. Incidentally, this happens very seldom after the rule of participation is established. We find mostly that all want to come, if they sense that we really mean to work on the family difficulties. It is when a family member feels that we are singling out an individual for especial attention and concern that he will show strong pressures to leave.

This same principle of working with the group governs the therapist when one family member wants to remove him to one side and establish a little private group with him. This happens so commonly that I refer to it as the most characteristic resistance in family group therapy. I am absolutely firm about my unwillingness to meet with a part of the family privately. I make it a rule that all relations between me and the family members must be in the group and known to all of them. Being alerted to the deviousness of their efforts to break this rule, I am prepared to affirm and reaffirm my position without apology as the need may arise. This is immeasurably reassuring to the group and protects its solidarity.

A further illustration of this principle may be found when the family begins to talk about relationships with others who are outside the group. Even though the therapist may recognize with the family that difficulties with these others are important, he brings the center of discussion back to the family group immediately in front of him. He points out how we cannot talk about these other relationships since the other people are not present to tell about how things look to them. He reminds the family that they are here to clarify what goes on among themselves.

In this same direction, I would not engage in activities with the family other than those required in the conferences. I would not have dinner with the family, I would not visit family members at work, school, in the home or the community. For even though I might learn from such occasions, I would be sacrificing the advantages and speed of treatment that follow a more disciplined and structured role for myself and a more consistent emphasis on the family group.

Towards this goal of keeping the boundaries around the family group as intact as possible, and towards strengthening them, I try to avoid intruding myself into the family group, except in line with a role that is defined for the family group and for me as demanded by the therapy. Essentially, this means that the therapist avoids, where possible, taking over functions that any family member performs for the family or may be expected to perform. Family members try to push the therapist into assuming family responsibilities. One of the places this is peculiarly evident is when we are working with a family group from which one of the parents is missing. In this case a mother may try, particularly, to seduce the therapist into acting as a father for the children and a husband for herself. Or, if the parent is the father, he may evidence his need for a wife and a mother for the children, by pressing the therapist towards acting out his conception of how this missing parent should function.

This pressure on the therapist also occurs when a complete family is in front of him. This is commonly seen when one of the family turns to the therapist and says: "What would you do?" If mother is asking the question, we have to ask if father would feel displaced if the therapist were to answer it. Very likely he would. Quite often such a question conveys a covert criticism of another family member, saying to him, in effect, that the question would not be needed if he were playing his appropriate part. Telling what you would do then takes on the implication that you concur with the devaluation of the other family member. But turning the question back to the group preserves family roles, strengthens or adjusts them, and works towards improvement of the interrelationships between them.

The above illustrations grow out of the application of the first principle of treatment that follows identification of the family as a problem. In essence the principle states that as a primary method of treatment the therapist relates to the identified family group so as to strengthen the boundaries surrounding the group as a group.

THE TASK FOR THE FAMILY

A second principle specifies that the task on which the family group is to work during the course of the treatment must be group oriented. The task falls into three areas: (1) identification of the family problems; (2) analysis of the problems and of factors that create them; and (3) development and testing of solutions to the problems. More narrowly the task is to examine the interrelationships among the family members to determine how they may be handled better. The therapist and the family must keep the task focus on that which is to benefit the group. The therapist puts this task into words and promotes the set to work on group issues.

Requisite to the identification and analysis of the family problem is the expansion of the communication between the family members. An immediate task is to put into words what before has been left unexpressed or said in such circuitous ways that its meaning has not been transmitted. Part of this is accomplished by putting into words that which is spoken in the private language which all families use and which normally excludes the therapist from understanding what is being said, at least in its nuances. I refer to all the little gestures, facial expressions, and personalized uses of words whose special meaning was created during the family's private history. Important as is the therapist's under-standing, it is even more important that the family members understand; this happens in new ways as they express themselves afresh, as they translate their messages from the easy shorthand of the private family tongue into the public language appropriate for talking with outsiders like the therapist. Towards the all-embracing goals of revision of the family group functioning, an immediate and instrumental task is to develop new forms and intensity of communication.

The group emphasis in communication demands that each family member have an equal chance to take part in the discussions. This does not mean that each will talk an equivalent amount but rather that he will have the chance to talk if he wishes to contribute to the analyses of the problems or the proposal of solutions. Further, he will participate in the decisions about solutions and thus identify them as his own solutions as well as those of the group as a whole.

The therapist tries to promote such equivalence and to maximize individual participation. He listens for the signs that persons wish to take a more active part. He helps to provide the chances for such partici-pation, even when what one family member wishes to say may not be relished by the others, as during some of the stormy battles that we expect at certain stages of the treatment.

We find that the communication will increase in the family, but this is purposeful only as a means towards accomplishing the task of solving the family problems. If you say to a family "What are your problems, and how can we solve them?" the family normally finds these questions appropriate for it and has a clear idea of what is being asked, even if the means by which the questions may be answered seem not to be at hand. In exploring the scope of these questions through improving communi-cation, the family usually begins to narrow the scope of the problems it wishes to talk about. This does not represent necessarily a solution of the other problems or a sign that there is a greater urgency about the issues selected. Most frequently one, two, or a few problems are sifted out for discussion as symbols of the full range of problems. They are concrete representations of the areas of tension, ambiguity, indecision, and breakdown of solidarity in the group. Around these concrete issues the ways in which the group members are functioning may be studied and revised towards a better structure for the group and better articu-lation among the group members in reaching for individual and group goals. Family group therapy taps the motivation of the family group to improve itself.

The therapist is an agent who works to start and keep alive this problem solving program. He works with the family on the means of study and of problem solving. Consistent with keeping outside the family group, he does not determine the goals for the family nor make its decisions for it. He helps them into the position where they recognize their goals and are free to make such decisions as are demanded in the movement towards attaining them. I have found that the family in treatment is more concerned with attaining goals that are represented in its present value system than in reaching out for new values. Most families with whom I have worked are discouraged about reaching the goals they know and respect; they want the experience of success in reaching some of these before seeking new values. The family in treatment is in crisis and is seeking a way out of the crisis first. Then may come a grappling with new and larger questions of value. At this state, it would be appropriate to call on the assistance of educational and religious agencies.

The group orientation of the task on which the family is working is reflected further in the way in which the therapist handles decisions. He will participate if these are decisions about the therapy conferences themselves. If, for instance, the family desired to change the time of the therapy hour, the therapist would work jointly with them in making the decision about the appropriate time. If, on the other hand, the decisions deal with the family life, such as deciding on a new time for the dinner hour, the therapist would remove himself openly from the decision. The therapist's task is the therapy; the family's task is solving the family problem. The therapist consciously maintains his distance from the group task, at a defined peripheral position.

No outsider therapist has enough information nor could secure enough to decide the course for the family, even though he might be tempted to attribute such omniscience to himself. If he desists, he will find that one family may elect decisions that seem diametrically opposite to those of the next family. For example, in one family a father decides that he must be the disciplinarian; in another, he decides that he must turn over this responsibility to the mother. It is not appropriate to expect the therapist to decide which solution is right. Each family must seek out and attain its own answers to its questions, for only in this way can the family enhance its own identity and solidarity.

THE THERAPIST'S TASK

Now I wish to return to the point that the therapist's task is the therapy, for there is a third principle involved. It is a correlate of the two previously defined. If the family is to maintain its group status and to work on the group problem, the therapist must keep his distance, stay out of the family, and restrict his work to the therapy. He relates *to* the family, not within the family. He communicates how he will relate to the family from the beginning of the first session and tries to make his actions accord with the rules he imposes on himself. He orients the family to the limits he will adopt and then holds to them firmly and unambiguously. Having described the orientation and other techniques elsewhere,[1] I will not take the time to discuss them here. Let me illustrate, however, by one example the attitude and role of the therapist.

I insist on holding the conferences in an office rather than in the home. In the latter the therapist is a guest, subject to the conventions of that status. His freedom for determining the conditions of the conferences is restricted. In an office he can take direction of the situation. The setting there supports the authority of his actions. It cleanly separates the authority of the therapy from the authority in the home, where the therapist should not aspire to be an authority. As director of the therapy sessions, he can predetermine his role, communicate it to the family, relate to the family accordingly, and thereby facilitate the therapy in ways he chooses.[2]

The Struggle Towards Change

In a moment we will examine briefly how, from his distant position, the therapist makes the impact upon the family that produces change. First, however, we should note that change does not come easily. When the family seeks the help of a therapist, it is caught between a need to change and a need to preserve its current organization. All families, as all natural groups, experience this bind at various periods of their history, and most of them revise their interactions without outside assistance. When change and stability are desired at one and the same time, and there is no resolution of the ambiguity, anxiety and emotional disturbance follow. Under these circumstances it is common to take advantage of some personal "oddities" of an individual in the family, to conclude that the situation could be rectified if that individual would change, and to divert the attention from the group to him—a process that perpetuates the individual's difficulties, since the other choice, change in the group, is more painful.

When a family seeks out therapy for one of its members, it is facing a crisis. The balance by which the family group has operated has been disturbed. Under these conditions the family may seek ways to reinforce the scapegoat mechanism, to call in outside strength to support the projection of responsibility on to one family member and to give backing to the demand that this individual change. We had better be alert to this when one family member refers another. Unfortunately, individual therapy too often fits right in with this scapegoating, by concurring that the individual is sick. While the family wishes the individual to change, we must remember that it has found a means of preserving its group stability through the individual's difficulties, so there are probably strong unconscious pressures to keep the individual disturbed. These may be strong enough to defeat therapeutic progress and to preserve the behavior that the family says it wants to change. The simplest response to a crisis precipitating the family towards change is to strengthen the pressures towards keeping the present organization.

A second way of handling the difficulty is to isolate the disturbed individual—to remove him from the group to the outside, so that a new family group may be formed without him. The family may not seek this openly but demonstrates its motivation in this direction by the readiness with which it accepts plans to reduce or break the individual's ties to the family. It is no accident that various forms of institutionalization have been devised to care for the disturbed. We tend to think of these as methods that professionals have arranged, and also as society's way of taking care of problem persons. I suspect, however, that our hospitals, clinics, foster-homes, and other such institutions are outgrowths as much as anything of family pressures.

A third way of regaining balance in the group is to change the internal social structure and to incorporate new behavior into the group interactions. We use individual therapy to accomplish this, and it often results in positive changes in the whole family of which the patient is a part. More frequently than desirable, however, it results in the family's transferring the scapegoat status to a new family member, so that the over-all organization remains comparable, although disturbance is now shown by a new individual. Family group therapy begins with the aim of changing the structure of the family group, but hopefully with a change that involves the interactions between the members, not just a rotation of the scapegoat pressures to someone new.

The Process of Family Group Therapy

If family group therapy is able to accomplish reorganization, by what means does it seem to do so? Have we any explanations for the ways it works? For myself, I have set forth my thesis about how the therapist effects change in the family group in five propositions:

1. In all social groups, and particularly the family, the communication and interaction is structured within certain operational limits that produce stereotyped patterns of reactions between family members and a restriction on the permissible ranges of individual behavior. These are normal consequences of belonging to the family. They often result in mutual depreciation of the potentialities of the other, a kind of cynicism about what can be expected of him, and an unrealistic appraisal of what he might accomplish. Such limits are an obvious consequence of any group membership, are consistently evident in the family, and are necessary to establishing and maintaining the group operations of the family.

2. Most older children and their parents have available to them potential patterns of behavior beyond those they use in the family. These are revealed in the community in relation to persons outside the family. I refer to these as public patterns, as separate from familial patterns.

3. The therapist is a community figure in relation to whom the individual family member may show behavior that extends beyond what he normally reveals in the family. He may react in these ways towards the therapist without engendering the intense anxiety that would follow venturing these new behaviors alone in the family. The therapist seeks such public behavior from each of the family members. For the family this introduces change.

4. In response to the new patterns revealed, the rest of the family members must revise their stereotypes about the family member, must re-evaluate him, must respond to him with new attitudes, and new accommodations of their own behavior. Together they test out, thereby, potentialities for relationship, incorporating changes that prove useful, and rejecting those that fail.

5. Having developed new modes of interacting, supported by mutual commitment that they are better and should be continued, the family consolidates these new patterns. They work in common to inhibit or eradicate the old outworn patterns, and to strengthen the new. A whole field of research in learning could be spread out before us through study of the methods by which the family members act upon one another to reinforce the patterns they have newly achieved.

Reviewing these propositions, we may say that the treatment process depends on a therapist engaging each family member in a relationship in which the individual is encouraged to express himself distinctly and differently from his customary behavior in the family, and to do this in the presence of the family. It accomplishes no instructive purpose for the family if he does this alone with the therapist. The extended range of his behavior needs to be visible to the family.

Probably we can see how the clarity of definition of the therapist's role aids this process. It is designed to reduce the anxiety of each family member. It stimulates each to respond to the therapist and gives clues about how he expects him to act, which also contributes to a reduction of anxiety. It is designed to prevent intrusion of the therapist into roles already pre-empted by family members so that he may draw forth new public behavior from each individual. If the therapist takes on a family role he calls up the stereotyped family patterns; only as he separates himself from family functions and patterns does he challenge the family members to show their extra-familial behavior, to make it potentially of use in the family, and to stimulate thereby family reorganization.

Out of such social engineering comes a new family, carrying over that which is respected from the past, incorporating the new that is to its profit. The changes are changes in depth, but depth is defined first by group change rather than by intrapsychic change. This does not mean that the changes fail to touch individuals. Just as the group changes, so also do the individual members, through a learning experience that is so intense that the changes are deep. But the intrapsychic changes are secondary to changes in the relational processes, the truth of which those who have mastered individual therapy also recognize. This, then, is how I see family group therapy solidifying the family group, solving the interactional problems, and providing the individual family members with a secure status in the family, the primary condition for self-respect, true independence of spirit, and freedom for accomplishment.

NOTES

1. Bell, John E., Family Group Therapy. *Public Health Monograph 64*, 1961, p. 52.
2. Recent experiences with lower class families that include delinquents suggest that with them treatment in the home may be preferable. It appears that the therapist may assume more control over the situation for therapy in the lower middle class home than he could in the home of a middle or upper class family.

CHAPTER 13

Conceptual Issues and Clinical Implications of Family Therapy

James L. Framo

With the advent of family therapy over the past decade or so, a quiet revolution has been taking place in psychopathologic thought. Although the genesis of family therapy was rooted in practical, clinical considerations, it has come to be less significant as a form of treatment than as a conceptual shift in a view of man. Family therapy experience has enriched and widened the concept of man as not just a personality constellation with his own defined boundaries but as being linked to and shaped by the transactional context within which he is involved, feels, and behaves. Such a shift in focus has profound implications not only for clinical practice but for the general study of human behavior; indeed, family system theory not only promises to provide "a bridge from the personal to the social" (see Coffey's review of *Intensive Family Therapy*, 1967) but also has connotations for general systems theory as it applies to different fields.

John Bell, one of the early workers in the family therapy field, was one of those who foresaw some of the wider implications of the family approach when he stated in one of his first publications that

. . . the developmental process in personality is of much greater complexity and of much longer duration than is implied in much current psychological theory; also, . . . the sensitivity of the person to his situation continues to determine his responses in a substantial way through much of life [1961, p. 50].

The family therapy investigations of the writer were undertaken at the Family Therapy Project of the Eastern Pennsylvania Psychiatric Institute, Philadelphia, Pa.; Ivan Boszormenyi-Nagy, M.D., Director. Thanks are due Dr. Boszormenyi-Nagy for reading this paper and offering suggestions. This chapter is a discussion-commentary, written especially for the present volume, of Chapter 12: "A Theoretical Position for Family Group Therapy," by John Bell.

Before we begin the discussion in depth of John Bell's "A Theoretical Position for Family Group Therapy" (1963), an introduction to family therapy findings and concepts is necessary for the benefit of those readers who are not familiar with this area. Before the introduction of the family approach there was a sensible rationale behind the decision of the psychoanalyst or psychotherapist to involve himself as little as possible with the family of the patient he was treating. While to some extent this policy, which took its cue from Freud's dicta regarding relatives, was unrealistically rigid at times, it was based on accumulated experience and is still valid for many cases: the transference field would be contaminated; the focus of interest was on the intrapsychic realities of the patient and their elaborations rather than the external realities of his family life; even when it became apparent that the patient was caught up in a web of sick relatives, the rationale was that when the patient's ego grew stronger he would be better able to handle the family pathology, as well as other reality problems. These principles, essentially based on the psychoanalytic model, had their analogue even in the treatment of the psychotic when the goal was to help the patient separate from the family by individual treatment, peer group therapy, or hospitalization; there was a phase when, in order to relieve the hospitalized patient from family pressures, contacts with the family were temporarily not allowed (e.g., the family was not permitted to visit "because the visits upset the patient too much"). Implicit in this latter approach was that the family made the patient crazy so you had to get the patient away from the noxious influence in order to cure him; there were always misgivings, moreover, about sending the patient back to that same deleterious family environment. (This approach ignores the patient's contribution to the family pathology and also shows lack of awareness of how family systems operate—but more of this later.) Psychotherapists, and even psychoanalysts, treating adults on an outpatient basis often find themselves engaged in various kinds of maneuvers in handling family members who try to intrude themselves into the treatment process. The dynamics of the interaction between therapist and family members who are not part of the treatment are highly complex and have a life of their own even when the therapist does not permit any contact between himself and the family; the fantasies of each about the other, with the patient as the communicator between the two, can have a strong influence on the course of the treatment. In those instances where the therapist allows occasional contact with the family, often consenting to see them without the patient, a host of new problems arises, running the gamut from open or suppressed angry feelings on both sides, to uncertainty about questions of confidentiality, conflicts about where loyalties lie, competition for the patient, and even, at times, surreptitious coalitions between therapist and family members, both fancied and real.

The one area where there has been wide agreement on the involvement of family members is in the treatment of children. The child guidance movement, however, has not dealt with system or interactional aspects of the family as a unit; rather, the emphasis has been on the treatment of the child, and therapeutic work with other family members, primarily mothers, has been considered as ancillary or peripheral to the main purpose. According to this model, the child is referred to a child therapist while the mother or both parents are seen by a social worker (who, really, has to deal with the bulk of the pathology), and then the social worker and child therapist meet collaboratively to compare observations. The inherent weaknesses in this approach were seen only gradually as perplexing treatment failures accumulated. There is a parallel here to the way juvenile offenders are handled. When an adolescent commits an offense the mother is usually called in to discuss the situation with the probation officer, and the focus of the discussion is on the child. Rarely is the mother asked about her marriage (she is not likely to mention either an emotional divorce from her husband or constant battling); the "well" siblings are usually not brought into the picture (even though they may have far graver pathology than the delinquent has); and fathers are seen infrequently. When one considers that children committing an offense are usually responding to some unbearable family situation—how they have had to settle arguments between parents or provide for parents what parents should be providing for them, or they have parents who get vicarious gratification from their acting out—these omissions which prevent focus on the heart of the process which fosters the delinquency are difficult to fathom. Unwittingly, too, the mental health associations, which stress early recognition of signs of emotional disturbance so that the "loved one" can get professional help, have fed one of the main resistances of the family, namely, to isolate the patient's problems from the rest of the family's problems so he can be changed by the professional to fit into some preconceived family notion of what he should be (e.g., the family failure, the adhesive for the parent's marriage, the family healer, the family actor-outer, etc.). Increasing recognition of the patient's inability to change in the face of absence of change in the family was one of the key stimulants to work with the whole family. For over a century professional psychotherapists either did not see the family together or if they did have an occasional meeting with various members there was no focused attention on the transactional aspects of the interacting unit of the marriage or family itself. While the difference may seem to be casual or subtle the change of emphasis in seeing the family as the patient was a giant step in the history of psychopathology.

When family members were observed interacting with each other a variety of fascinating, unique phenomena became available for study by the psychological sciences for the first time. The transactional operations observed between those in close relationship have been particularly instructional. Take, for example, the principle that the referent point of feeling and behavior of a person is almost always an Other who is important to the Self. For instance, whenever two people are in close relationship they carry psychic functions for each other in an unconscious trade which not only permits vicarious experiencing but comes to characterize the functioning of the dyad as a unit (e.g., "I will be your bad self if you will be my weak self." Or, "If you will be over-conscientious, I can be irresponsible."). Related to this phenomenon is one wherein people in intimate relationship often split their intrapsychic conflicts, project the negative part onto the Other, and then battle it in the Other (a common manifestation in marriage situations of chronic conflict where there is no chance that the partners will ever permanently separate). An intriguing theoretical sidelight of this sampling of transactional operations is the realization that the thinking of Melanie Klein (1950) and Ronald Fairbairn (1952) about splitting of mental processes, although constructed within an intrapsychic framework, presaged a personal social psychology. It is true that some of these phenomena had been observed before, in systematic studies of ad hoc groups and in group psychotherapy, but because of the aforementioned taboos the psychology of *intimate* relationships and interactions had never before been examined in depth, and this psychology has been found to have distinct qualities and laws of its own. There is a special, real quality in one's dealings with one's mate, parents, siblings, and children which does not apply to one's other social relationships. The development of oneself as a person is embedded in blood ties of long duration and deeply rooted in innumerable affect experiences. One pretty much *has* to be involved with one's family, whether one wishes to or not, even if one does not actually see the family members very often or at all. One's parent may not be the sort of person one would have chosen to be associated with; even if one's father is an embarrassingly coarse, vulgar loudmouth always playing the fool in public or one's mother is flagrantly promiscuous or one's parent is a depressed martyr, always arousing pity and anger, or a con artist manipulating others, or a sycophant, or if one has to be a marriage counselor to one's parents' marriage, one cannot easily give parents up the way one could give up an acquaintance. Friends and colleagues are replaceable; nothing can change the fact that one's mother and father will always be one's mother and father. The stakes are higher and the consequences graver when one deals with one's family members because they have the wherewithal to affect the core of one's being; perhaps these realizations help explain why disappointment and frustration are so much more intense among family members, the hostility much more hurting, the sacrifices so compelling, and the gratifications so fulfilling. Because expectations are so high and the feelings so potentially explosive, family members have great difficulty stating their intentions and motives to each other or telling each other how they really feel. To be sure, people carry over into other relationships the rational and irrational feelings derived from family relationships, and skillful observers can often reconstruct the family origins of these feelings as they observe the way people handle each other. On the other hand, one can speculate that because people have such profound needs to preserve a good or bad fantasied relationship with a parent, they may have to act out and live through the negative or positive with others, thus giving a false picture of the nature of the relationship with the parent. Family therapists prefer to work at a level which brings investigation back to where it all began, and they believe that it is far better, for example, for a son to be helped to work out something with his real father than through a therapist, a parental surrogate whose association with the patient is necessarily professional and limited.

When families as a unit were treated it was learned, further, that each family is an exceedingly intricate system with implicit rules that govern the roles and the ways in which each member will reciprocally behave toward the other; these roles or constellations of attitudes (particularly those assigned the children by the parents) are often irrational projections rooted in past conflictual, unresolved relationships and perpetrated by myths, distorted communications, and secret alliances. The lack of individuation, the fusion of the personalities, created such phenomena as family regression (e.g., no contact with the outside world), parentification of children, lack of commitment to the marriage, and blurring of generational differences, as well as the kind of narcissistic relating whereby other family members, rather than being viewed as persons in their own right, are seen as mourned but recaptured introject representatives or clay objects to be molded to one's needs. Although it was learned that the symptoms of the child are merely the surface manifestation of a deep, family-wide pathology and that the child's symptoms are often the passport for the parents to get treatment, it was also learned that the child is not just a victim and makes his own offerings to maintain the family homeostasis. In essence, the focus of some family therapies has been to deal with the family members' transference distortions *to each other*.

What has been summarized thus far represents a distillation of the ideology and findings of some family therapists, particularly those of the present writer. While there are areas of agreement among all family therapists, there are areas of diversity in rationale, premises, and techniques. Take, for example, the question of who is the family, or the nature of the unit to be treated; some family therapists insist on seeing the entire family at each meeting, whereas others will work with subunits (parents alone, just the children, a parent and child, etc.), and at least one family therapist, Murray Bowen, will see one family member, not for individual therapy, but for the purpose of raising the level of differentiation of an entire family (Bowen, 1966). It should come as no surprise that various workers in a field develop diverse ways of looking at their data. Theoretical differences in all fields of endeavor are not only inevitable but necessary, because sometimes these differences lead to systematic research. Certainly, then, at this stage of knowledge, it is presumptuous for any family therapist to say that his way is best. As someone once said, "The damnedest things help people." On the other hand, I can write in this paper only from the vantage point of my own experience and compare it to that which Dr. Bell describes, hoping that useful information will be drawn from the comparison.

Despite the fact that it is not easy to distinguish between matters of rationale and therapeutic technique, it does seem as if the bulk of Dr. Bell's article deals with technique. One is always on shaky ground in evaluating someone else's psychotherapy techniques; to mention just a few of the complications involved:

1. It is suspected that every therapist has a particular style of doing psychotherapy, a way that is most comfortable for him, and that he develops a rationale for what he does.

2. There is often a wide gap between what a therapist actually does (as seen by outside observers) and what he says he does.

3. An outside observer, on the other hand, not being present in the living therapy situation and not having the responsibility for making therapeutic decisions, makes his evaluations on the basis of a psychological atmosphere quite different from that of the therapist.

4. Because he is caught up in his own feelings and reactions a therapist may have much more, or less, effect on patients than he thinks he does.

5. There may be disparities between what a therapist believes he is doing with patients and the way the patients perceive or interpret the therapist's behavior.

6. One therapist may provide a rationale for one principle and another for the opposite principle; yet because much is communicated which goes beyond words, the two therapists may actually function similarly.

Keeping the foregoing in mind and remembering that no therapist can adequately describe what he does, the present writer will attempt an in-depth discussion of Dr. Bell's work. Dr. Bell's approach to family therapy appears to be based on the rationale that when the therapist does not become embroiled in the family conflicts and avoids having himself placed in one of the family roles, he comes to represent a community reality figure. In their interaction with the therapist the family members, unable to involve the therapist in their usual way, are thereby forced to manifest extrafamilial behavior which has not been evident to the rest of the family, and, consequently, when the members depart from their characteristic family roles, family reorganization can take place. This construct of family therapy does seem to describe one important dimension of the therapy process. When Dr. Bell specifies that "the therapist must keep his distance, stay out of the family . . . relate *to*, not within the family," this stance of the therapist, while it may seem detached, seems logically consistent with the rationale. It is often of great value for a family to observe a member's interaction with the therapist and to see that member behave in a way the family had never seen before. Children may be pleasantly surprised to see their mother or father interact with an outsider in a more mature way than the parents behave with each other. A parent may observe his mate handling the therapist in a way which reveals heretofore unexhibited personality strengths. The children may gain something important when they may learn things about their parents which they did not know before (e.g., that their parents, whom they have always seen as unhappy with each other, were, at one time, very much in love). Parents observing a child's interaction with the therapist may see assets in the child which they had not noticed before, or they may learn about certain aspects of the sibling world which the children had concealed (e.g., that a brother and sister have an especially close or distant relationship of which the parents were unaware). Most people find it very difficult or impossible to tell certain members of their family how they really feel, and often in the family therapy situation they can relate events and feelings to an outsider (therapist) for the first time, even in the presence of the rest of the family. The rules of the family do set up, not only what things can be talked about, but the channels of communication which must be followed; these channels provide many clues about the family dynamics (e.g., son goes to mother to discuss his problems and mother transmits the information to father). Our own work, we feel, provides some further understanding about why family members are so circumspect in revealing to each other deeper feelings having to do with the special qualities of relationships within the family, with maintaining the family system status quo, and with the transference distortions which the members have toward each other—a concept to be elucidated below.

There do, however, seem to be both a contradiction in Dr. Bell's rationale and a disregard of other inherent features of all psychotherapies which suggest that Dr. Bell's description represents a limited aspect of a very complex process. According to the rationale which Dr. Bell proposes, the therapist maintains a neutral position and separates himself from family functions, yet at the same time engages each family member in a relationship, in the presence of his family, in order to encourage the individual to express himself differently from his customary behavior with his family. One wonders how the therapist keeps his distance yet at the same time makes himself the key figure in the transaction. Making the relationship with the therapist a central part of the therapy gives far greater weight to the activity or inactivity of the therapist than would techniques, say, which encourage interaction among family members themselves. Maintaining neutrality in the face of the kind of highly charged emotional transactions which occur in family therapy is no mean feat, especially when one considers that therapist neutrality is pretty much of a myth anyway. Every therapist shows his feelings and expresses his opinions, whether he does this by specific direction, by selecting aspects of the material to focus on, by consistent avoidance of some issues or implications, by his tone of voice, by innuendo or facial expression, or the like. Perceptive patients, even of very inactive psychoanalysts, can often tell how the analyst feels about something by noting his breathing patterns.

Another complication which is involved in these matters is the traditional phenomenon of transference to the therapist. It has become fashionable these days to devalue or negate psychoanalytic concepts and to abandon such terms as transference, but one wonders whether a phenomenon becomes nonexistent if it is no longer recognized or dealt with. Whether or not a therapist chooses to conceptualize the phenomenon or deal with it in treatment, and whether one describes it in such terms as unrealistic feelings, illogical expectations, or projections onto the therapist, patients do view the therapist in a multitude of idiosyncratic ways (as someone to be feared, admired, castigated, shamed, reified, depended upon, respected, hated—as someone who will judge, rescue, persecute—the range is infinite), and these perceptions, while irrational at this time, toward this therapist, are quite rational when understood as the final destiny of a dynamic past. The therapist can, of course, try to ignore these feelings and attend to other matters, but the feelings are going to be there, and they are going to have a powerful effect on what takes place in the treatment; as a matter of fact, if there is any one area most therapists are likely to avoid dealing with, it is this area of transference, as Breuer and Freud discovered long ago. With transference taken into account, then, the question can be raised as to whether family members *will* display characteristic behavior while interacting with a therapist who is so magically endowed; patients do not ordinarily behave with therapists the way they do with others. While family members can benefit from observing other members' assets in interacting with the therapist, it is also common, because of transference factors, for the liabilities, the neurotic or psychotic features of the personality of the interacting member, to become revealed or accentuated. (E.g., it is not unusual in family therapy for parents to compete with their children for the therapist; they become more infantile than they characteristically are, and, as a consequence, the children may become increasingly disgusted and demoralized.) The family therapy treatment situation itself, moreover—the physical setting, the uniqueness of the occasion, the apprehension that family members have about sitting together, as well as the fantasies about treatment—are all factors which at least temporarily work against the display of typical behavior.

One point of view about family therapy holds that the focus of investigation should be on current, immediate family interaction, whereas another espouses a more comprehensive approach by including, in addition to current interactions, the dynamic past as part of the therapeutic process. While the distinction between these points of view might not warrant the conclusion that they represent two schools of family therapy, nonetheless the difference in emphasis obviously affects one's theory and practice of treatment. (For a more complete statement of the present writer's position see Framo, 1965a.) The question can be posed: do the behaviors observed in family therapy have a unique quality of their own, discontinuous with the past and explainable on the basis of an interactional psychology alone, or are the behaviors more understandable when one takes into account what has gone before and utilizes, in addition to current interactional concepts, all that has been learned about individual and depth psychology? (Although a dynamic therapist may use the past in making his own constructions, it is recognized that some patients will use a flight into the past as a major resistance, in which case it is necessary to focus on what is currently going on.) We have found, for example, in a number of marriages in the families we treat that the mates are not able to commit themselves emotionally to their marriage because their deeper involvement is with their parents (e.g., the only time they become alive or can talk sensitively with genuine feeling is when they are discussing their parents). These people go through the motions of married life, and their present marital relationship is shadowy, unreal, and dream-like because the only meanings they attach to the marriage are a function of the living through of the symbolic programming imprinted many years ago. (The mate was selected on the basis of the prospectus—as someone who lent himself to be revenged upon, a detached person who would not make demands, someone who was to make up for old wrongs, etc.) The exploration and working through of these deeper motivational levels, which involve historical relationships, represents another approach to therapy with the family.

Another area about which there has been some controversy in the family field has to do with the focus and extent of exploration of individual members of the family. We are in full agreement with Dr. Bell that private sessions with individuals outside the family sessions feed one of the characteristic resistances of family therapy and that individual therapy which is concurrent with the family therapy is likely to diffuse and undermine the family treatment (as well as raise the sticky issue of confidentiality). There have been occasions where we did not discourage members from obtaining concurrent individual help, but this treatment is given by outside therapists and not by the family therapists. It has not been uncommon, however, for individual therapy for one or more members of the family to precede or follow family therapy. Temporary work with family subsystems has also been useful because we have found that family members often will reveal certain behaviors only when in the presence of certain other members of the family (e.g., the father can relate to his son only when his wife is not present). We believe, moreover, that there is a basis on which intrapsychic exploration of individual members of the family, in the presence of the family, is therapeutic for the whole family; such "individual" therapy is transitory and is utilized in the overall strategy of treatment for the whole family. Often the family cannot progress unless one key member undergoes a change first; when one member's attitudes and behavior change, the others are forced to change vis-à-vis this person (e.g., if one member no longer invites scapegoating, the other members cannot really scapegoat that person). Experiences such as these provide the basis for the assertion that the best way to bring about change in another person is to change yourself—a seemingly simple formula which is exceedingly difficult to effect.

Dr. Bell is consistent with his principle of relating to the family as a group when he discourages the family members from talking about relationships with others who are not present in the sessions. Another point of view, however, is that a case can be made for the changing of attitudes in the present members about the absent members. In view of the fact that a person does not respond, say, to mother as she is today but to a distorted image of mother, i.e., to the introject, therapeutic work on the internal image is necessary before the person can handle mother differently. Furthermore, if a grandparent or family lawyer or aunt exercises great influence on this present family, yet does not come to the sessions, not only would it seem artificial to inhibit discussion about this significant peripheral person, but there may be indications for changing this family's attitudes about and relationship to this outside person. (One adolescent boy said that his grandmother was the colonel and his mother the sergeant because his mother called her mother every morning to get her instructions.) We have found it useful to invite the outside influential person to the sessions, but sometimes their existence and the nature of their power is concealed for a long time, and, further, sometimes this significant absent person refuses to attend sessions. Factors such as these led Speck (1967) to involve the wider social network of the family in the therapeutic process. An additional reason for attempting reconstructive change in one or other individuals in the family is that it promotes one of the goals of family therapy—the separateness and differentiation of the members from the "family ego mass" (Bowen, 1966) and the taking of personal responsibility. Contrary to popular thinking, it is not "love" which makes people want to be involved with one another; the more pathogenic and conflictual the relationship the more the parties *have to* be fused and involved with one another: it is not safe to be too close or too distant and the homeostatic emotional temperature must be regulated at a tolerable level. Adolescents can separate from parents and form families of their own only when things have been settled somewhat; the worse the relationship with the parents the harder it is for the adolescent to separate (except, say, by joining the hippies, self-destructively).

Shifting now to a different dimension of family therapy, the concept mentioned earlier—namely, the transference distortions which family members have toward each other, some family therapists have noted that irrational feelings are not just misdirected onto therapists but are even more likely to occur among close relationships. A family member is not just a person with a certain instrumental role for another member; he or she is one who fills or does not fill powerful human needs. Struggles over love, disappointments, gratifications, hurts and jealousies, whether real or in fantasy, constitute the hidden substance of family life, as novelists and playwrights have known for centuries. The motivational fits, misalignments, and cleavages in the family can represent one of the most important avenues of exploration for family therapy. The full emotional impact of family systems is subject to ready denial, especially when one considers how everyone, including professional family therapists, are stuck in the morass of their own family systems. When one explores the family from this vantage point, one learns that family members feel toward and react to other members as mother, father, grandparent, or sibling—but not with the member with this natural role; daughter may be seen as sister by her mother; wife may be seen as mother by her husband; and the small child may be seen as little mother. Parentification of the child, an important concept developed in family therapy, is a striking example of a way that intrafamilial transference attitudes are expressed. Parentification is a complicated phenomenon which can assume many different forms and can operate under many guises. Many parents who suffered loss of one or both parents in their early years became fixated in significant aspects of their personality development at the time of their loss; when these people have children they often relate to them unconsciously as if they were the lost parent, and in this way they delay further the mourning process and thus avoid the pain of the loss. Parentification may be obvious, such as when a parent invites the child to intervene in a battle with the mate; it may also be disguised in the form of overgiving to the child, not being able to set limits, or letting the child take over the household. One mother we saw could not understand why her child would go into a rage when she presented him with a menu for dinner every night offering him a wide choice of food; this same mother said to her child during a therapy session, "Tell me what kind of mother you want me to be, and I'll be it." Because the parents are still attempting to perpetuate or master old conflicts from their family of origin they project onto selected children qualities or traits which often are not even remotely connected with the actual personality of the child (although the child is often trained to acquire that trait). The child must be seen as lazy, oversexed, affectionate, mean, as mother's protector, as father's antidepressant, as a bum, as an offering to God, as brilliant, as sick, or what have you, and these views are impervious to reality considerations. The children also project their own fantasies onto parents inasmuch as they, too, deal with introjects of the parents as well as the real parents. Since working with these underlying, subjective realities of family life is extremely demanding on the therapists, many family therapists work as cotherapy teams.

When Dr. Bell refers to the "problem-solving function of the family therapy" and says that "the family must keep the task focus on that which is to benefit the group," I recognize that he had to use a kind of shorthand to describe an intricate process; nonetheless I find it difficult to connect this description with my own experiences of how problems are presented or handled by a family. The construct "problem" is one about which there is a great deal of confusion in psychotherapy. From an individual point of view, a person has a problem when there is something about himself that he wishes to change but cannot, i.e., he is in conflict, has a symptom which gives him pain, wishes he were more outgoing, or any one of the thousands of ways people are dissatisfied with themselves. If this person's "problem" is someone else's behavior (e.g, a parent who is disturbed by her child's firesetting or a man who says he is unhappy because of his wife's nagging), then one has to think of "problem" in a different kind of way. The complaint is a problem for the complainer but may not be one for the object of the complaint. (The wife may say, "What my husband calls 'nagging' is not a problem to me. That's *his* problem.") When therapists ask the family, "What is your problem?" the response may be blank looks or a kind of paralyzed silence, because many families cannot put their difficulties into words, even though inferentially they present a host of dilemmas. Often a family spokesman labels some one person in the family, usually the family scapegoat, as "the problem." Once the scapegoating mechanism is out of the way, however, there is rarely unanimity among the family members as to what the problems are. As in all forms of therapy, the definitions of the problems undergo frequent change as therapy progresses and awareness widens. The situation is usually that one person in the family wants another person to change in some way—be more loving, take a stronger stand, change an attitude, etc. Once the family members come to trust the therapists each will relate his secret strategy for what he hoped to get out of the therapy, and these secret agendas usually call for change to take place in others in the family which will benefit himself. Once family therapy is underway it is difficult for me to conceive that there will be a "group problem" for the family to be focused upon and whose task it is to solve. Aside from scapegoating, which is promoted with the explicit or implicit concurrence of the entire family, including the scapegoat, the only other kinds of families I have seen who maintain a group position are the "pseudo-mutual" ones described by Wynne et al. (1958) who cling to the myth that they are together on issues.

Another major level in the definition of problems resides in the therapist who makes his own dynamic constructions. In general, the problems that patients find easiest to talk about are not the important ones as viewed by the therapist. Parents can be very disturbed by their child's stealing, yet be indifferent to his being withdrawn or friendless. (For example, one parent said to her sexually promiscuous daughter, "What do you need friends for? You have me.") If a child refuses to attend school, objectively the problem is one of truancy; dynamically it may represent an attempt by the child to save his parents' marriage or to stay home to protect a husbandless, lonely mother. If a father can only complain about his child's stealing or destructiveness, yet gives many clues that he is "suggesting" the acting out and fostering it, what is the problem? A dyad, triad, or whole family can share a myth as to the nature of "the problem"—e.g., by agreeing that father is bad and mother is good and that, if mother drinks a great deal, it's because "she needs it for medicine." One wife initially could only see the family's problem as arising from her husband's not showing enough attention to her son, and her husband agreed, but as the material developed and she stated, "I can't be a mother to this boy," the therapists were able to show her how she had been projecting onto her husband her own rejecting feelings about her son. The presenting problems of many people seem trivial or pointless at first: one husband and wife said they had argued for twenty years over the fact that the wife would not put soap in the bathroom, and that one of them would always forget to put the cap back on the toothpaste tube. The therapist needs to relate the feelings to the real issues. This principle reminds me of the Sid Caesar skit in which the husband comes into a room and sees his wife kissing another man; at this point he adopts a reasonable attitude about the incident, saying that, after all, they are civilized people and can discuss it intelligently, but later he gets into a tremendous argument with the man about the way he makes martinis. One family presented as one of their main problems the fact that the family never ate a meal together. Mother complained that she had to cook separate dinners and serve them at different times, but she went along with the situation; father complained that his wife did not have dinner ready when he got home, but he would arrive home at different times; the children said that mother wanted to serve dinner before they were hungry. When the suggestion was made that the family work it out on their own so they could eat together (a seemingly simple task), left to their own devices they floundered, could not come to a joint agreement, and kept bringing in extraneous issues. When the therapists attempted to work it out with the family, they found their heads spinning and wondered if they were going crazy when they ran smack up against the massive rationalizations and use of the game of "Yes, but" (Berne, 1965). Until the therapists dealt with the conflicts which underlay the superficial problems (e.g., collusive avoidance of intimacy and closeness, withdrawal from controversies which were regarded as even more deadly), the conflicts were expressed in another area (e.g., mother and father gave many reasons why they could not sleep together). There is often a common element which connects apparently dissimilar conflicts. As Dr. Bell warns, it is not so much that the therapist should define a course for a family based on his own omniscience but rather that he intervene in order to make sense out of the productions, that he try to discover the experiential realities of the family relationships. When Dr. Bell states that "the therapist's task is the therapy; the family's task is solving the family problem" (a distinction I have some difficulty understanding), it does seem that he would be less likely to work at these levels of activity and interpretation. Still, in an earlier publication (Bell, 1961) he does specify modes of interpretation that he uses (the reflective, the connective, the reconstructive, and the normative), which leads me to suspect that in the actual therapy situation we may function similarly. Dr. Bell, I am sure, is more humanly involved and less technique oriented than he sounds in his writings.

Dr. Bell indicates that in his strategy of staying out of the family group he avoids making decisions for the family. While we may evade the question, "What would you do?" or turn it back to the questioner, we have found it useful at times to state our view clearly; this technique, appropriately timed, not only makes the therapist more real as a person who takes a stand but often helps the family members question their behavior and motives, and this in turn can lead to deeper exploration. For example, one father told the male therapist that he came home every day from work to wash the dishes and clean the house because his wife claimed she wasn't feeling well, and when he asked the therapist, "What would you do?" the therapist replied that he wouldn't do it except in an emergency. This interchange then led to exploration of the father's background, and it was learned that he had played the role of housewife with his mother after his father died. The wife was also led to questioning her motives in always being ill when her husband got home. To be sure, there are greater risks and complications when the therapist gets more involved with the family; feelings are stronger and transference and countertransference phenomena are intensified as underlying motivations are explored and the substance of the family system is threatened. Indeed, we would find the therapy task extremely difficult without the help of a cotherapist who can pull his colleague out of the family mass entanglement. An additional important point to be kept in mind is that it is insufficient and may be antitherapeutic to interpret, to expose myths, and to open up walled-off areas; in our judgment it is necessary to follow through and do the painstaking "working through" which constitutes the bulk and real labor of therapy.

Utilizing a variety of techniques to facilitate open communication in the family so as to tap the family's inherent motivation to improve itself, Dr. Bell indicates that he avoids determining goals for the family, and that he stays close to the family's present value system. When the family gets to the point where it grapples with larger questions of value he advocates calling on the assistance of educational and religious agencies. Dr. Bell raises here an intriguing question of the extent to which family goals and values can or should be modified in family therapy. Considerable controversy has surrounded this issue in individual psychotherapy. Value issues concerning the family, the basic unit of society, are even more loaded and deserve extended discussion beyond the purposes of this paper. We find that in our intensive, extended work with families their value systems are shaken up and often do undergo fundamental reorganization, but until more investigation is done on what constitutes a healthy family in the context of a given culture we would defer judgment on what a family should be. We have relied, instead, on such operational criteria as defining generational boundaries, strengthening marital ties, increasing the members' capacities to love and relate closely without suffocation and at the same time to be free to separate and explore an individual definition of self (which may be quite different from one's role as formerly viewed by the family), lessening of family or individual pain, and enlarging of the family's capacity to enjoy life. It is necessary to stress that this ideology does not mention "insight" as a major goal, although insight may be involved. No one really knows what the critical ingredients of improvement are for any form of psychotherapy, much less the more intricate family therapy situation (e.g., whether the ingredients involve the experience itself, improvement of communication, identification with the therapist, etc.).

During the past decade or so family therapy has moved from relative obscurity and controversy to a position of major significance in psychotherapy. For a long time the field was under the same kind of attacks as was the field of psychoanalysis in its early years. The family field is respectable now and has become a part of the standard armamentarium of psychotherapy. The growth of the field has been tremendous. The workshops and seminars on family therapy at professional conventions continue to be crowded, and numerous articles and books on the subject are appearing. Local family institutes have been established, and attempts to create a national organization have been undertaken. The movement has been interdisciplinary from its beginnings, with social workers, psychiatrists, and psychologists working together in a model of interdisciplinary cooperation. To some extent, however, the family approach has been overbought by some and has been applied inappropriately at times. There is general agreement that prior experience in individual and conventional group therapy, while prerequisite, is insufficient for the practice of family therapy; specialized training is necessary, and already a number of family therapy organizations around the country are offering training programs.

Because the foundation of any field is its research findings, a whole new area of systematic investigation of family interaction has begun, both in the family therapy situation and in the laboratory. Family interaction research relies on responses of family members to each other rather than to the investigator, and in the laboratory studies the family is typically presented with a standard task or game, and coded measurements are taken on how the members collectively handle the task. (For a survey of the field of family interaction research the reader is referred to Framo, 1965b.) Not only do such studies provide information about basic family processes, but they have practical clinical implications. For example, there is agreement that traditional methods of one-to-one psychological testing are not only inefficient timewise and unable to meet the evaluation needs of the community mental health centers, but individual testing also reinforces designation of one individual as the patient. There have been some developments in research methods which evaluate groups of related people—e.g., the Family Rorschach (Loveland, Wynne, & Singer, 1963). A national conference on Systematic Research on Family Interaction was recently held at the Eastern

Pennsylvania Psychiatric Institute and the proceedings are being prepared for publication (Framo & Boszormenyi-Nagy, in press).

Technical issues of the *therapy* of the family aside, Dr. Bell and I agree on the potential contribution of the principles of family system theory, not only in clinical practice but as a fundamental reorientation toward psychopathology and thinking about the nature of man. By recasting the nature of emotional disturbance in concepts which recognize that behavior which seems disturbed or maladaptive from an individual point of view may be seen as not only adaptive but necessary when viewed in its natural familial habitat, a meaningful alternative is offered to the medical model predicament of psychiatry which requires a *patient* with an *illness*. There are numerous practical consequences which result from slavish adherence to the individual theory of illness. How often will we see situations where one child after another from the same family will be taken for treatment by the parents, without anything essentially changing? How many unnecessary divorces will there be because husband and wife seeing two therapists separately never had an opportunity to examine the interlocking and transactional nature of their dyadic pathology? Dr. Bell has very wisely pointed out that isolation and institutionalization of problem persons—placement in hospitals, foster homes, delinquent institutions, homes for the aged, etc.—may be outgrowths of pressures from families who utilize professionals to lend the stamp of official authenticity to their extrusion process. It is suggested that with increasing realization of the real meaning and impact of the family point of view, the community mental health centers will in time become family centers. (For example, family therapy principles will be useful in the training of nonprofessional community workers going into people's homes.) The value of family diagnostic interviews as a routine intake procedure has been discovered as the best way of evaluating what is really going on, even in those situations where family therapy is not indicated or feasible. The practice of seeing families in the midst of an acute crisis can result in better-aimed therapeutic intervention, as for example in suicide attempts; marital crises; sudden personality changes or outbreaks of symptoms; after an adolescent has been arrested, been truant, been taking LSD, become a hippie, etc. The family approach lends itself as a central integrative process for the entire scope of clinical services in a community mental health center. After several family evaluation sessions the team is in a better position to determine which of a variety of treatment methods are indicated— such as hospitalization, day hospital, group therapy, family therapy, individual therapy, etc. Those therapists who have had experience in seeing families together find that they approach individual therapy in a different way thereafter.

The family approach is likely to have an impact in areas unforeseen at this time. For instance, the educational system of this country is over-burdened because the expectation of the community is that schools should counteract and make up for deficiencies in the home life; too many problems are seen as school problems which are really family problems. The family approach has implications for the poverty programs and civil rights movement, considering especially the Moynihan report on the Negro family. It should be emphasized, however, that we have hardly begun to understand the dynamics of transpersonal motivational systems, that the theoretical constructs of family therapy are still in the stage of hypothesis formation, and therapeutic techniques are still rudimentary. Although a body of knowledge does exist, most family therapists espouse the position of searching inquiry, exploration, and investigation in their efforts at achieving greater understanding. A personal social psychology is the portent of the future, since what a person is to, and for, himself is intertwined with what he is to, and for, others who are close to him.

REFERENCES

Bell, J. E. *Family group therapy*. Public Health Monograph 64. Washington, D. C.: United States Department of Health, Education, and Welfare, 1961.

Berne, E. *Games people play*. New York: Grove Press, 1965.

Bowen, M. The use of family theory in clinical practice. *Comprehensive Psychiatry*, 1966, 7, 345–374.

Coffey, H. S. Review of *Intensive family therapy*. *Contemporary Psychology*, 1967, 12, 358–359.

Fairbairn, W. R. D. *An object-relations theory of the personality*. New York: Basic Books, 1952.

Framo, J. L. Rationale and techniques of intensive family therapy. In I. Boszormenyi-Nagy & J. L. Framo (Eds.), *Intensive family therapy*. New York: Hoeber Medical Division of Harper & Row, 1965. (a)

Framo, J. L. Systematic research on family dynamics. In I. Boszormenyi-Nagy & J. L. Framo (Eds.), *Intensive family therapy*. New York: Hoeber Medical Division of Harper & Row, 1965. (b)

Framo, J. L., & Boszormenyi-Nagy, I. *Research on family interaction: An encounter between family researchers and family therapists*. Palo Alto: Science & Behavior Books, in press.

Klein, M. *Contributions to psycho-analysis*. London: Hogarth Press, 1950.

Loveland, N. T., Wynne, L. C., & Singer, M. T. The family Rorschach: A new method for studying family interaction. *Family Process*, 1963, 2, 187–215.

Speck, R. V. Psychotherapy of the social network of a schizophrenic family. *Family Process*, 1967, 6, 208–214.

Wynne, L. C., Ryckoff, I. M., Day, J., & Hirsch, S. I. Pseudomutuality in the family relations of schizophrenia. *Psychiatry*, 1958, 21, 205–220.

CHAPTER 14

A Constant Frame of Reference for a Therapist with a Family

Robert MacGregor

In his article "A Theoretical Position for Family Group Therapy" John Elderkin Bell gives a fine exposition of the freedom to be gained by the exercise of discipline. He shows how he ensures maximum usefulness to the family in treatment by invoking a number of rules. These are rules of group and individual therapy by which the therapist holds the scene steady enough that he can view the figure-ground relationships of complex behavior. "The therapist must keep his distance, stay out of the family, and restrict his work to the therapy; . . . [he] tries to make his actions accord with the rules he imposes on himself. He orients the family to the limits he will adopt and then holds to them firmly and unambiguously." He regards requests to see the therapist separately as a resistance: "We will insist on having all members of the family come to all sessions. I expect attendance and postpone meetings if someone cannot come."

The theoretical position is simply that "the family is the problem," implying a social and psychological orientation. Such an orientation is a significant achievement, as may be seen in the work of Alfred Friedman and the Philadelphia Psychiatric Center, in *Psychotherapy for the Whole Family* (1965), in which a group of psychotherapists report their struggle to move from the intrapsychic view of psychopathology toward a view that would deal with the family as a malfunctioning social organism. Bell finds extra strength for the influence of family group therapy as he differentiates it from group therapy. It is in part *because* the group existed before the therapy and may move into the future as a

This chapter is a discussion-commentary, written especially for the present volume, of Chapter 12: "A Theoretical Position for Family Group Therapy," by John E. Bell.

group that change initiated in a therapy hour may have more pervasive effect. He sees this as due to twenty-four-hour-a-day support and
reinforcement.

Bell conceptualizes the problem for which a family seeks therapy as
a disturbance in the balance of forces by which the family operates.
Family group therapy aims at changing the structure and balance of
the family by permitting the inclusion of new patterns of behavior in the
family system. Patterns with which some family members have some
outside contact are allowed entrée to the family repertoire, because the
therapist represents the outside community's influence. The process is
described in terms of communications work, but it does seem to be
more a matter of breaching a relatively closed and defensive system so
that it may receive nurture from without and become a relatively open
system, able to grow. It seems likely that the growth experience that Bell
describes for himself may have come from moving with his special
view into the family from the closed-system notions that speak only of
a changed balance of forces or homeostatic change (Jackson, 1957)
toward those of dealing with the living system. Therapy for the system
is at times needed so that it will not defensively ward off the information and new experience necessary to growth, as another living system
may protect a cancer or reject a transplanted organ.

Family group therapy as developed by Bell has, in common with
other forms of family therapy conducted by a single therapist, the expensive requirement of therapist neutrality and a format of scheduled
sessions of about an hour one or more times per week. This reviewer has
found (MacGregor, Ritchie, & Serrano, 1964) that a team can afford
its members the opportunity to experience the family system more
directly, particularly when the work is scheduled to include both group
and individual sessions in the same day. The meeting as a group and
never separately seems to be necessitated by the one-therapist con-
straint. Most therapists who have not excluded family contact from
their work will recognize the economy of Bell's self-imposed rules.
Multiple-therapist methods which allow one team member to monitor
another's involvement are difficult to schedule and expensive in professional personnel. Their economy lies in fewer and more widely spaced
sessions, but sessions of greater length. An answer to the question of
whether one or another method produces lasting results in an overall
shorter period of time awaits improvement in psychotherapy research
methodology.

The importance of this contribution lies in its evidence that Bell, who
in his pioneering 1961 Public Health Monograph on a family in treat-

ment, has been able to use this application of group therapy as a constant frame of reference and a special entrée to the family. He has thus demonstrated the greater appropriateness to clinical work of socio-psychological notions, and in particular the usefulness of those notions which relate systematic thinking in general to the problems of living systems.

Family therapy is meanwhile being developed in many directions, starting from procedures that therapists have already mastered. In this case the procedure is called family group therapy, and the disciplines of individual and group therapy provide the points of observable departure. Others have used the developing methodology and rationale for crisis intervention as a frame of reference. Frank S. Pittman (1966) and his team from the Family Treatment Unit at the Colorado Psychopathic Hospital in Denver combine in many ways to circumvent the crisis of impending hospitalization. Minuchin (1965), using a conflict-resolution model, divides the family between alternating groups of participant and observers. Norman Paul (1967), perhaps influenced by Lindeman's study of those bereaved by the Coconut Grove fire (which study spawned the crises theory), used the grief process as a model for a family therapy procedure called "Operational Mourning."

A number of systematically small steps amounting to a big leap have moved family work from the tape recorder in the room to the video-tape playback. Minuchin, in the study cited above, had family members join him behind a one-way mirror, and Paul, in the study already cited, had families listen to the playback of crucial sections of the tape of the current session. Another pioneer is Charles Fulweiler (1959), who, during the 1950s, had families meet in front of a one-way mirror to discuss their problem. When the discussion reached an impasse, Fulweiler would knock on the door, enter, straighten out the discussion or reorient it, and leave so they could continue.

Another direction, related to the need for a constant frame of reference, has set families at home, in the clinic waiting room, and, as in Fulweiler's probation department, behind a one-way mirror. Generally described as the "Revealed Differences" method (Titchener & Golden, 1963), its users propose rather standard problems to the family and use a variety of techniques for analysis of the recorded results. Strodtbeck (Bales & Strodtbeck, 1953) has used it in homes in a wide variety of cultures and subcultures, scoring the recorded interview with Bales' Interaction Process Analysis. In contrast, Haley (1965) had family therapists listen to tapes of families deciding on the color of an automobile to find out whether from interaction, intonation, or other cues they could tell which family yielded a psychotic or a delinquent. Ravich and his colleagues (1966) have been studying marital discord using the standard scene and hardware of a model electric truck on a track, a problem designed by Deutsch to study decision making.

There appears to be a gap between the clinical researchers who tend to express their innovations in the form of treatment methods, syndromes, proposed typology, and interpersonal patterns ranging from the "charge nurse syndrome" to the "absent patient maneuver," and the research methodologists who take a "lesser included offense," give it operational statement, and then set up a simulated situation from which quick measurable phenomena can be observed. The method of clinical research is that of controlled description and repeated observation. Holding some of the scene constant is crucial, but the measurability of the result is less.

More in the manner of applied scientists, in contrast to clinical researchers, those of us who have tested our ideas by organizing the viewing mechanism into a pattern of therapy also have a constant frame of reference. MacGregor (1964) and his colleagues in Galveston developed standard multiple-therapist procedures to be used in a variety of ways predictable according to a proposed typology. If the method can be pursued according to the typology, it is a vote for either the method or the typology.

Much of the family work so far has held typology constant, because the studies have been of families with a schizophrenic member. While the older studies of family process were derived from sociological and anthropological approaches and left the dynamic core of the family as an unexplained "black box," the newer studies have used schizophrenic processes as the model for what is in the "black box." Bowen's "Family Ego Mass" (1965), Lidz's "Transmission of Irrationality" (1965), Wynne's "Pseudomutuality" (1958), Jackson's "Family Homeostasis" (1957), and Ivan Boszormenyi-Nagy's effort (1965) to extend the psychoanalytic language to account for family processes all reflect this.

Bell's work with family group therapy, as presented to the American Psychological Association in Boston, April 1953 (Bell, 1961), started out as a "method for treating children" and seems to have been more clearly associated with the development of methods of intervention and diagnosis which appeared later in the work of Nathan Ackerman (1958). Ackerman also developed his method of diagnosis and treatment as a one-man family therapist working with outpatients who did not usually present a schizophrenic family member.

Family therapy as a window to the family offers many possibilities for revision of the view from the outside. This view has affirmed much that we see in society: that parents seem concerned about competitive behavior and that sibling rivalry is evident. The view from within exposes the tender processes which society prefers not to notice. Collusion, cooperation, and collaboration are much more apparent (MacGregor, 1965). The future of family therapy may be bound up with the future of psychotherapy in moving away from a model based on illness discussed in the detached climate of the doctor's office. Rather, the future may perhaps be in multiple-therapist methods scheduled in ways to which present practice has difficulty adjusting. "The Growing Edge" is the title of an interview with Carl Whitaker (Haley & Hoffman, 1967), who has developed multiple-therapist techniques begun by Rudolph Dreikurs (1957) to their present subtlety as a way of opening a closed system rather than as an invasion of privacy. Certainly, current child guidance clinic practice has overwhelmingly adopted the team family interview as an intake, a diagnostic and treatment planning session.

REFERENCES

Ackerman, N. W. *The psychodynamics of family life.* New York: Basic Books, 1958.

Bales, R. F., & Strodtbeck, F. L. Phases in group problem solving. In D. Cartwright & A. F. Zander (Eds.), *Group dynamics: Research and theory.* Evanston: Row, Peterson, & Co., 1953. Pp. 386–400.

Bell, J. E. *Family group therapy.* Public Health Monograph 64. Washington, D. C.: United States Department of Health, Education and Welfare, 1961. Also reprinted as Family group therapy—a new treatment method for children. In *Family Process*, 1967, 6, 254–263.

Boszormenyi-Nagy, I., & Framo, J. L. (Eds.) *Intensive family therapy: Theoretical and practical aspects.* New York: Harper & Row, 1965.

Bowen, M. Family psychotherapy with schizophrenia in the hospitals and private practice. In I. Boszormenyi-Nagy & J. L. Framo (Eds.), *op. cit.*, pp. 213–243.

Cohen, I. M. (Ed). *Family structure dynamics and therapy: Psychiatric research report #20.* Washington, D.C.: American Psychiatric Association, 1966.

Dreikurs, R. Family counseling. In R. Corsini, *Methods of group psychotherapy.* New York: McGraw-Hill, 1957. Pp. 180–197.

Friedman, A. *Psychotherapy for the whole family.* New York: Springer, 1965. See review by R. MacGregor in *Contemporary Psychology*, 1967, 12, 86–87.

Fulweiler, C. Panel presentation. In Family oriented diagnosis and psychotherapy. Symposium presented at the American Psychological Association, Cincinnati, September 1959.

Haley, J. Panel presentation at the University of Kansas Eighth Annual Institute, Research in family group therapy, April 1965.

Haley, J., & Hoffman, L. *Techniques of family therapy*. New York: Basic Books, 1967. Pp. 265–360.

Jackson, D. D. The question of family homeostasis. *Psychiatric Quarterly Supplement*, 1957, *31*, 79–90.

Lidz, T., Fleck, S., & Cornelison, A. R. *Schizophrenia and the family*. New York: International University Press, 1965.

MacGregor, R., Ritchie, A., Serrano, A. C., et al. *Multiple impact therapy with families*. New York: McGraw-Hill, 1964.

MacGregor, R. Competition, compromise and collusion. Paper presented at the University of Kansas Eighth Annual Institute, Research in family group therapy, April 1965.

Minuchin S. Conflict resolution family therapy. *Psychiatry*, 1965, *28*, 278–286.

Paul, N. L. The role of mourning and empathy in conjoint marital therapy. In G. H. Zuk & I. Boszormenyi-Nagy (Eds.), *Family therapy and disturbed families*. Palo Alto: Science and Behavior Books, 1967. Pp. 186–205.

Paul, N. L. Effects of playback on family members of their own previously recorded conjoint marital therapy. In I. M. Cohen (Ed.), *Family structure dynamics and therapy: Psychiatric research report #20*. Washington, D.C.: American Psychiatric Association, 1966. Pp. 175–187.

Pittman, F., et al. Family therapy as an alternative to hospitalization. In I. M. Cohen (Ed.), *op. cit.*, pp. 188–195.

Ravich, R. A., Deutsch, M., & Brown, B. An experimental study of decision making. In I. M. Cohen (Ed.), *op. cit.*, pp. 91–94.

Titchener, J. L., & Golden, M. Prediction of therapeutic themes from observation of family interaction through the "revealed difference" technique. *Journal of Nervous and Mental Diseases*, 1963, *136*, 464–474.

Wynne, L. C., Ryckoff, I. M., Day, J., & Hirsch, S. I. Pseudomutuality in the family relations of schizophrenics. *Psychiatry*, 1958, *21*, 205–220.

CHAPTER 15

American Psychotherapy in Perspective

Jerome D. Frank

Human beings spend most of their lives interacting with each other. In the process they influence each other powerfully for good or ill. This book has singled out for study one particular class of influencing procedures—the psychotherapy of adults. This is a help-giving process in which a professionally trained person, sometimes with the aid of a group, tries to relieve certain types of distress by facilitating changes in attitudes. As a relationship in which one person tries to induce changes in another, psychotherapy has much in common with child-rearing, education, and various forms of leadership. Its closest affinities, however, are with time-limited interactions between a sufferer and specially trained persons that stress either healing or attitude change. The former include therapeutic rituals in primitive societies and healing religious shrines in our own, the latter religious revivalism and Communist thought reform.

This chapter attempts to recapitulate the main points emerging from our survey, with special reference to their implications for psychotherapy in America today. Features that American psychotherapies share with other forms of interpersonal healing and influence are stressed. The justification for relative neglect of characteristics that might distinguish them from each other and from other healing methods is that such characteristics would gain significance only to the extent that the results produced by them cannot be accounted for by their common features. Despite the voluminous literature delineating differences between schools of psychotherapy, convincing evidence is lacking that these correspond to any important differences in the immediate or long-term

This chapter was voted, by the Editorial Board of the present volume, as one of the creative developments in psychotherapy, 1958–1968. From Jerome D. Frank, *Persuasion and Healing*, (Baltimore: The Johns Hopkins Press, 1961).

results. Perhaps when common features of different psychotherapies and their effects are better understood, certain of their divergencies will become important.[1]

PSYCHIATRIC ILLNESS AND PSYCHOTHERAPY

Psychiatric illnesses and psychotherapies are intimately interwoven with their sociocultural settings. The illnesses are the results or expressions of disharmonies within a person and between him and his society. Because a person's patterns of perceiving and relating to others reflect his internal psychic state, and affect it in turn, these are two sides of the same coin. Moreover, the cause-effect sequence runs both ways. A person's internal harmony or conflict affects his relationships with others, and his interpersonal experiences influence his internal state. They may disorganize him, as seen in the primitive who dies from a witch's curse, or help him to reintegrate himself, as in religious conversion.

Cultural factors determine to a large extent which conditions are singled out as targets of the influencing process, and how they manifest themselves. The same phenomena may be viewed as signs of mental illness in one society, of demoniacal possession in another, and as eccentricities to be ignored in a third. Moreover, the behavior of the afflicted person is greatly influenced by culturally determined expectations as to how persons so defined should behave.

Since the distress is related to the behavior of the person in his totality, it involves all levels of his functioning. Purely psychic and purely bodily disorders exist only as logical extremes of a continuum. Although the locus of the major disturbance may differ considerably in the different types of distress with which we have been concerned, the biological, psychological, and social components are always all involved to some degree.

The aim of psychotherapy is to relieve distress by encouraging beneficial changes in all aspects of personal functioning. Emotionally it tries to produce an optimal level of excitation to facilitate change, quieting the overexcited patient and stimulating the apathetic or complacent one. At a combined cognitive-emotional level it tries to engender his hopes and strengthen his self-esteem. In the cognitive realm it attempts to supply him with new information and new ways of perceiving what he already knows, to enable him to straighten out his assumptive systems concerning himself and persons close to him. Socially, it tries to foster improvement in his interpersonal behavior, so that he gains more satisfaction and suffers less frustration in his interactions with others.

Attainment of these goals is sought through the performance of certain prescribed activities in the context of a particular relationship between the healer (often assisted by a group) and the patient. Both activities and relationship are determined in part by aspects of the culture, especially its assumptive world and the culturally sanctioned training of the healer.

In all cultures, however, the relationship seems to have three features. First, the influencer (and group) genuinely care about the sufferer's welfare. They are deeply committed to bringing about the kind of change they deem desirable and expend considerable effort in the attempt. Second, the influencing figures have a certain ascendancy or power, which may rest on a variety of interrelated attributes. These may include their socially determined role and status, their ability to inspire the sufferer's expectation of relief, and their control of means of coercion. Their ascendancy enables them to exert more or less direct pressure on him and sometimes encourages him to imitate or emulate them. Third, the influencer mediates between the person being influenced, the influencing group (if there is one), and the larger society. In many cases he also represents suprapersonal—often supernatural—forces that are postulated by the group's world view and that the sufferer must appease or win over.

The specific means of guidance is a ritual or task that is viewed as the way by which the sufferer is brought to see the errors of his ways and correct them, thereby gaining relief. The task requires the active participation of all involved and is typically repetitive. Some therapeutic or influencing tasks closely prescribe the sufferer's activities; others impel him to take the initiative and the influencing figures reward statements that accord with the requirements of the treatment scheme and discourage those that do not.

The influencing process expresses and is guided by a conceptual system that includes illness and health, the deviant and the normal. It explains the cause of the sufferer's distress and specifies desirable goals for him. It cannot be shaken by him or by his failure to gain relief. Acceptance of it gives him a means for understanding his distress and of regaining a sense of unity with his fellows, so that it becomes a way of promoting both internal and external harmony.

American psychotherapy is colored by certain interrelated features of American society, notably its diversity, the high value it places on democracy and science, and the methods of training psychotherapists.

The diversity of American society permits the co-existence of various therapies based on differing conceptual schemes representing the value systems of different subcultures. This may have certain virtues. A patient whose outlook is at variance with one group may find acceptance in another, that is, he need not conform to one particular life style in order to gain healing group support. Moreover, variations among different groups enable the psychiatrist to represent attitudes and values differing from those of the patient. If the differences are not too great, they may help the latter to gain some new and useful perspectives on his problems. On the other hand, differences in world view of psychiatrist and patient, based on differences in their backgrounds, may more or less seriously impede communication between them. In addition, the absence of a single, all-embracing world view shared by the patient, the therapist, and the larger society limits the amount of pressure the therapist can mobilize to help the patient change his attitudes. No form of American psychotherapy can approximate the influencing power of primitive healing or thought reform in this respect, though perhaps an ideal therapeutic community, which completely immerses the patient in a culture expressing a self-consistent assumptive world, could approach it.

Despite the variety of American culture, almost all segments place a high value on democracy and science. The democratic ideal assigns a high worth to individual self-fulfillment. It regards behavior that is apparently self-directed as more admirable than behavior apparently caused by external pressures. Thus it values independence of thought and action, within limits, and the rebel or deviate, if not too extreme, may continue to count on group tolerance and even respect. The whole concept of the therapeutic community, with its view of the hospital inmate as a responsible person entitled to kindness, understanding, and respect, is an expression of the democratic world view.

The scientific ideal reinforces the democratic one by valuing lack of dogmatism. It also values objectivity and intellectual comprehension, and these features may not be entirely advantageous for psychotherapy. They tend to result in an overevaluation of its cognitive aspects. From the patient's standpoint, "insight" in the sense of ability to verbalize self-understanding may be mistaken for genuine attitude change. From the therapist's standpoint, the scientific attitude may lead to undue stress on the niceties of interpretation and avoidance of frankly emotion-arousing techniques such as group rituals and dramatic activities, even though there is universal agreement that in order to succeed psychotherapy must involve the patient's emotions.

Both democratic and scientific ideals tend to cause many American therapists to underestimate the extent to which psychotherapy is an influencing process. Members of a democracy do not like to see themselves as exercising power over someone else, and the scientist observes —he does not influence. So the most prestigious forms of psychotherapy in America are termed scientific and permissive though in many respects they are neither.

Within the broad framework of the democratic, scientific world view, American psychotherapy embodies the values of the medical tradition on the one hand and psychoanalysis on the other. Since psychoanalysis was founded by a physician, it shares some aspects of the medical orientation, but also differs in certain respects.

The physician's role is an exception to the over-all democratic pattern of relationships in America. He is expected to be authoritarian with his patients. Psychoanalysis rejects this aspect of the medical orientation and also diverges from it in stressing psychological rather than bodily causes of distress. It shares the medical viewpoint that the physician's primary obligation is to his patient, with its corollary insistence on the privacy of the doctor-patient relationship. In this regard it also accepts, though with reservations, the medical conceptualization of illness as residing primarily in the patient.

Actually, psychiatric illness often seems to be the expression of a disturbed interactional system involving several persons. The one who comes to treatment becomes labeled as the patient by this act, but the major locus of the disturbance may well lie elsewhere.[2] Acceptance of the medical view of mental illness has led to neglect of group and community forces in production and relief of distress and maintenance of beneficial changes. Although theories of psychotherapy increasingly recognize that disturbed interpersonal relationships in childhood are related to maladaptations of adult life, they regard the causal sequence as running primarily from the adult patient's internal disharmonies to his external ones. This results in an undue emphasis on helping him to resolve his internal conflicts in the belief that resolution of the external difficulties will necessarily follow. Exploration of the potentialities of the reverse procedure, namely trying to resolve external conflicts as a means of facilitating resolution of inner ones, or working at both levels simultaneously, has received considerable impetus from group therapy and the therapeutic community, so this one-sidedness may soon be rectified.

The divergent views of medicine and psychoanalysis with regard to the major etiological factors in illness may have contributed not only to the relative neglect of bodily factors in mental illness and of physical and pharmacological remedies by psychologically oriented psychiatrists, but also to their overemphasis by medically oriented ones. This split bids fair to be resolved by advances in neurophysiology and psychopharmacology, which should eventually make it possible to trace out in some detail the interplay between bodily and mental states.

Differences between medical and psychoanalytic conceptualizations of the role of the therapist are reflected in the division of American psychotherapies into directive and evocative approaches. The former, favored by psychiatrists who have maintained their primary identification as physicians, use the conventional authoritarian physician-patient relationship to instigate behaviors that will expose the patient to corrective experiences. As in the rest of medical practice, treatment is directed towards alleviation of a particular symptom or symptom-complex. Evocative therapies, used by psychiatrists who see themselves primarily as psychotherapists, are modeled on a democratic pattern of relationship and try to evoke a wide range of the patient's attitudes in the treatment situation. The therapist guides the course of therapy to some extent by subtle cues of approval or disapproval.

Long-term evocative therapy involves detailed scrutiny of many aspects of the patient's present and past life, including his reactions to the therapist himself. This may mobilize a variety of emotions, such as resentment, anxiety, and guilt, which may supply incentives for change. The therapist tries to guide the process at a cognitive level by his interpretations.

It is interesting that evocative therapies are usually termed "permissive," which reflects the adherence of therapists using this method to the democratic world view and their corresponding reluctance to recognize the extent to which they influence their patients. A further incentive to overlook the persuasive aspects of this type of treatment lies in the therapist's natural desire to use the patient's productions as independent confirmation of his theories. It is easy to do this because the influencing cues are often so subtle as to escape awareness of both therapist and patient.

In short, American psychotherapy, when viewed against the background of other methods of persuasion and healing, appears to embody certain biases related to the scientific, democratic values of society and to its own medical and psychoanalytic ancestry. These biases have virtues and disadvantages. They imply respect for the patient's individuality, which strengthens his self-esteem, and emphasis on self-understanding, which helps most persons to deal more effectively with the problems of life. On the other hand, they may result in inadequate attention to emotional aspects of the therapeutic process, the role of group forces, and the influencing power of the therapist.

The popularity of religious healing and healing cults in America may be related to the fact that they stress the very areas in which conventional forms of psychotherapy are deficient. Their therapeutic procedures operate in the framework of an infallible theory that explains the patient's troubles and prescribes the methods of cure. The healer glories in his claimed powers and exerts them unabashedly. His own attitudes, in many cases shared and reinforced by a group of believers, strongly mobilize the patient's hopes, and the group helps to sustain any beneficial changes.

Mention of beneficial changes leads to the knotty question of the effectiveness of psychotherapy. This is extraordinarily difficult to evaluate. Nevertheless, a few very tentative generalizations may be ventured. Since the forms of suffering treated by psychotherapy involve all levels of a person's functioning as well as his relations to his group, the effectiveness of these methods is limited by externally and internally fixed boundaries to the patient's adaptive capacities. Externally the benefits of treatment may be limited by unmodifiable environmental stresses, such as serious illness in a family member. Limits to therapeutic benefit are also set by stresses induced by the assumptive systems of the patient's society or by conflicting assumptive systems of the groups to which he belongs. No amount of psychotherapy, for example, can abolish certain stresses confronting a Negro in parts of the South, or those impinging on a child one of whose parents is a militant atheist and the other a devout Catholic.

Resolution of culturally induced stresses lies beyond the psychiatrist's powers. The best he can do is improve the patient's ability to deal with them; their correction lies in the hands of political, social, and religious leaders. He may be able to affect social stresses indirectly by offering insights that help shape the aims and guide the activities of these leaders, but this becomes preventive psychiatry rather than psychotherapy.[3] Internally set limitations to psychotherapeutic effectiveness include biological deficiencies and very deeply ingrained maladaptive patterns resulting from severely damaging life experiences.

To be a good prospect for psychotherapy, a person must have a certain adaptive capacity and flexibility, often referred to as "ego-strength." Qualities like verbal facility and intelligence seem related to ability to profit from most forms of American psychotherapy, partly because these qualities make it easier to play the psychotherapeutic game and also because they go with assumptive systems valuing self-knowledge. Other personal attributes that make persons good candidates for psychotherapy are similar to those related to general accessibility to influence— a high degree of distress, anxiety, self-dissatisfaction, and feelings of social or personal insecurity.

There is a bit of evidence that methods of psychological healing have nonspecific and specific effects. The former are of the nature of symptom relief and seem to result from mobilization of the patient's expectation of help. They therefore usually appear fairly promptly and are unrelated to the type of therapy. The specific effects lie in the realm of changes in attitudes and behavior, and these presumably would differ to some extent depending on the conceptual scheme and method underlying the type of therapy used.

The long-term effects of psychotherapy are especially hard to evaluate because of the fact that the patient continues to be exposed to a bombardment of experiences with beneficial or noxious potentialities during and after treatment.

Whether or not the changes initiated by psychotherapy are sustained depends on the nature of these new stresses and whether the gains achieved through psychotherapy enable the patient to cope with them more successfully than before. Moreover, the extent to which he receives group support for his new attitudes and behavior is probably crucial. Here the existence of many groups with a wide range of ideologies may be an advantage, for if the patient after therapy can no longer find support from his former group, he may be able to get it from a new one. Group support need not be expressed as increased liking. What really counts is whether his new self achieves recognition and respect. He may gain this through being able to embody the group's values more successfully, or, on the contrary, in line with our democratic values he may win increased respect for being able to think and act more independently. In any case, he can more readily maintain changes induced by therapy to the extent that they enable him to feel less derogated and isolated.

Every experienced psychotherapist has treated cases in which therapy seemed to have far-reaching and permanent effects, enabling the patient to reach a level of comfort and effectiveness that he would have been most unlikely to attain without treatment. By and large, however, the effect of successful psychotherapy seems to be to accelerate or facilitate healing processes that would have gone on more slowly in its absence. This is, of course, the function of most medical treatment. If psychotherapists did no more than reduce duration of suffering and disability, this would be well worth their efforts.

It seems that patients come to psychotherapy when they are under internal or external pressures to modify their feelings and behavior, and the psychotherapist assists in the process much as a midwife might at the birth of a baby. What he does may make a lot of difference in how smoothly or rapidly the process occurs, but the extent to which he causes it is uncertain.

IMPLICATIONS FOR RESEARCH

As this survey has made evident, though there is an abundance of clinical lore, the amount of experimentally verified knowledge about psychotherapeutic processes is disappointingly meager. This is not through want of trying, as psychotherapy has absorbed the attention of many able investigators and been amply supported financially during the past decade.[4] Though this is not the place for detailed consideration of research aspects of psychotherapy, a brief attempt to make explicit some of the major areas of difficulty and the most promising directions of progress seems appropriate.[5]

One set of problems arises from the conditions of psychotherapeutic practice. Most experienced psychiatrists have a considerable emotional involvement in the efficacy of their methods. Each has become expert in a particular mode of psychotherapy as the result of long and arduous training. His self-esteem, status, and financial security are linked to its effectiveness. Under these circumstances he can hardly be expected to be an impartial student of his own method, and any data he reports cannot escape the suspicion of bias. Theoretically there is an easy solution to this dilemma, which is to separate the roles of researcher and therapist. The psychiatrist would permit himself to be observed by trained researchers through a one-way vision screen or by means of sound films and tape recordings of interviews. Unfortunately, many of the most sophisticated and experienced psychotherapists are unwilling to submit their work to this sort of systematic impartial scrutiny.

The obvious objection that such an examination would constitute an unacceptable infringement of the psychiatrists' confidential relationships with their patients is reinforced by other less clearly articulated misgivings. Objective study of psychiatrists' methods entails certain risks. It might turn out that what they actually do differs from what they say they do, that changes in the patients are not caused by the maneuvers to which they attribute them, and that their results are no better than those obtained by practitioners of other methods. All in all, they can hardly be blamed for subscribing to a bit of wisdom attributed to Confucius, "A wise man does not examine the source of his well being." But the effect of his prudence is to force researchers in psychotherapy to study treatment as carried out by younger therapists who are often still in training, and the results obtained are always open to question on the grounds that the therapists were insufficiently experienced.[6] Although reluctance of experienced psychiatrists to participate in research has been a serious obstacle, it is gradually yielding to the persistent blandishments of researchers.

A similar type of superficial but troublesome hindrance to psychotherapy research arises from the fact that its subjects are human beings who can be disciplined only up to a point. Therapists chafe at the restrictions imposed by research requirements and are tempted to circumvent them when they believe that they interfere with treatment. Captive patients in hospitals can be fairly easily controlled, but outpatients are another matter. They break appointments, drop out of treatment without warning, and take vacations at the wrong times. Another practical obstacle lies in the fact that certain forms of psychotherapy involve prolonged, frequent contacts with the patient, so no one practitioner can accumulate an adequate sample for study in a reasonable period of time. This consideration tends to cause researchers to stick to the study of short-term psychotherapy to increase the available sample of patients, with inevitable neglect of long-term methods of equal theoretical interest.

Difficulties for research presented by personal qualities of therapists and patients and aspects of the methods are surmountable in principle. Another type of obstacle presents a more serious problem because it is inherent in the very nature of psychotherapy. Being concerned with all levels of human functioning from the biological to the social, psychotherapy raises all the issues concerned with human nature and the communication process. The range and complexity of this subject matter create difficulties of conceptualization. Some formulations try to encompass all its aspects. Many of these have been immensely insightful and stimulating and have illuminated many fields of knowledge. To achieve all-inclusiveness, however, they have resorted to metaphor, have left major ambiguities unresolved, and have formulated their hypotheses in terms that cannot be subjected to experimental test.

The opposite approach has been to try to conceptualize small segments of the field with sufficient precision to permit experimental test of the hypotheses, but these formulations run the risk of achieving rigor at the expense of significance. The researcher is faced with the problem of delimiting an aspect of psychotherapy that is amenable to experimental study and at the same time includes the major determinants of the problem under consideration. He finds himself in the predicament of the Norse god Thor who tried to drain a small goblet only to discover that it was connected with the sea. Under these circumstances there is an inevitable tendency to guide the choice of research problems more by the ease with which they can be investigated than by their importance. One is reminded of the familiar story of the drunkard who lost his keys in a dark alley but looked for them under the lamp post because the light was better there. This has led to a considerable amount of precise but trivial research.

In spite of these obstacles, certain areas of research in psychotherapy are beginning to look promising. Individual and group sessions afford excellent opportunities to study human communication systems. The most basic questions in this area, such as the effect of the bodily presence or absence of the therapist on the productions of the patient, require elucidation.[7] Interesting research is being done on the formal properties of the interaction system formed by therapist and patient, such as how much each speaks, how this changes over time, and how changes in the speech patterns of one participant affect the patterns of the other.[8]

Especially pertinent to psychiatry are studies of the means by which therapist and patient can influence the content of each other's productions through subtle, nonverbal, cues. Experimental studies of verbal conditioning have demonstrated that if a person cares what another thinks of him, his verbalizations are readily influenced by cues of approval or disapproval. Therefore if the therapist has an hypothesis in mind—and he could not do research without one—he might well unwittingly convey it to the patient, who might oblige by producing supportive material. Obviously, this type of confirmation is of dubious value. Until the personal and situational conditions determining the influence of the therapist's expectancies on the patient's productions, and the kinds of material most susceptible and most resistant to this type of influence are better understood, hypotheses about human nature supported solely by patients' productions in psychotherapy must be considered to be unproven.

The demonstration of the conditionability of patients' verbalizations leads directly to a fundamental question about which very little is known—the relationship between what a person says and what he actually feels. An experimental approach to this problem is afforded by a study of patients' emotional responses to what transpires in the interview, as revealed through various physiological measures.[9] These methods may help to define the personal and situational factors arousing patients' anxieties on the one hand and hopes on the other, as well as personal differences in emotional responsivity, which have formed the basis of personality classifications since the days of Hippocrates. Some patients are too phlegmatic, others too excitable, and the optimal degrees of therapeutically useful tension for them may be quite different.

Better understanding of the types of therapy that most effectively mobilize patients' favorable expectations is especially needed. One promising experimental approach has been the investigation of conditions determining responses of psychiatric patients to inert medications whose therapeutic properties lie in their symbolization of the physician's role. This proves to be quite a complex matter involving the interaction of personality characteristics, attitudes towards physicians and medication, and properties of the therapeutic situation.

Studies of the effects of patients' emotional states on their progress must include the question of the definition of improvement. Although investigation of the therapeutic process can illumine many theoretical issues of human interaction, their practical value depends on solution of this question. For without adequate criteria of improvement there is no way of deciding which of the processes in psychotherapy are relevant to its goal and which are not. Decision as to what type of change constitutes improvement rests on considerations of value rather than scientific pertinence, and this has tended to confuse the issue. It seems possible to approach the problem from a research standpoint by using the same criteria of improvement as do all healing arts—reduction of distress and improvement of functioning. Since symptoms of distress are subjective, one must rely on the patient's report, which may be strongly colored by the impression he may wish to make on the researcher. Physiological measures offer hope of gaining more objective criteria of distress. Successful functioning is not merely a matter of behavior but of attitudes, so evaluation of this criterion must take into account not only the patient's behavior, but its meanings for himself and those who are important to him. Despite these and other methodological problems, the question of the effects of psychotherapy proves to be researchable and is leading to the accumulation of interesting data on the effects of duration of treatment, amount of therapeutic contact, and presence or absence of other patients in the treatment situation.[10]

A special problem in the evaluation of psychotherapy lies in the fact that the psychotherapeutic interview is only a tiny fraction of the patient's encounters with others, and it is therefore hard to disentangle its effects from those of other personal contacts. Therapy may be given credit for improvement really due to a change in the patient's living pattern such as getting married or, conversely, its potentially beneficial effects may be wiped out by a personal catastrophe. To complicate matters further, because of the reciprocal nature of human behavior, improvement in the patient started by therapy may lead to favorable changes in the attitudes of others. Therapy may have given him the courage to ask his girl to marry him. Questions of this type loom especially large with respect to long-term treatment, which requires some way of determining whether the patient handles stress he meets subsequent to undergoing therapy more comfortably and effectively than before.

Ultimate elucidation of the effects of psychotherapy thus depends on success in conceptualizing human interactions, at both personal and social levels. For the sociocultural determinants of mental illness and its treatment must also be taken into account. All in all, considering the theoretical and practical problems involved, it is easy to see why research on psychotherapy has not yet registered any major triumphs. Many hopeful leads are now appearing, however, so that significant progress along many fronts may be confidently anticipated.

IMPLICATIONS FOR PRACTICE

The practice of psychotherapy cannot wait until research has yielded a solid basis for it. In the meanwhile, this survey has suggested certain implications for practice that may be worth explicit mention. The pattern of psychotherapeutic practice in America is seriously imbalanced in that too many of the ablest, most experienced psychiatrists spend most of their time with patients who need them least. This has been the unfortunate, though probably inevitable, consequence of the concept of mental illness as personal malfunctioning, which in itself represents a great gain in understanding. The trouble is that this view makes it impossible to draw the line, so that many persons who are showing essentially normal responses to the wear and tear of life or who are unhappy for reasons other than personal malfunctioning see themselves —and are seen by others—as proper candidates for psychotherapy.

Those candidates for psychotherapy who have education and money naturally seek out psychiatrists with the most prestige. Since in our society the highest prestige attaches to psychoanalytic training in its broadest sense, candidates gravitate towards the best practitioners of evocative therapy. Because analytic training has the highest prestige, it attracts the ablest young psychiatrists, who, having completed it, settle down in the largest cities and devote themselves largely to the long-term treatment of the patients just described. They would have to be super-human to resist this temptation. They cannot very well turn away persons who come to them for help, especially when they are personally congenial (being on the whole of the same intellectual and social level as themselves), pay their bills, are seldom worrisome during the course of treatment, and show a gratifying response.

In the meantime, there are not nearly enough trained psychiatrists to care for the less attractive lower class, seriously ill patients who crowd outpatient clinics and state hospitals and who, from both a medical and a social standpoint, present by far the greater challenge.

Obviously there is no easy remedy for this state of affairs, for which no one can be blamed. Trends that may gradually rectify it are the steady increase in trained nonmedical psychotherapists on the one hand, and the elucidation of the biological components of mental illness on the other. These trends will in time modify the public image of both mental illness and psychotherapy. It may be hoped eventually that the situationally distressed or morally perturbed will come to seek sources of help other than psychiatrists, who then will be free to devote themselves to the treatment of the severely mentally ill, for which their medical training uniquely qualifies them.

Our survey has suggested that much, if not all, of the effectiveness of different forms of psychotherapy may be due to those features that all have in common rather than to those that distinguish them from each other. This does not necessarily mean that all therapies are interchangeable. It may well turn out, when types of patients and effects of therapy are better understood, that certain approaches are better for some types of patients than for others and that they differ in certain of their effects, which have not as yet been specified. Until these questions are clarified, the advance of both knowledge and practice is probably better served by members of different schools defending their own positions, while being tolerant of other schools, than by being uncritically eclectic. For the therapist's ability to help his patient depends partly on his self-confidence, and this in turn depends on mastery of a particular conceptual scheme and its accompanying techniques. Since the leading theories of psychotherapy represent alternative rather than incompatible formulations, it is unlikely that any one of them is completely wrong. As an eminent philosopher has wisely said: "A clash of doctrines is not a disaster—it is an opportunity."[11] The activity stimulated by the clash of psychotherapeutic doctrines will eventually yield sufficient information either to prove that they are to all practical purposes identical or to clarify and substantiate differences between them.[12]

A further implication of this survey for psychotherapy is that the emotional components of the process deserve more attention. At a physiological level, certain drugs seem to have promise as the means of producing optimal emotional excitation. It may be possible through their use to stir up overapathetic patients, relax overinhibited ones, and dampen those who are too excited, in each case improving their accessibility to the therapist and creating a favorable state for the production of change.

At a symbolic level, it is important to mobilize the patient's expectancy for help, or at least to do nothing to counteract it. The psychiatrist should therefore be prepared to modify his approach, within limits possible for him, to meet his patients' conceptions of therapy, insofar as he can discern them. For patients who cannot conceive of a treatment that does not involve getting a pill or injection, it may be advisable to offer a prescription as a means of establishing and solidifying a therapeutic relationship. Once this has occurred, it is often possible to help the patient modify his expectations and the medication is dispensed with.[13]

The question of how far a physician should go to meet a patient's expectations is a thorny one. Obviously he cannot use methods in which he himself does not believe. Moreover, reliance on the healing powers of faith, if it led to neglect of proper diagnostic or treatment procedures, would clearly be irresponsible. On the other hand, faith may be a specific antidote for certain emotions such as fear or discouragement, which may constitute the essence of a patient's illness. For such patients, the mobilization of expectant trust by whatever means may be as much an etiological remedy as penicillin for pneumonia.

It is important for the psychiatrist to accept the fact that he inevitably exerts a strong influence on his patients. He cannot avoid doing so; therefore it is better that he exert his influence consciously than unconsciously. It has been said that "in all therapy trouble is apt to follow the ignorant application of important forces,"[14] and this applies particularly when the important force is the therapist himself. This leaves open, of course, the question of how the therapist should best use his influence—for example, whether with a particular patient he should ostensibly be directive or permissive. But he will be better able to reach the correct decision if he remembers that in either case he significantly affects what transpires.

Finally, this review emphasizes the desirability of exploiting group forces more fully to produce and sustain therapeutic change. This means not only the use of group therapeutic methods, but the inclusion of persons important to the patient in his treatment. For hospitalized patients it means full use of the potentialities of the "therapeutic community." For outpatients it implies more attention to the resources in the patient's environment that might be mobilized to facilitate and perpetuate his improvement. "No man is an island," and the degree and permanence of change in any individual will depend in part on corresponding changes in those close to him and on support from his wider milieu.

NOTES

1. Masserman (1957) offers an interesting, broadly conceived consideration of psychotherapy from historical and comparative standpoints.

2. This point has been elaborated by Bateson and his coworkers (1956) and Haley (1959), and also by Lidz *et al.* (1957).

3. An excellent example of a socially effective psychiatric document is Group for the Advancement of Psychiatry (1957). See also Frank (1958, 1960).

4. In 1958, the United States Public Health Service alone spent about two million dollars for research in psychotherapy.

5. An excellent discussion of research problems in psychotherapy is to be found in Group for the Advancement of Psychiatry (1959). See also Frank (1959).

6. The contributions of Carl Rogers and his group (C. R. Rogers and Dymond, 1954), based mainly on studies of therapy conducted by experienced psychologists, represent an important exception to this statement. Strupp (1960) has devised ingenious indirect methods for studying attitudes and techniques of experienced medical and nonmedical psychotherapists.

7. Dr. K. M. Colby is currently experimenting with this (personal communication).

8. See, for example, Lennard and Bernstein (1960) and Saslow and Matarazzo (1959).

9. The literature on measurement of human autonomic functioning, with

special reference to psychotherapy, is superbly summarized by Lacey (1959).
10. See, for example, Shlien (1957).
11. Whitehead (1925), p. 266.
12. Dreikurs (1960).
13. Frank (1946).
14. Modell (1955), p. 56.

REFERENCES

Bateson, G., Jackson, D. D., Haley, J., & Weakland, J. Toward a theory of schizophrenia. *Behavioral Science*, 1956, *1*, 251–264.

Dreikurs, R. Are psychological schools of thought outdated? *Journal of Individual Psychology*, 1960, *16*, 3–10.

Frank, J. D. Psychotherapeutic aspects of symptomatic treatment. *American Journal of Psychiatry*, 1946, *103*, 21–25.

Frank, J. D. The great antagonism. *Atlantic Monthly*, 1958, *202*, 58–62.

Frank, J. D. Problems of controls in psychotherapy as exemplified by the Psychotherapy Research Project of the Phipps Psychiatric Clinic. In E. A. Rubinstein & M. B. Parloff (Eds.), *Research in psychotherapy*. Washington, D.C.: American Psychological Association, 1959. Pp. 10–26.

Frank, J. D. Breaking the thought barrier: Psychological challenges of the nuclear age. *Psychiatry*, 1960, *23*, 245–266.

Group for the Advancement of Psychiatry. *Psychiatric aspects of school desegregation*. New York: Group for the Advancement of Psychiatry (Report No. 37), 1957.

Group for the Advancement of Psychiatry. *Some observations on controls in psychiatric research*. New York: Group for the Advancement of Psychiatry (Report No. 42), 1959.

Haley, J. The family of the schizophrenic: A model system. *Journal of Nervous and Mental Diseases*, 1959, *129*, 357–374.

Lacey, J. I. Psychophysiological approaches to the evaluation of psychotherapeutic process and outcome. In E. A. Rubinstein & M. B. Parloff (Eds.), *Research in psychotherapy*. Washington, D. C.: American Psychological Association, 1959. Pp. 160–208.

Lennard, H. L., & Bernstein, A. *The anatomy of psychotherapy*. New York: Columbia University Press, 1960.

Lidz, T., Cornelison, A. R., Fleck, S., & Terry, D. The intrafamilial environment of schizophrenic patients: 2. Marital schism and marital skew. *American Journal of Psychiatry*, 1957, *114*. 241–248.

Masserman, J. H. Evolution vs. 'revolution' in psychotherapy: A biodynamic integration. *Behavioral Science*, 1957, *2*, 89–100.

Modell, W. *The relief of symptoms*. Philadelphia: Saunders, 1955.

Rogers, C. R., & Dymond, R. (Eds.) *Psychotherapy and personality change.* Chicago: University of Chicago Press, 1954.

Saslow, G., & Matarazzo, J. D. A technique for studying changes in interview behavior. In E. A. Rubinstein & M. B. Parloff (Eds.), *Research in psychotherapy.* Washington, D.C.: American Psychological Association, 1959. Pp. 125–157.

Shlien, J. M. Time-limited psychotherapy: An experiential investigation of practical values and theoretical implications. *Journal of Counseling Psychology,* 1957, *4,* 318–322.

Strupp, H. H. *Psychotherapists in action.* New York: Grune & Stratton, 1960.

Whitehead, A. N. *Science and the modern world.* New York: Macmillan, 1925.

CHAPTER 16

Commonalities, Differences, and Directions in Contemporary Psychotherapy

Arnold P. Goldstein

At regrettably rare intervals in American psychiatry there appears a book which in scope of scholarship, originality of appraisal and clarity of presentation deserves the sincere appreciation of the entire profession. Jerome Frank has written such a volume. . . .

American Journal of Psychiatry

Professor Frank's book will take its place among the classics of psychiatric literature.

The Psychiatric Quarterly

The march toward an understanding of what makes the many diversified forms of psychotherapy "work" has been slow, sometimes halting, but persistent. *Persuasion and Healing* is another milestone along the road.

American Catholic Psychological Association Newsletter

Jerome Frank has indeed written a magnificent book. With compelling eloquence and disarming simplicity, he moves us several giant steps toward the advancement of psychotherapy. In several ways he has presented us in this book with both new vision about psychotherapy as it already exists and new perspectives around which to frame our plans for its future growth.

Psychotherapy, in its most basic aspect, is an interpersonal influence process. Despite the apparent diversity of contemporary psychotherapeutic approaches, all seek to reduce suffering through persuasion mediated by interpersonal influence. As such, psychotherapy shares important features in common with many other historical and contempo-

---

This chapter is a discussion-commentary, written especially for the present volume, of Chapter 15: "American Psychotherapy in Perspective," by Jerome D. Frank.

rary forms of persuasion and healing—healing in primitive societies, miracle cures, religious revivalism, communist thought reform, placebo effects in medical practice, and so forth. Frank's distillation and examination of these commonalities during change processes provides a major contextual perspective for contemporary psychotherapy. These shared characteristics include: initial subjective distress experienced by the sufferer; the arousal of favorable expectation for change through dependence upon a socially sanctioned healer; a circumscribed ritualistic relationship with the healer; a socially shared series of assumptions about illness and the healing process that cannot be disproved by the sufferer's failure to respond; a detailed review of the patient's past life; the mobilization of guilt; the heightening of self-esteem; and changes in attitude and social reinforcement of these changes.

Throughout his book, and in many of his other writings, Frank (1958, 1959) places particular emphasis upon expectancy and relationship commonalities as prime movers of patient change in psychotherapy. We wish here to strongly underscore this emphasis, for it is precisely these two variables, expectancy and relationship, which we have pointed to earlier in a discussion of therapy outcome research:

As the first means of bringing outcome research "out of storage" we urge continued focus upon process variables—but with more discriminating attention to those for which there now exists growing evidence of an association with therapeutic outcome. We need less focus on psychotherapy as a functionally autonomous research endeavor and renewed interest in process variables as they relate to therapeutic outcome [Goldstein & Dean, 1966, p. 142].

Thus Frank has, by his examination of change process commonalities, given a focus to the change process itself which can serve in important ways to increase its efficiency.

Frank's emphasis on commonality provides much more, however. One of the major historical obstacles to the advance of psychotherapy has been its conceptualization in terms which emphasized its relative uniqueness. Both economic and ego-syntonic forces have served to perpetuate this myth, a myth which Frank destroys by his brilliant demonstration that psychotherapy is but one set of change processes in a historical and contemporary sea of many. But he does much more than destroy, for knowledge of change-relevant commonalities can provide the building blocks for more discerning, and potentially more successful, attempts at improving the efficacy of psychotherapy. Greater research and clinical attention to expectancy and relationship considerations are but two such building blocks. Frank directs us to many others by his skillful examination of social-psychological studies of persuasion for their relevance to psychotherapy. Social and experimental psychology have provided vast amounts of information regarding other change processes which have equally great potential relevance for psychotherapy. Studies of interpersonal influence, interpersonal attraction, attitude change, cognitive consistency, group dynamics, and the immense learning research literature are but a few examples of where Frank's focus encourages us to turn in our efforts aimed at improving psychotherapy.

One further direction for the advance of psychotherapy may be abstracted from Frank's focus on commonality. Bergin (1966) has noted that

. . . effective variables cut across schools of treatment and thus provide the basis for applying techniques on the basis of known effects rather than on doctrines promulgated by warring factions. This also indicates that titles, degrees, or years of training should not define the psychotherapist, but rather what the individual can do.

The spirit reflected in Frank's focus on the *therapeutic* in psychotherapy and the unbinding by writers such as Bergin of our diploma-tied helping hands has been evidenced in the large number of so-called nonprofessional therapists recently appearing on the therapeutic scene. Thus, at an ever-increasing rate, research reports are appearing which demonstrate the therapeutic potency of nurses (Ayllon & Michael, 1959; Daniels, 1966), aides (Ayllon & Haughton, 1964; Carkhuff & Truax, 1965), patient's parents (Allen & Harris, 1966; Guerney, 1964; Straughan, 1964; Wahler, Winkel, Peterson, & Morrison, 1965), college undergraduates (Poser, 1966; Schwitzgebel & Kolb, 1964), psychological technicians (Catell & Shotwell, 1954; Poser, 1967), convicts (Benjamin, Freedman, & Lynton, 1966), housewives (Rioch, 1966), auxiliary counselors (Costin, 1966; Harvey, 1964), human service aides (MacLennon, 1966), and foster grandparents (Johnston, 1967). Surely we do a gross disservice to the large numbers of unseen but real therapy candidates if we fail to be responsive to implicit messages such as Frank's and Bergin's for greater use of nonprofessional change agents. Frank further underscores this message by drawing our attention to the manner in which, while focussing our therapeutic efforts upon the YAVIS patient—young, attractive, verbal, intelligent, successful (Schofield, 1964)—we have failed to serve the "less attractive, lower class, seriously ill patients who crowd outpatient clinics and state hospitals and who, from both a medical and a social standpoint, present by far the greater challenge."

Thus, Frank's attention to commonalities in therapies and other change processes has helped us point to significant variables for further study, encouraged us to turn to nonclinical psychological research for the development of hypotheses relevant to psychotherapy, and suggested that much greater therapeutic use be made of persons not traditionally considered psychotherapists. It is possible, however, that within the very importance of Frank's emphasis on commonality lies an almost equally important danger; that differences also exist between therapies, and that in certain respects these differences may be as significant for patient change as are Frank's commonalities. To some extent, Frank is in accord with this position:

Our survey has suggested that much, if not all, of the effectiveness of different forms of psychotherapy may be due to those features that all have in common rather than to those that distinguish them from each other. This does not necessarily mean that all therapies are interchangeable. It may well turn out, when types of patients and effects of therapy are better understood, that certain approaches are better for some types of patients than for others and that they differ in certain of their effects, which have not as yet been specified. Until these questions are clarified, the advance of both knowledge and practice is probably better served by members of different schools defending their own positions, while being tolerant of other schools, than by being uncritically eclectic [p. 256].

Yet therapists displaying such tolerance are clearly in the minority today, and instead we find the prevalence of an essentially parochial operating assumption. It might be called the One True Light assumption, the either-or assumption, or, more generally, the assumption that eventually one and only one type of psychotherapy will prove "best" or will prove applicable to all patients. Bonded to this assumption is the corollary prediction that all other therapies will be proven "wrong," or less adequate, or, somehow, to be pseudotherapies. Contemporaneously, this assumption finds expression in the implicit or explicit feeling that psychotherapies can be hierarchically arranged on some sort of effectiveness, rightness, or goodness dimension for all patients. Is there a viable alternative assumption? We feel there is. It is the assumption, as Heller (1965) has put it, that we need precision rifles and not a shotgun, psychotherapies and not psychotherapy. Whether one subscribes to a medical model of psychotherapy or a learning-educative model of behavior modification in treating patients, one can find extremely few medical or learning problems which are universally resolvable for *all* persons experiencing the given problem by a single intervention technique. Hence, we would propose that psychotherapy should not be viewed as a potentially singular set of techniques. Maslow (1962), for example, has meaningfully distinguished between *deficit needs* and *being needs*. One need not necessarily subscribe to his essentially existential position to propose that the former may be more readily helped by a behavior therapy approach, the latter by therapies more focused upon actualization, fulfillment, and the like. This very same point regarding differences between psychotherapies is rigorously demonstrated by Frank's own research, reported in *Persuasion and Healing*. Here, patient improvement in social effectiveness is related to the type of therapy received—individual, group, or minimal—over the course of the six-month treatment course. In brief, therefore, we are urging here that Frank's very strong and highly appropriate emphasis on common features must not serve to obscure the real and likely consequential impact of differences between change processes.

REFERENCES

Allen, K. E., and Harris, F. R. Elimination of a child's excessive scratching by training the mother in reinforcement procedures. *Behavior Research and Therapy*, 1966, *4*, 79–84.

Ayllon, T., & Michael, J. The psychiatric nurse as a behavioral engineer. *Journal of the Experimental Analysis of Behavior*, 1959, *2*, 323–334.

Ayllon, T., & Haughton, E. Modification of symptomatic verbal behavior of mental patients. *Behavior Research and Therapy*, 1964, *2*, 87–98.

Benjamin, J. G., Freedman, M. K., & Lynton, E. F. *Pros and cons: New roles for nonprofessionals in corrections.* Washington, D. C.: United States Department of Health, Education and Welfare, 1966.

Bergin, A. E. Some implications of psychotherapy research for therapeutic practice. *Journal of Abnormal Psychology*, 1966, *71*, 235–246.

Carkhuff, R. R., & Truax, C. B. Lay mental health counseling. *Journal of Consulting Psychology*, 1965, *29*, 426–431.

Catell, R. B., & Shotwell, A. M. Personality profiles of more successful and less successful psychiatric technicians. *American Journal of Mental Deficiency*, 1954, *58*, 496–499.

Costin, S. B. Training nonprofessionals for a child welfare service. *Children*, 1966, *13*, 63–68.

Daniels, A. M. Training school nurses to work with groups of adolescents. *Children*, 1966, *13*, 210–216.

Frank, J. D. Some effects of expectancy and influence in psychotherapy. In

J. H. Masserman & J. L. Moreno (Eds.), *Progress in psychotherapy*. Vol. 3. New York: Grune & Stratton, 1958. Pp. 27–43.

Frank, J. D. The dynamics of the psychotherapeutic relationship. *Psychiatry*, 1959, *22*, 17–39.

Goldstein, A. P., & Dean, S. J. *The investigation of psychotherapy*. New York: John Wiley & Sons, 1966.

Guerney, B. Filial therapy: Description and rationale. *Journal of Consulting Psychology*, 1964, *28*, 304–310.

Harvey, L. V. The use of non-professional auxiliary counselors in staffing a counseling service. *Journal of Counseling Psychology*, 1964, *11*, 348–351.

Heller, K. A broader perspective for interview therapy. Paper presented at Midwestern Psychological Association, Chicago, 1965.

Johnston, R. Foster grandparents for emotionally disturbed children. *Children*, 1967, *14*, 46–52.

MacLennon, B. W. New careers as human service aides. *Children*, 1966, *13*, 190–194.

Maslow, A. H. *Toward a psychology of being*. Princeton: Van Nostrand, 1962.

Poser, E. G. The effect of therapists' training on group therapeutic outcome. *Journal of Consulting Psychology*, 1966, *30*, 283–289.

Poser, E. G. Training behavior therapists. *Behavior Research and Therapy*, 1967, *5*, 37–42.

Rioch, M. J. Changing concepts in the training of therapists. *Journal of Consulting Psychology*, 1966, *30*, 290–291.

Schofield, N. *Psychotherapy, the purchase of friendship*. Englewood Cliffs: Prentice-Hall, 1964.

Schwitzgebel, R., & Kolb, D. A. Inducing behavior change in adolescent delinquents. *Behavior Research and Therapy*, 1964, *1*, 297–304.

Straughan, J. H. Treatment with child and mother in playroom. *Behavior Research and Therapy*, 1964, *2*, 37–42.

Wahler, R. G., Winkel, G. H., Peterson, R. F., & Morrison, D. C. Mothers as behavior therapists for their own children. *Behavior Research and Therapy*, 1965, *3*, 113–124.

CHAPTER 17

Effective Ingredients in Psychotherapy: An Approach to Unraveling the Patient-Therapist Interaction

Charles B. Truax

The essential question to be asked about psychotherapy is "What do we as therapists do that makes for constructive personality change in our patients?" What are the essential effective ingredients in psychotherapy? It seems certain that not all of what happens actually contributes to the work of psychotherapy.

Psychoanalytic (Alexander, 1948; Halpern & Lesser, 1960; Ferenczi, 1930; Schafer, 1959), client-centered (Dymond, 1949; Jourard, 1959; Rogers, 1951; Rogers, 1957), and eclectic theorists (Fox & Goldin, 1963; Raush & Bordin, 1957; Shoben, 1949; Strunk, 1957; Strupp, 1960) have emphasized the importance of the therapist's ability to understand sensitively and accurately the patient's inner experiences. Also, they have stressed the importance of nonpossessive warmth and acceptance of the patient and have emphasized that the therapist be mature, integrated and genuine within the relationship. These three characteristics of the therapist behavior cut across the parochial theories of psychotherapy and can thus be considered as elements common to a wide variety of

The present findings are a part of an ongoing research program supported in part by NIMH Grant No. M 3496, and in part by a grant from the Office of Vocational Rehabilitation, No. RD–906–PM. This research was carried out with patients at Mendota State Hospital with the generous support of Dr. Walter J. Urben, Superintendent, and his staff. The total program, of which this present report is a part, has been directed by Carl R. Rogers, Eugene T. Gendlin, and Charles B. Truax. This chapter was voted, by the Editorial Board of the present volume, as one of the creative developments in psychotherapy, 1958–1968. From the *Journal of Counseling Psychology*, *10*, 1963, 256–263. Copyright 1963 by the American Psychological Association, and reproduced by permission.

psychoanalytic, client-centered, and eclectic approaches to psychotherapy.

Halkides (1958) and Barrett-Lennard (1959) have attempted to investigate the importance of these three therapist behaviors (or conditions) in a university counseling center population. Their evidence suggests the relevance of these three therapist conditions for success with counseling cases, although a replication of Halkides' (1958) study by Hart (1960) failed at confirmation. Recent research has also indicated the relevance of these therapist-offered conditions to effective group psychotherapy with hospitalized mental patients (Truax, 1961).

PSYCHOTHERAPY WITH SCHIZOPHRENICS

EMPATHY

Now a body of empirical knowledge is developing which shows the relationship of these three therapeutic conditions to psychotherapy with schizophrenics. This research involves attempts to relate measures of the three therapist conditions derived from tape-recorded psychotherapy sessions to measures of change in the patient's personality functioning derived from psychological pretests and posttests.[1] The evidence showing the relevance of accurate empathic understanding communicated by the therapist to personality growth in the patient will be considered first.

Our first step was the construction of a scale, the Accurate Empathy Scale (Truax, 1961a), on which trained judges could reliably rate the extent of empathic understanding by the therapist occurring in tape-recorded samples of psychotherapy. The scale was designed to measure a conception of empathy which involves the sensitivity to current feelings, and, the verbal facility to communicate this understanding in a language attuned to the patient's current feelings. At a high level of accurate empathy the message "I am with you" is unmistakably clear—the therapist's remarks fit with the patient's mood and content. The therapist's responses not only indicate a sensitive understanding of the apparent feelings but serve to clarify and expand the client's awareness of his feelings or experiences. This is communicated not only by language appropriate to the patient, but also by the voice qualities which reflect the seriousness, the intentness, and the depth of feeling. At a low level of accurate empathy the therapist may be preoccupied with his own intellectual interpretations and, so, be less aware of the client's "being." The therapist at this low level of empathy may have his focus of attention on the content of what the patient says rather than what the client "is" during the moment and thus may ignore, misunderstand, or simply fail to sense the client's current feelings and experiencings. Indeed, the therapist may be accurately describing psychodynamics to the patient but a lack of empathy is shown in the use of language not that of the client. A lack of empathy is also shown when dynamics are presented at a time when these are far removed from the current feelings of the client. Thus "accurate empathy" has much in common with the "good" psychoanalytic interpretation.

To see if this conception of empathy was related to therapeutic progress in the initial stages of psychotherapy, four patients who showed clear improvement and four patients who showed deterioration on a battery of psychological tests after six months of therapy were selected. The 384 samples of tape-recorded psychotherapy were randomly selected from the first six months of therapy and then coded so that raters would not know whether a sample came from a test-improved case or a test-deteriorated case, or, from an early or a late interview.

The findings clearly indicated the relevance of accurate empathy to the kind of personality change occurring in the patient: the psychotherapy involving test-improved patients rated consistently higher on accurate empathy than tape-recorded psychotherapy with test-deteriorated cases ($p < .01$).

A second study involving 14 hospitalized schizophrenic cases and 14 counseling cases from the University of Chicago and Stanford University was completed using 112 samples of recorded psychotherapy from early and late interviews. Analysis of this data indicated that accurate empathy ratings were significantly higher for the more successful cases than for the less successful ($p < .01$). Also, the positive relationship between accurate empathy and outcome of therapy held for hospitalized schizophrenics and for counseling cases. The same condition seemed relevant for both populations. The more successful cases received higher accurate empathy ratings, while the less successful cases have many more average and low accurate empathy ratings ($p < .05$).

More recently, trends in the levels of accurate empathy for schizophrenics covering a time span from six months to three and one-half years have been investigated. One 4-minute tape-recorded sample was taken from every fifth interview for each of 14 schizophrenic cases, giving a total of 358 samples to work with. Analysis of these data showed no tendency for therapists to systematically change over time in the level of accurate empathy offered to the patient. As predicted, however, the therapists of the more improved patients were judged to have offered significantly higher levels of accurate empathy throughout the course of therapy than was received by the unimproved patients ($p <.05$).

These studies suggest that the level of accurate empathy is indeed related to the outcome of constructive personality change. Thus the question of *who* is causing empathy to be high or low in therapy becomes crucial. Is it the therapist, or is it the patient who determines the level of accurate empathy that will occur in a given psychotherapy relationship?

One way of answering this question is to have a group of therapists see each member of a group of patients and have each patient see all therapists. If the level of accurate empathy is different for different patients, this would show that patients determine accurate empathy levels offered by the therapists. If the level of accurate empathy is different from different therapists, this would show that therapists determine levels of accurate empathy. A study has been completed using data from a group of 24 patients living on one continuing-treatment ward where eight different therapists offered psychotherapy to all patients on a demand basis. From the tape recordings of all interviews, samples were selected in which the same eight therapists saw the same eight patients according to a balanced incomplete block design. This research design allowed us to find out if the therapists had an effect upon the level of accurate empathy and, separately, if the patient had an effect upon the level of accurate empathy.

Analysis of ratings indicated that different therapists produced different levels of accurate empathy when interacting with the same set of patients ($p <.01$). In sharp contrast, different patients did not receive different levels of accurate empathy when interacting with the same set of therapists ($p <.40$).

The data, then, suggest that it is the therapist who determines the level of accurate empathy. While it is likely that with extreme patients (such as comparing very talkative with very quiet patients) it would be possible to show effects on accurate empathy of patients, the present findings indicate that the therapist is primarily responsible for the level of accurate empathy occurring in psychotherapy.

In summary, these findings say that the level of accurate empathy occurring in the patient-therapist interaction is higher for more successful cases than for less successful cases; and that this relationship holds not just for outpatient neurotics, but also for severely disturbed schizophrenic patients; and that the therapist is the principal determinant of the level of accurate empathy offered in psychotherapy.

UNCONDITIONAL POSITIVE REGARD

As a precondition for the therapist's ability to deeply and accurately sense the patient's current feelings and experiences and for the patient's ability to use this accurate empathy in the process of his own self-exploration and experiencings, the therapist's nonconditional warmth has seemed theoretically crucial. A scale (Truax, 1962) designed to measure the degree of nonconditional warmth has been devised for use with tape-recorded psychotherapy sessions. At its highest levels, unconditional positive regard involves only the condition that the patient talk of personally relevant material; the therapist is willing to share equally the patient's fears and hopes or achievements and failures, without placing conditions upon the warm acceptance of the patient's inner self. Briefly, unconditional positive regard requires a nonpossessive caring for the patient as a separate person with the inherent right and responsibility of self-determination.

In a study applying this scale of unconditional positive regard to the 358 samples of psychotherapy taken from every fifth interview with 14 schizophrenic patients, it was predicted that the therapists of the more improved cases would be rated as higher than those of unimproved or failure cases. This prediction was supported by the data which showed that samples from improved cases were consistently higher in unconditional positive regard than samples from unimproved or failure cases ($p < .05$).

Viewed in tandem, accurate empathy and unconditional positive regard intertwine in a logical fashion that suggests that the achievement of a high level of accurate empathy is dependent upon first obtaining at least a minimally high level of unconditional positive regard for the patient. To be deeply sensitive to the moment-to-moment "being" of another person requires of us as therapists that we first accept and to some degree unconditionally prize this other person. However, neither of these two conditions could function properly without the therapist being himself integrated and genuine within the therapeutic encounter. At high levels of self-congruence this means that the therapist does not deny feelings and that he be integrated within the therapy hour: it does not mean that the therapist must burden the patient with overt expression of all of his feelings—only that he not be ingenuine.

SELF-CONGRUENCE OF THERAPIST

Self-congruence is not taken to mean only the element of self-awareness, but also the presentation to the patient of a real person in the encounter.

There is always the temptation to present a facade, a mask of professionalism, or some type of confessional-professional screen; the temptation to be incongruent with the self or ingenuine as a person.

A scale (Truax, 1962a) has been developed to measure the degree to which this conception of therapist self-congruence occurs within tape-recorded therapeutic sessions. In a very recent study this scale of therapist genuineness or self-congruence was used on the 358 tape-recorded therapy samples taken from every fifth interview of the 14 cases described above. Analysis of the data showed a significant tendency for the therapist in improved cases to be rated higher in self-congruence during the therapeutic sessions than therapists in nonimproved or failure cases ($p < .05$).

It should be noted that the ratings on each condition under study were done "blind" in the sense that the judges were given coded samples so that they did not know whether the sample came from early or late in therapy, or from a successful or unsuccessful case. Also, the last three studies employed naive lay raters who had no systematic knowledge about psychology or psychotherapy and so would have few of the biased preconceptions often found in judges. They simply rated randomly coded 4-minute samples of psychotherapeutic interaction according to the specific definitions of the scales.

CONTROL STUDIES WITH SCHIZOPHRENICS USING ALL CONDITIONS COMBINED

Thus, the above studies seem strong evidence to support the theoretical view that each of these three therapist-offered conditions is related to constructive change in patients. Since all three conditions, however, are considered by theory to be essential ingredients for successful psychotherapy, research has been completed comparing therapy cases rated high on all three conditions with both control patients receiving no therapy and therapy cases rated relatively low on levels of accurate empathy, unconditional positive regard and therapist self-congruence.

A total of 14 schizophrenics receiving therapy, and 14 matched controls were selected for analysis of over-all change in psychological functioning. Patients had been randomly assigned to either therapy or control conditions and complete batteries of psychological tests had been given initially and later.

All accurate empathy, unconditional positive regard and therapist self-congruence ratings from the studies reported earlier were examined and mean values computed. A total of eight patients were judged to have received relatively low levels. The hypothesis was that patients receiving high levels would show greater constructive personality change, while patients receiving low levels of conditions in therapy and the control patients would show less constructive personality change.

The initial test battery and the latest test battery for both therapy and matched control cases were given to two clinical psychologists[2] for a "blind" analysis of change in level of psychological functioning.

Primary emphasis was placed upon the Rorschach and secondary emphasis upon the MMPI in the assessing of change although the total test battery included the Thematic Apperception Test, the Wechsler Adult Intelligence Scale, the Anxiety Reaction Scales, the Stroop Tests, the F Authoritarian Scale, the Q Sort, and the Wittenborn Psychiatric Rating Scales.

Patients receiving high levels of conditions showed an over-all gain in psychological functioning (mean change of 6.0 where 5.0 represents no change) whereas, patients who received relatively low levels of accurate empathy, unconditional positive regard and self-congruence showed a *loss* in psychological functioning. Control patients evidenced moderate gains. These differences proved statistically significant ($p < .05$).

In terms of number of patients at or above the median change ratings, the control group had a rough 50–50 split while *all* patients in the group receiving low levels of conditions were below the median. Those patients receiving relatively high levels of conditions from the therapist are six of the eight patients at or above the median of positive change in psychological functioning.

Thus the data suggest that high conditions facilitate constructive personality change as predicted. However, the findings also say that patients who received relatively low conditions showed negative personality change.

Another study with the same design was conducted to specifically check the relation between conditions offered in therapy and change in anxiety experienced by the patient. The Anxiety Reaction Scale consisting of three factors of Interpersonal Anxiety, Somatic Anxiety, and General Anxiety had been administered to each patient both early and late.

The data of all three subscales show a clear tendency for those patients receiving high conditions to show a drop in anxiety level, while those patients receiving low conditions show an increase in anxiety level. The controls show almost no change. The differences between the three groups reached statistical significance on both the measure of Interpersonal Anxiety and on the measure of General Anxiety ($p < .05$).

When the Q Sort for self data on the same patients was analyzed an even more disquieting finding appeared: the self concept of the patients receiving high levels of conditions and the self concept of the control patients receiving no therapy both show a slight tendency toward better adjustment from early to late, but the patients receiving low conditions in therapy show a significant change toward less well-adjusted self concept ($p < .01$).

Similar analyses were carried out on subscales of the MMPI, the F Authoritarian Scale, the Wittenborn Psychiatric Rating Scales, and the Wechsler Adult Intelligence Scale. Statistically significant differences ($p < .05$) in the direction of the hypothesis occurred on the Sum of Clinical Scales, the Depression Scale, the Psychopathic Deviate Scale, the MF Scale, the Schizophrenia Scale and the Social Introversion Scale of the MMPI. Statistically significant differences occurred on only three of the 14 submeasures of intelligence; in each case the low conditions group showed a decrease in intellectual functioning. Differences were not found to be statistically significant on either the F Authoritarian Scale or upon any of the subscales of the Wittenborn Psychiatric Rating Scales. The scores from each instrument did, however, tend to show a consistent pattern: the patients receiving high therapy conditions tended to show improvement either slightly greater than or equal to that of the no therapy control group, while patients receiving low levels of therapeutic conditions tended to show negative personality change.

A final study involved the Constructive Personality Change Index which uses items from early and late MMPI tests as the measure of personality change. On this measure the control group showed moderate positive changes, the low conditions therapy patients showed moderate negative changes, and the high conditions therapy patients showed large positive changes in personality functioning ($p < .05$). Next the therapy patients were ranked on conditions received in psychotherapy and these rankings were compared with their Constructive Personality Change Index scores. The rank order correlation *rho* was computed between the ranking on all conditions combined and the Constructive Personality Change Index, yielding a correlation of .87 ($p < .01$). Rank correlations with each of the separate conditions ranged between .67 and .90 ($p < .05$).

The comparisons of patients receiving high and low conditions in therapy with control patients receiving no therapy has a special significance. If comparisons had been made only between the therapy cases and the control cases, there would have been no differences in outcomes and it would have been erroneously concluded that all psychotherapy was ineffective as a treatment procedure with hospitalized schizophrenics. This certainly raises the intriguing question of whether or not the studies that have reported no effect of psychotherapy with neurotics have made such conclusions because they have lumped together psychotherapy involving high conditions with therapy involving low conditions.

The unexpected finding that the change in personality functioning is largely negative when conditions are lower is a very sobering one. It seems to say that low conditions lead schizophrenic patients to become more disturbed. Psychotherapists have, perhaps naively, held to the belief that even when psychotherapy did not prove therapeutic, it at least did not facilitate negative change in personality functioning.

One possible interpretation of the negative change in the low conditions patients is based upon the observation that all psychotherapy focuses upon the malfunctioning or life-failures of the patient. When the therapist is sensitively and accurately able to understand the patient and communicates this understanding in a relationship involving both genuineness and nonpossessive warmth, then life-failures can be explored and attempts at new modes of living can be tried. However, when these elements are not sufficiently present in psychotherapy, we would expect that the schizophrenic patient is left only with a greater realization of his life-failures. This reinforced realization of malfunctioning combined with an inability to resolve life-failures could be expected to produce negative change in personality functioning.

It may very well be that a lack of these three conditions in the patient's environment is what led him to become schizophrenic in the first place. If so—and the reverse of accurate empathy, unconditional positive regard and self-congruence certainly fits with what we know of the Schizophrenogenic Mother—then the present findings with psychotherapy show that more poor conditions continue to make the patient worse, not better.

To summarize the research, the evidence seems to clearly point to the importance of accurate empathy, unconditional positive regard, and congruence in successful psychotherapy with even the most difficult patient population—the hospitalized schizophrenic.

IMPLICATIONS OF THESE FINDINGS

What meaning might these findings have for the future of psychotherapy? The evidence does suggest possible future directions for research, for the training of therapists, and for the practice of psychotherapy.

These findings reflect the fruitfulness of focusing upon the therapy behavior of the therapist. The attempts to newly conceptualize and measure the complex concepts of accurate empathy, unconditional positive regard, and therapist self-congruence have led to more explicit definitions.

The task ahead for research, then, is to further specify the separate types of therapist behaviors and evaluate their relevance to successful outcomes. Thus, since it now appears that communication of a sensitive accurate understanding of the patient's current feelings and experiences is related to positive personality change, it becomes important to know *which* therapist behaviors among all those now labelled as empathic are doing the actual work of therapy. For example, is the tonal quality of the voice that the therapist uses to communicate his deep understanding a significant factor, or is it only the understanding? Does it matter whether the therapist uses the patient's own words to communicate his understanding? Is the understanding more effective when it is expressed concretely or abstractly?

Present research, then, in isolating therapist-offered conditions effective in successful psychotherapy leads to even more specific questions for future research aimed at clarifying what we as therapists do that produces constructive change in our patients.

The unexpected finding that when patients receive low conditions in therapy, they show negative personality change, would, if confirmed by future research, raise a host of very serious ethical and practical questions. Since very large sums of both public and private funds are yearly spent upon psychotherapeutic treatment, there is a pressing social need for research to further investigate the validity and generality of these findings—to test this out both with schizophrenic and neurotic populations, and to experimentally vary the conditions.

As the research evidence becomes more specific and solidly founded, it will be possible to rely less on the learning of general concepts and more upon the teaching of specific behaviors in training therapists for the practice of psychotherapy. Research rating scales can be directly applied to training programs. Tape-recorded samples of psychotherapy rated very high on accurate empathy, for example, can be selected to provide concrete examples for the beginning therapist.[3] Beyond this, rating scales such as the Accurate Empathy Scale can be used to rate samples of therapy from the trainee's own early cases. This will give the trainee immediate and concrete informational feedback about how well he is learning the practice of the concepts. Finally, by selecting random samples of actual tape-recorded cases seen by the trainee and then having them rated along research scales designed to measure the concepts that were taught, a more objective evaluation of outcomes of training programs can be made. This means that evaluations of how well a trainee has learned could be objectively based upon how he behaves in therapy instead of merely how well he remembers and can intellectualize the concepts.

While the present findings are only beginning attempts to specify therapist behaviors which lead to successful psychotherapy, they point strongly to the importance of the therapist's ability to understand sensitively and accurately the patient and to communicate this understanding in a language attuned to the patient's current feelings. They point strongly also to the importance of a relationship that involves both genuineness and nonpossessive warmth.

What might these consistent research findings mean for us as therapists? (1) As therapists, we might aim toward a more clear and sensitive awareness of the patient's inner being; towards a greater ability to deeply understand the patient's moment-to-moment feelings and experiencings and to thus make more accurate meaning out of the shifts in posture, the slight inflections in tone, or the empty silences. It would mean that as therapists we would concentrate less upon developing skill at highly intellectualized diagnostic formulations and more upon developing skill at the moment-to-moment diagnosis of the patient's "being." (2) As therapists we could allow ourselves to express more openly our deep caring for the *person* who comes to us for help: to do this unconditionally would be to set no conditions on the prizing of the person. (3) As therapists we can afford risking confrontation with the patient as a person rather than as an institution. Our open or nondefensive intactness, our human genuineness encourages the patient to also deeply "be" himself within the relationship.

Finally, these research findings might mean that when we are not able to offer these therapeutic conditions to a particular patient, then we would best serve the interest of that patient by helping him to find another therapist.

NOTES

1. Brief mimeographed research reports of the individual studies reported here by the author are available at the Wisconsin Psychiatric Institute, University of Wisconsin.

2. John V. Liccione, Chief Psychologist, Milwaukee Mental Health Center,

and Marshall Rosenberg, Director of Clinical Services, Psychological Associates, Clayton, Missouri.

3. Such attempts are now underway at Wisconsin by Eugene T. Gendlin and Marjorie Klien, and at the Psychotherapy Center, University of Kentucky, by Charles B. Truax and Robert R. Carkhuff.

REFERENCES

Alexander, F. *Fundamentals of psychoanalysis.* W. W. Norton, 1948.

Dymond, Rosalind. A scale for the measurement of empathic ability. *J. consult. Psychol.,* 1949, *13,* 127–133.

Ferenczi, S. The principle of relaxation and neocatharsis. *Internat. J. Psycho-Analysis,* 1930, *11,* 428–443.

Fox, R. E., & Goldin, P. C. The empathic process in psychotherapy: A survey of theory and research. Unpublished manuscript, 1963.

Halkides, G. An experimental study of four conditions necessary for therapeutic change. Unpublished doctoral dissertation, Univer. of Chicago, 1958.

Halpern, H., & Lesser, Leona. Empathy in infants, adults, and psychotherapists. *Psychoanalysis Psychoanalytic Rev.,* 1960, *47,* 32–42.

Hart, J. T. A replication of the Halkides study. Unpublished manuscript. University of Wisconsin, 1960.

Jourard, S. I—thou relationship versus manipulation in counseling and psychotherapy. *J. Individual Pyschol.,* 1959, *15,* 174–179.

Raush, H. L., & Bordin, E. S. Warmth in personality development and in psychotherapy. *Psychiatry: J. Study of Interpersonal Processes,* Vol. 20, No. 4, November, 1957.

Rogers, C. R. *Client centered therapy.* Cambridge, Mass.: Riverside Press, 1951, 73–74.

Rogers, C. R. The necessary and sufficient conditions of therapeutic personality change. *J. consult. Psychol.,* 1957, *21,* 95–103.

Schafer, R. Generative empathy in the treatment situation. *Psychoanalytic Quart.,* 1959, *28,* 342–373.

Shoben, E. J., Jr. Psychotherapy as a problem in learning theory. *Psychol. Bull.,* 1949, *46,* 366–392.

Strunk, O., Jr. Empathy: A review of theory and research. *Psychological Newsletter,* 1957, *9,* 47–57.

Strupp, H. H. Nature of psychotherapist's contribution to the treatment process. *Arch. Gen. Psychiat.,* 1960, *3,* 219–231.

Truax, C. B. The process of group psychotherapy. *Psychol. Monogr.,* 1961, *75,* No. 14 (Whole No. 511).

Truax, C. B. A scale for the measurement of accurate empathy. *Discussion Paper,* No. 20. Wisconsin Psychiatric Institute, University of Wisconsin, September 26, 1961. (a)

Truax, C. B. A tentative scale for the measurement of unconditional positive regard. *Discussion Paper*, No. 23. Wisconsin Psychiatric Institute, University of Wisconsin, January 16, 1962.
Truax, C. B. A tentative scale for the measurement of therapist genuineness of self-congruence. *Discussion Paper*, No. 35. Wisconsin Psychiatric Institute, University of Wisconsin, May, 1962. (a)

CHAPTER 18

A Commentary on the Effective Ingredients in the Patient-Therapist Interaction

Jerome D. Frank

The central significance of this report, the first of a series, is that it demonstrates it was possible to define subjective, therapeutically relevant, aspects of the psychotherapeutic relationship in objective terms and to show that the extent to which these features were present was related to the outcome of treatment.

Research on psychotherapy has long suffered from difficulties in defining both the outcome and the process of treatment. Both are influenced by many factors outside the therapeutic encounter, including aspects of the patient's and therapist's personalities, the former's current life situation, and the setting in which therapy is conducted. Improvement, as has long been recognized, is not unitary, and the goals of therapy may differ for different types of patients and are defined differently by therapists of different theoretical persuasions.

Furthermore, like all intense, intimate human relationships, the course of therapeutic interaction is subtle and complex. It is transmitted at many levels—verbal and nonverbal, conscious and unconscious. Indeed, until the advent of electronic recording devices there was a real question as to whether it could be studied objectively at all. Much of what transpired in the therapeutic relationship was entirely subjective and could only be learned by quizzing patient and therapist. Doing this repeatedly might well influence or destroy the relationship. It would be as if one tried to study the functions of the living cell by killing and staining it so that it could be seen under the microscope. Although this objection was

---

This chapter is a discussion-commentary, written especially for the present volume, of Chapter 17: "Effective Ingredients in Psychotherapy: An Approach to Unraveling the Patient-Therapist Interaction," by C. B. Truax.

used as an excuse by therapists who were unwilling to submit their work to critical scrutiny, it deserved to be taken seriously. Electronic recording methods made it possible to allow therapy to progress without interference and to study what went on retrospectively from the tapes, as well as to eliminate many sources of observer bias, for the evaluators could be kept in ignorance of the sequence of the tapes as well as of the hypotheses. The mere existence of material available for analysis, however, does not guarantee that significant categorizations will be found. In his study here Truax singles out three aspects of the therapeutic relationship that would be assumed to be rewarding in any human interchange: sensitive awareness of the other person's feelings, deep concern for his welfare, and willingness to be honest about one's own reactions. He shows that they can be reliably rated from short segments of tapes of interviews and correlated with certain measures of outcome.

One outstanding contribution of this report is its demonstration that the amount (if one can use such a word) of the relationship present in a psychotherapeutic interview depends primarily on the therapist. All that would have been demonstrated otherwise is that patients who elicit these qualities have a better prognosis than those who do not.

But from this report alone it would not be possible to determine how far the results could be generalized. The findings depend on work with hospitalized schizophrenics, except for brief mention of a confirmatory study of the effects of accurate empathy with counseling cases. Moreover, almost all the measures of outcome are subjective, that is, are based directly or indirectly on self-reports. The only behavioral measure, the Wittenborn Psychiatric Rating Scales, did not show any significant difference between patients receiving the high or low therapy conditions. Perhaps this simply means that in a mental hospital schizophrenic behavior may be adaptive; that is, it may be the best way to gain the attention of the staff and avoid painful interactions with them and other patients. Subsequent work by Truax and his colleagues, however, has shown that the results may be generalized, at least in part, for other categories of patients.

Another, more disturbing, finding is that the absence of warmth, empathy, and genuineness in the therapist can make certain patients more anxious and damage their self-esteem, something that might have escaped notice had the patients not been schizophrenics (who are especially sensitive to the nuances of personal contacts and are easily crushed by rebuffs, even when unintentional) and the therapists presumably inexperienced. Although they are not described, I assume that they were graduate students in clinical psychology, many of whom would be likely to be made anxious by psychotics and therefore to become preoccupied with controlling their own feelings. As a result they might be expected to be relatively self-protective and obtuse to the feelings of their patients. Had Truax used more experienced therapists and less vulnerable patients, the evidence that some patients can be harmed by "therapy" might not have emerged.

It seems probable that the general finding that experienced therapists achieve better results than inexperienced ones may result in large part from the increasing self-confidence that comes with experience, enabling them to offer more empathy, warmth, and openness to their patients. Also a self-selection process probably operates to cause unsuccessful therapists (presumably low in these qualities) to move to more rewarding fields of work, while those who become experienced have profited from on-the-job training. These considerations mitigate the alarm that a reader might feel at the finding that inept psychotherapists can make some patients worse.

These findings have important implications not only for research but also for training. Most training programs in psychotherapy have not focused sufficiently on teaching young therapists to achieve greater skill in projecting the kinds of attitudes that are therapeutic; the trainees have been left to pick these up from the precept and example of their supervisors. Truax and his colleagues have gone on from the work reported here to demonstrate that the efficiency of training programs can be greatly enhanced by deliberate focus on cultivating the therapeutic qualities they have identified.

In the long run, perhaps the greatest significance of this report is that it finally freed students of interview forms of psychotherapy from nagging doubts that there might really be nothing worthwhile to investigate. They could only deny that those who claimed that the effectiveness of psychotherapy had not been proven had conclusively shown that it was ineffective. In the meanwhile, perhaps researchers in psychotherapy were simply studying the various ways in which it did not work. To surmount this hurdle, it was necessary to show that what went on in psychotherapy did make a difference to some patients, that some of the sources of this effect could be reliably identified, and that they came from the therapist, not the patients. Since this demonstration, researchers have been pushing ahead with renewed confidence to identify other features of the interactions between therapist and patient and investigate their relation to the outcome.

CHAPTER 19

Further Commentary on the Effective Ingredients in the Patient-Therapist Interaction

Sol L. Garfield

In my view, C. B. Truax's paper on the patient-therapist interaction has significant implications for the practice of psychotherapy as well as for research and training. As pointed out by Bergin (1963), it is one of the first published studies to throw some light on the often beclouded and emotion-provoking problem of the effectiveness of psychotherapy. Before elaborating on the more substantive features of the paper, however, it may be worthwhile to present a brief synopsis of the major findings reported.

The main body of data reported in the paper was secured from a sample of hospitalized subjects diagnosed as schizophrenic, although a small group of cases from two university counseling centers was also studied. The earlier studies utilized the "Accurate Empathy Scale" developed by Truax and appeared to show a relationship between the level of accurate empathy on the part of the therapist and the type of outcome secured in therapy. Two additional scales were then developed, "Unconditional Positive Regard" (or Warmth) and "Self-congruence of Therapist." When these scales were applied to data secured from fourteen schizophrenic patients, results comparable to those secured for the empathy scale were obtained. "Thus, the above studies seem strong evidence to support the theoretical view that each of these three therapist-offered conditions is related to constructive change in patients [p. 272]."

This chapter is a discussion-commentary, written especially for the present volume, of Chapter 17: "Effective Ingredients in Psychotherapy: An Approach to Unraveling the Patient-Therapist Interaction," by C. B. Truax.

On the basis of the work mentioned above, a controlled study of schizophrenic patients was then carried out utilizing the three scales of therapeutic conditions. Patients were randomly assigned to either therapy or control conditions and a battery of tests was given initially and later. On most test measures, the most frequent pattern was the following: (1) Those patients receiving high levels of the therapeutic conditions showed the most positive changes; (2) the controls showed modest positive changes or no change; (3) those patients receiving low therapeutic levels tended to show negative findings.

Clearly, these findings are of real significance for persons engaged in psychotherapy practice or research. In the first place, the often-reported finding that no change occurs as a result of psychotherapy can be viewed and interpreted from a different perspective. In the past, much has been made of the fact that if one studies a group of clients receiving psychotherapy and compares them with an untreated control group, the two groups will show somewhat comparable outcomes. This has been the recurrent theme of Eysenck's evaluations of the effectiveness of psychotherapy (1952, 1960, 1966), and while psychotherapists have not been happy with such evaluations, they have not been able to refute them in any really satisfactory way. The present paper clearly suggests another and quite compelling interpretation. Psychotherapy (at least, what is presumed to be the client-centered approach) does have an impact on the client, but this impact can be a positive or a negative one. The mixing of cases with positive and negative outcomes can thus be seen as producing the kind of result which has been emphasized by Eysenck. Rather than no effect, it would now appear that psychotherapy does indeed have an effect and, like that of any potent drug, the effect may be good or bad.

This seems to me the basic finding presented in the paper and one whose importance should not be underestimated. The isolating of basic therapeutic conditions which appear to be related to therapeutic outcome is, of course, also of significance. However, the aforementioned conclusion is one which should make all of us who are involved in various aspects of psychotherapy take notice and ponder its implications. Most of us who have worked in clinical settings have probably come into contact with some clients who appeared to have become worse or whose difficulties became magnified as a result of some experience in psychotherapy. Sometimes this has been inferred when we have begun working with a client who had had some previous therapy with someone else. (Rarely, of course, do we note such negative results with the cases with whom we work.) These, however, are usually clinical impressions of temporary duration, and most psychotherapists, in my own experience, tend not to be overly sensitive to the occurrence or likelihood of negative results. In this connection, I recall an experience of mine in an outpatient clinic many years ago. I was attempting to get the staff of the clinic interested in initiating some kind of evaluation of the effectiveness of our clinical work. I mentioned to them that we operated primarily on the basis of one hypothesis: that any contact we have with a client is beneficial to the client. In the absence of data to support this hypothesis, however, we also had to consider the plausibility of two other equally tenable hypotheses—one, that our contacts with a client produced no change in him, and the other, the very upsetting possibility that some clients were actually made worse. The response of my colleagues to these latter possibilities was one of marked amazement and incredulity. One of them replied immediately by stating, "How can you say that? You know we help these patients."

Although a few studies have been reported which can be interpreted as lending some credibility to these speculative comments (Bergin, 1963), the findings reported by Truax were the clearest on this problem available at that time. The paper highlights the possibility that therapy can have no effect or a negative effect on the client and presents some of the therapeutic variables which appear to be related to positive or negative outcome.

In helping to isolate and specify process variables which are related to outcome in psychotherapy, Truax adds to the significant advances in research begun and fostered by Carl Rogers and his collaborators. It is a further indication of how research in psychotherapy can deal with significant aspects of the psychotherapeutic process, can relate process and outcome variables in a meaningful manner, and can secure findings of vital concern to those who practice psychotherapy as well as to those who are involved in the training of individuals who will be engaged in psychotherapy. This is no mean achievement.

Another aspect worth mention is that the study reported by Truax illustrates how clinically derived insights about the therapist's role and impact in psychotherapy can be fruitfully investigated by means of research. The results obtained help us to sharpen some of our clinical impressions and alert us to problems that were only vaguely perceived previously. The investigation of psychotherapeutic phenomena by means of research, while still at an early stage, can be viewed increasingly as a necessary and vital component of the field of psychotherapy. While some practitioners may still claim that psychotherapy is mainly an art and cannot be studied scientifically, the present research can be viewed as a rebuttal of this point of view. Not only *can* psychotherapy be investigated by means of scientific procedures, but it is vitally necessary that active research be fostered and encouraged if the field is to grow and develop along productive paths. It is the writer's own belief that the diversity of schools of psychotherapy will diminish and some commonly accepted techniques of therapy will develop with the increase in our tested knowledge of what kinds of counseling and psychotherapy foster positive change. Such developments will depend on how productive and successful our research endeavors have been.

In planning my comments on Dr. Truax's paper, I had, as a good psychologist, noted a number of possible criticisms which might be made of the paper. While I will make some reference to these shortly, it seems to me much more important to emphasize the positive features of the paper and to view it in its historical perspective as another in a long line of important contributions which owe their impetus and inspiration to Carl R. Rogers. Rogers has been unusually successful in attracting students and collaborators who reflect his own dedicated interest to *both* the practice and the research investigation of psychotherapy. The results reported in the paper are part of a larger report and study in which Rogers was involved. Since the publication of the paper under discussion, more comprehensive reports have been published (Rogers, Gendlin, Kiesler, & Truax, 1967; Truax & Carkhuff, 1967), and it is difficult to omit reference to them or be uninfluenced by them. These reports, of which the present paper is an excerpt, not only illustrate the significance of research for psychotherapy but also indicate that psychologists, by virtue of their training and skills, can be expected to play a leading role in such research endeavors.

I would also like to mention two other implications available from the present report which I feel are worthy of some emphasis. One of these pertains to the frequent discussions in the past concerning the relative merits of process and outcome research (Astin, 1961; Rubinstein & Parloff, 1959; Strupp, 1963). There is no need to debate this somewhat unproductive issue here. While I have long been biased in favor of outcome research, it seems to me that the best solution to this controversy is apparent in the type of research exemplified in the present paper. In the long run, the most fruitful and productive research has to be concerned with both process and outcome variables. Research on process variables which is not linked or related to outcome measures is not likely to have any pronounced impact on the field. At the same time, pure outcome research will be of limited value unless outcome criteria are closely tied to clearly defined process variables. The present report, and the project which it represents, clearly show the superior utility of this type of research strategy. I, for one, hope that it will become a model for future research in psychotherapy.

The other implication upon which I would like to comment concerns the matter of the selection and training of psychotherapists. It seems quite obvious to me, and this has already been emphasized by Truax and his colleagues in subsequent reports (Carkhuff & Truax, 1965; Truax & Carkhuff, 1967) that the findings reported in the present paper have important implications for education and training in this area. If the therapeutic conditions identified are indeed related to therapeutic outcome, then the training of psychotherapists and counselors should explicitly take cognizance of these conditions and strive to develop high levels in would-be therapists. By the same token, students who display low levels of these therapeutic conditions may be evaluated in terms of their lack of aptitude for this type of endeavor. It is also conceivable that with more direct means of selecting and training psychotherapists, the time of training such persons could be shortened significantly. I am of the opinion, based on the results of Truax and Carkhuff (1967), and Rioch and others (1963), that quite competent psychotherapists could be trained in two-year programs directed toward that end and utilizing appropriate selection procedures. Regardless of how much of this may come to pass, the isolation and evaluation of some significant variables relating to outcome does suggest the likelihood of their being utilized more directly in the training and evaluation of psychotherapists.

The comments and observations which have been offered testify to the value and stimulating quality of Truax's paper. Like most papers it also contains some flaws. I would have liked to see some tables of data so that the actual amounts of change would have been evident. Also missing is any specific indication of the amounts of the therapeutic conditions offered the patients receiving therapy. These are important aspects of the problem of change in psychotherapy, and the impact or value of the paper is diminished by their absence. Nor is this just an academic matter. What kinds of changes occur as a result of psychotherapeutic intervention and the extent of change are clearly of clinical and social significance. For example, if a patient's scaled score on the Schizophrenic Scale of the MMPI improves from 88 to 80, how "significant" is such a change? While it seems fairly evident that the therapeutic conditions do have an effect, the extent of this is, for all practical purposes, not clear. In this connection it is stated that "patients receiving high levels of [the therapeutic] conditions showed an over-all gain in psychological functioning (mean change of 6.0 where 5.0 represents no change) whereas, patients who received relatively low levels of accurate empathy, unconditional positive regard and self-congruence showed a *loss* in psychological functioning [p. 273]." We are not informed of the extent of loss in the one group, nor does the reader have any frame of reference to evaluate the gain for the other group. The fact that no statistically significant differences were obtained on the Wittenborn Scales is also of concern, since scales of this type deal with psychopathology and disturbed behavior, and they have been used extensively and rather successfully to evaluate changes in patients undergoing drug therapy.

Thus, one can respond favorably to Truax's paper while still offering criticisms and having some reservations about it. I regard it as a historically significant paper, one which points up some important problems for investigation in psychotherapy and which also has value as a model. It should also be added that Truax has not been content to let matters rest where they are, in terms of the present paper, but has used these results as a springboard for an extensive and impressive series of studies which have been reported recently in book form (Truax & Carkhuff, 1967). If the test of any research project is the kind of research which it appears to have generated, then, indeed, this has to be viewed as an unusually successful and stimulating research report.

REFERENCES

Astin, A. W. The functional autonomy of psychotherapy. *American Psychologist*, 1961, *16*, 75–78.

Bergin, A. E. The effects of psychotherapy: Negative results revisited. *Journal of Counseling Psychology*, 1963, *10*, 244–250.

Carkhuff, R. R., & Truax, C. B. Training in counseling and psychotherapy: An evaluation of an integrated didactic and experiential approach. *Journal of Consulting Psychology*, 1965, *29*, 333–336.

Eysenck, H. J. The effects of psychotherapy: An evaluation. *Journal of Consulting Psychology*, 1952, *16*, 319–324.

Eysenck, H. J. The effects of psychotherapy. In H. J. Eysenck (Ed.), *Handbook of abnormal psychology*. New York: Basic Books, 1960. Pp. 697–725.

Eysenck, H. J. *The effects of psychotherapy*. New York: International Science Press, 1966.

Rioch, M. J., Elkes, C., Flint, A. A., Udansky, B. S., Newman, R. G., & Silber, E. National Institute of Mental Health pilot study in training mental health counselors. *American Journal of Orthopsychiatry*, 1963, *33*, 678–689.

Rogers, C. R., Gendlin, E. T., Kiesler, D. J., & Truax, C. B. (Eds.) *The therapeutic relationship and its impact.* Madison: University of Wisconsin Press, 1967.

Rubinstein, E. A., & Parloff, M. B. *Research in psychotherapy.* Washington, D. C.: American Psychological Association, 1959.

Strupp, H. H. The outcome problem in psychotherapy revisited. *Psychotherapy,* 1963, *1,* 1–13.

Truax, C. B. Effective ingredients in psychotherapy: An approach to unraveling the patient-therapist interaction. *Journal of Counseling Psychology,* 1963, *10,* 256–263. Reprinted in this collection, pp. 267–279; page numbers cited in the text refer to *Creative developments in psychotherapy.*

Truax, C. B., & Carkhuff, R. R. *Toward effective counseling and psychotherapy.* Chicago: Aldine, 1967.

CHAPTER 20

The Person Who Is the Psychotherapist

J. F. T. Bugental

It is a familiar observation that the psychotherapist is the latest de-
scendant of a line which traces back to prehistory. The psychotherapist's
ancestors are the medicine man, the wizard, the priest, the family
doctor. In every age man has needed to have someone to turn to help
him in contending with the awful unknownness of his fate. Inevitably,
invariably, the one turned to has been invested by others and by himself with supranormal vision and potency. This has usually been both
his greatest reward and his most terrifying burden. Certainly this is so
for the psychotherapist today.

The practice of psychotherapy, as well as the training and research
for such practice, has increasingly become an area of attention for
clinical psychology specifically and, to some extent, for psychology in
general. There can be little doubt that the prime variable affecting
psychotherapy (outside of the patient himself, of course) is the psychotherapist. Psychotherapy may in time take forms which reduce the
essential significance of the individual psychotherapist, but at least as
of today the personality, sensitivity, and skills of the therapist are of
crucial importance. Despite this fact (and with a major exception of the
area of psychoanalysis), little study has been made in depth of the

Presented as a part of a symposium on "The Psychologist's Identity as a Psychotherapist," sponsored by the Division of Clinical Psychology at the American
Psychological Association annual meeting in Philadelphia, August 30, 1963.

This paper is adapted from one of a similar title first presented to the Fifth
Annual Post-Doctoral Workshop in Clinical Psychology at the Arizona State University, Tempe, April 26–27, 1963.

This chapter was voted, by the Editorial Board of the present volume, as one of
the creative developments in psychotherapy, 1958–1968. From the *Journal of
Consulting Psychology*, 28, 1964, 272–277. Copyright 1964 by the American Psychological Association, and reproduced by permission.

qualities in the psychotherapist which most favor or militate against successful therapeutic outcomes in his work. The present paper addresses itself to this matter, employing the method of description based on observations of varied psychotherapists in a variety of settings and examining some of the principal influences within the psychotherapist which seem likely to influence the therapeutic process importantly.

It is the intent of this presentation to provide sufficient description of the important variables that future studies may be able to derive hypotheses as to the nature of the therapist's subjective contributions to the therapeutic process. Working from the raw data of the therapeutic interaction in this fashion hopefully makes possible research dealing with more significant variables in that process.

Concurrently, the sort of description which is here advanced may well be useful in planning and conducting programs for training and supervision of psychotherapists by providing variables for the attention of the teachers and supervisors and for the self-observation of the student-therapists.

It can hardly be debated that there is a selective process, operating largely at unconscious levels, which determines those who will come into the field of psychotherapeutic practice. By no means does this recognition imply that this is altogether a bad thing; nor does it reassure that it is altogether a good thing. For the moment let it rest that a great many psychotherapists have sought through becoming psychotherapists to deal with their own anxieties, both existential and neurotic.

NEUROTIC GRATIFICATIONS TO THE PRACTICE OF PSYCHOTHERAPY

It seems that anyone who becomes involved in the practice of intensive psychotherapy finds gratifications which are deeply and personally meaningful. Some of these are clearly neurotic or destructive; others are more "synergic." The following are among the less constructive.[1]

ONE-WAY INTIMACY

Allen Wheelis (1958) has described what he feels is a powerful selective factor operating in determining who will become a psychoanalyst. This is a hunger for closeness, a great desire for affective intimacy, and a great fear of it. The practice of psychotherapy makes possible a kind of one-way closeness of great intimacy, quite frequently with more affective expression than is to be found in any other relationship, not excluding the marriage relationship (Warkentin, 1963). Yet it is in many ways "safer" to the therapist in that he is enjoined by his ethics and training to withhold himself from the commingling which is potential. How beautifully, then, this practice fits the needs of those with a great affect hunger, a great desire for intimacy, and a great fear of affect in intimacy.

OMNIPOTENCE

Second, the practice of intensive psychotherapy provides rich nourishment for one's omnipotence and omniscience strivings. Most people today have these. Many who feel frightened and impotent in their own lives find in the practice of therapy a kind of splendid calm which they and their patients conspire together to believe the benign influence of the therapist's perspective. A frequent, special instance of the omnipotence striving is the myth of the curative effect of the therapist's love. A great many therapists at one time or another seem to pass through a phase where they become convinced that a vast amount of unquestioning, undemanding love from the therapist for the patient is the curative agent which can produce profound changes. This seems to come about because many patients are emotionally deprived people who seek the kind of concern from their therapists that they feel they never received from their parents. The response of the patient to seeming to gain that caring from the therapist is often dramatic and pervasive, for a period. Only when the therapist has worked with a truly dependent personality over a period of years, does he begin to recognize, if he is wise, that while the patient may indeed achieve remarkable reorganizations of his life through the benign influence of the therapist's love, these are all fragilely hung on the relationship. The patient resists with frightening ruthlessness any attempt by the therapist to reduce that dependence. It is not unusual for the work of months and years, all the hard won gains in life effectiveness which the patient and therapist have worked out, to be brought crashing down in a relatively short space of time when the therapist begins to try to free the patient of his dependence upon the sustenance of the therapist's concern.

CONTINGENCY MASTERY

A third, important gratification in the practice of psychotherapy is the opportunity the therapist has for a vicarious and seemingly safe way of dealing with contingency, with the basic realities of life. Therapists sometimes say they have found themselves using the patient as "a guide dog to go through the mine field" of certain threats first in order to reassure themselves that it can be negotiated. One may respect the therapists who recognize this and be quite confident that nearly all therapists so use their patients in some measure, all too often without such candid recognition. We live in anxiety; we seek to become more self-trusting; we never achieve this fully. When, with full recognition of the patient's needs, we can encourage him to confront that which breeds anxiety within ourselves, we are heavily invested in the outcome.

GIVING TENDERNESS

A fourth neurotic gratification in being a therapist is that it provides an opportunity to give tenderness, compassion, and love in a completely masculine way. A great many who are drawn into this field have fears of their own emotions, fears that these feelings represent weakness and perhaps effeminacy. Often these fears are completely unconscious, and may even be counter-phobically concealed by the therapist being overly expressive of his emotions. We document with research and learned papers the healthfulness of emotional expression and the disasters attendant upon emotional inhibition. And in the therapeutic hour, secure in our masculinity of being doctors and healers, we can dispense tenderness and love without arousing our own anxieties.

REBELLIOUSNESS

A fifth, very frequent gratification in the practice of psychotherapy is that it gives an opportunity to attack authority and tradition while armored in all the prerogatives of position. Study and observation confirm how the needless inhibitions of society complicate the lives of all: the taboos about sexual talk and actions; the guilts about ambivalence toward parents, spouses, and others; the shame of death wishes and other hostile impulses. With the authority of being a therapist, one can strike back at these influences. Notice how often psychotherapists, particularly in their earlier years of practice, become great users of the four-letter words (Feldman, 1955). Notice how often they are flagrant in their expressions of sexual and hostile impulses. It seems quite clear that this may be an acting-out, a counter-phobic kind of behavior which represents the celebration of the licenses of being a therapist. Thus one may pay back society, hit back at authority. It is not a matter of chance, for example, that most therapists tend to be political and social liberals. We would like to think that this is chiefly because they have had an opportunity to see the crippling effect of social ills, and this is one significant reason. On the other hand, the person who is in some revolt against what he feels is social injustice may find in the practice of psychotherapy a relatively safe way to express his rebellion.

SYNERGIC GRATIFICATIONS

Having listed some important aspects of the practice of psychotherapy which provide neurotic gratifications, it will be useful to describe now some creative gratifications which are also realized in such work. Maslow's (1962) term, "synergy," best delineates the common property these have. In a truly synergic relation that which most contributes to the fulfillment of one of the participants is most fulfilling of the other also. It should be evident that the present writer does not hold with the view that the psychotherapist has no needs seeking satisfaction in his work. To the contrary, the therapist must find important fulfillment if he is to be able to mobilize his total resources for the task, as he must frequently do. Some of the incentives to his doing so seem to be the following.

PARTICIPATION

To the psychotherapist is offered the opportunity to participate with unique immediacy in the business of life itself. In psychotherapeutic practice one deals daily with the life *and* death of human personality and potential. This phrase intends no play on words, and the melodrama implicit in this characterization is that of the human experience itself. As the therapist accompanies his patient in his efforts to confront the minor and the great issues of his life, to contend with the ever-present unknownness of choices and their consequences, to meet and live with the multiple emotional seekings and stresses of human relationships—as the psychotherapist visits the heights of elation and self-affirmation, the depths of confusion and madness, the brink of suicide, the bleakness of relinquishment, and on and on—then the therapist must know at once his own humble gifts and his privileged situation in viewing the human condition.

PERSONAL GROWTH

A good therapeutic relation is growth inducing in both participants. Growth potential is infinite, and the therapist who is an authentic participant in his work with his patient has repeated stimulation and opportunity to increase his realization upon his own potential. In a climate in which genuineness is requisite and yet always sought anew, that which is false and self-defeating in the therapist himself must ever and again be illuminated for the shoddy self-deception it is. The therapist who has come to love the realization of human potential—

and I am convinced this is a distinguishing characteristic of the dedicated therapist—will be continually renewed in his own growth.

PSYCHOLOGICAL PROCESSES

A high proportion of psychologist-psychotherapists entered their parent discipline of psychology because, among other reasons, of a fascination with psychological processes which may be likened to that some people show with mechanics, others with color and form in the arts, and still others with mathematics and quantitative processes. There is no other opportunity in all the world like that of intensive psychotherapy for a person with this orientation to immerse himself in the working of psychological processes in their natural condition. All our familiar psychological topics of learning, motivation, attitudes, emotions, attention, remembering, perception, and so on—all of these are displayed in endless variation and exquisite detail.

PATIENT'S GROWTH

Most patients who come to the psychotherapist show improvement. The doubters to the contrary, the psychotherapeutic experience is generally one in which there is a gain in human effectiveness and satisfaction (although, albeit, not the magical one frequently initially expected). It is for the therapist, once he has adjusted his own sights to realistic dimensions, a deeply meaningful experience to have participated in his patient's emergence. There are, of course, the failures, the disappointments, the questionable outcomes. However, with experience, constant self-development, and much learning just to wait, the proportion of favorable outcomes increases, the pervasiveness of the changes becomes more evident. It is, then, an enriching feeling to have been an intimate participant in this growth.

Maturity of the Therapist

We will describe now some characteristics which are found in the mature psychotherapist and which, it is believed, portray what this field means to the psychologist who dedicates his career to it.

HUMILITY

Probably one of the first forms of genuine maturing in the therapist is his acceptance of the fact that he has but limited knowledge of his patient. Since, as a therapist, he gets to know his patients so much more thoroughly than he knows any other human beings in his life, he may often feel that he really knows the patients fully. This is a myth; this is the omniscience fantasy being enacted. As a therapist one never knows all about his patients, only some aspects. These may be terribly important aspects and certainly significant to know, but one needs to recognize they are but a part of what could conceivably be known about these patients.

SELECTIVE PARTICIPATION

A second mark of the maturing therapist is his selective use of his own participation. This is to say he is able so to modulate when and how he intervenes that his participation is maximally effective in a restricted area. The maturing therapist participates verbally sparingly, but with precision. A very common fault of the tyro-therapist is that he talks too much or too little or at the wrong times.

ENCOUNTER

A third characteristic of the maturing therapist is his willingness genuinely to encounter his patient. This does not mean a kind of exhibitionism or display of himself. It does mean a willingness to "be there" with his patient, to confront his patient directly when appropriate, to take responsibility for his (the therapist's) own thinking, judgments, feelings; and to be authentic in his own person with the patient. Sidney Jourard[2] suggests that this is indeed one of the main things that has a curative effect in the therapeutic relationship, that is, the therapist serving as a model of authenticity for the patient.

EVOLVING CONCEPTUUM

A further evidence of growing maturity in the therapist is that he has an evolving set of constructions about himself, his world, the nature of psychotherapy, and what he means by the concept of personality. One may be mistrustful of the therapist who believes he has reached final answers on any of these points. Recognition of the dynamic quality of knowledge, of the continuing learning experience of therapeutic work demands that one be changing if one be dedicated and aware.

GUILT ACCEPTANCE

One of the most difficult aspects of therapeutic maturity is the acceptance of the guilt of being a therapist. Certainly all that has been said above about the neurotic gratifications of being a therapist will have indicated that there is inevitably a load of guilt in being a therapist.

We will not re-elaborate on these points. Going further, however, we are saying that there is guilt for our failure to be all that we can be as therapists to these people who come and give us their lives and trust.

The other day I saw Jack again for the first time in five years. Initially I saw Jack eleven years ago; that was for vocational guidance. He came back a year later because he was having trouble with his marriage, and I was able to be of some help in patching up a shaky relationship. Seven years ago when he came to me the marriage had collapsed at last, and he was readjusting his life to a new pattern of living. At that time we attempted intensive psychotherapy, and I saw him for several years. I think Jack was helped by the experience. However, I put it in this somewhat tentative fashion because I can see so many ways today that he could have been helped so much more. I look at Jack in my office today, and I see a man with the gray coming in at his temples. I see in him also virtually a boy of 29 as I first saw eleven years ago. The prime years of his early maturity are embraced by our relationship. As I look at Jack, I think of Louis, who I am currently seeing and who is about the age Jack was when he first came to me. Louis is going to have a much fuller life than Jack has had because I am so much more able to meet him and to help him in becoming himself. To look at Jack is to look at my own guiltiness for not having been all that Jack needed. I comfort myself that I served him with sincerity with the best of my skill at that time. I comfort myself even that many another therapist might have done no more for him than I did, but this does not give Jack back his lost years.

This is a story of the therapist's guilt. If I am to be a growing, evolving person, each old patient I see again is an accusation; each patient of former years will be in some measure someone who trusted me, and whom I failed by today's standards. If I become despondent or self-punitive, I am acting out a neurotic type of guilt; but if I recognize the legitimate responsibility I had in this matter, I am revitalized in my own growth.

But there is yet one further way in which this guilt operates. When I recognize that I am continuing to try to grow, to increase my awareness, skill, and competence in effectively being in the relationship with my patients, then I must look at my patients today and know that each one of them is getting less than I hope I will be giving his successor 5 years hence. There is guilt in this too.

The reader may protest, "This all sounds very masochistic and self-punishing. It's just the way things are. There's no need to expend guilt, regret on it." In one sense this protest is very right; in another, it's very wrong. Yes, this is the way things are; but the fact that a condition is so does not mean that it is unladen with emotional significance. It is so that I can only do so much for my patients now and that that seldom is all I potentially can do, even today. If the sense of guilt becomes an interference with my effective use of myself rather than part of a heightened sensitivity, then it is clearly becoming a neurotic guilt and an attempt to forestall other anxiety. The kind of guilt that I am trying to characterize here is not forestalling of anxiety, nor yet laden with additional anxiety, but is an emotional fact of being.

CONCLUSION

I want to conclude by saying very briefly what it means to me to be a psychotherapist. I feel like one of the fortunate ones. I feel more fortunate than most. The men and women who come to see me entrust me with that which is most deeply meaningful in all their experience. They offer me the awesome privilege of participating in the very essence of their lives. When I am most authentic, I am most humble in my appreciation of this opportunity.

As I started this paper, I called attention to the lineage from which we psychotherapists take our vocation: medicine man, wizard, priest, and family doctor. This is a proud line, and we may be proud to be part of it. These are the bearers of man's hope and man's faith. These are the personifications of man's courage and creativity in confronting the immensity of the unknown. We are, for our brief time, hoisted on the shoulders of our fellows that we may catch some glimpse of the yet untouched reaches of what it means to be truly man.

NOTES

1. In all of these observations, the writer recognizes that he is certainly describing himself as well as other therapists.

2. S. M. Jourard, personal communication, 1963.

REFERENCES

Feldman, M. J. The use of obscene words in the therapeutic relationship. *Amer. J. Psychoanal.*, 1955, *15*, 45–48.

Maslow, A. H. Notes on synergy. In A. H. Maslow (Ed.), *Summer notes.* Del Mar, Calif.: Non-Linear Systems, 1962. Pp. 48–58.

Warkentin, J. The therapist's significant other. *Ann. Psychother.*, 1963, 4(1), 54–59.

Wheelis, A. *The quest for identity.* New York: Norton, 1958. Pp. 206 ff.

CHAPTER 21

Person into Therapist

Frederick Wyatt

I have been asked to comment on Dr. Bugental's paper. Does my assignment imply criticism? If so, I happen to find myself mostly in agreement with his observations concerning the motives of therapists. Clearly, Dr. Bugental's paper rests on a great deal of experience with therapy. To quibble about details would only detract from a point of view representing both a highly complex experience over many years and the reflection which guided and accompanied it. Critical strictures do not fit a comprehensive attitude toward life and work. It will be more appropriate, therefore, to expand on some of Dr. Bugental's points and add to them where it seems useful. The concluding section of Dr. Bugental's paper deals with the obligations of the therapist and presents, in a manner of speaking, Dr. Bugental's *apologia pro vita sua.* Here I differ with him, but will speak of it only in order to focus on a question which all therapists have to consider at various stages of their careers.

Dr. Bugental's paper treats of the therapist's subjective contribution to the therapeutic process, resulting as it must from his motives for becoming a therapist. Among the less constructive reasons for making this vocational choice, such as hunger for intimacy and the need for omnipotence and omniscience, is also what Dr. Bugental calls *contingency mastery.* It refers to the inclination, usually comfortably rationalized and otherwise concealed, of therapists to use their clients for vicarious experience.

In this way patients sometimes become a cast of alter egos for the therapist, impersonating his own limitations and unmastered repres-

---

This chapter is a discussion-commentary, written especially for the present volume, of Chapter 20: "The Person Who Is the Psychotherapist," by J. F. T. Bugental.

sions. Nobody is quite satisfied with the limitations of his own self, and the detachment of the therapeutic position is likely to hide a lot of unstilled desire. In general it holds a potential for envy. The search for vicarious gratification leads the therapist to delegate to the patient experiences he cannot realize for himself. The specific idiosyncratic relevance which the patient's report thereby attains is, however, only one aspect of the much larger scope of the therapist's vicariousness.

But how does this vicariousness work? This brings us to a concept which I should like to call the *hypomanic adaptation*. By this arrangement the patient becomes the naïve, or helpless, or foolish part of the therapist's self. The other part, the knowing and self-assured one, laughs at the wayward and ignorant child, thus settling, at least temporarily, memories of defeat and embarrassment, of secret inadequacy and dissatisfaction with himself. The hypomanic adaptation is obviously a version of Freud's structural explanation of humor and mania. The unconscious attraction of this arrangement is that it affords the therapist the opportunity over and over again to "rise above himself." At least in his therapeutic activity he can behave (or imagine himself behaving) as he always wanted and expected himself to. While realizing an ideal deeply rooted in our culture he can be, at the same time, both the needy patient *and* his own ideal, elevated self.

Under the protective cover of this elaborate and sometimes very subtle maneuver the therapist can also experience vicariously what the patterning of his own life precluded him from experiencing. As he indulges himself he also "understands," and so has not only an excuse but a way of detaching himself from the strains which open vicariousness would cause him. To speak of this stratagem so baldly may be chilling, even for therapists. However, once we get accustomed to the idea that the pursuit of therapy must have its unconscious motives no less than other engagements do, we will recognize that the unconscious gains of doing therapy may be no less functional and productive than humor is in life. The idea of therapy entirely directed by reason and performed by a detached and puritanical intellect does not seem realistic. Even if it were possible, the prospect would not be appealing. As in other adaptive-defensive sets the question is not so much from what instinctual needs it derives but how it is being used, that is, in a more theoretical formulation, how it has become integrated into the ego.

There is yet another aspect to the therapist's vicarious investment in his patient. The conflicts which beset the patient at times are not too different from those the therapist knows from his own experience. In assisting the patient to cope with his anxieties the therapist (as Dr.

Bugental observes) also has him fight his own psychological battles. I would describe this aspect of the therapist's involvement as the *counterphobic motive* for doing therapy. Here, too, the therapist, using the patient as an instrument, continues his own adaptive efforts. It will not surprise us too much that this process resembles the maturation inherent in being a parent as Benedek (1959) has described it. By guiding the patient through the wasteland of unredeemed conflict the therapist also attempts to resolve his own unsettled problems. Here again we have no reason to be concerned with the origins of this motive as long as we can be sure that the therapist is aware of it. The vicarious involvements of the therapist will become a technical defect as well as an ethical liability only when he remains unaware of his own motives and hides his aims behind highflown pretenses.

Therapists also use the therapeutic situation, Dr. Bugental suggests, for giving tenderness and love without threat to their masculinity, which is safeguarded by the seeming detachment and vaunted objectivity of the therapeutic role. Dr. Bugental is right; surely this is foremost among the unofficial motives of therapy. There is, however, a deeper reason why the therapeutic situation becomes an opportunity for many therapists to give affection and tenderness under carefully guarded conditions. People so obviously crave love that we tend to overlook—we have, in fact, overlooked it in our theories—that there is a need for *giving* tenderness, as well as for receiving it. This need is not so demonstrative or petulant in expression as the need for love, which may be the reason that it has not been more fully acknowledged. The therapeutic endeavor as a whole is in this sense a paradigm of giving affection, even though in a low key and with a reasoned restraint. The therapist's effort at its best belongs structurally, therefore, to what Erikson (1950) has called *generativity*, the capacity for giving and passing on to the younger generation what one has learned oneself, without expecting to be rewarded for it. Both psychotherapy and generativity, however, are related to the process which I have called hypomanic adaptation. Elsewhere I have described this model as the *mechanism of inner duality* (Wyatt, 1967), suggesting that the therapist treats his patient in some respects as he wishes he had been treated when he himself was a child. The aims of therapy, and above all its routine, will of course keep the responsible therapist from imposing his own needs upon the patient. Generativity implies the capacity for incorporating the desire to give love to others into a larger scheme of life; and therapy is a highly specialized, as well as special, occasion for generativity—at least when we consider its potential.

Finally we come back to the question: what makes vicariousness so attractive and so important in therapy? Dr. Bugental mentions, among therapists' more creative, or integrative, motives, the *synergic* one, according to which "the therapist participates with unique immediacy in the business of life itself": another way of saying that vicariousness is a fundamental motive for doing therapy. It may be truly syntonic, or it may represent merely an illicit gratification for the therapist, and the distortions and rationalizations following it do more harm, one can be sure, than gratification itself. Synergic means here that what fulfills one participant in this dyadic interaction will also fulfill the other one. Therapist and patient generally have the same aims but define them differently, through their respective roles. One of the mechanisms which brings about the synergic mutuality of therapy must, therefore, be located in the vicarious inclinations of the therapist, or perhaps we should say, rather, in his potential for vicariousness, thereby acknowledging the fundamental importance of this disposition for the therapeutic enterprise as a whole.

Dr. Bugental argues that "there is inevitably a load of guilt in being a therapist." Moreover, "there is guilt for our failure to be all that we can be as therapists to these people who come and give us their lives and trust. . . . If I am to be a growing, evolving person, each old patient I see again is an accusation, . . . someone who trusted me and whom I failed by today's standards." The therapist who becomes self-punitive in this matter would only act out a neurotic type of guilt, but he would further his growth if he recognized his legitimate responsibility.

Here I differ from Dr. Bugental. As he did not have the space to state his premises I must attempt to reconstruct them here as well as I can. Giving his best to his patients is so much of an inner obligation that the therapist is bound to feel sorry when his best efforts today must be outdone by tomorrow's ordinary good ones. Dr. Bugental is aware that all this may sound very masochistic and warns against extremes. This issue is so complex, however, that it needs some clarification.

There is, first, the distinction between *norm* and *practice*: how therapists should ideally behave and what they actually do. As usual, reality is not up to the lofty standards of the ideal. But when we speak about the conduct of therapists, we must at once acknowledge that a great variety of personalities and circumstances is involved here, and, as usual, reality confounds the ideal with a profusion of uncharted eventualities. If we consider for the moment the actual behavior of therapists, we note that they differ not only among each other but also within themselves. Whether they want to or not, they behave differently with different patients. Age and experience seem to influence the therapist's work. As a rule we do therapy more competently, and therefore more effectively, later on in our careers. This has, of course, to do with the accumulation of experience and with maturation. We become more detached and are less concerned with principles. True, by the same token, our enthusiasm is tempered too. If therapists are candid they will admit to being less often involved and more often bored at the height of their competence than they were at an earlier stage of their career (Berman, 1949). Then, every hour was a contest, a quest for the ultimate, significant far beyond its immediate purpose; and the young therapist, brave soul, pitted himself against the forces of repression and guilt, and fought for the recovery of his patient as he would fight for his own autonomy. In fact, the two must often have merged into one great task. Later on, however, the therapist learned to husband his energies and to protect himself against too much exposure. The slow, steady drip of disappointment does its part, too. The accumulation of experience sobers the mind as it improves it. Enthusiasm always presupposes a certain limitation of scope, but it also endows us with an inestimable power. There is simply nothing better than good will, says Kant.

When Dr. Bugental concludes that the therapist should feel bad because, even though he does his best at this moment, he still is not good enough because some day he will be better, he relies not so much on an ethical as on a logical paradox. He condenses the real present with an imaginary future in matters of commitment and guilt, but keeps them properly apart with regard to acquiring competence. Speaking more concretely, I may reflect today that at some future date I shall be more competent than I am now, although, as a rule, such thoughts do not occur often and by definition must remain vague and schematic. For how can I really know what it is like to be "more competent" unless I recognize at once that I am not doing the right thing even as I am doing it, or unless I have already become more competent and compare what I am doing now with what I did at an earlier stage? I can experience myself, even in Dr. Bugental's special, invigorating sense, as "not good enough" only when I know that I am *not* doing the right thing *now*, but not because I anticipate now that I *shall*, in an unspecified way, do better at some unspecified date in the future. The thought would perhaps be more plausible if it were stated in this way: I am now reflecting on patients I have treated some time ago. On the basis of what I have learned in the meantime both about therapy and myself, I *must* admit to myself that, had I picked up that cue at a critical period and responded to it with that therapeutic intervention, I *might* have helped the client more than I actually did. Note, however, the auxiliaries which I have italicized.

Therapists at all stages of their careers will feel inadequate with one client or another. Our prototypical therapist finds himself thinking: "I really don't understand him; I don't know why he behaves that way"; or: "He makes me uncomfortable"; or: "I don't like him much"; or, even more plainly: "He bores me"! At any rate, I know I am not doing the right thing. It may not be pleasant to admit, but this surely is a common experience for most of us. It does not even mean that the therapy so questioned must of necessity be a failure. Such underlying despair will often signify a crisis of transition at a certain phase of therapy. Here, too, the dawn may be near when the night is darkest. As things go, though, the therapist most needing to question his competence is usually the one least encumbered by doubt. Every therapist has reason to scrutinize his performance and recognize past or present shortcomings. This does not mean, however, that he should perpetually fret over his shortcomings while doing his work as well as he can right now.

There is a silent assumption in all this that the therapist is somehow metaphysically committed not only to do his actual but his potential best, and also that he has a quasi-predetermined responsibility for the salvation of his patient. This suggests its own dangers. At any rate, such an image of his function could be meaningful only *if* it corresponded with the absolute relevance of therapy by a particular therapist for the patient's life. Such relevance, however, is highly doubtful, as we shall see in a moment. This view of therapy implies that, unless the therapist is at his existential best, the client will lose his only, precious chance. But will he really? Do we know so well what it is that will change the course of his life? The right interpretation, the right therapeutic attitude? The birth of a child; the death of an obnoxious parent; a promotion due to the heart attack of somebody else—something completely outside the therapeutic effort, but fit to create an opportunity for the client where it is least expected? Perhaps even an act of renunciation, long due and beneficial, but prompted by external circumstances rather than by the therapist's intervention?

Let there be no misunderstanding: the planned interventions of the therapist matter a great deal, and his sober, efficient sympathy, his "good will," matters even more. From the patient's point of view, what is important is the experience of a relationship with a person competent without needing to be superior, sensible without becoming priggish, and well-meaning without taking sides. If the therapist succeeds in communicating to his client an incorruptible sense of reality, he will have great impact even if we cannot say afterwards what, exactly, it was that brought about the beneficial change. The scope of therapy is limited, and there are always the vicissitudes of life. We can easily see that an adaptive and flexible person will be better able to cope with the slings and arrows of outrageous fortune than a rigid and neurotically inept one, although even here we note a surprising latitude of possibilities and outcomes. By far the greater portion of the forces whose reverberations we sense in therapy never come into its grasp, even though they clearly promote or obstruct it. In fact, the therapist is no less subject to them than the patient.

Jack's story, which Dr. Bugental cites as a paradigm, might not have been much different had he previously enjoyed the benefits of the professional experience which his therapist offered him a decade later. It is quite possible that even a very seasoned therapist could not have done more than help Jack to manage his marriage for the time being. We have every reason to insist that therapists be as well trained, as competent and responsible as we can possibly make them. But we must not expect that therapists can transcend their mundane selves at every stage of their careers. This is reserved to the founders of religions and the makers of myth, who have something stronger than therapy to offer to the needy. (If these tried to perform therapy, however, they might not be so good at this much more modest and limited enterprise.)

In short, behind the encompassing obligation which Dr. Bugental requires of therapists there is a hint of omnipotence. The therapist and his competence are of critical importance, but in a different, less exclusive, less saintly way. We should not expect of him the impossible, that he be more ideal, less needy than other men. This sounds too much like the images patients have of their therapists at certain stages of the transference, usually before the patient is able to reveal to the therapist some of the greed and anger which hitherto he kept under the wraps of reaction formation and self-tormenting symptoms. It sounds too much like the fantasies which the child, and the enduring regressive child in the adult, has of his parents: generous without limit toward him, but abstinent with regard to their own needs. We cannot expect the therapist to be more virtuous than other people; but we can expect him to have some knowledge of the conditions of virtue—the common predicament of instinctual urges and narcissistic preoccupation. We also can and must expect of him that he can control his own needs and affects when he does therapy. We cannot demand of him that he relate to his client with a metaphysical commitment, like a guardian angel. We expect of him, rather, that he assist his patients without exacting awe and without enhancing those magical fantasies of which they need to be disabused; but he will be able to do this only if he can also accept his own limitations calmly.

REFERENCES

Benedek, Therese. Parenthood as a developmental phase. *Journal of the American Psychoanalytic Association*, 1959, *7*, 389–417.

Berman, Leo. Countertransference and attitudes of the analyst in the therapeutic process. *Psychiatry*, 1949, *12*, 159–166.

Erikson, H. E. *Childhood and society*. New York: W. W. Norton & Co., 1950.

Freud, S. Humour (1927). Standard Edition, Vol. 21. London: Hogarth Press, 1961. Pp. 162–163.

Wyatt, F. Clinical notes on the motives of reproduction. *Journal of Social Issues*, 1967, *23*, 29–56.

Part III

The Working
Processes of
Psychotherapy

CHAPTER 22

The Working Processes of Psychotherapy: Creative Developments

Alvin R. Mahrer and *Leonard Pearson*

Part III deals with creative developments in the working processes of psychotherapy, the concrete methods and techniques which make up what Matarazzo calls the art or practical craft of psychotherapy. We will summarize these creative developments by discussing the articles included in this section, with some reference to articles from other sections of the volume.

THE NEED FOR WORKING INTRASESSION GUIDELINES

Psychotherapy is a recent offshoot of an ancient enterprise, the study of personality (Frank; Whitaker), which today still rests upon meager experimentally verified and generally accepted information (Frank). Indeed, at the practical level of working guidelines for intrasession operations, Matarazzo considers it premature to expect any of our theories to provide systematic rules of procedure. Psychoanalytic approaches offer relatively explicit therapeutic procedures which are being abandoned largely because they do not work (Alexander), whereas other approaches such as existentialism do not possess a set of specifically articulated working techniques (May). A good part of the popular appeal of client-centered and behavior-modification approaches lies in their provision of specific guidelines for the psychotherapist. At present, Matarazzo concludes, the intrasession guidelines constitute an art, a practical craft, with fragmentary rules of thumb passed on from master to apprentice; it is a myth to treat psychotherapy as a science.

It is our conviction that sets of working guidelines must be found and articulated, whether these are considered artistic or scientific. While there is value in the construction of comprehensive personality approaches and mini-theories of personality change, the future of psychotherapy hinges on the development of working guidelines to intra-session operations, of specific techniques to bring about specific effects. If these can be articulated and found to possess regular demonstrable effects leading to constructive change, our conviction is that theory, research, and practice will all profit.

THE WORKING DATA OF PSYCHOTHERAPY

IDENTIFICATION OF ACTUAL WORKING DATA

A 27-year-old male patient, in his fifteenth session with a private practitioner, says the following: "I rode the greatest horse. Gee, was he spirited. Bam, and he was away. He was just great . . . uh . . . [coughs]. Where is your Kleenex? I remember when I was a kid I used to ride for hours with my father, but now I have to p-p-pay for it, and I can't afford it two or three times a week. Should I t-t-tell you a dream, or do you want to know more about what happened?"

The data may be construed to yield inferences that the patient is showing some slippage in his thinking, making overtures toward a closer relationship with the therapist, stuttering, defending against aggressive impulses, becoming childish, manifesting anxiety, providing information about his father, manifesting a lack of masculine identity, showing an inability to form attachments, revealing subtle signs of underlying schizophrenic thinking, avoiding meaningful material, attempting to seduce the therapist, fighting homosexual impulses, being passive-dependent—among many other potential inferences.

It is obvious that there is no one conceptual framework for identifying the working data of psychotherapy, for defining what is going on at a given moment (Alexander; Auld; Frank; Garfield; Matarazzo; McQuown; Scheflen). Different guidelines, principles, and theories aid the therapist, depending upon his theoretical orientation, training, and background, in naming the critical elements out of the total complex of data.

There is vigorous interest in the systematic analysis of the actual events of psychotherapy in order to study the minute processes in step-by-step detail (Alexander; Auld; Frank; Garfield; Matarazzo; McQuown; Scheflen; Truax). In part, this involves the intensive study of effective psychotherapy. Sometimes it involves the application of different kinds of conceptual frameworks to the ongoing process of psychotherapy—verbal analyses, transactional analyses, dynamic analyses, and the like. Primarily, it involves research investigation of patient-therapist interactions. According to Matarazzo, sound work on this problem is more likely to emerge from practitioner-theorists than from writer-theorists. Here is one area in which effective integration is required between practice and research, with the hope of effective inter-stimulation (Garfield), as, for example, in the work of Rogers and his collaborators (e.g., Truax).

THE PAST AND THE PRESENT AS WORKING DATA OF PSYCHOTHERAPY

The therapist may attend to the data of the ongoing present—how the patient is in the given here-and-now moment. Or the therapist may construe the same data as providing information about the past. For example, the data of the 27-year-old patient may be understood as indicating here-and-now attempts to ward off the therapist, or the data may be construed as providing information about his childhood relationships with his father. Similarly, the therapist may elect to work with whatever the patient is doing right at the current moment, or the therapist may be geared to enter into the patient's past. Do the working data consist of present or past material?

The personality model as a determinant. Mowrer points to the personality model as one determinant of whether the present or the past constitutes the working data. For example, within a psychoanalytic framework, whether the problem arises from an early-formed severe superego or a here-and-now ego deficiency will determine whether the working data are those of the past or of the present. Some personality models lean toward the past and others lean toward the present.

The past as etiological backdrop for the present. One position is that the past cannot be ignored; it provides the template for current behavior, the backdrop for etiological understanding of the present (Alexander; Framo). However, psychotherapy is to focus on the patient's current life situation, while acknowledging the historical roots of current behavior. Even when treatment goes into the past to work out early conflicts, therapy must then refocus on current life functioning. This position warns against a wholesale targeting upon the past (Alexander), and calls attention to the danger of missing current functionings by following the patient into a discussion of childhood-infantile material (Alexander).

The past as fused with the present. The entire past may be construed as a currently ongoing process. With regard to etiology, the past provides data upon which is constructed an understanding of the patient's current personality functionings. But in addition, past modes of relating, tendencies, and ways of being are understood as continuing to operate in the ongoing present (May). The current dynamics constitute the data, whether the referent content is the present, the past, or the future; the immediately current moment is the complete source of data (May). The patient's early relationship with a parent is understood, according to this position, as operating here and now in the current moment. He is, right now, being a little boy who is fearful of offending the parental figure. He is being a certain way, right now, as he tells of an incident from his childhood. The ongoing past is fused with the present.

THE LEADING EDGE OF PERSONALITY

For some therapists, the primary working data are the immediate personality forces and experiencings, rather than the deeper personality forces or the individual experiencings which are "next" (Gendlin; Wyatt). For example, an individual's immediate experiencings may consist of a fear of rejection, of being turned away. The hierarchy includes a deeper personality force or "next" experiencing having to do with safe and comfortable affection, but the focus of therapy must be on the fear of rejection or whatever is the leading edge of personality. Deeper motivations, available or accessible feelings, potential tendencies, fundamental personality processes, and next experiencings are of critical importance in understanding the immediate ongoing personality functionings, but they do not constitute the immediate working data of the psychotherapeutic process.

The role of the therapist. According to Auld, the role of the therapist is underemphasized in approaches such as behavior modification and psychoanalysis. The patient's crying is only half the data, for the patient is crying in the psychotherapeutic situation, in the relationship with the other person—the therapist. Consequently, the data includes the patient's behavior in relationship to the therapist. The therapist is underemphasized by considering him as an external interpreter or receiver of the data—the behavior of the patient. Similarly, the therapist is underemphasized when he is considered a blank screen, instead of a distinct and concrete human being, acutely reacted to by the patient (Alexander). Auld further asserts that the role of the therapist is overemphasized in approaches along client-centered lines. Auld's resolution is simply to identify an interactional complex involving both patient and therapist and to understand the working data as events occurring within this interactional complex.

Transference as a data-decoy. The concept of transference serves to protect both patient and therapist against the (more anxiety-provoking) current ongoings between the two persons (May). The patient's terrible hate is thereby attributed to the transference of her unconscious feelings toward her father; it is not personally invoked because of the therapist. By invoking the transference concept, the therapist is led away from an identification of the here-and-now, ongoing data occurring in the current interaction with the therapist.

The ongoing interactional complex as data-source. The data refer to the here-and-now, ongoing verbal and nonverbal interactional complex between two actual persons in the current moment (Alexander; Matarazzo; May; McQuown). The data are interpreted through the continuous asking of a question such as: What is the patient doing (feeling, behaving, showing, communicating, wanting, seeking) right at the current moment in his interaction with the therapist?

Sheflen highlights the value of a communicational framework in identifying the ongoing interactional data. A communicational framework involves the careful observation of whether a behavior results in some communicated behavior change in the other person. It is critical to identify units of communication, involving all the sense modalities. The context might be part of a session, a full session, or a series of sessions. The meaning of a single communicational event, Sheflen says, must be understood within its own natural context.

Therapist feelings as working data. The therapist's feelings and reactions with and toward the patient are powerful data components of the psychotherapeutic interaction (Alexander; Matarazzo). Previously, when viewing working data of psychotherapy, the therapist's own feelings and reactions were commonly considered confounding interferences, intrusions of the therapist's personal involvement or countertransference. We are referring, for example, to the rise of internal bodily tension, a scary feeling in the stomach region, a heightened tempo of pulsing blood. Now, two guidelines bring these feelings of the therapist into the realm of working data. First, to the extent that the patient's behavior is understood as goal directed (or in interaction with the therapist, or involved with the therapist, or motivated toward an impact upon the therapist), the therapist's feelings serve as a data-base for inferences. What is the patient doing (feeling, behaving, showing, communicating, wanting, seeking) right at the current moment in his interaction with the therapist? The answer is that the patient is affecting the therapist so as to bring out tension, a scary feeling, anxiety. In this manner, the therapist's feelings provide working data about the patient. The patient is bringing out these particular feelings in the therapist, as the therapist is the object or target of the patient's behavings and manner of being.

Second, the therapist's own immediate feelings provide data about what is also occurring within the patient at the moment. For example, as the patient is beginning to confront his own aggressive tendencies, or as the patient is beginning to function in an aggressive manner, the therapist's feelings are a source of inferences about the patient's own feelings toward his aggressive tendencies or behavior; namely, the patient is scared, tense, and anxious about them. The therapist's feelings provide inferential data about the immediate ongoing feelings within the patient himself. The therapist is, therefore, more than the object or target of the patient's behavings; he is, in addition, the ally (spokesman, colleague, interpreter) of the patient's motivations, drives, next experiencings, or behavioral tendencies.

THE FLOW OF BODILY FEELINGS AS WORKING DATA

According to Gendlin, some of the primary data of psychotherapy are the inwardly sensed, bodily felt events—the flow of bodily sensing or feeling. These bodily felt feelings make up what is meant by "experiencing." They are what is ongoing at the moment and accessible to awareness. Although others have pointed to the patient's feelings as psychotherapeutic data (Alexander; Auld; Framo; Frank; Matarazzo; May; Rogers; Truax; Whitaker), Gendlin offers an explicit system for identifying and analyzing these data as the richest source of inferences—indeed the very subject matter—of psychotherapy.

BEHAVIOR AS WORKING DATA

It is simply not enough to assert that the data consist of the patient's behaviors. Psychotherapists whose approaches highlight behavior are not defining what their data are so much as they are identifying what their data are not. That is, they are asserting that their data do not consist of some mysterious entity labeled the patient's condition or intrapsychic state or neurotic condition or weak ego or inadequate defense. One must still identify the behavior of a given patient at a particular moment. As Scheflen points out, the quest for the explicit identification of behavior is faced with a near infinity of potential behavioral units, ranging across all levels of abstraction.

Scheflen suggests that the first step, in selecting and identifying which of the myriad of potential behaviors are to be treated as data, lies in the use of some conceptual system for organizing the relevant behaviors and behavioral units. Particular theories of communication, behavior modification, and psychoanalysis may equally seek behavioral data, but they will select different behaviors as their focus. Similarly, a particular social-learning theory and a particular school of existential psychology will name different patient behaviors as their subject data. The answer to the question of which behaviors constitute the data depends upon the theoretical system of personality used.

As an interpretive summary, we propose the following guidelines for the identification of the working data of psychotherapy: (a) The data include presently ongoing behaviors, occurring in the immediate moment. This means that the data refer to the behavior of the patient right now, rather than the behaviors which he describes or talks about. It means that we exclude the behaviors which were present during the last session and whatever behaviors we believe are latent, potential, or available in the future within the patient's personality. (b) The data include those behaviors characterized by motivation, goal-directionality. The question is, what is the patient doing (seeking, wanting, needing, communicating)? It is here that different personality theories will select different behaviors on the basis of their own construct systems. (c) The data include behaviors occurring within a given situational context, the immediate relationship with the therapist or a parental relationship with an accepting mother figure. Thus, the patient is reaching out for understanding, but this behavior is occurring not in a vacuum or in a "transference" context; it occurs with regard to the therapist, or toward a specific paternal individual, or within a situational context of acceptance and understanding. (d) The data include the immediate ongoing flow of bodily felt feelings.

Returning to the fifteenth session of the 27-year-old male patient, for example, one way of construing the data is as follows: (a) at the present moment, the patient (b) is impulsively but hesitantly making overtures to give to, to be with, to have contact with (c) the therapist, and, through the therapist, with a father figure, (d) with internally felt bodily feelings of dizziness or tension or fear.

PSYCHOANALYTIC METHODS OF PSYCHOTHERAPEUTIC CHANGE

THE PRESENT STATUS OF PSYCHOANALYTIC METHODS

With regard to techniques and methods, Alexander observes that psychoanalytic treatment has remained essentially unchanged in the last fifty years. With regard to the effectiveness of its methods and techniques in bringing about psychotherapeutic change, Mowrer finds psychoanalysis vulnerable to severe criticisms and succinctly declares its methods "therapeutically inert." After extensive research on relative effectiveness, Strupp finds it disconcerting, especially when one considers the rigorous selection procedure for accepting candidates into formal psychoanalysis, that up to one third of psychoanalytic patients were unimproved or only slightly improved. With regard to its former predominance in therapeutic appeal, Matarazzo comments that psychoanalysis (both Freudian and non-Freudian) has shrunk to the point where it is no longer dominant in therapeutic theory, research, and practice; substantive new models dominate the marketplace. Alexander states that the emerging principles of psychotherapeutic *treatment* can no longer be encased within psychoanalytic ideology, whereas Mowrer is equally firm in asserting that if changes in psychoanalytic *theory* are transformed into practice, surprisingly little would remain of traditional psychoanalytic treatment methods.

Psychoanalytic writers are apparently faced with several dilemmas: (a) If psychoanalysis is identified with its traditional treatment methods, the whole psychoanalytic approach is heading toward therapeutic atrophy. (b) If psychoanalysis adopts the newer emerging therapeutic principles and techniques, it will lose its ideological identity as psychoanalysis. (c) If significant modifications in contemporary psychoanalytic theory produce their own distinctive treatment methods, then the classic psychoanalytic approach will have completed its own dissolution, for neither theory nor treatment will bear resemblance to what traditionally has been recognized as psychoanalysis.

Insight as a working method of psychotherapeutic change. Gendlin is a representative spokesman for two cogent comments against insight as a working method of psychotherapeutic change. First, insight (interpretation, explanation) is unable to effect personality change because, in itself, knowledge of one's problem and its nature does not in any way invoke a theoretical process of personality change. Second, insight, as traditionally understood, is an indication that personality change has already occurred. A theme of the present volume is the requiem for insight as a major working agent of therapeutic change.

PERSONALITY THEORIES: FOR OR AGAINST PERSONALITY CHANGE

Some personality models, according to Gendlin, posit a personality structure which allows and provides for a process of change. Gendlin asserts, however, that a personality model which conceives of a personality structure housing static elements serves only to describe what the person is like in the static present. Not only do such models fail to provide a theoretical basis for personality change but their constructs lead to a stout resistance to change. Instead, says Gendlin, personality change is theoretically impossible in such models. Accordingly, in order to maintain itself, the personality must distort, avoid, resist, and repress any material which might threaten to alter it. When a theory such as psychoanalysis postulates a personality structure composed exclusively of such static elements, change is impossible.

METHODS OF PSYCHOTHERAPEUTIC CHANGE: INTERNAL INTEGRATION

Methods of psychotherapeutic change based on clinical methods fall into two categories. In this section, we will review the methods which focus on the feelings which constitute the interaction between the person and his avoided (repressed, narrowed, denied, disintegrated, distantiated) needs (personality processes, drives, motivations). These therapeutic methods aim at the assimilation or acceptance of one's own needs or personality processes and the full experiencing of the heightened positive feelings which characterize the changed interactional relationship. This, then, brings about internal integration. Later in this section, we will discuss the clinical methods featured in the second approach, actualization of behavior.

THE FOCUS ON EXPERIENCING

The specific target during therapy is to overcome, in Alexander's and Matarazzo's words, the patient's resistances to his own unconscious material. Gendlin conceptualizes the resistance to internal personality processes as a state in which the experiencing feeling has been stopped, incompleted, or narrowed. The way out of resistance or avoidance or repression is through the reactivation of the experiencing process (Gendlin; May). This process refers to the person's feelings as the relationship between his immediate clinical state and the deeper personality processes. The aim is for these immediately ongoing feelings to be fully and completely experienced. Only through such a process of experiencing will there occur a change in the interactional feeling relationship; only through experiential acceptance will the avoided deeper personality processes change in the direction of assimilation, becoming part of the self, toward a state of internal integration.

Psychotherapeutic change involves the experiencing of immediate and momentary bodily felt feelings (Gendlin). At any moment internal feelings are going on; they are to be experienced. The locus of these feelings is at or within the body. Accordingly, the appropriate focus includes what is going on at or within the body (Gendlin). Experiencing means that the patient is to have or to let occur the bodily feelings going on at the moment. The patient whose eyes are starting to water is to experience the bodily feelings surrounding open sobbing. Internal bodily trembling, shaking, and quivering are to be felt and experienced. The continuous focus is on the full experiencing of these internal bodily felt feelings.

The role of the psychotherapist. The therapist's role is to maintain and facilitate a continuing focus on the ongoing process of experiencing bodily felt feelings (Gendlin). The experiential process cannot occur unless there is a continual maintaining of such a focus. In addition, Gendlin describes a detailed method of concretizing the immediate bodily feeling: the therapist is to help specify the nature of the immediate ongoing bodily experiencing. By continuing precise references to the bodily felt feeling, the process of experiencing is deepened (Gendlin).

Truax reports that one critical ingredient of effective psychotherapy is the ability to understand, sensitively and accurately, the patient's inner experiencings. The therapist who is sensitive to the current feelings of the patient and who possesses the verbal fluency to communicate this understanding in a language attuned to the patient's current feelings apparently has one major quality of what is termed the successful psychotherapist (Truax). We suggest that one reason for the effectiveness of empathic understanding is that it facilitates concrete experiencing; the therapist who is sensitively understanding of the patient's feelings is helping the person to undergo the process of therapeutic experiencing.

PSYCHOTHERAPEUTIC CHANGE: EXPERIENCING OF FEELINGS IN
CONJUNCTION WITH EXPERIENCING OF NEEDS

The sheer existence of bodily feelings is insufficient to effect personality change (Gendlin). The person must experience bodily feelings as interacting with an ongoing personality process. Gendlin describes this personality process as a *felt meaning*, or as that about which we have the bodily feeling. To May and O'Connell, the personality process is a need, motivation, or drive. Thus, personality change is brought about by the experiencing of ongoing bodily feelings in interactive relationship with ongoing personality needs (motivations, felt meanings, or drives). There must be an experiencing of both the personality need and the accompanying internal bodily feelings. Thus, for example, as you experience your own need to destroy your marriage, you simultaneously experience the internal bodily feelings of wrenching sobs; as you experience the need to reveal personal problems to another person, you give in to the experiencing of the internal bodily tension, fear, and tightness. Personality change requires both the experiencing of behavioral tendencies (needs, motivations, felt meanings, drives) and the accompanying internal bodily feelings. These two processes must occur in interaction with each other.

Reduction of disturbing feelings. The full confronting (having, focusing upon, or experiencing) of the deeper need, implying as it does the acceptance of the need, results in a reduction of disturbing feelings. Gendlin, May, and O'Connell argue that these "bad feelings" occur as an avoidance of the underlying need or felt meaning and that such bad feelings are reduced through the apparently paradoxical method of a full and interactive experiencing of this very same underlying need or felt meaning. Disturbing feelings are a sign that the person is getting close to experiencing the underlying need or felt meaning, and these are replaced with more integrative feelings when the person no longer avoids the underlying need.

Truax reports that characteristics of an effective psychotherapist include nonpossessive warmth and caring and unconditional acceptance of the patient. We see this kind of feeling relationship between therapist and patient as the model of the optimal feeling relationship between the patient and his own deeper needs or felt meanings; the patient is to approach acceptance of himself as unconditionally as the therapist accepts him. If the patient maintains respect, caring, and acceptance toward his own deeper personality processes, the disturbing feelings may be replaced by positive integrated feelings. The process of the therapeutic relationship becomes an internalized living process for the patient. We propose this primary explanation for the reported effectiveness of therapists with the characteristics described earlier.

THE LOCI OF EFFECTIVE EXPERIENCING

The patient and current external events. The patient's own needs or felt meanings may occur in the form of current events external to the patient-therapist situation. Thus, the locus of experiencing may be a current interaction with a spouse or friend or employer in some other clearly defined situation. Effective experiencing begins with the bodily feelings which started to occur in interaction with these external occurrences (Gendlin; May; O'Connell). These moments afford the patient the opportunity to proceed forward into a full experiencing of his internal bodily felt feelings in conjunction with his own needs or felt meanings (Gendlin; O'Connell). The felt meanings which relate to the open expression of affection, for example, may be accompanied by an internal state of bodily fear as they start to, or almost, occur in interaction with another individual; this external event is the locus of the beginning of experiencing. Psychotherapy provides the opportunity for proceeding forward into a full experiencing of such current external events.

The patient and past external events. The locus of what is to be experienced may be set within the context of the past. For example, this may include a vividly recollected partial-experience in which other girls teased and taunted the patient on the school playground. Effective therapeutic experiencing occurs within the context of that teasing and taunting by the other girls on the playground, together with the internal bodily feeling which started to occur. The external event (i.e., the taunting and the teasing) is to proceed toward an intensification and completion during the current moments of the therapy hour. Similarly, the internal body feelings which only started to occur are, finally, to occur to completion.

Experiences which arose in the past can be treated as still occurring: we go back into the past in order to further the experiencing of partial-experiences, and the experiencing occurs in the ongoing present. We resolve the past by undergoing present experiencings in a reasoned direction which is far more than an abortive, truncated recurrence of the past (Alexander).

The patient and the therapist. The critical interaction between the patient and his own deeper needs or felt meanings may occur within the context of the relationship between patient and therapist. This is facilitated by the occurrence of a personal feeling between patient and therapist, especially as it is determined by the invested personality needs and felt meanings of the patient himself (Alexander; Bergin; Gendlin; May; O'Connell; Rogers). The deeper need or felt meaning may include the development of open hostility or rejection toward the therapist. Effective experiencing includes the complete occurrence of internal bodily feelings in interaction with the experiencing of the rejection event. Psychotherapy provides the context for proceeding forward into the full experiencing of whatever internal bodily feelings occur in the interaction with the external event, including negative attitudes toward the therapist (Gendlin).

FUNCTIONS OF THE THERAPIST

The therapist facilitates the patient's effective experiencing of internal bodily feelings conjointly with deeper needs or felt meanings. The following are utilized by the therapist in this function:

Facilitation of experiencing of externalized needs. The therapist facilitates the patient's accepting, assimilating, and integrating externalized fragments of his own personality (May), aspects of himself which he may avoid by externalizing them or projecting them onto other persons. This is accomplished by enabling the patient to experience those parts of himself which he has imposed upon other individuals. The therapist facilitates the experiencing of the externalized need or felt meaning by a process of "focused referring" between the patient and the other person (Gendlin). If the other person represents the patient's own sexual expressiveness, the therapist is to intensify the patient's interaction with that external person. While maintaining the interaction between the patient and the sexually expressive other person in fantasy, the therapist seeks to bring the need toward the level of full experiencing. He penetrates the experience by exactly and concretely referring, not only to the patient's internal bodily feelings, but also to the other person's sexual sighings, physical reachings out, verbal overtures, or sexually provocative body postures, all in a direct verbal interactive relationship with the patient.

Bodily feelings as a tracking guide. The therapist utilizes the patient's bodily feelings as a working guide in the search for the true nature of the external need or felt meaning. Since the bodily feelings manifest the relationship between the patient and the deeper need, an increase or decrease in bodily feeling indicates whether tracking is proceeding in the right or wrong direction. If, for example, the patient describes the other person as laughing at him, and these words reduce the level of experiencing of bodily feelings, the error is to be corrected by trying out other precise references (e.g., the other person is inviting you to put your arms around her) until bodily feelings are reawakened and intensified. In this manner, bodily feelings serve as tracking guides toward the full experiencing of the external need or felt meaning (Gendlin; May).

Penetrating the experienced feeling. The patient's unintegrated feelings stand between him and his own deeper need or felt meaning (Gendlin; May; O'Connell). Effective experiencing requires that the therapist accept the patient's feelings so that the patient can penetrate beyond that feeling to the need about which the patient has the feeling. For example, if the patient is experiencing a sense of dread, the therapist must accept and explore that, so that the patient can go beyond that feeling. He can then bring out, for example, the underlying deeper need or felt meaning about which he experiences dread (e.g., a behavioral tendency to express sexual desire for another person).

Maintaining the experiential process. The therapist must maintain the experiential process over continuous shiftings and changings. Gendlin provides rules for following the patient, even though the content becomes hard to follow and even bizarre, even though the patient begins to talk in highly symbolic terms or plunges into silence. The therapist must nevertheless encourage the patient to maintain the flow of experiencing, both with regard to the ongoing bodily feelings and to the deeper need or felt meaning. When the patient overemphasizes the bodily feeling, the therapist must focus on the underlying personality need; when the patient gives himself over to the deeper need or felt meaning, the therapist must balance experiencing by focusing upon the ongoing bodily feeling. When the experiencing process reaches a crescendo and personality change occurs in the form of pervasive internal integration, the therapist goes along with the patient toward whatever bodily feelings and deeper needs or felt meanings are next. In short, the therapist helps the patient maintain a steady course during this experiential process.

METHODS OF PSYCHOTHERAPEUTIC CHANGE:
BEHAVIORAL ACTUALIZATION

The second category of working clinical methods focuses on the behavioral actualization of the person's motivations and needs. These methods seek to bring into the world of experiential actualization the patient's potentiality. The emphasis shifts from the feelings, which mark the relation between the person and his deeper needs, to the behavioral needs of the functioning personality. This is a shift from therapeutic methods of achieving internal integration to the methods of behavioral actualization.

MODES OF THERAPEUTIC CHANGE AND THE STRUCTURE OF PERSONALITY

Two major schools of personality change dominate the current psychotherapeutic scene. One school stresses affect-experiencing, and rests on the assumption that personality change requires affect change, emotional involvement, and the experiencing of feeling (Bergin). Perhaps the best representative of this school is Rogers and the burgeoning existential-humanistic-experiential movement. The second school assumes that personality change is based upon the realm of thought, problem-solving, planning, cognitive change (Bergin). Theories of learning and behavior modification are representative of this second school. A major controversy hinges on the relative emphasis to be given to these two major schools in the achievement of therapeutic change.

We do not view these two schools as contradictory, but as intermeshing approaches, both at the level of working therapeutic techniques and methods, and also at the theoretical level of personality structure. Deeper personality needs (or drives, potentialities, capacities, behavioral tendencies, or felt meanings) bear a definable relation to the functioning or operating or behaving personality, a relation which is manifested in the form of feelings, internal bodily felt feelings. The first category of working clinical methods (*internal integration*) aims for optimal change in the feeling relationship between the person and his deeper personality needs. Two associated kinds of personality change occur as a result of the process of internal integration. First, the feeling relationship is changed from unacceptable to acceptable, from bad to good, from one characterized by disintegration to internal integration, from inner turmoil to internal peace, from disruption to internal harmony, from self-hate to self-acceptance, from a disjunctiveness to a sense of internal wholeness. Second, the deeper need is acknowledged and brought into the person; it is closer to being experientially actualized; it is assimilated into the self and becomes available to the functioning personality; it becomes what the person is, rather than what the person potentially can be; the deeper need is now behaviorally available. These two changes are accomplished by means of the experiencing of bodily feelings in interaction with deeper (including externalized) personality needs. The existential-humanistic-experiential school of therapeutic change is appropriate for this kind of structural personality change, i.e., for accomplishing internal integration.

The second category (*behavioral actualization*) deals, not with the person's feeling relationship with his deeper personality needs, but instead with the direct behavioral actualization of personality needs, drives, behavior potentials, or motivations. The emphasis is upon the evoking of behavior, the facilitation of goal-directionality, the manifestation of behavior, the expression of behavioral personality processes. Personality structure is conceptualized in terms of processes, needs, motivations, potentials, capacities, and tendencies which are to be expressed behaviorally. This change is accomplished by working therapeutic methods of eliciting (evoking, modifying, changing, educing) the occurrence of behavioral change. For these purposes, the school which stresses thought, problem-solving, planning, and cognitive change is highly relevant.

In our view, a single conception of personality structure may encompass both schools of personality change. Both affect-feeling-experiencing and cognitive change (problem-solving, thought, etc.) are major means of effecting psychotherapeutic change. The former category is appropriate for certain personality change processes and the latter for others; they are both, we believe, of major importance and may be used to complement each other rather than being viewed as antagonistic schools of psychotherapeutic change.

METHODS OF BEHAVIORAL PSYCHOTHERAPEUTIC CHANGE

Matarazzo conceptualizes the patient-therapist relationship as falling within a larger category of two-person interactions including teacher-student, mother-child, or experimenter-subject. Effective behavioral change is brought about through the use of psychological principles of two-person interactions, influence, cognitive dissonance, or decision-making. Research with direct bearing upon principles of behavioral change is being conducted in such areas as interpersonal attraction, attitude change, cognitive consistency, group dynamics, and the immense learning literature (Goldstein). We believe that highly creative contributions to the psychology of psychotherapeutic change are occurring in these areas. As we indicated in the introduction to this volume, it is our view that many working techniques of behavioral-modification approaches have direct implications for other psychotherapeutic theories. The following techniques and methods of behavior actualization are taken from the contributors to the present volume, who, generally speaking, are not behavior modificationalists but whose therapeutic methods disclose a common ground which constitutes an area of future creative developments in psychotherapy.

Experiencing of behavioral change. Behavioral change is achieved by undergoing a behavioral experience within the therapeutic setting but directed toward persons in the patient's current life situation. A motivational need or capacity for being assertive implies assertive behavior in a given situation and in interaction with particular other persons in the patient's real life. Accordingly, the patient is to experience this assertive behavior in the therapy situation, to feel the full bodily experience of carrying out the implied behavior in concrete detail. The patient is to enter into the situation with the significant other individual, for example, a husband, and to undergo in minute detail what it is like to sit him down and to insist that he share with her some of the events of the day. Such a detailed living-through brings the motivational need toward behavioral actuality. The process requires the following elements: (a) moving from the therapy situation to the meaningful extratherapy current situation (e.g., in the patient's bedroom, alone with the husband); (b) moving from an interaction with the therapist to an interaction with the significant other figure (e.g., the husband); (c) detailed and minute living-through of the assertive behavior; and (d) experiencing the bodily feelings which accompany the new behavior.

Responding to the deeper need. The therapist enables new behavior by responding to the deeper motivational need which lies behind the actual behavior. This requires an accurate understanding of the patient's deeper needs and a keen hold on what is occurring at the given moment. A man who lauds the business acumen of his partner may be indirectly expressing a deeper need to criticize the partner's continual obstructionism. The therapist brings out the criticism by responding to the patient as if critical behavior were actually occurring. The therapist accomplishes this by such means as detailed interpretation ("You are complaining about the way he resisted all your ideas at the last directors' meeting"); sharing induced feelings ("My stomach is all tied up, like it is hard to complain openly about him"); expressing the patient's new behavior for him ("I have had enough of your petty remarks; if you can't help us, get out!"); or any other method of bringing into actuality the behavior implied by the ongoing deeper need.

Adopting the values of psychotherapy. A psychotherapist achieves behavioral change through the adoption of implicit or explicit values which facilitate certain ways of behaving. When psychoanalysis was dominant, its therapeutic values induced patients to behave in characteristic ways outside of therapy. Frequently these persons became skilled at offering interpretations of their own behaviors and the behaviors of others. In a similar way, the contributors to the present volume maintain at least two major therapeutic values which fashion patients to behave along two defined pathways.

One value is to behave on the basis of continually deeper needs, without defenses, avoidances, or indirections. The therapist almost uniformly structures the patient to behave in this manner, and he himself adheres to this value whether he is serving as a model for the patient, selectively responding to the patient, or actively describing and influencing the way the patient is to be during the treatment hour. By adopting this value for both himself and his patients, such psychotherapists tend to induce behavioral change marked by openness, candor, and freedom from defenses, avoidances, or indirections.

A second value is to share what is going on within oneself. What was initiated by psychoanalysis ("Tell me whatever thoughts occur to you; do not censor any whatsoever") has been deepened and extended by writers such as those represented in the present volume. Both therapist and patient are to share the entire internal world of immediately ongoing experiencings. The patient is carefully schooled to attend to internal bodily feelings and to share these with the therapist. One's internal feelings become premium coin of interpersonal relationships, both for patient and therapist. Such a mutual sharing of what is occurring within is far more than a treatment technique to effect personality change within the therapeutic session; it also serves as a major psychotherapeutic value and guideline for extratherapeutic behavior. The patient achieves major behavioral change by sharing with appropriate others his immediate internal experiencing in the form of internal bodily sensations ("I guess you can't tell, but I'm trembling all over"), internal reactions to oneself ("That felt just right; I'm glad I said that!"), or feelings in relation to another person ("I get all tied in knots when you start cross-examining me like that." "Yes, you are right; it feels just right; go ahead").

Behavioralizing the personality potential. A patient is unable to actualize such abstract entities as potential, capacity, personality process, need, or felt meaning. This is much too lumpy an assignment, nearly always accompanied by a muted plea for help in identifying exactly how one goes about the process of actualization. A part of the therapist's role is to spell out exactly what behavior is to be actualized by the patient. The therapist may be confident that the major burgeoning potential in a 29-year-old married woman may relate to the providing of nurture and comfort. This is consistent with her clinical history, her presenting problems, three months of intensive treatment, and a thorough understanding of her dream world. However, the personality potential cannot be experienced until it is translated into specific and concrete behaviors, a task which demands the highest clinical skills of the therapist. The behavior may be that of embracing her husband openly and spontaneously, or taking a real interest in the thoughts and feelings of her 7-year-old daughter, or complimenting her husband on small expressions of thoughtfulness, or helping a neighbor, or making love in a different way, or having another child.

A thorough understanding of the patient may lead to behavioral change simply by helping the patient find the critically effective behavior for the appropriate situation. Months of intensive treatment may culminate in the distilling of the specific behavior which both patient and therapist "know" is the right behavior in the right situation to provide the right experiential actualization. At that point, the denouement consists of a simple nod: Go ahead; be this way; carry it out; yes.

Any personality process (need, drive, capacity, felt meaning) has direct implications for the person's behavioral change. It is a proper and necessary area of clinical study and investigation to inquire exactly what new behaviors are implied by this particular personality process in this particular person. Behavioral change follows the sequence of identifying the critical personality process (need, drive, capacity, or felt meaning), translating it into critical specific behaviors, and mutually implementing its occurrence.

Facilitating the goal-directionality of behavior. Facilitating the goal-directed component of behavior opens up a wide range of methods of achieving experiential actualization. To the extent that behavior is characterized by intentionality, drive, or motivation, it is directed toward goals. Behavioral change comes about after the therapist facilitates that goal-directionality.

A woman's depressed behavior may be carefully understood as directed toward a withdrawal, a pulling away. It takes the form of a withdrawal into herself, away from her family. The initial phase of treatment reveals that she is anxious to free herself of her role of caretaker for her mother and aunt. She works to support them, and the three live together in the mother's small apartment. To the extent that the depression is directed toward the goal of pulling herself away from such an arrangement, behavioral change involves the salutary withdrawal from the role of caretaker. Behavioral change is brought about by the experiential actualization of the deeper need, drive, or motivation which accounted for the goal-directed depression. Thus, a new job, a new freedom, a new marriage, or other new behaviors are experientially actualized by facilitating the goal-directionality of the manifested behavior. Any manifested behavior, from nail-biting to low grades, from militant protest to having visions of Jesus Christ, may be understood in terms of a goal-directionality which may be further facilitated by a wide spectrum of techniques. These methods vary from empathic acceptance of the valued goal to directed change in living arrangements, from allowing the patient's goal-directed behavior to "reach" the therapist, to assigning a particular role to him in a hospital setting.

Acquiring the locus of control. Another pathway toward the actualization of behavioral change involves the patient's acquiring control by becoming the activator, director, initiator of his own behavior. Two kinds of behavioral change are involved: the trying out of new behaviors and the controlled elimination of disturbing behaviors. The emphasis, however, is on the control or direction of the behaviors so that the patient is to be the activator or initiator of the behavioral change. The occurrence of the new behavior or the elimination of the disturbing behavior is not the sole aim; the locus of control shifts to the patient himself as he gains the ability to initiate or to stop a behavior because he is determined to do so, not because he is driven by forces in the external world or deeper needs, motivations, drives, or felt meanings beyond his control.

For the patient to actualize affectionate behavior so as to acquire her own locus of control, the patient must be able to carry out the concrete behavior under her own direction and initiation. She must be the one who reaches out for her grandfather's hand and tells him that she loves him. The sense of activation continues until the close, when she is the one to end or complete the behavior in any way which is fitting to the moment. In this manner the good internal bodily feelings are a blend of (a) those which accompany the behavior of being affectionate, and (b) those which accompany the gaining of control, initiation, activation, and determination of one's own behavior. In a similar fashion, the patient acquires the locus of control over disturbing behavior, from masturbating to excessive alcoholism, from interrupting others to having visions of one's deceased mother. It must be up to the patient whether these behaviors are to occur, not up to external variables or alien, deep impulses. At the point when he senses the urge to masturbate or to drink, he must resist until he is flooded with internal bodily feelings which proclaim that *he* is the determiner, the one who is in control of this behavior. This aim is also achieved by carrying out the disturbing behavior under his own direction and initiation. Under conditions activated by the patient, he is to masturbate or drink or interrupt others or have a vision of his deceased mother even though external forces are not inducing him or the internal impulses are not present. It is the patient who determines both the occurrence and the cessation of the behavioral act, both phases contributing to the enhancement of his own control and the acquisition of determination.

The psychotherapeutic process varies along a line from external control to internal control. At the external pole are those treatment modalities in which the responsibility for bringing about personality change lies within the therapist or external agency. This is the case when the therapist of a child brings about change by seeing the parents, or a therapist assumes the burden of responsibility for effecting change. It is the therapist who does the directing, the advice-giving, who brings in the spouse for treatment, hospitalizes the patient, gives interpretations, and in general operates as the repository of external direction and control over the patient's change processes. At the internal pole are those therapeutic modalities in which the person himself is the source of direction, control, initiation, and activation of the process of personality change. This is the case when the process is one of self-integration, self-actualization, self-analysis, self-contemplation. The burden of responsibility for effecting personality change lies within the person himself. Between these two poles lie most of our conventional modes of psychotherapies, distributed closer to one or the other of these two poles.

CHAPTER 23

The Dynamics of Psychotherapy in the Light of Learning Theory

Franz Alexander

Most of what we know about the basic dynamic principles of psychotherapy is derived from the psychoanalytic process.

One of the striking facts in this field is that the intricate procedure of psychoanalytic treatment underwent so few changes since its guiding principles were formulated by Freud between 1912 and 1915 (7–11). Meanwhile substantial developments took place in theoretical knowledge, particularly in ego psychology. Moreover, in all other fields of medicine, treatments underwent radical changes resulting from a steadily improving understanding of human physiology and pathology. No medical practitioner could treat patients with the same methods he learned 50 years ago without being considered antiquated. In contrast, during the same period the standard psychoanalytic treatment method as it is taught today in psychoanalytic institutes remained practically unchanged.

It is not easy to account for this conservatism. Is it due to the perfection of the standard procedure which because of its excellence does not require reevaluation and improvement, or does it have some other cultural rather than scientific reasons?

Among several factors one is outstanding: to be a reformer of psychoanalytic treatment was never a popular role. The need for unity among the pioneer psychoanalysts, who were universally rejected by outsiders, is one of the deep cultural roots of this stress on conformity.

Read at the 119th annual meeting of The American Psychiatric Association, St. Louis, Mo., May 6–10, 1963. This chapter was voted, by the Editorial Board of the present volume, as one of the creative developments in psychotherapy, 1958–1968. From the *American Journal of Psychiatry*, 1963, *120*, 440–448. Copyright 1963, American Psychiatric Association.

The majority of those who had critical views became "dissenters" either voluntarily or by excommunication. Some of these became known as neo-Freudians. Some of the critics, however, remained in the psychoanalytic fold.

(Some analysts jocularly expressed the view that the stress on conformity was a defense against the analyst's unconscious identification with Freud, each wanting to become himself a latter day Freud and founder of a new school. Conformity was a defense against too many prima donnas.) Another important factor is the bewildering complexity of the psychodynamic processes occurring during treatment. It appears that the insecurity which this intricate field necessarily provokes creates a defensive dogmatism which gives its followers a pseudosecurity. Almost all statements concerning technique could be legitimately only highly tentative. "Tolerance of uncertainty" is generally low in human beings. A dogmatic reassertion of some traditionally accepted views—seeking for a kind of consensus—is a common defense against uncertainty.

In spite of all this, there seems to be little doubt that the essential psychodynamic principles on which psychoanalytic treatment rests have solid observational foundations. These constitute the areas of agreement among psychoanalysts of different theoretical persuasion. Briefly, they consist in the following observations and evaluations:

1. During treatment unconscious (repressed) material becomes conscious. This increases the action radius of the conscious ego: the ego becomes cognizant of unconscious impulses and thus is able to coordinate (integrate) the latter with the rest of conscious content.

2. The mobilization of unconscious material is achieved mainly by two basic therapeutic factors: interpretation of material emerging during free association and the patient's emotional interpersonal experiences in the therapeutic situation (transference). The therapist's relatively objective, non-evaluative, impersonal attitude is the principal factor in mobilizing unconscious material.

3. The patient shows resistance against recognizing unconscious content. Overcoming this resistance is one of the primary technical problems of the treatment.

4. It is only natural that the neurotic patient will sooner or later direct his typical neurotic attitude toward his therapist. He develops a transference which is the repetition of interpersonal attitudes, mostly the feelings of the child to his parents. This process is favored by the therapist encouraging the patient to be himself as much as he can during the interviews. The therapist's objective non-evaluative attitude is the main

factor, not only in mobilizing unconscious material during the process of free association, but also in facilitating the manifestation of transference. The original neurosis of the patient, which is based on his childhood experiences, is thus transformed in an artificial "transference neurosis" which is a less intensive repetition of the patient's "infantile neurosis." The resolution of these revived feelings and behavior patterns—the resolution of the transference neurosis—becomes the aim of the treatment.

There is little disagreement concerning these fundamentals of the treatment. Controversies, which occur sporadically, pertain primarily to the technical means by which the transference neurosis can be resolved. The optimal intensity of the transference neurosis is one of the points of contention.

This is not the place to account in detail the various therapeutic suggestions which arose in recent years. Most of these modifications consisted in particular emphases given to certain aspects of the treatment. There are those who stressed interpretation of resistance (Wilheim Reich, Helmuth Kaiser), while others focussed on the interpretation of repressed content. Fenichel stated that resistance cannot be analyzed without making the patient understand what he is resisting(6).

It is most difficult to evaluate all these modifications because it is generally suspected that authors' accounts about their theoretical views do not precisely reflect what they are actually doing while treating patients. The reason for this discrepancy lies in the fact that the therapist is a "participant observer" who is called upon constantly to make decisions on the spot. The actual interactional process between therapist and patient is much more complex than the theoretical accounts about it. In general there were two main trends: 1. Emphasis on cognitive insight as a means of breaking up the neurotic patterns. 2. Emphasis upon the emotional experiences the patient undergoes during treatment. These are not mutually exclusive, yet most controversies centered around emphasis on the one or the other factor: cognitive versus experiential.

While mostly the similarity between the transference attitude and the original pathogenic childhood situation has been stressed, I emphasized the therapeutic significance of the difference between the old family conflicts and the actual doctor-patient relationship. This difference is what allows "corrective emotional experience" to occur, which I consider as the central therapeutic factor both in psychoanalysis proper and also in analytically oriented psychotherapy. The new settlement of an old unresolved conflict in the transference situation be-

comes possible not only because the intensity of the transference conflict is less than that of the original conflict, but also because the
therapist's actual response to the patient's emotional expressions is
quite different from the original treatment of the child by the parents.
The fact that the therapist's reaction differs from that of the parent, to
whose behavior the child adjusted himself as well as he could with his
own neurotic reactions, makes it necessary for the patient to abandon
and correct these old emotional patterns. After all, this is precisely one
of the ego's basic functions—adjustment to the existing external conditions. As soon as the old neurotic patterns are revived and brought into
the realm of consciousness, the ego has the opportunity to readjust them
to the changed external and internal conditions. This is the essence of
the corrective influence of those series of experiences which occur during treatment (2, 3). As will be seen, however, the emotional detachment of the therapist turned out under observational scrutiny to be less
complete than this idealized model postulates.

Since the difference between the patient-therapist and the original
child-parent relationship appeared to me a cardinal therapeutic agent,
I made technical suggestions derived from these considerations. The
therapist in order to increase the effectiveness of the corrective emotional experiences should attempt to create an interpersonal climate
which is suited to highlight the discrepancy between the patient's
transference attitude and the actual situation as it exists between patient and therapist. For example, if the original childhood situation
which the patient repeats in the transference was between a strict
punitive father and a frightened son, the therapist should behave in a
calculatedly permissive manner. If the father had a doting all-forgiving
attitude towards his son, the therapist should take a more impersonal
and reserved attitude. This suggestion was criticized by some authors,
that these consciously and purposefully adopted attitudes are artificial
and will be recognized as such by the patient. I maintained however
that the therapist's objective, emotionally not participating attitude is
itself artificial inasmuch as it does not exist between human beings in
actual life. Neither is it as complete as has been assumed. This controversy will have to wait to be decided by further experiences of
practitioners.

I made still other controversial technical suggestions aimed at intensifying the emotional experiences of the patient. One of them was changing the number of interviews in appropriate phases of the treatment in
order to make the patient more vividly conscious of his dependency
needs by frustrating them.

Another of my suggestions pertains to the ever-puzzling question of termination of treatment. The traditional belief is that the longer an analysis lasts the greater is the probability of recovery. Experienced analysts more and more came to doubt the validity of this generalization. If anything, this is the exception; very long treatments lasting over many years do not seem to be the most successful ones. On the other hand, many so-called "transference cures" after very brief contact have been observed to be lasting. A clear correlation between duration of treatment and its results has not been established. There are no reliable criteria for the proper time of termination. Improvements observed during treatment often prove to be conditioned by the fact that the patient is still being treated. The patient's own inclination to terminate or to continue the treatment is not always a reliable indication. The complexity of the whole procedure and our inability to estimate precisely the proper time of termination induced me to employ the method of experimental temporary interruptions, a method which in my experience is the most satisfactory procedure. At the same time it often reduces the total number of interviews. The technique of tentative temporary interruptions is based on trusting the natural recuperative powers of the human personality, which are largely underestimated by many psychoanalysts. There is an almost general trend toward "overtreatment." A universal regressive trend in human beings has been generally recognized by psychoanalysts. Under sufficient stress every one tends to regress to the helpless state of infancy and seek help from others. The psychoanalytic treatment situation caters to this regressive attitude. As Freud stated, treatments often reach a point where the patient's will to be cured is outweighed by his wish to be treated.

In order to counteract this trend a continuous pressure on the patient is needed to make him ready to take over his own management as soon as possible. During temporary interruptions patients often discover that they can live without their analyst. When they return, the still not worked out emotional problems come clearly to the forefront.[1]

Furthermore, I called attention to Freud's distinction between two forms of regression. He first described regression to a period of ego-development in which the patient was still happy, in which he functioned well. Later he described regressions to traumatic experiences, which he explained as attempts to master subsequently an overwhelming situation of the past. During psychoanalytic treatment both kinds of regression occur. Regressions to pre-traumatic or pre-conflictual periods —although they offer excellent research opportunity for the study of personality development—are therapeutically not valuable. Often we find that the patient regresses in his free associations to preconflictual early infantile material as a maneuver to evade the essential pathogenic conflicts. This material appears as "deep material" and both patient and therapist in mutual self-deception spend a great deal of time and effort to analyze this essentially evasive material. The recent trend to look always for very early emotional conflicts between mother and infant as the most common source of neurotic disturbances is the result of over-looking this frequent regressive evasion of later essential pathogenic conflicts. Serious disturbances of the early symbiotic mother-child relation occur only with exceptionally disturbed mothers. The most common conflicts begin when the child has already a distinct feeling of being a person (ego-awareness) and relates to his human environment, to his parents and siblings, as to individual persons. The oedipus complex and sibling rivalry are accordingly the common early sources of neurotic patterns. There are many exceptions, of course, where the personality growth is disturbed in very early infancy.

Another issue which gained attention in the post-Freudian era is the therapist's neglect of the actual present life situation in favor of preoccupation with the patient's past history. This is based on the tenet that the present life circumstances are merely precipitating factors, mobilizing the patient's infantile neurosis. In general, of course, the present is always determined by the past. Freud in a rather early writing proposed the theory of complementary etiology. A person with severe ego defects acquired in the past will react to slight stress situations in his present life with severe reactions; a person with a relatively healthy past history will require more severe blows of life to regress into a neurotic state(12). Some modern authors like French, Rado, myself and others feel that there is an unwarranted neglect of the actual life circumstances(1, 15). The patient comes to the therapist when he is at the end of his rope, is entangled in emotional problems which have reached a point when he feels he needs help. These authors feel that the therapist never should allow the patient to forget that he came to him to resolve his present problem. The understanding of the past should always be subordinated to the problems of the present. Therapy is not the same as genetic research. Freud's early emphasis upon the reconstruction of past history was the result of his primary interest in research. At first he felt he must know the nature of the disease he proposes to cure. The interest in past history at the expense of the present is the residue of the historical period when research in personality dynamics of necessity was a prerequisite to develop a rational treatment method.

These controversial issues will have to wait for the verdict of history. Their significance cannot yet be evaluated with finality. One may state, however, that there is a growing inclination to question the universal validity of some habitual practices handed down by tradition over several generations of psychoanalysts. There is a trend toward greater flexibility in technique, attempting to adjust the technical details to the individual nature of the patient and his problems. This principle of flexibility was explicitly stressed by Edith Weigert, Thomas French, myself and still others.

While there is considerable controversy concerning frequency of interviews, interruptions, termination and the mutual relation between intellectual and emotional factors in treatment, there seems to be a universal consensus about the significance of the therapist's individual personality for the results of the treatment. This interest first manifested itself in several contributions dealing with the therapist's own emotional involvement in the patient—"the countertransference phenomenon." Freud first used the expression, countertransference, in 1910. It took, however, about 30 years before the therapist's unconscious, spontaneous reactions toward the patient were explored as to their significance for the course of the treatment. The reasons for this neglect were both theoretical and practical. Originally Freud conceived the analyst's role in the treatment as a blank screen who carefully keeps his incognito and upon whom the patient can project any role, that of the image of his father (father transference), of mother (mother transference), or of any significant person in his past. In this way the patient can reexperience the important interpersonal events of his past undisturbed by the specific personality of the therapist. The phenomenon called "countertransference," however, contradicts sharply the "blank screen" theory.

It is now generally recognized that in reality the analyst does not remain a blank screen, an uninvolved intellect, but is perceived by the patient as a concrete person. There is, however, a great deal of difference among present day authors in the evaluation of the significance of the therapist's personality in general and his countertransference reactions in particular.

Some authors consider countertransference as an undesirable impurity just as the patient's emotional involvement with his therapist (transference) originally was considered as an undesirable complication. The ideal model of the treatment was that the patient should freely associate and thus reveal himself without controlling the train of his ideas, and should consider the therapist only as an expert who is trying to help him. Later, as is well known, the patient's emotional involvement turned out to be the dynamic axis of the treatment. So far as the therapist's involvement is concerned, it is considered by most authors as an unwanted impurity. The therapist should have only one reaction to the patient, the wish to understand him and give him an opportunity for readjustment through the insight offered to him by the therapist's interpretations. The latter should function as a pure intellect without being disturbed by any personal and subjective reactions to the patient.

The prevailing view is that the analyst's own emotional reactions should be considered as disturbing factors of the treatment.

Some authors, among them Edith Weigert, Frieda Fromm-Reichmann, Heimann, Benedek and Salzman, however, mention certain assets of the countertransference; they point out that the analyst's understanding of his countertransference attitudes may give him a particularly valuable tool for understanding the patient's transference reactions (5, 13, 14, 16). As to the therapeutic significance of the countertransference, there is a great deal of disagreement. While Balint and Balint consider this impurity as negligible for the therapeutic process (4), Benedek states in her paper on countertransference that the therapist's personality is the most important agent of the therapeutic process (5). There is, however, general agreement that a too intensive emotional involvement on the therapist's part is a seriously disturbing factor. Glover speaks of the "analyst's toilet" which he learns in his own personal analysis, which should free him from unwanted emotional participation in the treatment. This is, indeed, the most important objective of the training analysis; it helps him to know how to control and possibly even to change his spontaneous countertransference reactions.

I believe that the countertransference may be helpful or harmful. It is helpful when it differs from that parental attitude toward the child which contributed to the patient's emotional difficulties. The patient's neurotic attitudes developed not in a vacuum but as reactions to parental attitudes. If the therapist's reactions are different from these parental attitudes, the patient's emotional involvement with the therapist is not realistic. This challenges the patient to alter his reaction patterns. If, however, the specific countertransference of the therapist happens to be similar to the parental attitudes toward the child, the patient's neurotic reaction patterns will persist and an interminable analysis may result. There is no incentive for the patient to change his feelings. I recommended therefore that the therapist should be keenly aware of his own spontaneous—no matter how slight—feelings to the patient and should try to replace them by an interpersonal climate which is suited to correct the original neurotic patterns.

One of the most systematic revisions of the standard psychoanalytic procedure was undertaken by Sandor Rado, published in several writings, beginning in 1948(15). His critical evaluation of psychoanalytic treatment and his suggested modifications deserve particular attention because for many years Rado has been known as one of the most thorough students of Freud's writings.

As years went on, Rado became more and more dissatisfied with the prevailing practice of psychoanalysis, and proposed his adaptational technique based on his "adaptational psychodynamics." As it is the case with many innovators, some of Rado's formulations consist in new terminology. Some of his new emphases, however, are highly significant. He is most concerned, as I am, with those features of the standard technique of psychoanalysis which foster regression without supplying a counterforce toward the patient's progression, that is to say, to his successful adaptation to the actual life situation. He raises the crucial question: is the patient's understanding of his past development sufficient to induce a change in him. "To overcome repressions and thus be able to recall the past is one thing; to learn from it and be able to act on the new knowledge, another(15)."

Rado recommends, as a means to promote the goal of therapy, raising the patient from his earlier child-like adaptations to an appropriate adult level—"to hold the patient as much as possible at the adult level of cooperation with the physician." The patient following his regressive trend "parentifies" the therapist but the therapist should counteract this trend and not allow himself to be pushed by the patient into the parent role. Rado criticizes orthodox psychoanalytic treatment as furthering the regressive urge of the patient by emphasizing the "punitive parentifying" transference (the patient's dependence upon the parentalized image of the therapist)(15). Rado points out that losing self-confidence is the main reason for the patient to build up the therapist into a powerful parent figure. Rado's main principle, therefore, is to "bolster up the patient's self-confidence on realistic grounds." He stresses the importance of dealing with the patient's actual present life conditions in all possible detail. Interpretations must always embrace the conscious as well as unconscious motivations. In concordance with mine and French's similar emphasis (1) Rado succinctly states: "Even when the biographical material on hand reaches far into the past, interpretation must always begin and end with the patient's present life performance, his present adaptive task. The significance of this rule cannot be overstated."

Rado considers his adaptational technique but a further development of the current psychoanalytic technique, not something basically contradictory to it. It should be pointed out that while criticizing the standard psychoanalytic procedure, Rado in reality criticizes current practice, but not theory. According to accepted theory, the patient's dependent—in Rado's term—"parentifying" transference should be resolved. The patient during treatment learns to understand his own motivations; this enables him to take over his own management. He assimilates the therapist's interpretations and gradually he can dispense with the therapist, from whom he has received all he needs. The therapeutic process thus recapitulates the process of emotional maturation; the child learns from the parents, incorporates their attitude, and eventually will no longer need them for guidance. Rado's point becomes relevant when one points out that the current procedure does not always achieve this goal, and I may add, it unnecessarily prolongs the procedure. The reason for this is that the exploration of the past became an aim in itself, indeed the goal of the treatment. The past should be subordinated to a total grasp of the present life situation and serve as the basis for future adaptive accomplishments.

At this point my emphasis is pertinent, that it is imperative for the therapist to correctly estimate the time when his guidance not only becomes unnecessary but detrimental, inasmuch as it unnecessarily fosters the very dependency of the patient on the therapist which the latter tries to combat. I stated that deeds are stronger than words; the treatment should be interrupted at the right time in order to give the patient the experience that he can now function on his own and thus gain that self-confidence which Rado tries to instill into the patient by "positive interpretations." No matter, however, what technical devices they emphasize, the goal of these reformers is the same: to minimize the danger implicit in the psychotherapeutic situation, namely, encouraging undue regression and evasion of the current adaptive tasks. It is quite true that regression is necessary in order to give the patient opportunity to reexperience his early maladaptive patterns and grapple with them anew to find other more appropriate levels of feeling and behavior. The key to successful psychoanalytic therapy is, however, not to allow regression in the transference to become an aim in itself. It is necessary to control it.

In view of these controversies the need for a careful study of the therapeutic process became more and more recognized. Different research centers initiated programs from grants given by the Ford Foundation to study the therapeutic process. At the Mount Sinai Hospital in Los Angeles under my direction, we undertook a study of the therapeutic process, in which a number of psychoanalysts observed the therapeutic interaction between therapist and patient in several treatment cases. All interviews were sound recorded and both the participant observer—that is, the therapist—and the nonparticipant observers recorded their evaluation of the process immediately after each interview. Our assumption was that the therapist being an active participant in the interactional process is not capable of recognizing and describing his own involvements with the same objectivity as those who observe him. His attention is necessarily focussed on patient's material and being himself involved in this complex interaction cannot fully appreciate his own part in it. This expectation was fully borne out by our study.

As was expected the processing of the voluminous data thus collected proved to be a prolonged affair which will require several years of collaborative work. Yet even at the present stage of processing, several important conclusions emerge. The most important of these is the fact that the traditional descriptions of the therapeutic process do not adequately reflect the immensely complex interaction between therapist and patient. The patient's reactions cannot be described fully as transference reactions. The patient reacts to the therapist as to a concrete person and not only as a representative of parental figures. The therapist's reactions also far exceed what is usually called countertransference. They include in addition to this, interventions based on conscious deliberations and also his spontaneous idiosyncratic attitudes. Moreover, his own values are conveyed to the patient even if he consistently tries to protect his incognito. The patient reacts to the therapist's overt but also to his non-verbal hidden intentions and the therapist reacts to the patient's reaction to him. It is a truly transactional process.

In studying this transactional material I came to the conviction that the therapeutic process can be best understood in the terms of learning theory. Particularly the principle of reward and punishment and also the influence of repetitive experiences can be clearly recognized. Learning is defined as a change resulting from previous experiences. In every learning process, one can distinguish two components. First the motivational factor, namely, the subjective needs which activate the learning process and second, certain performances by which a new behavioral pattern suitable to fill the motivational need is actually acquired. In most general terms unfulfilled needs no matter what their nature may be—hunger for food, hunger for love, curiosity, the urge for mastery—initiate groping trial and error efforts which cease when an adequate behavioral response is found. Adequate responses lead to need satisfaction which is the reward for the effort. Rewarding responses are repeated until they become automatic and their repetition no longer requires effort and further experimentation. This is identical with the feedback mechanisms described in cybernetics. Every change of the total situation requires learning new adequate responses. Old learned patterns which were adequate in a previous situation must be un-learned. They are impediments to acquiring new adequate patterns.

I am not particularly concerned at this point with the controversy between the more mechanistic concepts of the older behaviorist theory and the newer Gestalt theory of learning. The controversy pertains to the nature of the process by which satisfactory behavior patterns are acquired. This controversy can be reduced to two suppositions. The older Thorndike and Pavlov models operate with the principle of con-tiguity or connectionism. Whenever a behavioral pattern becomes asso-ciated with both a specific motivating need and need satisfaction, the organism will automatically repeat the satisfactory performance when-ever the same need arises. This view considers the organism as a passive receptor of external and internal stimuli, which become associated by contiguity. The organism's own active organizing function is neglected. The finding of the satisfactory pattern, according to the classical theory, takes place through blind trial and error.

In contrast, the Gestalt theoretical model operates with the suppo-sition that the trials by which the organism finds satisfactory behavioral responses are not blind but are aided by cognitive processes. They are intelligent trials which are guided by certain generalizations arrived at with the aid of the memory of previous experiences. They imply an active organization of previous experiences. This organizational act amounts to a cognitive grasp of the total situation. I am not concerned at this juncture with the seemingly essential difference between the connectionistic and Gestalt theories of learning. Probably both types of learning exist. The infant learns without much help from previous ex-periences. In this learning blind trials and errors must of necessity prevail. Common basis in all learning, whether it takes place through blind trials and errors or by intelligent trials, is the forging of a con-nection between three variables: a specific motivating impulse, a spe-cific behavioral response, and a gratifying experience which is the reward.

Accepting Freud's definition of thinking as a substitute for acting, that is to say, as acting in phantasy, the reward principle can be well applied to intellectual solutions of problems. Groping trials and errors in thought—whether blind or guided by cognitive processes—lead even-tually to a solution which clicks. Finding a solution which satisfies all the observations without contradictions is accompanied by a feeling of satisfaction. After a solution is found—occasionally it may be found accidentally—the problem solving urge, as everyone knows who has tried to solve a mathematical equation or a chess puzzle, ceases and a feeling of satisfaction ensues. The tension state, which prevails as long as the problem is not solved, yields to a feeling of rest and fulfillment. This is the reward for the effort, whether it consists of blind or intelligent trials. The principle of reward can be applied not only to a rat learning to run a maze, but to the most complex thought processes as well. The therapeutic process can be well described in these terms of learning theory. The specific problem in therapy consists in finding an adequate interpersonal relation between therapist and patient. Initially this is distorted because the patient applies to this specific human interaction feeling-patterns and behavior-patterns which were formed in the patient's past and do not apply either to the actual therapeutic situation or to his actual life situation. During treatment the patient unlearns the old patterns and learns new ones. This complex process of relearning follows the same principles as the more simple relearning process hitherto studied by experimental psychologists. It contains cognitive elements as well as learning from actual interpersonal experiences which occur during the therapeutic interaction. These two components are intricately interwoven. They were described in psychoanalytic literature with the undefined, rather vague term "emotional insight." The word "emotional" refers to the interpersonal experiences, the word "insight" refers to the cognitive element. The expression does not mean more than the recognition of the presence of both components. The psychological process to which the term refers is not yet spelled out in detail. Our present observational study is focussed on a better understanding of this complex psychological phenomenon—emotional insight—which appears to us as the central factor in every learning process including psychoanalytic treatment. Every intellectual grasp, even when it concerns entirely non-utilitarian preoccupations, such as playful puzzle-solving efforts, is motivated by some kind of urge for mastery and is accompanied with tension resolution as its reward. In psychotherapy the reward consists in less conflictful, more harmonious interpersonal relations, which the patient achieves first by adequately relating to his therapist, then to his environment and eventually to his own ego ideal. At first he tries to gain the therapist's approval by living up to the supreme therapeutic principle—to the basic rule of frank self-expression. At the same time he tries to gain acceptance by living up to the therapist's expectations of him, which he senses in spite of the therapist's overt non-evaluating attitude. And finally, he tries to live up to his own genuine values, to his cherished image of himself. Far-reaching discrepancy between the therapist's and the patient's values is a common source of therapeutic impasse.

This gradually evolving dynamic process can be followed and described step by step in studies made by non-participant observers. Current studies give encouragement and hope that we shall eventually be able to understand more adequately this intricate interpersonal process and to account for therapeutic successes and failures. As in every field of science, general assumptions gradually yield to more specific ones which are obtained by meticulous controlled observations. The history of sciences teaches us that new and more adequate technical devices of observation and reasoning are responsible for advancements. In the field of psychotherapy the long overdue observation of the therapeutic process by non-participant observers is turning out to be the required methodological tool. This in itself, however, is not sufficient. The evaluation of the rich and new observational material calls for new theoretical perspectives. Learning theory appears to be at present the most satisfactory framework for the evaluation of observational data and for making valid generalizations. As it continuously happens at certain phases of thought development in all fields of science, different independent approaches merge and become integrated with each other. At present, we are witnessing the beginnings of a most promising integration of psychoanalytic theory with learning theory, which may lead to unpredictable advances in the theory and practice of the psychotherapies.

NOTE

1. This type of "fractioned analysis," which was practiced in the early days of the Outpatient Clinic of the Berlin Institute, is an empirical experimental way to find the correct time for termination.

BIBLIOGRAPHY

1. Alexander, F., and French, T. M.: Psychoanalytic Therapy. Principles and Application. New York: Ronald Press, 1946.
2. Alexander, F.: Psychoanalysis and Psychotherapy. New York: W. W. Norton & Co., 1956.
3. ———: Behav. Sci., 3: Oct. 1958.
4. Balint, A., and Balint, M.: Int. J. Psychoanal., 20: 1939.
5. Benedek, T.: Bull. Menninger Clin., 17, 6, 1953.

6. Fenichel, O.: The Psychoanalytic Theory of Neurosis. New York: W. W. Norton, 1945.
7. Freud, S.: The Dynamics of the Transference (1912). Collected Papers, Vol. II. London: Hogarth Press, 1924.
8. ————: Recommendations for Physicians on the Psychoanalytic Method of Treatment (1912). Collected Papers, Vol. II. London: Hogarth Press, 1924.
9. ————: Further Recommendations in the Technique of Psychoanalysis on Beginning the Treatment. The question of the first communications. The Dynamics of the Cure (1913). Collected Papers, Vol. II. London: Hogarth Press, 1924.
10. ————: Further Recommendations in the Technique of Psychoanalysis. Recollection, Repetition and Working Through (1914). Collected Papers, Vol. II. London: Hogarth Press, 1924.
11. ————: Further Recommendations in the Technique of Psychoanalysis. Observations on Transference-Love (1915). Collected Papers, Vol. II. London: Hogarth Press, 1924.
12. ————: New Introductory Lectures on Psychoanalysis. New York: W. W. Norton, 1933.
13. Fromm-Reichmann, F.: Principles of Intensive Psychotherapy. London: Allen & Unwin, 1957.
14. Heimann, P.: Int. J. Psychoanal., 31: 1950.
15. Rado S.: Psychoanalysis of Behavior: Collected Papers. Vol. I (1922–1956); Vol. II (1956–1961). New York: Grune & Stratton, Vol. I, 1956, Vol. II, 1962.
16. Weigert, E.: J. Am. Psychoanal. Ass., 2: 4, 1954.

CHAPTER 24

Alexander's "Psychotherapy and Learning Theory": Critique and Commentary

O. Hobart Mowrer

If others have the same experience as this commentator, they will emerge from a first reading of Franz Alexander's 1963 article "The Dynamics of Psychotherapy in the Light of Learning Theory" with mixed reactions: with surprise and interest that this author, an eminent psychoanalyst, should here speak so positively about learning theory, but also with perplexity and disappointment that he does not make his argument more explicit, pointed, and powerful. During his professional lifetime, Alexander was known as a lucid and seminal writer; but at first blush, this paper seems to exhibit neither of these qualities.

Despite the emphasis given to "learning theory" in the title of this paper and the conclusion that "learning theory appears to be at present the most satisfactory framework for the evaluation of [psychotherapeutic] observational data and for making valid generalizations [p. 343]," there is little reference to learning theory per se until the last three pages; and there one finds not a single allusion to the pertinent learning literature. Various conceptions of the learning process are discussed only in the most general (one might almost say "layman's") terms, and there is no mention of the relatively numerous efforts which have already been made to utilize learning principles in reformulating and testing psychoanalytic concepts and procedures (Burnham, 1924; Dollard, et al., 1939; Dollard & Miller, 1954; Eysenck, 1959; Mowrer, 1939, 1940, 1948, 1950a, 1950b, 1952a, 1952b, 1953a, 1953b, 1954, 1964a, 1965, 1966a, 1966b, 1968; Mowrer & Ullman, 1945; Mowrer & Whiting,

---

This chapter is a discussion-commentary, written especially for the present volume, of Chapter 23: "The Dynamics of Psychotherapy in the Light of Learning Theory," by Franz Alexander.

1940; Shaw, 1948; Shoben, 1959; Wolpe, 1958, 1961; Wolpe, Salter, & Reyna, 1964).

What, then, gives this article its special significance?

I

The article is remarkable, first of all, in that a psychoanalyst of Alexander's stature has, near the end of his life, come out so bluntly with the proposal that the psychology and language of learning should replace psychoanalytic theory and terminology. Such a suggestion would be made, surely, only in the face of extreme disenchantment with traditional psychoanalytic notions; the author quickly confirms this surmise and provides the reader with some understanding of the basis of his dissatisfaction. Near the beginning of his paper, Alexander notes that although psychoanalytic theory has evolved and changed during the last half-century, psychoanalytic treatment methods have remained virtually unaltered since the classical guidelines were laid down by Freud in the period between 1912 and 1915. In no other field of medicine, says Alexander, are physicians today using technical procedures which are so "dated"; toward the end of the paper Alexander points out that even in the preliminary stages of the study conducted on psychoanalytic therapy at Mount Sinai Hospital in Los Angeles, it became apparent that learning principles would have to be introduced to order the accumulated data at all adequately. He says:

As was expected the processing of the voluminous data thus collected proved to be a prolonged affair which will require several years of collaborative work. Yet even at the present stage of processing, several important conclusions emerge. The most important of these is the fact that the traditional descriptions of the therapeutic process do not adequately reflect the immensely complex interaction between therapist and patient. The patient's reactions cannot be described fully as transference reactions. The patient reacts to the therapist as to a concrete person and not only as a representative of parental figures. The therapist's reactions also far exceed what is usually called countertransference. They include in addition to this, interventions based on conscious deliberations and also his spontaneous idiosyncratic attitudes. Moreover, his own values are conveyed to the patient even if he consistently tries to protect his incognito. The patient reacts to the therapist's overt but also to his non-verbal hidden intentions and the therapist reacts to the patient's reactions to him. It is a truly transactional process.

In studying this transactional material I came to the conviction that the therapeutic process can be best understood in the terms of learning theory [p. 340].

Although Alexander makes no reference to the now fairly numerous studies (Brody, 1962; Dollard, 1945; Eysenck, 1952, 1961; Freud, 1937; Knight, 1941; Mowrer, 1961, 1964b; Wilder, 1945) which have brought the therapeutic value of psychoanalysis sharply into question, the possibility—indeed, probability—that psychoanalysis is therapeutically inert must have played an important role both in instigating the Mount Sinai investigation of psychoanalytic treatment procedures and in prompting Alexander to suggest a further shift from prevailing psychoanalytic concepts to learning theory. In light of such radical proposals for change and the mounting empirical research, it would seem that psychoanalysis is today under much criticism and pressure (from both within and without). The question is: Can changes as radical as those Alexander proposes be made in psychoanalysis, both as theory and as technique, without its losing all distinctiveness, indeed its very identity?

II

It is easy to misread the Alexander article and infer that the author is saying that psychoanalytic technique has evolved and changed over the years and that the conservatism is in the area of *theory*. As a result of including the term *learning theory* in the title of his article and of suggesting that it be substituted for conventional psychoanalytic concepts and principles, Alexander might seem to be saying that there is a transcendent need for changes in theory. Moreover, in the body of the article he seems, at certain points, to be indicating widespread satisfaction with psychoanalytic treatment methods:

> There is little disagreement concerning the fundamentals of treatment. Controversies, which occur sporadically, pertain primarily to the technical means by which the transference neurosis can be resolved. The optimal intensity of the transference neurosis is one of the points of contention. [p. 332].

Thus one may be led to infer that the main area of disagreement and controversy is not that of treatment procedures but of theory; this impression is further strengthened by some of the concluding statements which have already been quoted. However, as one reflects upon the situation, it seems likely that exactly the opposite is the case: that theory *has* changed whereas therapeutic procedures have remained relatively static. Then one recalls that this is, in fact, precisely what Alexander says (perhaps not too consistently with respect to other passages just quoted) at the outset of his paper:

One of the striking facts in this field is that the intricate procedure of psychoanalytic treatment underwent so few changes since its guiding principles were formulated. . . . Meanwhile substantial developments took place in theoretical knowledge, *particularly in ego psychology* [p. 330, italics added].

Despite the place of importance thus given to it, there are only a few other brief references to ego psychology until page 335, where we read:

In general, of course, the present is always determined by the past. Freud in a rather early writing proposed the theory of complementary etiology. A person with severe *ego defects* [italics added] acquired in the past will react to slight stress situations in his present life with severe reactions; a person with a relatively healthy past history will require more severe blows to life to regress into a neurotic state (Freud, 1933). Some modern authors like French, Rado, myself, and others feel that there is an unwarranted neglect of the actual life circumstances (Alexander & French, 1946; Rado, 1962).

This passage seems to involve a basic confusion or at least one emphasis where another is more appropriate. Here the accent is upon past vs. present determinants of psychopathology. Does not the more basic question pertain to the *nature* of psychopathology, as it is reflected in the individual's personality structure? The classical assumption in psychoanalytic circles has been that the problem lies in overseverity of the superego; but Alexander, in the article under discussion, seems to take it for granted that the problem is today seen as one of "ego defects." Although relatively speaking, the two conditions—superego excess on the one hand and ego deficiency on the other—may seem to be mirror images of each other, there is a radical difference in therapeutic implications. If, as was formerly supposed, the neurotic's basic problem is overseverity and unrealism on the part of the superego, then therapy becomes essentially a *subtractive* procedure: some part of the personality is overdeveloped or distortedly developed and needs to be removed or at least pared down to size; whereas if the neurotic's basic problem is ego weakness, the thrust of therapy must be in the direction of fostering greater ego strength and character development. The one procedure is essentially negative, subtractive; the other is positive, additive, and calls for very different methods: *learning* rather than extinction, *education* rather than "desensitization."

By way of summarizing this section, let it be said that, despite some apparent inconsistency on this score, the situation to which Alexander primarily addresses himself is one involving a need for change in psychoanalytic treatment procedures rather than in theory, and that in trying to explicate the change which has already occurred in theory, he somewhat misleadingly stresses past as opposed to present rather than superego excess as opposed to ego deficiency. The issues involved here are manifestly complex and still somewhat obscure, but at least this much can be said. The traditional emphasis upon *the past* in the causation of neurosis is a corollary of the belief that superego over-severity is the basic problem, since this part of the personality is presumably laid down, formed, early in life. On the other hand, the emphasis upon *the present*, i.e., "actual life circumstances," is congruent with the notion that much of the neurotic's trouble comes from ego inadequacy and weakness, which shows itself in here-and-now (or at least relatively recent) decisions which are poorly made or, if well made, poorly kept.

III

If, within the domain of psychoanalytic theory, there has been a major shift from the early emphasis upon an overdeveloped and too-harsh superego to the present-day emphasis upon ego inadequacy and weakness, then why is it that corresponding readjustments have not been made in psychoanalytic technique? Near the outset of his article, Alexander suggests possible reasons for the "conservatism" which analysts have shown in this regard; an alternative possibility is that if analysts systematically translated the implications of ego psychology into practice, very little would remain of psychoanalysis as Freud originally propounded and practiced it.

In response to Alexander's suggestion that ego psychology is a development from within the classical framework of psychoanalysis itself and thus not antithetical or foreign to that system, one recalls Freud's 1911 article entitled "Formulations Regarding Two Principles of Mental Functioning," in which the author made a clear distinction between what he called the *pleasure principle* and the *reality principle*: here psychological health presupposed the capacity on the part of an individual to restrain infantile, animalistic tendencies toward immediate impulse gratification (pleasure) as a means of insuring greater long-term gratification and security (the reality principle). Repeatedly, in *A General Introduction to Psychoanalysis* (1920), Freud alluded to personality development, or progression, and to regression. In his *New Introductory*

Lectures on Psychoanalysis (1933), Freud epitomized the objectives of psychotherapy in a now famous slogan: "Where id was there shall ego be." And in *An Outline of Psychoanalysis* (1949), published posthumously, he also appears to take a decidedly benevolent attitude toward the superego when he quotes Goethe, thus:

> What thou hast inherited from thy fathers,
> Acquire it to make it thine [p. 123].

Then with the publication of Anna Freud's book *The Ego and the Mechanisms of Defense*, in 1937, ego psychology was given another push forward. In Chapter 1 she observes:

There have been periods in the development of psychoanalytical science when the theoretical study of the individual ego was distinctly unpopular. Somehow or other, many analysts had conceived the idea that, in analysis, the value of the scientific and therapeutic work done was in direct proportion to the depth of the psychic strata upon which attention was focused. Whenever interest was transferred from the deeper to the more superficial psychic strata—whenever, that is to say, research was deflected from the id to the ego—it was felt that here was a beginning of apostasy from psychoanalysis as a whole [p. 3].

From the beginning analysis, as a therapeutic method, was concerned with the ego and its aberrations: the correction of these abnormalities and the restoration of the ego to its integrity [p. 4].

In the id the so-called "primary process" prevails; there is no synthesis of ideas, affects are liable to displacement, opposites are not mutually exclusive and may even coincide and condensation occurs as a matter of course. The sovereign principle which governs the psychic processes is that of obtaining pleasure. In the ego, on the contrary, the association of ideas is subject to strict conditions, to which we apply the comprehensive term "secondary process"; further, the instinctual impulses can no longer seek gratification without more ado—they are required to respect the demands of reality and, more than that, to conform to ethical and moral laws by which the super-ego seeks to control the behavior of the ego [p. 7].

It is therefore not incorrect to say that ego psychology represents the fruition of ideas which date well back into the past. But at the same time it must be observed that the notion that "neurosis" results from ego weakness is not altogether compatible with the better known and more characteristic psychoanalytic assumption that this condition arises because of overdevelopment of the superego. Here are two passages which are representative of a very large literature in which this notion is repeatedly set forth:

> Conscience is a function we ascribe, among others, to the superego; it consists of watching over and judging the actions and intentions of the ego, exercising the function of a censor. The sense of guilt, the severity of the superego, is therefore the same thing as rigour of conscience. . . . It [conscience] is the direct expression of the dread of external authority [Freud, 1930, p. 127].

> In our investigations and our therapy of the neurosis, we cannot avoid finding fault with the super-ego of the individual on two counts: in commanding and prohibiting with such severity it troubles too little about the happiness of the ego and it fails to take into account sufficiently the difficulties in the way of obeying it—the strength of instinctual cravings in the id and the hardships of external environment. Consequently in our therapy we often find ourselves obliged to do battle with the super-ego and work to moderate its demands. Exactly the same objections can be made against the ethical standards of the cultural super-ego [Freud, 1930, p. 139].

IV

The question of whether a neurotic person is suffering from ego deficiency or from superego excess may, from one point of view, seem trivial. If the objective of therapy were simply to make the ego stronger *relative* to the superego, this could, in principle, be accomplished by any of three procedures: (1) the superego could be weakened, (2) the ego could be strengthened, or (3) both procedures might be carried out simultaneously or successively. And since psychoanalysis has had much to say about how the superego can be weakened (through interpretations, the transference, etc.), and has said very little about how the ego can be strengthened, we see why psychoanalytic technique has remained relatively unmodified through the years: early theory, established methodology, and entrenched training procedures all tended to focus upon superego modification, in the direction of greater leniency and "acceptance," rather than upon ego development.

But since conscience is a product of the sustained efforts of parents, teachers, clergymen, judges, and others to make it strong and reliable, psychotherapy along the lines just indicated runs counter to these efforts and arouses, not only in the individual himself, but also in society at large, more or less massive resistance. There are certain rules and values which *must* be observed if a given society is to function satisfactorily; any attempt to bring inner peace to neurotic persons by inducing them to take these rules and values less seriously than society in general holds necessary will either be ineffective or, if effective, will promote morally or socially objectionable behavior in the patient.

If, on the other hand, an attempt is made to strengthen the ego relative to the superego, not by weakening the latter but by supporting, encouraging, and developing the former, this type of "therapy" will be congruent with the overall objectives of human socialization and education, rather than antithetical to them, and should be welcomed by the mentors of the young instead of opposed by them. Thus it is by no means a matter of indifference whether a condition of ego-superego imbalance is rectified by superego shrinkage or by ego encouragement and growth. In order for a human being to function adequately in his society (whatever that may be), there are certain external requirements or "standards" which are supposed to be "introjected" by all persons; and any attempt to help neurotic, maladjusted individuals by systematic derogation of these internalized values and controls will be strenuously opposed by the society—or, if not opposed, will undermine the stability and integrity of the society itself.

Elsewhere more than a dozen empirical studies have been reviewed (Mowrer, 1967a) which consistently indicate that, on a socialization continuum or scale, neurotic individuals fall, on the average, well *below* normal persons—rather than above them, as the theory of superego overdevelopment would suggest. These studies thus give further support to the supposition that "therapy" calls for a strengthening, rather than a weakening, of some part or parts of the neurotic's personality structure—and thus qualifies as a form of *education*, rather than "treatment" in any reductive sense of the term. Logically, the deficiency with which we are here concerned might be in either the superego or the ego, or in both. There is, however, no indication that either of these agencies is too strong and ought to be weakened. So the relevant question becomes: Is a "neurosis" corrected by strengthening the ego, or the superego, or both? Until recently there was little or no empirical evidence as to which of these procedures is the correct one. Fortunately, we now have clear indications that in most, if not all, neurotic persons what is needed is not a weakening of the superego but instead a decided increase in the strength and effectiveness of the *ego*. Inner harmony is thus achieved when a revitalized and energized ego brings the individual's behavior up to the requirements of the superego (and of the social order which the superego represents), *not* by encouraging the ego to act in disregard of the behests of conscience and community.

V

For some time there has been increasing evidence that "socialization," as it impinges upon the human young, is not a unitary process but is instead comprised of two (possibly more) component parts: a component which leads to *temptation fear* (or anxiety) and a component which results in *guilt.* The first of these is the capacity to experience fear *before* the occurrence of a highly motivated but previously punished act, whereas guilt is the fear an organism experiences *after* the performance of a forbidden act, while punishment is still impending. Temptation fear may reasonably be thought of as an ego function: here the organism still has "freedom of choice," i.e., the capacity to act in either an approved or a disapproved way. Such power of decision is usually thought of as residing in the ego. On the other hand, guilt is usually conceived as a superego function: here an organism, in the face of temptation, has yielded, the fact of his culpability is now irrevocable, and punishment is his due—unless restitutive measures of some kind can be taken.

Solomon (1960) describes a series of experiments that led to such operational definitions of guilt and temptation fear. Puppies were starved for two days, then admitted singly to a room where, set before their trainer, there were two dishes of food, one highly preferable to the other. Most puppies chose the more attractive food within a few seconds, and when they touched it, they were hit with a folded newspaper until they withdrew. After several days, the puppies went immediately to the less preferred food. This was called a *taboo-training* situation. Then came a *temptation-testing* phase. The puppies, again starved for two days, were admitted singly to the room, again supplied with the two foods but with the trainer absent. Some puppies would circle the dish of preferred food; some would avoid looking at it; some would crawl toward it, barking and whining. The time elapsed before the puppies yielded to the temptation to eat the preferred food was measured. The intervals ranged from six minutes to sixteen days. Solomon feels that resistance to temptation should be clearly distinguished from guilt. Although the evidence was not clear, owing to uncontrolled factors in the training process, it seemed inferable that puppies that were punished as they approached the food would exhibit signs of emotional stress when exposed to temptation but not after they had yielded to it. On the other hand, other puppies, allowed to eat some of the preferred food and then punished, would show emotional disturbance after eating the food: a guilt reaction. Ability to resist temptation and strength of guilt reaction appeared to depend both on the intensity and the timing of the punishment.

These experiments have a parallel in the two major techniques used in the socialization of children: observation of the child's behavior, with punishment when he attempts to commit a tabooed act, and entrapment into the commission of the act, followed by punishment. The "conscience" appears to include two elements, resistance to temptation and guilt reactions, and its development in the individual depends upon the relative strengths of both. Solomon assumes that, with suitable variations in training procedures affecting the relative strengths of these two elements, he could have produced four basic types of "conscience" in puppies.

Here is an example of how learning theory and research can be used to clarify clinical concepts and to suggest new research. This is not to say that temptation fear (anxiety) and guilt, as experienced at the human level, are identical with these reactions as they occur in lower organisms. One obvious difference is that in human beings there is usually an element of consent or commitment to social rules or morality not found in a laboratory animal (cf. Mowrer, 1968). But here is a good foundation on which to build a sound structure of clinical theory and practice.

VI

Stimulated by the investigations of Solomon and associates which have just been reviewed and by prevailing controversy concerning the nature of psychopathology, Johnson, Ackerman, and Frank have carried out research with human subjects which they report in a paper entitled "Resistance to Temptation, Guilt Following Yielding, and Psychopathology (1968). They begin with a contrast of my view of the basis of mental illness with that of Freud, quoting from my paper of 1950 my view that "anxiety comes, not from acts that the individual would commit but dares not, but from acts which he has committed and wishes he had not. . . . a 'guilt theory' of anxiety rather than an 'impulse theory.' " Rather than allowing psychoanalysis to reduce the strength of the superego, which Freud regards as generating "neurotic guilt" without a basis in reality, the patient, whose guilt is based on an awareness of having transgressed certain rules, should either confess his sins or, if he believes the rules to be wrong, openly disavow them. The authors are somewhat critical of my interpretation of Freud, since Freud often appeared to be concerned with strengthening the ego rather than weakening the superego, but they tend to agree that the influence of Freudian theory has tended in the direction that I attributed to Freud himself. (Jourard [1958] and Eysenck [1960] suggest furthermore the existence of several types of neurotic and/or psychotic disturbances with varying id-ego-superego balances.) They admit, though, that my "about-face in ideas regarding mental disturbance" (1967a) has received "a fair amount of empirical support."

The authors emphasize, once again, the constituent elements of the "conscience," citing studies of children (Rebelsky, Allinsmith, & Grinder, 1963) and puppies (Solomon, 1960) as suggesting that resistance to temptation and guilt feelings both are present, though "only minimally related to one another." Acting on this assumption, the authors proposed to investigate these two factors in their relation to mental health. Institutionalized psychiatric subjects and a control group were given projected story-completion tasks. Some stories required the subject either to yield to or resist temptation, while others began with the subject yielding to temptation and were intended to discover the subject's tendencies to feel guilt, to confess, or to make restitution. The psychiatric subjects had a greater tendency to allow the story subjects to yield to temptation than the control group did, but the pattern of guilt behavior was not significantly different from that shown by the control group. In a second experiment with such tasks the psychiatric patients were replaced by noninstitutionalized neurotic patients, and similar results were obtained. In a third experiment, the group under study were "college students varying in adjustment," and "measures of stability-neuroticism, internal vs. external control, and of openness in self-disclosure" were added to the projective story tasks. Their conclusions, the authors report, imply that

the person whose locus of control and responsibility is internal rather than external, and who shows ability to resist temptation, is more likely to be mentally healthy according to the indices of mental health used herein. The results suggest that two aspects of conscience—resistance to temptation and guilt following yielding—are only minimally related, and that resistance, but not guilt, is related to mental health.

Johnson, Ackerman, and Frank tend to identify both resistance to temptation and guilt capacity as superego functions, but they would presumably not object if resistance to temptation were made an ego function and guilt capacity assigned to the superego. In fact, they imply as much when they say: "Freud himself, at least at many points in his career, appeared chiefly concerned with strengthening the ego, not with reducing the absolute strength of the superego." Resistance to temptation and guilt capacity are, to be sure, both related to the overall phenomenon of socialization. And if we identify resistance to temptation as an ego function and guilt capacity as a superego function, we derive the diagram shown in the table below.

	"PUNKS"	SUC. CRIM.	NEUROTICS	NORMALS
Superego	W	W	S	S
Ego	W	S	W	S

Schematic representation of the phenomenon of human socialization (from left to right), as a function of ego and superego strength (S) and weakness (W). The abbreviation "Suc. Crim." stands for "Successful Criminals." "Punks" are the lowest, least effectual type of criminal, who are disdained by Successful Criminals.

If this conceptualization is correct, variation in strength of superego does not differentiate normal and neurotic persons, but it does differentiate both of these personality types from "successful criminals" and "punks." Where neurotics and normals apparently differ is in regard to *ego strength*, not superego strength. If this is the case, then therapy for neurotic persons should consist of helping them develop greater resistance to temptation (and any other characteristics that may be properly identified as ego functions). It is conceivable that there is a type of (classically Freudian) neurotic whose ego is essentially normal and who has an abnormally strong superego, which needs to be weakened, brought down to size. But the empirical findings reported by Johnson, Ackerman, and Frank (1967) and by Mowrer (1967a) suggest that ego weakness, not excessive superego strength, is the problem of greatest importance in so-called neurotic persons.

If an individual shows sociopathic (criminal) tendencies, then superego strengthening becomes the major task of rehabilitation (cf. Glasser, 1966; Shelly & Bassin, 1966). But from the sources here cited, as well as from some contemporary psychoanalytic literature, it now appears that ego development, rather than either a weakening or a strengthening of the superego, should be the primary objective in the treatment of neurotics. This position is congruent with Alexander's emphasis upon "ego defect" in the neurotic and the need for greater "ego strength." Alexander makes only indirect allusion to neurotics in whom there may be a need for superego weakening. If the schematization proposed in the table is correct, this (in contrast to the prevailing thought of an earlier day) is rarely if ever the basic desideratum.

VII

After what may have seemed a digression, we now return to the Alexander article, hopefully with a better basis for appraising and clarifying the somewhat ambiguous argument advanced therein. Now it is clear why Alexander has suggested that the central consideration in therapeutic endeavor with psychoneurotic individuals is *learning*, rather than unlearning or extinction, and why learning *theory* can be expeditiously used for conceptualizing the "therapeutic" ("educational") process. In classical psychoanalysis, it was commonly assumed that there were two types of clinical problem: *sociopathy*, which called for education; and *neurosis*, which called for extinction, de-education. It is doubtful that this is a valid distinction. If the table is correct, *all* therapeutic and rehabilitative problems (in the entire spectrum of functional disorders or personality failure) are developmental or educational and call for positive teaching and learning. The neurotic's need, according to this view, is for learning in the realm of ego strength and control; the "punk" and the "successful criminal" both need teaching and learning in the realm of "values" (superego); and the "punk" also requires education and change with respect to the ego.

It has been generally recognized that sociopaths are untreatable by psychoanalytic and other conventional psychotherapeutic procedures. Perhaps we should note that as long as neurotics were perceived as having a superego excess, they too were "untreatable," i.e., therapeutic effort was ineffective, if not actively harmful. If we now accept the schema suggested in the table, the treatment of neurotics calls for methods which will encourage the development of ego strength rather than superego weakening; and that of sociopaths, of whatever stripe, calls for superego strengthening (and, in the case of the "punk," for ego strengthening as well). Classical training in psychoanalysis has not, it seems, specifically equipped its practitioners for *either* of these enterprises.

Alexander acknowledges that psychoanalysis is often unsuccessful in its therapeutic thrust and, worse than that, can even be detrimental. He says:

The traditional belief is that the longer an analysis lasts the greater is the probability of recovery. Experienced analysts more and more came to doubt the validity of this generalization. If anything, this is the exception: very long treatments lasting over many years do not seem to be the most successful ones. . . . A clear correlation between duration of treatment and its results has not been established. There are no reliable criteria for the proper time of termination. Improvements observed during treatment often prove to be conditioned by the fact that the patient is still being treated. . . . A universal regressive trend in human beings has been generally recognized by psychoanalysts. Under sufficient stress everyone tends to regress to the helpless state of infancy and seek help from others. The psychoanalytic treatment situation caters to this regressive attitude [p. 334].

If the table is valid, then to the extent that psychoanalysis (operating on the premise that the neurotic's superego is too strong and needs to be weakened) succeeded in its avowed therapeutic objective, it did indeed produce "regression," not only toward infantilism and helplessness, but also toward sociopathy. And since this type of change is not what the neurotic needs (his need is for ego strengthening, not superego weakening), one can see why "very long treatments lasting over many years do not seem to be the most successful ones." In fact, one might even infer that the *less* of this kind of "treatment" the neurotic person receives, the better off he is! Alexander's "diagnosis" of neurosis as an "ego defect" suggests interventive methods of a very different nature, and we can readily understand his observation that:

In order to counteract this trend [toward regression] a continuous pressure on the patient is needed to make him ready to take over his *own management* as soon as possible. During temporary interruptions [of therapy] patients often discover that they can live without their analyst. When they return, the still not worked out emotional problems come clearly to the forefront. This type of "fractional analysis," which was practiced in the early days of the Outpatient Clinic in the Berlin Institute, is an empirical experimental way to find the correct time for termination [p. 334, italics added].

When Alexander posits a "universal regressive trend in human beings," perhaps the danger is not so much a return to helplessness (or "pregenital" sexuality) as a loss of responsibility and integrity in the adult, mature sense of these terms. This "universal regressive trend" seems to be not too far removed from the concept of Original Sin, not in the sense that "in Adam's fall we sinned all," but in the sense that morality, whatever its ultimate advantages, always calls for restraint and sacrifice, here and now; and we human beings apparently need support and encouragement in following the behests of conscience, rather than in ignoring them. Ego strength is needed by the neurotic and the "punk" and superego strength by both types of sociopath.

VIII

Now one sees why Alexander was so intrigued by the work of Rado:

> One of the most systematic revisions of the standard psychoanalytic procedure was undertaken by Sandor Rado, published in several writings, beginning in 1948. His critical evaluation of psychoanalytic treatment and his suggested modifications deserve particular attention because for many years Rado has been known as one of the most thorough students of Freud's writings.

> As years went on, Rado became more and more dissatisfied with the prevailing practice of psychoanalysis, and proposed his adaptational technique based on his "adaptational psychodynamics." . . . He is most concerned, as I am, with those features of the standard technique of psychoanalysis which foster regression without supplying a counterforce toward the patient's *progression*, that is to say, to his successful adaptation to the actual life situation. He raises the crucial question: is the patient's understanding of his past development sufficient to induce a change in him. "To overcome repressions and thus be able to recall the past is one thing; to learn from it and be able to act on the new knowledge, another" (Rado, 1962).

> Rado recommends, as a means to promote the goal of therapy, *raising the patient from his earlier child-like adaptations to an appropriate adult level—* "to hold the patient as much as possible at the adult level of cooperation with the physician." [p. 338, italics added].

But then there follows an apologetic note, which seems to be somewhat inconsistent with the passage just quoted:

> Rado considers his adaptational technique but a further development of the current psychoanalytic technique, not something basically contradictory to it. It should be pointed out that while criticizing the standard psychoanalytic procedure, Rado in reality criticizes current practice, but not theory [pp. 338–339].

In some ways it would seem that both Alexander and Rado underestimate the extent to which their position is "basically contradictory" to classical psychoanalytic theory as well as technique. As we have seen, "ego psychology" has a long history in psychoanalysis, but it has been decidedly a minor theme in comparison to the notion that the neurotic is a victim of *too much* "education," particularly in the moral area, and that such a person needs to *get rid* of his "inhibitions" and "repressions." Traditional psychoanalytic treatment procedures have been predicated far more on this view of the neurotic state than upon the tenets of "ego psychology." As psychoanalytic writers like Alexander began to change their conception of neurosis, established therapeutic methods became largely irrelevant; yet no alternative treatment methodology was immediately forthcoming. More than ten years ago, the present writer recalls hearing a prominent psychoanalyst say, in effect: "We are now in the process of moving away from the classical emphasis upon interpretation and superego change, toward ego psychology; but at present we know very little about the ego and are even further from knowing how to modify it in a positive, healthy direction."

Although one must be careful not to read into the Alexander article more than the author intended, it seems likely that the author wrote this extraordinary paper largely in response to the need to find treatment procedures which are genuinely congruent with the newer ego psychology. This may be why both Alexander and Rado stress *learning* (rather than extinction) and *progression* (rather than regression).

According to present indications, the best way for a neurotic person to acquire greater ego strength is for him to enter an appropriate form of *group* therapy (cf. Mowrer, 1964a, 1967b); and it has also recently been discovered that where (as in the case of the sociopath) there is need for development of superego strength, this too can best be accomplished in group therapy, of a particularly intensive, *continuous* nature (Casriel, 1963; Shelly & Bassin, 1965; Yablonsky, 1965). Since the sociopath is further removed from normality than is the neurotic (see the table), it follows that the rehabilitative efforts called for in his case will have to be particularly intensive. But what is now also clear is that regardless of whether the problem is neurosis or sociopathy, the need is for *progression, growth, learning, education*—primarily in the realm of the ego for neurotic persons and in the realm of superego, or ego and superego, in sociopaths.

The Alexander article usefully contributes to this conceptual and practical reorientation.

REFERENCES

Alexander, F. The dynamics of psychotherapy in the light of learning theory. *American Journal of Psychiatry*, 1963, *120*, 440–448. Reprinted in this collection, pp. 330–344; page numbers cited in the text refer to *Creative developments in psychotherapy*.

Alexander, F., & French, T. M. *Psychoanalytic therapy: Principles and applications*. New York: Ronald Press, 1946.

Brody, M. W. Prognosis and results of psychoanalysis. In J. H. Nodine & J. H.

Moyer (Eds.), *Psychosomatic medicine*. Philadelphia: Lea & Febiger, 1962.

Burnham, W. H. *The normal mind*. New York: Appleton-Century, 1924.

Casriel, D. *So fair a house: The story of Synanon*. Englewood Cliffs: Prentice-Hall, 1963.

Dollard, J. The acquisition of new social habits. In R. Linton (Ed.), *The science of man in world crisis*. New York: Columbia University Press, 1945.

Dollard, J., Doob, J., Miller, N. E., Mowrer, O. H., & Sears, R. *Frustration and aggression*. New Haven: Yale University Press, 1939.

Dollard, J., & Miller, N. E. *Personality and psychotherapy: An analysis in terms of learning, thinking, and culture*. New York: McGraw-Hill, 1950.

Eysenck, H. J. The effects of psychotherapy: An evaluation. *Journal of Consulting Psychology*, 1952, *16*, 319–324.

Eysenck, H. J. Learning theory and behaviour therapy. *Journal of Mental Science*, 1959, *61*, 105.

Eysenck, H. J. *Behavior therapy and the neuroses*. New York: Pergamon Press, 1960.

Eysenck, H. J. The effects of psychotherapy. In H. J. Eysenck (Ed.), *Handbook of abnormal psychology*. New York: Basic Books, 1961. Pp. 697–725.

Freud, A. *The ego and the mechanisms of defense*. London: Hogarth Press, 1937.

Freud, S. *A general introduction to psychoanalysis*. New York: Liveright, 1920.

Freud, S. *Civilization and its discontents*. London: Hogarth Press, 1930.

Freud, S. *New introductory lectures on psychoanalysis*. New York: W. W. Norton & Co., 1933.

Freud, S. Formulations regarding two principles of mental functioning (1911). In *Collected papers*. Vol. 4. London: Hogarth Press, 1934. Pp. 13–21.

Freud, S. *An outline of psychoanalysis*. New York: W. W. Norton & Co., 1949.

Freud, S. Analysis terminable and interminable (1937). In *Collected papers*. Vol. 5. London: Hogarth Press, 1950. Pp. 316–357.

Glasser, W. *Reality therapy—a new approach to psychiatry*. New York: Harper & Row, 1965.

Jourard, S. *Personal adjustment—an approach through the study of healthy personality*. New York: Macmillan, 1958.

Johnson, R. C., Ackerman, J. M., & Frank, H. Resistance to temptation, guilt following yielding, and psychopathology. To be published.

Knight, R. P. Evaluation of the results of psychoanalytic therapy. *American Journal of Psychiatry*, 1941, *98*, 434–436.

Mowrer, O. H. A stimulus-response analysis of learning and its role as a reinforcing agent. *Psychological Review*, 1939, *46*, 553–565.

Mowrer, O. H. An experimental analogue of "regression" with incidental observations of "reaction-formation." *Journal of Abnormal and Social Psychology*, 1940, 35, 56–67.

Mowrer, O. H. Learning theory and the neurotic paradox. *American Journal of Orthopsychiatry*, 1948, 18, 571–610.

Mowrer, O. H. *Learning theory and personality dynamics.* New York: Ronald Press, 1950. (a)

Mowrer, O. H. Pain, punishment, guilt, and anxiety. In P. H. Hoch & J. Zubin (Eds.), *Anxiety.* New York: Grune & Stratton, 1950. (b)

Mowrer, O. H. Neurosis and its treatment as learning phenomena. In L. Abt (Ed.), *Progress in clinical psychology.* New York: Grune & Stratton, 1952. (a)

Mowrer, O. H. Learning theory and the neurotic fallacy. *American Journal of Orthopsychiatry*, 1952, 22, 679–689. (b)

Mowrer, O. H. (Ed.) *Psychotherapy—theory and research.* New York: Ronald Press, 1953. (a)

Mowrer, O. H. Neurosis: A disorder of conditioning or problem solving? *Annals of the New York Academy of Sciences*, 1953, 56, 273–288. (b)

Mowrer, O. H. Ego psychology, cybernetics, and learning theory. In Kentucky symposium on learning theory, personality theory, and clinical research. New York: John Wiley & Sons, 1954.

Mowrer, O. H. *The crisis in psychiatry and religion.* Princeton: Van Nostrand, 1961.

Mowrer, O. H. Freudianism, behavior therapy, and "self-disclosure." *Behavior Research and Therapy*, 1964, 1, 321. (a)

Mowrer, O. H. *The new group therapy.* Princeton: Van Nostrand, 1964. (b)

Mowrer, O. H. Learning theory and behavior therapy. In B. Wolman (Ed.), *Handbook of clinical psychology.* New York: McGraw-Hill, 1965.

Mowrer, O. H. The basis of psychopathology: Malconditioning or misbehavior? In C. Spielberger (Ed.), *Anxiety and behavior.* New York: Academic Press, 1966. (a)

Mowrer, O. H. The behavior therapies, with special reference to modeling and imitation. *American Journal of Psychotherapy*, 1966, 20, 439–461. (b)

Mowrer, O. H. New evidence concerning the nature of psychopathology, 1967. In N. Feldman (Ed.), *Studies in psychotherapy and behavior change.* Buffalo, N.Y.: University of Buffalo Press, 1968. (a)

Mowrer, O. H. Loss and recovery of community—a guide to the theory and practice of integrity therapy. In G. M. Gazda (Ed.), *Theories and methods of group psychotherapy and counseling.* Springfield, Ill.: C C Thomas, 1967. (b)

Mowrer, O. H. The psychoneurotic defenses (including deceptions) as punishment-avoidance strategies. In B. Campbell & R. Church (Eds.), *Punishment and aversive behavior.* New York: Appleton-Century-Crofts, 1969.

Mowrer, O. H., & Ullman, A. D. Time as a determinant in integrative learning. *Psychological Review*, 1945, *52*, 61–91.

Mowrer, O. H., & Whiting, J. W. M. Habit progression and regression—a laboratory study of some factors relevant to human socialization. *Journal of Comparative Psychology*, 1943, *36*, 229–252.

Rado, S. *Psychoanalysis of behavior: Collected papers.* Vol. 2 (1956–1961). New York: Grune & Stratton, 1962.

Rebelsky, F. G., Allinsmith, W., & Grinder, R. E. Resistance to temptation and sex differences use of fantasy confession. *Child Development*, 1963, *34*, 955–962.

Shaw, F. S. Some postulates concerning psychotherapy. *Journal of Consulting Psychology*, 1948, *12*, 426.

Shelly, J. A., & Bassin, A. Daytop Lodge—a new treatment approach for drug addicts. *Corrective Psychiatry*, 1965, *11*, 186–195.

Shoben, J. E., Jr. Psychotherapy as a problem in learning theory. *Psychological Bulletin*, 1959, *46*, 366.

Solomon, R. L. Preliminary report on temptation and guilt. In O. H. Mowrer, *Learning theory and the symbolic processes.* New York: John Wiley & Sons, 1960.

Wilder, J. Facts and figures on psychotherapy. *Journal of Clinical Psychopathology*, 1945, *7*, 311.

Wolpe, J. *Psychotherapy by reciprocal inhibition.* Stanford, Calif.: Stanford University Press, 1958.

Wolpe, J. The systematic desensitization treatment of neurosis. *Journal of Nervous and Mental Diseases*, 1961, *132*, 189.

Wolpe, J., Salter, A., & Reyna, L. J. *The conditioning therapies.* New York: Holt, Rinehart & Winston, 1964.

Yablonsky, L. *The tunnel back.* New York: Macmillan, 1965.

CHAPTER 25

The Practice of Psychotherapy
Is Art and Not Science

Joseph D. Matarazzo

During the month of March, 1964, I was in self-imposed seclusion on the Oregon coast reading and reviewing, for the following year's *Annual Review of Psychology*, the books and articles on psychotherapy which had been published during the previous twelve months. Coincidentally, but quite prophetically in view of this invitation to prepare a discussion of Franz Alexander's paper, my office forwarded a note from him, dated March 3, in which Professor Alexander replied to a letter I had earlier written him requesting a copy of his forthcoming Karen Horney lecture. In this note he included the following comments: "I have changed the topic of my Karen Horney lecture to Neurosis and Creativity. I scarcely think that this would fit into your chapter on psychotherapy. . . . I am enclosing, however, a reprint of my paper on "Dynamics of Psychotherapy in the Light of Learning Theory," which probably would be suitable for your purposes . . . ." As the reader remembers, Franz Alexander died on March 8, 1964, five days after mailing this letter.

This excerpt from his note shows the importance he attached to this paper, which had been published five months earlier, in November, 1963. I was not surprised, because I felt it represented a major contribution to psychotherapy literature, as well as a turning point for psychoanalytic theory and practice, at least in our country. A full page of my annual review chapter was devoted to this single article. I will deal first with some of the passages which impressed me then and now, and then propose more general, evaluative comments.

This chapter is a discussion-commentary, written especially for the present volume, of Chapter 23: "The Dynamics of Psychotherapy in the Light of Learning Theory," by Franz Alexander.

PSYCHOANALYTIC DOGMA: A DEFENSE AGAINST
THE THERAPIST'S OWN ANXIETY

In my opinion, Franz Alexander, like Freud, during his entire career was to psychoanalysis as practiced by physicians what Carl Rogers is to psychotherapy as practiced by many psychologists, psychiatrists, and social workers. He was one of the first representatives of his discipline to modify, innovate, develop, and, most importantly, to expose to public (scientific) view what he actually was doing, always encouraging his colleagues to try to validate or improve upon what he had done or was then doing in psychotherapy. Thus it is not surprising that Alexander begins his article with a candid declaration of psychoanalysis' failure to reflect the clinical and scientific developments of the past half-century. He states that from 1912 to 1962 the practice of medicine underwent radical changes, in keeping with clinical and scientific advances. However, psychoanalytic theory and practice as taught in our psychoanalytic institutes in 1962 was little different from that taught by Freud in 1912. Alexander declares this to be due in great part to the bewildering complexity of the psychodynamic processes occurring during treatment. Since human beings, therapists included, typically have a low tolerance for uncertainty, and since the psychotherapy interaction is so ambiguous and bewildering, the dogmatic theory and technique which is still taught in psychoanalytic institutes is a helpful defense for the otherwise anxious beginning psychoanalyst.

In my opinion, as well as Alexander's, this understandably human, but unfortunate, aspect of psychoanalytic teaching, more than any other single factor, has caused the decline, if not demise, of classical psychoanalysis. Today it is clear to everyone, including the leaders in American psychoanalytic practice, I believe, that Freudian (and neo-Freudian) psychoanalysis is no longer the dominant theme in psychotherapy theory, practice, or research that it was during the past three decades. The many important contributions of psychoanalysis (e.g., the role of unconscious factors in human behavior and the vast richness and complexity of interpersonal phenomena) have been assimilated, quietly and imperceptibly, into many areas of Western intellectual life (psychology, sociology, psychotherapy, medicine, philosophy, literature, etc.). Those aspects of psychoanalysis which did not survive close scrutiny, such as many aspects of symbolism and the exaggerated role of primary instincts in everyday behavior, have been downgraded to a position of rapidly diminishing influence. As with the nearly extinct Hullians and other important but seemingly premature global theorists in experimental psychology, the psychoanalyst-theoretician appears to be little in evidence today—a situation clearly envisioned by Alexander. Franz Alexander's life, writings, and teachings were the very antithesis of this premature closure and rigidity in theory and practice. The Chicago Institute for Psychoanalysis, which he founded in 1932, with its dedication to experimentation was an important, but unfortunately relatively powerless, challenge to organized American psychoanalysis to change with the times for its own good. Another such challenge, national in scope, was the Academy of Psychoanalysis, in which Alexander played a major role, serving at one time as president. One of the main purposes of this academy was to further research in psychoanalysis and to this end admitted to membership a class of non-psychoanalysts, called "scientific associates."

Probably no other single feature of classical psychoanalysis offended other scientists and university educators as much as the ecclesiastical aura which pervaded organized psychoanalysis during the 1930s, '40s, and '50s. With the exception of Alexander's Chicago Institute for Psychoanalysis and a few other places (e.g., the Menninger Foundation and the Washington School of Psychiatry), formal psychoanalysis has been taught in a score of American psychoanalytic institutes which are immune to the checks and balances of academic scrutiny. Making observations on this fifty-year-old guild type of specialty education, I wrote in my *Annual Review* chapter, just a few years ago:

Unless the teaching of psychoanalysis is carried on in the future as a post-psychiatric residency specialty program in selected medical school departments of psychiatry, or selected university departments of psychology, it is my opinion that training (and thus specialized practice) in psychoanalysis will disappear completely. Rapid advances in knowledge, as well as a changing social order, require the abandonment of parochial teaching based on the six decades' old clinical observation of one sensitive and brilliant man—no matter how insightful his clinical observations nor how fertile his extraordinary mind [Matarazzo, 1965, p. 217].

In the five years since this was written, my informal "soundings" around the country have led me to conclude that (1) universities and medical schools are still not interested in launching *formal* psychoanalytic teaching programs, and (2) more psychoanalysts are leaving this field of practice than are entering it. Thus, for all practical purposes, psychoanalysis, including the refreshing brand taught by Alexander first in Chicago and then, after his 65th birthday, in Los Angeles, is rapidly becoming a matter of history. Today one rarely encounters a student-in-training in psychology, psychiatry, or social work who has *formal* psychoanalytic training as his goal. I am convinced that this would not be the case if other psychoanalysts had heeded Franz Alexander's prophetic conclusion in his 1948 book, *Fundamentals of Psychoanalysis*: "Finally, it should be emphasized that psychoanalytic theory and practice are in process of development. To further this development a continuous revision of theoretical assumptions and generalizations, as well as experiments with therapeutic procedure, is imperative [p. 300]." It is unfortunate that so few psychoanalysts other than Alexander himself heeded this plea. In my opinion, the opening comments in the preceding article reflect Alexander's disillusionment that, fifteen years later, the teaching in most American psychoanalytic institutes had changed little since 1948 or, worse still, since 1912.

2. PSYCHOANALYTIC PRACTICE: FOUR AREAS OF UNIVERSAL AGREEMENT

Nevertheless, Alexander continues this article by stating that despite the fact that psychoanalytic theory and dogma became prematurely rigidified as the therapist's defense against the uncertainty he encountered in the therapeutic interaction, psychoanalysts of different (but still dogmatic) theoretical persuasions all appeared to agree on four basic principles: (1) during treatment repressed, unconscious material becomes conscious; (2) free association and the patient's emotional interpersonal experience (transference) are the methods for aiding this material to become conscious; (3) the patient will show resistance to uncovering this unconscious content; and (4) use of the patient's reaction to the therapist (transference) is the key factor to overcoming this resistance and to a better understanding and resolution of early, repressed experiences and traumas (pp. 331–332). Alexander acknowledges the universal acceptance of these four principles, and generously notes in passing that some psychoanalytic theorists emphasize one or another of these points, and then unobtrusively introduces a discussion of his own concept of the "corrective emotional experience [pp. 332–333]." This major innovation within Freudian theory, first introduced by Alexander and French in 1946, challenged the very essence of the basic concept of transference. For other psychoanalysts the transference neurosis consisted of an abreactive reliving of the actual emotional experiences of childhood for the parent. But Alexander felt that the current transference reaction of the patient was different and less intense than in the original conflict, and that the therapist's response to the patient's emotional expressions was quite different from the original treatment of the child by the parents.

While formal Freudian psychoanalysis was at its level of greatest influence in this country (through the powerful influence of the Boston and New York psychoanalytic institutes), Alexander was suggesting innovations at the very core of the theory. Concurrently, Harry Stack Sullivan in Washington, D.C., and the Menninger brothers in Topeka were stressing the same point: that psychotherapeutic interaction is an important experience in itself and should be examined, utilized, and understood for its own distinctive features. (On the European continent and in the British Isles, as well as in other parts of the United States, such ego psychologists as Hartmann, Kris, Lowenstein, Rapaport, and Gill were similarly showing signs of replacing the classical Freudians.) These developments in America, including Alexander's emerging views, soon found expression in a union (tenuous at first) between American neo-Freudianism and the investigative energy made available to psychology and sociology by the flood of post-World War II graduate students into these two disciplines, as well as the tremendous amounts of federal and private money then becoming available for research into two-person interpersonal processes. In his twenty-four years at the Chicago Institute of Psychoanalysis (1932–1956), Alexander had focused his own research efforts primarily on the study of psychosomatic phenomena while concurrently aiming his theoretical writings at the innovations in psychotherapeutic theory and practice mentioned above. In 1956, in his new position as head of the Psychiatric Department at Mount Sinai Hospital in Los Angeles which was then being formed, he found an opportunity and a setting wherein he, himself, could do research on the psychoanalytic two-person interaction. His move from Chicago thus ended the era of his investigations of asthma, essential hypertension, and emotional stress and its effects on bodily functioning generally, and he switched to a study of the behavioral interaction of therapist and patient.

Although twenty years earlier he had highlighted the differences and necessary interrelationships between the *cognitive insights* and *emotional experiences* which take place in psychoanalysis, Alexander apparently had come to suspect in his final days at Chicago that what therapists *say* they do in psychoanalytic practice (for example, "I follow formalized classical theory and practice quite faithfully as the analysis unfolds") was very probably quite different from what they in fact *did* in therapy. He had written earlier, and summarized in this article (p. 333), that psychoanalysts and other therapists could not be the same tabula rasa with each and every patient. To this he added that the therapist should be flexible and adapt his person (his role, or self in the language of William James) to accommodate the idiosyncratic needs of each patient. His earlier innovations (cutting the frequency of visits from five times to once or twice weekly; paying attention to the patient's early history primarily in order to understand his present situation; concurrent focus on both the intellectual and emotional aspects of the patient's problems and new learnings; temporary as well as ad-lib terminations in treatment, etc.) had been greeted with only cautious suspicion by followers of traditional Freudianism. However, his challenge to the classical and invariant neutral role to be played by the analyst was met, as can be guessed, with considerable alarm. Alexander responded that the classical requirement that the therapist be an objective, unemotional, and nonparticipating member of the dyad was itself an artificial stance, "inasmuch as it does not exist between human beings in actual life [p. 333]."

Other practicing psychoanalysts, notably Glover in England, had suspected that analysts were not invariant carbon copies of each other, and of themselves, in their work with different patients. Alexander, too, verbalized this heresy in print and, after leaving Chicago for Los Angeles, began to investigate whether or not his idea could be validated by experimental evidence. He also guessed that practicing psychoanalysts did not all rigidly and systematically explore the early history of each patient. In this article, again in a theoretical vein, he wrote: "The past should be subordinated to a total grasp of the present life situation and serve as the basis for future adaptive accomplishments [p. 339]"; and also that ". . . the therapist should never allow the patient to forget that he came to him to resolve his present problem. The understanding of the past should always be subordinated to the problems of the present. Therapy is not the same as genetic research [p. 335]." Having repeatedly stated this theoretical pronouncement as a basic tenet of his own school of neopsychoanalysis, Alexander set out to examine it in Los Angeles. He appears to have asked himself, "Do psychoanalysts focus principally on the past, as classical theory dictates? It is a straightforward precept. How well and how uniformly is it followed?"

3. A RAY OF LIGHT IS INTRODUCED INTO PSYCHOANALYSIS: A LOOK AT WHAT PSYCHOANALYSTS ACTUALLY DO

In the forties and early fifties, while Alexander was still writing research papers on psychosomatic phenomena, an active and energetic group of graduate students and colleagues gathered at the nearby University of Chicago Counseling Center where Carl Rogers was submitting himself and other "nondirective" (later, "client-centered") therapists, with their patients and clients, to scientific study. Rogers (1942) had written a book on his theory of psychotherapy and included in it a verbatim transcript of an actual therapeutic encounter so that the reader could check Rogers' theory (and, of course, his personal dogma of the moment) with his, Rogers', actual therapeutic behavior. Two decades later, Rogers and Dymond (1954) and their colleagues followed this up with a description of a large-scale research undertaking into psychotherapeutic interaction. Concurrently, psychoanalytically oriented university therapists, such as Mahl and Redlich at Yale, Strupp at North Carolina, and Bordin at Michigan, also began to study the actual behavioral interventions of their own variety of psychotherapist. The 1956 move to Los Angeles appears similarly to have provided Alexander with the appropriate administrative and personal circumstances to carry out a comprehensive study of what the psychoanalyst actually did in his practice. In the late 1950s I was fortunate to be a member of a team which site-visited Alexander at Mount Sinai Hospital while he was embarking upon his series of studies of the therapist-and-patient interaction. Behind a one-way mirror, I watched Alexander conduct one of his psychoanalytic interviews, and saw it filmed and recorded for later transcription and study.

In the article under review I glimpsed what Alexander would soon be learning from his very elaborate, Ford Foundation-supported, long-term study of the therapist: namely, that psychotherapists are, first and foremost, individual human beings and only secondarily members of a particular class called psychotherapists. Parenthetically, I would like to point out that, as followers of Rogers' research at Chicago will remember, the early research done by the Rogers group focused primarily upon client characteristics (including client changes following psychotherapy). Only with Rogers' own move to Wisconsin, in the mid-fifties, and his joining up with a new team of colleagues (Rogers, Gendlin, Kiesler, & Truax, 1967; Truax & Carkhuff, 1967) did the client-centered movement change its focus from study of the client to study of the therapist and his impact. This Wisconsin research led, among other things, to the sobering discovery that, in glaring contradiction to the universally held "blank screen" conception of the neutral therapist, some psychotherapists appear to make patients worse (Truax, 1963; Bergin, 1966; Truax & Carkhuff, 1967; Rogers et al., 1967). In view of the now well-accepted view that therapists can have a negative impact, a caution first systematically promulgated in the early nineteen-sixties by Betz at Hopkins, Lorr in the Veterans' Administration, and Truax and his colleagues at Wisconsin, Alexander writes almost prophetically, in the present article:

At this point my emphasis is pertinent, that it is imperative for the therapist to correctly estimate the time when his guidance not only becomes unnecessary but *detrimental*. . . . No matter, however, what technical devices they emphasize, the goal of these reformers [the neo-Freudians] is the same: *to minimize the danger implicit in the psychotherapeutic situation*, namely, encouraging undue regression and evasion of the current adaptive tasks. [p. 339; my italics].

He makes this last point only in passing and it is significant primarily because it allies him, a Neo-Freudian, with the potentially dangerous aspects of psychotherapeutic intervention which were becoming obvious to therapists of still other persuasions in such centers as Wisconsin, Baltimore, and Chicago.

On pp. 339–340 Alexander describes one of the most important discoveries emerging from his Los Angeles studies of the therapeutic process. This was that neither patient nor psychoanalyst behaved, in fact, as he and other theorists and practitioners had believed they did.

4. A REVOLUTIONARY "DISCOVERY": NO TWO PSYCHOTHERAPISTS PRACTICE ALIKE!

Alexander's revolutionary findings uphold my contention that he was to psychoanalysis what Carl Rogers is to psychotherapy. Looking back, it seems strange to me that only a few years ago no university or psychoanalytic institute training program with which I was familiar emphasized the point that therapists are vastly different from each other.[1] Despite psychology's long history of concern with individual differences in almost all facets of human behavior, some six decades of writings on the theory and practice of psychoanalysis and psychotherapy failed to recognize adequately that, even with the prescribed personal psychoanalysis which was to make each graduating therapist an objective, emotionally neutral carbon copy of every other one, no such result was possible in the complete set of attitudes and interpersonal skills which characterize the practicing psychotherapist. We have all undoubtedly been dimly aware that, even following the more formalized lock-step education of medical and graduate school, no two graduate physicians, psychologists, surgeons, or teachers practice their art, science, or profession in the same way. We have dimly realized also that some members of each of these professions are more proficient than others and, yes, that, in medicine, for example, some were even noxious enough that there came to be a term for physician-created or physician-exacerbated illnesses or conditions, iatrogenic disease.

Alexander did not deal with or even suggest this extension and elaboration of his findings in this preliminary report of 1963, although he did insist that the therapist's guidance can become "detrimental" or even dangerous (p. 339). Appropriately and unemotionally, he wrote that research on the therapist and his patient clearly reveals that neither behaves in real life as our clinical and theoretical writings dogmatically assert he will. Rather, it appears that each therapist and each patient behaves as anyone knowing him would expect: namely, he is more like himself than he is a caricature of some mystical entity labeled "patient" or "therapist." The implications for theory and training of this preliminary finding are profound, especially if corroborated by researchers in other centers which still subscribe to a formal theory of the practice of psychotherapy as a universal and invariant phenomenon, unfolding in a prescribed and predictable manner for each patient (and therapist). It would be an unfortunate error for the several psychotherapy professions not to deal with the full implications of this preliminary observation by Alexander, one that threatens the very core of classical as well as neoclassical Freudianism, as well as all other formalized theories (and practices) in psychotherapy, including that of Rogers. That Rogers is aware of this is clear (1963, pp. 5–7). I have faith, based on the intellectual and scientific revolutions in psychology and psychiatry of the past two decades, that the challenge will in fact be faced (e.g., Bergin, 1966, 1967; Ellis, 1958; Frank, 1961; Kiesler, 1966; Rogers et al., 1967; Schofield, 1964; Strupp, 1960, 1967; Thorne, 1950; Truax & Carkhuff, 1967).

While we face the full implications of the challenge posed by Alexander's findings, we cannot help but bring some aspects of the theory, research, and practice of psychotherapy into the mainstream of other more fully developed, science-based professions. A mutually beneficial tie-in between psychotherapy research and research in basic psychology will inevitably result in a cross-fertilization in both directions. Psychotherapy interaction is a potentially rich field in which to apply some of the vast store of knowledge in social psychology that appears to have immediate relevance to psychotherapy theory, practice, and research, for example, the social psychology of "influence" or "decision-making" as seen in two-person (and group) behavior, or the social psychology of "communication processes," the psychologies of "affiliation" or of "cognitive dissonance," etc. Those psychotherapists who heretofore have seemed to make a fetish of such concepts as "the process" of psychotherapy or who have exalted the "transference" relationship to a position of almost religious preeminence will learn, to their surprise I believe, that such mystical phenomena are probably little more than what occurs in most, if not all, social interactions; and that the same general laws and principles which are relevant to the study of other behavior (e.g., parent-child, peer-peer, teacher-student, experimenter-subject, and other important human pairings) also apply to the study of psychotherapy (Matarazzo, 1965, p. 218). In addition, while some general laws or principles will emerge from the study of such human interactions, individual differences undoubtedly will continue to attenuate these general laws and thus will force psychology to look still further for individual and interactional variables not yet identified or fully isolated.

5. A REEXAMINATION OF PSYCHOANALYSIS'
THEORETICAL FOUNDATION AND SUBSTRUCTURE

With the preliminary empirical observation that therapists and patients behave in the psychotherapeutic interaction much like two human beings in other kinds of human encounters, Alexander fully realized that neither a biological-genetic (unconscious) nor a neo-socio-bio-genetic model of unconscious-conscious unravelings and reexaminations could serve as the theoretical structure for understanding and explaining psychoanalytic theory and practice. Consequently, in the last three pages of his 1963 article (pp. 341–343) Alexander discards all earlier allegiance to psychoanalytic models (including his own neo-Freudian ones) and, in their stead, embraces what he calls *learning theory* as his explanatory model. For me this is the weakest part of an otherwise exceptionally lucid paper. Not surprisingly, in view of his presumed lack of formal contact with the theoretical and empirical controversies that raged among psychologist-learning theorists of the 1930s, '40s, and early '50s, Alexander's conception and use of the term learning theory appears to me similar to the unsophisticated view of learning theory held by writers of popular magazine and newspaper articles. Nevertheless, although somewhat elementary in its exposition, his conception of learning theory (and the role of reward and punishment) is, in its general aspects, refreshingly similar to the learning theory framework earlier promulgated for psychotherapy by Laurance Shaffer, Norman Cameron, Dollard and Miller, and, in all fairness, by Freud many years earlier.

My disappointment with Alexander's theoretical concept is not that he used a theory the intricacies of which he could hardly have been expected to be conversant with but, rather, that he should feel he needed a theoretical framework at all. On the first page of his article (p. 330), he candidly suggests that it was the traditional psychotherapist's low tolerance for the bewildering ambiguity of the therapeutic encounter which led him to embrace tenaciously each and every theoretical pronouncement of the leader and prophet of his own particular professional and clinical ideology. Yet, in the same article, after having just taken his first fleeting glimpse at what therapists and patients actually do in the therapy encounter, and publicly chronicled his surprise at some of his research findings, Alexander, perhaps unwittingly, demonstrated his own continuing "need" for a theory when he used these still fragmentary research glimpses to throw out completely his earlier theoretical scaffolding and, in its stead, substitute a new framework—one which, as mentioned above, he hardly understood. Perhaps, if he had been familiar with the basic controversies among the several, widely disparate learning theories of the pre- and post-World War II era, no longer viable today, he would have been less likely in 1963 to have embraced a general, and still clearly mythical, "learning theory" as the theoretical scaffolding for psychotherapy theory and practice.

Although the seemingly evangelistic followers and disciples of Hull, Tolman, Guthrie, and others each plunged into the task of erecting (collectively with their master) an all-encompassing learning theory from 1930 to 1945, subsequent events (1945–1955) revealed that such a hope was not to materialize for any of these competing groups. As a consequence, a "theory of learning," or "learning theory," or, more realistically, a number of "learning theories," no longer appears as a viable and imminent goal for the experimental psychologist of today (1955–1967). Rather, eclecticism and the search for empirical relationships, especially as they apply to the more modest "miniature systems" (being investigated by offshoots of the older generalist-learning theorists such as Miller, Mowrer, Spence, Estes, Harlow, Solomon, Kimble, Prokasy, R. F. Thompson, Underwood, and others), seem to be in vogue today.

It is of interest to me that around 1950–1955, the time when the theorists and scientists in experimental psychology were divesting themselves of their clearly premature search for a learning theory (or theories), writers and practitioners of psychotherapy "discovered" that this same mythical and illusory learning theory might be more scientifically respectable as a framework for understanding early and later human development and for applying this theoretical understanding in the practice of psychoanalysis and psychotherapy. Just before this turn of events I found myself, in my graduate school days, profoundly impressed with the systematic attempt of Dollard and Miller (1950) to wed psychoanalysis to learning theory and thus give both theories a new breath of life. These two authors had such an extensive breadth of knowledge, scholarship, and practical experience in psychoanalysis and learning theory that, if such a translation had been possible, they surely could have accomplished it and, in the process, advanced both fields. Now, in retrospect, except as a stimulating intellectual exercise, we see that their book did not have the effect that many had hoped for it. Numerous other writers of the same period attempted to erect a similar bridge between psychotherapy practice and behavior theory, but they did so less systematically and with less relative success even than the minimal level achieved by Dollard and Miller.

6. PSYCHOLOGY IN THE 1950S: A TIME OF FERMENT

Such attempts by psychologists to make learning theory the theoretical framework for psychotherapy during 1950–1955 would today be a matter of history, in my opinion, except for several developments in psychology shortly thereafter: (1) the emergence of a neo-Skinnerianism; (2) the coalition of some aspects of social and experimental psychology; and (3) the emergence of Wolpe, a psychiatrist-psychotherapist, upon the scene. Beginning unobtrusively and inconspicuously in 1958 with what appears to have been only minimal experience in animal research (and that only tangentially related to the earlier-mentioned classical learning theories of the thirties and forties) and, aided shortly thereafter by Eysenck (1960) and others, Wolpe (whom I consider an excellent and sensitive clinician) has managed to keep alive the hope in many quarters that learning theory can serve as the theoretical explanatory model both for guiding psychotherapeutic practice and for furthering scientific advance (Wolpe, 1958, 1963; Wolpe, Salter, & Reyna, 1964). The neo-Skinnerians have aided the followers of Wolpe in this enterprise, as have the experimental-social psychologists.

In my opinion, purely speculatively, the viability and vigor currently associated with Wolpe's explicit views regarding a rational (theoretical) basis for psychotherapy is a product of several factors. First, with the decline of the aura and magic of psychoanalysis which began in the early 1950s, dynamic (applied) psychology needed a new theoretical model (dogma, if you will) around which to rally. In the opening paragraphs of his article Alexander aptly describes the anxiety experienced by practitioners working "blindly" in the deeply emotional encounter called psychotherapy. Clinical psychology in the early fifties, searching for a substitute for psychoanalysis, seems to me to have vacillated between Rogers' nondirective and client-centered neo-existentialism, on the one hand, and experimental psychology's learning theory (e.g., Dollard & Miller), on the other. Rogers' views clearly were more phenomenological and "mentalistic" than "behavioral" (a characteristic not in harmony with the strong behavioral emphasis then emanating from the emerging conflict between "experimental" and "clinical" psychology and the influence of the National Institute of Mental Health, which was supporting programs of teaching and research oriented toward a more objective basis for psychotherapy). Thus Rogers' client-centered theoretical framework, revolving around such concepts as "becoming" and "experiencing one's self," did not for long serve to guide the increasing numbers of somewhat helpless ("anxious") new psychotherapists entering the ranks of psychology (and sociology and possibly psychiatry as well). Since the posthumous writings of Harry Stack Sullivan (1953, 1954) were being published at this time, many clinical psychologists and younger psychiatrists, including me, attempted to substitute Sullivan's ideas for Rogers'. Alas, creative as were his ideas, Sullivan's writings, like Rogers', did not provide the step-by-step map for psychotherapeutic practice which many new practitioners earlier had erroneously felt were provided by Freudian and neo-Freudian psychoanalysis. Also in the mid-1950s, impressed by the flood of post-World War II doctoral dissertations, characterized by negative results, which had focused on the "projective hypothesis" in the study of personality, academicians in clinical psychology, nudged by their experimental-psychologist colleagues, were discouraging their students from continuing to attempt to validate Freudian or other equally dynamic hypotheses and "theories." In addition, the provocative attack on the alleged results of psychotherapy by Eysenck (1952), although admittedly overstated at the time (Strupp, 1964), could not be overlooked by any serious student or practitioner of psychotherapy.

In summary, then, the following forces seem to me to have been influential between 1950 and 1960: (1) the beginnings of disillusionment with the projective and other Freudian hypotheses and the resultant switch by personality researchers to "safer," laboratory-derived, empirical studies; (2) Eysenck's provocative challenge; (3) the failure of the otherwise brilliant dynamic ideas of Rogers or Sullivan to allay the anxiety of neophyte psychotherapists as psychoanalytic theory had earlier done (and also the failure of Dollard and Miller's equally brilliant attempt to save it); (4) the need to present both an adequate (behavioral?) theory and a scientifically sound research strategy and methodology in order to qualify for the research funds, by then abundant, from the National Institute of Mental Health and other sources; and, finally, (5) the almost complete lack of awareness by most clinical psychologists and other practitioners of psychotherapy that the search for single or multiple "learning theories" had been all but abandoned by experimental psychologists—the same group that the clinical psychologist was being forced by these other circumstances to attempt to emulate.

The effect on psychology and psychiatry of all these forces was, in my opinion, to give rise in clinical psychology (especially its academic components) to still other developments, such as operationism, which characterized the "older" sciences (including experimental psychology) before and during this time. I remember only too well my own anxieties as a beginning teacher, psychotherapist, and researcher from 1950 to 1955. Having anxiously attempted to learn, and then to embrace, consecutively Freudian, Rogerian, and Sullivanian theory to guide my beginning practice and research in dynamic psychology and failing to find the necessary "closure" and resulting relief most of us need in such enterprises, I desperately sought solace in a new religion (operationism) then being discovered by psychology but, alas, even at that time being discarded by physics and the related disciplines from which it first emerged (Oppenheimer, 1956, pp. 134–135). During the early and mid-1950s Freud, Alexander, Rogers, Sullivan, and similar idols were being displaced for my Boulder-spawned generation of clinical psychologists by the desperately welcomed prophets of the so-called philosophy of science. Percy W. Bridgman (1927, 1959), Hans Reichenbach (1951), Phillip Frank (1950), and other proponents of this "new" framework for understanding science, including happily the fledgling "science" of human encounter, offered hope to our generation of psychologists that not only could such difficult concepts as "length," "magnetism," and "time" be better understood by recourse to this framework, but also such ephemeral concepts as "ego," "transference," "unconditional positive regard," and "personality change." Although I was one of the many who heard the disquieting 1955 San Francisco address to the American Psychological Association by Oppenheimer, I could not really believe at the time that physics, too, must of necessity, in the last analysis, rest upon subjectivity and not upon the almost total objectivity which my generation had been led to believe that "operationism" and a vast store of mathematico-scientific developments had provided for it. But this is another chapter, and I had best return to my speculative description of the resurgence in the late 1950s of interest in the possibility of a realliance between learning theory and psychotherapy. Wolpe (1963, 1964) seems to personify the zeitgeist of this last era, just as Dollard and Miller (1950) and others had personified it a decade or two earlier.

Just as nature abhors a vacuum, so do practitioners of psychotherapy seem to abhor the lack of a theory to guide them or possibly even to lend them a cloak of scientific respectability. Wolpe's views went relatively unnoticed when first published (Wolpe, 1958). Yet, along with the many other developments catalogued above, two others were unfolding in, of all places, experimental psychology: a new and younger breed of experimental psychologist was rediscovering Skinner, and other experimental psychologists began to team up in research with social psychologists. The new Skinnerian psychologist, trained in his graduate school days in a methodology utilizing rats and pigeons, soon began to apply his technology to human subjects with surprising success (Lindsley, 1956; Krasner & Ullmann, 1965; Ullmann & Krasner, 1965). Concurrently, the study of the "small group" in its natural environment, an early interest of the naturalist breed of social psychologist, soon gave way to the interest of a new breed of experimental-social psychologist in the experimental and systematic injection of variables under the control of the experimenter. The results of the latter development clearly revealed that the behavior of humans in experimentally contrived small groups could be brought under the control of the experimenter. It was only natural that readers of reports on this small group research would soon recognize that patient and therapist in psychotherapy constitute merely a two-person "group," and that many of the same variables which were found to be operating in other small groups also might be operating in the extensively studied but poorly understood two-person psychotherapy encounter. Thus, as the 1960s arrived, increasing numbers of Skinnerians abandoned animals and began to try to apply similar methodologies to humans while social-experimental psychologists began to show interest in the two-person group in psychotherapy. The research of Ferster (in Maryland), Bijou (in Washington), and Patterson (in Eugene, Oregon) with parent-child interactions, and Lovaas (with autistic children at the UCLA Medical Center), to take several examples, seemed to serve as a bridge between the Skinnerians and the experimental-social psychologists.

In my review of the 1964 psychotherapy literature I classified all these groups roughly as "behavior therapists" and indicated that Wolpe and Eysenck (strange bedfellows in many ways) were emerging as their theoretical leaders. (Anyone familiar with Skinner and his writings readily recognizes why he refuses to be the head of any "theoretical" movement in psychology, be it behavior therapy, teaching machine applications, or the other related movements upon which, in Alexander's words, the "anxious" psychotherapist or educator-revolutionary could build a theoretical scaffolding for his practice.) Today it is clearer to me that the single classification utilized in 1964 is too crude and that the three groups identified above are emerging as quite distinct.

However, to emphasize once again why "theories" (Wolpe's, Eysenck's, and Skinner's included) to guide psychotherapeutic practice or research are premature even in 1967, I refer the reader to the sharp attack by Breger and McGaugh (1965) on the Wolpe-Eysenck, or "Skinner," brand of learning (and behavior) theory as a possible scaffolding for psychotherapy theory and practice. Although the not unexpected rejoinder by Rachman and Eysenck (1966) and the highly scholarly reply by Wiest (1967) highlight what appear to be glaring shortcomings in the Breger and McGaugh arguments, an uninvolved and, hopefully, objective reader cannot but conclude that, even today, no viable learning theory exists to guide the understandably anxious psychotherapist as he attempts to help a fellow human reach a higher level of effectiveness and/or happiness. Parenthetically, as a thoroughly refreshing example and reminder that some clinically-oriented psychologists can make contributions to the fledgling science and practice of psychotherapy that are equal in their heuristic power to the very best products which have come from experimental psychology, the reader is referred to the stimulating book by Goldstein, Heller, and Sechrest (1966). These extensively read and experienced scholars have presented clinical psychology, and psychology in general, with a set of 35 "research hypotheses" around which they chart a "miniature system" for further research (and practice) in psychotherapy. Theirs is not a rehash of earlier "systems of psychotherapy"; rather, it is a completely new look at psychotherapy and behavior change which results from their desire to reunite these two subjects with the mainstream of research in social and experimental (as well as clinical) psychology. If Wolpe and Eysenck remain as the personification of one of today's three streams of what I labeled "behavior therapy" in 1964, and Lindsley, Ferster, Krasner, and others emerge as the personification of the neo-Skinnerians, then Goldstein, Heller, and Sechrest without question will soon be identified as the intellectual leaders of the third tributary (social-experimental psychology) of the current stream. (Gendlin et al., 1968, will quite probably serve as an excellent additional representative of this third tributary in spite of Gendlin's having been initially identified with the more clinical, Rogerian, brand of research.) To their credit, unlike earlier writers, Goldstein, Heller, and Sechrest have proposed a "miniature system" to aid their understanding of a somewhat limited and heuristically circumscribed phenomenon ("behavior change"), rather than trying to encompass globally such phenomena as "psychoanalysis," "psychotherapeutic practice," "global personality," etc. Although Wolpe, in my opinion, occasionally writes as if he were interested in a learning theory basis only for his psychotherapeutic approach to "phobias," at other times he seems interested in a theoretical scaffolding for the same global phenomena which earlier interested Freud, Rogers, Alexander, and other personality theorists.

On the opening page of the article here reproduced Alexander quite clearly sees that in our present primitive understanding of the psychotherapeutic interaction the need for a global "theory" was a defense against the psychotherapist's own anxieties. One might well ask why, then, did he forget caution in the last two pages and substitute "learning theory" for his own neo-Freudianism as a scaffolding for the practitioner. My guess, again highly speculative, is that, not being a student of the field, he held learning theorists in awe. As a result, and as many neophytes (especially undergraduates) did and do with psychoanalytic theory, Alexander appeared to accept as gospel all that was written by respected leaders in the field of learning.

7. A PERSONAL CREDO: ALL GLOBAL THEORIES IN PSYCHOTHERAPY ARE STILL PREMATURE

I am aware that there will be readers who will disagree with both the specific thesis suggested by the present heading and my earlier more general argument. In order to amplify and, hopefully, to clarify my argument, I would like to state that I am not atheoretical in my own philosophy of science; nor am I pessimistic in my attitude toward the ultimate role that the usual canons of science will play in psychology generally and in psychotherapy more specifically.[2] However, as an individual who has tried to divide his time among reading about psychotherapy (and psychology more generally), doing research in psychotherapy and related areas, and practicing the art of psychotherapy, I find that theory helps me very little either in practice or in research. (I believe, too, that few practitioners will disagree with this statement.) To summarize my argument, because I apply it to the role of theory in both research and in psychotherapeutic practice, I will refer the skeptic to the 1959 volume of the *American Psychologist* (pp. 167–179) in which some of this country's leading experimental scientists in psychology discuss how they actually do research in contrast to what writers of textbooks on research (or science) say scientists do. They write:

We approached the question of formal training (for research in psychology) by asking first what content could be standardized in view of the characteristics of established and successful researchers. It was here that we collided head on with the stereotype of the scientist as one who begins with a thorough knowledge of the literature in his field, master of the technical skills related to it, a systematic worker, open-minded in his observation, and responsive to opposing evidence or an opponent's cogent argument. It appears instead that the productive man is often narrow, preoccupied with his own ideas, unsystematic in his work methods or in his reading of the literature, and it even seems sometimes that he is productive because he is illogical and willing to follow his hunches instead of the implications of existing knowledge and methods. It seems clear to us that the characteristics that make for inventiveness and originality bear little relation to those that can be developed by formal course work, given a certain level of intellectual ability and background knowledge [pp. 178–179].

Although the above quotation is a remarkably apt description of how I and, I now suspect, how most of us have conducted research, I invite the reader to reread the quotation and to substitute the words psychotherapy and practitioner for research and scientist. When this is done one sees a striking similarity between what these psychologist-scientists wrote about how scientists actually do research and what Alexander wrote in 1963 about how psychotherapists actually do psychotherapy.

In conclusion, I believe the search for a theory to guide the intrasession (or full series) practice of psychotherapy is as premature and doomed to failure *today* as would be the search for a theory to guide us when we and others deliver a lecture, drive an automobile, or date and court a sweetheart. It might be interesting for the reader to speculate why our beginning "science" of human behavior (psychology) has not evolved a theory of love behavior, even a rudimentary one, to help provide a scaffolding to guide the romance relationship. One can easily understand why, if such a theory existed (no matter how primitive its development), many young (and self-admittedly anxious) lovers would swarm to it. The crudeness of its development would hardly be noticed by the bewildered participants, each of whom would be anxiously searching for any framework (valid or invalid) that would promise to bring order out of chaos. Similarly, even a crude, admittedly speculative, theory of how to drive an automobile, or swing a golf club, or deliver a lecture, if one existed for these human activities,[3] would be embraced as anxiously, one can speculate, as would one which purported to serve as a guide for young lovers.

I do not believe these last examples to be either overly dramatic or far-fetched. I am guessing that many readers, if they will review their own early (and possibly even current) gropings for a theory to aid their psychotherapeutic practice (and courtship or teaching experiences), will see a description of themselves and their own histories in this section. Alexander surprised me by his espousal of learning theory so long after he became an experienced practitioner. My guess is that he included this passage more as an index of the growing respect he was developing for the psychologist-scientists he had encountered in the 1940s and 1950s than as a reflection of what he actually did, or what "theory" he was, in fact, guided by in his practice of psychotherapy. The research-based description he provided of what the psychoanalyst-clinician actually did in the practical encounter applied no less to him than to the other Los Angeles colleagues he studied.

8. THE APPRENTICESHIP: A TIME-TESTED SOLUTION
FOR THE ABSENCE OF SCIENTIFIC SCAFFOLDING

Possibly no one has put this general argument more succinctly than Colby (1962, p. 95), a practitioner-scientist, when he candidly discusses the science versus art issue in psychotherapy: "Psychotherapy is one of the practical arts. It is not a science, it is not even an applied science. It is a practical art, a craft like agriculture or medicine or wine-making in which an artisan relies on an incomplete, fragmentary body of knowledge and empirically established rules traditionally passed on from master to apprentice."

All but a few practitioners appear to me to have known this, yet it has been difficult for us to admit. We are aware that there exist few useful textbooks to guide the practice of psychotherapy. However, by a type of professional schizophrenia, akin to that which Kelly (1954) ascribed to the Rorschach-as-a-panacea psychologist of an earlier day, we refuse to admit that the *practice* of psychotherapy is an art, and may long remain one. I make these statements even though I know that I, along with other investigators, see the psychotherapy interaction as an excellent setting in which to do research on basic, person-to-person processes (i.e., on the subject matter of general psychology). The fruit of such research hopefully will enrich our understanding of both general psychological processes and of those processes arising uniquely in the psychotherapy setting.

If psychotherapy is an art, how do we avoid the chaos which could result if each practitioner learned and practiced this art completely idiosyncratically? The answer, as we all are aware from our own histories, is the apprenticeship. This institution has been as useful in guiding the development of psychotherapy practice as it has been in guiding the development of other arts and practices. In these arts a more experienced member of the profession helps each beginner, through active supervision, to make the most of his individual idiosyncratic potential for such practice.

At this point it might be appropriate to ask the reader whether he feels that he and I and our colleagues are ready to give up theories in psychotherapy until science provides at least a few more validated observations and hopefully first- and second-order functional relationships of the type envisioned by Goldstein, Heller, and Sechrest (1966). For some years now I have been trying to help young graduate student-scientists in experimental psychology, on the one hand, and clinical psychology student-practitioners, on the other, to recognize that the so-called science of psychology is a myth, perpetrated by writers who themselves in most instances do neither research nor psychotherapy, and that quite probably no such science, even moderately developed, will emerge to guide their research or practice for decades to come. Alas, few graduate students will listen to me, I suppose because the ever-waiting doctoral dissertation committee seems to continue its pretense (despite the 1959 article, which was by this country's best psychologist-scientists) that all dissertations must evolve from "theory" (not miniature systems mind you—that level of sophistication I would accept) and because fifty minutes in an interview room with your first psychotherapy client or patient is an agonizing eternity—even with a "theory" to guide you! Yet I continue to meet each year's group of graduate students with a faith that among them I will find, as before, that occasional believer or, better yet, skeptic who will challenge or test my admittedly clinical observations by empirical refutation (and/or confirmation) of them. It is he, of course, who makes your efforts and mine fun and worth continuing.

9. CONCLUDING REMARKS: SOME ISSUES IN PSYCHOTHERAPY WHICH CAN NO LONGER BE AVOIDED

I would not experience closure in this attempt to articulate my own appraisal of where the art and practice of psychotherapy is and has been if, before concluding, I did not share with the reader a few problem areas which I, as a practitioner and teacher, believe we must all face openly and candidly in the next few years. One group of these problem areas has in common that each of its elements may hold back unnecessarily the teaching (supervision), research (basic psychology), and practice (art) of psychotherapy unless we more explicitly and deliberately identify its common denominator. This is the group of beliefs surrounding psychotherapy which Kiesler (1966), extending the observations of Colby (1964), labelled as myths and recently exposed so aptly. Among these are the myths still evident in most theoretical and research papers in psychotherapy, which suggest that all patients are alike (which even the neophyte psychotherapist-practitioner quickly realizes is not true) and all therapists are alike and interchangeable. (Several earlier sections in my present paper have added to Kiesler's arguments relating to these two myths. The recent book by Truax and Carkhuff, [1967] contains many excellent descriptions of the variation presented by individual patients and individual therapists and should help remove once and for all these two myths from writings on psychotherapy.)

Akin to these two "uniformity myths" are other rarely challenged tacit assumptions. One of these, although ludicrous when identified, is that all psychotherapy is conducted in more or less identical surroundings. The reader need only imagine the differences among such broad classes of settings for the practice of psychotherapy as an office in a Park Avenue apartment in New York City, a crowded outpatient psychiatry clinic, a university professor's campus office, a private practitioner's consulting office in his own home, a prison psychotherapist's conference room, a practitioner's office in a professional building (not to mention the infinite variations within each of these broad classes) to understand that most theoretical writers on psychotherapy, each of whom appears to identify it as a single, uniform process, are woefully unaware of many of what may be the most relevant variables of the phenomena they are attempting to describe. Would anyone for a moment doubt, a priori and without the admittedly necessary empirical demonstration, that the setting, *qua* setting (as the crucial variable), in which a director of a psychoanalytic institute or the chief of a famous medical school's psychiatry or psychology service practices, with all of its visible signs of his "expertness," probably sets a different stage for the subsequent psychotherapy sessions in which he participates and the results he and his patient achieve, than do the often barren surroundings which serve as a context for the newly graduated psychologist, psychiatrist, or social worker? More to the point, contrast these two highly disparate classes of settings with those in which the neophyte psychotherapist-in-training practices his art; remember also that it is these neophytes, practicing in just such teaching settings, on whom so much of the published research in psychotherapy is collected! Even a rudimentary knowledge of the basic research findings which have emerged from studies in the experimental-social psychology of perception (e.g., Rosenthal, 1966, 1967) should lead theoretical writers on psychotherapy to realize that the vast differences in perceptual stimuli which distinguish one psychotherapist from another must in all probability mask, submerge, or distort whatever uniformities among psychotherapists he (the writer) is postulating or describing, at least in our current "scientific" understanding of the practice and phenomena of psychotherapy. If one now adds to this guess on my part that each individual practitioner in each of the broad classes of psychotherapist here being highlighted is himself highly different in numerous, potentially important, personal characteristics from every other member of his own broad class (along with his own particular practice setting), one may better understand why I have repeatedly stressed above that theoretical writers seem to me to be out of step with the actual realities of the phenomena they purport to describe and conceptualize.

Still another tacit assumption in theoretical writings needing discussion is the myth that psychotherapy as practiced by experienced therapists, especially the more dynamic ones, more or less consistently and uniformly involves score upon score, if not hundreds upon hundreds, of hours. On the basis of personal observation solely, I gained the impression that psychotherapy generally includes fewer than ten sessions in all (Matarazzo, 1965, p. 218). Since that time, two reports constituting preliminary validations of my hunch have appeared in the literature. The first, by Ryan (1966), will be presented below. The second was published (also in 1966) by the National Center for Health Statistics (Washington, D.C., 1966, Public Health Service Publication No. 1000, Series 10, Number 28) under the title *Characteristics of Patients of Selected Types of Medical Specialists and Practitioners: United States, July 1963–June 1964*. Based on data reported by a large, representative sample (134,000) of Americans, the survey revealed that (1) a total of 979,000 Americans (about 0.5 per cent of the civilian, noninstitutionalized population) consulted a psychiatrist during this twelve-month period of time; (2) they did so for a total of 4.7 visits per person during the twelve-month period; and (3) they showed surprisingly little variation in this (small) average frequency as a function of either sex (4.6 and 4.8 visits, respectively, for males and females) or family income (4.1 versus 5.4 visits per psychiatric patient from families with annual incomes of under $2,000 and over $10,000, respectively). Of today's still all-too-typical writer of theoretical or systematic treatises on the practice of psychotherapy, I again ask: How much uniform following of a model based on Freud, Rogers, et. al., or on "learning theory" can a practitioner do in a mere five hours? Clearly our textbooks on the practice of psychotherapy, as well as our articles on the most effective research methodologies and strategies to use in programs of research on psychotherapy, must meet the challenges that these empirical findings pose to their assumptive positions.

Will practitioner-readers and writer-theoreticians really find it so hard to believe that today's typical general practicing psychotherapist and even an occasional example of the rarer psychoanalyst-specialist has with very few exceptions a time-limited "crisis" type of practice, one which, for the bulk of his patients, requires under ten hours and is more like that of the attorney or minister who offers professional counsel than it is like the layman's (and writer-theoretician's) stereotype of a reconstructive psychoanalysis requiring hundreds upon hundreds of hours? I trust such a reader will not, and I am hoping that he will begin to incorporate this seeming empirical truth into his own future teaching and writing.

Another fundamental issue which I want to highlight is an extension of the last, namely, that only a few, and a very few at that, residents of each community can afford more than the average of five psychotherapy sessions which the bulk of today's clients and patients appear to be receiving. The reader need only ask if he knows many families, including his own, which can easily write a check for a new refrigerator or a new stove. Yet the cost of one of these necessary appliances is the equivalent of from five to ten hourly visits to the majority of today's private practicing psychotherapists! Few families in our whole nation can afford one, let alone ten, refrigerators in a year; still fewer can bear this latter burden (equal to ten new refrigerators) annually for two to five years. Consequently, despite the fact that most treatises on psychotherapy tacitly follow a mythical model of the practice of this art which suggests that it universally requires hundreds upon hundreds of hours to unfold, the empirical fact appears that such long-term practice is rare, if for no other reason than that few families in our nation can afford 100 to 500 hours of private psychotherapy (equivalent to ten to fifty refrigerators) for one of their members. (That indigent or low-income outpatient clinic patients also receive, on the average, only five hours of psychotherapy is too well known for me to document extensively here; see Matarazzo, 1965, pp. 202–203.)

Since many practitioners of psychoanalytically oriented psychotherapy do occasionally get a long-term client or patient in their own practice, even though he or she is the exception in such a practice, it might be well to ask who such clients are. It is generally assumed that a fair proportion of such long-term patients come from the most affluent segment of our society, while still others are middle income, students (graduate and professional), or young adults. In a recent, disturbing book, Ryan and his colleagues (1966) surveyed the complete mental health resources of a total community (Boston, Massachusetts) and, while documenting this assumption, extended it to one of its necessary corollaries, thereby providing another insight into who provides services for the remaining "poorer," less affluent members of our society. They found that even in a community with more psychiatric personnel per capita than postulated as ideal by the American Psychiatric Association, the distribution of such helping resources is grossly uneven—much more uneven than many of us could have realized. In answer to their research question, "Who sees a psychiatrist?" the community-wide survey of Ryan and his team revealed it to be

the group of patients with the most clear-cut and distinguishable characteristics. These patients cover a relatively narrow age range, half of them falling between the ages of 22 and 36. About two-thirds are female; four out of five have gone to college or are now college students; occupations are generally consistent with education, reflecting a class level in the middle and upper ranges. Only about one patient in five is diagnosed by his psychiatrist as psychotic or even borderline psychotic, the great majority being seen as suffering from chronic neurosis or character disorder. Close to half of these patients have had previous psychiatric care. The average patient is described as a person with a chronic character disorder having symptoms reflecting anxiety, depression, or both.

Of considerable interest is the unusual residential distribution of these patients. Slightly over half of Boston residents in private psychiatric treatment live in 4 contiguous census tracts (out of Boston's 156 census tracts). This area contains less than four per cent of the total Boston population. It is bounded approximately by the Charles River, Boston University, Boylston Street and the Public Garden. If to this small strip of land is added the rest of Back Bay and the front of Beacon Hill (this enlarged area including about 7 per cent of Boston's population), over 70 per cent of Boston patients in private psychiatric treatment will be included.

It is probable that this residential distribution is partially due to a generalized class factor. It is, after all, necessary to be fairly well off financially in order to afford the fees of a psychiatrist. On the other hand, however, other sections of the city with high social rank (for example, Hyde Park and West Roxbury) contribute only a tiny handful of private patients.

Additional analysis of this interesting phenomenon by the survey staff indicated that the patients who live in this small strip of the Back Bay are younger and more frequently female than other private patients. Four-fifths are female and almost two-thirds are between the ages of 20 and 34. In other words, about one-quarter of all Bostonians who are private patients are young women in their twenties and early thirties who live within an area of less than 100 blocks. The total number of young women in this age range (within this 100-block area) is fewer than 6,000, of whom about half have the general educational and economic characteristics of the private patients. In other words, this tiny group of approximately 3,000 young college-educated women in their twenties and early thirties furnishes one-quarter of the Boston patients in private psychiatric treatment [pp. 19–20].

In contrast, to the related research question, "Who goes to the public mental hospital?," Ryan and his colleagues' extensive survey of the Boston population revealed that

over 3,000 Boston residents are admitted to public mental hospitals each year. In this group men outnumber women and patients tend to be in the older age ranges. Only one out of every three to four patients admitted is in the diagnostic category that is usually thought of as the typical one for a psychotic hospitalized patient, that is, the category of schizophrenia. About 20 per cent of the patients are diagnosed as suffering from alcoholism, not usually with sufficient disfunction to be considered psychotic. In total, not many more than half of admitted patients are ultimately given a diagnosis of psychosis.

In addition to being usually poor and no longer young, these patients tend also to be lacking in environmental supports, often living alone, isolated from any social connections. The majority have never married.

The residential pattern of admissions is also quite striking, showing that the greatest proportion of patients are admitted from those sections of the city blighted by poverty, family disorganization, slums and racial segregation, such as the South End. Middle-class white residential sections of the city tend to have relatively low rates of hospital admissions [pp. 20–21].

Will we, the practitioners, investigators, and teachers in the field of psychotherapy, acknowledge these startling findings and be challenged by them to the new conceptions of our art that they, and our society, demand? Even before Ryan's study, one psychotherapist-writer (Schofield, 1964) acknowledged some of them and explicitly challenged us to review our assumptions and practices in this field. Will we now join Schofield? Again, I firmly believe we must and we will. I have confidence that the Ryan finding of four to five visits per year will also be true in other cities. (Actually, my own published hunch was based on personal observations I had made over a fourteen-year period in Boston, St. Louis, and Portland.) If it is found to be true in other cities and if it is confirmed elsewhere that a particular group of young females constitutes the largest segment of the long-term therapy patient group, then I am certain that our theories and training practices will be revamped. Needless to say, sociologists will also be interested in aspects of these emerging findings since they may constitute a unique chapter in the sociology of professions.

There are four additional strands in today's zeitgeist in the art and beginning science of psychotherapy upon which this hope and faith of

mine that we shall meet the challenges of the Ryan findings are founded:
(1) the recent scholarly, and thoroughly illuminating and refreshing,
book on psychotherapy theory and research by Truax and Carkhuff
(1967), two researchers who also practice psychotherapy; (2) the
candidly stated research findings of Alexander (1963), which served as
the stimulus for the first half of this essay; (3) Rogers' (1963) corollary
discovery that each psychotherapist and his views of the nature of the
psychotherapeutic interaction are unique; and (4) the just-published
findings by Koegler and Brill (1967) at the UCLA Medical School
(well known for its belief that psychoanalytically oriented psychotherapy was the treatment of choice for all intrapsychic and interpersonal difficulties) that, on follow-up, there were no differences among their
clinic groups of psychiatric outpatients receiving psychotherapy, drug
therapy, and placebo. Koegler and Brill, in common with Ryan, emphasize the extent to which pressure is growing to extend psychiatric service
to groups to whom it has been unavailable and the corresponding overwhelming societal need for the development of less expensive and less
time-consuming psychotherapeutic and other treatment methods. Koegler and Brill also candidly allude to the resistance their young residents
in training (originally highly biased toward a psychoanalytically
oriented psychotherapy for all psychiatric patients) exhibited in facing
the full implications of the similar findings emerging from their own
equally successful use of the three treatment approaches.

Since Freud first began to systematically develop psychotherapy as an
art, too many of its practitioners, theoreticians, and investigators have
written as if they appear to have conceived of it as a unitary process,
universally applied by a uniform agent, over a universally lengthy period of time, to an easily described and uniform supplicant. It is my hope
that the evaluation I have made in this paper of the past and present
status of the art of psychotherapy, with all its myriad variations and
increasingly public revelations, will be interpreted by the reader as the
exciting challenge to our art and young science that I wholeheartedly
believe it is. I for one am enjoying the practice of psychotherapy more
with each passing year because pioneering individuals like Rogers,
Alexander, Hollingshead, Redlich, and, now, Ryan and his associates
have had the courage to describe what they and we *do*, and not what
writers have *said* we do.

1. It was only three years ago that I first described my own attempt to
utilize this insight systematically in my teaching of novice psychotherapists
(Matarazzo, 1965, p. 219). With the patient's permission, I invited them to
sit in while I conducted psychotherapy, while they were sitting in also with

other faculty colleagues. They quickly became aware that each psychotherapist is a *unique* practitioner of his art.

2. Although I am far from a Skinnerian, a very scholarly exposition of my own view of why theories are currently premature in psychology (and psychotherapy) has been given by Skinner (1950).

3. My guess is that such theories would, in fact, exist today if any of the writers on these subjects of the past half-century had been as provocatively persistent and convinced, in their writing on such a subject, as was Freud about psychoanalysis. In my opinion, if Freud had been a minister, then religion, and not psychology and psychiatry, would today be the legatee of psychotherapy.

REFERENCES

Alexander, F. *Fundamentals of psychoanalysis.* New York: W. W. Norton & Co., 1948. (Published in paperback, 1963.)

Alexander, F. The dynamics of psychotherapy in the light of learning theory. *American Journal of Psychiatry,* 1963, *120,* 440–448. Reprinted in this collection, pp. 330–344; page numbers cited in the text refer to *Creative developments in psychotherapy.*

Alexander, F., & French, T. M. *Psychoanalytic therapy.* New York: Ronald Press, 1946.

Bergin, A. E. Some implications of psychotherapy research for therapeutic practice. *Journal of Abnormal Psychology,* 1966, *71,* 235–246.

Bergin, A. E. An empirical analysis of therapeutic issues. In D. Arbuckle (Ed.), *Counseling and psychotherapy: An overview.* New York: McGraw-Hill, 1967.

Breger, L., & McGaugh, J. L. Critique and reformulation of "learning theory" approaches to psychotherapy and neurosis. *Psychological Bulletin,* 1965, *63,* 338–358.

Bridgman, P. W. *The logic of modern physics.* New York: Macmillan, 1927.

Bridgman, P. W. *The way things are.* Cambridge, Mass.: Harvard University Press, 1959.

Colby, K. M. Discussion of papers on therapist's contribution. In H. H. Strupp & L. Luborsky (Eds.), *Research in psychotherapy.* Vol. 2. Washington, D. C.: American Psychological Association, 1962, 95–101.

Colby, K. M. Psychotherapeutic processes. In P. R. Farnsworth, O. McNemar, & Q. McNemar (Eds.), *Annual review of psychology.* Palo Alto: Annual Reviews, Inc., 1964, *15,* 347–370.

Dollard, J., & Miller, N. E. *Personality and psychotherapy: An analysis in terms of learning, thinking, and culture.* New York: McGraw-Hill, 1950.

Ellis, A. Rational psychotherapy. *Journal of General Psychology,* 1958, *59,* 35–49.

Eysenck, H. J. The effects of psychotherapy: An evaluation. *Journal of Consulting Psychology,* 1952, *16,* 319–324.

Eysenck, H. J. (Ed.) *Behavior therapy and the neuroses.* New York: Pergamon Press, 1960.

Frank, J. D. *Persuasion and healing: A comparative study of psychotherapy.* Baltimore: John Hopkins Press, 1961.

Frank, P. *Modern science and its philosophy.* Cambridge, Mass.: Harvard University Press, 1950.

Gendlin, E. T., Beebe, J., Cassens, J., & Oberlander, M. Focusing ability in psychotherapy, personality, and creativity. In J. Shlien et al. (Eds.), *Research in psychotherapy.* Vol. 3. Washington, D. C.: American Psychological Association, 1968, in press.

Goldstein, A. P., Heller, K., & Sechrest, L. B. *Psychotherapy and the psychology of behavior change.* New York: John Wiley & Sons, 1966.

Kelly, E. L. Theory and techniques of assessment. In C. P. Stone & Q. McNemar (Eds.), *Annual review of psychology.* Palo Alto: Annual Reviews, Inc., 1954, 5, 281–309.

Kiesler, D. J. Some myths of psychotherapy research and the search for a paradigm. *Psychological Bulletin,* 1966, 65, 110–136.

Koegler, R. R., & Brill, N. Q. *Treatment of psychiatric outpatients.* New York: Appleton-Century-Crofts, 1967.

Krasner, L., & Ullmann, L. P. (Eds.) *Research in behavior modification: New developments and implications.* New York: Holt, Rinehart & Winston, 1965.

Lindsley, O. R. Operant conditioning methods applied to research in chronic schizophrenia. *Psychiatric Research Reports,* 1956, 5, 118–139.

Matarazzo, J. D. Psychotherapeutic processes. In P. R. Farnsworth, O. McNemar, & Q. McNemar (Eds.), *Annual review of psychology.* Palo Alto: Annual Reviews, Inc., 1965, 16, 181–224.

Oppenheimer, R. Analogy in science. *American Psychologist,* 1956, 11, 127–135.

Rachman, S., & Eysenck, H. J. Reply to a "critique and reformulation" of behavior therapy. *Psychological Bulletin,* 1966, 65, 165–169.

Reichenbach, H. *The rise of scientific psychotherapy.* Berkeley: University of California Press, 1951.

Rogers, C. R. *Counseling and psychotherapy.* Boston: Houghton Mifflin, 1942.

Rogers, C. R., & Dymond, R. F. *Psychotherapy and personality change.* Chicago: University of Chicago Press, 1954.

Rogers, C. R. Psychotherapy today or where do we go from here? *American Journal of Psychotherapy,* 1963, 17, 5–16.

Rogers, C. R., Gendlin, E. T., Kiesler, D. J., & Truax, C. B. *The therapeutic relationship and its impact.* Madison: University of Wisconsin Press, 1967.

Rosenthal, R. *Experimenter effects in behavioral research.* New York: Appleton-Century-Crofts, 1966.

Rosenthal, R. Covert communication in the psychological experiment. *Psychological Bulletin,* 1967, 67, 356–367.

Ryan W. *Distress in the city: A summary report of the Boston Mental Health Survey (1960–1962).* Boston: Jointly published by Massachusetts Association for Mental Heath, Inc., Massachusetts Department of Mental Health, and United Community Services of Metropolitan Boston, Inc., 1966.

Schofield, W. *Psychotherapy: The purchase of friendship.* Englewood Cliffs: Prentice-Hall, 1964.

Skinner, B. F. Are theories of learning necessary? *Psychological Review,* 1950, 57, 193–216.

Strupp, H. H. *Psychotherapists in action: Explorations of the therapist's contribution to the treatment process.* New York: Grune & Stratton, 1960.

Strupp, H. H. The outcome problem in psychotherapy revisited. *Psychotherapy: Theory, Research and Practice,* 1964, 1, 1–13 (also 1964, 1, 100).

Strupp, H. H. Overview and developments in psychoanalytic therapy: Individual treatment. In J. Marmor (Ed.), *Frontiers of psychoanalysis.* New York: Basic Books, 1967, in press.

Sullivan, H. S. *The interpersonal theory of psychiatry.* New York: W. W. Norton & Co., 1953.

Sullivan, H. S. *The psychiatric interview.* New York: W. W. Norton & Co., 1954.

Thorne, F. C. *Principles of personality counseling.* Brandon, Vt.: Clinical Psychology Press, 1950.

Truax, C. B. Effective ingredients in psychotherapy: An approach to unraveling the patient-therapist interaction. *Journal of Counseling Psychology,* 1963, 10, 256–263. Reprinted in this collection, pp. 267–279; page numbers cited in the text refer to *Creative developments in psychotherapy.*

Truax, C. B., & Carkhuff, R. R. *Toward effective counseling and psychotherapy: Training and practice.* Chicago: Aldine, 1967.

Ullmann, L. P., & Krasner, L. (Eds.) *Case studies in behavior modification.* New York: Holt, Rinehart & Winston, 1965.

Wiest, W. M. Some recent criticisms of behaviorism and learning theory. *Psychological Bulletin,* 1967, 67, 214–225.

Wolpe, J. *Psychotherapy by reciprocal inhibition.* Palo Alto: Stanford University Press, 1958.

Wolpe, J. Psychotherapy: The non-scientific heritage and the new science. *Behavior Research and Therapy,* 1963, 1, 23–28.

Wolpe, J., Salter, A., & Reyna, L. J. (Eds.) *The conditioning therapies.* New York: Holt, Rinehart & Winston, 1964.

CHAPTER 26

Natural History Method in Psychotherapy: Communicational Research

Albert E. Scheflen

THE SEARCH FOR APPROPRIATE METHOD

Since 1956 our research group at Temple University Medical Center has been studying the processes of psychotherapy. We originally attempted two approaches: (1) isolating and counting variables; and (2) clinical observation, group discussion, and formulation through consensual validation.

The statistical approach did not yield information about the continuity of the processes or the relationships of the events we were studying.

Discussion failed to reach any consensus. First of all, each of the investigators used a different conceptual framework. One formulated in topographic terms: ego, id, superego. Another used psychosexual frameworks. Another thought in terms of interpersonal relationships, and so on. But the problem was deeper than this. Even when two investigators *were* able to reach common conceptual ground it was generally found that they did not agree; they conceived of different intrapsychic processes to account for what they had observed and often they had been watching different behaviors.

This was a serious problem. All theories of intrapsychic processes are based upon inferences made from the visible behavior. Even if various

The work was done in daily collaboration with Dr. Ray L. Birdwhistell, who generously declined co-authorship; but so inseparable are his contributions that the pronoun "we" is used throughout the paper. This chapter was voted, by the Editorial Board of the present volume, as one of the creative developments in psychotherapy, 1958–1968. From: *Methods of Research in Psychotherapy*, edited by Louis A. Gottschalk and Arthur H. Auerbach. Copyright © 1966 by Meredith Corporation. Reprinted by permission of Appleton-Century-Crofts.

researchers could get themselves to observe precisely the same behavior they still had multiple conceptions about its intrapsychic roots or concomitants. The trouble was that we were *dealing in methods based upon psychodynamic inference applied to processes that could not be observed directly.* The degree of consensual validation seemed to depend upon how similarly the various observers had been trained.

There is also a serious mixing of levels in most clinical studies. Research in psychotherapy is, at one level, research in social processes, i.e., research in interaction and communication. Such social level phenomena fall in the province of the social scientist. In order to use his skills in making inferences about intrapsychic processes, the clinician is apt to unwittingly reduce group processes to personality operations, thereby producing in the research a great confusion in levels. When these difficulties became apparent we split our research staff into two subteams. A clinical, psychoanalytic group was to continue the study of intrapsychic processes. The other team was to find means of systematically studying the interactional processes of psychotherapy. This development in our thinking occurred at the time that context analysis was being developed for the purpose of studying the interview by natural history methods. In 1958 we brought Dr. Birdwhistell, who had pioneered this development, to the Temple University project in research in psychotherapy. In 1959 a collaborative project for research in human communication was established at the Temple Research Division of the Eastern Pennsylvania Psychiatric Institute.

Ultimately researchers will have to integrate the intra-organismic (intrapsychic) and the social (communicational) processes for a holistic understanding of psychotherapy. This integration will depend upon the development of research methods which can deal with the complexity and organization of interaction and communication. Since modern natural history methods show promise of filling this need, this chapter will describe one variant of modern natural history research which is being applied to communication and psychotherapy.

CONTEXT ANALYSIS: A NATURAL HISTORY METHOD

THE MODERN EVOLUTION OF NATURAL HISTORY METHOD

For centuries it has been a fundamental step in scientific methods to select some element of an item under study, separate the element from the larger whole, and examine the abstracted element in isolation. The isolate is often measured or analyzed and its frequency is counted or correlated with other selected isolates. This quantitative approach was introduced into psychiatry from chemistry and experimental psychology. Since World War I it has so dominated formal psychiatric research that two generations of psychiatric researchers have grown up believing it is the *only* method of *scientifically* approaching human behavior.

Applied to research in psychotherapy this tradition has produced, in the name of science, a plethora of counts and correlations of isolated variables such as words per minute, noun-verb ratios, foot taps, therapist's interpretations, and so on. It is not surprising that such data and their analyses have tended to divide the psychiatric clinician and the psychiatric researcher. Such scores and statistical categories seem unfamiliar and unsatisfying to the clinician who has experienced the unity and flow of the psychotherapeutic session. This world of bits and pieces does not represent the richness of his experience. Concepts like rapport or empathy are destroyed rather than captured or sharpened by such dissection.

Yet the pressure in psychiatry to be "scientific" silences the clinician's protests. He withdraws from formal research or he reluctantly bows to quantitative procedures. All too often he abandons productive insights about methodology to obtain a grant or to achieve status as a "scientific" researcher.

It is not our purpose to deny the value of isolating variables and of treating them statistically. The value of this procedure has been amply demonstrated in the modern history of science. The point is that this approach is not appropriate to *all* kinds of research. In particular, as Brosin has said, it is not appropriate to many questions in research in psychotherapy (Brosin, 1966). In situations where the larger picture is clear and the relations within an element established, it is useful to use isolation and quantification to analyze some specific detail. But analysis into components is not useful if a research question involves relations and integration *per se*. For example, such techniques have dubious value in studying how a doctor and patient are related or how an interpretation relates to the history and/or to transference behavior. Quantitative techniques may tell us about the incidence of components but they will tell us little about meaning, function, and reference. In other words, quantification will not allow us to reconstruct ideas of systems, interaction, or processes. Such reconstruction is possible only through synthesis (Schneirla, 1949).

The clinician's objection to much current research procedure has substance. He wants to know how his actions are integrated and how they affect the patient and the relationship. It does not help him to know *how many* verbs or scowls he uses. He turns from research not solely because he fears scrutiny. In part, his research colleagues have alienated him by the rigidity and impoverishment of their techniques. His identity becomes machine not sentient organism.

But this criticism of quantification is not an endorsement of traditional clinical approaches to research. The dissatisfaction with statistics does not mean we can place our reliance on anecdotes nor upon team judgments about them. The clinical appraisal is capable of dealing with complexity and integration and it may be empirically accurate. However, a research method which relies upon free association and intuition is incomplete from another direction. Science demands that its operations of exploration and test be explicit and reproducible.

To deal with psychotherapy we must have research strategies which avoid atomism, on the one hand, and purely intuitive search operations on the other. There must be a way to deal with a complex structure systematically. Perhaps we can turn to other sciences for methodological suggestions. They have dealt with analogous problems. Not only human relationships, but all phenomena in nature exist in an integrated universe. *Life* is not found in atoms, but *emerges* only with their organization into macromolecules which are in turn organized into cells. It is in the cell that we can trace those processes we term *life*. Mobility by means of musculature is not a cellular activity but exists two levels above in the behavior of total organisms which are complex organizations of organ systems.

During the past century broad outlines of human behavior have been sketched. By 1900, the place of man in society had been tentatively formulated in a way which at least gave lip service to the monistic, deterministic canons applicable in the older sciences. Psychology, anthropology, sociology, and psychoanalysis had been formulated in a general way. Data, facts, details, confirmations were demanded by both teachers and students. The focus of investigation and self-justification as "sciences" prompted the movement to the study of elements and components. Perceptual experiments, isolated stimulus-response correlations, demographic counts, and skeletal measurements were needed to fill in and test the sweeping generalizations of the previous century.

Thousands of counts of percepts, concepts, attitudes, responses, stimuli, and associations now have been made. We have learned much about the individual isolated human being out of the context of society, his natural milieu. Now there is need to re-examine ideas of intrapsychic processes in terms of interpersonal processes, social organization, and culture. Greater sophistication and the exhaustion of detail seem to be reasons for the return of science after science to concepts of organization, relations, i.e., to the larger picture. With this trend has come a necessary revival of the natural history method, vastly advanced through systems concepts, capable of testing relations and determining organization seen in equilibrium and in change.

Astronomy has moved from concepts of gravitation (in relationship to individual bodies) to a unified field theory. Cybernetics was deliberately formulated as a science for dealing with complexity (Ashby, 1956). Anthropologists deal not only with cultural elements but with patterns of culture (Benedict, 1946). General systems theory (Bertalanffy, 1950), modern molar biology (Simpson, 1962; Novikoff, 1945), structural linguistics (Gleason, 1955; Hockett, 1958), field theory (Lewin, 1951), and gestalt theory (Koffka, 1935) emphasize the integrated system and the organization of parts in the whole. Freud, for psychoanalysis, emphasized that dream elements are not interpretable apart from their relation to the current life, the past history, and the relationship of patient and analyst (Freud, 1913).

Despite this trend, the adoption of systems concepts and natural history observation of them has been very slow in the psychological sciences. The dogmatic insistence upon quantitative procedures is only one manifestation of this resistance. Authors conversant only with the methods of isolation and/or quantification insist that we have no way to deal scientifically with nuance or subtlety in psychotherapy; no way to deal with complexity and integration in psychotherapy research. Many psychiatric and psychological researchers and officials of granting agencies misunderstand natural history methods, and seem to believe that such methods are based on purely clinical description, intuition, and consensual validation.

Natural history methods are used today, *when appropriate*, in every science (including the physical sciences). It should not be surprising that specific types have been developed to study human interaction: psychotherapy, human communication, and interviewing.

In 1956 the Palo Alto group[1] formulated a natural history method specifically for study of communication in the interview and Birdwhistell and Scheflen have further developed this method. This approach is called "Context Analysis."[2]

THE APPLICATION TO HUMAN COMMUNICATION

Theoretically the basic principles of context analysis apply in the study of any natural phenomenon. We have applied them to human small group behaviors abstracting those which belong to a communicational frame of reference.

Given a field of behaviors, the investigator chooses a frame of reference and abstracts only those elements that are demonstrably part of this framework (Scheflen, 1963). For example, suppose he is studying the behaviors of a group of college students. He may observe that in a day's time they carry out a great many diverse kinds of activities. The investigator may choose some particular set of their activities as part of a particular context in which he is interested. For example, he may study only the courtship behaviors of the students. The context chosen determines which behaviors he will use. (In this sense of the term, frame of reference, it is a context.)

The observer notes that the students walk and talk. The behavioral components of these activities are in the service of multiple frames of reference (they walk to get to class, to have lunch, to engage in campus activities, and to entertain coeds). The behaviors that the investigator will abstract (courtship being his frame of reference) are those that demonstrably belong to the context, courtship.

Similarly, we can conceptualize the behavior of a patient in psychoanalysis in any of several frames of reference. We may look at his actions from a standpoint of the level of psychosexual development and characterize them as oral, anal, or genital. We may look at patient behavior in terms of his apparent libidinal objects, abstracting those that indicate narcissism or object love (Freud, 1933). We could, furthermore, differentiate his behaviors on the basis of whether they appeared motivated by or reflective of various affects like guilt, shame, or anxiety.

The Communicational Frame of Reference. In this chapter context analysis will be applied to behavior in the communicational frame of reference, especially as it is seen in that specific variant of the communicational system, psychotherapy.

Our communicants will be patients and therapists. The criteria for abstracting given elements will be that they are communicative. We will not, however, decide a priori that a given behavior is communicative. *The crucial criterion for calling a behavior communicative is that its presence or absence accompanies an observable relation to the presence or absence of some particular behavior of an interactant or relationship.* In this sense, context analysis is operationalism. If a given behavior regularly is related to a given pattern of activity, then it has presumably been perceived or experienced by the membership at some level. Communication has taken place.

Let me hasten to say that, while we abstract the communicative quality of a behavior, this does not mean that the behavior does not have other functions and implications. The behavior is still an expression of a motive or defense or other intra-organismic process. An action can be a message in the communicational frame of reference and also represent a motive or a defense or a technique in the psychoanalytic frame of reference (Gottschalk, 1961; Strupp, 1957). A behavior is communicative at the social level; it is subject to intrapsychic inference at the organismic level. In communication research in psychotherapy, it is the social effect we study, while the psychoanalysts in our group work with the personality implications of the behavior. It is important to realize that communicational theories are in no way competitive or alternative to personality theories. They are complementary and methodologically they are at a different level of description. As Freud suggested, the observer's feelings may offer some clue to meaning (Freud, 1940) but the criteria we have established are *observable* relations between occurrences. In this way, the final reliance upon inference is reduced and we have made a tactical gain in research method.

Communication as an Abstract System. Our view of communication differs from the one ordinarily held in the psychological sciences. Generally, the psychologically oriented researcher necessarily begins with examination of the *performers* in an interaction. He focuses upon the view that Mr. *A* sends a message to Mr. *B*, which *B* decodes and so on. Such models, based on S-R theory and statistical information theory (Shannon and Weaver, 1949; Cherry, 1961), can be called interactional or action-reaction or coder-decoder models. Menninger has described psychotherapy in this model, speaking of party of the first part, party of the second part and so on (Menninger, 1958). This is also the model of Colby's machinomorphized version of communication in psychoanalysis (Colby, 1960).

We agree with Percy, who suggested that his colleagues ask what communication is instead of trying to force it into an S-R model (Percy, 1961). We approach human communication from a different direction beginning with the communicational system itself. Using a systems view, we see communication as an organization of abstractable structural units, standard, and shared by members of a common culture. These structural units are related in a hierarchy of levels. This system gives continuity, generation to generation. Each child born into the culture must learn these units and how to arrange them in order to communicate.

In a particular situation, certain of these units are selected out of the repertoire and arranged in certain ways. Another situation will call for a different set of units and a different organization of them. For example, courtship calls for different units and order from those of a court trial. Psychotherapy is a unique but regular system whose units are borrowed from the language and kinesic patterns of a given culture and from other institutionalized forms like doctor-patient, teacher-student, and parent-child reciprocals. A given session of psychotherapy will show some type of deployment of these standard units. Each psychotherapy is unique, to be sure, but we seek to abstract the commonalities. We try to reconstruct through comparative studies the basic ground rules, the units, and the arrangement characteristic of this institutionalized and transmissible interaction.

BASIC ASSUMPTIONS OF CONTEXT ANALYSIS

These ideas can be formulated as a set of basic assumptions which underlie the research. These are:

1. That communication (for a given group or culture), like all natural phenomena, has a regular, ultimately predictable structure consisting of definite units arranged in particular ways.
2. That the structural units of communication have a regular set of components and organization which must be performed the same way (within a given range) by all members of an ingroup or else communication will not occur. For example, of billions of possible combinations of phonemes, only a relatively small number actually constitute English words; and these are shared with some minor variations by all English speakers.
3. That these structural units, consisting of communicational behaviors, are themselves merely components of larger units in a hierarchy of levels. For example, in language, phonemes are organized into morphemes which are organized into syntactic sentences.
4. That institutionalized activities like psychotherapy use the basic communicational system of the culture modified in certain specialized but lawful ways.
5. That all participants have learned and know (mostly without consciousness) the system of communication for the groups in which they have membership.
6. That the communicative system of any type of group can be abstracted by context analysis.

This paper will describe how the communication system is derived, illustrating the procedure with excerpts from the Temple Experimental Film. Four steps will be described: (1) recording and transcribing; (2) ascertaining the structural units; (3) synthesizing the larger picture to determine meaning or function; and (4) setting up the natural history experiment.

STEP 1. RECORDING AND TRANSCRIBING

SOUND MOTION PICTURE RECORDING

Since context analysis requires that we search and research the data and deal with each element of a unit, it is essential that we have a complete and consistent record. We cannot depend upon our memories or those of the therapist or patient because many components may be forgotten or distorted in these recollections. We cannot use a tape recording alone because the non-linguistic behaviors are not picked up. At present, a sound motion picture is the necessary record for a context analysis.

This record of the interaction must be complete. Often the vital interchange at some second may involve the hands or feet of the interactants. In context analysis all actions are examined in terms of all others present. Accordingly, the cameraman must not pan the room or move in for a closeup, thereby cutting off some of the scene. These principles are described by Mr. Jacques Van Vlack in a paper in *Methods of Research in Psychotherapy*.

TRANSCRIBING DATA FROM FILM

Not only must we record all of the scene we wish to study, but we must include all the communicative elements in the analysis. The very behavior we think can be dispensed with may be the signal to take all of the other behaviors metaphorically and our omission of it may make it impossible to comprehend the meaning of the whole. The element we neglect may signal that one unit has been completed and another begun or it may be a parameter that changes the implications of all that will follow. *Just as we must not decide a priori what to leave out of the film we must not select arbitrarily what can be omitted from the analysis and synthesis.* We do not decide beforehand what is trivial, what is redundant, or what alters the system. This is a *result* of the research.

Not only must we record elements of language but of posture, body movement, touch, facial expression, dress, and decor. If we could record odors, vibration, and pressure we would do so. The communicational system uses all of the sensory modalities.

The recording of so many behaviors becomes feasible because we can record structural units as single entities (see below). Most of the larger structural units of communication have not yet been described but units of the size of the syntactic sentence and smaller are already well known through twenty-five years of linguistic research and ten years in kinesic research.

What we end up with in such microrecordings[3] are transcripts of syntactic sentences and familiar units of kinesics and posture for each interactant recorded on a time graph. Those elements of behaviors which we do not find familiar cannot be plotted in the beginning but will first have to be studied (see below). Such a plot shows us the order in which the communicative behaviors occurred. We can use it in several ways. If we attend to which person performed the behavior, we can reconstruct the interaction of the session through time. We can examine the time graph to spot patterns and repetitions. But such a description of sequence is not a determination of structure and system. It tells us only that events were or were not contiguous in time. It does not tell us the function of any behavior. It does not reveal how behaviors are integrated into a larger system. To do this we will have to use a synchronic approach determining the structural units and how they are put together. This approach will now be described.

STEP 2. ASCERTAINING THE STRUCTURAL UNITS

THE CHARACTERISTICS OF A STRUCTURAL UNIT

The structural unit can be defined as a regular organization or complex of components occurring in specific situations or contexts. A structural unit, then, has: (1) a given set of component parts; (2) a definite organization; and (3) specific location in a larger system. For example, an immediate family consists of a mother, father, and children with prescribed relationships and a definite position in a larger family or kinship system. Morphemes (words) consist of given phonemes arranged in regular ways and having set locations in the sentence.

A structural unit is recognized by three criteria. These are: (1) its components; (2) their arrangement; and (3) the neighborhoods or contexts in which it occurs.

Sometimes a component or unit is so well known and so characteristic that we can identify it by itself, i.e., even when it is not located in a larger unit or in a context. The anatomists would have no difficulty identifying the human brain in isolation. There are people we know so well that we would immediately recognize them no matter where we saw them; others we would be uncertain about unless we saw them in some familiar context such as in their shop or at the office.

Structural units can be seen as entities belonging to larger systems or they can be looked at in terms of their components. To look at a unit as a set of components is to analyze it. To examine a unit in relation to the larger systems to which it belongs is called syntheses (Simpson, 1962). In context analysis we both analyze and synthesize. Analysis in this usage does not merely mean to break down into components as the term often is used in chemistry or psychology. Analysis here, as in logic and in psychoanalysis, means to separate into units which are seen in relation to the whole.

Structural units, then, are parts of larger units, which are parts of still larger units, and so on. Such an arrangement is called a hierarchy of levels (Bertalanffy, 1950, 1960; Feibleman, 1954; Simpson, 1962; Scheflen, 1963). This relation of units in a hierarchy of levels can be represented schematically as seen in the next diagram.

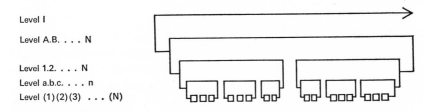

One example of a hierarchy of levels is the ascending order of complexity and inclusiveness of electron, atom, molecule, cell, organ, organism, and group. Another is phoneme, morpheme and syntactic sentence (Gleason, 1955; Hockett, 1958).

HOW UNITS ARE IDENTIFIED AND TESTED

The method for ascertaining or identifying the structural unit is based upon its three characteristics, i.e., its components, their organization, and the context(s) in which they occur. We begin by inspecting the behaviors and grouping, as a tentative unit, those that occur together in time. We then test this tentative formulation by three tests, reformulating the unit over and over by trial and error until we have determined the relations of components. When we have found the combination that is a structural unit each of its components will occur together every time. They will have consistent arrangement and appear invariably in the same context. If not we must begin again. The procedure becomes simple with practice and experience in the nature of communication units.

Three aspects of the relations of communicative behaviors are tested. They are:

1. *Delineation*: which components invariably occur together.
2. *Contrasting*: which components are not interdependent in this way.
3. *Testing in Context*: which context(s) or shifts in context regularly accompany the occurrence of each tentative unit.

The relations are determined by what in mathematics is called the *Method of Agreement and Difference* (also formulated as *Mill's canons*).[4] Simply stated, if A appears every time B appears, and vice versa, and if A does not appear when B is absent, then A and B have relations of interdependence and represent an entity. These relations are examined by direct observation of multiple instances of occurrence and non-occurrence.

Identity and Substitutability. All units which have the same components and arrangement and which occur in the same situations are said to have relations to identity. They are merely different performances, or occurrences of the same structural unit. Units which do not have identical components or arrangements but which occur in the same contexts, i.e., their occurrence has the same *effect*, are substitutable for each other in communication.

ILLUSTRATING THE OPERATIONS WITH A
SAMPLE OF PSYCHOTHERAPY BEHAVIORS

Operation 1
Delineation or Formulation of the Tentative Unit

Three times in the experimental session the therapist engaged in a behavior that looked like it might be a structural unit. She lit a cigarette. Each time this action was followed by a consistent change in the patient's behavior.

Cigarette-lighting occurred as follows:

1. From 00 minutes, 00 seconds–00 minutes, 20 seconds
2. From 12 minutes, 18 seconds–13 minutes, 36 seconds
3. From 20 minutes, 30 seconds–21 minutes, 31 seconds

The tentative unit can be described through time as follows:

The doctor reached to a table on her left and took up a pack of cigarettes and matches. With her right hand she removed a cigarette which she eventually placed between her lips. Holding the match cover in her left hand, she struck a match with her right hand, applied it to the cigarette, inhaled, and blew a puff of smoke. She then shook out the match with her right hand, transferred it to her left hand, and discarded it in an ash tray on the table to her left.

There are many things that we can do with this tentative unit. We can make a linguistic analysis of the associated speech (Pittenger, Hockett, and Danehy, 1960). We can measure the actions in any of several ways. Since we have motion pictures, we can superimpose standard grids and measure excursions of movement or distance between participants or measure any other dimension that interests us, for that matter. Since each motion picture frame is numbered, and there are twenty-four frames per second, we can accurately measure the duration of each act or pause or comment. There is, however, no point in making any detailed description of a tentative unit. We wait until we are sure we are dealing with a structural unit.

How do we determine whether the complex cigarette-lighting *is* a structural unit? We first analyze cigarette-lighting into its component behaviors at the level below.

The components of cigarette-lighting were:

1. Taking out a cigarette and bringing it and a pack of matches to her lap.
2. Waiting until the patient has finished a story.
3. Putting the cigarette in her mouth.
4. Waiting until the patient looks away.
5. Lighting up.
6. Discarding the match.

Each of these elements can, in turn, be analyzed. For example, *lighting up* has the following elements:

1. Holding match cover in left hand.
2. Removing a match.
3. Watching the patient until he diverts his eyes.
4. Striking the match with her right hand.
5. Applying the match to the cigarette.
6. Inhaling and exhaling smoke.

Operation 2
Contrasting or Distinguishing Between Units

Reciprocal to the procedure of finding what elements go together is the operation of finding what elements are not part of the tentative unit.

An example will clarify the concept. Suppose we are observing a colony of bees and have a chance to witness the fascinating dance by which these insects communicate the distance and direction of food supplies (Von Frisch, 1953). The dancing bee will carry out a series of movements in a given set of directions. If we test the relations of these movements we will find them interdependent; they invariably occur together. We have found a structural unit that occurs in a given context, i.e., when the unit occurs the bees will fly in a given direction. Another dancer will move in a different set of directions on the hive frames. These movements also prove interdependent and make up a unit which occurs in a context of flying in some other direction. In the same dance, the bee does not intermingle behaviors of Unit A and Unit B or his message would be ambiguous. We can distinguish Unit A and Unit B by the component movements of each, by the configurations of each whole dance, and by the context of each, i.e., the subsequent directions of flight.

There were several units on the same level as cigarette-lighting but which are contrasting and distinguishable from it. Consider at the moment only one other example.

Looking up: Frequently the therapist extended her neck and looked upward at the ceiling. She adopted a quizzical look, furrowing her brows and staring off into space as though deep in thought. In a second or two she looked back at the patient and started to speak.

Sometimes contrasting units have the same elements but they are organized differently. Other contrasting units have a similar set of components and a very similar organization, only one component being different. Yet these similar units are functionally different and occur in different contexts. For example, the one additional element may be a signal not to react to the unit. To consider structural units together just because they appear similar is to court the kind of trouble we had when when we considered all psychoses to be the same or when all renal disease was called Bright's disease. Appearance is deceptive. We must test each structural unit and contrast those we delineate.

Contrasting provides us with a second test of our tentative unit. That a unit X is not unit Y is part of distinguishing its characteristics. Later we will see that units at the same level which contrast in their structure are likely to be co-components in a larger structural unit.

Operation 3
Examining in Context(s)

It is possible to use an approximate and a definitive concept of the context. Loosely, we can define the context in terms of some aspect of it; some single component of the larger system which appears whenever the structural unit appears. For example, the earth appears in the context Solar System, but the earth might be identified for some space explorer by locating it in relation to Mars or Venus. The occurrence of some aspect of context in conjunction with the unit is useful in identifying the unit. Later we will have to define and determine contexts more precisely.

We now test the tentative unit's relation to an element of the context. The technique is already familiar. If the tentative unit, $(a.b.c.d. . .n)$ occurs each time in the same context and it does not occur without this context, then the tentative unit and the contextual event are interdependent.

A shift was noticed after cigarette-lighting. Let, for a moment, a single event stand for the context. The patient stopped relating anecdotes from his current life and spoke more of his feelings and attitudes. In doing so his manner changed from expansive bravado with over-loud and editorial paralanguage to a more hesitant, slightly childlike presentation. He began to speak of more personal matters. In clinical terms, the patient stopped acting like a conversationalist and adopted a stance more typical of the psychotherapy patient.

We carefully observed the relation of this shift to each occurrence of cigarette-lighting. *The test failed. The shift did follow cigarette-lighting but was not interdependent with it.*

We will have to search the data again and reformulate.

The tentative unit, cigarette-lighting, did have interdependent components and gave every evidence of being a structural unit,[5] but it was not in reliable relation to the shift in the patient's behavior. There are two possibilities: (1) that cigarette-lighting is not a *complete* unit because we have overlooked elements of it that do relate to the shift of the patient; or (2) that cigarette-lighting is a unit, but one that belongs to another context, a context that we have not yet uncovered. This second possibility proved to be the case.

Cigarette-lighting belonged to a context in which the therapist temporarily stopped conversing and began to try to interrupt the patient's story. Also the patient began to talk more rapidly and use more single bar junctures (a linguistic activity that discourages interruption).

We can now diagram the tested structure unit as follows:

Cigarette-lighting:	Occurring in a context A:
a set of regular interdependent behaviors in a given arrangement.	in which therapist shifts to refraining from conversation and tries to interrupt the patient's stories.

RECORDING AND VISUALIZING BECOME FEASIBLE

Context analysis is not a simple progression of steps, but a moving backward and forward through operations. The last step makes it possible to complete the first. Now we know how to go back and finish recording. We have the key which makes the transcribing of data from the motion picture film feasible. You may remember that our method called for inclusion of all the communicative behaviors. Without comprehending the structural units this task seems absurdly arduous. The micro-recording of communicative elements involves 120 variables each $\frac{1}{8}$th second for each participant; over 100,000 elements a minute.

What are we to record? Therapist blinks right eye, mutters "ah," looks down, wiggles toes. Patient sighs, looks up, flushes, says "a," then "d." How can we deal with such complexity let alone make any sense out of it?

The secret is that we do not have to record or examine each bit. The pieces are organized into standard structural units, many of which are known through other research, recognizable at a glance and recordable with a stroke. This is the nature of a communicative system. If its units were not highly regular with little deviation there would be no mutual recognition and therefore no communication.

This standardization may strike the psychiatrist as incredible. He is used to looking for individual differences, not similarities. He has always focused upon the *content* of the syntactic sentence. There are hundreds of thousands of different words that can be placed in this structural unit, but the truth is that all syntactic sentences follow one of a mere half-dozen forms. There are probably no more than thirty American gestures.

An analogy may help explain the point. Suppose you are at a baseball game and you are to record every behavioral event. If you do not know the structural units of the game you will have to record thousands and thousands of fragments, e.g., Player Number 1 opens mouth, scratches arm, lifts bat, looks at player Number 7, and so on. But if you do know the units and the system of notation you can codify the entire game on a single sheet of paper and later reconstruct the game in sufficient detail for a lengthy newspaper account. You note hits, walks, and outs and you codify just how each was made.

But you have to be willing to abstract similarities. If you dwell on the individuality of human behavior and see each communicative behavior as a piece of creative inventiveness you will have an endless list of units. Actually, it takes conformity to be a communicant. The forms of a communicative unit have only the narrowest allowable deviation. Exceed this range and you will not communicate. If I make up one new word I will get a questioning letter from the editor. If I ask for another martini in a creatively novel pitch pattern I will be likely to be served coffee. There are, to be sure, stylistic and dialectical variations but the sine qua non of communicative behavior is its reliability. As an American I can recognize lawn mowing, embarrassment, and the New York skyline at a glance. I can sense the slightest deviation in stress or pronunciation. *This regularity in the communicative system permits the researcher to recognize known structural units quickly and to record them with a single symbol.*

It is true that we do not know all the units of the communicative system, but those that are unfamiliar can be determined by context analysis.

STEP 3. SYNTHESIZING THE LARGER PICTURE: THE APPROACH TO MEANING

THE CONCEPT OF CONTEXTS

If we were interested only in defining the one structural unit, cigarette-lighting, we might stop here—short of knowing more about its context and therefore of knowing accurately about its meaning or function. Since we have only three instances we might go on to study other sessions to accumulate a larger number of cigarette-lightings for a more creditable sample. We might also make conjectures about cigarette-lighting, e.g., maybe it is part of the therapist's self-discipline in refraining from conversation with her patient.

If, however, we wish to determine the structure of other units and the organization of the larger picture, if we wish to accurately determine the meaning of these actions, we must go on. We will have to identify the other contrasting units and the more complete contexts. We are already familiar with how this is done. We again formulate tentative units and test them. All such units, once identified, that are interdependent with each other (at the same level) are the components of the larger unit at the next higher level in the hierarchy. At the same time such units constitute the immediate context for any one of them. The *immediate* context, then, of any unit is the more inclusive unit at the level above.

The *mediate* context is the unit at the next higher level. The units at still higher levels constitute the *remote* contexts of a unit. The immediate context of a therapy session, for example, might consist of other sessions in the course of a particular psychotherapy or psychoanalysis. The mediate contexts might prove to include all psychotherapy and psychoanalysis, the institutional environment, and schools of psychiatric thought. Remote contexts might turn out to include the evolution of cultural ideals, middle-class values, and the economic situation in the community.

OTHER UNITS AT THE LEVEL OF CIGARETTE-LIGHTING

There were two other tested structural units at the level of cigarette-lighting. These were:

1. *Interpreting*: You remember that I described the therapist's tendency to look up at the ceiling with a quizzical expression. The action was interdependent with the lexical actions typical of the clinical technique of interpreting and with actions that encourage the patient to discuss the point. This unit I will call *interpreting*.

2. *Tactical Shifting*: The shift in the patient's behavior from bravado and story-telling to acting like a patient was related to three activities of the therapist.

(a) *Discarding ashes and shifting the cigarette to the left hand*: In the act of taking a drag on the cigarette and discarding the ashes in the ashtray on her left, the therapist would shift the cigarette from her right to her left hand. This shift presumably made it easier for her to reach the ashtray. It is important to note that she sometimes took a drag without discarding ashes. Therefore, discarding and dragging were not interdependent. They were separate elements that belonged to different structural units. It was discarding that occurred with shifting the cigarette that is part of the unit we are now reconstructing.

(b) *Shifting posture*: After the therapist lit her cigarette she shifted her entire body in two ways. First, she would rotate slightly to her left (away from the camera) and more directly face the patient. Second, she would slouch slightly, becoming less erect in the chair. This postural shift brought her pelvis forward and nearer the patient. It would have brought her upper body farther from him except that she also bent slightly at the waist and inclined toward him.

We have already told you that in the act of discarding her match she shifted from a position of arms or hands crossed to one of uncrossed upper extremities. Collectively, these shifts bring a person slightly closer to and more open or accessible to a vis-à-vis. The shift also gives a person the appearance of greater ease and relaxation.

This postural shift was either durable or transient. Either she made this postural shift only to quickly go back to her original position or she maintained this new position until she finished smoking. *Only the maintained shift* was associated with the shift in the patient's presentation.

(c) *Instructing the patient*: During this sequence of behaviors the therapist made a comment to the patient. Either she told him to talk about his problem, or she asked him about it, or she talked about an anecdote from her own life as if providing him with an example of what to talk about.

None of these elements was new to us. We have seen them all before in our research in psychotherapy. Instructions to act more like a patient we have called *structuring maneuvers* (Scheflen, 1960). The use of the left, rather than the right, hand in holding a pipe proved to be an important signal of rapport and openness in the Whitaker and Malone method (Scheflen et al., 1965). Postural shifts of this same type and context have been observed in each of twelve psychoanalytically oriented psychotherapies that we have studied. In each case unfolding the arms and/or the legs and moving toward the patient was associated with an offer to help or an invitation to talk about personal problems. *Postural shifting, then, is a regular element in offering rapport.*

Often two of these elements would occur but not the others. The configuration was, therefore, not complete. *When all of the components had been complete and when the therapist was smoking, the shift in the patient's presentation invariably and immediately occurred.* These actions are the components of a tested structural unit. We will call the unit *tactical shifting*.

It was like putting together a puzzle consisting of four pieces. It does not matter which piece is put down first. The gestalt appears when all four have been placed.

The doctor often delayed in supplying one of the three pieces or performed a component and then retracted it. It was as though she was hesitant to complete the unit that would prematurely signal the patient to shift. For example, she might transfer the cigarette to her left hand, instruct the patient, shift toward him, and then shift back again. A moment later, she would again shift forward and repeat her instruction, but she would delay discarding the ashes and shifting the cigarette to her left hand. In either case, this configuration remained incomplete.

It was apparent that these delays and backtrackings were related to the patient's refusal to accept interruption and his insistence on prolonging his stories and his anecdotes. Later, the therapist reported that her principal preoccupation during the session was her difficulty in getting the patient to relate to her and talk about himself. In reading the transcript it is evident that he kept talking about his previous therapist and avoiding the subject of his relationship to her, a fact that she commented upon and interpreted. Presumably, she delayed completion of the unit until she picked up some readiness in her patient. The cue appeared to be a pause in his narrative.

The multiple false starts in this sequence of behaviors, however, were useful to the context analysis. Unlike the cigarette-lighting, where there were only three instances, there were recurrences of the discarding, postural shifting, and instructing components of tactical shifting. There is considerably more evidence of a relation between tactical shifting and the patient's modification.

Whenever the therapist finished her cigarette she tamped it out in the ashtray and then step by step undid or reversed the steps in tactical shifting. She moved back to her erect posture (more distant from the patient) and again folded her arms across her chest. As she did so, she also stopped her passive listening and began a period of active interpreting to the patient. He promptly responded to the reversal of her sequence by again reverting somewhat to his non-patient behavior.

This sequence of behaviors could be diagrammed as follows:

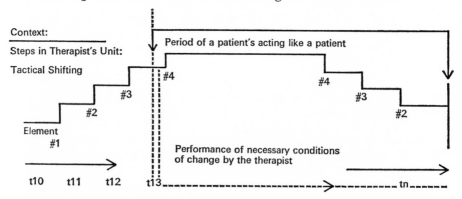

You will note an analogy in these findings to the work of the ethologists in animal interaction, where the innate releasing mechanisms are dependent upon exact configurations of behavior. You will also note that our method is quite parallel to those the ethologists have used (Klopfer, 1963; Lorenz, 1952). Apparently the human infant smiles at four to six months in response to, and only in response to, the eye-nose-mouth configuration (Spitz, 1951). This is one example of a precise configuration acting as a signal or releasor.

Now that the structural unit has been tested, it is possible for us to describe it in great detail. We could describe it diachronically as a series of components in sequence as they occurred through time. Or we could describe synchronically the organization of components, the duration, the contextual conditions for its occurrence, variations in its form, its regulation by the patient's behaviors, and so on. But you have suffered enough detail. Those qualities of the unit have been recorded for future comparison with similar structures in other psychotherapies.[6] We can now put the parts together.

THE LARGER UNITS (OR THE CONTEXTS) TO
WHICH CIGARETTE-LIGHTING BELONGS

Lighting up, tactical shifting, and interviewing proved to be interdependent. They belong to a shift in context in which patient and therapist change from conversation to the typical psychotherapy relationship involving free association and interpretation. Suppose I call this unit *structuring therapist-patient reciprocals.*

The unit can be diagrammed as follows:

UNIT I STRUCTURING THERAPIST-PATIENT RECIPROCALS							
A. Refraining from Conversation		B. Tactical Shifting			C. Interpreting		D.*
1. Cigarette-lighting	2. Smoking etc.	1. Shift to left hand	2. Postural shift	3. Instructing	1. Looking up	2. Offering interpretation	1. etc.

*Unit 1 also seemed to contain another unit or two which were not tested. It also often contained more than one repetition of unit C and an occurrence of tactical shifting in reverse (see above).

There is something else we can say about this unit. Like other units, it has *markers*, i.e., definite actions which indicate its beginning and end (Scheflen, 1964). It begins with lighting a cigarette and ends with extinguishing the cigarette.

In this way, we synthesize *upward*, level by level in successive contexts, as if we were building a pyramid, until the multiple events of an interaction come together as components of a single overall unit.

By gross inspection the structural unit, structuring therapist-patient reciprocals, seemed to contrast to three other tentative units which in clinical terms appeared like "working through," "telling anecdotes," and "discussing advice." These units, however, were not tested.

In this way the synthesis continues repeating the same operations until a whole session has been described or until certain units have been studied comparatively in multiple sessions.

Meaning. Only when we know the organization of the systems and the relation of components to larger entities can we systematically determine the meaning or function of any unit. In clinical work we often seek meaning by intuiting what we have observed about the organization of behavior. There is little doubt about the intuitive abilities of the experienced clinician but his operations are private.

Meaning can be defined operationally as the relation of a specific unit and its context or contexts (Bateson, 1966). The meaning of a unit x is that it is not y or z and that it regularly occurs in the contexts X or Y, but not in contexts A or B. For example, the meaning of psychotherapy, it might be postulated, is that it is not child-rearing or courtship, and it occurs in the contexts of correction of deviancy and treatment of psychophysiological disorder, but not in evangelism or political indoctrination. The operations for confirming this guess would be: determination of the structural units and contexts of each of these large social units and making the necessary contrasts.

The concept of meaning can be explained in another way. Consider meaning as a relative quality. Bateson (1966) has said that meaning increases as ambiguity decreases. Operationally then, the meaning of a unit is approached by decreasing the ambiguity of its relations to contexts. For example, if the tentative unit, psychotherapist behavior, were to be found only in the context correction of deviancy systems, then the ambiguity would be small. A specific role interdependent with a single specific context (precisely defined) would not allow for possible alternatives to the fact that psychotherapy behavior was an activity in deviancy correction.

Here is another application of the idea that meaning is inversely proportional to ambiguity. Suppose we were given the letters *b.b.* and asked about their meaning. The great ambiguity would lead us to throw up our hands. If we were supplied contextual elements (e.g., that *b.b.*

occurred as part of the phrase "big boy") we could start making guesses about contexts: gangster movies, large artillery, child-rearing, and so on. If we, then, learned that the word was said by a father to his son upon viewing a job well done, the ambiguity is considerably reduced. We would then only need to know whether the paralanguage indicated sarcasm or approval and the meaning would be determined through excluding other possibilities.

If an event is stripped out of the context in which it actually occurred, its meaning is at the mercy of the imaginary contexts that we supply for it. In Langer's terms, we form a conception rather than a concept (Langer, 1953). We may try to objectify free associations about meaning by using judges and correlating their guesses, but the fact that they may agree may mean little. Fifty million Frenchmen *can* be wrong. If a particular understanding is shared by a group, it may be a doctrinal or cultural misconception rather than a private illusion; the number of people in agreement do not verify the understanding. In the past, consensual validation has been achieved about phlogiston, N-Rays, witches, a flat earth, and a geocentric universe. Today some researchers in psychotherapy seem to examine all events in psychotherapy in the light of a private conception of morality or proper practice. Meaning, thus, becomes little more than value judgment.

The answer to the problem of meaning lies in not ripping events out of context in order to study them. To avoid the ambiguity that results from the replacement of known contexts by imaginary ones we must *observe the units in the contexts in which they actually occurred.*

Function. We can also translate the language of context analysis into the more familiar terms of experimental medicine. The principles were laid down a century ago by Bernard (1927). The development of the modern concept of the adrenal will serve as an example. Based on the anatomy, the adrenal gland was once conceived of as an entity, even though the type of components (cells) and their arrangements were known to differ in the two sections of the adrenal, the medulla, and the cortex. When the cortex of the adrenal was selectively extirpated a very different physiology obtained from when the medulla was removed. These two parts of the adrenal were then known to have different functions in the physiological system. The context of the unit, cortex, we could then say, is different from that of the unit, medulla.

If, however, we are examining a stream of events or structures which we cannot manipulate, we may not have information about what happens when one event is removed. What we can see is that A occurs in given contexts. We can observe through time (as we did with the tactical shifting) and wait until *A* does not occur at its expected place in the pattern. We then learn what happens in its absence. Thereby, we can gain information analogous to that of the extirpation experiment. We can confirm such relations by natural history experimentation (see Step 4).

In this way the meaning or function of any unit is found by examining its relation to the larger system or contexts to which it belongs. Thus we find the transforms between three ideas: meaning, function, and place in the larger system. We are also warned against reductionism: the tendency to explain a thing in isolation or in terms of its parts or mechanisms. Reference and explanation require examination of the level above, of the larger picture.

STEP 4. SETTING UP THE NATURAL HISTORY EXPERIMENT

When we have ascertained the structural units and their relations in a hierarchy of levels, we can experiment to determine more exactly their role in a system. We can find out what will happen in the larger picture if we remove a unit or if it changes or fails to occur. In this sense, the natural history method ultimately uses a classical technique. But after a natural history description has been made, relations and organization have been determined systematically and the smallest change becomes quickly apparent when a system is thoroughly known.

SUMMARY

1. Some shortcomings (in terms of research in psychotherapy) of quantitative methods and clinical evaluation are described.

2. The growth of modern natural history methods is traced, and basic concepts of one type of natural history research are described. It is called *context analysis.*

3. The application of this method to studying communication in psychotherapy is elaborated.

4. The operations of context analysis are described and explained, using illustrations from the experimental psychotherapy film.

NOTES

1. G. Bateson, R. L. Birdwhistell, H. Brosin, F. Fromm-Reichmann, C. Hockett, N. A. McQuown, at the Center for the Advanced Study in the Behavioral Sciences.

2. *Context* analysis must be distinguished from *content* analysis, a method of studying words and ideas only.

3. Birdwhistell (1952, 1966) has published details of more refined and exact microrecording of kinesics and the structural linguistics have developed exact recording for speech modalities (Gleason, 1955; Hockett, 1958).

4. Ordinarily in the psychologic sciences we think of determining relations by scattergram or product moment correlation. This would be possible in context analysis. We could take more film to obtain a larger n, set up intervals, and determine the frequency of each component. We could then determine the correlation. But this procedure is unnecessary. We are interested in occurrence and non-occurrence, not in measuring degrees of difference. We want to know what pieces go together. In pattern and natural structure, co-occurrence is not probabilistic. We do not bother to assess the probabilities that human beings have hearts or that the word *heart* has an *a* in it.

5. There are two exceptions to the generalization that a given communicative unit invariably contains the same elements. First, a unit may be "incorrectly" performed, whereupon it does not have its customary effect in context and it will "fail" communicationally. Second, in established human relationships there tends to be abbreviation of units as members develop short-cuts and private languages. The units in such a relationship may be incomplete or lack some of their usual components. Such incomplete units are nonetheless regular for *that* relationship.

6. There is every indication so far that psychotherapists who smoke use their cigarettes or pipes as important props in regulating and signalling their tactics. For the most part, this relation appears to be nonconscious. It may be borrowed from general communicational practices or learned by identification in psychiatric training.

REFERENCES

Ashby, W. R. *An introduction to cybernetics.* New York: Wiley, 1956.

Barker, R. G., and Wright, H. F. *The midwest and its children: The psychological ecology of an American town.* New York: Harper & Row, 1954.

Benedict, R. *Patterns of culture.* Mentor MD 89, 1946.

Bateson, G. The message, "This is play." In B. Schaffner (Ed.), *Group processes*, Vol. II. Madison, N.J.: Madison Printing Co., 1955.

Bateson, G. Chapter I. Communication. In N. McQuown (Ed.), *The natural history of an interview.* New York: Grune & Stratton, 1964.

Bernard, C. *An introduction to the study of experimental medicine.* New York: Abelard-Schuman, 1927.

Bertalanffy, L. V. An outline of general systems theory. *Brit. J. for Phil. of Sci.*, 1: 134, 1950.

Bertalanffy, L. V. *Problems of life.* New York: Harper & Row, 1960.

Birdwhistell, R. L. *Introduction to kinesics.* Louisville, Ky.: University of Louisville Press, 1952.

Birdwhistell, R. L., Chapter 3, in N. McQuown (Ed.), *The natural history of an interview.* New York: Grune & Stratton, 1964.

Brosin, H. In N. McQuown (Ed.), *The natural history of an interview*. New York: Grune & Stratton, 1964.

Butler, J. M., Rice, L. N., and Wagstaff, A. K. On naturalistic definition of variables. In H. H. Strupp and L. Luborsky (Eds.), *Research in Psychotherapy*. Washington: Psychological Association, Inc., 1962.

Cherry, C. *On human communication*. New York: Science Editions, Inc., 1961.

Colby, M. K. *An introduction to psychoanalytic research*. New York: Basic Books, 1960.

Feibleman, J. K. Theory of integrative levels, *Brit. J. Phil. Sci.*, 5: 59, 1954.

Freud, S. *The interpretation of dreams*. New York: Macmillan, 1913.

Freud, S. *New introductory lectures in psychoanalysis*. New York: Norton, 1933.

Freud, S. A note upon the mystic writing pad. *Int. J. Psychoanal.*, 21: 469, 1940.

Gleason, H. A. *An introduction to descriptive linguistics*. New York: Holt, Rinehart and Winston, 1955.

Gottschalk, L. A. *Comparative psycholinguistic analysis of two psychotherapeutic interviews*. New York: International Universities, 1961.

Hockett, C. F. *A course in modern linguistics*. New York: Macmillan, 1958.

Langer, S. K. *Introduction to symbolic logic* (2nd ed.), New York: Dover, 1953.

Lewin, K. Field theory in social science. In *Group Dynamics: Research and Theory*. Cartwright, D. (Ed.), New York: Harper & Row, 1951.

Lorenz, K. *King Solomon's ring*. New York: Crowell-Collier, 1952.

Klopper, P. H. *Behavioral aspects of ecology*. Englewood Cliffs, N.J.: Prentice-Hall, 1962.

Koffka, K. *Principles of gestalt psychology*. New York: Harcourt, Brace & World, 1935.

Menninger, Karl. *Theory of psychoanalytic technique*. New York: Basic Books, 1958.

Novikoff, A. B. The concept of integrative levels and biology. *Sci.*, 101: 209, 1945.

Percy, W. The symbolic structure of interpersonal process. *Psychiat.*, 24: 39, 1961.

Pittenger, R. E., Hockett, C. F., and Danehy, J. J. *The first five minutes*. Ithaca, N.Y.: Paul Martineau, 1960.

Scheflen, A. E. *A psychotherapy of schizophrenia: A study of direct analysis*, Springfield, Ill.: Charles C. Thomas, 1960.

Scheflen, A. E. Research in psychotherapy. In J. Masserman (Ed.), *Current phychiatric therapies*, New York: Grune & Stratton, 1963.

Scheflen, A. E. Context analysis. In *Strategy and structure in psychotherapy*. English, O. S. (Ed.) In press.

Schneirla, T. C. Levels in the psychological capacities of animals. In E. W. Sellars, *et al.* (Eds.), *Philosophy for the future.* New York: Macmillan, 1949.

Shannon, C. E., and Weaver, W. *The mathematical theory of communication.* Urbana, Ill.: Univ. of Illinois Press, 1949.

Simpson, George Gaylord. The status of the study of organisms. *Amer. Scientist,* 50: 36–45, 1962.

Spitz, R. *No and Yes.* New York: International Universities, 1951.

Strupp, H. H. A multi-dimensional system for analyzing psychotherapeutic techniques. *Psychiat.,* 20: 293, 1957.

Von Frisch, K. *The dancing bees.* New York: Harcourt, Brace & World, 1953.

ADDITIONAL REFERENCES RELATED TO CONTEXT ANALYSIS

1. ON LEVELS OF ORGANIZATION AND INTEGRATION

Bertalanffy, L. V. General systems theory: A new approach to unity of science. *Human Biology,* 23: 302–312, 1951.

Grobstein, C. Levels and ontogeny. *Amer. Sci.,* 50: 46–58, Mar. 1962.

Hawkins, D. *Design for a mind.* Daedalus, 1962.

Koehler, W. Gestalten problems und Anfaenge Einer Gestal and theorie. *Jakresber ges Psychiol.,* 3, 1925.

Miller, G. A., Galanter, E., and Pribram, K. H. *Plans and the structure of behavior.* New York: Holt, Rinehart and Winston, 1960.

Novikoff, A. B. The concept of integrative levels and biology. *Sci.,* 101: 209–215, 1945.

Redfield, R. (Ed.) *Levels of integration in biological and social systems.* Symposium No. 8. Lancaster: Cottell Press, 1942.

2. ON NATURALISTIC OBSERVATION

Barker, R. G. *The stream of behavior.* New York: Appleton-Century-Crofts, 1963.

Bateson, G. *Naven* (2nd ed.), Stanford: Stanford University Press, 1958.

Bernard, G. *An introduction to the study of experimental medicine.* New York: Abelard-Schuman, 1927.

Bock, P. B. *The social structure of a Canadian Indian reservation.* Doctoral Thesis, Harvard University, 1952.

Evans-Pritchard, E. E. *Social anthropology.* London: Cohen and West, 1951.

Harris, Z. *Methods in structural linguistics.* Chicago: Univ. of Chicago Press, 1951.

Lorenz, K. *King Solomon's ring.* New York: Crowell-Collier, 1952.

McQuown, N. A., Bateson, G., Birdwhistell, R. E., Boronsen, H. W., and Hockett, G. F. *The natural history of an interview.* (To be published).

Tinbergen, N. *Social behavior in animals.* London: Methuen, 1953.

3. ON INFORMATION THEORY, COMMUNICATION AND CYBERNETICS

Bavelas, A. Communication patterns in task-oriented groups. *J. Acoust. Soc. Amer.*, 22: 725, 1950.

Berlo, D. K. *The process of communication.* New York: Holt, Rinehart & Winston, 1960.

Deutsch, K. On communication models in the social sciences. *Public Opinion quart.*, 16: 356–380, 1952.

Dewey, J., and Bently, A. F. *Knowing and the known.* Boston: Beacon Press, 1949.

Lawson, C. A. Language. Communication and biological organization. In L. Bertalanffy and A. E. Rapoport (Eds.), *General systems*, 8: 107–115, 1963.

Latil, P. de. *Thinking by machine.* Boston: Houghton-Mifflin, 1957.

Maruyama, M. The second cybernetic: Amplifying mutual causal processes. *Amer. Scientist*, 51: 164–180 (June), 1963.

Ruesch, J., and Bateson, G. *Communication, the social matrix of psychiatry.* New York: Norton, 1951.

Weiner, N. *Cybernetics.* New York: Wiley, 1948.

4. ON LANGUAGE

Birdwhistell, R. L. Paralanguage: 25 years after Sapir. In H. Brosin (Ed.), *Lectures on experimental psychiatry.* Pittsburgh: University of Pittsburgh Press, 1961.

Bloomfield, L. *Language.* New York: Holt, Rinehart & Winston, 1933.

Duckert, A. R. The acquisition of a word. *Lang. and Speech*, 7: 107–111, 1964.

Harris, Z. S. *Structural linguistics.* Chicago: Univ. of Chicago Press, 1951.

Harris, Z. S. Discourse analysis. *Language*, 28: 1, 1952.

Joos, M. Description of language design. *J. Acoust. Soc. Amer.*, 22: 701–708, Nov., 1950.

Mandelbaum, D. G. (Ed.) *Selected writings of Edward Sapir.* Berkeley: Univ. of Calif. Press, 1949.

McQuown, N. A. Linguistic transcription and specification of psychiatric interview materials. *Psychiat.*, 20: 79, 1957.

Osgood, C. E. (Ed.) *Psycholinguistics: A survey of theory and research problems.* Baltimore: Waverly Press, 1954.

Pike, K. L. *Language.* Glendale, Calif.: Summer Inst. of Linguistics, 1954.

Pittenger, R. E., and Smith, H. L., Jr. A basis for some contributions of linguistics to psychiatry. *Psychiat.*, 20: 1, Feb., 1957.

Trager, G. L. Paralanguage: A first approximation. In W. M. Austin (Ed.), *Studies in linguistics 13*: 1 and 2 Spring, 1958.

5. ON KINESICS, POSTURE AND TACTILE COMMUNICATION

Birdwhistell, R. L. Contribution of linguistic-kinesic studies to the understanding of schizophrenia. In A. Auerback (Ed.), *Schizophrenia.* New York: Ronald, 1959.

Birdwhistell, R. L. Kinesic analysis in the investigation of the emotions. *Address:* Amer. Ass. Adv. Sci., Dec., 1960.

Birdwhistell, R. L. Kinesics and communication. In E. Carpenter and M. McLuhan (Eds.), *Explorations in communication.* Boston: Beacon Press, 1960.

Birdwhistell, R. L. Body signals: Normal and pathological. *Address:* Amer. Psychol. Ass., Sept., 1963.

Charney, E. J. Postural configurations in psychotherapy. (In press.)

Darwin, C. R. *The expression of emotion in man and animals.* New York: Philosophical Library, 1955.

Deutsch, F. Analytic posturology. *Psychoanal. quart.,* 21: 196–214, 1952.

Frank, L. K. Tactile communication. In E. Carpenter and M. McLuhan (Eds.), *Explorations in communication.* Boston: Beacon Press, 1960.

Hewes, G. W. The anthropology of posture. *Scientific Amer., 196:* 123–132, Feb., 1957.

Scheflen, A. E. Communication and regulation in psychotherapy. *Psychiat.,* 26: 126, May, 1963.

Scheflen, A. E. On the significance of posture in communication systems. *Psychiat., 27:* 316, 1964.

6. ON MEANING OR SEMIOTICS

Bar-Hillel, Y. Logical syntax and semantics. *Language, 20:* 230–277, Apr.– June, 1954.

Carnap, R. *Meaning and necessity.* Chicago: Univ. of Chicago Press, 1947.

Ogden, C. K., and Richards, J. A. *The meaning of meaning.* London: Routledge, 1949.

Sebeok, T. A., Hayes, A. S., and Bateson, M. C. *Approaches to semiotics.* London: Mouton and Co., 1964.

7. ON RESEARCH IN COMMUNICATIONAL BEHAVIOR IN PSYCHOTHERAPY

Bellak, L. An experimental exploration of the psychoanalytic process. *Psychoanal. quart.,* 25: 385, 1956.

Chapple, E. D., and Lindemann, E. Clinical implications of interaction rates in psychiatric interviews. *Appl. Anthro., 1:* 1–11, 1942.

DeMascio, A., Boyd, R. W., Greenblatt, M., and Solomon, H. C. The psychiatric interview. *Dis. nerv. sys., 16:* 2–7, 1955.

Eldred, S. H., and Price, D. B. A linguistic evaluation of feeling states in psychotherapy. *Psychiat., 21:* 115–121, 1958.

Jaffe, J. Language of the dyad. *Psychiat., 21:* 249–258, 1958.

Gottschalk, L. A. (Ed.) *Comparative psycholinguistic analysis of two psychotherapeutic interviews.* New York: International Universities, 1961.

Gottschalk, L. A., and Gleser, G. C. Distinguishing characteristics of the verbal communications of schizophrenic patients. In *Disorders of communication*, Vol. XLII. Research Publ. ARNMD, 1964.

Pittenger, R. E., Hockett, C. F., and Danehy, J. J. *The first five minutes*. Ithaca, New York: Paul Martineau, 1960.

Pennicker, R. E. Microscopic analysis of sound tape. *Psychiat.*, *23*: 347, Nov., 1960.

Shakow, D. The recorded psychoanalytic interview as an objective approach to research in psychoanalysis. *Psychoanal. quart.*, *29*: 82, 1960.

Strupp, H. H. A multidimensional system for analyzing psychotherapeutic techniques. *Psychiat.*, *20*: 293–312, 1957.

8. ON MOTION PICTURE RECORDING FOR RESEARCH

Michaelis, A. R. *Research films in biology, anthropology, psychology, and medicine.* New York: Academic, 1955.

Spottiswoode, R. *Film and its techniques.* Berkeley and Los Angeles: Univ. of Calif. Press, 1951.

Van Vlack, J. D. The research document film. *J. Society of Motion Picture and Television Engineers*, Spring, 1964.

CHAPTER 27

The Communication Process
in Psychotherapy

Frank Auld

Scheflen's paper is not the first one to be concerned with the role of non-verbal responses in the therapeutic interaction. But it is the first to demonstrate convincingly the importance of such nonverbal responses. Since reading Scheflen's paper I have learned about other equally fascinating studies of the gestures and facial expressions of patients and therapists—the studies of Mahl (1967) and Ekman (1967); when I first read Scheflen's paper, however, the findings he presented came to me as fresh and surprising.

I had been accustomed to hearing and reading arguments for the importance of nonverbal communication phrased about like this: "Obviously you are misguided to study typescripts of psychotherapy interviews, because everybody knows that you can't tell what a person means unless you can hear the inflections he speaks in." (Here the critic would add some made-up example to buttress his argument. He did not consider it necessary to find a real-life instance, from actual therapeutic interchanges.) "But even more important," the critic would continue, "you can't see the patient's gestures. And we all know how important *they* are."

In response to such an argument, one could only sputter helplessly, "Well, I do seem to have been able to find some regularities in the behavior of therapist and patient in spite of all the difficulties you mention." There is really no arguing with a person who doesn't need facts to justify his position. Thus, I approached Scheflen's paper with considerable skepticism, and, when I discovered that he had taken the trouble to gather data and that he had presented a convincing case for the im-

---

This chapter is a discussion-commentary, written especially for the present volume, of Chapter 26: "Natural History Method in Psychotherapy," by A. E. Scheflen.

portance of nonverbal cues in the therapeutic communication, I was delighted.

How is it that Scheflen can provide us with facts where none were available before? He can do this because he has taken the methodology of linguistics, developed for the study of ordinary spoken language, and has applied it to the larger, interactive-communicative structures of the psychotherapeutic interaction—including the nonverbal structures. In doing this, Scheflen had the close collaboration of Ray Birdwhistell, a cultural anthropologist with a thorough training in linguistics. Applying linguistic methodology to the behavior of therapist and patient is by no means a mechanical task; though the methods are already at hand, the categories are not. Scheflen and Birdwhistell had to invent them.

The methodology of linguistics is based on the principle that actions taken by an observer to be equivalent in significance perform the same communicative function, i.e., are signals which can be substituted for each other. It is also assumed that when two actions of a person lead an observer to respond in one way to the first action and in a different way to the other, the two actions are not substitutable but differ in some way that is critical to their communicative function. It is further assumed that communicative units are hierarchically arranged, with smaller units functioning as constituents of larger ones and the larger ones providing context in which the smaller units must be understood. Application of these principles requires the investigator to observe communicators (both senders and receivers) who are familiar with the language, and it requires also a functional analysis of the interactive behavior of these communicators. As I was reading Scheflen's paper, I was often struck by the similarity of his approach to the approach of the investigator of learning, or of perception, who attempts to make a functional analysis of the behavior of his subjects.

In pondering Scheflen's approach, I wondered whether the idiosyncratic elements in the communicative transaction would not give him trouble or at least necessitate some modification of his method at critical junctures. This method has been designed to discover the way of communicating that is common among all members of a "language community," i.e., among all who understand and respond similarly to a shared stock of signals, but the phenomena of neurotic distortions in understanding and of neurotic transference presuppose a departure— in the therapist-patient dyad—from understandings of the culture-wide "language community," and yet a consistent adherence by the patient to *his* way of misunderstanding. In other words, within the language community of a particular dyad, acts of the therapist have a particular meaning to this patient which they ordinarily are not considered to have; within the framework of the particular dyad, at that particular point in time, there is no way empirically to identify these distortions. It is precisely because the therapist keeps as his reference point the understandings of the larger, culture-wide language community that he can recognize the neurotic distortions and can, bit by bit, demonstrate these distortions to the patient.

To give an example: A 35-year-old man, who entered psychotherapy because of depression, anxiety, and various physical complaints, at one point in the psychotherapy said to his therapist: "I feel you're looking at me with eyes that are hard, that lack compassion. You remember, I told you before . . . when I first came to you . . . that I thought you looked at me that way. I realize that it's unlikely that the way your eyes actually look changes from time to time; yet I *feel* that the expression in them changes, and right now I feel that you're looking at me without compassion." (This striking comment, we may note, was not considered by the therapist to be evidence of psychotic ideation—rather, to be a striking example of a neurotic distortion.) In analyzing the interactive behavior of patient and therapist in this example, the present author would not attempt to discover the supposed changes in expression of the therapist's eyes which led the patient to judge that the therapist was looking at him with harshness. For even if there were some identifiable physical characteristic of the therapist's eyes that could be correlated with the patient's judgment of "harshness"—such as, say, a narrowing of the pupils, or a crinkling of the skin in the corners of the eyes, or a fixation of therapist's eyes on patient's forehead—we should not have discovered, necessarily, a way in which the therapist was attempting consciously or unconsciously to give signals to the patient. The therapist's act may have been only expressive—in the sense that Mahl (1967) has used "expressive" to distinguish acts that are not communicative from gestures that are intended as communications, or the therapist's act may have been uncorrelated with any relevant mental activity—may only have indicated, for example, how much sleep he had the preceding night. The patient's seizing upon this piece of the therapist's behavior as a sign of the therapist's harshness could be utterly without relevance, therefore, to any organized interactive, communicative transaction between them, despite the patient's consistency in assigning meaning to it.

Is not the patient in such an instance behaving like Skinner's "superstitious" pigeon? Primed to expect harshness from the therapist, the patient will accept any sign which has the slightest plausibility and respond to this act in terms of his expectation. So much the better if there is a slight element of validity in the patient's excessive, inappropriate response; one would expect that a person sensitive to harshness will magnify any actions that hint of less than overwhelming acceptance.

Despite the reservation I have just expressed, I believe that the method Scheflen has presented will be extremely valuable to psychotherapy researchers. The problems of transference do not destroy the value of the method; they only make clear that the method needs to be extended and modified to take care of these problems. With such extensions and modifications the method will become a powerful way of showing these very distortions in communication, which according to psychoanalytic theory are at the heart of the neurotic process.

IMPORTANCE OF THEORY

In my judgment, Scheflen's work demonstrates the importance of theory in guiding the search for new principles, making possible new discoveries, and arriving at new understandings. Scheflen's paper emphasizes the methodological side—the importance of linguistic methodology, the importance of analyzing behavior in terms of its natural shapes, the importance of observing naturally occurring instances of the therapeutic process. Not discussed in the paper, but equally important, is the contribution that Scheflen's thorough grounding in psychoanalytic theory made to his joint work with Birdwhistell. For example, the importance of the therapist's "tactical shifting" could hardly have been suspected without a sharp awareness of the importance of *resistance* in the therapeutic process. When the patient could not bear to confront his own affects—his own wishes, his own fears—he was in the habit of "not acting like a patient," of avoiding the self-investigative activity that therapists of a psychoanalytic persuasion expect, or hope for, in their patients. And this behavior of the patient instigated the therapist to tell the patient, by various nonverbal signs, that she wished him to get down to business.

The most powerful investigative methodology is useless without a mind to guide it, to pick out those aspects of the complex situation under observation that are likely to prove significant. Much of the history of content-analysis of psychotherapy attests, as Murray and I pointed out (1955), to the sterility of a mechanical application of methodology to any items that happen to be handy. Mere counts of adjectives and adverbs, of personal pronouns, of references to past and to present, or of new words and words used before, have not led investigators very far. The method of linguistics, which is in effect a species of the functional analysis of behavior, allows us to demonstrate functional relationships, provided we have chosen categories which will yield such relationships. The relationships discovered in this way will be related to other relationships, forming part of a comprehensive, powerful theoretic system, when we have chosen the categories wisely.

THE VALUE OF COLLABORATION

We could not have a better instance of the value of collaboration. To their joint work, Scheflen brought (among other things) a thorough knowledge of psychoanalysis, a dedication to searching investigation of the therapeutic process, a willingness to have his own activity as a therapist made the object of investigation. Birdwhistell brought a grounding in the methodology of linguistics, long experience in applying this methodology to the nonverbal aspects of face-to-face communication, and the objectivity of the anthropologist, who tries dispassionately to understand what is going on without allowing his likes and dislikes to warp his observations and interpretations.

The fruitfulness of this collaboration has a lesson, I believe, for psychological research in general. Psychoanalysts have been in possession of a fertile theory, while lacking the methodological skill to investigate its implications effectively; social scientists, including academic psychologists, have had the needed methodological skills but usually have lacked pertinent and powerful theories. It is the combination of fertile theory and appropriate methodology that leads to effective scientific work.

STUDY OF BOTH PARTICIPANTS IN THE INTERACTION

Scheflen's work brings out clearly the fully interactive, mutually influencing nature of the therapeutic dyad. Many previous investigators have been disposed to direct their attention to either the therapist or the patient, neglecting the part played by the other. Adherents of the so-called behavior therapy approach seem inclined to consider the therapist a person who is programmed to provide reinforcements and nonreinforcements to the patient, rather than an individual who is participating in a human interaction and may himself be influenced by it. The psychoanalytic theory of therapeutic technique, as expressed by some authors, similarly neglects the therapist's participation as a real person. A necessary corrective to this omission is seen in the discussion of analysts like Reich (1951), Weigert (1954), and Tower (1956), who have written about "countertransference." On the other hand, some researchers on client-centered therapy have given so much attention to the therapist's activity that they have barely noticed that the patient does specific things, that his "growth" and increased self-acceptance involve specific responses to specific actions of his therapist.

Scheflen did give equal attention to both participants, and did make the assumption that these people are fully interactive and mutually influencing. Refusing to abandon this point of view until he had pushed it to its limits, he discovered that much that would otherwise have gone unnoticed came to light. For example, it looks as though the therapist (in the dyad which Scheflen studied intensively) backs off from pressing the patient for more open communication and for more direct confrontation of feeling when she senses that the patient has had as much stress as he can bear. On the other hand, the patient responds to the therapist's encouragement of, and demand for, more open expression by attempting to be more expressive—until the therapist lets up the pressure.

EMPHASIS ON GESTALTS

In his paper Scheflen lays great stress on the context in which behavior occurs, on the organized, patterned properties of behavior. At first blush, such stress seems unnecessary and overdone. One asks: Doesn't everyone believe in studying behavior in meaningful units, not in units that are torn out of their proper setting? Didn't B. F. Skinner himself show great concern for the functional analysis of behavior and for choosing a concept ("the reflex") that would have natural, appropriate boundaries? However, as one scans the scene of current research activity, one notices that in fact researchers often neglect the gestalt properties of the interactions they are studying. Furthermore, reductionism —particularly physicalistic reductionism—is running rampant in American psychology. Concepts that can be connected with physiological observations are frequently thought to be "more real" than concepts that are inferred from reports of experience or from gross-behavioral observations, even if such physicalistic concepts do not fit naturally with the shape of interpersonal behaviors. The habit of investigating isolated response systems, out of the context of the organism's adaptive task in the situations that are studied, is prevalent. Battalions of researchers do studies of nonsense-syllable learning without ever asking why the subjects agreed to participate in the experiments in the first place and how this may make a difference in their responses. Studies of so-called behavior therapy are made in which the subjects learn to handle rats, submitting themselves to this learning process in order to meet the course requirements of introductory psychology, and the investigator never seems curious about the influence of this motivational context on the behavior that is observed. Studies having very little relevance, either practical or theoretical, to the problems of human adaptive functioning, are made mostly because these particular studies can conveniently be carried out; there is apparently the hope that somehow all of these fragments will one day provide material for the framing of a new science.

But how is one to know what is an adequate gestalt for the purposes of behavioral research? It seems to me than one can know this only by insisting on a comprehensive theory of the domain that is under investigation, allowing oneself to be guided by such a theory in carrying out the investigation, and then judging, from the results of the study, whether the concepts chosen do in fact slice the world of observation in a way that is helpful to scientific explanation. The concepts that will seem natural after the results are in are the concepts that lead to valid predictions, the concepts that are productive of hypotheses about observable behaviors.

SUMMARY

Scheflen has made a beginning toward elucidating the role that nonverbal behaviors play in the communication between therapist and patient. He is able to make this contribution because, with the collaboration of Ray Birdwhistell, he has brought the methodology of linguistics to bear on the communicative process in psychotherapy, and because he has been able to apply the insights of psychoanalysis effectively. The fruitful collaboration of Scheflen and Birdwhistell not only shows the value of a collaboration in which the members of the team have complementary skill and knowledge; it also demonstrates strikingly the importance, for therapy research, of both *theory* and *methodology*. Finally, Scheflen has made two points well worth making: that the therapeutic transaction is truly interactive, involving both parties; and that the investigator of this process would do well to discover truly natural units, gestalts, in which to cast his theory of the therapeutic process.

REFERENCES

Auld, F., Jr., & Murray E. J. Content-analysis studies of psychotherapy. *Psychological Bulletin*, 1955, 52, 377–395.
Ekman, P. Communication through non-verbal behavior. In John M. Shlien

(Ed.), *Research in psychotherapy*. Vol. 3. Washington, D.C.: American Psychological Association, 1967.

Mahl, G. F. Gestures and body movements in interviews. In John M. Shlien (Ed.), *Research in psychotherapy*. Vol. 3. Washington, D.C.: American Psychological Association, 1967.

Reich, A. On counter-transference. *International Journal of Psycho-Analysis*, 1951, *32*, 25–31.

Tower, L. E. Countertransference. *Journal of the American Psychoanalytic Association*, 1956, *4*, 224–255.

Weigert, E. Counter-transference and self-analysis of the psychoanalyst. *International Journal of Psycho-Analysis*, 1954, *35*, 242–246.

CHAPTER 28

Natural History Method— A Frontier Method

Norman A. McQuown

The rediscovery of what Albert E. Scheflen terms the natural history method in his article "Natural History Method in Psychotherapy: Communicational Research" is a phenomenon typical of the scientific frontier, and particularly of the often belated recognition, in a given field of scientific endeavor, of the frontier nature of a particular discipline. Frequently, after decades of sporadic, intuitive delving, of half-blind groping in the unimagined depths, some few workers reach such a level of frustration and dissatisfaction with the methods previously employed in such delving that they decide to undertake a boot-straps operation: they embark on a step-by-step exploration of those depths, employing fully explicit discovery-conducive frames and fully specified discovery-facilitating procedures, in an open-ended series of fully retraceable discovery-producing steps. The provisional, ever-expanding, open-ended result is a natural history of the phenomena to the study of which that discipline directs itself. The natural history method in scientific research is, accordingly, constantly being rediscovered.

Although such rediscovery constitutes a point of departure for Dr. Scheflen's article on communicational research within the context of psychotherapy, his article attempts much more: it attempts a preliminary map of the general characteristics of the structure of the behavior undergoing description and a concomitant outline of research methods adequate to such description. He reminds us that research in psychotherapy focuses, not merely on intrapsychic processes, but also, and necessarily simultaneously, on social processes and that all inferences as

---

This chapter is a discussion-commentary, written especially for the present volume, of Chapter 26: "Natural History Method in Psychotherapy," by A. E. Scheflen.

to both derive from observations made on external behavior. He points out, further, that such behavior, whether viewed as a process of inter-action or as the result of such interaction (or communication) is both highly complex and highly organized and that its study will depend on the development of similarly highly complex and similarly highly or-ganized research methods.

Among such research methods he outlines one which he labels con-text analysis, a method for ferreting out systematically, within a com-plex, highly organized structure, the parts, their interrelations, and their integration into the complex whole. Context analysis necessarily limits in some fashion, initially in accordance with some arbitrarily chosen criterion (such as a communication channel, a cultural concern, or a social situation), ultimately in accordance with the structural limits between the various systems which context analysis uncovers, the field of behaviors to which its methods are applied. Context analysis requires as its initial tool a highly structured meta-system whose components are so chosen as to match in the number and complexity of their interrela-tions those of the behaviors for which they are to furnish a description, and which are so flexible as to permit their rearrangement in a way that will ultimately match the arrangement of the elements in the system of behavior whose structure is to be described. Such meta-systems must be so flexible as to be extensible or contractable, as the requirements of the behavioral system under description demand, and so adaptable as ultimately to provide a perfect diagram of the structure points and point interrelations of the behavioral system to which context-analytic methods are applied. In a given social group, whose members in their day-to-day behavior single out the units representative of cultural con-trasts and trace out the web of the interrelations of such units in the larger cultural system, communication is on occasion effected only be-cause such systems are "organizations of abstractable structural units, standard, and shared by" participants in a common culture. Applied to a particular medium of communication, context analysis tries "to recon-struct . . . the basic ground rules, the units, and the arrangement char-acteristic of this institutionalized and transmissible interaction."

Scheflen states his assumptions with respect to the nature of the medium through which communication takes place:

(1) It "has a regular, ultimately predictable structure consisting of defi-nite units arranged in particular ways";
(2) Such "structural units of communication have a regular set of com-ponents and organization which must be performed the same way (within a given range) by all members of an ingroup";

(3) These "structural units, consisting of communicational behaviors, are themselves merely components of larger units in a hierarchy of levels";

(4) "Institutionalized activities like psychotherapy use the basic communicational system of the culture modified in certain specialized but lawful ways";

(5) "All participants have learned and know (mostly without consciousness) the system of communication for the groups in which they have membership";

(6) "The communicative system of any type of group can be abstracted by context analysis."

These assumptions clearly make the method which Scheflen calls context analysis central to the analysis of communication. What then does the method consist of? Scheflen describes four steps involved in the application of the method to communication as recorded in sound motion pictures: (1) recording and transcribing; (2) ascertaining the structural units; (3) synthesizing the larger picture to determine meaning or function; and (4) setting up the natural history experiment.

At present, a sound motion picture is the means of recording the speech and body-motion components of a communicative interaction. (In the near future, it will doubtless be a videotape.) If, as Scheflen suggests, "the communicational system uses all the sensory modalities," a full record of all its components would involve a full battery of recording devices capable of giving a full account of input and output through all of these modalities. Furthermore, if visceral events are integral with those externally observable, a full battery of visceral taps would provide a full record of visceral changes correlatable with, and on occasion furnishing clues to, externally observable events: "This record of the interaction must be complete." Clearly, these requirements for mechanical or electronic recording place demands on currently available equipment which current technology cannot satisfy. But if technology is to supply the indispensable starting point for context analysis, it must become cognizant of the nature and scope of these requirements and devote the necessary effort to developing the necessary recording tools.

Transcribing, the second part of Scheflen's first step, makes demands which are even harder to satisfy. He insists that "not only must we record all of the scene we wish to study, but we must include all the communicative elements in the analysis." Recording requires only a mechanical or electronic means for registering the behavior. Transcribing requires the isolation of the structural elements and the determination of their interrelations, level-by-level in all of the media and in all of the systems of communicational behavior manifested in them. It further requires the conventional assignment of symbology representative of elements and interrelations and the setting down of such symbology in such a way as to be both expeditious and permanent. Even when such isolation of elements and determination of interrelations is limited to only one level of one system manifest in one medium and is only preliminary and provisional there, the procedures necessarily used are part and parcel of those involved in the full-scale definitive analysis and representation of the total system. The first half of the second part of Scheflen's first step involves, then, all the remaining steps, in a constantly recurring dialectic. Step 4, the natural history experiment, cannot even be set up until the first three steps have been carefully (and exhaustively) carried through.

In practical terms, if the behaviors of which we undertake an analysis are English-language behaviors produced by Americans of a certain social level, performed in accordance with the cultural rules privy to certain subgroups within that social level, in order successfully to carry out the transcribing substep of Scheflen's procedures for context analysis, we need to know more than the philologists and linguists in all our departments of English in all our universities have thus far been able to tell us about the internal structure and salient differences of the regional and social varieties of American English, more about the structure of American society and the salient differences between levels, and more about the cultural characteristics peculiar to particular subgroups and the salient differences from group to group within these levels, than our sociologists have thus far been able to discover for us. The successful isolation of a particular element and the successful determination of its interrelations with another on one level of one system manifest in one medium may well require the previous linguistic structural placement, within a particular dialect and cross-dialectally, of that element and the social and cultural placement of the individual speaker who makes use of it in his speech. Even step 4, the experimental introduction of such an element into an otherwise known situation, could be at best inconclusive, at worst utterly fruitless, in the absence of such knowledge of its placement in the linguistic structural and sociocultural matrices. What is now true of the linguistic portion of the speech medium in the communication package is, of course, even truer of the other portions of that package where only the first attempts at structural description are currently available, and the establishment of socially and culturally correlating norms has not even been begun. The *prior* requirements imposed on the raw materials to which the natural history method is to be applied are severe.

As though this were not enough, Scheflen insists that we exercise no *prior* selection among the raw materials to which we apply the method: "Just as we must not decide a priori what to leave out of the film, we must not select arbitrarily what can be omitted from the analysis and synthesis." Judgments as to relevance are results of research, not guides to prior depuration of the raw materials on which research is performed.

Minor problems are created by the very complexity of the graphic representation of the transcriptions of the multileveled, multichanneled behaviors produced from the recordings by the full (often microscopic) representation of these behaviors on a time graph. Such a time graph helps us to locate these behaviors in their succession and simultaneity. But Scheflen is careful to point out that sequence or simultaneity are clues to, not determinants of, structure and system. Structures may manifest themselves at particular times and in particular places, but structures as such are neither synchronic nor diachronic: they are achronic. How they are to be uncovered is considered in Scheflen's step 2.

A structural unit, says Scheflen, "has: (1) a given set of component parts; (2) a definite organization; and (3) specific location in a larger system." Every structural unit, then, faces two ways: inward, toward its components, and outward, toward the larger matrix of which it is, as a unit, an undifferentiated component. Rephrasing this, Scheflen says that a structural unit is recognized by three criteria: (1) its components; (2) the arrangement of these components; and (3) the neighborhoods or contexts in which the unit occurs. These criteria are general and apply to structural units on any level, in any system, in any modality, or in any combination of levels, systems, or modalities. Some structural units are so *sui generis* that they may be identified upon inspection, even in isolation; others are so ambiguous or multivalent as to be recognizable only in context and to be differentially identifiable only in different contexts. Context "analysis," accordingly, involves both *analysis* and *synthesis* (looking at a unit both as a set of intra- and as a set of extra-related components). Structural units, regarded both inward and outward, both upward and downward, participate in a larger arrangement which constitutes a hierarchy of levels.

The specific methods leading to the identification of a structural unit derive directly from its three characteristics: its components, the organization of the components, and the wider contexts in which it occurs. *Delineating* establishes which components invariably occur together. *Contrasting* establishes which components are not interdependent in this way. *Testing-in-context* establishes which context(s) (or shifts in context) may regularly accompany the occurrence of each tentative unit.

All units that have the same components and arrangement and that occur in the same situations are merely *different* performances or occurrences of the *same* structural unit. Units that have similar but nonidentical components or arrangements but that occur in analogously different contexts with the *same* effect are, on a particular level, substitutable for each other in communication. Units that have neither the same components nor arrangements and occur in the same contexts with *different* effects are not only not substitutable for each other on any level—they constitute *different* units. These three situations are the ones to which linguists have applied the labels *identity, complementary distribution,* and *contrast.* A variant of the second situation, in which units with nonidentical components or arrangements may *freely interchange* with each other in the same contexts with, *on that level,* the same effect, constitutes an instance of a situation which linguists have labeled *free variation.*

Neither variant of the second situation is generally viable: both complementary distribution and free variation are level-limited within a particular structure, or situation-limited in a wider context. Put somewhat differently, *any* difference on *any* level between a pair of units is potentially exploitable, either on another level of the same system or in a cross-cutting system which employs the same medium.

Relations of identity and of contrast, on the other hand, *are* more generally viable. Differences among the various manifestations of what is the *same* unit (both as to components and as to arrangement) are not, on *that* level and in *that* system, exploitable for purposes of contrast. Differences (both as to components and as to arrangement) between two (or among several) units are not, on *that* level and in *that* system, ignorable; they must be utilized as instances of contrast.

With respect both to *delineating* and to *contrasting,* Scheflen observes that delineated units which contrast on a particular level are likely to be co-components in a larger structural unit on the next level.

Testing in context requires an identification of context; it is often possible to make such an identification in terms of some restricted portion of it. If the tentative unit to be so tested occurs each time in the same context so identified and does not otherwise occur, we have established the *inter*dependence of the unit and its context, on the one hand, and, on a lower level, the *in*dependent existence, at least, of the tentative unit.

Referring to the apparent great complexity of microrecordings of communicative elements, Scheflen points out that such complexity is apparent only if all such elements are treated as structurally co-equal. When, however, their packaging and hierarchical organization are taken into consideration, large packages, and even whole levels, may, on occasion and for particular purposes, be handled as units and their internal complexity bypassed. The general principles of analysis and synthesis are valid for units of any size. When units of a particular size prove to be explanatorily inadequate, however, one must proceed either (1) to break them up into their components and search for differential correlations for different components or (2) to look at the larger structures within which the units of this size differentially participate in the hopes of a rebound which will force an internal differentiation of such units. In either case the result of such forced internal differentiation may reveal either (1) greater internal systemic complexity than previously suspected or (2) the involvement in such new internally differentiated units of cross-cutting systems which make use of selected components of such units for their own manifestation. All such units, large or small, single-system, or cross-systemic, are standardized, behaviorally repetitive, quickly recognizable, and immediately transcribable. The price of effective communication is precisely the enforced employment of such preexisting and prerecognized units. Creative inventiveness may flourish, and individual personalities may freely express themselves, but only if they are willing to pay this price. Those who are unable or unwilling are inescapably intuition-bound and inevitably tongue-tied.

In proceeding to his step 3, Scheflen makes a rough distinction between *immediate, mediate,* and *remote* contexts. Units may be tested within the context of the larger units of the next level above, among these and those of a further higher level, or among these and those of still higher levels. These are very rough distinctions, and the ultimate determinants of the length of the context chain are, on the one hand, the nature of the unit and of its relations to more inclusive (or less inclusive) units, and on the other, the detail and precision with which other context-providing units and systems have been described. The search for the larger picture is once again part-and-parcel of the same procedure that was pursued within narrower limits. In summarizing the procedures, Scheflen observes: "In this way we synthesize *upward,* level by level in successive contexts. . . ." Since one inevitably plunges into the *middle* of a cultural structure, not knowing where the bottom is, it might be suggested that the progression resulting from the application of the method of context analysis is both upward and downward, both outward and inward, "until the multiple events of an interaction come together as components of a single overall unit."

Having reached his goal (the provisional establishment of the outlines of a cultural structure: the identification of its units and the specification of their interrelations and overall integration), Scheflen now suggests, at last, that experimental manipulation of our postulated units and relations may give us clues as to their more precise identification and specification. At this point too, statistical manipulation of structure points and structural relations might furnish additional clues as to points at which to apply anew the natural history method.

Careful pursuit of the full consequences of Scheflen's contentions with respect to substantive prerequisites and methodological procedures will provide a new and useful breadth to the description of the materials of communicative activity and will make such materials available not only to those interested in research in psychotherapy but also to those who engage in research in other kinds of human communicative activity. It will, finally, break down stereotypy in research styles and will, inevitably, lead to a new fertility in the communication sciences.

CHAPTER 29

A Theory of Personality Change

Eugene T. Gendlin

After a few pages which state two main problems and two observations, a theory of personality change will be presented. The theory is another step in the continuing work on "experiencing" (Gendlin, 1957, 1962*b*; Gendlin and Zimring, 1955). The theory of experiencing provides a frame of reference in which theoretical considerations are viewed in a new way.

A theory requires terms, defined words with which to specify observations, and a formulation of a chain of theoretical hypotheses. The theory presented here is developed within this basic structure, and special notice should be given to the new terms which are introduced and defined. These terms are pointed out and numbered. (We can have a genuine theory only with carefully defined terms, and only by using defined terms can we later modify, improve, and extend theory.)

PROBLEMS AND OBSERVATIONS

In most theories, the static content-and-structure aspects of personality are primary, and therefore personality change is an especially difficult problem. The present theoretical frame of reference is especially suited to account for change, since it employs concepts that apply to the experiencing process, and to the relationships between that process and content aspects of personality.

Author's note: I am grateful to Malcolm A. Brown for many helpful and clarifying discussions, which greatly aided the process of writing this chapter, and to Dr. Sidney M. Jourard, Marilyn Geist, Dr. William Wharton, Joe T. Hart, David Le Roy, and Ruth Nielson for their valuable comments and editorial help.

This chapter was voted, by the Editorial Board of the present volume, as one of the creative developments in psychotherapy, 1958–1968. From Philip Worchel & Donn Byrne (Eds.) *Personality Change.* New York: John Wiley & Sons, Inc., 1964.

Personality theories have chiefly been concerned with the factors that determine and explain different individuals' personalities as they are, and the factors which have brought about the given personality. What is called personality maintains its character despite circumstances. Aspects of an individual fail to puzzle us if his current situation explains them. We do not even attribute it to his personality when an individual shows all sorts of undesirable behavior under overwhelmingly bad circumstances, or when he becomes likable and secure under the influence of events which (as we say) would make almost anybody likable and secure. What we do attribute to personality is the reverse: when an individual remains likable and secure under overwhelmingly bad circumstances, and when an individual remains afraid and in pain despite apparent opportunities and good luck. Thus, it could be said that, far from explaining personality change, our theories have been endeavoring to explain and define personality as that which tends not to change when one would expect change.

To some extent this view of personality as factors which resist change is justified. We usually think of a person as involving identity and continuity through time. However, the contents and patterns in the theories are a *type of explanatory concept* which renders change impossible by definition. The structure of personality (in theories) is formulated in such a way that it is said to maintain itself against all new experience which might alter it. The individual is viewed as a structured entity with defined contents. These explanatory concepts can explain only why an individual cannot change.

Personality theory, then, has concentrated upon the factors which explain why an individual is as he is, how he has become so, and how these factors maintain him so, despite circumstances, fortunes, and opportunities. Such explanatory concepts of content and structure tell us what prevents an individual from being changed by experience, what factors will force him forever (by definition) to miss or distort everything that might change him unless (as we commonly say) his personality (somehow) changes first.

Since structure and content do tend to maintain themselves and distort present experience, we can account for personality change only if we can show exactly how this change resistance yields to change.

Theories in the past have not wanted to portray personality change as impossible. On the contrary, the theories assert that change does actually occur. The chief personality theories have sprung from psychotherapy—that is to say (when psychotherapy is successful), from on-going personality change.

Quite paradoxically, as personality change occurs before their eyes and with their participation, therapists find their minds formulating what has been wrong. Even the individual, himself, as he searches into his feelings and expresses these, speaks as if the whole endeavor were to investigate what has been wrong—what has constituted the aspects of his personality which have prevented ordinary adaption and change. And, usually, such an individual becomes aware of much which, he then says, has been true all along but of which he has not been aware.

Thus, psychotherapy regularly gives us this observation of an individual "uncovering" or "becoming aware" of these stubborn contents and his previous inability to be aware of them. So well have the various personality theories formulated these contents and this self-maintaining and censoring structure that, while we have concepts to explain what makes an individual as he is, we cannot formulate how he can change. Yet all the time the individual has been changing just these "uncovered" factors which we formulate in terms of static explanatory contents.[1]

I will now present in more detail the two main ways in which much current formulation of personality makes change appear theoretically impossible. I call these two impossibilities "the repression paradigm," and "the content paradigm."[2]

Since these theories, nevertheless, also assert that change does occur, I will then take up the two main ways in which theories attempt to account for change. I will try to show that theories usually cite two observations: *a feeling process*; and a certain *personal relationship*.

TWO PROBLEMS

The "Repression Paradigm." Most personality theories (in different words and with somewhat different meanings) share what I call the "repression paradigm." They agree that in an individual's early family relations he introjected certain values, according to which he was loved only if he felt and behaved in certain ways. Experiences which contradicted these demands on him came to be "repressed" (Freud), or "denied to awareness" (Rogers), or "not me" (Sullivan). Later, when the individual encounters experiences of this contradicting sort, he must either distort them or remain totally unaware of them. For, were he to notice the contradictory experiences, he would become intolerably anxious. The ego (Freud), or self-concept (Rogers), or self-dynamism (Sullivan), thus basically influences awareness and perception. This influence is termed "resistance" (Freud), or "defensiveness" (Rogers), or "security operation" (Sullivan), and a great deal of behavior is thereby explainable. A personality is as it is, and remains as it is, because it cannot take account of these experiences. Or if, somehow, repression is forcefully lifted and the individual is made to become aware of these experiences, the ego will "lose control," the self will "disintegrate," and intolerable "uncanny emotions" will occur. In psychosis, it is said, the individual is aware of such experiences and the ego or self-organization has indeed broken down.

If the individual needed merely to be reminded, or to have the "repressed" factors called to his notice, he would soon be straightened out. There are always helpful or angry people who attempt this, and many situations grossly demand attention to these factors. The individual, however, represses not only the given factors within him but also anything outside him which would relate to these factors and remind him of them.[3] He misunderstands or reinterprets so as to prevent himself from noticing the aspects of events and persons which would bring these factors to his awareness.

Thus the specific personality structure maintains itself and change is theoretically impossible. Whatever would change the individual in the necessary respects is distorted or goes unnoticed just to that extent and in those respects in which it could lift the repression and change him.

Now, this explanation (shared in some way, as I have tried to indicate, by the major personality theories of the day)[4] is based on the striking way in which the individual during psychotherapy becomes aware of what (so he now says) he has long felt but has not known that he felt. Moreover, the individual realizes how powerfully these previously unaware experiences have affected his feelings and behavior. So many individuals have now reported this that there is no longer much doubt that it is a valid observation. The open question is how we are to formulate it theoretically.

Once we formulate theory along the lines of the repression paradigm, we cannot then blithely turn around and "explain" personality change as a "becoming aware" of the previously repressed. Once we have shown how anything will be distorted which tends to bring these experiences to awareness, we cannot then consider it an explanation to simply assert that personality change is (by definition supposedly impossible) a becoming aware. Change happens. But, to say that is not to offer an explanation—it is only to state the problem. We may take the "repression paradigm" to be one basic aspect of personality change—one of the two basic factors with which this chapter will be concerned. To account for personality change, we will have to account for how this crucial be-coming aware really does occur, and then we will have to go back and reformulate our theory of repression and the unconscious.

The "Content Paradigm." The second basic aspect of personality change (and the second way in which current modes of formulating make change theoretically impossible) concerns the view of personality as made up of various "contents." By "contents" I mean any *defined* enti-ties, whether they are called "experiences," "factors," "S-R bonds," "needs," "drives," "motives," "appraisals," "traits," "self-concepts," "anx-ieties," "motivational systems," "infantile fixations," "developmental fail-ures," or whatever.

If we are to understand personality change, we must understand how these personality constituents can change in nature.

To account for this change in the nature of contents, we need a type of definition (explanatory constructs) which also can change. We can-not explain *change* in the nature of the *content* when our theory spe-cifically defines personality only as content. Such theory can formulate what needs to be changed, and later it can also formulate what has changed, and into what it has changed; but it will remain theoretically unexplained how such change is possible, so long as all our explana-tions are in terms of concepts of this or that defined content.

We require some kind of more basic personality variable to formulate an account of how, under what conditions, and through what process, change in the nature of contents can occur.

Thus, for example, chemistry defines the elements in terms of more basic activities of electrons and protons, and thereby we can account for the subatomic processes by which elements engage in chemical change reactions, and through which an element can be bombarded with subatomic particles and turned into a different element. Without these concepts, which view elements as motions of something more basic, we could not explain the chemical and atomic *change* we observe, nor operationally study and define the conditions under which it occurs. We could state only that at t_1 the test tube had certain contents A, B, while at t_2 the contents were C, D. Only if A, B, C, D, are not themselves the *ultimate* explanatory concepts can we expect to explain changes from one to another. And so it is with personality change. If our ultimate explanatory constructs are "contents," we cannot explain the change in the nature of just these contents.

Our conclusion here is not simply that defined contents of personality do not exist. Rather, it is that if we define personality as contents and in no further, more basic way, then we cannot expect to use the same concepts to explain just how these contents change. And, inasmuch as it will have been just these contents which define the personality (and the respects in which change must occur if it is to be important personality change), exactly this theoretically impossible task is posed when personality theories come to explain change.

For example, during psychotherapy the patient finally comes to realize these essential contents (they will be conceptualized in whatever the vocabulary of the particular theory the psychotherapist uses). He realizes now that he has been full of "hostility," or that he has felt and acted from "partial, fixated sexual desires," or that he "hates his father," or that he is "passive-dependent," or was "never loved as a child." "Now what?," he asks. How do you change such contents? No way is given. The fact that these contents actually do change is our good fortune. The theories explain the personality in terms of these defined contents, these "experiences," or "needs," or "lacks." The theories cannot explain how these contents melt and lose their character to become something of a different character. Yet they do.

Our second basic problem of personality change, then, is this "content paradigm." The question is, "In what way should the nature of personality definitions change so that we can arrive at a means of defining that will fit the process of change in personality contents?" In answering this, we will describe something more basic or ultimate than defined contents. Then we will consider how defined contents arise in this more ultimate personality process.

TWO UNIVERSAL OBSERVATIONS OF PERSONALITY CHANGE

Now that two basic *problems* of personality change have been stated (becoming aware and change in the nature of contents), we will turn next to two basic *observations* of personality change. In contrast to the aforementioned *theoretical* impossibilities, most theories of personality cite two *observations*, which they assert are nearly always involved in personality change.

1. Major personality change involves some sort of intense affective or feeling process occurring in the individual.

2. Major personality change occurs nearly always in the context of an ongoing personal relationship.

The Feeling Process. When major personality change occurs, intense, emotional, inwardly felt events are usually observed. I would like to give the name "feeling process" to this affective dimension of personality change. The word "feeling" is preferable to "affective," because "feeling" usually refers to something concretely sensed by an individual. In personality change the individual directly feels an inward reworking. His own concepts and constructs become partly unstructured and his felt experiencing at times exceeds his intellectual grasp.

In various contexts it has been noted that major personality change requires not only intellectual or actional operations, but also this felt process. For instance, psychotherapists (of whatever orientation) often discuss the presence or absence of this feeling process in a particular case. They discuss whether the individual, in a given psychotherapy hour, is engaged in "merely" intellectualizing, or whether (as they phrase it) he is "really" engaged in psychotherapy. The former they consider a waste of time or a defense, and they predict[5] that no major personality change will result from it. The latter they consider promising of personality change.

Now, although this difference is universally discussed, it is most often phrased so unclearly, and the words following "merely" ("merely" intellectualizing, defending, avoiding, externalizing, etc.), and the words following "really" ("really" engaged, facing, dealing with) are so undefined that we may as well simply refer to this difference as the difference between "merely" and "really." Although it may not be phrased well, what is always meant or referred to by "really" is a *feeling process* which is absent when something is termed "merely."

A similar distinction between "merely" and "really" is talked about in education: There has always been much concern with the contrast between "mere" rote learnings of facts and "really" learning something (making it one's own, becoming able to "integrate," "apply," and "creatively elaborate" it).

"Really" learning is predicted to result in observable behavior changes, while "mere" rote learning is predicted to result in little (or different) behavior change. The learning process is said to differ in the two instances, depending upon the degree of the individual's "internal motivation," his way of "taking the new material in," his "application of himself to what he learns," his genuine grasp of meanings. These metaphoric phrases indicate that, here again during learning, the difference between "really" and "merely" refers to a certain participation of the individual's feelings in the learning process.

Let me give some further aspects of this observation from psychotherapy.

An Adlerian therapist some years ago told me: "Of course interpretation is not enough. Of course the person doesn't change only because of the wisdoms which the therapist tells him. But no technique really expresses what makes the change itself. The change comes through some kind of emotional digesting; but then you must admit that none of us understand what *that* is."

Therapists often miss this fact. They labor at helping the individual to a better explanation of what is wrong with him, yet, when asked how the individual is to *change* this now clearly explained maladaption, nothing very clear is said. Somehow, knowing his problem, the individual should change, yet *knowing* is not the process of changing.

A good diagnostician, perhaps with the aid of a few psychometric tests, can often give a very accurate and detailed description and explanation of an individual's personality. Therapist and client often both *know*, after such testing and a few interviews, a good deal of what is wrong and what needs to be changed. Quite often, after two years of therapeutic interviews, the description and explanation which was (or could have been) given at the outset appears in retrospect to have been quite accurate. Yet it is clear that there is a major difference between knowing the *conceptual* explanation of personality (which one can devise in a few hours) and the actual *feeling process* of changing (which often requires years). Relatively little has been said about this process,[6] how one may observe and measure it, and just in what theoretical way this feeling process functions to permit personality change.

The Personal Relationship. Just as the feeling process is observed as essential in personality change—while little is said to delineate, observably define, or theoretically account for it—so also the personal relationship is always cited. Can theory define this enormous and critical difference which it makes to the individual to live in relation to another person?

We observe that when the individual thinks about his experiences and emotions by himself, there is often little change. We observe that when he speaks about these things to *some* other people, equally little change occurs. However, when we come to the "therapeutic" or "effective" personal relationship, we say that "suggestion," or "libidinal support," or "approval and reinforcement," or the other person's "therapeutic attitudes," or the "conversation between the two unconsciousnesses," somehow obviates the factors which otherwise shape all his experiences and personal relations to keep the individual as he is. Somehow, now, he is said to "become aware" of what he previously could not be aware of, he is "influenced" by suggestions, he "overcomes" the transference, his "libidinal balance" is altered, he somehow now "perceives the attitudes" of the therapist, where he has always distorted and anticipated the attitudes of others. This is really the problem, not the explanation, of personality change.

But we do *observe* that almost always these changes occur in the context of a personal relationship. Some definitions of the kind of relationship which does (and the kind which does not) effect personality change have been offered (Rogers, 1957, 1959*b*). Very little has been said about how relationship events affect the conditions making for repression and the nature of contents, so that these alter.

So far we have formulated two problems of personality change and we have then cited *two observations*: the feeling process in the individual; and the personal relationship.

Our two observations and our two problems are related: simply, we may say that, while it is *theoretically* impossible for the individual to become aware of what he must *repress* and to change his personality *contents* into other *contents*, we *observe* that both occur *when* the individual is engaged in a deep and intense *feeling process* and in the context of a *personal relationship*. We need a theoretical account of this observed possibility, and we need to reformulate the theory of repression and the definitions of personality constituents, so that observed changes can be theoretically formulated.

The Theory

BASIC CONCEPTS—WHAT ARE PSYCHOLOGICAL EVENTS?

1. *Experiencing.*
(*a*) The "ing" in the term "experiencing" indicates that experience is considered as a *process.* (We will have to define the theoretical conceptions which go to make up a process framework.)

Now, of course, the above is not really a definition, since the usage of the word "experience" is currently confused and various. The field of psychology lacks a theory of experience. However, the theory of experiencing (Gendlin, 1962*b*) attempts to provide a process for determining a theory of experience.

Since the term "experiencing" is extremely broad, more specific terms will be defined for specific aspects of experiencing. Anything in particular which we may consider will be a particular *manner* or *mode* of experiencing, or a particular *function* of it, or a particular logical pattern we choose to impose. The term "experiencing," then, denotes all "experience" viewed in terms of the process framework.

(*b*) The word "experience" in psychology, wherever employed, means concrete psychological events. The same is the case here. Experiencing is a process of concrete, ongoing events.

(c) Finally, by experiencing we mean a *felt* process. We mean inwardly sensed, bodily felt events, and we hold that the concrete "stuff" of personality or of psychological events is this flow of bodily sensing or feeling.

Experiencing is the process of concrete, bodily feeling, which constitutes the basic matter of psychological and personality phenomena.

2. *The Direct Referent.* Both in social talk and in theory we so largely emphasize external events and logical meaning that it almost seems as if it were difficult to notice that, in addition to external objects and logic, we also have an inward bodily feeling or sensing. This is, of course, a commonplace that can be readily checked by anyone.

At any moment he wishes, one can refer directly to an inwardly felt datum. Experiencing, in the mode of being directly referred to in this way, I term the "direct referent."

Of course, there are other modes of experiencing. Situations and external events, symbols, and actions may interact with our feeling process quite without any reflexive attention paid to the direct referent. We are aware and feel without this direct attention as well as with it.

One can always refer directly to experiencing.

3. *Implicit.* It is less apparent, but still easily checked by anyone, that this direct referent contains meaning. At first it may seem that experiencing is simply the inward sense of our body, its tension, or its well-being. Yet, upon further reflection, we can notice that only in this direct sensing do we have the meanings of what we say and think. For, without our "feel" of the meaning, verbal symbols are only noises (or sound images of noises).

For example, someone listens to you speak, and then says: "Pardon me, but I don't grasp what you mean." If you would like to restate what you meant in different words, you will notice that you must inwardly attend to your direct referent, your *felt* meaning. Only in this way can you arrive at different words with which to restate it.

In fact, we employ explicit symbols only for very small portions of what we think. We have most of it in the form of *felt* meanings.

For example, when we think about a problem, we must think about quite a number of considerations together. We cannot do so *verbally*. In fact, we could not think about the meaning of these considerations at all if we had to keep reviewing the verbal symbols over and over. We may review them verbally. However, to think upon the problem we must use the *felt* meanings—we must think of how "this" (which we previously verbalized) relates to "that" (which we also previously verbalized). To think "this" and "that," we employ their *felt* meanings.

When felt meanings occur in interaction with verbal symbols and we feel what the symbols mean, we term such meanings "explicit" or "explicitly known." On the other hand, quite often we have just such felt meanings without a verbal symbolization. Instead we have an event, a perception, or some word such as the word "this" (which represents nothing, but only points). When this is the case, we can term the meaning "implicit" or "implicitly felt, but not explicitly known."

Please note that "explicit" and "implicit" meanings are both *in awareness*. What we concretely feel and can inwardly refer to is certainly "in awareness" (though the term "awareness" will later require some reformulations). "Implicit" meaning is often confusingly discussed as if it were "unconscious" or "not in awareness." It should be quite clear that, since the direct referent is felt and is a direct datum of attention, it is "in awareness." *Anything termed "implicit" is felt in awareness.*

Furthermore, we may now add that even when a meaning is explicit (when we say "exactly what we mean") the felt meaning we have always contains a great deal more implicit meaning than we have made explicit. When we define the words we have just used, or when we "elaborate" what we "meant," we notice that the felt meanings we have been employing always contain implicitly many, many meanings—always many more than those to which we gave explicit formulation. We find that we employed these meanings. We find they were central to what we did make explicit, that they made up what we actually meant, yet they were only felt. They were implicit.

4. Implicit Function (In Perception and Behavior). So far we have thought of implicit meanings as existing only in the direct referent; that is to say, only if and when we directly refer to our experiencing as a felt datum. However, quite without such direct reference to experiencing, most of life and behavior proceed on implicit meanings. (Explicit meanings serve only a few special purposes.) We say, for example, that our interpretation of and reactions to present situations are determined by our "past" experiences. But in which way are our past experiences here *now*? For instance, if I am to observe an immediate situation and then describe it, in what way are there present my knowledge and experiences of past events, my knowledge of language, and my memories of this situation which I have just observed so that they function now? To describe the situation I just observed, my words will arise for me from a felt sense of what I have observed, reacted to, and now mean to say. Rarely, if at all, do I think *in words* what I now observe. Nor do I think each of the past experiences which function in this observing. Rarely do I think in explicit words what I will say. All these meanings *function implicitly as my present, concretely felt* experiencing.

5. *Completion; Carrying Forward*

6. *Interaction.* Implicit meanings are *incomplete.* Symbolic *completion* —or *carrying forward*—is a bodily felt process. There is an *interacting,* not an equation, between implicit meaning and symbols.

I must now make it quite clear that "implicit" and "explicit" meanings are different in nature. We may feel that some verbal statement says exactly what we mean; nevertheless, to feel the meaning is not the same kind of thing as verbal symbols. As we have shown, a felt meaning can contain very many meanings and can be further and further elaborated. Thus, the felt meaning is not the same in kind as the precise symbolized explicit meaning. The reason the difference in kind is so important is because if we ignore it we assume that explicit meanings are (or were) already in the implicit felt meaning. We are led to make the felt, implicit meaning a kind of dark place in which countless explicit meanings are hidden. We then wrongly assume that these meanings are "implicit" and felt only in that they are "hidden." I must emphasize that the "implicit" or "felt" datum of experiencing is a sensing of body life. As such it may have countless organized aspects, but this does not mean that they are conceptually formed, explicit, and hidden. Rather, we *complete* and form them when we explicate.

Before symbolization, the "felt" meanings are *incomplete.* They are analogous, let us say, to the muscle movement in my stomach which I can call "hunger." This sensation certainly "means" something about eating, but it does not "contain" eating. To be even more graphic, the feeling of hunger is not a repressed eating. It does not contain within itself the search for an animal, the killing and roasting of this animal, the eating, digesting, and absorbing of food particles, and the excretion and burying of wastes. Now just as all these steps (some of them patterned in the newborn organism, some of them learned) do not exist within the hunger sensation of muscle movement, so also the symbolic meaning "hunger" does not exist within it. Symbols must interact with the feeling before we have a meaning. The verbal symbol "hunger," just as "food," must interact with it before we carry forward the digestive process. The symbol "hunger," like other aspects of the search for food or my sitting down at a table, is a learned step of the digestive process and carries that process forward. Before that occurs, the feeling of the muscle movement implicitly contains the body's patterned readiness for organized interaction but not the formed conceptual units. Implicit bodily feeling is *preconceptual*. Only when *interaction* with verbal symbols (or events) actually occurs is the process actually carried forward and the explicit meaning formed.[7] So long as it is implicit, it is *incomplete*, awaiting symbols (or events) with which it can interact in preorganized ways.

Thus, to explicate is to *carry forward* a bodily felt process. Implicit meanings are *incomplete*. They are not hidden conceptual units. They are not the same in nature as explicitly known meanings. There is no equation possible between implicit meanings and "their" explicit symbolization. Rather than an equation, there is an *interaction* between felt experiencing and symbols (or events).[8]

THE FEELING PROCESS—HOW CHANGE TAKES PLACE IN THE INDIVIDUAL

7. *Focusing.* "Focusing" (or, more exactly, "continuous focusing") will be defined in terms of four more specific definitions (8–11) below. "Focusing" is the whole process which ensues when the individual attends to the direct referent of experiencing.

We noted earlier that direct reference is one mode of experiencing. The feeling process we term "experiencing" also occurs in an individual's awareness without direct reference to it as a felt datum. In these other modes, also, experiencing has important functions in personality change. We will discuss them later.

"Focusing" refers to how one mode of experiencing, the direct referent, functions in ongoing personality change.

The foregoing definitions (1–6) will be employed in the following discussion, and four more definitions concerning focusing will be formulated.

Focusing will be analyzed in four phases. The division into these phases is more a result of my way of formulation than of any inherent four-step divisibility in the process. Although it may occur in these clearly separable phases, more often it does not.

8. *Direct Reference in Psychotherapy (Phase One of Focusing).* A definitely felt, but conceptually vague referent is directly referred to by the individual. Let us say he has been discussing some troublesome situation or personal trait. He has described various events, emotions, opinions, and interpretations. Perhaps he has called himself "foolish," "unrealistic," and assured his listener that he really "knows better" than to react

in the way he does. He is puzzled by his own reactions, and he disapproves of them. Or, what amounts to the same thing, he strongly defends his reactions against some real or imaginary critic who would say that the reactions make no sense, are self-defeating, unrealistic, and foolish. If he is understandingly listened to and responded to, he may be able to refer directly to the felt meaning which the matter has for him. He may then lay aside, for a moment, all his better judgment or bad feeling about the fact that he is as he is, and he may refer directly to the felt meaning of what he is talking about. He may then say something like: "Well, I know it makes no sense, but in some way it does." Or: "It's awfully vague to me what this is with me, but I feel it pretty definitely." It may seem as if language and logic are insufficient, but the trouble is merely that we are not used to talking about something which is conceptually vague, but definitely and distinctly *felt*.

If the individual continues to focus his attention on this direct referent (if he does not break off attending to it because it seems too foolish, or too bad, or too doubtful whether he isn't just coddling himself, etc.), he may become able to conceptualize some rough aspects of it. For example, he may find: "I feel that way whenever anyone does such-and-such to me." Or: "I think there is something about that kind of thing which could make something completely terrible and frightening happen to me, but that's silly. You have to accept things like that. That's life. But that's the way it feels, kind of a terror."

Having conceptualized some such rough aspect of "it," the individual usually feels the felt meaning more strongly and vividly, becomes more excited and hopeful about the process of focusing within himself, and is less likely now to settle for the conceptual explanations, accusations, and apologies. It is a profound discovery for most people when they find it possible to continue direct reference. It comes to be deeply valued as "I am in touch with myself."

As the individual continues to focus on such a direct referent, he may puzzle over what a funny kind of a "this" he is talking about. He may call it "this feeling," or "this whole thing," or "this is the way I am when such-and-such occurs." Very clearly it is an inwardly sensed referent in his present experiencing. Nothing is vague about the definite way he *feels* it. He can turn to it with his inward attention. Only *conceptually* is it vague.

A very important and surprising fact about direct reference to felt meanings is that if the matter under consideration is anxiety producing or highly uncomfortable, this felt discomfort *decreases* as the individual directly refers to the felt meaning. One would have expected the opposite. Certainly the opposite is true, for example, when the individual chooses between various topics for discussion. The prospect of talking about this difficult, anxiety-provoking matter certainly makes the person more anxious than the prospect of talking about some neutral or pleasant subject. Thus, he may be in quite a lot of inward pain as he decides to bring the matter up at all. However, once into the topic, the more directly he attends to the direct referent, the felt meaning, the less his discomfort and anxiety. If he momentarily loses track of it, the anxiety flares up again, and the diffuse discomfort of the topic returns.

As the individual symbolizes some aspect of the felt meaning, he senses its rightness partly by the degree of *easing* of the anxiety which he feels.

In contrast to the anxiety or discomfort, the felt meaning itself becomes sharper, more distinctly felt, as he refers to and correctly symbolizes what it is. In fact, his sense of whether or not he has "correctly" symbolized is partly just this sense of increased intensity of the felt meaning.[9]

This decreased anxiety is a very surprising fact, much against the general assumptions about anxiety-provoking material. We generally assume that to focus directly on the experiencing makes us more anxious. My observations indicate that increased anxiety comes from topic choice, and it is this which we generally expect. On the other hand, given the topic, the more we focus directly upon the felt meaning, and the more of it we symbolize correctly, the more relief we feel. Even a little error in symbolizing ("no, what I just said isn't quite it") again increases the anxiety.

We may theoretically interpret this observation in terms of definitions 5 and 6 and our use of the work of Mead and Sullivan. To symbolize a directly felt implicit meaning carries the organismic process a step forward. It is felt so. It also appears from this that we should consider the direct reference (or the giving of attention), as itself, already a kind of symbolizing. Direct reference, as well as the resulting symbolizations, involves bodily felt tension relief.[10]

There are other ways of describing the individual's focusing on a direct referent of experiencing. We may say that, at such moments, his experiencing is "ahead of his concepts." It "guides" his concepts. He forms concepts and "checks them against" his directly felt meaning and, on this basis, decides their correctness.

As he continues to refer directly to the felt meaning (he is probably calling it "this"), he may find that his previous formulation which felt correct must be replaced by another which now feels more correct. The listener can help by pointing his words also at "this" and by helping to find words and concepts that might fit it.[11] The listener, of course, cannot judge the correctness. Not even the individual himself judges it but, we might say somewhat poetically, his direct referent does the judging. Both persons may thus be surprised by the direction which the symbolizing takes.

The above has been a description of how an individual may directly refer to or "focus on" a direct referent of experiencing which, for him, constitutes the felt meaning of some topic, situation, behavior, or personality aspect.

9. *Unfolding* (*Phase Two of Focusing*). Sometimes, in focusing on a directly felt referent, there is a gradual step-by-step process of coming to know explicitly what it is. Yet, it may "open up" in one dramatic instant. Most often there is both a gradual coming to know it better and some instants during which there is a very noticeable "opening up." With a great physical relief and sudden dawning, the individual suddenly knows. He may sit there, nodding to himself, thinking only words such as "yes, I've got it" quite without as yet finding concepts to tell himself what it is he "has got." However, he knows that now he *can* say. It is possible that, if he is now suddenly interrupted, he may "lose it," so that later he can only say, "I really felt I knew what it was at that moment, but I've lost it now." Usually, however, he will as swiftly as possible find concepts and words to say what has opened up. It is almost always a number of things. For example:

Yes, *of course* he is afraid, he realizes. He has not permitted himself even to think about dealing with *this* and *this* aspect of the situation, and this has been because he has not believed that these aspects really existed. Well, yes, he did realize they existed, but he also felt compelled to blame himself for them as if he merely imagined them. And if they do exist (and they do), he does not know how he could possibly live with them. He has not allowed himself to try to deal with them (he now realizes) or even to consider them anything other than merely his imagination, because, my God, if they are really there, then he is helpless. Then there is *nothing* he can do! But they are there. Well, it is a relief to know at least that.

This example illustrates the multiplicity one generally finds in an implicit meaning which was felt as one "this." It may, as in the example, be a multiplicity which can still be thought of as "one thing." Experiencing has no given definite unit experiences.

The example also illustrates that, often, the meanings one finds with such great relief are not at all pleasant or good. The problem is not at all resolved. Quite the contrary, now it *really* looks impossible. Now it seems clear why one has been so anxious. It *does* seem hopeless. Yet it is a great and physically experienced tension reduction when the directly felt referent "unfolds" in this way.

The unfolding of a direct referent always involves a surprising and deeply emotional recognition of the good sense of our own (previously so seemingly irksome) feelings. "*Of course,*" we say over and over, "Of course!" Or, we say, "Well, what do you know, that's what that was!"

Because what was previously felt now actually "makes sense," problem resolutions can occur at this stage. For, we may see that *given this or that judgment,* or perception, or event, or situation, "of course" we felt as we did, but we do not now judge it in the same way. However, my example illustrated that even when the solution seems further away than ever, still the physiological tension reduction occurs, and a genuine change takes place. I believe that this change is really more basic than the resolution of specific problems.

A whole vast multiplicity of implicit aspects in the person's functioning and dysfunctioning is always involved. For, when a direct referent of experiencing "opens up," much more change has occurred than the cognitive realization of this or that. This is most dramatically evident when, after the "unfolding," the individual still sees no way out. He says, "At least I know what it is now, but how will I ever change it or deal with it?" Yet, during the following days and in the next therapy hour, it turns out that he is already different, that the quality of the problem has changed and his behavior has been different. And, as for a good explanation of all this resolution . . . "well, it just seems all right now." There is a global change in the whole manner of experiencing in this regard. From this *felt change,* with its lack of logical description, come some of our simple-minded notions: "Just accept it," we tell ourselves and others. We can recall that we have observed individuals, such as I just described, *report* a basic change in such a simplistic way:

"How is everything different?"

"Well, it just seems OK now!"

"Do you still feel that such-and-such might happen and you couldn't deal with it?"

"Yes, but now I kind of feel, well, that's life. That's the way it is, you have to accept things like that."

And that is just what he had said to himself over and over again, *without any effect,* before the process in which he focused on the felt meaning and it unfolded!

Thus, as I have said, only sometimes does *what* is unfolded lead to a solution in an explicable way. More often, deep global feeling change occurs as one unfolds the direct referent, even when it seems to open into something which sounds worse and more hopeless than one had expected. Whether or not some specific resolution is noticeable, the change appears to be broad and global. It is not just this problem resolved, or that trait changed, but a change in many areas and respects. We can say that the broad multiplicity of aspects which are implicit in any felt meaning are all of them changed—thus the global change. Or we can say that meanings are aspects of the experiencing process and that the very *manner of* experiencing changes, hence also the quality of all its meanings.

As one client put it: "Until now I always saw this problem in black and white terms, and I struggled for a solution that would be gray. But now, this new way isn't black or white, *or* gray. It's in color!" Thus the unfolding of a felt referent does not just inform one about what was involved, but, rather, it changes the whole manner in which one experiences.

10. *Global Application (Phase Three of Focusing).* This global way in which the process of direct reference and unfolding affects many aspects of the person is noticeable not only in his later reports of the resulting difference, but also in the moments which immediately follow the unfolding of a felt referent. The individual is flooded by many different associations, memories, situations, and circumstances, all in relation to the felt referent. Although conceptually they can be very different, they share the same felt meaning with which he has been dealing. Except for this they may concern quite different and unrelated matters.[12] "Oh, and that's also why I can't get up any enthusiasm for this-and-this." "Yes, and another thing about it is, this comes in every time somebody tells me what to do or think. I can't say, well, what *I* think is more important, because, see, this way of making myself wrong comes in there." "Oh, and also, back when this and this happened, I did the *same* thing."

During this "wide application" period which often follows the unfolding of a felt referent, the individual may sit in silence, only occasionally voicing some of the pieces from this flood.

I realize that some of the foregoing observations have been termed by others as "insight." I believe that is a misnomer. First, the global application is in no way a figuring out, nor is it chiefly a better understanding. Rather, insight and better understanding are the results, the by-products, of this process, as a few of its very many changed aspects call attention to themselves. One can be sure that for every relation or application the individual here explicitly thinks, there are thousands which he does not think of, but which have, nevertheless, just changed. Not his thinking about the differences which the unfolding has made, but the unfolding itself, changes him in all these thousands of respects. The change occurs whether or not he thinks of any such applications, and whether or not he considers the unfolding to be a resolving. For, as I emphasized, he may well walk out saying, "I have no idea what I can do with this, or how I change it." But, it has already changed, and the great multiplicity of respects in which "it" *implicitly functions* have all changed.

11. *Referent Movement* (*Phase Four of Focusing*). A definite alteration or movement in the direct referent is felt. This "referent movement" often occurs after the three phases just described. When there has been *direct reference*, dramatic *unfolding* occurs, and when the flood of *global application* subsides, the individual finds that he now refers to a direct referent which feels different. The *implicit* meanings which he can symbolize from this direct reference are now quite different ones. It is a new direct reference; and so the four-phase process begins again.

But focusing is not always such a neatly divisible four-phase process. As noted before, *unfolding* can occur with or without a noticeable flood of *global application*. Unfolding can also occur quite undramatically, in very small steps of successive symbolization. And, even without unfolding, even without any symbolization which feels "correct," the individual's direct reference can *carry forward* the feeling process and is experienced with bodily tension relief. What we are here calling the fourth phase of focusing, the *referent movement*, can occur at any of these times. Usually, direct reference alone does not change or move the direct referent, but does make it stronger, sharper, and more distinctly felt. It increases its intensity as a feeling and diminishes the diffuse tension, discomfort, and anxiety. However, sometimes the mere process of continuous direct reference will change or "move" the direct referent. More often, such a movement occurs after at least some unfolding and symbolizing, and especially after the felt flooding of global application.

The individual distinctly feels a change in the quality of the felt referent. It is not only a change but a directly experienced "give" or "movement" which feels right and welcome. Its tremendous importance lies in the fact that after such a referent movement (even very small), the implicit meanings are now different. The "scenery," as it were, which one confronts, changes.

It is just this referent movement which is usually missing when one *talks at* oneself, when one has recited all the good reasons, considerations, and ways one should feel and would be more sensible to feel, etc.

458 / A THEORY OF PERSONALITY CHANGE

Most often, thereafter, the *same unchanged* felt referent is still there, and the same diffuse anxiety as well. From this lack of referent movement, one knows that nothing has really changed.

Conversely, after referent movement, the meanings and symbolizations one formulates are different. The relevant considerations are different. The whole scene is different. Of course, most often in one such step one does not find "solutions." The individual may say: "Well, that doesn't help me either, because now this helpless feeling, it just seems like the worst crime in the world to be helpless, weak, just let everything happen to you. I can't stand that either. I don't know what is so bad about it, I mean, if actually, in reality, I can't do anything about it anyhow." Here we see that there is no hint of anything like a solution, but the relevant surrounding considerations have now changed. What he looks at and symbolizes is different as the felt referent to which he directly refers is different.

Reference movement gives direction to the focusing process. The individual's attention and symbolizing tends to follow that direction which produces referent movement.

Without reference movement, what is said is "merely" talk, "merely" intellectualization, "merely" hair splitting, or "merely" reporting.

Reference movement is the direct experience that something more than logic and verbalization has occurred. The movement can often be logically analyzed (that is to say, logical relationships can be formulated between what he said earlier and what he says now). However, such logical analysis can be made between any verbalizations, whether or not there has been reference movement. And, often, for a small bit of reference movement the logical or conceptual shift is extremely large. Even a *slight* reference movement can make for what conceptually looks like a totally different vantage point.

Reference movement is a change in the felt meaning which functions in symbolizing.

I hope I have conveyed something of the overlapping character of what I call the four phases of focusing. To summarize them: phase one, *direct reference* to a felt meaning which is conceptually vague but definite as felt; phase two, *unfolding* and the symbolizing of some aspects; phase three, a flooding of *global application*; phase four, *referent movement*, and the process can begin again with phase one.

These four definitions (8–11) define "focusing."[13]

12. *The Self-Propelled Feeling Process.* As the individual engages in focusing, and as *referent movement* occurs, he finds himself pulled along

in a direction he neither chose nor predicted. There is a very strong impelling force exerted by the direct referent just then felt. The individual may "get off the track," "talk about something else," or put up with considerable distracting comments and useless deductions by his listener; and still the given felt, direct referent remains strikingly as the "next thing" with which he must deal.

If the listener's responsiveness makes it possible, the individual finds himself moving from one referent movement and unfolding to another and another. Each time the inward scene changes, new felt meanings are there for him. The cycles of the four phases set into motion an overall feeling process. This feeling process has a very striking, concretely felt, self-propelled quality.

As a psychotherapist I have learned that I must depend on this self-propelled feeling process in the client. This is an important principle, because I have the power to distract him. When I do so (by too many explanations or insights of my own into what he says), then this feeling process does not occur. On the other hand, I have also learned that my questions and self-expressions can be useful, provided I always intend what I say to refer to the individual's felt referent and I show that I would like him to continue to focus on it.

In order to permit the feeling process to arise, we must sometimes remain silent, at least for some brief periods. If either he or I talk all the time, little direct reference can take place. Therefore, when he has stopped talking and I have stopped responding, I am glad if there is a little silence in which he can feel the meaning of what we have been saying. I am especially glad if the next thing he then says follows not simply and logically from what we have said, but shows that he has been immersed in something felt. In this way I can notice that a felt referent has provided the transition from what he did say to what he now says. This "descent" into himself, this focusing, and the overall feeling process which arises, give verbalization to the underlying flow of events of personality change. This self-propelled feeling process is the essential motor of personality change.

Once this feeling process has arisen, it continues even between the times the individual engages in the four-phase focusing process I have outlined. Thus, during the several days between two psychotherapy hours, the client may find important thoughts, feelings, memories, and insights "coming" to him. He may find a generalized "stirring," an inward "eventfulness," even without a specific symbolized content. Thus the overall *feeling process* comes to be self-propelled and broader than just the four phases of focusing I have described.

We tend to be so concerned with content (symbolized meanings) that
we sometimes discuss psychological questions as if personality were
nothing but contents. We forget the obvious differences which exist not
only in *what* an individual's experience is at a given moment, but also in
how he experiences. Thus we ask a question such as this: What difference does the personal relationship make, since the individual can think
and feel the same contents when he is alone as he can when he talks to
another person?

Often a psychotherapist (or any listener who wants to be helpful)
will feel that he must "do something," "add something," bring in some
new content or insight, so that he will be helpful and make a difference.

Yet, there is already all the difference between *how* one thinks and
feels *alone* and *how* one thinks and feels *with another person*. The conceptual content may (for a time) be the same as the individual can
think and feel by himself; but, the *manner* of experiencing will be totally
different. Consider, for example, the type of listener who interrupts with
his own concerns and is inclined to be annoyed and critical long before
he understands what is said. With him, my manner of experiencing will
be quite constricted. I will think of less and feel less than I do when I
am alone. I will tend to say what I must in round, general, swiftly finished terms. I will *not* tend to feel deeply, or intensely, or richly. Certain
things will never occur to me when I am with him or, if they do occur
to me, I will save them for the time when I am alone, and can feel them
through without the constricting effects of his responses. We all know
this difference between the manner of our experiencing with certain
persons as compared with when we are alone.

Similarly, there are others (we are fortunate to know one) with whom
we feel more intensely and freely whatever we feel. We think of more
things, we have the patience and the ability to go more deeply into the
details, we bear better our own inward strain when we are speaking to
this person. If we are sad and dry-eyed alone, then with this person we
cry. If we are stopped by our guilt, shame, and anxiety, then with this
person we come to life again, inwardly, as being more than these emotions. If we have showered disgust and annoyance on ourselves to the
point of becoming silent and deadened inside, then with this person we
"come alive" again. As we tell this person some old, familiar, many times
repeated story, we find it richer and freshly meaningful, and we may

not get all the way through it for the many facets of personal meaning which now unfold.

How shall we theoretically explain these differences in the *manner* in which we experience in different relationships and alone?

13. *Manner of Experiencing.* Whatever the content which we are said to experience, there is also the manner in which we experience. Few terms in our formal psychological language denote differences in *manner of experiencing*. Let us, therefore, define some more terms. (These terms overlap, so that fully explicating one of them would give us the others.)

Immediacy of Experiencing. Immediacy can be contrasted with dis-association or postponement of affect. Descriptive and poetic terms are usually invented by individuals to describe immediacy and its opposites: "I do everything right, but I'm not in it"; or "I am a spectator of my own behavior"; or "What it means to me so occupies me that I don't feel what is going on at all"; "Life is going on all right, but I'm in some back room. I merely hear about it, I'm not living it."

Presentness. Am I reacting to the present situation? Am I feeling a *now*, or is the present situation merely an occasion, a cue for a familiar, repetitious, structured pattern of feeling?

Richness of Fresh Detail. Any moment's experience has a host of fresh details that I experience implicitly, some of which I could symbolize and differentiate. In contrast, the structured feeling pattern consists of only a few emotions and meanings. Sometimes, however, I have none of the richness of the present, only the same old, stale feeling pattern. In such instances psychologists are inclined to notice chiefly the content of the stale pattern. We say: "This is a protesting reaction against authority," or "this is a need to dominate," or a "partial" infantile sex drive such as "voyeurism," or "exhibitionism," or a "passive-aggressive need." We tend to neglect the fact that such feeling patterns are also different in *manner* from an immediate, present, and richly detailed experiencing. It is not only that I react poorly to authority. Rather, I react this way to *every* person whom I perceive as an authority. And, more important, I react *only* to his being an authority, not to him as a person, and to the very many present facets of him and our situation which are different from any other situation. The "authority pattern," or any similar pattern, is really only a bare outline. My experiencing is *structure-bound* in manner, when I experience only this bare outline and feel only this bare set of emotions, lacking the myriad of fresh detail of the present. I might resent my boss's behaviors even if my manner of experiencing were optimal. Too much time and attention is wasted in deciding whether my reaction to him is to be blamed on me or on him. It does not matter. What does matter is the *manner* of my experiencing. No matter how obnoxious he may really be, if my experiencing is structure bound, I do not even experience *his* obnoxiousness except as mere cues for the experience of my old bare structure.

Frozen Wholes. We often speak of contents or "experiences" as if they were set, shaped units with their own set structure. But this is the case only to the extent that my experiencing is structure bound in its manner. For example, when I listen as you tell me something of your feelings I may occasionally think of my own experiences. I need the feelings and meanings of my own experiences in order to understand yours. However, if I must keep thinking of my experiences explicitly as such, then I cannot grasp the meanings yours have to you. I will then insist that your experiences are the same as mine (or, if I am wise, I will know that I am not understanding you). Unless *my* experiences *implicitly function* so that I can newly understand *you*, I cannot really understand you at all. Insofar as my experiencing is structure bound, it does not implicitly function. It is not "seamlessly" felt by me with its thousands of implicit aspects functioning so that I arrive at some fresh meaning, something you are trying to convey to me. Rather, in this regard, my experience is a "frozen whole" and will not give up its structure. Whatever requires the implicit function of experiencing in these regards makes me feel my whole frozen structure and nothing new.

Repetitive versus Modifiable. Since within the bare structured *frozen whole* experiencing does not function in interaction with present detail, the structure is not *modified* by the present. Hence, it remains the same, it repeats itself in many situations without ever changing. So long as the manner of experiencing remains structure bound, the structures themselves are not *modifiable* by present occurrences.

Optimal Implicit Functioning. It is clear from the above that, to the extent the manner of experiencing is structure bound, the implicit functioning of experiencing cannot occur. Instead of the many, many implicit meanings of experiencing which must interact with present detail to interpret and react, the individual has a structured feeling pattern.

These terms define *manner of experiencing.*

14. *In Process Versus Structure Bound.* Experiencing is always in process and always functions implicitly. The respects in which it is *structure bound* are not experiencing. The conceptual content *in an abstract way* can *appear* to be the same with different manners of experiencing. However, in the structure-bound manner the experiencing process is,

in given respects, missing. By "missing" we mean that from an external viewpoint we may notice that the implicit functioning of experiencing ought to be there, but there is only the process-skipping structure, *and the experiencing surrounding it and leading up to it.* Thus we say that *structure-bound* aspects are not *in process.*

15. *Reconstituting.* Earlier we said that symbols, or events can *carry forward* the process of experiencing. Experiencing is essentially an *interaction* between feeling and "symbols" (attention, words, events), just as body life is an *interaction* between body and environment. In its basic nature, the physical life process is interaction. It requires not only the body's respiratory machinery but also oxygen. And the body's respiratory machinery itself consists of cells which again are chemical processes involving oxygen and food particles. If we apply this conceptual model of interaction process to experiencing, we can consider it an *interaction* of *feeling* and events ("events" here includes verbal noises, others' behaviors, external occurrences—anything that can interact with feeling).

If we formulate the theory of experiencing in this way, we can formulate why the other person's responses so basically affect the individual's manner of experiencing. [14] For, *if there is a response, there will be an ongoing interaction process.* Certain aspects of the personality will be *in process.* However, without the response, there will not (in these respects) be a process at all.

Subjectively, phenomenologically, people describe this as "coming alive inside," or as "feeling many more facets" of oneself. *Responses* can *reconstitute* the experiencing process in respects in which, before the response, there was no process (no interaction between feeling and something else and hence no *ongoing* interaction process).

The peculiar condition of "experience" which is not *in process* has puzzled psychology for many years. It has been called "unconscious,"[15] "repressed," "covert," "inhibited," "denied," etc. The fact is that we observe individuals awarely and actively feeling (in ways which were missing before) when they are responded to in certain ways. The individual feels that the feelings "have always been there in some sense, but were not felt." Psychology cannot deny this common observation. One way of formulating it is as the *reconstituting* of the experiencing process.

16. *Contents Are Process Aspects.* What is a "content" of experience (or "*an* experience," when that is meant to refer to a given content)? We noted (definitions 3 and 5) that the felt implicit meanings of experiencing can be put into interaction with verbal symbols. We then say that

the symbols "mean" or "represent" what the experience is "of" or, more simply, that the symbols symbolize the experience. Such a *symbolized unit is a content.*[16]

Thus, in order for there to be a content, some aspect of *implicit function* (see definition 4) must be ongoing in interaction with symbols.

But what if there are not, as yet, any *verbal* symbols? Is there then no ongoing experiencing either? The answer is that verbal symbols are not the only events with which feelings can be in an interaction process. External occurrences, other people's responses, even our own attention, can interact with feeling so as to constitute a process.

Therefore, it is often the case that there is an ongoing experiencing process without verbal symbols. In fact, most situations and behaviors involve feeling in interaction with nonverbal events. Experiencing *functions implicitly* with countless meanings which, as felt (without verbal symbolization), are aspects of the ongoing interaction.

The respects in which experiencing is ongoing are also those in which we *can* verbally symbolize contents. The respects in which it is not ongoing (no matter how it may appear externally) cannot be verbally symbolized. Only pale, useless, general meaning can be given to concepts of the supposed contents which are not at this instant process aspects. Contents are aspects of ongoing felt process. That is to say, contents are *process aspects.*

17. *The Law of Reconstitution of the Experiencing Process.* An individual can symbolize only those aspects which are *already* implicitly functioning in ongoing experiencing.

In any experiencing (that is to say, in any ongoing interaction of feeling and events) a great many implicit meanings are process aspects (so-called "contents"). Thus, for any moment's ongoing experiencing one can symbolize a great many contents. These are *incomplete* (definition 5) until some symbols (or events) *carry forward* the process in these respects.

Thus there are two different definitions: to *carry forward*, and to *reconstitute*. To "carry forward" means that symbols (or events) occur to interact with *already* implicitly functioning aspects of ongoing experiencing. To "reconstitute" means that the process has become ongoing and implicitly functions in respects in which it previously was not ongoing.

We can now state a *law of the reconstitution of experiencing process*: When certain *implicitly functioning* aspects of experiencing are *carried forward* by symbols or events, the resulting experiencing always involves *other* sometimes newly *reconstituted* aspects which thereby come to be *in process* and *function implicitly* in that experiencing.

18. *Hierarchy of Process Aspects.* If contents are viewed as process aspects—that is to say, as implicitly functioning aspects of ongoing experiencing—then *the law of reconstitution* implies that *certain* contents (process aspects) must be symbolized before certain *other contents* (process aspects) can thereby become process aspects that are capable of being symbolized.

This fact gives the individual's self-exploration an ordered or hierarchical character. It is as if he can "get to" certain things only via certain other things. We must let him travel his "own road," not because we believe in democracy, and not because we like self-reliance, but because *only* when the experiencing process has been reconstituted, so that certain aspects become implicit in it, can he symbolize these.

19. *Self-Process.* To the extent that experiencing does *implicitly function*, the individual may respond to himself and may *carry forward* his own experiencing. This interaction of the individual's feelings with his own (symbolic or actual) behavior,[17] we term "self." A more exact term: *self-process.*

To the extent that experiencing does not implicitly function, the individual cannot respond to himself and carry forward his experiencing. In whatever respects it does not function (is structure bound), responses are needed first to *reconstitute* the interaction process of experiencing in these respects.

Why is it that the individual himself does not *carry forward* his already *implicitly functioning* experiencing in ways which would newly reconstitute *structure-bound* aspects of it? Of course, he cannot respond to the structure-bound aspects, as such (they are not implicitly functioning), but neither can the psychotherapist. The psychotherapeutic response can be defined as one which responds to aspects of experiencing which *are* implicitly functioning, but to which the individual himself tends not to respond. More precisely, his own response is a whole frozen structure which does not carry forward the felt experiencing process in these respects.

20. *The Reconstituting Response Is Implicitly Indicated.* The response which will *reconstitute* the experiencing process (in some now *structure-bound* respect) is already implied[18] in the individual's experiencing. One must respond *to the functioning experiencing, not to the structure.*

In practice this means that one must take at face value and give a personal response to the *functioning* aspect of the person. No one is greatly changed by responses and analyses of how he does not function (though we are often tempted in this direction). We see that the individual's work behavior actually defeats his desire to work, that his sexual behavior turns away opportunities for genuine sexuality, that his desire to please makes him annoy people, that his way of reaching out to people actually turns people away, that his self-expression is dramatized and hollow. Yet these structures are his responses *to* his *actually functioning* desire to work, his actually functioning sexuality, his actually functioning desire to relate to people and be close to them, and his actual self-expressive urge. Only if we respond to these actually functioning aspects of his experiencing (despite the obviously opposite character of his behavior and symbolic self-responding) can we carry forward what is now actual and reconstitute the process where he himself had (symbolically and actually) responded only with structure.

21. *Primacy of Process.* We tend to neglect the fact that contents are process aspects. We pay the most attention to contents as symbolized meanings with specific logical implications (which they also are). Hence we often discuss self-exploration as if it were purely a logical inquiry in search of conceptual answers. However, in psychotherapy (and in one's private self-exploration as well) the logical contents and insights are secondary. Process has primacy. We must attend and symbolize in order to carry forward the process and thereby reconstitute it in certain new aspects. *Only then*, as new contents come to function implicitly in feeling, can we symbolize them.

In definition 9 we noted that "unfolding" can occur as a felt "now I've got it," quite without symbolization. This is a direct experience of *reconstituting*. The process is felt as ongoing in newly reconstituted respects. Reconstituting occurs when one symbolizes meanings which, in the previous moments, have already been implicit. The carrying forward of these implicit meanings turns out to involve the wider process which reconstitutes the new aspects.

In psychotherapy, therefore, the situation is not that first we figure out what is wrong with an individual and how he must change—and then, somehow, he does it. Rather, his experiencing with us is *already* vitally different with us than it previously could be. From this different experiencing arise the solutions of his problems. The changes are already occurring as he speaks. *Our* responses (as verbal symbols *and as events*) interact and carry forward *his* experiencing. Our gestures and attitude, the very fact that he is talking *to* us, the differences which each moment he makes to us—all of this interacts concretely with what implicitly functions in him, his felt experiencing. Conceptually it may look like a futile statement and restatement of problems. Or, conceptually, we may arrive at *the* most basic causes and factors—the ways in which an individual ought to change, the reasons and lacks which prevent him from so changing—but no genuine *solution* is *conceptually* arrived at. The conceptual search ends by shrugging and attaching some blameful label to the individual who, through bad will or constitution, is said to lack these or those basic essentials. Yet, *given certain interpersonal responses, he is already different.*

By *primacy of process* over conceptual content, we mean this fact:[19] The presently ongoing experiencing process must be *carried forward* concretely. Thereby it is in many respects reconstituted, made more immediate in its manner of experiencing, more full of differentiable detail. Thereby new process aspects (contents), "solutions," and personality changes arise. Most often these solutions seem terribly simple,[20] conceptually (see definition 9), and cannot possibly be the reason for the change. Rather, they are rough conceptualizations of a few aspects of a broadly different process.

22. *Process Unity.* There is a *single* process which involves all of the following: environmental interaction, body life, feeling, cognitive meanings, interpersonal relations, and self. The concretely occurring process is one, although we can isolate and emphasize these various aspects of it. Our "thing language" tends to present whatever we discuss as if it were a separable object in space. In this way we artificially separate environment, body, feeling, meanings, other people, and self.[21] When they are discussed as separable things, their obvious interrelations become puzzling: How can *feelings* be involved in (psychosomatic) body illnesses? How can *cognitive* thought be influenced by *felt* needs? How is it that expressing ourselves *interpersonally* results in changes in the *self*? At every juncture the "separate thing" view of these phenomena builds these puzzles into our discussions. Instead we can employ a frame of reference which considers the *one* process which concretely occurs. I want to give the name *process unity* to the way in which the one concrete process is basic to these various aspects.

We have tried to show that *feeling* is a bodily affair, an aspect of physiological process. We have shown that *cognitive meanings* consist not only of verbal or pictorial symbols, but also of a *felt* sense which is implicitly meaningful and must function in interaction with symbols. *Interpersonal responses* (like other types of events) can interact with *feeling* and carry forward the concrete process. Now we will try to show that the *self* (the individual's own responses to his implicitly functioning experiencing) is also an aspect of the one concretely felt process, continuous with body, feeling, meanings, and interpersonal relations.

23. *The Self Process and Its Interpersonal Continuity.* Throughout this discussion we have been dealing with one concretely occurring interaction process between *feeling* and *events.* Interpersonal events occur before there is a self. Others respond to us before we come to respond to ourselves. If these responses were not in interaction with feeling—if there were nothing but other people's responses as such—the self could become nothing but the learned responses of others. But interpersonal responses are not merely external events. They are events *in interaction with the individual's feeling.* The individual then develops a capacity *to respond to* his feeling. The self is not merely a learned repertoire of responses, but a response process *to* feeling.

If feeling did not have implicit meaning, then all meaning would depend totally on the events or responses which occur. Again then, the self could never become anything but the repetition of the responses of others. The individual would always have to interpret himself and shape his personal meanings just as others had interpreted him.

But feeling has implicit meanings. Therefore, to the extent that a feeling process is ongoing, we can *further* respond to it differently than others have. However, to the extent to which we respond to our own feeling so as to skip or stop the process rather than carry it forward, to that extent we need others to help us be ourselves. Not only the genesis, but the adult development of the self also may require interpersonal responses. Such responses are required not because of their appraisal or content, but because we need them concretely to reconstitute the feeling process. If in certain respects the process is not ongoing when we are alone, it does not help to recite to ourselves some content or happy appraisal which we may remember from a person with whom we felt "more ourselves"; that person's effect on us was brought about not by his appraisal or evaluation, which we can recite to ourselves. Rather, the effect occurred through his responses to our concrete feeling process and, in some respects, reconstituted it and carried it forward. If we can do *that* alone, we are independent selves in that respect.

Thus, personality change in us is not a result of our perceiving another's positive appraisals of us or attitudes toward us. It is true that rejecting attitudes toward us are unlikely to carry forward our implicit meanings. However, that is not because of the negative appraisal as such, but because rejection usually ignores the implicit meanings of my feeling. To reject is to turn away or push away. In contrast, someone's "unconditional positive regard" toward us is not only an appraisal or attitude. They respond and carry forward the concretely ongoing process with their responses.

We must, therefore, reformulate Rogers' (1959b) view that personality change depends on the client's *perception* of the therapist's attitudes. The present theory implies that the client may perceive the therapist's attitudes correctly, or he may not. He may be convinced that the therapist must dislike him and cannot possibly understand him. Not these *perceptions*, but the *manner of process which is actually occurring*, will determine whether personality change results. In many cases, the client can perceive positive therapist attitudes only after the concrete personality change process has already occurred.

The change-effective factor is not the perception of a content, an appraisal, an evaluation, or an attitude, considered apart from the concrete process.

Personality change is the difference made by *your* responses in *carrying forward my* concrete experiencing. To be myself I need your responses, to the extent to which my own responses fail to *carry* my feelings *forward*. At first, in these respects, I am "really myself" *only when I am with you.*

For a time, the individual can have this fuller *self-process* only in just this *relationship*.[22] That is not "dependence." It should not lead one to back away, but to fuller and deeper responses carrying forward the experiencing, which, for the time being, the individual says he can feel "only here." The continued *carrying forward* into *ongoing interaction process* is necessary to *reconstitute* the experiencing long enough for the individual himself to obtain the ability to carry it forward as *self-process*.

REPRESSION AND CONTENT DEFINITIONS REFORMULATED

24. *The Unconscious as Incomplete Process.* When "ego" or "self-system" are said to "exclude" some experiences from awareness, usually it is assumed that these experiences nevertheless exist "in the unconscious" or "in the organism." Our discussion, however, leads us to the conclusion that they do not. *Something* exists, to be sure, but it is not the experiences as they would be if they were optimally ongoing. Rather, what exists is a felt and physiological condition which results when, in some regards, the body interaction process is stopped—i.e., is not occurring. What kind of condition is that?

We have shown how the resulting dysfunction will be such that something is "missing," but we should not place what is missing into the unconscious (any more than we should place *eating* into the unconscious when someone is *hungry*). Rather, the unconscious consists of the body's stopped processes, the muscular and visceral blockage—just as a stopped electric current does not consist of a current that is going on under cover, but rather of certain electric potentials which build up in various parts (not only at the interruption) of the circuit. When a conductor re-establishes the electric current, different events occur than were occurring in its interrupted condition—yet, of course, the two are related. We say that this is the electrical energy which existed (in static form) before the current was reconstituted. This is "the unconscious."

When we say that certain experiences, perceptions, motives, feelings, etc., are "missing" from our awareness, it is not that *they* exist "below" awareness (somewhere under there in the body or in an unconscious). Rather there is a narrowed, or in some respects blocked, interaction and experiencing. The manner of experiencing which we have described is one in which, in a good many regards, the experiencing and body life process is *not* "completed" or fully ongoing.

Does this mean that there is no "unconscious"? Only what we are aware of exists? To put the matter in that too simple way ignores important observations. The present theory must be able to account for these observations.[23] Therefore, we are basically reformulating the theory of the unconscious rather than in any simple way throwing it out. The unconscious is redefined as *incomplete process.*

Since there is no sharp distinction between *carrying forward* what is implicitly felt, and *reconstituting* experiencing in previously stopped respects (the former will involve the latter),[24] the felt datum which *is* there, in a sense, contains everything. In what sense does it? In the sense that, *given fully carrying forward responses* to it, everything will be here as aspects of ongoing process.

Therefore, in practice the rule is: "Never mind what is not being felt. Respond to what is being felt."

25. *Extreme Structure-Bound Manner of Experiencing* (*Psychoses, Dreams, Hypnosis,* CO_2, *LSD, Stimulus Deprivation*). Throughout, we have been discussing the *felt, implicit functioning* of the interaction process we term "experiencing." We have been pointing out that all appropriate behavior and interpretations of present situations depend on this *felt* functioning. It constitutes the thousands of meanings and past experiences which determine appropriate present behavior. In addition, it is this felt functioning to which we can respond ourselves, and this is the *self-process.* The functioning I am discussing is *felt,* meaning that we can refer it to ourselves. For example, as we read this page the words are sound images for us. These sound images are all we explicitly have

in mind. However, we also have the *meanings* of the sound images. How? We do not *say* to ourselves what it all means. We *feel* the meanings of what we read as we go along. They function implicitly. This feeling process is an interaction between the symbols on the page and our feeling. This felt *interaction* process is now *ongoing* and gives us appropriate feelings and meanings.

When the *interaction process* is greatly curtailed (as in sleep, hypnosis, psychosis, and isolation experiments), the inwardly felt experiencing is thereby curtailed. The individual then lacks the implicit function of felt experiencing and loses both his sense of "self" and his capacity to respond to and interpret present events appropriately. Both require the felt process just illustrated.

The peculiar phenomena which occur under these circumstances are somewhat more understandable when they are considered in terms of curtailment or stoppage of the *interaction* process and *implicit function of felt* experiencing.

I would like now to state some of the characteristics of this (hallucinatory or dreamlike) *extreme structure-bound manner of experiencing.*

Structures Are Perceived as Such. Ordinarily, past experiences and learnings function implicitly in felt experiencing, so that we interpret and perceive the present, not the past experiences themselves. Yet under hypnosis, in dreams, and in hallucinations, we may perceive rigid structures and past events as such. Characteristically, we do not then have the relevant aspects of felt process which usually function. Thus hallucinations and dreams are not understandable to the present individual. He is puzzled or aghast at them. They often seem to him "not his." The felt experiencing that would give him a sense of their being "his," and would let him know their meaning, is not ongoing. Dreams and hallucinations are, so to speak, decomposed pieces of what would otherwise be a functioning, felt process. This interaction process with the present is not ongoing, and hence the felt meanings are not functioning.

Let me now trace through these several different kinds of circumstances how in each the interaction process is first curtailed, and how in each the function of felt experiencing is then missing.

Extreme Structure-Bound Manner Occurs Whenever the Interaction Process Is Greatly Curtailed. Dreams, hypnosis, psychosis, CO_2 and LSD, and stimulus deprivation share at least one factor, the curtailment of ongoing interaction.

In sleep there is a great reduction of external stimuli. Dreams occur with this curtailment of the usually ongoing interaction process with the environment.

In hypnosis, too, the subject must shut off his interaction with present stimuli, and must cease his own self-responsiveness. He must concentrate on a point.

Psychosis, as has often been remarked (for example, Shlien, 1960), involves both in its genesis and later, an "isolation," a curtailment of interaction between feeling and events. Also, physical isolation from people can, in some individuals, bring on hallucinations.

Certain poisons (CO_2, LSD) are inimical to the physiological interaction process of body life. CO_2 narrows (and eventually stops) the process of respiration.

Experiments in which individuals are placed in soundproof and light-proof suits that also prevent touch stimuli result (after a few hours) in psychotic-like hallucinations.

The peculiarly similar experiences which arise under these widely different conditions hint at something similar. At least one factor they all share is the curtailment of the ongoing interaction process which, as felt, is experiencing. We would thus expect a lack of the implicit functioning which ongoing experiencing usually provides.

And indeed this is shared by the phenomena which occur in all these circumstances. The peculiar character of these phenomena is understandable as a rigidity or lack of this *felt functioning* which usually interprets every present situation for us, and to which we respond in *self-process*. Thus appropriate interpreting of situations and sense of self are lost.

Lack of Implicit Function. The implicit function (see definition 4) of felt experiencing becomes rigid (not *in process*) or "literal" in all these conditions. In hypnosis, for example, when the individual is told to "raise your hand," he will lift the palm of his hand up by his wrist. He will not, as when awake, interpret the idiomatic phrase appropriately (it means, of course, to raise one's whole arm up into the air). The same "literal" quality occurs in dreams and in psychosis. Much of what has been called "primary process," "schizophrenic thinking," or the schizophrenic's inability to "abstract" his "concrete" thinking, his "taking the part for the whole" (Goldstein, 1951), really consists of this *literal* and rigid manner in which experiencing functions. As in dreams and hypnosis, the *felt* process of experiencing is curtailed and does not provide its implicit functioning.

The many implicit *felt* meanings that are needed for appropriate interpretations and reactions do not function, since the *felt* process (of which they are process aspects) is not ongoing. That is exactly what "literal" means: the lack of functioning of *other* meanings which should inform our interpretation of a given set of words or events.

"Loss of Self." Another characteristic shared by dreams, hypnosis,

psychosis, and the phenomena obtained in stimulus-deprivation and LSD, is the loss of a sense of self. In dreams what we perceive is beyond the control, interpretation, ownership, of the self (or ego). In hypnosis the individual specifically accepts another's suggestions for his own and totally permits them to replace his own self-responding. And in psychosis so often the patient complains: "I didn't do that. Something made me do it"; or "I'm not myself"; or "These voices are not mine"; or, "Inside me I'm nothing at all." The hallucinations, voices, and things in his head are not *felt* to be his own. He lacks the sense of self. If he does have a sense of self (an "intact ego"), this felt sense does not inform the hallucinatory phenomena. In regard to these, he has no sense of self that implicitly contains their meaning.

This loss of self is due to the missing felt functioning of experiencing. Just as outward events (to the extent of psychosis) are not interpreted and interacted with on the basis of felt experiencing, so also this felt experiencing is missing for self-responses.

We have defined the self as *self-process*. The self exists to the extent that the individual can carry his felt process forward by means of his own symbols, behaviors, or attention. Experiments with stimulus deprivation have found that individuals who develop psychosis more slowly have a greater capacity to respond to themselves (the most "imagination" and "creativity," it was called). The finding would corroborate our views since, to the extent the individual can carry forward his own experiencing, he will be maintaining (by symbols and attention) his interaction process. When the interaction process is greatly narrowed, not only do psychotic-like experiences occur, but the sense of "self" is lost. The felt process to which there can be self-response becomes static and the individual has *unowned* perceptions.

Static, Repetitious, Unmodifiable Manner. Insofar as the implicit function of felt experiencing is rigid, there is no way for present situations to interact with it, and to modify it so that it becomes an interpretation of the present situation. Instead we perceive a repetitious pattern that is not modified by the present situation. The sequence may "go off" as a result of being "cued" by present events, but it is not an interpretation of, or response to, present events.

The Universality of Psychotic "Contents." Experiences in the extreme structure-bound manner are not *process aspects*. They occur precisely to the extent that the felt process is not ongoing. It is striking how certain themes universally recur—usually the familiar "oral, anal, and genital" themes. It seems that this is the stuff of which we are all composed . . . and into which the usually ongoing process decomposes, insofar as it is not ongoing.

Psychotic Experiences Are Not "the Repressed." It is fallacious to consider these structure-bound manifestations as repressed experiences which have now "emerged" or "erupted." To so consider them raises the puzzling question: On the one hand many theories hold that adjustment requires awareness, and that repression makes maladjustment, but on the other hand they hold that the psychotic is "too aware" and needs to "rerepress" all these experiences.

A better formulation, I think, would be to interpret this observation as follows: Optimally these universal past experiences function implicitly in felt experiencing. When that ongoing process ceases, decomposed static patterns occupy the center of the sensorium.

The implications of this reformulation can be seen, for example, in the following. "The psychosis," in this view, is *not* these supposedly underlying contents (in that sense everyone is "psychotic"). Rather, *"the psychosis" is the curtailment or cessation of the interaction process of feeling and events.* When, therefore, we label an individual "border-line psychotic," this does *not* mean that certain dangerous *contents* lie down there in him. Rather, he is "isolated," "uninvolved," "not quite there," "withdrawn," or "out of touch with himself"; i.e., his *manner* of experiencing is highly structure bound. To prevent "the psychosis" from occurring, one must respond as much as possible to such feelings as do implicitly function, so as to carry forward and reconstitute ongoing interaction and experiencing.

The view of *"latent psychotic contents"* leads to two dangerous errors: either one decides that the individual's feelings of difficulty and trouble had better be ignored (lest they "blossom into" full psychosis), or one "interprets" them and "digs" them "out." Either decision denies and pushes away the personal interaction and the individual's *implicitly functioning* feelings. Either decision will result in psychosis—they involve the same self-verifying misconception that "contents" are psychotic.

There is nothing "psychotic" about any "underlying contents." What is psychotic is the structure-bound manner of experiencing, the absence or literal rigidity of felt experiencing and interaction.

Whether "borderline" or seemingly "gone," the person will "come alive" if interaction and experiencing[25] is reconstituted by personal responses which carry forward what does still function.[26]

26. *Content Mutation.* As *implicitly functioning* felt meanings are *carried forward* and the process is *reconstituted* and made more immediate in *manner*, there is a constant change in "content." As *referent movement* occurs, both symbolization and direct referent change. There is a sequence of successive "contents." Sometimes these successive contents

are said to "emerge" as if they had always been there, or as if the final basic content is now finally revealed. But I prefer to call this *content mutation*. It is not a change only in how one interprets but, rather a change both in feeling and in symbols. The contents change because the process is being newly completed and reconstituted by responses. What the contents will be depends greatly on the responses.

An example of *content mutation* has already been given (definitions 8–9). Here are more examples of content mutation:

The client is in terror. She says there will be "doom." The world will fly to pieces. Something awful will happen. There is a monster.

Here is "the psychosis," someone might say. At any rate, a common enough psychotic *content*.

She is awfully afraid, she says. I respond that she is afraid and that I want to keep company and be with her, since she is afraid. She repeats that she *is* afraid. No matter how much or little meaningful symbology there is to the "doom," she is *afraid now*.

Minutes or months later she can say:

"I'm afraid of being lost. I'm lost. I'm *so* lost!"

"For years I have had to know exactly what to do every moment. I'd plan to know exactly what to do so I'd be distracted. It's like blinders. I'd be afraid to look up, sort of. I need someone or something to hold on to, or I'll disappear."

This is more understandable than world doom. The *content* seems now to be "object-loss" or "passive-dependent needs." Whatever it is, the response needed must provide contact: I grasp her hand; or I talk gently, saying something, pertinent or not—something from me to maintain contact and not to talk away the fear of being lost. In terms of *process unity* such talking and such touching are really the same, in that they both *re-establish interaction*. To do so it must be personal and it must convert the *need* to "hold on" into a successfully *ongoing* contact, real or symbolic.

"I need to hold on, but I'm a monster. No one can love me. You must be sick of me. I need so much, all I do is need. I'm just selfish and evil. I'll suck you dry if I can. I'm just a horrible mouth."

Oral needs, oral incorporation, are now the contents that might be proposed.

But her need *does feel* endless, infinite, hungry. "Sure," I say, "It feels endless, bottomless, and awful to you. It's like you want to be fed and held forever."

Then, or some other time, she may say: "I'm just a baby. I hate that child. An ugly child. I *was* an ugly child. Nobody could like me the way I am."

But we have come a long way when the monster is now a child! A child is quite a nice thing. What became of the monster? A child is quite a human, every-day, daylight thing. What became of the terror? *The psychosis?*

Such *content mutation* can occur within a few minutes or over months. It may occur in such words and symbols as above or in purely socially acceptable language, or with bizarre incoherent words, or in silence. The point I am trying to make is that *the content changes as one responds* and thereby carries forward and reconstitutes an interaction process. Such interaction constitutes felt experiencing, and contents are always aspects thereof. As the process changes, the contents change. I term it *content mutation.*

Content mutation occurs strikingly with so-called "psychotic contents." The monsters, weird fears, infinite hungers, and doom-expectant terrors are so often aspects of isolation, loss of self and interaction. They are not psychotic "things" in a person, but a narrowed or stopped interaction process. As the interaction process is restored the contents change and, also, they become more understandable and commonly human.

But *content mutation* occurs not only with quite dramatic expressions, such as in the above example. It occurs equally with the often silent, unexpressive, and "unmotivated" individuals with whom we have so largely been working in the current research on psychotherapy with schizophrenics (Rogers et al., 1967; Gendlin, 1961, 1962a, 1962c), although these individuals often conceptualize so little of what they are feeling. The following is a further example of *content mutation*:

An individual talks about a chain of circumstances which disturb him. Numerous patterns, characteristics, and personality "contents" seem noticeable in his report of these circumstances.

Perhaps with the aid of responses, he goes on to find that this chain of circumstances really makes him very *angry.* That's it! He is furious. He wishes he could harm and destroy the people involved. He is afraid he will attack them when he next sees them. He hopes he will be able to control this destructive desire. He is amazed at his own *hostility* and his own fear of it. He hardly needs further to report the circumstances, so deeply true is his experience of this anger and destructive need. Again, now, we are tempted to consider personality "contents." Our first deductions now seem too broad. Here, really, we have some contents of this man's personality. We are familiar with this fear of one's own hostility and what some of the bases of the hostility probably are.

But let us say the man continues (and I continue to respond to his *felt meanings*). He imagines himself attempting to vent his anger at these people. He finds now that he is not afraid he will uncontrollably attack and harm them. It is more likely (of all things!) that he will not be able even to yell at them, because perhaps he will cry. His voice would choke up, he is sure. In fact, it is somewhat choked up right now. This thing is not really hostility, it now appears. It is rather that he feels so *hurt!* They should not have done this to him! They hurt him, and . . . what can he do? And now he feels, with some relief, that he finally is in touch with what all this really means to him. (We may now propose a third group of personality contents, again different.)

But, as he continues, it turns out that the circumstances as such do not really matter. No wonder! It seemed all along quite a petty thing to be so upset about. The content is really something else and that is what hurts. And he finds now it is not a hurt after all. Rather, it brought home to him that he feels weak and helpless. "I'm not really hurt" (he now finds), "it's more that it points up to me how I can't make it in the world" (passivity, castration, we may now say).

The term "content mutation" can be applied to this sequential shifting of what seems to be the "content." Contents are process aspects of ongoing feeling process. They can be symbolized because they function implicitly in that feeling process. As it is carried forward, there is referent movement and change in what can be symbolized. It is not merely a shifting of interpretation. There is *referent movement*—that is to say, *that which is being symbolized* is changing.

Content mutation does not imply that all our concepts are simply inapplicable. Often they are correct in terms of predicting the individual's other behaviors, and often they enable us to guess or be sensitively ready for a next content mutation. However, the concepts of personality contents are static and much too general[27] and empty. They are never a substitute for *direct reference, referent movement,* and *content mutation.*

NOTES

1. This tendency to view ongoing change in terms of the static contents it reveals can be seen also in the very many research projects which have employed psychotherapy and hospital situations to study diagnostic and classificatory aspects of people as compared with the very few researches which have employed these treatment settings to study change. Our psychometric instruments do not as yet have standardized or even defined indices of personality change, having been used so rarely before and after psychotherapy. This is another example of the way we tend to think most about the change-resistant contents of personality, even in treatment situations.

2. "Paradigm," or model, refers to the *theoretical* models used in these theories, regardless of whether they use the words "repression" and "content" or not.

3. The repression paradigm in its most oversimplified form can be noticed in use when person A insists that person B has some content he cannot be aware of, because it is "unconscious." B's own experiences and feelings are, by definition, undercut and "thrown out of court." No way to the supposed content exists which B can use.

4. S. Freud, 1914 (p. 375), 1920 (pp. 16–19). H. S. Sullivan, 1940 (pp. 20–21, 205–207), 1953 (pp. 42, 160–163). C. R. Rogers, 1957, 1958, 1959a and b, 1960, 1961, 1962.

5. Throughout, the new concepts and words defined here are intended to lead to new and more effective operational variables. Where research is cited, the theory has already led to some operational variables. One must distinguish *theoretical concepts* from *operational variables*. For example, above, "feeling process" is a theoretical concept. The operational variables (and there will be many specific ones) which a theoretical concept aids us to isolate and define are indices of behavior and exactly repeatable procedures whereby these can be reliably measured.

When it is held that the difference above between "really" and "merely" is a "subjective" difference, this only means that we have *not yet* defined the observable variables which enable a common-sense observer to predict differential behavioral results.

6. Rogers discovered how, in practice, the individual can be helped to overcome the repression model.

His discovery is that defensiveness and resistance are obviated when one responds to an individual "within his own internal frame of reference." This phrase means that the psychotherapist's response always refers to something which is directly present in the individual's own momentary awareness.

Rogers at first found that even if the therapist did nothing more than to rephrase the patient's communication—that is to say, if the therapist clearly showed that he was receiving and exactly understanding the patient's moment-by-moment communications—a very deep and self-propelled change process began and continued in the patient. Something happens in an individual when he is understood in this way. Some change takes place in what he momentarily confronts. Something releases. He then has something else, further, to say; and if this, again, is received and understood, something still further emerges which the individual would not even have thought of (nor was capable of thinking), had not such a sequence of expressions and responses taken place.

7. Experiencing is essentially an *interaction* between feeling and "symbols" (attention, words, events), just as body life is an *interaction* between body and environment. In its basic nature, the physical life process is interaction. (This is an application of Sullivan's basic concepts.) For example, the body consists of cells which are interaction processes involving the environment (oxygen and food particles). If we apply this concept of interaction to experiencing, we can view it as an interaction of feeling and events ("events" here includes verbal noises, others' behaviors, external occurrences—anything that can interact with feeling).

8. For the full theory of affect and meaning see Gendlin (1962*b*). As will be seen later (definitions 15–18 and 26), the discussion here lays the ground for a view of personality which avoids the "content paradigm"; i.e., the erroneous assumption that psychological events involve conceptually formed static units.

9. The word "correctly" here really refers just to this interaction between the felt referent and the symbols which we are describing. The fact that, a few minutes later, the *same* type of interaction with further symbols can again produce a very different, yet now "correct" further conceptualization shows that "correctness" does not imply that a given set of symbols means what the felt referent alone means. Rather, "correctness" refers to the experienced effect which certain symbols produce and which is described above, and in definitions 5 and 6.

10. Research (Gendlin and Berlin, 1961) employing autonomic correlates has borne out this observation operationally. Individuals were given tape-recorded instructions to engage in various processes. After each instruction there was a period of silence in which to carry it out. It was found that galvanic skin resistance (also skin temperature and heart rate) indicated tension reduction during the period when individuals were instructed to (and reported later that they did) focus inwardly on the felt meanings of a troublesome personal problem. It has continued to be difficult to define and check individuals' performances after this and other instructions. Therefore, this research remains tentative. Nevertheless, several replications have supported the observation that, while threatening topics in general raise tension, direct inward focusing involves tension reduction.

11. It is extremely important that the listener refers his words to "this" felt datum in the individual and that he shares the sense that the datum itself decides what is correct and what is not. It is much less important whether or not the listener's words turn out to be accurate.

12. We can always apply logic after the process and formulate the relationships implied, but we can almost never choose correctly ahead of time which of the thousands of possible relations between various problems and topics will function in a concretely felt process as described above.

13. I must now describe some common sorts of so-called "internal" attention which do not involve direct reference and thus are not *focusing*.

Since the term "experiencing" includes any kind of experience at all, so long as we consider it as inwardly *felt* and apply to it the theoretical formulation of *process*, misunderstandings have arisen concerning the mode of experiencing called the *direct referent*. By this latter, more specific term we do not at all mean just anything at all which can be called inward attention.

Especially since the direct referent is "felt," it has been confused with emotions. (Emotions are also said to be "felt.") But the direct referent is internally complex and an individual feels "in touch with himself" when he refers to it, while emotions are internally all one quality . . . they are "sheer." They often keep him from sensing that in himself which is the complex ground of the emotion.

This and other distinctions will become clearer in the following list of kinds of occurrences in an individual which are not direct reference and thus are not focusing.

Direct reference is not:

1. *Sheer emotions.* The emotions of guilt, shame, embarrassment, or feeling that I am "bad" are *about* me or this aspect of my experience and its meaning to me. These emotions are not themselves the experience and its meaning to me. The emotions as such are not a direct reference to the felt experiencing. I must, at least momentarily, *get by* these emotions *about it* (or about myself) in order to refer directly to what all this means to me, why and what makes me feel ashamed. For example, I must say to myself: "All right, yes, I *am* very ashamed; but for a minute now, although it makes me feel very ashamed, I want to sense *what* this is in me."

For example: One client spent many sleepless hours each night with anxiety, shame, and resentment. He blamed himself for his reactions to a certain situation. He felt foolish and ashamed of the whole thing. As he tried to resolve it, he alternately felt resentful (he would decide to confront them, fight it out, not back down, etc.), and alternately he felt ashamed (he was a fool, and humiliatingly so, etc.). Only in the psychotherapy hour did it become possible for him to focus directly on "this," what it was, how it felt, and where it "lived" in him. In "this" he found a good many valid perceptions concerning the other people and the situation which he had not been able to specify before, and a good many personal aspects of himself. During a number of hours he directly referred to successive direct referents and felt meanings. Yet between hours he was unable to do this alone, but felt only shame or resentment. Only by moving temporarily "on by" these emotions could he refer directly to "this," "what I feel," about which, granted, I also have these emotions.

It seems quite striking and universal that we feel guilt, shame, and badness, *instead* of feeling that concerning which we feel shame, guilt, and badness. It is almost as if these emotions themselves preclude our feeling what it all is to us—not so much because they are so unpleasant, as because they skip the point at which we might complete, symbolize, respond or attend to that which centrally we feel. I am inclined to hypothesize that guilt, shame, and badness are emotions which occur as responses instead of the response which, by action or symbolizing, we would otherwise give our felt referent. These emotions seem to complete but actually "skip" the incomplete implicit meanings. It is like an animal whose response to hunger is to bite itself in the leg. Instead of responding with a behavior which in some way "symbolizes" the hunger and carries forward the organismic digestion process, such an animal would be most aware of the pain in its leg and would behave accordingly. At any rate, the preoccupation with these emotions is not to be confused with the felt meaning which, though connected to these emotions, needs the focusing.

One client describes it in terms of a hurricane: "If you only go so far into something, it's like going into a hurricane and getting terribly blown around. You have to go into it and then keep going further and further *in* till you get to the eye of the hurricane. There it's quiet and you can see where you are." This beautifully expresses the fact that the direction of focusing is definitely into the emotions, not away from them, yet also that focusing involves something qualitatively very different than merely "being blown around" by the emotions. The illustration also captures something of the centrality, depth, and quiet which one finds—the quality which others have called "being in touch with myself." The felt referent, for the moment, *is* "me." It *unfolds* and is a thousand things. In comparison, the emotional tone which attaches to it and precedes it is not itself a thousand things. To remain with it merely feeds it. There is always a "breath-held," tense, tight quality about most of these emotional tones. Yet to turn away from the emotion is to turn away also from the direction in which one "finds oneself." Thus, one must "move into" and "through," or "on by," these emotional tones to the direct referent which is the *felt meaning* of it all.

The difference between focusing and "wallowing" or "being trapped in" certain emotions is most dramatically evident when one compares the usual experiences of an individual when he works on a personality difficulty alone and when he does so in the presence of an understanding other person. The difference is dramatic, because during many hours he has gone round and round, feeling the same series of emotions and lacking any *referent movement*. In contrast, often even just saying to the other person a little of what one has been feeling and thinking produces direct reference and referent movement. Later I will discuss this role of the other person in making focusing and other therapeutic processes possible. Another person's responses to the emotions, for instance, can make it possible to "grant them," "let them," and "get by" them, so as to refer directly to the felt meanings. It is often possible, though always unsteady and difficult, for the individual to focus by himself.

2. *Circumstantial orbit.* Just as one may get lost in the sheer emotions of guilt, shame, or badness, so one may also get lost in an inward recitation of circumstances, such as: what one ought to have done or did do; what others did, or might have done, or can be imagined to have done, etc. Such circumstantial play and replay, the inward repetitions of conversations, and dramatic re-enactings are clearly different from the felt meaning all this has and on which the individual could (perhaps, with help) focus. Often the client arrives for the therapy hour after sleepless nights and tired days of this kind of circumstantial "runaround" and finds, with a few responses to the felt meaning of "all this," that with great relief he now directly refers to and unfolds the felt meaning. No matter what a bad look it turns out to have, the physically felt and verbalized steps of focusing are clearly and relievingly different from the circumstantial orbit.

3. *Explanatory orbit.* Attempts at explanations are different from direct reference: "Is it just that I'm so hostile?" "It must mean that I'm projecting some latent homosexuality." "This means I have a need to fail." "It's just

that I'm trying to be right." "I'm just trying to get the love I didn't get as a child." "This is paranoid." "Other people don't get upset at this, so it must be that I'm not grateful for what I have."

Whether the explanatory concepts are simple and foolish, or sophisticated and quite correct, they are useless unless one employs them as pointers to momentarily name and hold onto a directly felt meaning. Without that, one cogitates in a vacuum and gets "no further." The explanatory "runaround" races the mental engine, disengaged from the wheels. It makes one tired and confused, and it is quite different from focusing on the felt meaning. Even one small step of the focusing process can change the inner scene so that one's whole set of explanatory concepts suddenly becomes irrelevant. In comparison with the felt meaning, explanatory concepts are so gross, so general, so empty, that even when they are accurate they are helpless abstractions.

4. *Self-engineering.* A fourth runaround consists in something that might be called "self-engineering." In this also one does not attend to one's felt meaning. Instead, one "talks at" oneself, inwardly. One is very active and constructive, arranging and rearranging one's feelings without stopping to sense quite what they are. This self-engineering is clearly different from focusing on a felt referent and the sensing and symbolizing of its implicit meaning.

Self-engineering is not always futile. In fact, it can succeed exactly to the extent to which one's experiencing in the given regard functions implicitly. The trouble with willpower and engineering is not, as Sullivan held and Rogers sometimes seems to assume, that there is no such thing. There is. One is not always automatically "wafted" into action or self-control. Willpower, decision, and self-engineering are often necessary. However, they cannot be effectively exerted at points where experiencing does not implicitly function. In such regards self-responses or the responses of others are required first, so that the process can be carried forward and experiencing then does implicitly function.

This focusing may be what has always been meant in religious terms by "listening to the still small voice." This has more recently been confused with conscience (and, only in very well-adjusted people can one identify conscience with direct reference). All but a few people have been puzzled as to where inside to "listen" and "hear" this "voice." The above indicates that to "listen" really means to keep quiet, to stop "talking at" yourself, and to sense just what is there, bodily felt, meaningful, and about to become clearer and then verbalizable.

The rule for focusing—a rule to be applied inwardly to oneself—is "Keep quiet and listen!" Then, by referring to the concretely felt referent, it will unfold; the sense of its meaning, and then the words, will come into focus.

14. Our formulation here may be seen as an extension of Sullivan's basic concepts referred to earlier at the beginning of our discussion of Sullivan.

15. Recall our earlier discussion of the repression paradigm. Also see later discussion of the unconscious, definition 24.

16. Compare our earlier discussion of the "content paradigm."

17. Compare George Herbert Mead (1938, p. 445): "The self . . . grows out of the more primitive attitude of indicating to others, and later arousing in the organism the response of the other, because this response is native to the organism, so that the stimulation which calls it out in another tends to call it out in the individual himself."

18. This point has been made by others. Freud said that the energy of the defense comes from the repressed—i.e., that the *concrete force* which motivates the behavior is the *real* one, despite the opposite and *unreal* nature of the *structure that determines the behavior*. Rogers said that the most therapeutic response is to take the basic, intended felt meaning of the individual's self-expression at face value, no matter how obvious the defensiveness and rationalization. But we may add specificity to these more general statements.

19. I call it a fact, because in psychotherapy we observe it. In the above context it is a matter of theoretical formulation, not of fact.

Some observable research variables have been defined: Assents to one set of descriptions of "immediacy" were found to increase significantly in successful psychotherapy (Gendlin and Shlien, 1961). One group of therapists observed significantly more of the above described new experiencing during the hour in success cases (Gendlin, Jenny, and Shlien, 1960). Successful clients were judged significantly higher on scale-defined variables called immediate manner of experiencing and expression (concerning self, personal meanings, the therapist, problems . . . any content), as compared with failure clients.

20. This is a trouble with most concepts about personality change and psychotherapy, as well as with most concepts of ideals, moral values, and life wisdom: The concepts tell a little something of how it seems when one has arrived at the aim, but they tell nothing of the process of getting there. Such concepts make all sorts of mischief because we tend to try to fit them without allowing ourselves the very different process of getting there. Better concepts about the process of getting there can remedy this age-old problem.

21. Many contemporary writers point to the essential interpersonal relatedness of the human individual. Daseinsanalyse, Sullivan, Mead, and Buber point out that individual personality is not a self-contained piece of machinery with its own primary characteristics which is *then* placed into interaction. Rather, *personality is an interacting*.

22. Only in verbal and conceptual content is "self-exploration" in psychotherapy distinguishable from the personal "relationship." As an ongoing experience process they are the same. The individual may say "only here am I myself" (showing the process to include both self and relationship), or he may speak mostly about the *relationship*, or mostly about *himself*. It is the same process whether the content seems to be mostly about self or mostly about the relationship.

One research finding (Gendlin, Jenny, and Shlien, 1960) employed some operational variables related to this point. Psychotherapists were asked to make ratings of the extent to which "therapy, for this client, focuses chiefly on his problems, or . . . on his relationship with you." These ratings were *not* associated with outcome.

On the other hand, outcome did correlate with the following two scales: "How important to the client is the relationship as a source of new experience? Examples: 'I've never been able to let go and just feel dependent and helpless as I do now'; or, 'This is the first time I've ever really gotten angry at someone.'" Another scale which also correlated with outcome was: "To what extent does the client *express* his feelings, and to what extent does he rather talk *about* them?" These findings indicate that outcome is not affected by whether the *content* (*topic*) is the self or the relationship. Rather, it matters whether the individual is engaged in a *manner* of ongoing interaction process which involves newly reconstituted aspects of experiencing.

This research illustrates the usefulness of process concepts as compared to content concepts to generate operational research variables. Earlier research (Seeman, 1954) had posed the problem by finding no significant association between success in psychotherapy and discussion of the relationship with the therapist. The finding seemed to contradict the importance of the relationship. New research replicated that finding and added scales concerning the ongoing interaction *process*.

We need theory to create operational definitions. The most effective kind of theory for that purpose is one which employs process concepts in reference to experiencing. We must carefully distinguish from theory the operational terms (to which it leads) that are then defined by procedure and observation, not by theory.

23. I will choose two observations and show how the reformulation accounts for them:

1. A sequence of words is flashed, each for fractions of a second, on a screen by means of a tachistoscope. When the individual is unable to read the word it is flashed again and again. Now, for example, an individual may be able to read the words "grass," "democracy," "table," "independence," with an average number of repetitions, but for the word "sex" he requires twice as many repetitions. The theories of the unconscious explain this as follows:

The organism can discriminate a stimulus and its meaning for the organism without utilizing the higher nerve centers involved in awareness.

The current theories have this assumption in common: Words such as "unconscious," "repression," "covert," "not me," "denial to awareness," "subception," all involve the uncomfortable but seemingly necessary assumption that there is a discrimination before an aware discrimination takes place, and that the experience or *content* which the individual misses in awareness actually exists somewhere in him. How else can one account for the above example and the many other observations just like it?

But we need not assume that something in the individual first reads the word sex, then becomes anxious about it, and then forces it to remain outside of awareness. Rather let us try to interpret this observation as a case where the individual does not ever read it until he does so in awareness. Why then does he take so long to read just that word when he could read the others in half the time? We have tried to show earlier (definitions 4 and 16) that, in order to read a word and to say what it is, the function of *felt* experiencing is necessary. We read without *explicitly* thinking the meanings of what we read. We have the sound images and *we have the felt meaning*. Now if for some reason our felt process cannot interact with the words, our eyes may continue, but we cannot say what we have read.

To explain the matter, process theory must take the place of content theory. The process of interacting with the symbols, of "reading them," requires the function of experiencing (the inwardly felt body process). If this felt process is not functioning in some regards, then the expected discriminating will not occur in these regards. Aspects which ought to be "implicit" will not function and, therefore, cannot interact and interpret the present situation. Hence, in these regards, the individual may misconstrue or simply miss (be unable to complete) the process, without this implying that he first interpreted these fully and then keeps them out of awareness.

The difference can be put simply: content theories assume that one completes the process of knowing, experiencing, interpreting, reacting, but that some of this process does not reach awareness. The present theory holds that the process does not completely occur.

2. A second observation:

An individual leaves a certain situation feeling quite happy. Four days later he becomes aware that really he has been quite angry about what happened. He feels that he "has been" angry all along but "wasn't aware of it."

Now, our theory denies that what he now calls anger was in his body all along, without awareness. Rather, *there was something, but not the process of being angry*. He calls it being angry *now*, because *now* he is engaged in that process, and he clearly feels the releasing (see definition 8) quality which physiologically lets him know that his present anger "satisfies," "discharges," "releases," "symbolizes," "completes"—in short, *has some deeply felt relation to*—the condition he physically felt during the four preceding days. The process *was not occurring*, and that made for a physiological condition which is *only now* altered. When "structure bound" experience "goes to completion," we feel that we *now* know what it was *then*; we did not know it then, because the ongoing process of now is different from the stopped condition of then.

Only by *completing* the process by response to the feeling or felt meaning that is there (and is *not* anger) does the individual then "become aware" of anger. If we view this in terms of content, it is all very puzzling. First the content is not there, and then, later on, it is said to have been there all along (hidden in there, somewhere). But in terms of process it is precisely this deeply felt relationship of the later anger to the previously felt condition that tells us that a previously stopped process has only now been completed.

We, therefore, need not assume that there are two minds in the individual —one being an unconscious mind that first perceives a content and then permits or prohibits the aware mind to perceive it. Rather, the aware feeling (whatever it is—let us say it is a tension or a dissatisfaction, not at all anger) must be responded to and carried forward. Only thereby does the process go to completion and anger (or whatever supposed content) come to be an aspect of the reconstituted process.

24. See definition 17, the law of reconstitution.

25. In the large research (Rogers, 1960, p. 93) into psychotherapy with schizophrenics in which I am now engaged, we are applying process variables to the behavior changes of psychotics. The findings so far (Rogers et al., 1967) indicate that improvement on diagnostic tests is associated with operational behavior variables of a less rigid, less repetitive, less structure-bound manner of experiencing, and a greater use of felt experiencing as a direct referent and as a basis for behavior, expression, and relating. These tentative findings are defined in terms of rating scale variables and rating procedures.

26. Therapist's self-expression used to reconstitute process:

When the client's verbalization or behavior gives us a sense of the implicit, felt meanings from which he speaks, then responding to that (even if it is not at all clear) carries the process forward and reconstitutes it as well. However, when the client is silent or speaks only of external matters, then *the therapist's* voicing his own feelings is an important mode of response which can reconstitute *the client's* experiencing process.

There are several other kinds of difficulties. Sometimes the client's talk is bizarre and hard to understand. If there are bits which do make sense, one must repeat these carefully, checking one's understanding. This gives the isolated individual a moment-by-moment sense of contact—something like the pier is for a drowning man. I do not want to be merely poetic in saying that. I want to point up the need for a concretely felt sense of the interacting listener which, where welcome to the client, should be given every few moments during talk that is hard to follow.

Sometimes there is no understandable *logical* content, but the symbolic images do add up to a feeling. (Client: "The Austrian army took all my possessions. They're going to pay me a million dollars." Therapist: "Somebody did you dirt? Took everything away from you? You want to make them pay back?").

Sometimes even less is understandable, but one can be sure the individual is suffering, lonely, hurt, having a rough time. The therapist can talk about any of these without needing any confirming response from the client.

Sometimes the therapist must simply *imagine* what *might* be going on in the client. If the therapist says he does not know, would like to know but need not be told, and imagines so-and-so, the therapist can speak about what he imagines and thereby an interaction process is restored.

The client may not say a word, but what is occurring is a felt interaction process in which articulation and symbolization is given his feelings. One person's behavior can *reconstitute* the interaction and experiencing process of the other person (see definition 23).

During silent hours the therapist can express what might go on in a troubled person uncomfortably sitting there; or, what goes on in the therapist as he wishes to help, wishes to hear, wishes not to pressure, hates to be useless, would be glad if he knew the silent time was useful, or imagines many feelings and perhaps painful ones going through the client's mind which he is not ready to talk about yet.

These therapist self-expressions require four specifications:

1. They are expressed explicitly *as the therapist's own*. If they imply anything about the client, then the therapist says he is not sure it is so, he imagines it, has this impression, etc. It needs no affirmation or denial from the client. It is the therapist, speaking for himself.

2. The therapist spends a few moments *focusing* on the feeling he might express. He seeks some aspect from all he feels, some bit which he can safely and simply say. No one can say all of the thousand *implicit* meanings he feels at one moment. One or two—especially those which, at the moment, seem too personal or bad or embarrassing—become, after a moment's *focusing*, an intimate and personal expression of present interaction.

Perhaps it is hard for me that we are silent and I am perhaps useless to him. There! That is something I can tell him. Or, I wonder if in this silence he is doing anything at all. I find that I am glad to be silent if that gives him time and peace to think and feel. I can express that. Such expressions are a warmly personal interaction. But they require a few moments of self-attention during which I *focus* on and *unfold* my present experiencing in this interaction.

3. The phrasings and meanings which arise in us are very strongly influenced by our overall feeling toward the person to whom we speak. The therapeutic attitude toward the client as a person is an attitude of being totally for him—Rogers' (1957) "unconditional regard." Whitehorn (1959) terms it being like the patient's "lawyer." It is an attitude that whatever we both dislike about this trouble, *the individual as a person is "up against" that in himself*. I can always truly assume that. (This attitude has nothing to do with an overall approval or agreement or liking for this or that behavior, trait, attitude, or peculiarity.) Often I must imagine the person inside, who is "up against" all this. Only months later do I come to love and know that person.

It is amazing what a definable and concrete attitude this is. One can depend on it. There is always a person *"up against"* anything dislikable in him.

4. When the client expresses himself, a response to *that* is needed. At such times therapist self-expression can get in the way.

When one has an opportunity to respond to the client's feeling, to *his* specific felt meaning, and the exact way of perceiving and interpreting something, responding exactly to that is the best and most powerful response. The self-expressive modes of responding fit those clients who give little to which one can respond.

Therapist self-expression as a mode of responding is important with those among the people labeled psychotic, who express little feeling, only externalized situational descriptions, or who sit in pure silence. However, there are many well-functioning persons with whom it is difficult to form a deep interaction because they do not express themselves. Kirtner and Cartwright (1958) found that individuals can be predicted to fail in therapy if their *first* interview shows little inward attention. Recently we are learning that therapist self-expression can help reconstitute the interaction and experiencing process of such individuals.

27. A note on the many new terms:

In the realm of personality *change* we largely lack sufficiently specific concepts to discuss and define observations. The present theory attempts to offer such concepts. It is hoped that with these concepts (and others) our thinking and discussing will be advanced and our ability to isolate and define observations sharpened.

There may be some difficulty in holding fast to new definitions such as *direct referent, referent movement, carrying forward, reconstituting, manner of experiencing, implicit function.* It cannot be hoped that all twenty-six definitions will succeed in entering the language. Nevertheless, we need these (or better) terms to discuss personality change.

REFERENCES

Freud, S. Recollection, repetition and working through (1914). In *Collected papers.* Vol. 2. New York: Basic Books, 1959. Pp. 375–376.

Freud, S. Jenseits des Lustprinzips (1920). In *Gesammelte Werke.* Vol. 13. London: Imago Publishing Co., 1940.

Gendlin, E. T. A process concept of relationship. *Counseling Center Discussion Papers, 3,* 2. Chicago: University of Chicago Library, 1957.

Gendlin, E. T. Initiating psychotherapy with "unmotivated" patients. *Psychiatric Quarterly,* 1961, *35,* 134–139.

Gendlin, E. T. Client-centered developments in psychotherapy with schizophrenics. *Journal of Counseling Psychology,* 1962. (a)

Gendlin, E. T. *Experiencing and the creation of meaning.* New York: The Free Press of Glencoe, 1962. (b)

Gendlin, E. T. Need for a new type of concept: Current trends and needs in psychotherapy research on schizophrenia. *Review of Existential Psychology and Psychiatry,* 1962, *2,* 37–46. (c)

Gendlin, E. T., & Berlin, J. I. Galvanic skin response correlates of different modes of experiencing. *Journal of Clinical Psychology,* 1961, *17,* 73–77.

Gendlin, E. T., Jenny, R. H., & Shlien, J. M. Counselor ratings of process and outcome in client-centered therapy. *Journal of Clinical Psychology,* 1960, *16,* 210–213.

Gendlin, E. T., & Shlien, J. M. Immediacy in time attitudes before and after time-limited psychotherapy. *Journal of Clinical Psychology,* 1961, *17,* 69–72.

Gendlin, E. T., & Zimring, F. M. The qualities or dimensions of experiencing and their change. *Counseling Center Discussion Papers, 1,* 3. Chicago: University of Chicago Library, 1955.

Goldstein, K. Methodological approach to the study of schizophrenic thought disorder. In Kasanin & Lewis (Eds.), *Language and thought in schizophrenia.* Berkeley: University of California Press, 1951. Pp. 17–41.

Kirtner, W., & Cartwright, D. Success and failure in client-centered therapy as a function of initial in-therapy behavior. *Journal of Consulting Psychology*, 1958, 22, 329–333.

Mead, G. H. *The philosophy of the act.* Chicago: University of Chicago Press, 1938.

Rogers, C. R. The necessary and sufficient conditions for therapeutic personality change. *Journal of Consulting Psychology*, 1957, 21, 95–103.

Rogers, C. R. A process conception of psychotherapy. *American Psychologist*, 1958, 13, 142–149. Reprinted in W. G. Bennis, K. D. Benne, & R. Chin (Eds.), *The planning of change.* New York: Holt, Rinehart & Winston, 1961. Pp. 361–372.

Rogers, C. R. A tentative scale for the measurement of process in psychotherapy. In E. Rubinstein (Ed.), *Research in psychotherapy.* Washington, D. C.: American Psychological Association, 1959. Pp. 96–107. (a)

Rogers, C. R. A theory of therapy, personality, and interpersonal relationships as developed in the client-centered framework. In S. Koch (Ed.), *Psychology: A study of a science.* Vol. 3. *Formulations of the person and the social context.* New York: McGraw-Hill, 1959. Pp. 184–256. (b)

Rogers, C. R. Significant trends in the client-centered orientation. In D. Brower & L. E. Abt (Eds.), *Progress in clinical psychology.* Vol. 4. New York: Grune & Stratton, 1960. Pp. 85–99.

Rogers, C. R. The process equation of psychotherapy. *American Journal of Psychotherapy*, 1961, 15, 27–45.

Rogers, C. R., Gendlin, E. T., Kiesler, D., & Truax, C. B. *The therapeutic relationship and its impact: A study of psychotherapy with schizophrenics.* Madison: University of Wisconsin Press, 1967.

Rogers, C. R. Toward becoming a fully functioning person. In A. W. Combs (Ed.), *Perceiving, behaving, becoming.* 1962 Yearbook, Association for Supervision and Curriculum Development. Washington, D. C., 1962. Pp. 22–31.

Seeman, J. Counselor judgments of therapeutic process and outcome. In C. R. Rogers & R. F. Dymond (Eds.), *Psychotherapy and personality change.* Chicago: University of Chicago Press, 1954. Pp. 99–108.

Shlien, J. M. A client-centered approach to schizophrenia: First appproximation. In A. Burton (Ed.), *Psychotherapy of the psychoses.* New York: Basic Books, 1960. Chapter 2.

Sullivan, H. S. *Conceptions of modern psychiatry.* New York: W. W. Norton & Co., 1940.

Sullivan, H. S. *The interpersonal theory of psychiatry.* New York: W. W. Norton & Co., 1953.

Whitehorn, J. C. Studies of the doctor as a crucial factor for the prognosis of schizophrenic patients. Paper from the Henry Phipps Psychiatric Clinic of the Johns Hopkins Hospital, 1959.

CHAPTER 30

The Outcome Problem
In Psychotherapy Revisited

Hans H. Strupp

For reasons which will become more apparent later, the outcome problem in psychotherapy has been receiving relatively scant attention in
recent years—not because the problem has lost its importance but rather
because of a realization on the part of researchers that a new approach
to the issue must be found, and that more pressing matters must be dealt
with first before we can address ourselves meaningfully to the question
of the effectiveness of psychotherapy. This rationale partly accounts for
the great interest in so-called process studies which have swept the
scene during the last decade. In this paper I have set myself the task of
reexamining the issue in the light of recent research evidence. Furthermore, I shall attempt to redirect attention to the therapeutic situation
proper as an important criterion situation; if true, this statement would
apply par excellence to the psychoanalytic situation. It appears that
in the furor for "easy" quantifications we have largely lost sight of the
rich potentialities for research in the transference situation, which unquestionably represents the greatest single methodological discovery
for interpersonal research in the twentieth century.

One of the major difficulties in psychotherapy research is that of
adequately specifying the independent variable—the psychotherapeutic
methods—to which therapeutic changes are being attributed. Knight

The writing of this paper was aided by Research Grant No. M–2171(C3), of the
National Institute of Mental Health, Public Health Service.

I am greatly indebted to Dr. Martin Wallach for a critical reading of the manuscript and for a number of valuable suggestions for improvement.

This chapter was voted, by the Editorial Board of the present volume, as one of
the creative developments in psychotherapy, 1958–1968. From *Psychotherapy:
Research, Theory and Practice*, 1963, *1*, 1–13.

(1941), for example, cites the following characterizations (among others):

(1) With regard to the preponderant attitude taken or influence attempted by the therapist; e.g., suggestion, persuasion, exhortation, intimidation, counseling, interpretation, re-education, re-training, etc.

(2) With regard to the general aim of the therapy; e.g. supportive, suppressive, expressive, cathartic, ventilative, etc.

(3) With regard to the supposed "depth" of the therapy—superficial psychotherapy and deep psychotherapy.

(4) With regard to the duration—brief psychotherapy and prolonged psychotherapy.

(5) With regard to its supposed relationship to Freudian psychoanalysis as, for example, orthodox, standard, classical, or regular psychoanalysis, modified psychoanalysis, "wild" analysis, direct psychoanalysis, psychoanalytic psychotherapy, psychoanalytically oriented psychotherapy, psychodynamic psychotherapy, psychotherapy using the dynamic approach, and psychotherapy based on psychoanalytic principles.

(6) With regard to the ex-Freudian dissident who started a new school of psychotherapy. Thus we have Adler's individual psychology with its Adlerian "analysis," Jung's analytical psychology with its Jungian "analysis," the Rankian "analysis," the Stekelian "analysis," and the Horney modifications (pp. 52–53).

What do these techniques have in common? What are their unique differences? What variance is introduced by the person of the therapist practicing them—his degree of expertness, his personality, and attitudes? These are staggering research problems, and the available research evidence by and large is insufficient. It seems to me that we shall not be satisfied with studies of therapeutic outcomes until we succeed in becoming more explicit about the independent variable. Thus the very extensive research efforts which are beginning to get under way in the area of the therapist's contribution, including his personality and techniques, are crucial as a prerequisite. I shall merely mention in passing that variables in the patient's life situation, social class and other environmental factors, are also increasingly being studied. This work is bound to have a cumulative effect.

Let us stay, however, with the method of treatment and consider further its relation to outcomes. For this purpose let us disregard (what in reality cannot be disregarded) therapist variables and socioenvironmental factors. Perhaps it can be agreed that some methods of psychotherapy are more intensive than others—in terms of effort, aim, duration, and the like. If we asked clinicians to rank order different methods of psychotherapy on this continuum, we would undoubtedly find that psychoanalysis, four times a week, for two or more years, would rank at the top and once-a-week supportive therapy in which the patient is seen for a total of 5–10 sessions would be rated somewhere near the bottom. Let us go a step further and predict that therapeutic outcome is (partly at least) commensurate with the effort expended—not an unreasonable assumption in education, training, and child-rearing. It would then follow that, other things being equal, the results achieved by psychoanalysis should be substantially greater than those resulting from minimal treatment methods. We shall for the moment set aside a specification of "greater" but merely suggest that even with crude measuring instruments (which is all we have at present) the demonstration of differences in outcome between the two methods should be a fairly simple matter. The literature, unfortunately, is replete with quasi documentation which has hopelessly befogged the issue.

A brief review of Eysenck's (1952) widely quoted survey, which capitalized upon and added considerably to the existing confusion, may be instructive. In order to make any meaningful statements about the effects of psychotherapy, Eysenck reasoned, it is necessary to compare psychotherapy patients with "untreated controls." The effects of psychotherapy, if any, would thus be demonstrated in terms of differences between the two major groups. The "base line" was provided by two studies, one dealing with the percentage of neurotic patients discharged annually as recovered or improved from New York state hospitals, the other a survey of 500 patients who presented disability claims due to psychoneurosis and who were treated by general practitioners with sedatives and the like. The assumption was made in these two studies that the patients did not receive psychotherapy, or, at least not anything resembling "formal" psychotherapy. The amelioration rate in both studies was in the neighborhood of 72 per cent. Typical criteria of recovery were: (a) return to work and ability to carry on well in economic adjustments for at least a five-year period; (b) complaint of no further or very slight difficulties; (c) making of successful social adjustments.

The results of these studies were compared by Eysenck with 19 reports in the literature dealing with the outcomes of both psychoanalytic and eclectic types of psychotherapy. Pooling the results he found that patients treated by means of psychoanalysis improved to the extent of 44 per cent; patients treated eclectically improved to the extent of 64 per cent; patients treated only custodially or by general practitioners improved to the extent of 72 per cent. Thus, paradoxically, it appears that there is an inverse relationship between intensity of psychotherapeutic treatment and rate of recovery.

A situation in which clinical experience is completely at variance with statistical data usually calls for a searching analysis to discover possible sources of error. However, Eysenck answered—to his satisfaction—the question that the "control" patients were as seriously ill as the treated patients, and that the standards of recovery were equally stringent for both groups. His paper also shows that contrary to the subsequent popularizations of his findings (by himself) he was well aware of the limitations of the comparison. However, he takes seriously his conclusion that "roughly two-thirds of a group of neurotic patients will recover or improve to a marked extent within about two years of the onset of their illness, whether they are treated by means of psychotherapy or not" (p. 322).

Several writers have taken Eysenck to task for his conclusions, pointing out numerous fallacies in his design. For example, his so-called untreated control groups are almost certainly deficient for the purpose; the criteria for discharge from a state hospital are undoubtedly very different from those of a psychoanalytic treatment center; and the "spontaneous recoveries" may, for all we know, be spurious. If this is true, or even if the "spontaneous recovery" rate is grossly overstated, Eysenck's uncritical acceptance of these figures and his unfortunate conclusion to abandon the training and practice of psychotherapy forthwith would be rash. Furthermore, if two-thirds of all people who suffer from a "neurosis" "recovered" within two years "after onset," emotional disorder would scarcely be the serious problem which manifestly it is. Finally, one may take issue with Eysenck's assertion that psychotherapists must do significantly better than 72 per cent before they can make any legitimate claim for the efficacy of their procedures.

Even if Eysenck's arguments are ill-founded, it behooves us to take a close look at the results reported by the psychoanalytic treatment centers, because it may be presumed that the most intensive, the most ambitious, and the most thoroughgoing form of psychotherapy is practiced there. Eysenck's data abstracted from published reports are given in Table 1.[1]

Eysenck points out that in this tabulation he classed those who stopped treatment together with those who were rated as not improved. This seemed reasonable to him on the ground that a patient who failed to finish treatment should be considered a therapeutic failure. However, if only those patients are considered who completed therapy— about one-third broke off treatment—the percentage of successful treatments rises to about 66 per cent (Eysenck). Although it may be true that errors in technique may have been responsible for some of the premature terminations, it seems quite unjustified to regard such cases as

TABLE 1 (*From Eysenck, 1952*)
SUMMARY OF REPORTS OF THE RESULTS OF PSYCHOTHERAPY

	N	CURED; MUCH IMPROVED	IMPROVED	SLIGHTLY IMPROVED	NOT IMPROVED; DIED; LEFT TREATMENT	% CURED; MUCH IMPROVED; IMPROVED
(A) *Psychoanalytic*[*]						
1. Fenichel (1930; pp. 28–40)	484	104	84	99	197	39
2. Kessel & Hyman (1933)	34	16	5	4	9	62
3. Jones (1936; pp. 12–14)	59	20	8	28	3	47
4. Alexander (1937; pp. 30–43)	141	28	42	23	48	50
5. Knight (1941)	42	8	20	7	7	67
All cases	760	353		425		44%

[*] Part B (Eclectic) omitted.

"therapeutic failures"; by the same token, the efficacy of insulin therapy is hardly adequately represented by including those diabetics for whom it was prescribed but who failed to adhere to the regimen.

Eysenck presented his tabulation of results from therapy under four headings: (a) cured, or much improved; (b) improved; (c) slightly improved; (d) not improved, died, discontinued treatment, etc. This criterion is undoubtedly crude; it may be unreliable; it may reflect an impossibly high standard of perfection; it may be entirely incomparable to the judgments made for the "control" cases or for the studies of "eclectic psychotherapy." But, over-all assessments are often the best we have, and in many areas of psychological measurement they have been shown to have a highly valid core. This would hold true on even stronger grounds where the raters have had ample opportunity to make observations and have intimate knowledge of the person being rated. Where would such conditions be met more perfectly than in psychoanalytic treatment? Irrespective of the validity or meaningfulness of Eysenck's comparisons, the statistics reported by the four[2] psychoanalytic treatment centers may be accepted as reasonable assessments. Still, there is the somewhat disconcerting fact that some 21 per cent of the patients treated were only "slightly improved" and 35 per cent fall into the limbo category "not improved, died, discontinued treatment, etc." However the data are analyzed, we are left with the conclusion that psychoanalysis was only slightly successful or unsuccessful for about 30 per cent of the patients who at one point were accepted for therapy. Since they were accepted for therapy we may presume that at that time, at least, they were considered suitable candidates for this form of psychotherapy. Apart from the fallibility of the criterion measure (which has been considered to be relatively slight), the lack of success may be attributed to the following factors, or a combination of these:

(a) errors in judgment about the analysand's suitability; (b) factors in the patient's psychopathology or character structure which emerged as insurmountable obstacles after therapy began; (c) deficiencies in the method of treatment; (d) inadequacies of the therapist's technical skills or shortcomings of his personality; (e) vicissitudes of the particular patient-therapist interaction which resulted in a therapeutic impasse; and (f) variables in the patient's (and/or the therapist's) life situation which produced adverse effects.

Some of these factors may have been predictable at the beginning of therapy provided more complete information had been available; others may have been completely fortuitous and beyond human control. For example, if we had precise information that patients with a certain character structure fail to benefit markedly from psychoanalysis 80 to 90 per cent of the time, and if we could be sure that Patient X is a member of that class, it would be unwise to recommend psychoanalysis for him. Or, if we had precise information that patients with a certain personality structure in 80–90 per cent of the cases come to grief when entering therapy with a therapist having a particular personality structure, one would advise them accordingly and help them select a more suitable therapist. Fortuitous circumstances (e.g., a fatal illness) need no further illustration. The point to be made is this: Considering the extremely important implications of the decision in advising a patient to enter or not to enter psychoanalysis (or, for that matter, any form of psychotherapy), it would be highly advantageous from the therapist's as well as the patient's point of view to have precise information about the outcome that might reasonably be expected. An increase in the power to predict the outcome of psychotherapy would indeed represent a tremendous advance: not only would it conserve money, energy, and professional manpower, but it would enhance the scientific status of psychotherapy to an unprecedented degree. In order to compete with other forms of treatment, psychotherapy and psychoanalysis need not establish that they are superior to anything else that is available: their claim to existence, survival, and development rests on the establishment of a large number of empirical, highly predictable relationships among key variables which are based on a coherent theory of demonstrable utility, that is, a theory which accounts for highly predictable *and* measurable therapeutic gains.

What is meant by "outcome"? In Eysenck's review and in many of the studies on which it is based, the term is used in extremely loose fashion. Eysenck himself treats neurosis in analogy to a form of physical illness, which allegedly one may contract at one time or another during one's lifetime, which seems to run an almost self-limiting course, and from which the patient somehow recovers through therapy or spontaneously. Anyone having the slightest familiarity with psychopathology and psychodynamics knows how erroneous and misleading such a conception is. I shall not pursue this point at the moment but plan to return to it in a somewhat different context. For the moment, it must be conceded that irrespective of our conception of neurosis or mental disorder there is such a thing as outcome from therapy. But, what kind of criterion is it?

Holt (1958), in an insightful and lucid article, tells us that there is a hidden trick in global predictions because they are not themselves a form of behavior but a judgment made by someone on a great deal of concrete behavior. This is true of grades in college, success in any type of treatment, and the like. "Because it is hidden by the label," Holt says, "there is a temptation to forget that the behavior you should be trying to predict exists and must be studied if it is to be rationally forecast." As long as one relies on global clinical judgments, like outcome, no matter how remarkable clinical judgments may sometimes be, one substitutes something for real information, and where there is no genuine information to begin with, none can be generated.

What needs to be done is "to decide what intervening variables need to be considered if the behavior is to be predicted [and] to deal with the inner constructs that mediate behavior and the determining situational variables as well. . . . The best practice seems to be to give explicit consideration to this step [the formation of clinical judgments], and to supply judgment with as many relevant facts as possible. This means studying known instances, comparing people who showed the behavior in question with others who in the same situation failed to" (p. 2).

To translate Holt's lesson to the therapy situation, it is futile to make judgments and predictions about outcome as long as we have paid insufficient attention to variables in the patient, the therapist, the method of therapy, the patient-therapist interaction, and the surrounding life situation. It is this realization, I believe, which in recent years has caused investigators in the area of psychotherapy to lose interest in "simplistic" (Luborsky's term) outcome studies of the kind we have been discussing and turned them to sustained research upon the psychotherapeutic process itself. Nevertheless, it seems to me, we shall again and again return, armed with more specific data, to the problem of outcome, no matter how arbitrary an end point it may represent.

In the following I shall attempt to deal with two areas having a bearing on the problem of outcome. Both represent important frontiers of research, although clearly they are by no means the only, or even the most important ones. But in both, researchers have had more than a modicum of success in mapping it out, in charting it, and in establishing the kinds of empirical connections of which Holt speaks. To be sure, the progress cannot be termed spectacular or a "breakthrough," but it represents the constructive, painstaking, gradual effort which is needed. I am referring to the area of the patient's motivation for therapy, including patient-therapist compatibility; and, secondly, to analyses dealing with the criterion problem. Progress in the former area is more impressive than in the latter, but both unquestionably represent cornerstones on which the scientific edifice of psychotherapy must ultimately rest.

From a fairly large body of converging empirical evidence, which I shall not review here, it is becoming increasingly clear that therapists have fairly specific—and presumably valid—notions about the kinds of attributes which a "good" patient should possess, as well as about those attributes which make a patient unsuitable for the more usual forms of investigative, insight-producing psychotherapy. Patients considered good prognostic risks tend to be young, physically attractive, well-educated, members of the upper middle class, possessing a high degree of ego-strength, some anxiety which impels them to seek help, no seriously disabling neurotic symptoms, relative absence of deep characterological distortions or strong secondary gains, a willingness to talk about their difficulties, an ability to communicate well, some skill in the social-vocational area, a value system relatively congruent with that of the therapist, and a certain psychological-mindness which makes them see their problems as emotional rather than physical. A number of these attributes appear to be statistically linked to social class. This linkage extends to the patient, the therapist, and the principles of psychotherapy to which he subscribes.[3]

Hence, therapists tend to select those patients whose attributes meet the above criteria. It is hard to say whether therapy is effective because therapists invest their best efforts when these conditions prevail or whether the existence of these conditions in itself presages favorable results. Both statements are probably true to some extent, although variables within the patient and situational variables may play a more important part than the therapist's attitudes and expectations.

Every neurotic patient is unconsciously committed to maintain the status quo, and psychotherapy, particularly if aimed at confronting the patient with his inner conflicts, proceeds against the obstacle of powerful unconscious resistances. Therefore, unless there is a strong conscious desire to be helped and to collaborate with the therapist, the odds against a favorable outcome may be insuperable. Motivation for therapy is a global and a highly complex variable; research has shown that it is made up of combinations of the variables in the patient which have already been mentioned. But, it represents a clinical judgment made by the therapist, which in turn is colored to a significant extent by his own personality and attitudes. Because psychotherapy demands great investments of time and emotional energy from the therapist, it is hardly surprising that his willingness to enter into a therapeutic relationship with a particular patient becomes highly selective. We know that different therapists, depending on their own personality, have highly individual preferences, which it would be important to elucidate. It seems reasonable to hypothesize that therapeutic relationships in which the patient is highly motivated to seek therapeutic help and in which the therapist in turn is highly motivated to put his skills at the patient's disposal have, other things being equal, the greatest chance of success.

For example, Kirtner & Cartwright (1958), studying 42 cases at the University of Chicago Counseling Center, found a significant association between treatment outcome and the manner in which the client conceptualized and presented his problem in the initial interview. Failure cases tended to intellectualize and discussed external manifestations of internal difficulties. Successfully treated cases, on the other hand, tended to deal with feelings in the therapeutic relationship and were eager to discover how they were contributing to their inner difficulties. No doubt, the second group was considered more suitable by the client-centered therapists. While it cannot be proven, it is entirely possible that those patients who felt they could be helped by client-centered therapy (and by client-centered therapists) continued to work on their problems, whereas those who did not, dropped out. One may also speculate that the therapist's motivation to help the latter group of patients, for a variety of reasons, was less. Thus, the therapist's attitude toward the patient may reinforce corresponding attitudes in the patient, leading to premature termination of therapy. There is no implication that this phenomenon is restricted to one form of therapy or to any one stage of therapy; however, the judgment of therapeutic failure, premature termination, therapeutic impasse, poor motivation for therapy, and the like, wherever it occurs, may signal an unwillingness or inability on the part of the therapist to work with a particular patient as much as it reflects limiting factors within the patient.

Empirical evidence bearing upon this problem has been adduced by our research group in a series of studies dealing with therapists' perceptions of patients, clinical judgments, treatment plans, and therapeutic communications. In some of these studies therapists were presented with a sound film of a therapeutic interview (Strupp, 1958); in others, they based their evaluations on patients seen in diagnostic interviews (Strupp & Williams, 1960); in still others, we presented therapists with written case histories (Wallach & Strupp, 1960). The findings have been remarkably congruent, and are corroborated by similar studies in the literature. Certain systematic differences in therapist responses were traceable to such variables as level of experience, theoretical orientation, and personal analysis. However, in all investigations the therapist's attitude toward the patient as rated by himself showed a highly significant statistical relationship to his clinical judgments and treatment plans, and, where we obtained such data, to the emotional tone of his communications. In recent studies, an item which inquired whether the therapist felt warmly toward the patient proved particularly predictive. For example: negative attitudes toward the patient were found to be correlated with a more unfavorable diagnosis and prognosis; with recommendations for greater strictness and activity on the part of the therapist; with recommendations for less frequent interviews; with greater unwillingness to treat him, etc. The reverse was also true.

With regard to the therapists' communications, there was a significant relationship between the degree of empathy shown toward the patient and the therapist's self-rated attitude, such that therapists who felt more positively toward the patient also communicated with him more empathically. The variable of personal analysis entered into this statistical relationship in a very interesting way: if the therapist had undergone a personal analysis he was more likely to reveal a high degree of empathy in his communications irrespective of whether he described his attitude toward the patient as positive or negative. This finding was particularly pronounced for the more experienced therapists. Thus it seemed that in the case of experienced therapists their personal attitude toward the patient was less likely to influence the emotional tone of their communications to the patient provided their training had included a personal analysis; if it had not, a negative attitude tended to be associated with lack of empathy.

The implications of these findings relate to the possibility that the therapist's attitude toward the patient, as conveyed by his communications, may bring about a realization of the therapist's conscious as well as unconscious expectations concerning the course and outcome of therapy. For psychotherapy the crux of the matter is not the perceptions and clinical evaluations or even the therapist's conscious attitude toward the patient; rather it is the manner in which these variables influence and structure the therapeutic relationship. This is one of the important problems requiring further exploration.[4]

It is as yet unknown to what extent the patient may fulfill the therapist's unverbalized prophecy. This much, however, is clear: In the absence of a keen and abiding interest and dedication on the part of the therapist, the patient cannot marshal the necessary strength and energy to fight his way to a healthier adaptation, or, to use Dr. Alexander's felicitous term, he cannot undergo a corrective emotional experience. This is particularly true in those situations in which the therapist aims at a thorough reorganization of the patient's personality by inducing him to relive his childhood traumas. Too, the infinite patience which dedicated therapists like Frieda Fromm-Reichmann, Otto Will, Harold Searles, and others have invested in therapy with schizophrenic patients bears eloquent tribute to the proposition that often therapeutic gains are commensurate with the efforts expended by the therapist, provided the patient possesses good basic personality resources.

On the experimental side, numerous studies attest that patients who appear to be motivated for psychotherapy (however the therapist understands this term) tend to be liked by therapists and the prognosis is seen as more favorable (Wallach & Strupp, 1960). Heine & Trosman (1960) have shown that mutuality of expectation is an important factor in the continuation of the therapeutic relationship. In this study, patients who continued in psychotherapy conceptualized their expectations of therapy in a manner more congruent with the therapist's role image, and may therefore have been more gratifying to the therapist. Similarly, Strupp & Williams (1960) found that patients who were judged nondefensive, insightful, likable, and well motivated for therapy were seen by therapists as most likely to improve. In the same vein, Sullivan, Miller, & Smelser (1958) summed up their findings by saying: "those persons who are least equipped to meet life challenges are the ones who stand to gain least from psychotherapy" (p. 7).

Now it may be conceded that a high level of motivation on the part of the patient as well as on the part of the therapist is auspicious for successful psychotherapy, but what about that large group of patients who fail to meet the above high criteria? What shall be done with them? Secondly, nothing has been said about a related question pertaining to the chronicity and severity of the personality disorder which the therapist is attempting to treat. Surely, no matter how highly a patient may be motivated to seek professional help and how eagerly he may consciously seek to do something about his difficulties, this desire may count for little if his personality structure poses insuperable difficulties to therapy.

To be sure, apart from the patient's motivation for therapy, there are clinical indicators which set limits to the therapist's best efforts. It will be recalled that Freud dealt with these most eloquently and exhaustively in his paper "Analysis Terminable or Interminable" and elsewhere.

The therapist cannot perform miracles, and he cannot exceed the limits set by constitutional and hereditary factors; nor can he always undo the crippling conditions brought about by extremely adverse childhood experiences. In this dilemma the therapist has essentially two choices: (a) he can attempt to select patients whom he considers promising candidates for psychotherapy, and with whom he feels he can work productively, rejecting all other applicants; (b) he can recognize the limitations imposed by reality and do his best even if he realizes that in such instances his success may be less than spectacular. What he must not do—and here we return to the experimental findings cited earlier—is to let *irrational* personal attitudes about the treatability or nontreatability of certain patients and clinical conditions influence the best technical efforts he might otherwise put forth. At the present state of knowledge, the dividing lines between clinical indicators and limitations on the one hand, and personal attitudes of the therapist on the other, are unfortunately not as clear as one would like them to be. If they could be disentangled and assessed more objectively, the prediction of therapeutic outcomes would be markedly enhanced, and the percentage of patients who emerge from therapy as "slightly improved" or "unimproved" might dwindle further to approach that ultimate, irremediable hard core contributed by "chance."

Undoubtedly there is no simple relationship between diagnostic indicators and therapeutic outcomes, and much remains to be learned about the problem; in principle there seems to be no reason why it should not be susceptible to conceptual analysis and empirical research—the kind of "job analysis" approach which Holt proposes. Traditionally, the "classical" neurotic conditions, like hysteria, have been considered ideally suited for psychotherapy and psychoanalysis, whereas severe character disorders and the psychoses have been relegated to the opposite end of the treatability continuum of psychotherapy. Partly such judgments are based upon clinical experience; but in part they also reflect subtle value judgments about the kinds of persons with whom psychotherapists prefer to work, as well as an appraisal in socio-cultural terms of the patient's character structure and symptoms. Consequently, a patient meeting the psychotherapist's explicit as well as implicit criteria of a "good" or "promising" patient not only has a better chance of finding a competent therapist, but he may from the beginning elicit greater interest from the therapist, who in turn may become more willing to make an emotional investment in the treatment program and to devote greater energy to the treatment. It is as yet unknown to which extent the patient may fulfill the therapist's unverbalized prophecy.

However, it may turn out that a great deal more can be done for certain patients psychotherapeutically once it is possible to approach them and their difficulties in living more objectively.

After many of the variables which need investigation and specification have been sorted out, we may find that only a relatively restricted band of the population meets the criteria for a "good" patient. The available evidence points to a convergent trend, which was aptly summarized by Luborsky (1959): "Those who stay in treatment improve; those who improve are better off to begin with than those who do not; and one can predict response to treatment by how well they are to begin with" (p. 324). It may be noted that the criteria of suitability which have been identified by research coincide remarkably well with those outlined much earlier by Freud. What about the much larger group of people who by these standards are unsuitable for the more common forms of psychotherapy practiced today?

From a practical point of view, the answer seems to lie not in making them more amenable to available methods of psychotherapy—sometimes this can be done, although it is a difficult and time-consuming effort—but in becoming more selective about making the limited facilities and the limited professional manpower available to those who can benefit from it the most. Rather than being "undemocratic," this appears to be a counsel of reality. Research might make an important contribution by refining the selection of particular patients for particular therapists and for particular therapeutic methods. The challenge for the development of alternative techniques and treatment methods for those who cannot readily benefit from customary psychotherapy of course continues and will have to be met. To return once again to the statistical results previously cited, there is a strong possibility that a segment of the failure or near-failure cases can be accounted for in terms of poor selection methods of candidates. In some cases it may be the better part of valor to acknowledge limitations imposed by reality, no matter how painful the consequences may be, rather than to attempt the impossible.

I shall turn next to another major stumbling block in psychotherapy research—the problem of criteria for evaluating results. Before the advent of the "modern era" in psychotherapy research, that is, before sophisticated methodologists and researchers versed in matters of objective investigation and experimental design concerned themselves with these matters, a group of prominent psychoanalysts, including such men as Fenichel, Strachey, Bibring, Bergler, and Nunberg (1937) addressed themselves to the issue. This occurred at the International Congress of Psychoanalysis at Marienbad, in 1936. While this group did not make any formal recommendation for judging outcomes, they dealt with the aims of psychoanalytic therapy and its modus operandi. Knight (1941), in a valuable paper, returned to the problem, listing three major groups of criteria, with several subheadings. Since this compilation has not been substantially improved upon, let me quote it in its entirety:

1. *Disappearance of presenting symptoms*
2. *Real improvement in mental functioning*
    a. The acquisition of insight, intellectual and emotional, into the childhood sources of conflict, the part played by precipitating and other reality factors, and the methods of defense against anxiety which have produced the type of personality and the specific character of the morbid process;
    b. Development of tolerance, without anxiety, of the instinctual drives;
    c. Development of ability to accept one's self objectively, with a good appraisal of elements of strength and weakness;
    d. Attainment of relative freedom from enervating tensions and talent-crippling inhibitions;
    e. Release of the aggressive energies needed for self-preservation, achievement, competition and protection of one's rights.
3. *Improved reality adjustment*
    a. More consistent and loyal interpersonal relationships with well-chosen objects;
    b. Free functioning of abilities in productive work;
    c. Improved sublimation in recreation and avocations;
    d. Full heterosexual functioning with potency and pleasure.

Knight, too, called attention to certain limitations, which may detract from the full effectiveness of the therapeutic method. These will be recognized as the counterparts of the "good patient" variables previously mentioned. Limitations may be due to: (1) the patient's intelligence; (2) native ability and talents; (3) physical factors, such as muscle development, size, personal attractiveness, physical anomalies, sequelae of previous injury or illness, etc.; (4) permanent crippling of the ego in infancy and childhood; (5) life and reality factors which might impose frustrations, privations, etc., against which the patient must do battle, and which might produce relapses; (6) the patient's economic status, whether there is too little or too much money.

It is apparent that Knight's enumeration of criteria goes far beyond a definition of disabling illness and in fact it attempts a definition of positive mental health. It is also clear that the objectives of psychoanalytic therapy have always aspired to this ideal, and the outcome statistics reported by the various psychoanalytic treatment centers leave no doubt on this point. As early as 1930, Fenichel stated in this connection:

We have defined the concept "cured" as rigorously as possible. We have included in this category only cases whose success involves not only symptom removal but which underwent character changes that are rationally and analytically completely understandable and which, where possible, were confirmed through follow-up. In view of this rigor, most of the cases designated as "much improved" are for practical purposes completely coordinate with the "cured" ones. "Improved" cases are those which have remained refractory in one form or another; in this category also belong those cases which for external reasons had to remain partial successes, as well as those which were discharged already in the phase of "transference cure," hence, psychoanalytically speaking they must be considered questionable [p. 19].

By contrast, Eysenck's survey implicitly adopted a much less rigorous standard, oriented around symptom removal. His compilation is a telling example of the confusion which arises when one uncritically mixes studies in which a variety of criteria, frequently unspecified, are adopted. This dilemma, however, cannot be resolved until we succeed in developing more specific empirical indicators of treatment outcomes. Among other things, this requirement entails operational definitions which can be agreed upon by independent observers. For example, there may be reasonable agreement on the meaning of "symptomatic recovery," but a moment's reflection will reveal the difficulties inherent in such judgments as "increased productiveness" or "achievement of sufficient insight to handle ordinary psychological conflicts and reasonable reality stresses."

Knight seems to take it for granted that the evaluations are to be made by the therapist. While it may be conceded that the therapist's knowledge of the patient's psyche is second to none, and that therefore he is in a unique position to perform the evaluative task, it must be remembered that his judgment is vulnerable on a number of grounds, including his personal involvement as well as the necessarily segmental view which he obtains of the patient's life.

In an effort to objectify the therapist's observations many attempts have been made during the last two decades to develop measures of the patient's intratherapy behavior. These have usually taken the form of quantifying aspects of his verbal behavior in therapy. Another large group of studies has followed the phenomenological approach, by asking the patient to evaluate his own status. A third approach has dealt with assessments by means of psychological tests. Zax and Klein (1960), following a review of several hundred investigations, conclude that the most serious failing of these approaches is that the criterion measures have not been systematically related to externally observable behavior in the life space of the patients. Their own proposed solution is to develop:

criteria of sufficient breadth that they are meaningful and representative of a wide range of functioning and yet, at the same time, circumscribed enough to be measured with reliability [p. 445].

They go on to say that the development of such criteria is in its infancy, largely because there is no unifying set of principles (a theory of "normal" behavior) to guide observations. Finally, they express the hope that it might be possible to develop "a relatively limited number of norms reflecting basic interpersonal environments which can be useful." The basic problem here seems to be one of bridging the gap between the person's inner psychic experience and his adaptation to an interpersonal environment.

Clearly, there can be no single criterion of mental health or illness. As Jahoda's ((1958) excellent review of current concepts points out, mental health is an individual and personal matter; it varies with the time, place culture and expectations of the social group; it is one of many human values; and it should differentiate between the person's enduring attributes and particular actions. One value prominent in American culture is that the individual should be able to stand on his own two feet without making undue demands or impositions on others.

From the research point of view, Jahoda discerns six major approaches to the subject:

1. Attitudes of the individual toward himself.
2. Degree to which a person realizes his potentialities through action (growth, development, self-actualization).
3. Unification of function in the individual's personality (integration).
4. Individual's degree of independence of social influences (autonomy).
5. How the individual sees the world around him (perception of reality).
6. Ability to take life as it comes and master it (environmental mastery).

In her searching and incisive discussion of the directions for further research Jahoda clearly indicates that we must develop better empirical indicators of positive mental health in all of the above areas; beyond this it is necessary to specify the conditions under which it is acquired and maintained. The development of outcome criteria in psychotherapy largely overlaps these requirements and must follow a similar course. The patient's behavior in therapy will scarcely suffice as an ultimate criterion, but it will occupy a central position in the cluster of criteria which will undoubtedly emerge. The therapy situation is a unique "test situation" in this respect, whose rich potentialities we have barely begun to exploit. I should like to outline briefly some of the unique advantages as well as some of the limitations.

1. By virtue of its particular structure, the therapeutic situation, and particularly the psychoanalytic situation, removes the conventional restraints in interpersonal communication and makes it possible to observe the patient's "real" feelings and emotional reactions with a minimum of distortions.

2. By inducing regression it uncovers invaluable data about the patient's most enduring patterns of interpersonal relatedness and facilitates the tracing of their genetic development.

3. It provides a penetrating view of the patient's motivational patterns, the manner in which basic strivings are bound intrapsychically, adapted to, and translated into action. Such microscopic observations are carried out over extensive periods of time. Thus it is possible to trace the relationship between an action and its underlying motivation, and to gain considerable information about the mediating processes. Hence the therapeutic situation avoids a frequent error in psychological research, namely the assumption of an invariant relationship between a behavioral act and the person's underlying motivation.

4. The therapeutic situation simulates an appropriately complex situation and thus meets the objections of oversimplification and artificiality frequently levelled against experimental analogues. (It has been said that the therapeutic situation represents a highly personal situation within a highly impersonal framework.)

5. In the therapeutic situation, the therapist gains important insights into the patient's inner experience, the manner in which he perceives himself, and his self-concept; but he also can assess the patient's social stimulus value—at least in relation to the therapist as a representative of the social environment, and observe discrepancies between inner experience and outward actions. Usually we are restricted in our knowledge of the other person and we can only make inferences from his actions, his verbal communications, and clues we get from his unwitting behavior. In individual therapy, by contrast, the patient himself, through the agency of his observing ego, adds important data about his inner experience to the aforementioned ones. Thus a unique, panoramic view is obtained.[5]

6. The therapeutic situation yields unique data on the manner in which a particular input (clarification, interpretation, etc.) is perceived, experienced, and reacted to on verbal as well as nonverbal levels. Thus, we may gain considerable information about the manner in which an

external stimulus is perceived and experienced, and we may note discrepancies between the "objective" aspects of the stimulus (at least as seen by the therapist) and the way in which it is experienced by the patient.

These are some examples to indicate the variety of ways in which the psychotherapeutic situation provides criteria—which in part have their own validity—about human mental functioning. But we demand that intratherapeutic criteria have a counterpart in the external world, that is, a validity beyond the therapeutic situation. It is noteworthy that in the various mental health criteria enumerated by Jahoda the therapeutic situation plays an important part in gathering more precise empirical indicators. It is my thesis, then, that the therapeutic situation itself should be used to a much greater extent than has been heretofore the case to generate and develop criteria of outcome. This conclusion follows from the belief that nowhere else do we have an opportunity to make as penetrating, intensive, systematic, and undistorted observations as in the therapeutic setting.[6] Furthermore, it is in keeping with one of the major working hypotheses of psychoanalysis, that the patient's relationship to the therapist (the transference) is the most faithful replica of the patient's capacity for intimate interpersonal relatedness; as a corollary it states that the patient's adaptation to his human environment outside the therapeutic situation "improves," that is, becomes less conflictual, and more satisfying to the extent that he is able to relate more effectively (in less conflictual ways) to the therapist. The skilled therapist is keenly aware of the shifts in the patient's patterns of relatedness (to him), and he regards them as sensitive indicators of therapeutic change and improvement. What I am advocating, then, is that as researchers we attempt to systematize and objectify these intratherapeutic observations and, wherever possible, relate them to the patient's interpersonal performances outside therapy.

In making this recommendation I am placing major emphasis upon the therapy situation as a miniature life situation, and I am stressing the alignment of psychic forces rather than specific behavioral acts in the outside world. This view is predicated on the (testable) assumption that there is a close association between the quality of the patient's relationship to the therapist and the quality of his relationships with others, including his adaptation to reality. I am also suggesting that the therapist, because he is in possession of incomparably fuller data about the patient's personality, is potentially in a superior position to assess the patient's "mental health." No therapist would maintain that the patient's behavior with close associates or his mastery of life's problems is unimportant, but he is probably correct in insisting that he (in collaboration with the patient) is better equipped to assess the patient's success in living than outsiders irrespective of the degree of their sophistication.

Among the difficulties of using the therapeutic situation as a criterion-generating situation we must note: (1) the problem of conceptualizing, specifying, and quantifying the multidimensional observations made in therapy; (2) the therapist's reliability as an observer (by which is meant more than countertransference); and (3) limitations inherent in the two-person setting, which provide representative, but incomplete, data about the patient's interactions with others. Because of the transference relationship, the therapist tends to get a more or less distorted perspective of the patient's current reality functioning and to some extent he is forced to accept the patient's view of reality, although he will generally be able to make appropriate corrections.

These recommendations, which need to be spelled out in much greater detail before they can be translated into research operations, are in keeping with my conviction that the transference situation, as defined by Freud, is the richest source for observing and studying interpersonal data, and that it has a unique validity of its own. Nowhere else is it possible to study interpersonal processes as systematically, intensively, deeply, and with as much control over extraneous influences. The task for the future is to find ways and means for ordering and quantifying the observations, and to aid the human observer in dealing more systematically and more objectively with the complex data in his auditory-visual field. "Validation" cannot come from experimental analogues and similar devices, and a naive faith in their seeming objectivity may merely serve to deprive us of the potentialities inherent in the transference relationship.

NOTES

1. I have reexamined the original sources quoted in Part A of Eysenck's Table 1 in an attempt to reconcile the two sets of data. I have been utterly unable to do so. To be sure, the various reports are not uniform, and it is difficult to bring the figures under common denominators. Nevertheless, on the basis of the published reports the therapeutic results are regularly more favorable to psychoanalysis than is suggested by Eysenck's tabulation—in some instances markedly so. There can be no doubt that Eysenck's zeal has led him to place the worst possible interpretation upon the results. It is also abundantly clear from the reports that exceedingly stringent criteria were employed in classifying outcomes. Thus, the standards employed in these sources were very different from the ones used elsewhere by Eysenck.

It is regrettable that in more recent years psychoanalytic institutes seem to have increasingly desisted from publishing such data, perhaps partly on the grounds that they are easily misinterpreted.

2. The study of Kessel & Hyman (1933) is out of place in Part A of Eysenck's Table 1, which focuses on psychoanalytic institutes and treatment centers. In contrast, the source of Kessel and Hyman's data is obscure, and no information is given about the characteristics of their sample. Most damaging is the fact that the evaluations of treatment outcome were made by unqualified judges (internists), who themselves disavow any competence in psychoanalysis.

3. This formulation readily lends itself to the misinterpretation that promising candidates for psychotherapy are not really "sick." This inference would be quite unwarranted, and it is in part a reflection upon the primitive status of currently available assessment techniques. By superficial behavioristic standards a person may be described as "mentally healthy" if he meets gross behavioristic criteria of performance, such as functioning in a particular social role, earning a living, absence of gross disturbances in interpersonal situations, absence of gross psychopathology, and the like. Yet, such conformity or seeming adaptation may be achieved at tremendous psychic cost; the individual may feel intensely unhappy, inhibited, conflicted, etc. It appears that, broadly speaking, psychoanalysis pays the closest attention to, and evinces the greatest respect for, the individual's intrapsychic organization and its function in the person's *fine* adjustment to himself and others. The latter is completely lost sight of in the statistical tabulations dealing with treatment outcomes. Unfortunately, there are no adequate measures of self-respect, a sense of worthwhileness as a person, emotional well-being arising from an ability to be at peace with oneself and others, a sense of relatedness, and identity—values which in this age of materialism largely seem to have lost their meaning. Unless we acknowledge that the integration and full unfolding of the human personality is worth striving for, no matter what the expenditure of therapeutic time and effort may be, and unless it becomes possible to reflect such achievements in tabulations of statistical results, we may be forced to concede that the future lies with tranquilizing drugs rather than with psychological techniques.

4. This discussion and the following paragraphs underscore the interdependence of "process" and "outcome" research and the importance of predictions at the beginning and throughout therapy.

5. Although it adds other complexities, group psychotherapy provides more than one representative of the social environment; and it permits the patient to test his motives, actions, inner processes, etc., against the background of the feelings of others.

6. This recommendation is far from original. Already a quarter of a century ago, in the first five-year report of the Chicago Psychoanalytic Institute, Dr. Alexander (1937) concluded that the analyst and the patient are in the best

position to judge the actual progress made and the weights to be assigned to analytic insight and the altered life situation in evaluating the therapeutic result. Unfortunately, very little has been done in the interim to design objective research investigations embodying this insight.

REFERENCES

Alexander, F. *Five year report of the Chicago Institute for Psychoanalysis, 1932–1937.*

Eysenck, H. J. The effects of psychotherapy: an evaluation. *J. consult. Psychol.*, 1952, *16*, 319–324.

Fenichel, O. Statistischer, Bericht über die therapeutische Tätigkeit 1920–1930. In *Zehn Jahre Berliner Psychoanalytisches Institut*. Vienna: Int. Psychoanalytischer Verlag, 1930. Pp. 13–19.

Glover, E., Fenichel, O., Strachey, J., Bergler, E., Nunberg, N., & Bibring, E. Symposium on the theory of the therapeutic results of psychoanalysis. *Int. J. Psychoan.*, 1937, *18*, 125–189.

Heine, R. W., & Trosman, H. Initial expectations of the doctor-patient interaction as a factor in continuance in psychotherapy. *Psychiatry*, 1960, *23*, 275–278.

Holt, R. R. Clinical *and* statistical prediction: a reformulation and some new data. *J. abn. soc. Psychol.*, 1958, *56*, 1–12.

Jahoda, Marie. *Current Concepts of Positive Mental Health*. New York: Basic Books, 1958.

Jones, E. *Decennial report of the London Clinic of Psychoanalysis, 1926–1936.*

Kessel, L., & Hyman H. T. The value of psychoanalysis as a therapeutic procedure. *J. Amer. med. Ass.*, 1933, *101*, 1612–1615.

Kirtner, W. L., & Cartwright, D. S. Success and failure in client-centered therapy as a function of initial in-therapy behavior. *J. consult. Psychol.*, 1958, *22*, 329–333.

Knight, R. P. Evaluation of the results of psychoanalytic therapy. *Amer. J. Psychiat.*, 1941, *98*, 434–446.

Luborsky, L. Psychotherapy. In P. R. Farnsworth (Ed.) *Annu. Rev. Psychol.*, 1959, vol. 10, 317–344.

Strupp, H. H. The psychotherapist's contribution to the treatment process. *Behav. Sci.*, 1958, *3*, 34–67.

Strupp, H. H., & Williams, Joan V. Some determinants of clinical evaluations of different psychiatrists. *Arch. gen. Psychiat.*, 1960, *2*, 434–440.

Sullivan, P. L., Miller, Christine, & Smelser, W. Factors in length of stay and progress in psychotherapy. *J. consult. Psychol.*, 1958, *22*, 1–9.

Wallach, M. S., & Strupp, H. H. Psychotherapists' clinical judgments and attitudes towards patients. *J. consult. Psychol.*, 1960, *24*, 316–323.

Zax, M., & Klein, A. Measurement of personality and behavior changes following psychotherapy. *Psychol. Bull.*, 1960, *57*, 435–448.

68137